Betty White on TV

From Video Vanguard to Golden Girl

By Wesley Hyatt

BearManor Media

Orlando, Florida

Betty White on TV: From Video Vanguard to Golden Girl
© 2021 Wesley Hyatt. All Rights Reserved.

No portion of this publication may be reproduced, stored, and/or copied electronically (except for academic use as a source), nor transmitted in any form or by any means without the prior written permission of the publisher and/or author.

Published in the USA by
BearManor Media
1317 Edgewater Dr. #110
Orlando, FL 32804
www.BearManorMedia.com

Cover Photo: Betty White in a publicity photo during the run of *The Golden Girls* in the 1980s. Courtesy of Everett Collection.

Softcover Edition
ISBN: 978-1-62933-657-2

Printed in the United States of America

Table of Contents

Acknowledgments	ix
Chapter One: Introduction: Thank You for Being a Friend	1
Chapter Two: Betty the Personality	9
Chapter Three: Betty the 50s Funny Lady	45
Chapter Four: Betty the Game Show Goddess, Part I	59
Chapter Five: Betty the Variety Star and Guest	95
Chapter Six: Betty the Game Show Goddess, Part II	123
Chapter Seven: Betty the Scene Stealer	167
Chapter Eight: Betty the Shining Star	193
Chapter Nine: Betty the Rose in Bloom	215
Chapter Ten: Betty the Boss and Grandmother	239
Chapter Eleven: Betty the Drama Queen	255
Chapter Twelve: Betty the Added Attraction	279
Chapter Thirteen: Betty the Omnipresent: Guest TV Acting Appearances 1956-2018	301 365
Epilogue	
Appendix: Betty By the Numbers	371
Bibliography	391
Index	397

Dedication

To Marion Carter, who loves to laugh at and with Betty White as much as anyone else I know.

Acknowledgments

Covering the career of a talent with a TV career stretching some eighty years is a daunting task. However, when the subject is as beloved and respected as Betty White, most people connected with her are more than happy to fill in the missing gaps. The following individuals graciously took time to be interviewed and recall their experiences related to a TV favorite: Hisham Abed (March 17, 2020), Ed Asner (Feb. 17, 2020), Steve Beverly (March 8 and March 19, 2020), Bruce Burmester (Jan. 13, 2020), Dick DeBartolo (Dec. 12, 2019), Bill D'Elia (March 27, 2020), Roger Dobkowitz (May 6, 2020), Mike Gargiulo (Jan. 13, 2020), Hal Gurnee (Nov. 19, 2019), Shelley Herman (Feb. 9, 2020), Michael Kagan (email May 1, 2020), Caren Kaye Temple (Sept. 26, 2019), Tom Kennedy (Aug. 24, 2019), Chris Korman (Oct. 9, 2019), Yvonne Lime Fedderson (Oct. 27, 2019), Jim MacKrell (Oct. 9, 2019), Suzanne Martin (email April 25, 2020), David Mathews (Jan. 25, 2020), Mark Maxwell-Smith (Aug. 28, 2019), Robert Noah (Sept. 24, 2019), Lex Passaris (March 14, 2020), Stewart Rafill (Feb. 14, 2020), Lew Retrum (Nov. 24, 2019), Andrew J. Selig (Jan. 13, 2020), Anne Serling (Feb. 19, 2020), Wil Shriner (March 18, 2020), Michael Stich (Feb. 3, 2020), Phoef Sutton (March 31, 2020).

Special thanks goes out to Steve Beverly and Chris Korman in obtaining overlooked material on Betty. Also going beyond their call of duty to offer extra help were Josh Jacobs, Bob Leszcsak (also known professionally as Bob O'Brien), Brendan McLaughlin, Adam Nedeff, Matt Ottinger, Rick Scheckman and Stu Shostak.

Additionally, Adam Nedeff supplied me with some rare photos of Betty. Other images came from Everett Collection courtesy researcher Michele Hadlow.

Those helping me find some rare TV and audio footage of Betty included again Adam Nedeff and Matt Ottinger along with Phil Gries of Archival Television Audio, Inc.; Rosemary Hanes, reference librarian for the Moving Image Section of the Library of Congress; Jim Hardy, Bob Hope's film archivist; Diana M. Moreno and Gary Necessary of George Schlatter Productions; and Bruce Remy of the Rock and Roll on DVD website. With their help, I was able to watch or listen to at least one episode of every national series where Betty was a regular or semiregular as well as about ninety-five percent of her guest acting shots.

Editing this manuscript was my work colleague Peggy Benson. I cannot thank her enough for agreeing to review my initial draft.

Last and never least, any author needs love, encouragement and understanding from family and friends about the time and resources needed to devote to a project. With that in mind, I offer my sincerest thanks to Gayle Willard Hyatt, Art Callahan, LuAnn Hyatt Martinson, Skip Martinson, Bennett Martinson, Brynn Martinson, Neil Alhanti, Aaron Bodnar, Marion Carter, Ellen Cooper, Todd Day, Alex Delaney, Amanda Downie, Renee Duncan, Anthony Evans, Kevin Grady, Linda Hill Guzman, Jeff Johnson, Kate Krayer, Jimmy Lancaster, Maggie Monahan, Ashley Sharp, Lexi Soberanis, Reggie Shuford and Veronica Summers.

Betty White on TV

From Video Vanguard to Golden Girl

Betty was already looking back at a considerable TV career in Los Angeles when she took a break from filming *Life with Elizabeth*, her first national TV series and first sitcom, running from 1952 to 1954. She would go on to have twenty-five more national series as a regular or semiregular over the next sixty-plus years. Courtesy of the Adam Nedeff Collection.

Chapter One
Introduction: Thank You for Being a Friend

"People love her. Animals love her. And if aliens arrive tomorrow from outer space, they would love her."

That's how the title hostess of *Barbara Walters' 10 Most Fascinating People* introduced Betty White when that TV special aired December 9, 2010. The statement wasn't just Barbara's opinion—it was fact. Voters in a Reuters/Ipsos survey a year later picked Betty as America's most popular and trusted celebrity. Not bad for a woman a few months shy of her ninetieth birthday.

Walters' words of admiration were a gracious compliment from one TV icon to another, especially given their shared connection. Betty had turned down the position of "girl Friday" on the NBC morning informational series *Today* in the 1960s. Walters took her place and began a career as a TV personality that lasted six decades.

But her impressive achievement still paled next to the incredible eight decades Betty would spend on the medium. That durability gained Betty the honor of longest TV career for a female entertainer in the book *Guinness World Records 2014*.

The Walters special highlighted Betty's many other accomplishments and summarized how successful 2010 had been for the actress and personality. "This year, Betty White seemed to be everywhere," Walters noted, followed by images illustrating her narration as she made these quick points.

• "In the mud." Viewers saw a clip of Betty's commercial for a candy bar where she was tackled to the ground during a pickup football game. A player said, "Mike, you're playing like you're Betty White out there!" "That's not what your girlfriend says!" Betty shot back. "Oooo!" went the players before Betty ate the candy bar and transformed back into a male receiver. The *USA Today* Ad Meter ranked it the most popular commercial to appear during Super Bowl XLIV. Surprisingly, BBDO, the ad agency for the candy maker, had recommended using Aretha Franklin, but the brand overruled that choice in favor of Betty.

• "On Facebook." The special showed a fan page from the social media website where David Matthews of San Antonio, Texas, set up a page demanding Betty host *Saturday Night Live*. The campaign generated so much publicity that executive producer Lorne Michaels capitulated to the demand and invited Betty to host the May 8, 2010 show. The appearance earned Betty her twentieth nighttime Emmy nomination—almost sixty years since her first one in 1951, when the annual ceremony was just three years old.

• "On her sitcom *Hot in Cleveland*." The bit shown on *Barbara Walters' 10 Most Fascinating People* featured Carl Reiner as her guest boyfriend. Reiner was the only living performer who had been a regular in nearly as many national TV series as White had, sixteen to her seventeen.

• "Being interviewed by everyone." Betty appeared on clips of *The View* (which Walters hosted), *Larry King Live*, *Good Morning America*, *Ellen*, and *Lopez Tonight*.

• "Winning awards." A shot showed Betty getting a standing ovation at the 16th Annual Screen Actors Guild Awards where she accepted the Annual Life Achievement Award from Sandra Bullock.

Overlooked in *Barbara Walters' 10 Most Fascinating People* was how time and technology had caught up with Betty. The explosion of websites hosting videos by 2010 gave computer users access to Betty's immense amount of TV work going back to the 1950s. Viewers had a chance to fully appreciate how Betty's marvelous wit and intellect had helped her through the decades. She was as sharp a personality as she was an actress whenever the camera shone on her.

Looking Back at Betty

Some of the old shows did make the montage of Betty's career on the special. The collection proved that for most Baby Boomers and later generations in America, Betty was always there for them to watch. The bits included Betty singing on *The Betty White Show*, her first network TV series on NBC daytime in 1954; *Life with Elizabeth*, her first national sitcom in which she starred and co-produced during the mid-1950s; *Password*, the 1960s game show where she stood out as a player and won host Allen Ludden's love; *The Mary Tyler Moore Show*, where she won two Emmys and got her first regular acting role on TV in fifteen years; and *The Golden Girls* (1985–92), which won her more awards and cemented her status as a TV icon.

After that montage, Barbara sat down with Betty and said, "Okay, Betty, describe this past year." "It's been a bear," Betty responded. "It really has been. It's been full and wonderful. But everybody says, 'Oh, Betty, it's so nice that you've had such a nice comeback …' I hate to say it, I've never been away, guys. I've been working steadily for the last sixty-three years."

That part was a little bit of an overstatement. Betty's career had some ups and downs since she joined deejay Al Jarvis as his on-air assistant on a daytime TV series, *Hollywood on Television*, airing in Los Angeles in 1949. She endured dry spells between jobs, particularly acting roles from the late 1950s through early 1970s.

But when Betty was hot, she had few peers in the medium. Consider this: Less than 200 scripted nighttime network TV series have run at least seven years. Betty was a regular on two of them—*The Mary Tyler Moore Show* and *The Golden Girls*—and both efforts are among the less than fifty Emmy winners for Outstanding Comedy Series.

She certainly did a lot of television. To watch all the holdings the Paley Center for Media alone has on Betty would take the equivalent of over six days nonstop.

Her busy work ethic helped overshadow her personal life, despite hundreds of talk show appearances. When she wed Allen Ludden in 1963, some publications had no idea she had two previous marriages. During the 1950s, some gossip outlets preferred portraying Betty as a bachelorette in love with actors Michael Rennie, Yul Brynner, and Michael Ansara instead of a determined double divorcée. To her fans, the former certainly seemed more believable.

Also, a few reporters accepted Betty's claim that she was born in 1926 rather than 1922, an approach she used like many other actresses during the 1950s and 1960s to combat ageism. Betty was more forthright with Barbara Walters on the 2010 special. When Barbara began a question with "At eighty-eight and a half-years old," Betty mockingly interjected, "I'm eighty-eight and three quarters!"

The Basics for Betty in This Book

The previous information is about as scandalous as *Betty White on TV* is going to get. This book's emphasis is on Betty's professional career. Having done literally tens of thousands of hours of television and film work seen by millions of people, there's plenty to explore.

Somewhat shockingly, chronicling Betty's legacy and importance to the television industry has been sparse. Outside of her memoirs *Betty White in Person* (1987) and *Here We Go Again: My Life in Television* (2010), she has been profiled in only a handful of TV encyclopedias and biographies. Since it's been a decade since her last book about her TV work, a follow-up is overdue.

Betty White on TV follows her career in chronological order when she came to prominence in various facets of television. She started as a talk show personality, then did sitcoms, game shows, variety shows, and so on, so the chapters follow that order. The one exception is guest acting, which she began in 1956. Since her primary acting career over the last two decades has been as a guest star, that phase of her life has been placed near the end of the book. Because they did not run on a network or pay channel, Betty's forays into direct-to-video projects like *The Lorax* are omitted.

Betty the Beloved

Getting back to the 2010 special, Barbara Walters noted that "This is the year Betty White felt the love." It's in this spirit that *Betty White on TV* is written. Simply put, in the eyes and ears of this author, while some properties in which Betty has appeared have been shaky to stinky, she's always giving 100 percent of herself to everything she's done. This approach has endeared her to millions across the political divide.

For example, when reviewing *Barbara Walters' 10 Most Fascinating People*, the left-leaning, now defunct website Gawker applauded the choice of Betty. So did Steven Krage, a self-described young Republican of Chicago Now blog aggregator website. "I absolutely adore actress Betty White!" he effused. "I even own a 'Betty White is my Homegirl' T-shirt."

Hollywood casts and crews fawned over her, as well. Gavin MacLeod, Betty's co-star on *The Mary Tyler Moore Show*, noted in a documentary on that series' second season DVD collection that "She's a favorite with the guys. The crews love Betty, because her humor is sensational." His own take was "She knocks me out. I mean, she is Miss Television."

Betty particularly earned popularity and longevity in game shows, spending an incredible sixty-one years in the genre. Game show historian Steve Beverly credited that run to her upbeat, gregarious personality and "the fact that she knew why she was supposed to be there, and that was to help those contestants win money." He added, "When Betty was on a show, even when she had a weak player against her, she would make that person better just because of her personality."

To be fair, not everyone has adored Betty. Some critics have found her spirit too blithe to bear. She has struck them as a Goody Two-shoes, a Pollyanna unwilling or unable to acknowledge the negative in the world. With her dimples, relentless smile and plucky attitude, her detractors view her less happy-go-lucky and more "happy-go-yucky."

Janet Kern of *The Chicago American* caustically commented in 1959, "*To Tell the Truth* remains one of our viewing circle's favorite programs [but] there are times when one panelist or another annoys me. Frequently it's Betty White whom I find too saccharine." In the 1970s, an anonymous actress groused to *TV Guide* about Betty's perpetually optimistic outlook and love of pets. (The general consensus is that the woman was Bea Arthur, later Betty's co-star on *The Golden Girls*.)

Still, for every detractor of Betty, there are many more defenders—some ardently so.

"You're talking about one of my favorite subjects," said Jim MacKrell, who worked with Betty on *The Golden Girls*, the game show *Celebrity Sweepstakes* and some telethons. "She's a fabulous comedienne. She's a great game player. She is a wonderful neighbor to many people and most of all, she is a friend to everybody, including the animals."

"She is a generous team player," said Ed Asner, her co-star on *The Mary Tyler Moore Show*. "She always delivers. She's a courageous little fighter. And she was very aggressive when the actors were on strike and they decided to strike game shows, as well. And she was a bewitching little tiger fighting for Allen's show [*Password*]."

"There's no artifice. There's no pretense with Betty," said Chris Korman, whose father Harvey Korman worked with Betty several times on *The Carol Burnett Show*, *Mama's Family*, and more. "But let's not kid ourselves. Betty can be more like Sue Ann Nivens than Rose Nylund. Don't let the sweet little grandma fool you. She can be bawdy."

"Betty is the epitome of the professional person," said director Mike Gargiulo, who worked with her on *Password* and other game shows in the 1960s. "She has a wonderful sense of timing. She's a lady. She never loses her cool."

"She's just the best," said Stewart Raffill, who worked with her on *The Pet Set* in the early 1970s. "And all the shows she's on, she has that personal kind of humor that is self-deprecating in a way and just catches everybody and you've got to watch it."

Perhaps the most amusing and appropriate assessment of Betty came from Johnny Carson when he hosted Betty on *The Tonight Show* on October 7, 1987. "I've known you a number of years, but I'm not sure that I really know you," he said. "I mean, sometimes you play this 'Hi, how are you?' And then underneath, these little … You're somewhere between Mother Teresa and a call girl, and I'm not quite sure where it is." As always, Betty just laughed and smiled.

In the decade since *Barbara Walters' 10 Most Fascinating People* first aired, people's love of Betty endured. She earned more than a dozen national award nominations, hundreds of flattering news articles and starred on two series, both of which earned her multiple Emmy nominations.

A measure of how much people treasure Betty came on December 27, 2016. The year piled up an unusually heavy amount of celebrity deaths for the public to endure. In response, Demetrios Hrysikos from Spartanburg, South Carolina, launched a GoFundMe campaign page to "Help protect Betty White from 2016." On the page, he wrote only slightly tongue in cheek, "Help 2016 catch these hands if it goes anywhere near Betty White! If she's okay with it, I will fly to wherever Betty White is and keep her safe till Jan 1, 2017."

Thankfully, he did not have to take such action. Nevertheless, the crowdfunding campaign surpassed its goal of $2,000 in less than a day and eventually surpassed $9,000. Hrysikos donated the money to the Spartanburg Little Theatre instead.

A few weeks later, during an interview with Katie Couric for Yahoo News, Betty was surprised, amused and humbled by the campaign. "How were they going to perpetuate me with money?" she asked Couric before adding how much she appreciated the devotion of her fans. "They spoil me rotten. Really, it's terrible, and I enjoy every minute of it and make the most of it."

Betty White on TV is meant to give Betty White fans even more enjoyment of their idol in the spirit of her own philosophy of life. "I hate to sound square, Barbara, but I always try to get the most out of what I'm living now," she said in 2010. "My beloved mother and dad would always say, 'We never want to hear you say, 'Oh, that's so wonderful, I didn't appreciate it at the time. I didn't realize it at the time.' Realize it right now, when it's special, as it's happening."

With that in mind, let's appreciate what Betty has accomplished in eight decades on television, because it is special.

Betty stood next to Eddie Albert and Mary Sampley as they did their daily chat show on KLAC in 1952. When this photo was taken, Betty had been doing a daily afternoon show on the station regularly for more than three years. Courtesy of the Adam Nedeff Collection.

Chapter Two
Betty The Personality

As a child, Betty White loved caring for animals and playing games. She would pursue those two passions for pleasure and profit throughout her life.

Betty later combined them with a third one—performing and appearing on television. The reason for that delay, in part, is that television did not really appear until Betty was in her late teens.

In 1939 in California, Betty debuted on experimental television in February, a month after graduating Beverly Hills High School. She sang in a version of the operetta *The Merry Widow* in a studio on the sixth story of a building in Los Angeles. Viewers were her family, friends, and other onlookers, watching on a small monitor on the ground floor showroom.

Betty was just seventeen when she first acted on TV. Oddly, that number was pivotal in her early TV career. Her first situation comedy, *Life with Elizabeth*, started on local television in Los Angeles on May 17, 1952. The filmed version of the series began September 17, 1953 and its first episode aired on October 17, 1953, starting on seventeen stations, as well.

But before that event transpired, seventeen figured prominently elsewhere in Betty's life. Her parents, Horace White and Tess Cachikis, were wed on February 17, 1921, and Betty Marion White was born on January 17, 1922, in Oak Park, Illinois. As the family moved to California when Bets (the Whites' nickname for their daughter) was two, Betty considered herself a native of the Golden State.

Growing Up Betty

Horace and Tess raised Betty to appreciate nature and animals at home and on vacation. By the time she was ten, Betty enjoyed such leisure activities as feeding the deer in Sequoia National Park. While traveling to and from destinations, the Whites played many games in the car with their daughter. Having this sort of fun, she never felt like a "lonely only child," just dearly loved.

Betty credited Horace for inspiring optimism in her early years. "One of Dad's favorite slogans is this: 'If you want to, you can worry about things three times: before they happen, while they're happening and after they're over. But why?'" she told Dorothy O'Leary in *Radio-TV Mirror*.

As a youngster, her diversions included going to the movies, where she idolized operatic singing stars Jeanette MacDonald and Nelson Eddy. "They were as important in my world almost as my mother and dad," she said in the 2018 PBS documentary *Betty White: First Lady of Television*.

Betty's interest in entertainment deepened when she helped organize a graduation play in middle school. "That's where the ham in me first showed," she told *The American Weekly* in 1954. "I wrote, directed, produced and starred in a tearjerker called *Land of the Rising Sun*. I could hardly wait to graduate and foist myself on a panting public."

Moving up to Beverly Hills High School, playing the role of Elizabeth in a production of *Pride and Prejudice*, solidified the acting bug in Betty. Her outgoing personality flowered, as well.

"Everybody loved Betty," former classmate Terrence O'Flaherty recalled in the *San Francisco Examiner* in 1985. He served as that paper's TV critic from 1952 until his retirement in 1986. "She was bright and bubbly, but underneath it was a tremendous vulnerability."

Her father wanted her to go into college after graduating high school, but Betty wanted to continue to develop an entertainment career. "That was a real blow to Dad—one of the few real storms we weathered," she told Dorothy O'Leary in *Radio-TV Mirror*. "But he finally said, 'You must make your own decisions. I won't force you to go to college.'"

Betty pursued a music career under the instruction of Felix Hughes, an opera singer. However, a six-week bout with strep throat hurt her voice, and Betty abandoned her operatic ambitions.

World War II soon arrived, and Betty spent the early 1940s volunteering to support the troops. As the war ended, she wed pilot Dick Barker in 1945. He expected Betty to enjoy a life of domesticity with him in the small town of Belle Center, Ohio. She hated the experience, so the couple returned to Los Angeles in a failed effort to salvage their marriage. They divorced before the year ended.

Telling her family that "I don't believe in defeat," Betty renewed acting and singing professionally after her marriage ended. Her parents supported her as she followed her dream.

"My mother and dad believed in me, and that helped," Betty told Jane Morris in *TV Star Parade*. "They never pushed me, but they were thrilled when any nice thing happened, and for me, nights I'd come home with a job, there was no stopping me! They shared my dream that someday something wonderful would happen." Betty lived with them as she went to find work.

Riding Into Radio

Betty tried to enter films but found only rejection. "The movie casting directors had the nerve to tell me I wasn't photogenic," she told *The American Weekly*. Undaunted, she studied performing at the Bliss-Hayden Little Theater Group. The drama school had several famous graduates, including Marilyn Monroe, before it became the Beverly Hills Playhouse in 1954.

For the Bliss-Hayden production of *Dear Ruth*, Betty won the lead part and the attention of Lane Allan, an agent from National Artists Corporation. He advised Betty to look for acting work on network radio. Allan also became romantically entangled with Betty. They wed in 1947.

Unable to work on radio unless she became a member of the American Federation of Radio Artists, Betty got assistance from Fran Van Hartesveldt, producer of *The Great Gildersleeve*. He gave her one line to say in a commercial on the hit comedy so she could join the union.

Betty scored more parts thereafter. Those roles included *Family Theater* on October 30, 1947 and April 27, 1949, and *This is Your FBI* on August 12 and 19, 1949.

"I got that by accident," Betty said of the latter appearance when interviewed on *Late Night with David Letterman* in 1985. "There was another actress Betty White, and I showed up and they said, 'Well, we wanted a blonde lady.' The other Betty White. ... But there was no time to recast. So that's how I got in."

This Betty White kept doing bit parts on other series, such as *Blondie*. Most parts paid her $5 apiece. On a good week, Betty had up to three radio roles. "It was kind of nice. I never had to worry about the income tax," she drolly remarked in *The American Weekly*.

But Betty knew that she had to do better than her measly activity and income to make a successful living. Her ultimate salvation turned out to be television.

TV Time

Commercial television began in Los Angeles in January 1947, with the opening of KTLA. The third station to open in the market was KLAC, which stood for Los Angeles, California, on September 17, 1948. KLAC shared the same call letters as a radio station, and its leaders wanted to transfer several of those top audio disk jockeys or deejays onto the new medium.

One talent was Dick Haynes for a TV variety special not long after KLAC launched. Producing the program was Joe Landis, who convinced Betty to sing two songs without payment.

"In those early days of TV, it was easy to persuade aspiring newcomers to sing for free. 'A showcase!'" Betty told Jane Morris in *TV Star Parade* in recalling her debut.

Haynes liked Betty's singing and repartee and recommended her to become a regular on *Tom, Dick and Harry*, featuring three vaudevillians doing sketches set at a hotel desk. Viewers were not wild about *Tom, Dick and Harry*, and the series went off the air after a few weeks.

Nonetheless, KLAC management offered Betty a regular job on *Grab Your Phone*, a game show hosted by Wes Battersea. "They'd ask a question and people would call in with the answers," she recalled to author Kliph Nesteroff in 2010. "I got ten dollars a week ... and they said, 'Don't tell the other girls because they're only getting five dollars, but [because] you can ad-lib with the emcee, you get ten.'"

As Betty's TV exposure increased, her marriage to Lane Allan fell apart. While he had supported her radio acting, he expected her to drop her ambitions in favor of homemaking and children. "And then suddenly he wouldn't have any part of a career lady, and I just couldn't give it up," Betty told Jane Ardmore in *TV Dawn to Dusk*. The couple divorced in late 1949.

But while *Grab Your Phone* helped cost Betty a husband, the series also gave her a key booster.

Enter Al Jarvis

Al Jarvis had a reputation in the radio industry as being the first radio host to play records regularly on the air. A native of Canada, he began his deejay career on Los Angeles radio in 1932. When commercial TV arrived in the city, he was ready to try the new medium.

Seeing how well Betty talked extemporaneously with Wes Battersea on *Grab Your Phone*, he offered her a role as a sidekick on his new series for KLAC called *Hollywood on Television*.

"I asked him what hour it was on," Betty recalled to Walter Ames in *The Los Angeles Times* in 1951. "When he told me the show ran five hours every afternoon, I thought he was kidding. I decided to try it, and here I am still trying it. All my friends thought I was crazy at first, and I think some of them still do."

On Monday, November 7, 1949, *Hollywood on Television* debuted live daily on KLAC. Jarvis soon learned more would be expected of him on daytime television than he initially envisioned.

"He just thought he would move his radio show to television," Betty said in the 2018 PBS documentary *Betty White: First Lady of Television*. "So we'd put on the records and oh, the phones would blow up! And people would write and say, 'We don't know what you're talking [about]. We see you talking but we can't hear you. We can hear the records on the radio. We want to know what you're talking about.' So after the first week, they deep sixed the records."

Betty's duties expanded quickly on *Hollywood on Television*, too. Soon, she did commercials, interviewed guests, sang, and danced. She even pushed props around when needed and had to do her own makeup. For all this effort, Betty received $50 a week.

Her main activity was to converse with Jarvis, who, at age forty and on his fourth marriage, had plenty of opinions to share on air. Betty did find one piece of advice he gave was invaluable.

"When I began my career as his assistant on a disk jockey show, he suggested I be different from other girls then on TV, who seemed to be vying with each other as far as tightness of sweater or depth of neckline were concerned," she told Grace Fischler of *TV Stage Magazine*. "I think this was very far-sighted of him, and I'm very glad I never decided to change."

Hollywood on Television came onto Los Angeles TV with no competition, as no technology existed then to carry live network programming. Also, the other TV stations were not on the air in the afternoons. Still, those who had TV sets overwhelmingly enjoyed the presentation, and advertisers clamored to get their products promoted on the series.

Flush with this success and impressed with what Betty provided, Jarvis told her good news after finishing their Thanksgiving show. First, KLAC would add another half hour of *Hollywood on Television* to the schedule and have the series start noon Mondays through Saturdays for five and a half hours. Second, he increased her salary to $300 a week, a small fortune in 1949 currency.

Ecstatic, Betty had finally found herself a home in an entertainment medium. She would be a regular on TV in some form for the next five years.

Hollywood on Television Gets Hot

By May 1950, *Hollywood on Television*, also known as *The Al Jarvis Show*, cut back an hour to run from 1 to 5:30 p.m. daily. That was still a lot of time to fill, especially with no holidays.

"I never spent a Christmas off the air in my life," Betty said of her schedule in her interview on *Late Night with David Letterman* in 1985. She and Jarvis also did commercials. "We did fifty-eight of them in one day," she told Letterman. The powers that be decided that amount was overkill and limited advertisements to no more than thirty per show by 1951.

The series also had a certain looseness. On the show *The Talk* on June 17, 2013, Betty recalled she once talked on air to a man on the street who accidentally walked through the studio door.

Hollywood on Television added more regulars, as well. Perhaps the wildest change was having Sam Balter, director of sports at KLAC, read the racetrack results while an attractive, giggling assistant named Mary Sampley wrote the finishes on a tote board. From there, Balter introduced Unity Minister Ernest C. Wilson for a closing homily. The reverend appreciated the spot because he had an attentive audience at neighborhood bars he otherwise could not reach.

Even with all the extras, Betty remained a star attraction on *Hollywood on Television* because she was vivacious, humorous and honest. The latter trait sometimes backfired. Once she said she loved almost any animal except spiders. In response, a viewer sent her a rubber tarantula in the mail as a mean prank. After opening the letter and seeing its contents, "That's the closest I've ever come to fainting," she told Johnny Carson on *The Tonight Show* on December 22, 1978.

Still, most of the audience respected and adored Betty. That devotion led to having her first regular nighttime series just eight months after *Hollywood on Television* premiered.

The First *Betty White Show*

From July 23, 1950 through January 7, 1951, Betty had her own Sunday show on KLAC from 7-8 p.m. along with *Hollywood on Television* daily. Using a living room set, the first of many series titled *The Betty White Show* included advice dispensed by Betty and her guests. For a change of pace, Betty would sing a few tunes joined by George Tibbles, her regular pianist.

Allen Rich of *The Valley Times* newspaper in North Hollywood, California assessed the series favorably overall in October 1950. "Miss White is far easier today than she was at the inception of the show not too long ago. It's an interesting format, too, with Betty and panel members discussing everyday problems sent in by viewers. These problems are things that might happen to you (and maybe have) and to me, too. .... A down-to-earth show that is pleasing."

But Betty's toughest critic was unimpressed. "Al Jarvis called and said, 'You don't want to do that show,'" she told Kliph Nesteroff in 2010. She agreed to work with him on another series in 1951.

However, the exposure secured Betty her first Emmy nomination for excellence in television in late 1950. She competed in the Best Actress category and lost to Gertrude Berg, star of the CBS sitcom *The Goldbergs*, at the awards ceremony held January 23, 1951.

Betty also ended 1950 with a raise. Her old union the American Federation of Radio Artists became the American Federation of Television and Radio Artists (AFTRA), and its pay standards increased Betty's salary by $100 weekly.

1951: A New Show Arrives and an Old Friend Leaves

On June 2, 1951, *The Al Jarvis Show* debuted with Betty on KLAC and ran Saturdays from 8:30-9:30 p.m. The series acted as a showcase for new talent to perform, with the winner getting to perform a week on *Hollywood on Television*. Thanks to the new

AFTRA rules, these winners got paid for their services rather than forced to work for free as Betty had done in 1948.

Also on the show was George Tibbles who, beside playing the piano, started writing sketches for Al and Betty to perform before Betty sang a number. The bits proved so popular that Tibbles moved into being the show's writer permanently, and Cliff Whitcomb assumed the role of pianist, as well as on *Hollywood on Television*. The sketches eventually would become a series in 1952, *Life with Elizabeth*, which will be discussed more in the next chapter.

Before the end of 1951, Jarvis announced he was leaving the show and *Hollywood on Television* to do a new series with his wife on rival station KECA. The series would run from 3-5 p.m. daily opposite *Hollywood on Television*.

Betty speculated that Jarvis may have made the move to keep peace with his fourth wife. Whatever the reason, his professional standing began to fade. By the summer of 1953, his afternoon show on KECA had shrunk down to run only from 3:30-4 p.m. daily before ending.

Thereafter, prospects worsened for Jarvis. When his radio show ended in 1957, he scrambled for work elsewhere. Desperate to regain his status as a deejay, Jarvis held a sign announcing "There must be a place for me in radio" in front of Los Angeles radio station KMPC in 1969. All he got was a job as a salesman for his old station KLAC. Jarvis held that position when he died of a cerebral hemorrhage on May 6, 1970, two months shy of his sixty-first birthday. Deejay Casey Kasem would recount Jarvis's tough later years as a tribute on Kasem's nationally syndicated program *American Top Forty* on five shows from 1976 through 1988.

Betty Goes Solo

When Jarvis left *Hollywood on Television*, an actor became the new host. *The Eddie Albert Show* ran on KTLA weekdays from 12:30-5:30 p.m. "It will take him some months to establish himself, but the man is a natural, judging from his opening day," opined *Daily Variety* of Albert on his debut on January 7, 1952. The publication added, "He got a fine assist from Betty White."

Joining Betty and Eddie as regulars were *Hollywood on Television* holdovers Sam Balter, Mary Sampley and Cliff Whitcomb along with newcomers Ed Lyon and Jimmy Boyd. The latter was a twelve-year-old singer and native of Missouri who would score a hit later in 1952 with his recording of "I Saw Mommy Kissing Santa Claus."

The emphasis of the show was still on casual chatter and entertainment, but not always. For example, on February 25, 1952, the show eschewed commercials in favor of a five-hour pitch live from an American Red Cross blood bank to donate blood for wounded Korean War veterans.

Although Betty enjoyed working with Albert, he remained in demand for cinematic roles. On June 13, 1952, he parted ways with the series to film the movie *Roman Holiday*, which earned him an Oscar nomination for Best Supporting Actor. Having lost yet another leading man, Betty inherited the reins of running the show and it became the third *Betty White Show*.

The Betty White Show ran from 12:30-5 p.m. until January 1953 through September 11, 1953, when the series ran from 12:30-2 p.m. and 3-4 p.m. Dick Haynes hosted a show between 2-3 p.m., the same Dick Haynes who had given Betty her first exposure on KLAC in 1948.

On September 14, 1953, KECA cut back its operating hours, so *The Betty White Show* now only aired from 3-4 p.m. weekdays. But a bigger opportunity was on the horizon for Betty. She was about to be seen on network television regularly for the first time.

The NBC "Brain Trust" and Betty
In 1953, NBC leaders charged four of its top executives with a daunting mission: Expand and improve the network's flailing daytime lineup.

The network was loaded with losers from the soap opera *The Bennetts* to *The Kate Smith Hour*, an expensive variety series fading in popularity. Meanwhile, rival CBS had hits with *Art Linkletter's House Party*, *Guiding Light*, and many more.

Coming into this situation were four men whom *Variety* dubbed a "brain trust": Mike Dann, Tom McAvity, Frederic W. Wile Jr., and Sam Fuller. The quartet adopted an aggressive policy of programming that the trade magazine dubbed "knock 'em off fast if they don't shape up as click potentials." To show that determination, they ended *Breakfast in Hollywood*, the replacement for *The Bennetts*, on February 5, 1954, after just four weeks, a daytime record then and now.

The "brain trust," all based in New York City, had heard reports about Betty's popularity on the West Coast. Wile, an NBC vice president, flew to Los Angeles and auditioned Betty personally. Suitably impressed, he helped create a deal for her to join NBC. He had no idea that Betty already had logged an estimated 4,800 hours on television in Los Angeles. After the deal was official, Betty did her last daytime show on KLAC December 17, 1953.

The Betty White Show Goes Network

The Betty White Show on NBC in 1954 provided the star with a bigger set and regular band than what Betty had received on KLAC for four years. Playing the violin in the background is orchestra leader and occasional foil Frank DeVol. Courtesy of the Adam Nedeff Collection.

The Betty White Show began on February 8, 1954, three days after *Breakfast in Hollywood* ended, although the series did not replace the latter. The show aired live daily from California at 9:30 a.m. so it would be seen on the East Coast at 12:30 p.m. On the West Coast, *The Betty White Show* ran three hours later on kinescopes, films made quickly from shooting a monitor camera carrying the live show. There was a small studio audience, as well.

Joining Betty were some old hands from KLAC, including writer George Tibbles as stage director and Don Fedderson, formerly the station manager, as executive producer. Betty's announcer and occasional on-air sidekick was Del Sharbutt. Frank DeVol and the Little Band provided music. Typically, Betty bantered with DeVol, who had conducted his own Saturday night program opposite *The Al Jarvis Show* with Betty in 1952.

Betty had twenty men on her crew on and off stage including producer Fred

Henry and director Bill Bennington. All were married except Bill Hamilton, who sang occasional love duets with Betty when he was not playing the clarinet and flute in the band. NBC played up Betty as a bachelorette among these men, with publicists claiming that she was never married. (Betty did not reveal her first two marriages until the 1980s.)

The show also featured one solo tap dancer who was black. Arthur Duncan would go onto bigger fame as a regular on *The Lawrence Welk Show* in the 1960s and 1970s, but in racially segregated 1954 America, his appearance caused a stir among some viewers.

On the NBC talent series *Little Big Shots: Forever Young* on June 21, 2017, eighty-three-year-old Duncan recounted to host Steve Harvey how Betty gave him his TV debut. "I was on the show, and they had some letters out of Mississippi and elsewhere that some of the stations would not carry the show if I was permitted to stay on there. Well, Betty wrote back and said, 'Needless to say, we used Arthur Duncan every opportunity we could.'"

When reunited with Betty on *Little Big Shots: Forever Young*, Duncan said, "God, I think I'm ready to go now!" Thankfully, he did not, as he energetically did a tap dance routine. Betty was her usual upbeat self, chiding him that "You never call!" and watching him perform.

The only other female contributor to the show was Helen Winston. She came up with the ideas for the regular "wishday" segment where every Monday Betty fulfilled requests from orphans in the Los Angeles area. One child got to meet cowboy stars Roy Rogers and Dale Evans.

The rest of *The Betty White Show* consisted of songs, letters from viewers, tips from Betty, and guest interviews. It was pretty much a casual affair along the lines of *Hollywood on Television*, albeit with a larger budget. Done in NBC studios in Burbank, California, *The Betty White Show* employed a standing set with five different backgrounds for transitions.

Because *The Betty White Show* aired at 9:30 a.m., it could be challenging to get show business types to appear that early in the morning. Betty handled such situations with her usual aplomb and honesty. "If a guest doesn't show up, I just look at the audience and say, 'This isn't the way I planned it, but this is it,'" Betty told a reporter with *The American Weekly*.

NBC executives must have liked what they had seen. A few weeks after her show debuted, Betty signed a contract with the network guaranteeing her $1 million over five years.

The Promotional Problem
While Betty's bosses were ecstatic about their new daytime star, national advertisers were wary. NBC offered four one-minute spots for sponsors to hawk their goods on *The Betty White Show*, yet the series had few takers. Executives decided having Betty appear as a spokesperson on a top-rated annual special might boost interest in commercial time on her series.

On March 25, 1954, NBC carried the 26th annual Academy Awards with hosts Frederic March in New York City and Donald O'Connor in Hollywood. After O'Connor sang the chorus to "In My Merry Oldsmobile," the cameras cut to a singing chorus introducing the sponsor's new convertible. Paul Douglas then introduced "Betty White, bright new star on NBC" along with announcer Bob LeMond. The dancers did a routine before Paul, Bob and Betty returned.

"Designed for the future, Oldsmobile is years ahead in every way," Paul said.

"And you wait till you drive it. It's even more terrific than it looks!" added Betty. She sang some before getting behind the wheel of the car prior to the commercial ending.

More advertising with Betty followed, but the effort to make her and the car likable backfired with some viewers. Writing in the advertising trade paper *Sponsor*, Bob Foreman noted the commercials brought groans from the studio audience watching the show in New York City. "And poor Betty White, a young lady who seems to have a certain naturalness and believability, was swamped by her copy and could only appear cloying and saccharine," he added.

Sponsor problems led to a change. The June 30, 1954 issue of *Variety* noted, "Betty White daytime TV show, which NBC brought in some months back with high hopes of grabbing a sponsor pronto, is still unsold. Web figures her upcoming switch from 12:30 to 4:30 will help toward a sale."

Shuffling Toward Cancellation
Efforts for Betty to get a sponsor at 4:30 lasted less than three months due to circumstances beyond anyone's control. When *The Betty White Show* moved on July 5, 1954, NBC added *The Bob Smith Show* from 12:30-1 p.m., starring the host of the hit

NBC daily show *Howdy Doody*. Besides his two daily TV series, "Buffalo' Bob Smith also hosted a morning radio show on NBC. The stress of the workload led to a heart attack on September 5, 1954, that left him unable to perform for weeks.

Worried about losing momentum in the time slot, NBC switched *The Betty White Show* to 12:30-1 p.m. and slotted *The Bob Smith Show* in the afternoon with guest hosts. After three weeks with no Bob in sight, *The Bob Smith Show* vanished from the lineup.

Meanwhile, *The Betty White Show* had moved to its third time slot in less than twelve months and lost much of its audience in the process. Worried about the viewer erosion and lack of sponsors, Betty flew to New York City in early December 1954 to convince NBC executives to give her series more time. Her pleas fell on deaf ears, as they announced *The Betty White Show* would end on December 31, 1954.

NBC officials' claim that Betty would come back to their daytime lineup in some form never occurred. Meanwhile, in February 1955 *The Betty White Show* became the shortest-lived daytime series ever to snag an Emmy nomination for Best Daytime Program. The series lost to *Art Linkletter's House Party*. By June 1955 ABC reportedly wanted her to host a show as part of its expanding daytime schedule for the fall. That plan never panned out either.

As it turned out, the cancellation was a long-term blessing to all concerned. Betty's replacement, Tennessee Ernie Ford, had a solid two-year run with his daytime show. Freeing herself from regular daytime exposure ultimately gave Betty better opportunities in the future, as well.

Indeed, as Betty cried on the finale of *The Betty White Show*, she managed to compose herself to remind viewers to watch her the next morning on the Tournament of Roses parade coverage on NBC. It was an assignment that she would handle for the next two decades.

Red Roses for a Blue Lady

Since 1890 the city of Pasadena, California, has hosted the annual Tournament of Roses parade the morning of New Year's Day. Its stunning floats and marching bands made a perfect spectacle for television. KTLA was the first station to cover the event in 1948. At the 1950 Emmys, presented January 23, 1951, fellow Los Angeles station KECA received a nomination for Best Special Events for its parade coverage.

In 1954, NBC presented the parade's first color transcontinental live broadcast.

While a *Billboard* reviewer remarked that the "colors lacked definition," his overall assessment was "the result was gratifying." The hosts were Roy Neal and Jimmy Wallingford. The latter was primarily a local radio announcer. Neal led NBC's West Coast news division. He specialized in science and space coverage for the network in the 1960s.

The following year, Betty and announcer Bill Goodwin appeared on the show to do commercials for Minute Maid while Wallingford and Jeanne Baird did the commentary. "Maybe NBC was feeling sorry for me because I'd just had my *Betty White Show* cancelled by them the day before," she recalled to Hal Humphrey in the *Los Angeles Times* in 1968. "Maybe they said to themselves, 'We ought to do something for this poor broad,' so they gave me the parade."

She and Goodwin kept pitching for the juice company for the next two parades. In 1957 NBC teamed Wallingford with the husband-and-wife acting duo of Anne Jeffreys and Robert Sterling to host the Tournament of Roses.

In 1958, Betty and Goodwin became parade hosts. Sadly, Goodwin died unexpectedly of a heart attack on May 9, 1958. Roy Neal returned to join Betty in 1959. In 1960 John S. Davidson (not the singer-actor John Davidson) made it a threesome with Betty and Neal. Only Betty and Neal hosted in 1961 and 1962, then they became a trio again in 1963 with the addition of Lee Giroux.

NBC paired Betty with Arthur Godfrey in 1964, an odd choice given his long association with CBS. The hosting became a debacle due to his performance.

"He mispronounced names, and there's nothing the hometown people are more irritated by than a mispronounced name," Betty told Humphrey. "I wound up doing the commentary for most of the two hours, and that was the longest two hours I ever put in." She denied rumors he was drunk.

In 1967, the Tournament of Roses parade became the first annually televised entertainment event seen on three networks when ABC added coverage along with NBC and CBS. Usually the networks covered only news stories simultaneously. Betty told Associated Press radio-TV writer Cynthia Lowry that this extra attention occurred "because it is unique in its field—more like an extravaganza than a parade."

Lowry noted how Betty and some 100 other NBC personnel would hold a four-hour production meeting New Year's Eve for the event. They had the blessing that New Year's Day fell on a Sunday in 1967, which meant that the parade would occur on January 2 instead, so they would have a rehearsal for timing the commercials and reading the float descriptions on cue cards.

After the parade, Betty and the crew reviewed a tape to see where they could improve coverage the following year. The process was effective at least in terms of audience. Betty's hosting of the Rose Parade consistently topped the ratings even with the increased competition.

Following two consecutive years of co-hosting the Macy's Thanksgiving Day Parade, Betty White and Lorne Greene teamed up again in 1965 to host that year's Tournament of Roses parade. Despite their obvious chemistry, they would do the parade together only once more three years later. Greene was the sixth of nine co-hosts Betty had for the parade from 1957 to 1973 on NBC.
Courtesy of the Adam Nedeff Collection.

Following Godfrey, Betty's Tournament of Roses cohosts were Lorne Greene in 1965 and 1968, John Forsythe in 1966, Bill Cullen in 1967 and Raymond Burr from 1969 to 1973. Betty told reporter Bob Martin she had a particularly fond memory of a blooper that occurred with the latter. "One time, as a float featuring giant chandeliers was rolling by, Ray said, 'Get a load of those chandeliers'—just as the camera closed in on a well-endowed young lady riding the float."

Betty's success with the Tournament of Roses secured her another job in describing the Grand Floral Parade in Portland, Oregon from 1969 to 1973. KGW was the home TV station broadcasting the event every June, but eleven other regional stations carried the parade, too. Print ads in 1971 promoting her participation dubbed Betty as "America's Miss Parade."

Taking a Ride on Another Network

Betty claimed her popularity in 1973 as a semiregular on *The Mary Tyler Moore Show* and *Match Game '73* led NBC officials to consider her a CBS star and drop her as parade hostess in 1974. News of her dismissal came out too late for CBS executives to add Betty to its coverage that year.

But in 1975, CBS installed Betty with Bob Barker as cohost and, in the process, removed June Lockhart who had been Bob's Tournament of Roses parade cohost on CBS since 1970. Directing Betty was Mike Gargiulo, who had worked with her previously on game shows in the 1960s.

"Do you realize that people take a week's vacation to volunteer to do the parade?" he said. Likewise, he and his crew made elaborate preparations in advance to meet the strict City of Pasadena requirements.

"We'd get there about 1:30 in the morning. It was set up the day before. The Rose Parade, you had to go there in October to ensure your location, and you have to itemize the equipment you were bringing, and if you get caught violating any of the precautions, you will not be covering the parade. For example, a cardinal sin is if you or any of your crew put a nail in a tree, that's it. You're finished."

As to what element was essential to have in place as part of the preparation, Gargiulo joked, "The most important thing to do in that parade is to have a portable bathroom with a lock! That bathroom was maybe five or six stalls, strictly for the control room and two celebrities. The commercial block was two minutes and thirty seconds, and you had to (use the facilities) then."

Betty's appearance on CBS marked twenty years of involvement with the parade and her last time with it. As she wrote in her book *Here We Go Again*, "I figured it was a nice round number and a good time to pack it in."

Another nice round number was ten. That figure was how often Betty hosted another parade.

Turkey Time for Betty

While carrying the Tournament of Roses parade, NBC also broadcast annually the Macy's Thanksgiving Day Parade from New York City, a tradition in that city since 1924. The network covered the event on radio starting in 1947 but did not secure national TV rights for the festivities until 1953.

Unlike the Tournament of Roses, NBC's telecast of the Macy's Thanksgiving Day Parade had turnover in hosts every year through 1962. Perhaps inspired by Betty's work on the Tournament of Roses parade, NBC assigned her the duties in 1963 along with Lorne Greene, star of the network's biggest hit series, the western *Bonanza*. Their coverage ran for ninety minutes. The next year, to increase advertising revenue, NBC added another half hour of the duo on the air.

The Rivalry with the Eye Network

In 1965, *Variety* headlined an article titled "Battle of Thanksgiving Parades; Tint Coverage Gives NBC an Edge." CBS had started covering the Macy's Thanksgiving Day Parade in 1959, but NBC had been drawing more viewers, and the story gave one reason why. While hosting on CBS, Arthur Godfrey moaned, 'If only you could see this in color!' Indeed, while CBS showed Macy's in black and white, NBC's presentation with Betty and Lorne in a full variety of hues made it a ratings winner again.

CBS switched to color for the parades in 1966. That accommodation was not the only one the network had to make for the event, according to director Mike Gargiulo, who handled the network's parade coverage from 1965 through 2002.

"The Macy's parade has got a deal with NBC in front of the store," he said. "They do not like anyone else to cover the parade. The location with CBS was Sixty-First Street and Central Park West, with our anchor area in the Columbus Circle on Fifty-Ninth Street. We had an arrangement with the city, with the police department primarily. We were very careful, and we had a wonderful relationship with the police department. They knew everything we were doing. And Macy did everything in their power to prevent us from being able to cover it."

Gargiulo said Macy's executives tried to stop CBS from providing seats for guests at its broadcasting location, even for physically challenged spectators. Macy's leaders also refused to give Gargiulo a rundown of the names and order of acts that would be appearing in the parade. He responded accordingly. "Two of my writers worked for NBC, and they were given the rundown and they would give it to me because they were freelance writers."

Macy's officials also created huge gaps between participating bands and floats after NBC featured the acts. This process meant CBS would get nothing but an empty street to show at times. "So, what we did was we started booking ice skating acts. And every time there was a lag in the parade, we would cut to a dance number. It was fun."

CBS also covered parades in Detroit, Philadelphia, Toronto, and other cities, some of which were taped in advance, to augment its coverage of the Macy's Thanksgiving Day Parade. The show aired as the *Thanksgiving Parade Jubilee* until 1967, *Thanksgiving Parade of Parades* from 1968 to 1971 and then *The CBS All-American Thanksgiving Day Parade* from 1972 onward.

"Look, we got our share of the audience. They [Macy's] got their coverage whether they liked it or not, and that was that," Gargiulo said. Still, Betty and NBC always had higher ratings.

The Spoof and the Fadeout

Betty and Lorne became so renowned for their Macy's parade coverage that they received a parody in America's leading comedy publication, *Mad Magazine*. The co-writer was Dick DeBartolo, who ironically had worked with Betty on the game show *The Match Game*.

DeBartolo said he scoured the Nielsen ratings to find programs that got huge audiences and pitch them as subjects for spoofs. "I said to [*Mad Magazine* editor] Al Feldstein, 'Al, we should do something on the Macy's Thanksgiving Day Parade because it's monstrous.' And he said, 'Great!'"

Co-written with Kedzie North, DeBartolo's piece, "Messy's Thanksgiving Day Parade" ran in January 1972 issue of *Mad*, which actually came out around Thanksgiving 1971. The takeoff made fun of many conventions of the coverage, such as the descriptions of the bands ("The group is 147 strong—and fourteen weak!").

Betty also got ribbed for her hosting reputation, as DeBartolo had her fall asleep and wake up muttering, "Where am I? The Orange Bowl Parade? The Rose Bowl Parade?"

The following year, Betty and Lorne got congratulations from Joe Garagiola on November 23, 1972 for their tenth consecutive time hosting the parade. "That means you're no longer guest stars, you're part of the big, big family," Garagiola said as he gave Betty a bouquet of roses.

"We're not at home—Lorne and I are not at home—but we feel that the Macy's parade is like a home for us, because we've spent so many Thanksgiving Days right here," Betty said at the top.

"That's right, Betty, and if for some reason you're unable to spend today with your family, we hope you'll consider sharing part of your Thanksgiving Day with us," said Lorne. "All of us here at the Macy's parade want you to know that even if you may not be home, you're not alone."

Entertainment included Freda Payne and Donna Fargo lip-syncing to their hits "Band of Gold" and "Funny Face" respectively, and performances by Broadway stars and school marching bands. And unlike in 1971 when winds grounded the attractions, many balloons of cartoon characters appeared, including a fifty-eight-foot-high Smokey the Bear and a Donald Duck balloon being retired after eleven years to be replaced by Mickey Mouse in a Disney tribute.

The hosts also provided clever commentary about many topics, including the frigid weather. "It's twenty-two degrees outside, Betty," Lorne said "Oh, it's warmed up!" she quipped.

After Santa came out and wished everyone a Merry Christmas, Betty said, "We hope you've enjoyed spending part of your Thanksgiving Day with us. And we hope that the rest of your day is everything you'd like it to be." She and Lorne then wished everyone a happy Thanksgiving.

However, in 1973 Betty and Lorne were no longer hosts. With Greene starring on the crime drama *Griff* on ABC and Betty being a semiregular on *The Mary Tyler Moore Show* and *Match Game '73* on CBS, NBC executives dropped them. Still, Betty's legacy was so strong that a 1985 episode of the sitcom *Who's the Boss?* used her voice for its fake Macy's parade coverage.

Betty had to satisfy herself with other activities, including being an excellent talk show guest. That reputation stemmed not from her work in early 1950s TV but rather from being a semiregular on the most popular and longest-running late night talk show from 1959 to 1962.

Betty Knows Jack (Paar)
NBC first telecast *The Tonight Show* with Steve Allen as host on September 27, 1954. Allen interviewed guests, did comedy bits with regulars, and performed music to eager albeit bleary-eyed Americans staying up late.

When Allen got his own Sunday night variety show on NBC in 1956, he ended doing *The Tonight Show* at the same time on January 22, 1957. Executives unwisely replaced Allen with *Tonight! America After Dark*, a dull mix of news and information that nearly ended the series.

Into this debacle stepped Jack Paar. He had hosted four different network talk and game shows in daytime and nighttime from 1952 to 1956 and made little impression. But joining *The Tonight Show* on July 29, 1957, Paar sparkled viewers as a comedian, interviewer, and raconteur. By 1958, the show had been renamed *Tonight Starring Jack Paar* in his honor and earned an Emmy nomination for Best New Show of the Year. Paar had his own Emmy nomination for Best Actor in a Musical or Variety Series.

Paar's star power on TV ascended as Betty's waned. After flopping with her sitcom *Date with the Angel*s and its successor *The Betty White Show* in 1958, Betty's acting career sank.

"I couldn't get arrested to do a dramatic or comedy role on television," she told game show historian Steve Beverly in an interview. "So I became 'TV personality Betty White.'"

Her first guest shot on *Tonight Starring Jack Paar* was on January 16, 1959. That show aired from New York City, but Betty did not mind making a round trip from southern California for the exposure on a top nighttime network series. The decision turned out to be a shrewd one.

Paar introduced Betty with "She's a favorite of mine, and I'm sure she will be of yours, Miss Betty White from Hollywood." Betty responded by telling him, "You know, in just twenty minutes, it will be my birthday, and I can't think of a nicer way to celebrate my birthday." In their initial chat, Betty discussed the differences between traffic and rude drivers in Los Angeles and New York City. "Out there, they're not bluffing. Out here, they mean it!" she said to laughter.

When guest Jonathan Winters came on stage, Betty said she first met him when emceeing an event in Detroit. "We were all in a great big group of about 1,500 men, heh heh," Betty and the audience giggled. In an ad-libbed sketch, Jack had Jonathan play a pilot while he and Betty were passengers on a plane, and the audience went into hysterics. Betty made passes at Jonathan and encouraged him to play a stewardess, as well, producing more laughter. To top things off, Betty even got some whistles from the audience for her outfit.

Betty's debut guest spot impressed Jack immediately, and she guest hosted the show on February 26, 1959 and March 20, 1959. Returning as a guest thereafter, Betty appeared on *Tonight Starring Jack Paar* an estimated sixty-five times the next three years.

"Betty was what you'd call a 'sure shot' when she came on," said Hal Gurnee, director of *Tonight Starring Jack Paar*. "Jack always knew that there would be a good segment and he could have fun with her. She was responsive and pretty, and you know, she was just a wonderful guest."

Gurnee said of his boss, "He was reliably undisciplined. He came in like mid-afternoon. He never rehearsed." Paar sought funny things to make the crew and audience laugh.

"I think Jack really invented the talk part of *The Tonight Show*," Gurnee added. "Before that was gags and all that. It was kind of funny. But Jack never finished high school. He just quit, went off and became an announcer. But he was very well read and very smart and very curious." Betty was one of what Gurnee called the "really interesting conversationalists" Jack used frequently.

"With Jack, all of a sudden you would say something in conversation, and he would pick up on it and take a turn either way over this way or way over that way. And you had to follow along. You had to go wherever he went," Betty said in the 2008 documentary *Pioneers of Television*.

Jack introduced decorated World War II pilot and bachelor Phil Cochran on one show to Betty the bachelorette. Romance sparked between the two to Paar's delight, and he would ask Betty for updates on their courtship during her appearances. However, Cochran had a booming trucking business in Pennsylvania that he refused to relinquish, while Betty remained resolute in wanting to live in Los Angeles. She turned down his offer of marriage.

By their fourth year of dating, Cochran had a rival suitor for Betty's hand—Allen Ludden, host of the hit daytime game show *Password*. Ludden got to work together more with Betty, including in California, and by January 1963, she told Cochran it was over between them.

Betty wed Ludden six months later. Ironically, after their honeymoon, their first professional job together was Allen hosting *Password* with Betty and Jack Paar as guest players. By then, Paar had left *The Tonight Show* in March 1962 for a Friday night show, which lasted until 1965.

Talking Without Paar

Betty popped up on many talk shows for a decade after *Tonight Starring Jack Paar*. Among them were *The Mike Douglas Show*, *The Steve Allen Show*, *That Regis Philbin Show*, *The Gypsy Rose Lee Show*, *The Woody Woodbury Show*, *The Donald O'Connor Show*, *Girl Talk*, and its successor *The Virginia Graham Show*, and *Joanne Carson's VIPs*. The latter was a 1972–1973 talk show hosted by Johnny Carson's ex-wife. As for Carson himself, who took over hosting *The Tonight Show* in 1962, he was reluctant to have any guest associated with Paar during the 1960s.

Betty also appeared in 1971 on *Juvenile Jury*, a talk show some sources categorize as a game show even though most of its elements reside in the former genre. Host Jack Barry let his panel of five preteens ask Betty questions rather than do the honors himself.

Though she was a popular guest, Betty acknowledged in her book *Here We Go Again* that "*The Merv Griffin Show* was the only one I actually enjoyed, as opposed to grinning and bearing."

This statement has some irony, as the first *Merv Griffin Show* flopped on NBC opposite *Password* daily from 1962 to 1963. Revived in syndication two years later, Betty made an early guest shot with Griffin in October 1965, describing how her mink got damaged by ink. On April 21, 1966, she returned to the program together with Allen Ludden. In a TV first, Ludden took off his glasses, and Betty said, "He looks like a blond Nelson Eddy!"

Betty did Griffin's show more as a solo performer until the series ended in 1986. She even was a guest host of *The Merv Griffin Show* on October 10, 1978 and July 17, 1979. Her last big appearance was on November 5, 1985, promoting her hit sitcom *The Golden Girls*. "The hair is blonde, the dress is gray, and that's as far as we will go," she joked at the outset. As her castmates joined her on the couch with Griffin, Betty still had time to get laughs, like when she said she didn't jiggle as high as she used to do.

Prior to that appearance, Betty got her own talk show, as well. This series was not the same as *The Merv Griffin Show* and the rest. Betty was talking to the animals as well as humans.

Bets Gets Set for Pets

"My favorite TV job was *The Pet Set*," Betty told Frank Bruni at the *Times Talk* interview recorded in 2011. The fact that she picked this series out of more than twenty series as a regular or semiregular and hundreds of acting jobs spoke volumes about her intense love for the project.

The concept took nearly two decades to become a reality. Betty first proposed the idea to Don Fedderson in 1951 when he was the station manager for KLAC and she was on *Hollywood on Television*. He was unenthusiastic, but Betty remained determined to sell the concept.

"I submitted brochures to every producer I could get in to see," Betty recalled to Don Page in *The Los Angeles Times* in 1971. "My original idea was called *Bandit and Me*, just a series based on me and my little poodle. But nobody wanted an animal show in those days."

When the obsession for *The Pet Set* hit Betty again, her husband Allen Ludden told her to make a formal series proposal. "Two years ago I was doodling with the idea, and a year ago, we ironed out the format," she told Steve Hoffman in *The Cincinnati Enquirer TV Magazine* in 1971.

Betty shot the pilot for *The Pet Set* in May 1970 with parade cohost Lorne Greene as her guest. The result convinced the Carnation dairy company to serve as sponsor for the syndicated series and promote its pet foods in some of the commercial time. In exchange, local stations got *The Pet Set* free and had time to add some of their own commercials during the show's breaks.

The Pet Set debuted in Los Angeles on January 10, 1971. Later that month, Betty and her crew had finished the first third of thirty-nine shows planned for the first year of production and appeared on fifty-three TV markets across the United States. Most stations aired the half-hour series on Saturday or Sunday late mornings or afternoons.

Betty researched each animal seen on *The Pet Set*. "Whatever writing there is, I do. I put together a skeleton script with the lead-ins and lead-outs and what we want to cover in each segment," she said of preproduction work to Jane Ardmore in *TV Dawn to Dusk*. To protect the animals, there was no studio audience, and crew members worked quietly and unobtrusively during tapings.

A typical episode of *The Pet Set* had four segments. The first was an interview with a celebrity joined with his or her companions. Guests included Michael Landon and his Poodle, Joey; Eva Gabor with her Yorkshire Terriers and a Siamese cat; Dennis Weaver and his part Poodle Heider and part Cocker Spaniel Mark Colby; Bob Crane and his Shih Tzu; and Eve Arden with a Lhasa Apso and Cockapoo. Betty and Beverly Garland even cuddled three cute Tibetan Lhasa Apso puppies. Other guests included Barbara Bain, Bob Barker and Betty's friend Mary Tyler Moore.

These spots usually were on the lighter side, such as Richard Deacon telling Betty the musical theater origins of his pets' monikers. He named his Sheepdog Nanette so he could scold her with "No, no, Nanette!" Deacon dubbed another Sheepdog he owned Marietta so that when she misbehaved, he could say, "Naughty Marietta!"

The other three segments of *The Pet Set* had Betty dispense information on a particular animal species, talk with an animal authority, and interact in some way with a wild animal. Betty also relayed pet-related items of interest, some of which firmly dated the series to the early 1970s. "You can now buy a waterbed for your dog for $25," she said on one show.

Ralph Helfer of Africa U.S.A. provided the domesticated animals on the set. For the wild ones and additional on-location work, Betty called on the assistance of film producer Stewart Raffill.

"We'd go out to some other stars' homes or we'd go out to the Channel Islands here to film with the elephant seals, things like that," Raffill recalled of his duties nearly a half century later. "I used to do it for quite a while. And I'd cut it together and incorporate it into the live show."

Raffill's weekly work on *The Pet Set* was shooting and editing five to ten minutes of film to incorporate in each episode. For visiting a celebrity, he said his work was "Just going out to these ranches and seeing their horses, their dogs, their homes. And we would shoot just short pieces communicating with people about the animals they loved. She was a good interviewer."

The other outdoors footage Raffill filmed himself in southern California. "We'd just get together and we'd get a boat and go out to the islands and film the sea lions or the elephant seals, I think she was interested in.

"And then on the way there we actually saw, one trip out there where we were going past this waterway—it must be twenty-five miles or something—this whole, incredible, huge pod of porpoises migrating north. Thousands and thousands of them. And we sailed through there. And on the way back, we went through a whole group of blue sharks, all going in the same direction. It was just so phenomenal. There were a lot more game around in those days."

Raffill did have help with his cinematography and editing. "I had a friend, a partner, and we shot two cameras on each so we could intercut footage. And then we'd just edit it together. That was shot at 16mm." Workers in the studio then transferred Raffill's edited film to video for final insertion in an episode of *The Pet Set*. "It actually wasn't much more difficult than that."

Of Betty, Raffill recalled, "She was very brave and always the most charming person there ever was. Never changed, never tired, always just smiling and humorous and easygoing. Her husband, Allen Ludden, was the producer of the show, and he handled the business and that sort of thing."

While *The Pet Set* was a labor of love for Betty, when Carnation removed its sponsorship in 1972, no other advertiser took its place to cover production costs. Though still airing in over fifty cities in the spring of 1972, *The Pet Set* vanished from most stations by September 1972.

Clips of *The Pet Set* resurfaced on *The Pat Sajak Show* on February 27, 1989, with Carol Burnett feeding milk to a baby elephant and Burt Reynolds affectionately describing his pet Basset Hound Bertha. "That was the happiest year I ever had," she told Sajak.

In 1996, Betty told Jan Curran in *The Desert Sun*, "There's always talk about redoing *The Pet Set* show, and I'm considering it again." According to Shelley Herman, her friend, talent agent Fred Wostbrock was helping Betty with an update until he died in 2016. "Betty was always very kind to him, and he was trying to set up deals to revive *The Pet Set* on some cable channel," she said.

But a revival never happened. Betty had to settle for being a busy talk show guest instead.

Playing with Dinah and Getting Back to *The Tonight Show*
After production ended on *The Pet Set*, Betty and Allen Ludden appeared on *Dinah's Place*, a morning talk show on NBC on March 2, 1972. Its hostess, Dinah Shore, was a longtime friend of the couple. When NBC cancelled the series, Shore started a daily

syndicated talk show called *Dinah!* in 1974. Betty showed up at least ten times, with and without her husband.

In June 1975 Betty and future *Golden Girls* co-star Bea Arthur danced and sang together briefly to "Forty-Second Street." For a 1977 Christmas show with Martha Raye and Rock Hudson, Raye and Hudson cracked each other up so hard that Dinah moved next to Betty on the other side of the couch. When Dinah started laughing hard too, Betty pleaded, "Oh, Dinah, don't you go! I don't want to be sitting here by myself!"

Then on the series' fifth-season opener in 1978, Betty put on a wig at the introduction and pretended to be Dinah to laughter. And Betty did one of Dinah's last shows on August 8, 1980.

Interestingly, Betty did two failed 1970s daytime talk shows with Dinah's companion, Burt Reynolds, as a fellow guest. *The Noonday Show* aired on NBC for a week in mid-December 1975 with David Steinberg as host. Betty and Burt were together again in September 1978 along with Carol Burnett for the debut of *The Jim Nabors Show*, which ran in syndication for a year.

Reynolds also gave Betty her first exposure on *The Tonight Show* since the days of Jack Paar. As guest host, Burt invited her to the series on Christmas Day 1974. Another substitute host, McLean Stevenson, had Betty as a guest during his *Tonight Show* stint on March 17, 1976.

Betty first appeared with regular host Johnny Carson on *The Tonight Show* on December 1, 1977. She visited next on August 16, 1978. Two months later, she and Carson did their first comedy sketch together.

On October 5, 1978, Betty played a woman reporter interviewing a baseball player in a locker room with lots of double entendres. "I must ask you, how did you ever get the nickname of Pee Wee?" Betty quipped before the bit ended with her entering the shower with Carson.

Betty became a sketch favorite with Carson thereafter. On *The Tonight Show* on December 22, 1978, she and Carson spoofed Yuletide variety shows with "The Andy Davidson Family Christmas Special." Playing a separated couple pretending to be friendly with each other, Betty and Johnny ended the skit fighting with the kids and Carson's parents to claim presents under the Christmas tree. Ironically, Betty had appeared in 1977 on *The John Davidson Christmas Special*.

On February 8, 1979, mocking Lee Marvin's recent palimony lawsuit, Betty and

Carson portrayed Adam and Eve in the same situation. As Eve, Betty demanded compensation for staying with Carson's Adam, noting that "I cooked, I cleaned, I took in the inseam on your fig leaf." "Why didn't you just give me a smaller fig leaf?" asked Carson. "They don't grow that small," sniffed Betty as the audience howled and she added, "I just called them as I see them." She ripped off Carson's fig leaf for the finale.

After the skit ended, Carson said, "And how about thanks for probably one of the best comedy actors in the business, Betty White? (audience clapping). It's a tough commodity to find, somebody who can really do comedy well." She was a guest on the show the following night.

On May 4, 1979, Betty played Linda Ronstadt opposite Carson's Governor Jerry Brown. When Betty came out later, Carson said, "I love working in sketches with you. You're so good and it's crazy and we don't have much time to work on them, but you're so good at it." Betty also got to show her first film clip on *The Tonight Show* for her TV-movie *The Best Place to Be*.

The Tonight Show audience applauded at the top of the August 14, 1981 show when Carson said Betty would play Jane opposite his Tarzan. This appearance was her first on TV since Allen Ludden's death in July. More clapping occurred during the sketch as Betty said, "Big king you are! That wasn't exactly a royal performance you gave last night, king!" "That never happen to Tarzan before!" retorted Carson. "Are you kidding? Even at your best, with you it's strictly wham, bam, thank you, bwana!" snorted Betty. At the end, Betty divorced Carson, but he got the last laugh, as a gorilla was revealed to be a Bo Derek impersonator.

That same show, Carson plugged an upcoming repeat of *The Best Place to Be* before introducing Betty, who talked about her work at the Los Angeles Zoo and its koala house under construction. Betty said so many people had sent donations for the koalas in honor of Allen Ludden that they were naming the plaza outside the koala house for her late husband.

On November 12, 1981, Betty's interview had more laughs on *The Tonight Show* than a so-so spoof about the legal implications of videotaping TV shows at home with her and Carson. Giving a nature quiz during her interview, fellow guest Dom DeLuise really lost his composure when Betty said, when cutting an earthworm in two, only its head part regenerates. "The thing you're left with is only a piece of tail!" DeLuise exclaimed. Betty nodded and added, "And you know that gets you nowhere!" "This show is degenerating into the pits!" said Carson in response.

The wettest piece Betty performed on *The Tonight Show* occurred September 7, 1983. She and Carson were a couple at a Malibu seaside restaurant amid stormy weather. After a violinist played "Ebb Tide," three waves came through an open window. Their impacts knocked a drenched Betty to the ground, and Carson pretended to do first aid to prevent her from drowning. After the skit, Carson said, "We rehearsed that a couple of times this afternoon without the water. We knew we were going to have water, but we didn't know we were going to have that much water!" Betty came out for an interview after he quipped, "The paramedics have now revived Betty White."

Beside Carson, Betty also visited *The Tonight Show* with several other guest hosts at least six times in 1979 and 1980. Betty also worked multiple times with Joan Rivers, who became the "permanent guest host" for *The Tonight Show* effective August 1983.

Joking With Joan, Hosting on Her Own

Betty had a great rapport with Joan Rivers on *The Tonight Show*, starting with their first interaction on December 2, 1982. Rivers called Betty "a really, genuinely funny, vicious lady" to laughter. Betty was ready to play, as she cracked up Rivers with, "I would like to say you look lovely, but unfortunately …" Betty said she had been without power and added, "You don't realize the number of things you do electrically," causing audience hysteria. "I'm so lonely!" Betty added. "I know my Christmas gift to you will be D-cell batteries!" Rivers responded.

On April 19, 1983, Betty showed her magazine cover posing next to a Norwegian Elkhound. "And if you daresay 'Who's the other bitch on the cover?' I will never speak to you again as long as I live!" she said, prompting laughter from Rivers and audience applause. Talking about her own magazine layout, Rivers said, "It's funny, because people wanted me to be topless, but I said no." "Oh, weren't you? It's so hard to tell," Betty sweetly responded to hysteria and applause. "Oh, I'd bet you'd be funny on a date if you ever had one!" shot back Rivers to Betty's amusement. After discussing the kind of men Betty likes, Rivers said, "For a woman your age, you're really doing so well!" Betty laughed and scored an imaginary point for Joan.

Rivers introduced Betty by saying, "Good mouth on her" on *The Tonight Show* on September 28, 1983. Betty told Joan she wanted to be Jeanette MacDonald when she grew up. "You're not going to believe this. I wanted to be Nelson Eddy!" cracked Joan. Betty also appeared with Rivers on *The Tonight Show* on June 1, 1984.

When Rivers got her own talk show on Fox in 1986, producers of *The Tonight Show* asked Betty to guest host as Carson got ready to go against Rivers. She only had a week and a half notice.

Game show producer Robert Noah recalled Betty's circumstances during this opportunity. "I'm doing this run-through, and I called Betty and asked her if she could spare some time and come in and do the presentation. She said, 'Great.' Then about two weeks later, she called and she said, 'Listen, I've got a question to ask you that I hate to ask, because once I commit to something, it's a commitment. Would I mess things up badly if I told you I would prefer not to do the run-through?' And I said, 'Absolutely not. Obviously something has come up.'

"And she said, 'Well, *The Tonight Show* has called me, and they want me to do the hosting.' Wow! Now, that's the kind of person Betty White was. She wouldn't tell me what the offer was, because she didn't want to influence me. If I had said, 'Boy, that's really tough, but I can't,' she would've told them no."

On September 8, 1986, Betty came out on *The Tonight Show* stage and received a rapture of applause and whistles. "As you will notice, all my guests are fellows," Betty said of her lineup. "And there's a reason for that. You see, I work with these three marvelous broads, uh, ladies all week long. And I adore them. I love them. Each and every one of them. But I thought tonight, as long as I had my druthers, it might be kind of fun, have a change of pace, and have men."

She added, "I like women. I do—in their place. No, that's a joke, no. The main reason is when you have men on the show, you don't have to ask them who they're sleeping with!"

After a commercial break, Betty said to laughter, "*People* magazine called me and said, 'Who's doing you for the show?' I said, 'They just called me and asked me. I didn't have to do anything like that to get on the show!' They said, 'No, we mean who is dressing you for the show!'"

Her guests formed a mutual appreciation society with their hostess. "You never hear anybody say a word against Betty White," said Jack Klugman. She flirted with William Devane, who said his best qualities were "designer clothes and rage." Paul Rodriguez agreed with Betty that his appearance on *The Golden Girls* was fun. And Charles Nelson Reilly needled his fellow guests.

"I have had an absolute ball," Betty said at the end to a hearty round of applause.

She added, "And for all you smart alecks who said I couldn't do a show without an animal, it just shows how much you know," and she brought out and cuddled a dog.

Betty resumed as a guest with Carson on *The Tonight Show*. On October 7, 1987, he said as she was an author promoting her book, *Betty White In Person*, she needed to be dignified. "A little dignified. Well, I don't blame you," Betty said and raised her skirt above her knee to laughter.

She told Carson she was a writer at age eight and brought along some writing when she was a child. "I ran across something I got a bang out of, I mean a kick out of—just reminiscing," she said in a sly double entendre. Reading her story, Betty noted one of her phrases she used that her dad loved was "'Why yes!' he ejaculated," and she never knew why, which made Carson grin. Running into plot trouble, Betty said she ended her story by saying it was all a dream by a character. "And do you know that they stole that idea?!" she said to audience applause.

Betty also did *The Tonight Show* with Carson February 18, 1986, April 1, 1987, February 3, 1988 and September 25, 1990 before he retired in 1992. Many thought his successor would be David Letterman, who Betty helped discover in Indianapolis and encouraged to come to Hollywood. Letterman instead got another talk show where Betty was happy to visit him.

Sitting in with Letterman

In the late 1970s Letterman's star rose with guest shots on *The Tonight Show*, and Carson used him as a frequent guest host. Then NBC programming head Fred Silverman gave Letterman a ninety-minute morning talk show. Debuting June 23, 1980, *The David Letterman Show* needed a director after Bruce Burmester left. Interviewing for the job was Hal Gurnee, who, after directing *Tonight with Jack Paar* and other shows in the 1960s, lived in Ireland. Returning to New York City, he ran into Letterman's manager on the street who mentioned the opening.

Gurnee told Letterman about how he made sauerkraut while living in Ireland. "My father used to make sauerkraut," Letterman said. After a fifteen-minute discussion about the process, Letterman told Gurnee, 'Why don't you come in Monday and do the show?'"

"We got along right away," said Gurnee, who would direct Letterman's shows through 1995. "I was able to do crazy stuff I always wanted to do, to take a chance."

But not everyone at NBC wanted to take risks, admitted Gurnee. "We would be called into the program office and have a meeting with the program director of all daytime programming, and she'd say, 'You need more cooking shows. That's what women are looking for. Why don't you do more cooking shows, shows about repairing houses, that kind of thing?' Then Dave and I would go away and start laughing." Unimpressed with the series' direction and low ratings, NBC executives canned *The David Letterman Show* on October 24, 1980.

Letterman returned with the more successful *Late Night with David Letterman*, which followed *The Tonight Show* from 12:30 to 1:30 a.m. starting February 1, 1982. "I loved it," said Gurnee, who also enjoyed Letterman intentionally calling him "Gurtner" on air. "It was like being home, sitting around for your family. And the crew was just great, getting along with everyone."

Betty debuted on *Late Night with David Letterman* on October 1, 1985. Letterman was impressed when Betty said she had been dancing in New York City until three in the morning. He brought out a copy of *Celebrity Sleuth* magazine purporting to show a naked photo of Betty when she was younger, which amused Betty. "My folks don't have nude pictures of me as a little kid because they didn't think it was that cute!" she said.

Late Night with David Letterman ended June 23, 1993 after NBC executives picked Jay Leno to take over hosting *The Tonight Show* from Johnny Carson. Letterman went to CBS to host his own series opposite *The Tonight Show*, *The Late Show with David Letterman*. Betty did that series on May 8, 2000 and on January 18, 2011. The latter appearance occurred before Betty's eighty-ninth birthday. Letterman said his mother was the same age, which prompted Betty to crack, "The last thing in the world that I want to think of is being your mother!"

On the same show, when Letterman asked, "What do you like to do in your free time?" Betty answered, "I like to do most anything, play with animals mostly. And, uh, vodka's kind of a hobby ..." The audience howled and applauded as Letterman brought out two glasses with ice and poured a round. Betty pretended to spit her vodka out while Letterman drank from the bottle. She also hugged a man from Camden, New Jersey, who begged Letterman to let him do so.

Betty returned to *The Late Show with David Letterman* on May 4, 2011. The host praised her so much that Betty asked, "Are you coming onto me, David?" Having noted again Betty sharing his mother's age, he replied, "Yes Mom, here I come!" "That's, I think it's a form of incest, but it's a harmless one!" she joked. "Wow, that would be, uh ..." he laughed.

Discussing her love life more, Letterman asked, "But do you ever, like, date? There's no reason why you couldn't or shouldn't." "Why do you make it sound like such a remote possibility?!" Betty responded. He laughed and apologized. "Of course I am!" she added. "Waste not, want not is the way I look at it! ... I never know what I mean when I'm talking to you!"

Best of all, while promoting her book *If You Ask Me (And Of Course You Won't)*, Letterman asked, "What's the deal on that?" and showed a photo of Betty talking with his late night rival Jay Leno. "I'm so sorry, I lost a bet," she said, cracking up Dave and his audience.

On June 13, 2011, Betty delivered her comic "Top Ten Hints for Living a Long and Happy Life" on *The Late Show with David Letterman*. He seemed to like the most her responses to Number Nine ("Exercise. Or don't. What the hell do I care?"), Seven ("The best way to earn a quick buck is a slip-and-fall lawsuit"), Five ("Schedule nightly appointment with Dr. Johnnie Walker"), Four ("Take some wheatgrass, soy paste and carob, toss in the garbage and cook yourself a big-ass piece of pork") and One ("Don't waste your time watching this crap").

Her last time on *The Late Show with David Letterman* was May 16, 2012. Regarding her enduring popularity, Betty quipped, "I'm a major rock star. We all have to bear the burden."

The Eighties Lady

Apart from Carson and Letterman, in the 1980s Betty appeared on *Hour Magazine*, *The Toni Tennille Show*, *The John Davidson Show*, *The Mike Douglas Show*, *The Regis Philbin Show*, and even *The Richard Simmons Show* and *Donahue*, hosted by Phil Donahue. Betty also appeared on *The Love Report*, a collection of fluffy pieces about romance introduced by Chuck Henry and Tawny Schneider that was more of an informational than talk show. She filed supposedly comic bits on June 19 and 26, 1984, a month before the series vanished from ABC's morning lineup.

Conversely, among Betty's most touching talk show outings were with Sally Jesse Raphael in 1985 and 1988. On the latter, the hostess said, "I might even ask that you put children in front of the television set. Besides her spicy mouth, I think they will get a very good role model today from our guest." During the hour, Betty got applause when she said, "I get mad at people sometimes who go through life angry. I think it's a big excuse to blame everything on somebody else. I think you've got to take your own shot at it." This appearance was one of Betty's best in showing her humanity along with her humor.

By the end of the 1980s, Betty did some nighttime talk shows opposite *The Tonight Show*, including *Nightlife*, *The Arsenio Hall Show*, and *The Pat Sajak Show*. She also visited the daytime series *Live with Regis and Kathie Lee* several times starting in 1988.

A Shrine to Shriner

Not all of Betty's 1980s talk show appearances made the air. In 1986, she did an unaired pilot with one newcomer she knew only from a few mutual game show guest shots.

Wil Shriner was the son of 1950s TV humorist Herb Shriner. "I started doing comedy in 1977, and then at the Comedy Store I met [David] Letterman," he recalled. "And Letterman was starting to host *The Tonight Show*. We had become friends, and he liked what I did. So he took me on *The Tonight Show* with him. The first three times, I did *The Tonight Show* with him. And then eventually I got on with Johnny [Carson] and did about a few more shows.

"When I went to New York in 1980 to work on *The David Letterman Show*—the genesis of David's career—Barry Sand, the producer, once said to me, 'Pay attention, because if David doesn't show up one morning, I'm putting you in that chair.' And I went, 'Oh, okay. I better pay attention!' So I started kind of studying what the prep work was and things like that. Because always in the back of my head, I kind of wanted to be like a Johnny Carson."

Shriner learned in 1986 of an opportunity to host a daily talk show on the Westinghouse TV station lineup. Leaders there sent Shriner to member stations to fill in for local hosts. "It went very well, so Westinghouse said, 'We like this. We're going to shoot a real pilot.'

"So, we were shooting these test shows to get ready, and that's where Betty came into play. Betty was going to be one of the guests on one of the non-broadcast pilots, which is a tough ask. She liked me, I think she knew my work. And so she said, 'Yeah, I'll do it. I don't care if it's never going to air.'"

Betty's appearance helped sell *The Wil Shriner Show* nationally. "We launched on 107 stations," he said. As the top-selling new talk show for the fall of 1987, its only competition was a new show with Geraldo Rivera.

"Well, as it turned out, Geraldo was doing tabloid television, and we were at the back end in, like, feel-good television, so we kind of got caught, even though we were on for a year and did 200 hours," said Shriner. "And also, the heads of Westinghouse were all let go during my tenure." The new management refused to renew *The Wil Shriner Show*, so the program ended after one year, even with Betty as an on-air guest in the series' fifth week on October 14, 1987.

Jon Stewart and Other Talkers
Betty worked the 1990s talk show circuit with *The Home Show*, *One on One with John Tesh* (and its successor *John and Leeza from Hollywood*), *Later* with Bob Costas, *Vicki!* with Vicki Lawrence, *The Howie Mandel Show*, *The Late Late Show with Tom Snyder*, and *The Martin Short Show*. She also did the syndicated animal show *ZooLife with Jack Hanna* in 1992.

Betty was better served as a guest on the satirical nightly program *The Daily Show with Jon Stewart* on Comedy Central. Host Jon Stewart avoided canned questions and responses too often used by other interviewers, which inspired Betty to have some lively discussions with him.

When Betty first appeared on May 11, 2000, Stewart said, "It's very exciting to meet you. I've been a huge fan of yours." "Well, may I return the compliment?" said Betty. He shot back "No." Betty laughed and they were off and running.

Betty said Fred Astaire was one of the most fabulous folks she met in the entertainment industry, then Jon interjected, "He looked a bit like a banana to me." "But a banana who could move like a dream!" Betty shot back. She cracked up Stewart by saying when Astaire danced with Rose Marie when Betty had to go into her kitchen, "I wasn't going to give her any dinner!"

At the end, Stewart asked Betty to come back and she said she would. But it was over a decade later before she returned on June 14, 2010. Stewart joked he was worried her recent success would go to her head. She gave some facial indications that would have made any diva proud.

Then Jon asked, "Are there people in your life who can still say 'No' to a Betty White, or is it …?" "I haven't found him," she replied, tickling Jon and his audience. Jon praised her comic timing as exquisite, and she told the crowd, "Would you look who's talking? You invented it!"

Returning November 29, 2011, Betty got much applause when she said she was turning ninety soon. "Guys, it isn't anything I accomplished, it just happened!" she said. "When you get to be that old, you can't remember the guys you've had!" Jon called her new book *Betty and Friends* "an exotic cookbook," which cracked Betty up. He ended by telling her, "You're the best."

Winding Up the Conversations
In the early 2000s, Betty was more durable than most of the daytime talk shows she did. Her appearances included *The Ainsley Harriott Show*, *Donny & Marie* (not to be confused with the latter's 1975-1979 variety series of the same name), *The Wayne Brady Show*, and *The Tony Danza Show*.

One exception was *Ellen* with Ellen DeGeneres, where Betty appeared in nine enjoyable visits from 2003 to 2010. Talking about her upcoming birthday in 2005, Betty said to applause and laughter, "I'm going to be eighty-three. That's only around my boobs!" In 2010, when Ellen congratulated Betty for the huge number of likes on Facebook for the veteran performer to host *Saturday Night Live*, Betty said, "Five hundred thousand people! That's more than I've dated!"

Her many talk show appearances in 2010 included *Lopez Tonight*, where when host George Lopez asked Betty about working so much, she said, "Well, I'm such a whore, I can't say no." Other shows were *The Bonnie Hunt Show*, *The Oprah Winfrey Show*, *Late Night with Jimmy Fallon* (where she played *Password* with studio audience members between 2009 and 2013), and *The Tonight Show with Jay Leno*, where she once shared a shower scene with Hugh Jackman.

Speaking of *The Tonight Show*, while Betty appeared seventeen times from 2007 to 2014 with Leno, their interactions were much less enjoyable than hers with Carson, Letterman, and even Joan Rivers. Leno used her in an irritating recurring spot called "Can We Make Betty Blink?" An audience member wagered if Betty would close her eyes briefly with something shot at her while protected by an acrylic divider. Betty candidly described the routine in *Here We Go Again* as "Not the classiest bits in the world but Jay and I have fun."

Other late-night talk shows Betty visited in the 2010s included *The Late Late Show with Craig Ferguson* and its successor *The Late Late Show with James Corden*, *Jimmy Kimmel Live!*, and *Conan* with Conan O'Brien. Her daytime talk appearances included *Live with Kelly and Michael*, *The Talk*, and *Queen Latifah*. On the latter in

2014, after a monkey defecated on camera, Betty brought out tissues and quipped, "This is not the first time I've cleaned up crap on a show!"

Betty did *The View* at least four times in the 2010s, including serving as guest co-host on May 3, 2011. When guest Rob Lowe said his infamous 1988 "sex tape" was the best thing to happen to him, she interjected, "She must've been great!"

Betty put her perspective on being a TV personality when she accepted a lifetime achievement award at the 2015 Daytime Emmys with the following comments: "I have been in this business for a long time. You may not have noticed that (laughter), but when I started, 1949, I had no idea that I would still be around at this point, for one thing (laughter). But that I'd still be privileged enough to still be in this business. And it is such a privilege.

"And the bottom line, I think, to the television business is that unless you're a real bad head, it is such fun. It really is. Thank you, thank you from the bottom of my heart. All those years, that I had no idea I'd still be working through, is so much thanks to you, and your mothers and fathers, grandmothers and grandfathers (laughter and applause). And a couple of great-grandfathers when I was younger! (more laughter) Thank you again with all my heart."

Betty was much more than a personality on TV, of course. She was also an actress, with a regular series that helped bring her to national prominence in the 1950s. Another sitcom followed that decade, which taught Betty some tough lessons about TV comedy, as well.

Chapter Three
Betty the 50s Funny Lady

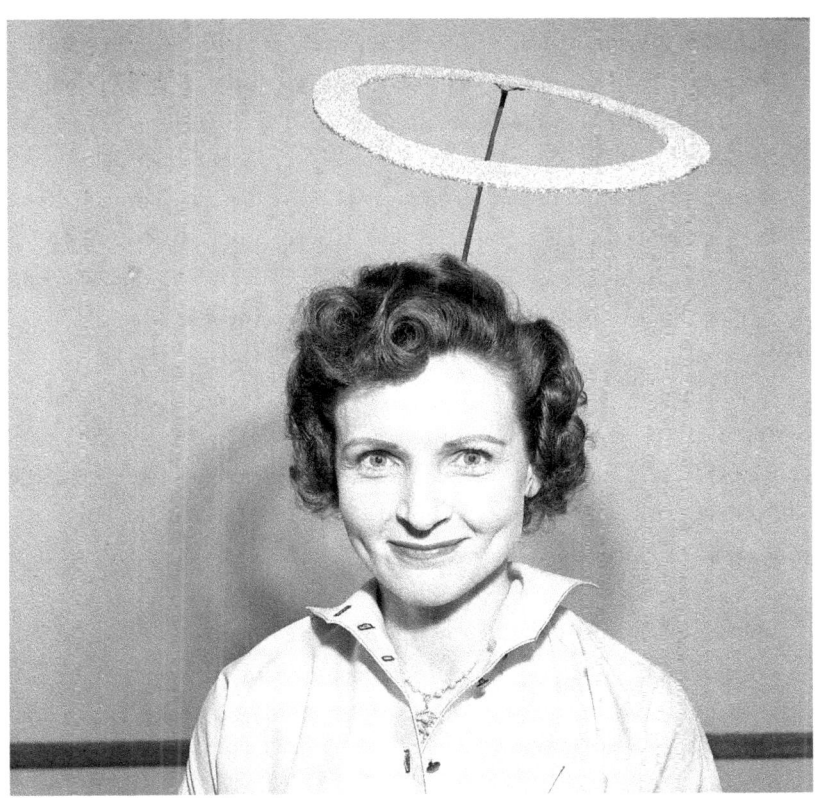

Betty posed with a fake halo over her head to promote *Date with the Angels* in 1957.
The prop never appeared on the show thankfully.
Courtesy of the Adam Nedeff Collection.

When *The Al Jarvis Show* started on June 2, 1951 Saturday nights on KLAC, Al and Betty found they needed more than just having amateur talent perform. Their pianist, George Tibbles, wrote sketches for Al and Betty playing a married couple with a tagline leading into Betty's musical number. The characters' names were variants of their own—Alvin for Al and Elizabeth for Betty.

Response to the Alvin and Elizabeth bits was positive, and soon Tibbles devoted his energy to writing more of the skits each week. When Jarvis left for a new series on KECA, Betty took over his old Saturday night show on KLAC on January 12, 1952, and continued the sketches under the title *The Betty White Show*.

On *The Betty White Show*, Betty worked opposite actor Del Moore as Alvin. Tibbles recommended Moore from having worked with the latter in a stage revue. Moore coupled a strong, towering build with a rubbery face that reacted exaggeratedly and exasperatedly to any mischief Betty caused as Elizabeth. Offstage, Betty affectionately called the actor nearly six years older than her "Delsey," but his full name was actually Marion Delbridge Moore. With Moore, the sketches became even more well received.

"So, one day, Don Fedderson, the manager of the station, called us in and said, 'Could you stretch that into a half-hour show, that little husband-and-wife thing that you do? Could you make that into a series?'" Betty recalled in the 2008 PBS documentary *Pioneers of Television*. "And George Tibbles, who was writing the little sketches, said, 'I guess we could.'

"And I, in my wisdom—I really was on top of everything—I said, 'Well, it won't work. A half hour stretched, the jokes won't last that long. You can't do a half hour.' That's how much I knew. I said, 'If we do them like anecdotes the husband and wife will tell in an evening ... but if you stretch that into a half hour, it goes flat in the middle. No, it won't work.' Well, he said, 'Try it.' We did. That was my first series, *Life with Elizabeth*."

Fedderson came up with the title, apparently to give Betty top billing subtly. She, Fedderson, and Tibbles formed a production company with equal ownership in the series. Dubbed Bandy Productions in honor of Betty's Pekinese Bandit, one of three dogs the animal lover Betty had at the time, the setup made Betty the first female television producer in Hollywood.

The trio agreed somewhat with Betty and designed the half-hour show with three sketches per episode. Stories focused on the trials and tribulations of Alvin and Elizabeth. Elizabeth usually was the instigator in the plots, befuddling or irritating

Alvin or both until the sketch resolved. She was a fun-loving housewife but not as wacky as, say, Lucy Ricardo on *I Love Lucy*.

Betty would rehearse *Life with Elizabeth* Fridays after her daily show *Hollywood on Television*. A run-through would occur Saturday afternoons before doing the show live in the evening.

Life with Elizabeth debuted on May 17, 1952, airing on KLAC Saturdays from 9:30 to 10 p.m. from the Music Hall Theatre in Beverly Hills. Its scenery was bare bones, with Betty and Del playing against a flat background with a couch and a few chairs to represent their home. Beside starring and producing the series, Betty also warmed up the audience prior to each show's start by climbing a ladder and using a megaphone to address those seated in attendance. It was a hit.

The new series also brought Betty an Emmy award in 1952. Betty had been up for an Emmy previously for Best Actress in 1950. The awards then split to have national awards plus local ones for Los Angeles television. That latter ceremony was a memorable one for Betty.

"True, I was nominated [for my first series, *Life with Elizabeth*], but Zsa Zsa Gabor was a shoo-in for her series *Bachelor's Haven*," she recalled to Morrie Gelman and Gene Accas in *The Best in Television: 50 Years of Emmys*. "It was exciting for me just to hear my name read as a nominee. When they read it again as the winner, my brain went into slo-mo, like one of those dream sequences. Everyone else was as shocked as I, including Zsa Zsa. We've laughed about it since."

Seeing Elizabeth Everywhere

The success of *Life with Elizabeth* coincided with a booming market of filming TV series for sale to individual TV stations across the United States. A top distributor was Guild Films, which went into production in late 1952 with *The Liberace Show*. That series became an immediate smash. Noting the achievement, Fedderson talked with Guild Films president Reub Kaufman about trying to do the same for *Life with Elizabeth*.

By the start of July 1953, Kaufman and Guild Films announced a deal to film and syndicate thirty-nine shows of *Life with Elizabeth* to TV stations. The budget was $10,000 per episode to allow for bigger and better sets than the live version, plus one guest per show. George Tibbles would be the producer and primary writer with a few other scribes, such as Milt Kahn and Roxy Roth, contributing to scripts as needed.

Rather than film *Life with Elizabeth* in front of a live audience with multiple cameras, as with *I Love Lucy*, the decision was to film the show at the Music Hall Theatre with no audience. While still doing her live daily afternoon show on KLAC, Betty rehearsed *Life with Elizabeth* Thursday nights in preparation for recording the episode Friday evenings.

The finished film then would be shown to a live audience to record their laughs and get shots of audience members clapping at the end. The only problem was that Betty and Del Moore had to anticipate when and how the studio audience would react to their lines, and sometimes the laughter drowned out their dialogue.

Filming on the syndication version of the series began September 17, 1953. This version of *Life with Elizabeth* made its TV debut on October 17, 1953, and in keeping with its numeric quirk, the series started out on seventeen stations, too.

Elizabeth in Action

When viewers across America saw *Life with Elizabeth*, the series began with a woman elegantly plucking a harp before an image of a woman in a cameo appeared. "Betty White in *Life with Elizabeth*!" proclaimed announcer Jack Narz as Betty turned from a side angle to face the camera, grin and wink. Canned applause appeared before the ending faded.

Narz appeared on screen and talked to Elizabeth at the start of "Incident Number One" while addressing the audience for each show. He set up the situation and asked Elizabeth questions about the event, to which she pantomimed her answers before Alvin showed up. The sketch typically ended with Elizabeth fooling Alvin, prompting Jack to say in voiceover, "Elizabeth! Aren't you ashamed?" and Elizabeth would shake her head to indicate no. Two other "incidents" would follow.

The plots for the young couple living in California typically took place in their suburban home. A cute exception was a flashback to their first kiss on the porch swing at Elizabeth's parents' house. Sketches included planning for parties or visits by family and friends, playing ping pong and board games (with Elizabeth cheating), and trying new hobbies. Like Betty White in real life, Elizabeth and Alvin had two pet dogs, Stormy and Bandy.

A few recurring visitors joined Alvin and Elizabeth. They included Elizabeth's effusive old flame Jack (played by Hal March), Alvin's diminutive bald boss Mr. William J. Fuddy (Ray Erlenborn) and their opinionated, older, nosy next-door neighbor Mrs. Chloe Skinridge (Loie Bridge). Elizabeth also endured Alvin's backwoods, unsophisticated friend "Moosie" Moosefield (LeRoy Lennart) and pal Richard (Dick Garton), a man so dumb he didn't know which of his legs was the left one.

The most frequently seen guest actor, Frank DeVol, appeared as several different characters. Betty had a comic ad-lib session with DeVol at a Kiwanis club that went so well that she told Don Fedderson and George Tibbles to add him to *Life with Elizabeth* whenever possible. Only one guest showed up per episode to save costs.

The third and final sketch of each show usually ended with Alvin, Elizabeth, and possibly a guest talking at the same time until Narz interrupted them to say goodbye. After a commercial break, each episode ended redundantly with Narz announcing "And now, here's the lovely star of our show, Betty White." She came out from behind a curtain to applause and said words along the lines of "Thank you, Jack. And thank you, everybody, thank you. Until we see you once more, goodbye everybody!" A shot of audience members applauding appeared before the credits rolled.

Attending one filming in 1953 was Tom Kennedy, who would later work with Betty on several game shows. At the time, Tom was going by his birth name, Jim Narz.

"I first met her through my brother on her first show, which was called *Life with Elizabeth*," he said. "I was just out from Louisville, Kentucky, looking for work. My brother was the announcer on that show, and so he said, 'Would you like to go down and see a live television show?' Or rather a filmed television show. I said, 'I would love it.'

"So, he took me down to see this show, and I got to meet Betty White, Del Moore—her co-star—and I was absolutely enthralled. I was on cloud nine. Not only meeting her, but going into the studio and watching them film and all that. It was terrific."

Betty Gets Kudos
The national critical reaction to *Life with Elizabeth* was very favorable to Betty. Assessing the series in 1954, Sid Shalit of *The New York Daily News* wrote, "It's been many an electronic moon since a new and refreshing TV comedienne has dented the ranks of the top rated. But a girl named Betty White seems, as of now, to have a fine chance to make it in the big time. ….

"With an eye-twinkle, a chuckle and an arched eyebrow, she can get more out of a modestly amusing line than most TV comediennes can extract from an epigram by George Bernard Shaw. On the basis of what we've seen of her, she's ready for bigger and better things.

"The situation plotting on this series is, sad to say, cliché stuff. Moore fixes the roof of their house and then makes a mess of it. Or he'll take work home from the office and is heckled by Betty as he tries to plow through it. .... But Miss White endows it with an attractive, winsome playing and it all, somehow, adds up to delightful chuckling."

In the second annual *Billboard* TV Film Awards poll of TV station operators, advertisers, ad agencies, film producers, and distributors in 1954, Betty nabbed two honors. She won Best Actress Appearing Regularly in a Non-Network Film Series Regardless of Type and Best Actress in a Comedy. *Life With Elizabeth* fared less well, as those surveyed about its overall quality put the series tied for twelfth place with *Annie Oakley* and *This Week in Sports*.

The acclaim for Betty and *Life With Elizabeth* led Guild Films to announce in May 1954 it planned to shoot sixty-five episodes of the series. Twenty-two shows already had been filmed at that point, with the series running in more than eighty markets, including Canada.

By June 1, *Life with Elizabeth* jumped to 102 TV outlets nationwide. That same day, production on the series resumed, and filming moved from the Music Hall Theatre to Filmcraft Studios. Most of the cast and crew had enjoyed a five-week break except Betty. She was doing *The Betty White Show* for NBC weekdays as she had since February.

Betty's workdays began with waking up at 5:15 a.m. to enjoy an early breakfast with her parents before arriving at NBC's Burbank studios at 7 a.m. for makeup and wardrobe. After doing *The Betty White Show* live from 9:30 to 10 a.m., Betty left for a second breakfast before returning to the studios to run through songs for the next *Betty White Show* with Frank DeVol and his band.

Following a late lunch, she rehearsed *Life with Elizabeth* in the afternoon before going home and studying her dialogue. Betty also reviewed her fan mail, which averaged 2,000 letters a week, and learned lyrics for new songs to perform on *The Betty White Show*. She aimed to be asleep by 10 p.m., but on Thursdays and Fridays, when she filmed *Life with Elizabeth*, Betty's workdays could stretch until two in the morning.

"The one salvation is that I love what I'm doing. I dream of leisure, but if leisure were offered to me tomorrow, I'd be sort of lost. I'm hooked, this business is fascinating," Betty said of her harrowing schedule to Jane Morris in *TV Star Parade* in 1954.

She had to take leisure sooner than she thought. Both shows would end before the start of 1955.

No More Life for Elizabeth

In late 1954, expenses for Guild Films' ten series in production reached $12 million. *Life with Elizabeth* was one of the series chosen to end for the company to stay financially viable.

Betty White flew to New York City in December 1954 to discuss future formats for *Life with Elizabeth* with Guild Films president Reub Kaufman and program chief Larry Menkin. As with her talks with NBC executives that same visit to keep *The Betty White Show* on the network's TV schedule, Betty failed to convince the duo to keep *Life with Elizabeth* in production. By early 1955, Betty had lost work both on *The Betty White Show* and *Life with Elizabeth*.

Life with Elizabeth continued to be popular once filming ceased. For example, by 1956, New York City viewers could see *Life with Elizabeth* reruns daily.

In 1959, Betty, George Tibbles, and Don Fedderson were plaintiffs in lawsuits charging breach of contract and wrongful conversion by Guild Films regarding *Life with Elizabeth*. They sought $50,000 in damages. Guild Films went into bankruptcy, and its films went into ownership through several different companies and mostly disappeared from TV stations in the 1960s.

Betty reprised her *Life with Elizabeth* character for the special *KCOP at 50* in Los Angeles on September 11, 1998. By that time, KTLA had changed its call letters to KCOP. Ten years later, in the PBS documentary *Pioneers of Television*, Betty said, "Nobody remembers *Life with Elizabeth*. They weren't born when *Life with Elizabeth* was on."

Yet talking to Larry King in 2014, Betty counted *Life with Elizabeth* along with *The Mary Tyler Moore Show* and *The Golden Girls* as the roles for which she would most like to be remembered. *Life with Elizabeth* remained a treasured experience that she appreciated—unlike her next role.

Making a Date with the Angels

In September 1955, Don Fedderson told *Motion Picture Daily* reporter Samuel

D. Berns, "Exhaustive preparation is the keynote to a successful TV show ... it is psychologically bad to make any major changes in a show or series once it has been launched. All this should be anticipated and corrected before the presentation."

Fedderson failed to follow his own rules when it came to Betty's second sitcom, *Date with the Angels*. The series altered its unique concept into something unexceptional and became a dud.

Betty, Fedderson, and Tibbles had stayed in touch after the end of *Life with Elizabeth*. Fedderson had a top ten hit producing the dramatic anthology *The Millionaire* on CBS in the fall of 1955 and got Betty a guest role on it. Meanwhile, Betty found potential in adopting the Broadway play *Dream Girl* as a series. She would play a newlywed housewife in southern California who fantasized about how she would redo disastrous situations for better outcomes.

By January 1956, Don Fedderson pitched his project for a fall launch on CBS, NBC or ABC. Betty filmed the test show, also known as a pilot, at Desilu Studios in April 1956.

For the male lead, Fedderson nixed Del Moore for fear of inviting comparisons with *Life with Elizabeth*. He auditioned several actors before an associate suggested he consider Bill Williams.

"But he's a cowboy!" protested Fedderson. The producer remembered Williams' role starring in *The Adventures of Kit Carson*, a syndicated series in production from 1951 to 1955.

"Thank goodness Don took time to interview me despite his split-second comment," Williams told Walter Ames in *The Los Angeles Time*s in 1957. "He auditioned me via one of his *Millionaire* TV shows and apparently liked what he saw because I got the job."

However, Williams had done little comedy acting and had to adjust to his new role, including working before a studio audience. "I discovered that while riding horses isn't the easiest task in the world, it was child's play compared to learning to deliver comedy lines. It opened my eyes and made me appreciate some of the comedy shows I had ridiculed in the past," he told Ames.

Though the pilot failed to make any network's fall lineup, filming of additional episodes was underway by October 1956. Fedderson had confidence in the premise. His persistence eventually paid off. *The Los Angeles Times* reported in November 1956 that NBC had bought the property, now called *Date with the Angels*, for a run in the summer of 1957.

Planning to sponsor *Date with the Angels* was Procter & Gamble, but its executives judged that the company was advertising on too many other nighttime shows and dropped the series. Car manufacturer Plymouth then snatched *Date with the Angels* to replace the faltering musical variety series *The Ray Anthony Show* on ABC. The powers that be at Plymouth launched *Date with the Angels* May 3, 1957, on Fridays from 10 to 10:30 p.m.

Joining as part of the deal was the newly dubbed Tom Kennedy. He had to change his name from Jim Narz in 1957 to stand out from his brother, Jack Narz, previously the announcer on *Life with Elizabeth*. "I made the call because there was an awful lot of confusion in the television audience, in the home audience, between my brother and I in our work, him being Jack Narz and me being Jim Narz. We didn't think we looked anything alike, but people actually confused us.

"So, I was about to sign with the Plymouth corporation as their spokesman and as the announcer on *Date with the Angels*. And so, the Plymouth people asked me if I wouldn't mind changing my name because Jack, my brother, was associated with the Ford Motor Company, doing commercials for them. So, anyway, I said, 'As a matter of fact, my brother and I have been considering this for some time.' So, the answer was yes. I went out to lunch with the agency people for Plymouth, and we sat and kicked around some new names and came up with Tom Kennedy."

Despite his title as announcer, Kennedy never saw Betty except when he visited her set at Desilu Studios. "The commercials that I did were done at ABC's lot down on Prospect and Talmadge," he said. So were his promos during the end titles of the show.

Nonetheless, Kennedy received billing on the series along with the personnel. "In those days, you got credit because they actually had a single sponsor for a whole show," he said. "So, you were part of the family, so to speak."

Entranced by the potential of *Date with the Angels*, Plymouth executives signed a contract to produce fifty-six episodes and eighteen weeks of repeats through October 1958, with an option to extend the deal to seven years. The company got the series in 137 TV markets, an impressive amount given the fewer number of affiliates ABC had compared to NBC and CBS in 1957.

Clouding these visions of success for Betty and crew was an edict from the sponsor to drop the series' fantasy element. The lead characters—Vickie and Gus, short for

Victoria and August respectively—could keep the Angel surname, but otherwise the show would be earthbound. The ominous development helped make *Date with the Angels* look more like hell than heaven.

The Angels Become the Bland Ricardos

Despite last-minute changes, the debut of *Date with the Angels* had the fantasy element of Vicki imagining how she would redo her approach at a fancy party to impress a rich client of Gus's. An unimpressed *Broadcasting* magazine reviewer wrote, "If the first show is a criterion, it tends too often to lapse into hackneyed lines and situations. Miss White handles her lines well, but often when a raised eye or puzzled expression should evoke a satisfactory chuckle, there is a disconcerting wave of audience roars."

The first twelve episodes of *Date with the Angels* often confirmed the cited tendencies. Helping George Tibbles write scripts were Bill Kelsay and Fran Van Hartesveldt, the latter being the same producer of *The Great Gildersleeve* on radio who helped Betty get her union card. The trio frequently lacked good lines for a revolving door of supporting characters. Among those popping up to join Vickie and Gus Angel were three married couples alone—George Clemson (Roy Engel) and Wilma Clemson (Natalie Masters), Carl Cates (George Neise) and Dolly Cates (Nancy Kulp), and Bert "Murph" Murphy (Richard Reeves) and Cassie Murphy (Maudie Prickett). The Murphys were the Angels' neighbors as were stuffy Roger Finley (Richard Deacon) and his father, Mr. Sidney Finley (Burt Mustin).

All got involved in various times and fashions with Vickie's well-meaning plans that produced complications and usually ended with Gus comforting her. To many observers, the setup reminded them of Lucy and Ricky Ricardo on *I Love Lucy*, only Lucille Ball and Desi Arnaz appeared more affectionate on screen than Betty and Bill Williams ever did on *Date with the Angels*. (Betty and Bill rarely kissed on the lips, for example.)

The plots often were trite and inane. Wilma Clemson's obstetrician pretended to be a general practitioner to treat Gus's illness. Vickie's mistaken belief the city was going to cut down a beloved tree led to her neighbors creating protest petitions to the city with crazy rumors attached. Gus and Vickie tried to mediate a feud between the Murphys and the Finleys.

The worst episode was probably "Chip Off the Old Block," which aired July 26, 1957. Macho Murph was disgusted that his son, Emmett Michael "Mike" Murphy (Paul Savage), was a flautist in the Navy. Gus and Vickie tried to smooth over the conflict. Eventually the couple devolved into arguing over the situation and other issues. Then two MPs arrived to arrest Mike for starting a brawl with the Marines when he docked at Long Beach, which amused Bert. "This is a day to remember," he laughed at the Angels. "You two kids are at each other's throat, and they drag my boy off to the brig! That's what I call a happy ending!" Before the episode was finished, Vickie said she never felt better in her whole life, capping off an unbelievable script.

Two good shows did emerge in this period. "The Wheel" on May 31, 1957, had Jimmy Boyd, Betty's former regular on *Hollywood on Television* in 1952, as Wheeler, her older sister's son visiting from Biloxi, Mississippi. Vickie set up Wheeler on a date with Joyce Bennett (Doreen McCann), the daughter of Gus's prospective client, Charlie Bennett (Hugh Sanders), and his wife Thelma (Paula Winslowe). Gus fretted at how clumsy and odd Wheeler was, but Joyce had a marvelous time with Wheeler, and his efforts helped convince Charlie to buy an insurance policy from Gus. Boyd had real comic presence, and the series might have survived longer if Gus and Vickie adopted him as their surrogate son.

Additionally, "Shall We Dance?" on June 21, 1957, provided a hilarious set piece with Roger Finley. Rehearsing interpretive dance for his psychology department's scientific portion of a charity show for a community boys club, Roger forced Vickie, Wilma Clemson and the Murphys to join his presentation. Roger then led very elaborate and amusing choreography for depicting a chain reaction using the participants. The dance included his father Mr. Finley dressed as an atom with balloons around his waist depicting electrons in a satisfyingly wacky entry.

When *Date with the Angels* ended its first season on August 2, 1957, Betty hoped the next episodes would fare better. Part of this belief came from ABC and Plymouth moving the series up a half hour in July to follow an anticipated new hit, *The Frank Sinatra Show*. Unfortunately, several scripts only made *Date with the Angels* appear even more like an *I Love Lucy* rip-off.

In "Everybody's Baby" on September 20, 1957, Wilma Clemson's childbirth had similar overtones of when Lucy had her baby in 1953, but with a sluggish pace. "The Train" on January 8, 1958 had the Angels arguing with the Cates on a locomotive ride which was much less funny and entertaining than the one the Ricardos took on the

1955 *I Love Lucy* episode "The Great Train Robbery." (For what it's worth, the episode revealed Vickie's maiden name was Morgan.)

Most glaring of all, "Star Struck" on October 25, 1957, had Vickie meeting Liberace and Hugh O'Brian at the Brown Derby while Gus and dinner companions, the Clemsons, missed both and didn't believe her. Any relation to when Lucy Ricardo spotted William Holden at the Brown Derby and made an idiot of herself on *I Love Lucy* in 1955 seemed purely intentional.

(Incidentally, Betty paid tribute to the show's inspiration in 1987 by hosting *We Love Lucy*, the title of two two-hour syndicated specials, each containing three episodes of the sequel to *I Love Lucy*. *The Lucille Ball-Desi Arnaz Show* was a series of thirteen hourlong specials that aired on CBS between the end of *I Love Lucy* in 1957 and the divorce of Lucy and Desi in 1960. The first *We Love Lucy* appeared in the spring of 1987 hosted by Lucille Ball's daughter Lucie Arnaz and actress Ann Jillian along with Betty. By June 1987, Betty hosted a follow-up solo.)

A few second season episodes escaped comparisons with *I Love Lucy* and worked well. "Return of the Wheel" on September 6, 1957, had Vickie's nephew Wheeler in a cute love triangle. His gum-chewing, plain girlfriend Laurie Olson (Sheila James) vied for his attention against Vickie's friend, glamorous blonde Jane Welles (Maureen Cassidy). Laurie won out while Betty was able to let loose more than usual and get laughs for mocking Jane and Wheeler at various points. "Wheeler at the Cabin" on January 1, 1958, was also enjoyable in watching Vickie's nephew unintentionally offend and make amends with mountain natives during a family retreat.

In "Catered Party" on September 27, 1957, Vickie and Gus relied on Mr. Finley and others to pretend to help at their Hawaiian luau designed to impress snooty guests. The mishaps flowed naturally and frequently. "Diane" on November 1, 1957, sparkled with Betty up against Cara Williams as Gus's old high school girlfriend Diane coming to dinner. "I want you to pretend I'm not even here," Vickie said. "Wonderful!" responded Diane. Gus lavished attention on Diane until he told her to go home for thinking she was still in high school in a fun outing.

Also, "Double Trouble" on January 15, 1958, offered Betty in a dual role. At a hotel resort, Stacey L. Stacey (Chuck Connors) was a rich but rough Texan obsessed with jaded resident lounge singer Honey Mitchell, a dead ringer for Vickie. When the Angels arrived at the hotel, guests and workers were appalled as they confused Vickie and Honey before they realized the truth and Gus and Vickie were never the wiser. Betty was great in both parts, naturally.

Still, ridiculous scenes predominated. "The Gorilla" on September 13, 1957, had Gus play a prank with a man in an ape suit. Vickie was unable to wake Wilma despite yelling directly into her ears in "The Burglar" on November 22, 1957. Wilma and Gus made stupid excuses to hide a birthday present from Vickie in "The Surprise" on December 6, 1957. Roger Finley was so intent on performing a psychological profile on Murph's dog Francis that he failed to realize his father had left home in "Francis Goes to School" on January 22, 1958. Collectively, the bits conveyed disrespect for the dwindling viewers of *Date with the Angels*.

Ending the Bad Date

If the results on air for *Date with the Angels* were mixed, backstage the turmoil was worse. The expected strong lead-in of *The Frank Sinatra Show* never occurred, as that series disappointed many viewers. Initial ratings showed the competition for *Date with the Angels*, *The Thin Man* on NBC and *Schlitz Playhouse of Stars* on CBS, had much bigger audiences.

Meanwhile, Bill Williams' constant complaints to network and sponsor executives irked those officials. For her part, Betty recognized the chemistry and comic timing she had with Del Moore on *Life With Elizabeth* was sorely missing with Williams.

Betty assessed the situation simply in her book *Here We Go Again*: "I think I can honestly say that that was the only time I have ever wanted to get out of a show."

Nevertheless, she remained a team player. To salvage the series' prospects, Betty made promotional efforts for Plymouth in the fall of 1957 when not filming *Date with the Angels*, visiting dealers and local media in eighteen cities. The tour didn't help the ratings. Betty then met with Plymouth leaders to see how they could salvage their contract, as there was no way the company would sponsor fifty-six more planned episodes of *Date with the Angels*.

In December 1957, news came that *Date with the Angels* would move to Wednesdays from 9:30 to 10 p.m. for five episodes starting New Year's Day. Its replacement would be *The Betty White Show*, a live comedy variety installment without Bill Williams, who rarely did comedies after *Date with the Angels* and got increasingly smaller parts before retiring in 1981 and dying in 1992.) The last episode of *Date with the Angels* on January 29, 1958 had the ironic title of "What an Opportunity."

Beside the new show, Betty also had time in 1958 to enjoy a genre in which she had already dabbled. It's time to take a look at an area where Betty had much more success in the long term, her work on game shows.

Chapter Four
Betty The Game Show Goddess Part I

As part of her activities on *Password* the week of July 23-27, 1962, Betty posed with her competing celebrity Jim Backus amid a backdrop of words as host Allen Ludden stood between them. Although Betty supposedly was checking out the passwords along with Backus, the direction of her eyes makes one wonder if she was more interested in looking at Ludden, who would become her husband less than a year later. Courtesy of the Adam Nedeff Collection.

While Betty's visit to New York City in 1954 failed to keep her series *The Betty White Show* and *Life with Elizabeth* in production, another appointment was more fruitful. She met with representatives of the Mark Goodson-Bill Todman game show production company about participating in their shows. Goodson-Todman, as it was commonly known, was the leader in nighttime network TV game shows using celebrities as guests.

"I was invited to be a panelist on *What's My Line?* And that started a whole pattern. That really started the game show pattern," Betty told her then agent Tony Fantozzi, interviewing her in 1997 for the Archive of American Television. She first replaced regular panelist Arlene Francis for two consecutive weeks in 1955.

Goodson also suggested Betty audition to host a new game show, *Make the Connection*. Sexist objections prevented her from securing the position, but Goodson picked her as a regular panelist.

Make the Connection ran only three months but led to four decades of Betty working for Goodson-Todman as a guest and regular. She appeared on most shows from the game show empire, which at times had more than ten shows in production.

Goodson-Todman director Mike Gargiulo said Betty was among "about fifty celebrities who had structurally strong names as game players" used for testing new concepts at Goodson-Todman. "And there was about eight or nine of us who were in the committee to come up with new ideas," he added. "What we would do is Mark Goodson would call a night, and usually it was when his girlfriends were out of town. Then we would have a meeting, it would usually average about once a month … From seven o'clock to three in the morning, we would play games. We would try something out and then, when we tried it out, we would do it again and then try one different part of it and do it again." The exhaustive process kept Goodson-Todman ahead of competitors.

However, Betty never signed an exclusivity contract, so other game show producers also booked Betty. As most network game shows aired from New York City through the 1960s, Betty would usually line up a spot on one when she visited *The Tonight Show* with Jack Paar. She became indelibly identified with the genre as a result.

This emphasis was a risk for Betty. Doing a game show was not held in esteem by certain members of show business and could backfire on an aspiring talent like herself.

"Once you do a game show, you kind of kill your career a little bit," said Wil

Shriner, who did *Just Men!* and *Wordplay* with Betty in the 1980s before hosting two game shows. "Once the buyers, the producers, the show biz community, sees you in a certain light, they don't see you in another light."

But Betty was more than happy to play games for money. She even made the field a family profession, and not just by marrying *Password* host Allen Ludden in 1963.

Until she died in 1985, Betty's mother Tess usually attended game shows tapings in Los Angeles when her daughter appeared. (Betty's father Horace died in 1963.) As Shelley Herman recalled when she wrote for *Liars Club* from 1977 to 1979, "I didn't have anything to do once the show was up and going, so I would sit with Tess, and there was usually somebody like Betty's assistant slash caregiver for Tess that was there. Tess wasn't ever seated by herself. I would sit out in the audience with them, and I had commented once to Tess how beautiful she looked.

"And it seems that, I'm not sure for every show, but at least for *Liars Club*, Betty and she would go to the Elizabeth Arden salon. And they would both get their hair done. And they would both get their nails done. And then they would come to the studio. So, they would have the same hairdo and the same nail polish. And I just thought, 'How lovely to have that kind of a relationship with your mother.' Not only that you would want to be kind of twins that way, but to be able to do that for your mother, to make her feel pretty and special, too."

Betty's work in game shows was so extensive that studying her achievements requires two chapters. This survey covers only national game show appearances, so no listings for, say, Betty's turns from 1968 to 1971 on *Lucky Pair*, which aired only in Los Angeles. Revivals of shows that aired after 1972 appear in this chapter for convenience except for *Password* and *Match Game* because of Betty's considerable impact on those series and vice versa.

Entries are chronological based on when Betty debuted, with the premiere and finale dates when Betty appeared in parentheses after the title. Where known, the exact dates of Betty's visits follow. For dates where she played against one celebrity, that person is listed in parentheses.

Betty probably did more than these game shows. For example, on *Hollywood Squares* in 2003, she claimed to have done *Celebrity Bowling*, but no record of it could be found. Only confirmed show appearances have been listed, which are still a staggering amount. Betty was busy, indeed.

What's My Line? (February 2, 1950–September 3, 1967; 1968–1975)
June 19, 1955; June 26, 1955; March 13, 1960; March 5, 1961; June 23, 1963; September 5, 1965; December 12, 1965; August 28, 1966; September 18, 1969; May 31–June 4, 1970; November 23, 1972

First seen on CBS Sunday nights, *What's My Line?* had four celebrities interrogate guests with yes-or-no questions to determine their professions. The quartet wore blindfolds to determine a Mystery Guest celebrity, as well. Though she didn't guess any right, Betty's game show debut on June 19, 1955 went well. Regular panelist Bennett Cerf complimented her appearance, and she got some applause for a clever quip referencing an early round of the game.

At the end, host John Daly said, "Betty, it's been real nice having you with us" and noted Betty would be back the following week. In that appearance, Cerf said Betty and regular panelist Dorothy Kilgallen had sung a duet backstage. If only there had been a recording of that!

Betty returned to *What's My Line?* to replace Kilgallen in 1960. A year later, Betty replaced Arlene Francis, and when learning a female truck driver only worked with people and not animals, she joked, "Mrs. MacDonald doesn't have a farm then, in other words." She nailed Genevieve as the Mystery Guest after Cerf ascertained that she was a regular on Jack Paar's show and Dorothy Kilgallen and fellow guest panelist Art Linkletter gave incorrect guesses.

Two years later, Betty and her husband, Allen Ludden, were the Mystery Guests. When guest panelist Martin Gabel asked, "Have you a regular television show?" simultaneously Allen said yes and Betty said no. Arlene Francis, Martin's wife, then identified the duo. Daly asked the newlyweds after the reveal, "And you're going to both do something together this summer, aren't you?" "Why, yes!" grinned Betty as John grimaced at his unintentional double entendre.

Allen and Betty returned as Mystery Guests in 1965, and Betty employed a Hungarian accent. When guest panelist Robert Q. Lewis asked if they were married, Betty cracked, "Most of the time." More laughs came when Arlene asked, "Do you do what you do together?"

Three months after that, fellow guest panelist Tony Randall introduced Betty as "the crown princess of television games." She made her last appearance a year before the series ended on CBS along with Ludden, their only joint time on the panel for *What's My Line?*

What's My Line? had a syndicated daily revival from 1968 to 1975. There, Betty was a panelist for a week in 1970 and showed up twice as the Mystery Guest in 1969 and 1972.

Make the Connection (July 7, 1955–September 29, 1955)
Regular panelist
Goodson-Todman employees spent more than 2,400 man hours on this game show from its conception to debut. Twenty-three women and twenty-four men underwent interviews for game playing ability, compatibility and balance in appearance, personality, and intelligence. The top ten candidates played more than 200 games concocted by the staff before the finalists were chosen. The end result, airing on NBC Thursday nights, was a lot of effort for little payback.

Jim McKay became host of *Make the Connection* after Betty missed the opportunity. He beat twenty other men considered as the emcee. Billed as "the star of *Life with Elizabeth*," Betty sat on a panel with deejay Gene Klavan and thespians Gloria DeHaven and Eddie Bracken. Their mission was to determine the relationship between two different subjects on stage by asking yes-or-no questions, with only a cryptic clue to help them.

For example, told that a man taught three girls an unspecified talent, Betty's questions included, "Is it something that you use when you're out on a date?" The girls jokingly agreed. The truth was they learned judo. For a child who gave her teacher the measles, Betty elicited laughs with saying, "You were the only one to have the nerve to do it?" She also got laughs asking a group of four expectant fathers helped by a woman, "Do you share the same kind of hobby?"

Best of all, for a policeman had given his wife a ticket, Betty learned that neither enjoyed what happened between them. "Well, if nobody enjoyed it, what did you do it for?!" she exclaimed.

A bell rang to end each panelist's queries, with guests earning $25 for each time they fooled a panelist and $150 for stumping all four. The third round usually involved a guest celebrity's connection. On the August 11, 1955 show, Betty correctly determined that songwriter Hoagy Carmichael appeared with the owner of the piano on which Hoagy composed "Stardust."

Gene Rayburn replaced McKay as host on August 4, 1955, with no explanation. Apart from Betty, generally the inquisitions on *Make the Connection* were tedious, and little chemistry occurred between panelists and the hosts. Betty would wait three years until she did another Goodson-Todman game show, *To Tell the Truth*.

To Tell the Truth (December 18, 1956–September 6, 1968; 1969–1978; September 3, 1990–May 31, 1991; June 14, 2016–present)

June 10, 1958–August 31, 1964 (forty-four times); April 20–24, 1964 (daytime); August 15–19, 1966 (daytime); spring 1974; September 24–28, 1990; November 26–30, 1990; February 4–8, 1991; regular in 2016

To Tell the Truth had three people appear on stage, but only one was really who he or she claimed. Sometimes the contenders were of different genders to add to the confusion. The host read aloud an affidavit before the four celebrities, who then grilled each of the trio roughly forty-five seconds apiece before guessing individually who was not lying. The real contestant then stood up and the other two bluffers revealed their true identities.

In her first guest shot, Betty replaced regular panelist Polly Bergen for three consecutive weeks. Betty returned for a two-week stint six months later starting December 23, 1958, where she got laughs asking a contestant what "depredations" are. She returned three weeks later and was the only one to identify the U.S. Mint superintendent.

On February 3, 1959, Betty again replaced Bergen, this time for seven weeks. During her tenure, Tom Poston replaced Hy Gardner as a regular panelist on February 17, 1959.

"Hy Gardner never really had any chemistry with anybody," asserted game show historian Steve Beverly. Gardner's two-year contract was up at the time. "Tom Poston was auditioned for a one-month contract, and they liked him so well that he stayed."

On Betty's visit on March 10, 1959, she began interrogating a circus performer and two imposters with "Number two, your mother and father were aerialists, and you were born in a wagon. You're lucky." The remark cracked up her fellow panelists and generated applause.

An emergency operation for Bergen led to Betty replacing her on May 5 and 12, 1959. Host Bud Collyer noted Betty flew into New York City the morning of May 5 to make the taping. Betty disqualified herself on the last round on May 12, as she had worked with caricaturist Gordon Curry on her Los Angeles TV series in the early 1950s. After his reveal, Curry said he would have captured Betty's "glorious personality" if he drew her and added, "I remember the fun we had when we appeared together in Hollywood."

Betty returned to the show on December 5, 1960, temporarily replacing Bergen while Johnny Carson made his series debut substituting for Poston. For three consecutive weeks beginning December 26, 1960, Betty appeared along with regulars Kitty Carlisle and Don Ameche. She had another extended run from March 27–May 1, 1961, this time replacing Carlisle.

"Kitty left the show because Moss Hart [her husband] was going to Hollywood," said Beverly. "He was going to be a screenwriter instead of a playwright. She left to go, and it was kind of odd, because they were flying Betty in to do the show from L.A., because she still lived there."

Betty's best moment in this period was on May 1, 1961. She reviewed the contenders for having rescued President John F. Kennedy when he was stranded on a Pacific island during World War II. Before questioning, Betty quipped, "Whichever one of you it is, you'll be happy to know when you do meet him, he has a good job now. He's working steady." She earned applause for that remark as well as when guest host Merv Griffin complimented her work on the panel.

Starting September 18, 1961, Betty did *To Tell the Truth* thirteen times over nine months. All but the last episode on June 25, 1962, paired her with Carson. Ironically, Griffin, Carson's future talk show rival, appeared on Betty's last go-round in this period. Betty guessed correctly in all three games for the first time on the November 20, 1961 show. Also, on her show with Griffin, a contestant claiming to be a former Miss America pageant winner pronounced the name of the contest's host Bert Parks with a deep Southern drawl. Following that, Betty cracked, "First of all, I think number three should be disqualified. We're not allowed to use a foreign language on this program," prompting laughter and applause and even a "Bravo!" from Griffin.

"Betty, nice to have you back with us, you've been away too long," Collyer said to Betty on November 19, 1962. On the first game involving a pilot for animals, she got guffaws for saying, "But I go for [contestant] three, because I know that they do transport fish in bags. And vice versa." When Betty returned on July 8, 1963 along with her new husband Allen Ludden, Collyer asked her how long she had been married. "Three weeks, three days, four hours and twenty minutes," Betty said. "Forty minutes," interjected Allen. Reviewing one contestant pretending to be a hypnotist,

Betty pleaded comically to Allen, "I look into his eyes, I get a funny feeling. I'm sorry, honey!" He feigned exasperation in reaction.

Two weeks later, Betty reappeared without Allen. When guest panelist Robert Q. Lewis said he had to disqualify himself for accidentally meeting beforehand an imposter posing as an exotic dancer instructor, Betty joked, "This is an old graduate on my right." Three months later on September 23, 1963, Betty tried to determine a real quarterback by asking one contestant, "Where were the goal posts in the All-Star game?" "At the end of the field," he said to laughter. "Nobody likes a bunch of smart alecks!" joked Betty as she added, "Were they behind the goal line or at the goal line?"

Betty last appeared on the nighttime *To Tell the Truth* in 1964 on April 4 and August 31. She was on the daytime version at least twice, in 1964 and in 1966. That version began on CBS June 18, 1962.

Steve Beverly said the daytime edition occurred primarily for economic reasons. "It was going to be one of the cheapest shows except for paying celebrities on television. The other thing, it fit well in doing the twenty-five-minute format, because that was when Douglas Edwards was doing a five-minute newscast. So, they could do two games rather than three in daytime with the added commercial breaks, and it fit very well into the twenty-five-minute slot rather than going the full half hour." The show used a different panel in daytime at first to distinguish itself, but by 1965, Poston, Carlisle, Peggy Cass and Orson Bean were daytime and nighttime regulars. *To Tell the Truth* ended in nighttime on May 22, 1967 and in daytime on September 6, 1968.

To Tell the Truth reappeared in syndication in 1969, hosted by Garry Moore. Bill Cullen joined Cass, Carlisle and Bean as regular panelists. Bean left in 1970, but the rest stayed until Joe Garagiola replaced Garry Moore as host in 1977. Betty appeared as a guest panelist at least once.

Other revivals appeared through 2002, but Betty did only the 1990–1991 NBC morning one. She appeared under a different host each time, first Gordon Elliott, then Lynn Swann, and finally Alex Trebek. Trebek's tenure began the same week Betty made her last visit in this incarnation.

To Tell the Truth returned in 2016 in nighttime hour episodes on ABC, louder, racier and dumber than ever. Host and co-executive producer Anthony Anderson said on its debut, "I've been a big fan of *To Tell the Truth* since I was a kid, and when we were deciding to bring this show back, I knew that there was one person I wanted to be on this show. And it is the lovely and talented Miss Betty White. (applause) She's appeared on this show more than fifty times over fifty years of *To Tell the Truth* and no one has played this game better."

Betty, fellow regulars Nene Leakes and Jalen Rose, and a guest panelist attempted to discern such imposters as which of three men dated singer Taylor Swift in high school. "Number Three, did you know her mom?" asked Betty. "Yes," he said. "How well?" asked Betty to laughter. In later shows, Betty and crew had to identify the right drag queen plasticware vendor; the maker of bras for big breasted women; an inventor of a bullet-resistant athletic supporter, which all three contestants had to wear; and an instructor who taught Channing Tatum how to strip. The latter bumped and grinded for the audience, which reflected the series' lowbrow standard.

This *To Tell the Truth* included snide comments and questions to contestants from Anderson and his mother, Doris Day Bowman. "Mama" or "Mama Doris" was TV's most opinionated scorekeeper. Combined with live music onstage from Cheche Alara and His Band of Liars and choppy editing of players asking questions, the show was a noisy, lumpy game to watch.

Betty was fairly accurate in guessing amid this forced fun. This success mattered because each show's losing celebrity had to tweet a lie on his or her Twitter account for a day without any denial. Betty avoided this fate until her sixth and last show. She had to tweet, "Nothing better than sharing a drink with a fan. If you see me out at the club, just tell the bartender to put it on my tab."

The audience clearly loved Betty, chanting "Bet-ty! Bet-ty!" at various points when she identified the correct competitive eater, led the panel in scoring, and told guest panelist Mike Tyson to shut up. "She'd probably kick his ass," Anderson added on that show.

Betty also landed a few amusing remarks. To a pretender claiming he held the record for longest tongue, she asked, "What are you doing after the show?" A man who supposedly crushed coconuts with his elbows led her to react with "Number Two, why do you do this?"

She had a rapport with panelist Jalen Rose. Told of a husband who was thirty-two years younger than the wife, he said, "Age shouldn't be a barrier" and held Betty's hands. She rubbed his hands back. Rose helped Betty out of her seat at the end of each show, as her mobility was limited.

The ABC *To Tell the Truth* aired with Betty through July 12, 2016. The show reappeared every summer without her thereafter through 2020. Her absence was probably wise on Betty's part.

I've Got a Secret (June 19, 1952–April 3, 1967; 1972–1973)
July 23, 1958; August 13, 1958; September 24, 1958; October 31, 1972; January 16, 1973

I've Got a Secret took the Goodson-Todman format for *What's My Line?* and emphasized more fun and laughs, as four celebrities had to discover what unusual event or activity involved each contestant. Its director in the 1960s, Mike Gargiulo, credited producer Chester Feldman and host Garry Moore as key to its success. Feldman determined when the buzzer would go off to end a celebrity's questioning period, based often on how much humor the discussion generated.

"He had a full staff of people just flushing out a secret," said Gargiulo. "And Garry Moore was very good at what he did. He was very good at laying out a spot. In other words, when you did a spot, you knew what you were going to do, and there was a beginning, a middle, and ending. And Garry Moore was excellent in setting up the secret, explaining the secret, doing the secret, and then paying off the secret. It was like every week we were writing a play. It was not phony."

Betty, whom Moore comically called "Twinkle Toes," replaced Jayne Meadows three times in 1958. Following questioning by regular panelists Betsy Palmer and Bill Cullen, Betty correctly guessed on just her second game that a female contestant had built her own home.

On September 24, 1958, guest Art Linkletter introduced three people, each of whom guessed the amount of money on each panelist. "Is this all you have with you?" an astonished Art asked Betty. She took a glance down her gown and then nodded yes to audience hysteria. Betty had only three dollars.

Besides Palmer and Cullen, the other regular with Betty in 1958 was Henry Morgan. "When he was a sweetheart, he was really great, but he could turn on a dime," said Gargiulo. "He wasn't mean or ornery or anything like that, but he also was not a 'neighborhood guy.'"

When *I've Got a Secret* returned with Steve Allen as host in 1972, Betty popped up, too, joining Alan Alda and semiregulars Pat Carroll and Richard Dawson. One secret was Milton Berle bringing jokes from his files for the panelists to read. Betty's gag was "A woman called up the police department and said, 'I have a sex maniac in my apartment. Pick him up in the morning!'" Animal lover Betty also enjoyed quizzing a man who ran a computerized dog dating service.

Betty's 1973 shot on *I've Got a Secret* placed her alongside Dawson again, plus Henry Morgan and Anita Gillette. She had an amusing spot trying to guess the connection between three men named Ex, Wye, and Zee. The trio stumped the panel. In the celebrity spot, Marty Allen changed hairpieces while the panel was blindfolded. The final spot had panelists guess what substance a contestant used to make jewelry (it was bread) in a boring bit.

Overall, this *I've Got a Secret* was a poor attempt to mimic the 1970s version of *What's My Line?* "It just didn't jell," production manager Andrew J. Selig said of the failure of the 1972–1973 *I've Got a Secret*. He disliked Steve Allen, who had hosted the CBS nighttime version from 1964 to 1967 after Moore left. "He wasn't much fun to work with. I don't think he understood the premise of the show." Selig's other headache was executives at the production studio, Los Angeles TV station KTTV, who dismissed some plans of showing the secrets on stage as unfeasible. The series had revivals in 1976, 2000–2001, and 2006, each without Betty.

Keep Talking (August 26, 1958–May 3, 1960)
July 1, 1959
Two celebrity trios, two male and one female, competed in this humorous outing. Each member of one trio spoke for a minute telling a story involving a topic and a secret phrase. When they all finished, the other team guessed what the phrase was and who said it. The setup encouraged participants to ad-lib wildly to disguise the phrase in their monologues. The loose atmosphere and players made the series a breezy half hour. *Keep Talking* earned an Emmy nomination for Best Panel, Quiz or Audience Participation Series in 1959, losing to *What's My Line?*

Monty Hall was host and Joey Bishop, Danny Dayton, Paul Winchell, and Ilka Chase were regulars when *Keep Talking* began. After six shows, Carl Reiner took over as host and Maury Amsterdam and Pat Carroll joined the show. On December 21, 1958, Peggy Cass replaced Chase. For Betty's guest shot, she and Nina Foch substituted for Carroll and Cass. The producer of *Keep Talking*, Herb Wolf, subsequently invited Betty to guest on his other game show, *Masquerade Party*, a month later.

Betty was in the second-to-last episode hosted by Reiner. On July 22, 1959, Vincent Price took over hosting *Keep Talking* for four weeks, followed by Merv Griffin.

The show ended its run on CBS September 23, 1959, after unimpressive ratings. *Keep Talking* switched to ABC on September 29, 1959, with Orson Bean replacing Joey Bishop as a regular. Tanking opposite *The Garry Moore Show* on CBS, *Keep Talking* stopped chattering less than seven months later.

Masquerade Party (July 14, 1952–September 23, 1960; 1974–1975)
August 6, 1959 (guest panelist); October 6, 1974 (mystery guest)
Masquerade Party was a long-running imitation of *What's My Line?* Its twist was to have celebrities appear in makeup and costumes for four panelists to guess who they were. The outfits served as a clue, like Ethel Merman disguised as a gas station attendant—"ethyl," get it?

Though it ran nearly a decade, *Masquerade Party* never was a hit. Part of the problem was the series was hard to follow as it ran in twelve different nighttime slots on NBC, CBS and ABC over eight years. Additionally, its seven regular emcees was a record for game shows until John O'Hurley became the eighth host of *To Tell the Truth* in 2000. Betty visited *Masquerade Party* when Bert Parks was the sixth host from 1958 to 1960, joining regulars Sam Levenson and Lee Bowman and guest panelist Dagmar.

During its syndicated revival in 1973, Betty returned to *Masquerade Party* as a mystery guest. with Richard Dawson as its final emcee. Executive producer Monty Hall revived the property because he wanted a game show to sell to stations for the early evening hours, according to game show historian Steve Beverly. "He was like a lot of these producers that were trying to get any property from the past, then maybe tweak it for the modern time," said Beverly. "He said that the problem with the show is that it was not well enough known to the younger audience." Other more successful game shows in syndication led *Masquerade Party* to be cancelled after one year.

Betty recalled on *The Pat Sajak Show* on February 27, 1989 that her elaborate disguise didn't fool at least one person. "*Masquerade Party*, they had me done up as an old, old man, whiskers, beard and a big, big pot like this [gestured to her belly] and a derby and a gray wig," she said. "And I walked down the hall at NBC and somebody said, 'Hi Betty!'"

Password (October 2, 1961–September 15, 1967)
October 16–21, 1961 (Don Ameche); January 29–February 2, 1962 (Barry Nelson); July 23–27, 1962 (Jim Backus); November 26–30, 1962 (Henry Morgan); February

17, 1963 (Shelley Berman); June 24, 1963 (Jack Paar); October 14–18, 1963 (all-star week with Allen Ludden, Jane Wyatt and Richard Boone); October 28–November 1, 1963 (Milt Kamen); December 30, 1963–January 3, 1964 (Allen Ludden); May 28, 1964 (Paul Anka); August 24–28, 1964 (Robert Reed); November 30–December 4, 1964 (Roddy McDowall); February 22–26, 1965 (Tom Poston); May 20, 1965 (Arlene Francis); July 26–30, 1965 (Wally Cox); October 25–29, 1965 (Frank Gifford); January 3–7, 1966 (Frank Gifford); March 21–25, 1966 (Frank Gifford); May 30–June 3, 1966 (Roddy McDowall); August 1–5, 1966 (Barry Nelson); January 9–13, 1967 (Ross Martin); March 5, 1967 (Frank Gifford); April 3–7, 1967 (George Grizzard); June 12–16, 1967 (Frank Gifford); September 11–15, 1967 (Frank Gifford)

Password came to CBS daytime after several duds followed when *Beat the Clock* moved to ABC after a year on CBS in the fall of 1958. The series unable to hold the audience between *As the World Turns* and *Art Linkletter's House Party* for more than six months were in order *The Jimmy Dean Show, For Better or Worse, Full Circle,* and *Face the Facts.* But *Password* was an immediate hit, surpassing *As the World Turns* as daytime's top program just eight weeks after its launch. In the process, *Password* revolutionized game shows and even gained Betty a husband.

For the first time on a game show, two pairs of a celebrity and a non-celebrity partner competed on *Password.* A member of each pair received a word in a wallet and gave one word as a clue to his or her partner. A correct answer netted the duo ten points. An incorrect one let a partner on the other team give another word to win nine points. The back and forth continued down to one point if needed.

The first team to twenty-five points played the Lightning Round. The celebrity had a minute to convey five words to his or her partner to win $250. Teams switched partners after that round for another game and Lightning Round, then both celebrities got new players.

The concept behind *Password* was deceptively simple. Although players could change vocal intonations to stress parts of a word, they could not use body language. Some common phrases seemed like one word when they were not, such as "hot dog." And homonyms were a constant danger. When one contestant gave "peers" as a clue for "equal" to Betty, on June 13, 1967, she thought he meant the word's definition of looking and responded with "peeks."

Hosting *Password* was genial Allen Ludden, who also was the intellectual, bespectacled emcee of *General Electric College Bowl* on CBS Sundays from 1959 to

1963. While he delivered rapid-fire questions on that show, Ludden took a more leisurely and engaging approach on *Password*.

As part of the Goodson-Todman stable of reliable celebrity players, Betty played *Password* its third week on the air. Ludden's wife, the former Margaret McGloin, was sick with cancer at that time and died two weeks later on October 30, 1961. When Betty returned to *Password* three months later, Allen was unsure about how he had treated her initially due to his preoccupation with Margaret's condition, so he talked with Betty some prior to taping. After that discussion, Allen told *Password* creator and executive producer Bob Stewart he planned to marry Betty.

Allen's pursuit of Betty was going strong when she did her first nighttime *Password* on February 17, 1963. The nighttime version debuted on CBS January 2, 1962. He used her nickname, Bets, and when he learned her second partner was a psychiatrist, he joked, "Betty, you should do very well!" "What does he mean by that?" she said in response. Still, their romance was low key.

Password director Mike Gargiulo had no idea of the blossoming courtship. "Allen Ludden was very quiet and reserved and dignified and standoffish, and Betty White was the total opposite of that," he said. "I mean, really?! The thing was a total surprise."

After Betty wed Allen on June 14, 1963, she joined him to play on the nighttime *Password* ten days later. "You gave her a nice ring. That's lovely," Betty's opponent Jack Paar told Allen before the start of the third game. As Allen thanked him, Jack interjected, "Were you on *The Price is Right*?" And when he learned one of Betty's partners was a theological candidate, Jack cracked, "Sneaky way to pay off the minister, isn't it, having him on!" to applause and laughter.

But it was Betty who stood out to many *Password* fans. She held the record among female celebrities for fastest time in the lightning round by 1964. Betty was a determined game player, too. On June 13, 1967, she spent thirty seconds giving nine clues to get her partner to say "marshmallow" during the lightning round. Allen himself complimented Betty for cleverly using "Jiminy" as a clue for "cricket" in the lightning round on September 13, 1967.

At the same time, she maintained her trademark sense of humor. "I'm not pregnant, to answer all your letters," she said at the outset of the May 28, 1964 nighttime edition. When Allen said he had to throw a word out of play on May 20, 1965, Betty chucked her wallet into the back of the set, as well. As the audience laughed, a nonplussed Allen said, "Gotta live with her." And in the second lightning round on September 13, 1967, she amused everyone by reacting with "Ah! Oh, there you are now!" to seeing "martini," indicating her fondness for the drink.

"What used to drive Allen Ludden crazy is that he was great for taking closeups after you said something humorous or whatever, and then he'd give you that closeup look, and everybody would laugh. She would do the same thing by raising an eyebrow," said Gargiulo. "So, she had an understated sense of humor."

Sometimes, others got the better of Betty on *Password*. On April 6, 1967, she broke up as announcer Jack Clark introduced her as "Allen Ludden's gin rummy nemesis." After Betty said on June 14, 1967, "I'll do anything to win," Allen shot back, "Even marry the emcee, huh?"

Password aired live and later on tape from New York City. From 1963 to 1967, Betty and Allen made thirty-nine round trips to and from Hollywood. "About three times, four times a year, we did a bunch of shows in LA," recalled director Mike Gargiulo. "We did four weeks of shows in a little less than two weeks and then go back to New York. We would fly out the table, because the table and the backstage of the table was the most important part of the staging of that show."

Gargiulo said this unusual procedure came directly from Mark Goodson, as did another change. "He wasn't interested in how much it would cost. So at one point, we built a second table just for use on the West Coast! To save shipping back and forth. Money meant nothing to him."

Betty was not on *Password* when its acknowledged top player, Lew Retrum, made his debut on April 18, 1967. "I had been watching as a kid in high school in 1961, when it first started broadcasting," he said. "Of course, it was in the daytime, so I didn't see it except in the summer. But we used to get together, friends of mine, and watch it. You know, cover our ears, cover the password. I was a big fan, so when I found out I could get on, I did that in 1967."

Described as a Princeton history major, Retrum was down 16–0 after the first two words until he and Connie Stevens roared back to win. She failed to convey "pine" to him in the Lightning Round to keep him from winning the maximum. Paired with Dick Shawn the next day, Retrum won that Lightning Round for a total of $650. He would return in the 1970s—as would *Password*.

Password went off CBS nighttime on May 22, 1967 and daytime on September 15, 1967. The latter cancellation was shocking, as *Password* was the second-highest rated daytime game show. Oddly, neither ABC nor NBC executives chose to add this solid performer to their schedules.

Instead, the show's last daytime season went into reruns in syndication and became a hit. Gargiulo credited Bill Todman, "the perennial dealmaker," with the novel idea. Its success encouraged Goodson-Todman to produce new shows to sell to local TV stations and later revive *Password*.

Play Your Hunch (June 30, 1958–September 27, 1963)
July 31, 1962 (daytime)
Play Your Hunch went through three networks—CBS its first six months, ABC its next five and then NBC when revived seven months after its ABC run ended—and four emcees. The series ran on NBC nighttime the summers of 1960 and 1962, too, all for a game director Mike Gargiulo described as "a takeoff on *To Tell the Truth*." Contestants asked questions to determine which of three people performing activities, each designated as "X," "Y," and "Z," was real. A celebrity appeared in one spot who was connected in some way to a subject to add to the supposed fun.

"We had a staff of about nine people to make up 'hunches,'" Gargiulo recalled. Original host Merv Griffin left the series a few months after Betty did her spot on the series. While Gargiulo found him delightful, "I would not say that he was structurally as adherent to the format. If he felt it was getting a laugh, he would play with something." The series ended a year after Griffin left and became the longest-running Goodson-Todman game show never to be revived.

Your First Impression (January 2, 1962–June 26, 1964)
September 24–28, 1962; December 24, 1962–January 11, 1963 (three consecutive weeks); April 8–26, 1963 (three consecutive weeks); June 10–21, 1963 (two consecutive weeks); September 30–October 4, 1963; January 6–17, 1964 (two consecutive weeks)

Your First Impression was a knockoff of *To Tell the Truth* and *What's My Line?* from Monty Hall-Art Stark Productions. Three celebrities quizzed a celebrity guest for information about a family member or friend, with leading statements for the guest to complete. Three contenders then appeared for the panel to give the same treatment and determine who was the correct relative or pal. The lines the panelists read were scripted, but the players' answers were not.

For example, Betty asked Dennis Day, "One thing my daughter hates to do is …" and he replied, "Study." When he left and three girls appeared, Betty said to one, "The thing I like best about my dad is …" and got the response, "He's funny." The panelist then revealed their choices without consultation and their reasons why, just as was done on *To Tell the Truth*. For the Dennis Day spot, Betty voted for a girl who said her father loved to kiss her mother. "And with eight children, I think that's a dead giveaway," she said to laughter. Betty guessed incorrectly.

In a second game, a mystery celebrity was in a soundproof room behind the panelists. They saw pictures of five possibilities and heard a filtered version of the guest's voice for each response. After one round of questioning, the studio audience learned the guest's identity followed by another round of questioning and then the panelists' picks. Betty correctly guessed Marty Ingels in one episode based on him saying he wanted to be a dentist and she remembered him talking about teeth a lot on *The Tonight Show*. Host Bill Leyden typically interviewed the guest briefly afterward before the show ended.

With only two games played per show and a lack of spontaneity during the inquisitions, *Your First Impression* moved rather slowly. NBC stuck with *Your First Impression* for two-and-a-half years despite ratings always lower than its CBS competition, the soap opera *Love of Life*. Game show historian Steve Beverly said part of the reason was that NBC officials wanted to placate the show's co-owner, Art Stark, who also produced *The Tonight Show Starring Johnny Carson*.

"Also, the other factor was NBC quite frankly just was going up against at that time a tremendous, almost unbeatable, soap opera lineup at noon," Beverly said. "And they just felt like they had nothing else that was in development that would have done better than *Your First Impression* did."

Betty played *Your First Impression* at least twelve weeks, more than any other daytime game show except *Password*, *Match Game* and *You Don't Say*. Even so, it's one of her lesser credits.

Missing Links (September 9, 1963–December 25, 1964)
November 11–15, 1963
Three celebrities attempted to fill in the blanks of a true story being told by a guest. If correct, they won money for a member of the studio audience. This Goodson-Todman effort ran the first six months on NBC with Ed McMahon as host and then nine

months on ABC with Dick Clark as host. Joining Betty during her sole week on the show were Robert Q. Lewis and Henry Morgan.

"It worked, but it wasn't structurally strong enough," said Mike Gargiulo, who directed *Missing Links* on NBC. "*Password* was foolproof. It's a good show. *To Tell the Truth* is a solid format. You have to say when playing the game, 'Who cares?' It was interesting, but not that interesting."

The Match Game (December 31, 1962–September 26, 1969)
January 28–February 1, 1963 (Darren McGavin); August 5–9, 1963 (Sam Levenson); September 2–6, 1963 (Rod Serling); November 18–21, 1963 (Shelley Berman); January 20–24, 1964 (all-star week); February 17–21, 1964 (Don Murray); April 27–May 1, 1964 (Pernell Roberts); June 15–19, 1964 (Pat O'Brien); August 3–7, 1964 (Pat O'Brien); September 14–18, 1964 (Jack E. Leonard); December 14–18, 1964 (Orson Bean); February 8–12, 1965 (Sidney Chaplin); April 19–23, 1965 (Gale Gordon); August 2–6, 1965 (Henry Morgan); December 6–10, 1965 (Ray Bolger); March 28–April 1, 1966 (Lloyd Bridges); June 27–July 1, 1966 (John Forsythe); November 28–December 2, 1966 (Alan King); December 26–30, 1966 (Roger Smith); March 13–17, 1967 (Robert Q. Lewis); July 24–28, 1967 (Sandy Baron); September 25–29, 1967 (Sheldon Leonard); November 27–December 1, 1967 (Allen Ludden); April 8–12, 1968 (George Hamilton); September 22–26, 1969 (Brian Keith)

When Robert Noah joined Goodson-Todman in 1962, he promptly helped to develop a game show classic. "Three of us sat down and met—Frank Wayne, Jean Kopelman and me," he said. "We were just pitching all kinds of wild notions, and Frank said, 'Okay, name something that weighs more than ten pounds.' So Jean wrote down, I think, 'An elephant.' And I wrote 'A bowling ball.' Well, Frank laughed. I guess there was something really funny about that. And we went on for about an hour or so and then went up to see Mark Goodson. He loved it, because he saw it as an opportunity to do a polling thing as the end game."

Noah added that the original plan was to have one contestant play against each other in matching answers. "Mark and Bob Stewart separately came up with the idea of a six-people panel with two contestants, and the other idea we came up was to make the questions a little stronger and sexier."

Writing many of those questions was Dick DeBartolo, a *Mad Magazine* contributor who was prolific in creating material for *The Match Game*. "He is a brilliantly funny guy," said Noah.

"Bob Noah, who was the executive producer, just as a joke, he would call me in and he'd say, 'Do the egg file,'" said DeBartolo. "And I'd say, 'Okay. Name something you do with an egg. Name an animal that lays an egg. Name an animal that doesn't lay an egg. Egg and BLANK. Name a sandwich you can make with an egg. Something you serve with an egg.'"

Answering these queries were two competing trios, each with a celebrity captain. After host Gene Rayburn read a question, players wrote down their answers and held up their hands to indicate they had finished. If two of the trio wrote the same answer, that team won twenty-five dollars. If all three team members matched, that team won fifty dollars. The first team to win $125 played the audience match, where three questions were asked of audience members and the team won fifty dollars every time they guessed the most popular answer.

Betty was a frequent celebrity contestant on *The Match Game*, including playing an all-star match in January 1964 with Peggy Cass and Joan Fontaine against Bennett Cerf, Robert Q. Lewis and Henry Morgan on behalf of the Girl Scouts of America and the Boy Scouts of America respectively. Questions included "Name something people do to show their disapproval of a performance," "To a rich man, BLANK dollars is nothing." and "Duke BLANK." For the latter, Betty wrote "of Windsor," Peggy "Ellington" and Joan "Wayne," resulting in no points.

DeBartolo also attended tapings of the show where a dicey situation came up unintentionally for him with Betty. "My Betty White story was, she was a lot of fun. We had a lot of laughs in the makeup room. So one day, *Mad* and NBC were just a block apart, and I was over at *Mad*. And I had just written my first *Mad* paperback book, and I took a bunch of them and I took them back to the studio. And I said, 'Hey Betty, I'm so excited. My first paperback book came out, and is it okay if I sign one to you?' And she said, 'Oh, that'd be great!' I did and didn't think about it anymore.

"And then on the show, Gene said, 'So Betty, what's new with you?' And Betty White said, 'Well, nothing's new with me, Gene, but guess what? Dick DeBartolo, who writes the questions, has a brand new book!' And she plugged the book and showed it. Well, this is back in the days of standards and practices, and after the show was over, on my headset [producer] Jean Kopelman said, 'Dick, you have to go down to standards and practices. They're really upset that Betty plugged your book.' I said, 'What?!'

"So, I went down, and they had an affidavit. 'Did you pay her? Did you tell her that she should do this?' I said, 'No! She's been on the show a lot, and we just clown around. And I thought she would enjoy a complimentary copy of my book, and no money changed hands.' 'And you gave her the book?' 'Yes!' 'All right. Well, we have to type all this up and you have to sign it.' So they typed it up and I signed it, and that was the end of that."

Never a hit, *The Match Game* nonetheless ran seven years on NBC. In 1973, the show returned in a newer, wilder version, and Betty was ready to go along for the ride.

You Don't Say! (April 1, 1963–September 26, 1969; July 14, 1975–November 26, 1975)

April 1–5, 1963 (Barry Sullivan); May 2–6, 1966 (Harvey Lembeck); October 24–28, 1966 (Bill Bixby); February 6–10, 1967 (Barry Sullivan); May 8–12, 1967 (Paul Lynde); October 30–November 3, 1967 (Allen Ludden); April 29–May 3, 1968 (Vincent Price); October 28–November 1, 1968 (Lorne Greene); March 10–14, 1969 (Mike Connors); July 28–August 1, 1969 (Charles Nelson Reilly); August 18–22, 1969 (Charles Nelson Reilly); four other times 1963–1969; July 21–25, 1975; July 28-August 1, 1975; August 11-15, 1975; November 3-7, 1975

Two pairs, each with a celebrity, competed on *You Don't Say!* The object was to get the partner to identify the name of a famous person, living, dead, or fictional, by conveying a word that sounds but is not spelled like any part of the name. Later, the game added places. Players made up a sentence and left off the last word as a clue, "the word that you don't say." The sentence could not refer to the person or place. To help their partners, players could indicate where to add syllables. Partners had five seconds to make guesses. Four turns occurred for each subject.

For example, during the debut week, Barry Sullivan received the name of singer Fabian. He tried to get his partner to say "fable" and failed. For her turn, Betty cleared her throat and said, "All right, ummm, if I have already gone to a place and someone invites me to go there and I say, 'No, I have already ____ .'" The contestant incorrectly guessed "gone," when she wanted him to say "been." Such miscommunication provided a good deal of humor to *You Don't Say!*

Correctly identifying the subject won a team one point. The first team to three points played the bonus board. The noncelebrity contestant picked one of three hidden clues to be revealed and had to guess the mystery person or place on the clues. A correct first guess won the contestant $300, $200 for the second and $100 for the third. Contestants could play until they lost two games.

Game show packager Mark Goodson vociferously claimed this offering from Ralph Andrews-Bill Yagemann Productions was a rip-off of Goodson-Todman's hit *Password*, recalled host Tom Kennedy. "He was very unhappy about it. The fact that it got on the air made him unhappy, and then we became a hit, he was livid. At one point, he sent out a memo to his bookers, 'Don't you ever hire a star who appears on *You Don't Say!* Don't ever book them on *Password*.'

"Well, that didn't sit too well with people such as Pat Carroll. She said, 'Mr. Goodson, bless you. I've enjoyed working on your shows. But don't ever try to tell me what shows I can and cannot do based upon what you think is a similarity.' And that was the end of that. She was the first one to speak up on it. Then others joined in and he quickly withdrew his edict. But that's how strongly he felt."

Andrews and Yagemann created *You Don't Say!* on KTLA in Los Angeles starting November 25, 1962, with Jack Barry as host. "But they decided they wanted to look at other people, as well, if they went network," said Kennedy. "They were looking for every possibility they could find.

"And so, they brought on, I think, just about everybody in town. One week at a time, they would bring various up-and-coming emcees, such as myself. And we'd go over to KTLA and do the show over one week and send the best of those shows to NBC and let them look at it. I was one of them, and NBC chose me, so that's how I got the show."

Debuting April Fools' Day, 1963, *You Don't Say!* was no joke, and neither was its debut female guest. "Betty was there to help kick us off, and I'm forever indebted to her for it. You can't get kicked off any better than that," said Kennedy. Ironically, *Password* host Allen Ludden was there, too. "Allen would come over and stand in the wings and wave and scream at Betty."

Betty returned often before NBC axed *You Don't Say!* despite being the network's highest-rated daytime game show. "To tell you how much I was caught off guard, I had just bought a new home and was having a new child at the same time," Kennedy said. "And all of a sudden, we were cancelled by a new, 'sweep-it-clean' vice president at NBC. He swept us right off the mat. In fact, he also swept NBC off the map." NBC sank to third in daytime for more than a year.

In 1975 ABC brought back *You Don't Say!* This time two players picked among a four-celebrity panel to give them clues. Airing 4-4:30 p.m. daily, not all ABC stations carried this version, which hurt the ratings and led to a quick cancellation despite four appearances by Betty.

You Don't Say! reappeared with the four-celebrity format in syndication in 1978 with Jim Peck as host. Betty didn't appear in this version, which ran a year.

The Price is Right (November 26, 1956–September 3, 1965; September 4, 1972–present)
February 14, 1964 (nighttime); July 12–16, 1965 (daytime); September 14, 1988 (daytime)

Debuting on NBC weekday mornings, *The Price is Right* was an instant smash. Developed for Goodson-Todman by Bob Stewart—he also created *To Tell the Truth* and *Password* for the company—the game show had four contestants perform a modified auction on various expensive prizes introduced by host Bill Cullen. The object was to estimate closest to the actual retail value of each item up for bid without going over after at least three rounds of bidding.

NBC added a nighttime edition from September 23, 1957–September 6, 1963. Thinking the series still had potential in prime time, Goodson-Todman moved *The Price is Right* to ABC in September 1963 for daily and nighttime installments. The series added celebrities to the mix of contestants in the nighttime version to boost ratings, one of whom was Betty in 1964.

"You've never done our show before, have you?" asked Bill Cullen. "No I haven't, except at home. And I'm very bad," she smiled and nodded.

Betty played for four studio audience members whose names she randomly picked from a bowl. During her first bid, the audience yelled "Freeze!" for her bid of $1,300 on outdoor furniture. Betty retorted, "Will you butt out?! I'm not asking you!" then sweetly said with a smile, "I freeze." She lost that game and the second one but, when she had the winning bid on the third game, Allen Ludden came out to surprise her with a kiss.

Betty's appearance was fun. However, *The Price is Right* ended in nighttime shortly thereafter on September 11, 1964. *The Price is Right* went off ABC daytime a year later.

In the fall of 1972, Goodson-Todman brought back *The Price is Right* in a daytime edition on CBS hosted by Bob Barker. Four players bid on a prize as before, only this time the winner played a different pricing game on stage. The top winners played in the Showcase Showdown for a bonanza of prizes they could claim if they were closest to the retail price without going over.

The Price is Right expanded to an hour on August 18, 1975. Three players in each half of the show spun "The Big Wheel" containing spots from five cents to one dollar. The player who came closest to or exactly tallied one dollar after two spins became one of the two playing in the Showcase Showdown. Installed permanently on CBS daily from 11 a.m. to noon on April 23, 1979, *The Price is Right* became the top daytime network game show for forty-plus years.

"What made it so easy was Barker," said production manager Andrew J. Selig of the production. "Barker was unbelievable. I mean, we would figure an hour to let him learn a new game, and he would have it down in twenty minutes."

Betty returned to the show in 1988, during the "Hole in One" game. She came on stage amid screams from the audience. "You look wonderful!" Barker exclaimed. "Well, I'm such a jock!" she joked. "They told me that you're the club champion up at Carmel," he added. "Yes, but not at golf necessarily," she joshed. "I assume so," he chuckled.

Betty pretended to line up her shot, then when she missed, she innocently asked, "It's supposed to go in?" Despite two tries, the contestant was too far away to win. Bob said everyone will be watching *The Golden Girls* as Betty departed.

Coincidentally, Betty intersected with the series one more time on an episode of her series *The Golden Palace*. In "A New Leash on Life," airing April 2, 1993, Sophia missed the chance to be in the audience for *The Price is Right*. She watched the show with Rose and Blanche and regretted not being there as announcer Rod Roddy called out her name and she was the first contestant not to come down to play with Bob Barker. It was a humorous storyline using Roddy and Barker's voices. Barker would stay with *The Price is Right* until retiring in 2007.

Get the Message (March 30, 1964–December 25, 1964)
March 30, 1964–April 3, 1964; June 1–5, 1964; August 31–September 4, 1964; September 21–25, 1964; October 26–30, 1964

"Mark Goodson, several years ago, was kind enough to think of me for a show called *Get the Message* and oh, I wanted that job so much," Betty recalled in 1975 on "The Great American Game Show," an *ABC Wide World of Entertainment* late-night special. "And I did several run-throughs, and it didn't work." As *Get the Message* ran only nine months, Betty didn't miss much.

"*Get the Message* was, I'm sorry to say, my idea," said executive producer Robert Noah. "It didn't work. That's all there is to it. It was too much like *Password* when we started. I didn't even realize how much like *Password* it was until we started to do it."

Two teams, each with two celebrities and one noncelebrity partner, competed in conveying a mystery phrase, slogan, name, expression, or book title. Each celebrity team member saw the hidden item and wrote one-word clues for their noncelebrity partners. An incorrect guess let the other contestant see what his or her celebrity partners wrote in addition to the previous clues. A miss by both teams allowed the celebrities to write another different one-word clue.

Obviously, the celebrities wanted to write down separate words from their partners to help them win. For example, when Betty teamed with Julia Meade to play against Bennett Cerf and Marty Ingels in June 1964, Betty wrote "president" and Julia wrote "Grover." Putting the two clues together, their partner correctly guessed the answer was "Cleveland."

The first team to win three points won $100 and played a game where the celebrities said clues aloud rather than written, with only one turn for each of three messages. Each correct answer won $50. Frank Buxton was host until Robert Q. Lewis took over on September 28, 1964.

Goodson attempted to modify the format using six celebrities in a pilot for NBC in 1986 entitled *Oddball*. The property failed to sell, so Goodson got the message and dropped it.

What's This Song? (October 26, 1964–September 24, 1965)/**Win with the Stars** (1968–1969)
January 25–29, 1965 (Morey Amsterdam); August 30–September 3, 1965 (Mel Torme); October 16, 1968 (Stubby Kaye); May 28, 1969 (Forrest Tucker)

With host Wink Martindale behind on a podium between two competing celebrity-civilian pairs who sang clues to win money, *What's This Song?* was a cross between *Password* and *Name That Tune*. In fact, the concept behind the series predated those game shows, as *What's the Name of That Song?* started on Seattle radio in the 1930s. In 1948, *What's the Name of That Song?* aired on TV on KTSL in Los Angeles and remained a local favorite into the 1950s.

Revived on KTLA in February 1964 as *What's This Song?*, NBC added the show to its morning lineup and billed the host as "Win" Martindale. Like *Jeopardy*, *What's This Song?* subtracted points with wrong answers. The show ran only a year opposite *I Love Lucy* reruns on CBS.

A revamped version emerged in syndication three years later as *Win with the Stars* with Allen Ludden as host. Betty showed up twice as she had on the network version. This effort added a band on stage to play the musical clues, but it couldn't add viewers, too, and vanished quickly.

Call My Bluff (March 29, 1965–September 24, 1965)

August 9–13, 1965

On January 29, 1965, Betty taped a trial run-through of *Call My Bluff*. The effort sold and began running on NBC at noon weekdays two months later. The concept was another knockoff of *To Tell the Truth*. Two trios competed, with two celebrities on each team. One team received a word to define. Two of the three opposing members gave a wrong definition. Picking the right answer from the opposition won a point, and two points won a game.

"Bill Leyden was a very excellent host. He was much better than the show," director Mike Gargiulo recalled of *Call My Bluff*, which was another Goodson-Todman production.

"He was very good, but the show depended on material that's very hard to get," added executive producer Robert Noah. "Words and their definitions. Well, it sounds like it's going to be difficult, and it was. Just didn't work. And nobody cared. That's the worst part."

Betty was on an all-celebrity week with actresses Vivian Vance and Rita Moreno and actors Darryl Hickman, Gene Rayburn and Elliot Reid. By the time they appeared, the show already was a goner in the minds of NBC executives and would end after only six months.

Concentration (August 25, 1958–March 23, 1973)

December 24, 1965

NBC's longest-running daytime game show had two players compete to match two hidden prizes on a board of thirty squares. To claim the prizes, a player had to solve a rebus revealed underneath the matched squares. In a Christmas Eve edition, Betty and Bill Cullen played for charity, with each disguised as Santa Claus. They revealed themselves at the end, and Betty plugged her hosting the Tournament of Roses Parade on New Year's Day.

Chain Letter (July 4, 1966–October 14, 1966)
July 4–8, 1966 (Hans Conreid)
Despite overtones of *The Match Game* and *Password*, *Chain Letter* came from Stephen Hatos-Monty Hall Productions and not Goodson-Todman. Competing pairs of celebrity and noncelebrity contestants received a topic and had to give an answer associated with it. The twist was that the last letter of a correct answer from one pair had to be the first letter for the next answer from the other pair. An invalid answer within ten seconds won the round for the other team. The show's pilot was taped in 1964 before selling two years later for a short run.

Betty kicked off the premiere for *Chain Letter*. Oddly, Betty was on *The Match Game* three days before *Chain Letter* debuted and on *Password* four weeks after this appearance.

Snap Judgment (April 3, 1967–March 28, 1969)
April 10-14, 1967 (Glenn Ford); June 5–9, 1967 (Soupy Sales); January 15–19, 1968 (Charlie Robinson); June 3–7, 1968 (Jack Cassidy)
Another *Password* derivative, *Snap Judgment* had two pairs of celebrities and noncelebrities alternate playing a word identification game. While one member of the pair was offstage, the other player chose five words or phrases associated with one word. The offstage players returned to the set and had twenty seconds to guess all five words, winning $50 for each correct guess. If the player guessed the bonus word or phrase, the total amount won would double.

According to game show historian Steve Beverly, Goodson-Todman had cut a deal with host Ed McMahon, offering him first refusal to host one of their daytime game shows on NBC. After *Missing Links* failed in 1964, *Snap Judgment* was McMahon's next opportunity. Beverly said the series ran two unremarkable years because NBC executives were uncertain if any other shows would fare better opposite CBS's repeats of *I Love Lucy* and, by 1968, *The Lucy Show*.

On December 23, 1968, the series' format became the same as *Password*. "It was desperation," said Beverly. McMahon was no Allen Ludden, and *Snap Judgment* ended three months later.

Liars Club (January–August 1969; 1976–1978)
Regular panelist (1969); frequent panelist at least 32 times (1976–1978)
On the original *Liars Club*, a panel of four celebrities told different stories about an odd object and its purpose. Three celebrities lied in describing the item. The $100 prize went to one of two contestants who deduced the truth most often, with usually four items per show. Betty did every show along with host Rod Serling, who swore to viewers he never saw any of the doodads in advance. Running daily, *Liars Club* managed to break into the New York City market in June 1969, but it was not a hit nationally and ended production two months later.

"I was on the show once," said Anne Serling, Rod's daughter. "The panel was guessing who I was. I can tell you this: If you look at the clips of my dad doing the show, I think it's clear he really enjoyed it. That's a genuine laugh. He loved Betty White, too. He took our Irish Setter Michael on her animal show [*The Pet Set*]."

In 1974, Los Angeles TV station KTTV revived *Liars Club* on Saturday nights, and Betty was a guest. This weekly revival went into syndication in 1976, and Betty appeared several times. Then midway through the 1976–1977 season, *Liars Club* had a creative overhaul, including the removal of its host, Bill Armstrong. His replacement was Betty's husband, Allen Ludden.

Also joining the production staff during this changeover was Shelley Herman as a writer. "They would have these different guys, part of the research team, who would go out to antique stores, look in catalogs, whatever it was," she said. "They would find the weird gadgets, and we would all sit in a room. Larry Hovis was producing then and he'd say, 'Okay, what is this?' And we'd sit around the room and just kind of spitball ideas and come up with silly stories about things. And that's how we came up with the stories for the celebrities to tell on the show.

"When it came time to brief the celebrities, we would go into their dressing rooms with them ahead of time before the show. And Larry would say, 'Okay, this is a Tibetan prayer wheel' or something. And it would be up to him and us to be with him going, 'Yeah, yeah, that's what it is!' We'd have to convince the celebrity of what it was and the story they were telling, too. That's how they would tell their stories to the guests that were there. And then they'd have to guess what it was. And then of course Allen Ludden was always left out of the loop of anything, because they would be afraid that he would tip off and go, 'Well, I know what it is!'"

Herman added there was a method in determining which celebrity was honest each round. "It was very deliberate, especially with somebody who was a good game player like Betty. All of them thought they were telling the right story. We would never say, 'Listen, this really isn't it, but you've got to sell it hard for the people.' But because Betty was so good as an actress and so believable, sometimes we would definitely give her something that was the hardest thing to describe, because we knew she could do it well. And like *The Hollywood Squares*, you tried to give someone an object that was in their wheelhouse to make it all the more convincing."

Although the product descriptions were scripted, celebrities did ad-lib funny asides. For example, when Buddy Hackett described a device as a "ball washer" and said that English balls are smaller, director Bill Rainbolt wisely did a two-shot with Betty nodding a deadpan approval.

In 1976, four players competed starting with $200. They could bet up to half their total every round except the final one, where any wager could occur. During each round, a player who solely guessed correctly doubled the amount he or she had bet. Payout odds were one to one the first round, two to one the second, five to one the third and ten to one the fourth.

The rules changed when Ludden became host so that three players started with $100. Doubling winnings any round no longer occurred, but spotting the right celebrity all four times won a player a bonus prize in addition to the money earned. Also, Ludden usually spent up to three minutes interviewing celebrities and contestants before playing the game.

The panelists sat in a distinctive set design by John C. Mula where stained-glass window panels, typically seen in pubs, appeared in the background. As producer and regular panelist, Larry Hovis sat on the far right seat, while Betty's position alternated as needed. Joining them included some friends of Betty and Allen's, including Burt Reynolds and David Letterman, who the Luddens encouraged to move from Indiana to try to make it as a comedian in Hollywood.

"I know that sometimes the celebrities on *Liars Club* were on there because Larry would book the show, and people would call to say they needed their health insurance for SAG or AFTRA," said Herman about the unions that required members to work a minimum number of hours each year to retain their insurance. "So, even though there might be somebody who's kind of a quirky person on the show, he would give them a week or two so they could get their health insurance."

The second *Liars Club* ran until 1979. Betty didn't participate in a 1989–1990 version taped in Canada. Other pilots for *Liars Club* popped up but failed to sell.

"I know they've tried doing it a few times since then," said Herman. "I've actually worked on a couple of versions. They knew I'd worked on the old version and called me in. And everybody thinks that they can reinvent the wheel. Just be a simple show. Don't try to conk it up with your own way of making it faster or better or hipper. It is like a parlor game. Just leave it at that."

It Takes Two (March 31, 1969–July 31, 1970)
July 28–August 1, 1969
Three pairs of celebrities, usually husband and wife, came up with their own numeric estimated answers to a question, such as how many barbers there are per American males. After revealing the average number for each couple, a studio audience member from an NBC affiliate made a guess via phone. Naturally, Allen Ludden appeared with Betty during her sole guest shot.

The future host of *It's Your Bet*, Dick Gautier, appeared on the show as a guest with his wife, actress Barbara Stuart at left, opposite Betty and Allen Ludden in February 1970. Tom Kennedy replaced original host Hal March, who died a few weeks earlier. Notice that host Tom Kennedy has his hand on his own phone, as do the players on theirs. Courtesy of the Adam Nedeff Collection.

Longtime Los Angeles Dodgers announcer Vin Scully hosted *It Takes Two*. Game show historian Steve Beverly attributed the run of this "celebrity takeoff of *The Newlywed Game*" to NBC executives' timidity. "They didn't have anything in development, so it managed to hang on for a year," he said. "And this is after *You Don't Say* became a big hit. They had a deal with [Ralph Andrews] to try to develop some more properties." Andrews also packaged *It's Your Bet*.

It's Your Bet (1969–1973)
October 13, 1969; February 9, 1970; January 3, 1972; May 8, 1972
Two celebrity couples competed on the syndicated *It's Your Bet* to win prizes for members of the studio audience. A divider went up between the couple at play as one spouse heard the question his or her partner would be asked. He or she bet up to 100 points on whether the spouse would answer correctly. If right, the couple earned the wager. The first couple to reach 300 points won.

It's Your Bet was based on *I'll Bet*, a game show on NBC daytime from March 29 through September 24, 1965. Betty and Allen Ludden appeared with each of its four hosts, the first time with Hal March, their second with Tom Kennedy, their third with Dick Gautier, and their last with Lyle Waggoner. Ironically, Kennedy's brother, Jack Narz, was host of *I'll Bet* in 1965.

"We taped it down in San Diego, which I enjoyed very much," recalled Kennedy. "But for me, it was sort of an interim show as far as I was concerned, until I got what I considered to be the next big show, or at least the next network show." By the time Betty's last program aired, he had that show and was hosting *Split Second* on ABC daily from March 20, 1972 through June 27, 1975.

He Said She Said (1969–1970)/**Tattletales** (February 18, 1974–March 31, 1978; 1977–1978)
November 23, 1969; April 13, 1970; March 25–29, 1974; May 13–17, 1974; August 13–17, 1974; October 14–18, 1974; February 9-13, 1976; January 31-February 4, 1977; September 19-23, 1977; November 20, 1977; January 9-13, 1978
On the syndicated *He Said She Said*, celebrity couples played for a prize for a different married couple in the audience. Four wives or husbands were on stage while their partners were in a soundproof room backstage. Host Joe Garagiola gave the spouses on stage a topic. The one who was the fastest to raise his or her hand would tell a personal

story related to that issue. That spouse also supplied a one- or two-word association which, hopefully, his or her partner would recognize. Joe then read the associated word or words to the backstage spouses via TV monitors, and the first spouse backstage to ring a button and give the correct explanation won twenty-five points. A wrong guess subtracted ten points. After two rounds, the spouses swapped positions.

Revived four years later on CBS daytime as *Tattletales*, the show originally was like *He Said She Said* except electronics replaced raised hands for players to make the word association. That process disappeared soon in favor of the offstage spouses hearing a question from host Bert Convy they had to answer and agree with their onstage spouses to win. On her first appearance on *Tattletales*, Bert asked Betty, "Do you believe that high school girls should be given the birth control pill if they ask for it?" "Oh, I think Allen would invariably say absolutely yes, if they ask for it, give it to them. And the pills too, yes," she said to audience applause and hysteria. Later in the same episode, Betty got more chuckles when she said, "We had our last, our tenth, not our last necessarily anniversary, although the jury's still out …"

This comic glimpse into marital life soon became a hit airing after *Match Game 74* on CBS 4-4:30 p.m. daily. As *Tattletales* alternated taping on the weekends with *Match Game 74*, many celebrities appeared on both shows. Often, they revealed how little they knew about each other. Betty and Allen spent one show with no matches. Dick DeBartolo, who served as creative consultant for the questions, said the same experience happened to other couples on the show.

"I used to think that was so funny, that the people you think would be locked together knew nothing about each other," he said.

The winners on *Tattletales* were studio audience members divided by sections where they sat. Each couple on stage represented a different colored section—red, "banana" (yellow) and blue. Whatever a couple won—say, $250—got split equally among audience members in the section represented by the duo. Production manager Andrew J. Selig said since tapings took place on Stage 41 at CBS Television City in Hollywood, its layout required relatively little setup. "All we had to do was just put up the banners to differentiate the three sections. It worked very well."

Audience members who attended didn't have to wait for their portion of the winnings either. "They got the checks right after the show. We had somebody from CBS there to use a check machine, and they got them right away," said Selig, noting that CBS executives came up with the system. "Otherwise they would've had to mail checks, and it would've been very cumbersome. This way, everything was right at the show."

Beat the Clock (1969–1974)
October 29, 1969; January 12, 1970; October 19, 1970
After airing on CBS nighttime March 23, 1950–February 16, 1958 and daytime September 16, 1957–January 27, 1961, with the first year on CBS and the rest on ABC, *Beat the Clock* returned in weekly syndication. A couple had to finish a stunt in a set amount of time, usually under a minute. Doing so before the clock ran out let a couple play for five dollars for each additional successful completion or fifty dollars for an especially challenging task. After a stunt, each of the two couples chose a letter in the show's title on the Cash Board. Host Jack Narz revealed how much money they earned behind that letter. Four letters hid twenty-five dollars, five hid fifty dollars, two hid $100, and one hid $200.

Betty turned up several times on a spot where a celebrity helped out one couple in a challenge and then did another stunt solo. For the latter, each couple bet for or against whether the star could complete the task in the allotted time.

Celebrities also participated in an "Either-Or" segment where three audience members joined the couples' spouses. The celebrity guessed what the majority chose from two possible answers to four questions, such as whether they preferred to drink coffee or tea. Each correct guess by the star won twenty-five dollars for both couples.

Gene Wood took over as host of *Beat the Clock* the last two years. Betty sat out the series revivals in 1979–1980, 2002–2003, and 2018.

Password (April 5, 1971–June 27, 1975)
August 16–21, 1971 (Johnny Mathis); January 10–14, 1972 (Ross Martin); August 28–September 1, 1972 (Tony Randall); January 15–19, 1973 (Rod Serling); April 9–13, 1973 (All-Star week, with Rod Serling, Carol Burnett and Elizabeth Montgomery); June 11–15, 1973 (Celebrity Charity Week, with Wayne Rogers as Betty's partner); September 24–28, 1973 (James Shigeta); November 26–30, 1973 (Greg Morris); March 11–15, 1974 (Joanna Barnes); June 24–28, 1974 (Joanna Barnes); July 15–26, 1974 (two weeks with Betty paired with Allen Ludden; Monty Hall guest host); September 16–20, 1974 (Greg Morris and Martin Milner versus Joanna Barnes and Betty White); September 23–27, 1974 (Allen Ludden; Monty

Hall guest host); January 27–31, 1975 (Password All Stars); February 17–21, 1975 (last week of Password All-Stars); March 10–14, 1975 (Vicki Lawrence); March 24–28, 1975 (guest host); June 27, 1975 (Kate Jackson and Sam Melville; Betty on finale)

Password returned to daytime TV due to ABC's declining fortunes in 1970. On March 25 that year, NBC debuted *Somerset* from 4-4:30 p.m., a spinoff of its top soap opera, *Another World*. The ratings of *Somerset* rose in the summer of 1970 while numbers declined for its ABC competition, *Dark Shadows*, and some ABC affiliates dropped *Dark Shadows* to run their own programming by September. ABC executives worried about losing the time slot permanently and thus a good amount of ad revenue from their daytime schedule. As *Password* was performing well in reruns syndicated to local TV stations for more than three years, the network suits asked for a revival of the property.

With Allen Ludden back as host, *Password* returned with a few new tricks. A pass or play option let the first person who received the word decide whether to force his or her opponent to go first. Passwords went down to five points before being thrown out. After the Lightning Round, a contestant could bet any or all winnings earned on whether he or she could convey one word within twenty seconds. Finally, players could play up to ten episodes. The changes worked. Within its first month, ratings for *Password* were five points ahead of what *Dark Shadows* had averaged previously.

Also returning on *Password* was a 1967 champ, Lew Retrum. "I decided I would make a little detour of the psychology grad schools, and I hitchhiked around the country. But I always had in mind—I remember calling my girlfriend at the time, saying, 'You know, I'm going to go to Los Angeles and win $10,000 on *Password*.' She said, 'Oh, yeah. Of course. Dream on.' So I ended up just practically with the last dollar in my pocket in Los Angeles."

Hitchhiking from Berkeley to Los Angeles, Retrum got on *Password*, taping shows Saturdays and Sundays. He won Saturday with Douglas Fairbanks Jr., and returned the next day with Jo Anne Worley opposite Tom Kennedy and his partner. Retrum lost when Worley gave the illegal clue of "Little Red Riding Hood" for "wolf." His shows aired June 26–30 and July 3–7, 1972.

"And so, I was knocked off the show, but I had just barely enough to qualify as the fourth highest money winner of the quarter," he said. *Password* had then implemented a quarterly tournament for its best-performing players to return. "As I said, I was out of money at that point, and I had to borrow money from [*Password* producer] Howard

Felsher to get to the next week. Luckily, it was the end of the quarter and they were going to do the quarterfinals the next week.

"So, I stayed in Los Angeles—I don't know what I planned to do if I lost—and the next week was the quarterfinals with George Peppard and Carolyn Jones." Winning there, Retrum got to return for the grand championship, taped on St. Patrick's Day in 1973 with Carol Burnett and Elizabeth Montgomery. He played opposite 1972 grand champion Martha Peukert.

"It was first to win seven games, and it came down to one game. It was six to six. I was playing with Carol Burnett." He said the word "lover" with a French accent, and Burnett correctly guessed "paramour." Retrum became the new grand champion of *Password*.

He returned with Montgomery June 11–15, 1973, to compete for charities against different celebrity pairs each day, including once with Betty and Wayne Rogers. The second week, Retrum was paired with Burnett. "We won every game. Nobody beat us. They were both fantastic players." Although the games were for charity, "I got to keep the money I won in the Lightning Rounds."

The week of April 22–26, 1974, Retrum successfully defended his grand champion title, again with Burnett and Montgomery as celebrity partners. By that time, he was receiving fan mail for his appearances on *Password*. As for Allen's wife, Retrum said, "I never really had a lot of contact with Betty. She was always in the audience. I remember her saying once, I came to see the quarterfinals at one point. By 1974, I had moved out here, and I remember her saying to her mother, 'Lew's come to check out the competition!'"

Betty was having her usual fun as occasional player and even substitute host on *Password* until ratings dropped precipitously in the fall of 1974. Having done reasonably well at noon Eastern since March 20, 1972, the competition of *The Young and the Restless* on CBS and *Jackpot* on NBC outdrew *Password* significantly and forced Goodson-Todman to make a drastic overhaul to stay on the air. The result, debuting November 18, 1974, was *Password All-Stars*, featuring only celebrity players and lots of gadgetry, gimmickry and noise—elements the series had avoided.

Password All-Stars displayed words on screen as if typed, with electronic sound effects indicating the display of each letter. Celebrities could play, pass, or try for double points on the first clue, but missing the latter meant the other team could get twenty points instead. A celebrity pair who won a round could get twenty more points if they each guessed the other's password within twenty seconds. Players switched partners after every round. Every point earned by a celebrity was credited to them individually.

Players with the most points during a week qualified for the Grand Master Tournament where $25,000 would go to his or her favorite charity. Betty qualified for the finale on February 21, 1975 along with Richard Dawson, Bill Bixby and Hal Linden. Dawson was the winner.

Retrum did *Password All-Stars* on February 3–7, 1975. "I didn't like it. You pressed a button, and an arrow shot up, a big red arrow. That's all I remember." Regular *Password* viewers hated the bells and whistles too, and *Password* reverted to its old format on February 24, 1975.

Actually, this *Password* had two celebrities like Betty and Vicki Lawrence opposite four, not two, contestants on stage. The contestants competed to be the first two to identify three passwords. A maximum of four clues were allowed for each password communicated between the celebrities and their partners. The Lightning Round now involved getting three words in thirty seconds, with twenty-five dollars for each identification and five dollars for every second left on the clock. The play, pass, or try for double points rule still existed and … well, this take was confusing and disappointing for viewers. ABC cancelled *Password*.

On June 27, 1975, Betty sat next to Allen onstage. He showed her a watch Mark Goodson gave to him as a farewell gift. "Can you believe he didn't have it engraved?" he joked. "That's why it says Mark Goodson on the back!" she jested in kind. But Betty got misty when Allen said, "I met this lady on this game fourteen years ago." He vowed *Password* would return.

Password did so in 1979, as did Betty on it. In the meantime, she occupied herself with a surprising development. By the end of 1975, in her fifties, Betty White became the hottest new guest on a TV variety series after flopping with her own show seventeen years earlier.

Carol Burnett sat left of Betty as they portrayed the surviving members of the Class of 1932 Waxahatchie University reunion on *The Carol Burnett Show*, which aired Dec. 11, 1976. Betty credited her three appearances on Carol's show for making her a hot property in the variety show genre in the late 1970s. Copyright CBS courtesy of Everett Collection.

Chapter Five
Betty, the Variety Star and Guest

Betty's work on *Hollywood on Television* and *The Al Jarvis Show* in the early 1950s had elements of variety shows, even though the former was more of a talk show and the latter more of a talent contest. Both series offered opportunities for Betty to sing, dance, do sketches, and interview guests. So, when talk centered on what programming should replace *Date with the Angels*, having Betty star in a variety series sounded reasonable to all parties.

Joining Betty would be some friends going back to *Life with Elizabeth*. Del Moore would play her husband again in sketches, joined by Don Fedderson as producer, George Tibbles as main writer and associate producer, and Frank DeVol as musical director and occasional performer.

Transferring from *Date with the Angels* would be Jimmy Boyd as a singer and comic support, and Tom Kennedy, who would do commercials again for the live show. Oh yes, *The Betty White Show* would air live from Hollywood to the East Coast Wednesdays 9:30-10 p.m. on ABC starting February 5, 1958. Alas, due to poor reviews and ratings, *The Betty White Show* would end in that slot less than three months later.

Themes and Schemes

The format behind every episode of *The Betty White Show* 1958 edition seemed rife with promise. Betty would introduce a blackout joke performed by members of her cast who, beside Moore and Boyd, include two top comic performers, full-figured, boisterous Reta Shaw and grinning, mustachioed Frank Nelson. Next, Betty would greet the audience and set up the show's theme for the night. From there, Johnny Jacobs would describe how Lydia Franklin (Betty) and her husband Willard Franklin (Del Moore) would face a complication related to that theme. The Franklins and the characters posed as if in freeze frame as Jacobs set up the scene before they commenced acting. After a musical number, another sketch relating to the episode's theme occurred before Betty said goodnight.

For example, "Jealousy" on April 9, 1958, began with Willard having some official papers left in his office. When his young secretary Ruthie (Sheila James) delivered the materials, Willard said of the papers, "It's quite a stack." "It certainly is!" Lydia interjected as she noticed Ruthie's figure. Lydia was placated when she learned Ruthie has a fiancé. Next, snooty movie star Laurie Brighton (Betty) was shooting a new film in rural Nebraska at the home of Ms. Peterson (Reta Shaw) and her son Sam (Jimmy Boyd). Studio head Frank Barnett (Frank Nelson) tried to smooth over Laurie's disdain for her surroundings. Due to misunderstandings, Sam thought Laurie loved him, so she told him Frank was her real love and swooned over the executive, much to Frank's confusion. Betty also sang a comic duet with Boyd.

Writing *The Betty White Show* with Tibbles were Si Rose and Seaman Jacobs, both with extensive comedy variety credits. Jacobs went back to *The Ed Wynn Show* in 1949, which won an Emmy for Best Live Show. Even so, their experience worked little magic into the new series.

"It was pretty apparent that the studio audience didn't think too much of *The Betty White Show*'s humor last Wednesday night," noted TV critic Bob Foster of the debut. "This was for everybody to see, for the director of the show had the poor sense to point the camera at the crowd at the end of each sequence—and it wasn't happy. After the first sequence, the cameras turned toward the audience to find them applauding ... on cue ... but there wasn't a smile on anybody's face."

Foster thought the show came off well despite the reactions, but assessed the sketches as falling short of their potential. He also believed the applause and laughter sounded coached. "If these little problems are worked out, *The Betty White Show* live might well make it," he concluded.

Unfortunately, *The Betty White Show* was hit or miss in subsequent episodes. To make matters worse, the series aired in the East and Midwest opposite *I've Got a*

Secret, a top ten hit in the 1957–1958 season. Seeing little potential for growth, the series ended on April 30, 1958.

That finale had the theme of "Vacation." Shaw played Willard's mother helping Lydia pack for a trip to Arizona until Willard changed vacation plans. The switch sparked an argument between husband and wife until Willard's colleague Frank (Frank Nelson) reversed his dates.

The other sketch had Betty as her recurring character Olga Novack, a cleaning lady with a goofy voice. Operators of a sporting goods store tried to impress Mr. Turnbull (Frank Nelson), but Olga kept getting in the way. This bit offered some good physical comedy from Betty as Olga cleaned a punching bag, parallel bars and a trampoline and got entangled by each device.

At the end, Betty told the audience, "Thank you so very much. I don't mean just from me, but from our whole cotton-picking group here. I did it again. I always swore I would never do it, and I did. I feel in love with each and every one of them. You start a new show and you say, 'Well, now, this is a business operation, and you're not going to get involved with all the personalities, you know? Boy, it's business!' We adore each other, and we don't care who knows it.

"As you've probably gathered by now, this is vacation time for all of us around here. In fact, we're all heading out in all sorts of different directions. And we're going to miss you very, very much while we're gone. And I sincerely hope you miss us a little bit, too. And don't forget, whatever you do while we're gone, to remember our fine, fine sponsor Plymouth." Then she and the cast sang the show's theme song to close the series.

The 1958 *Betty White Show* marked the last professional collaboration between Betty and producer Don Fedderson, who later had two hit sitcoms, *My Three Sons* (1960–1972) and *Family Affair* (1966–1971). Neither effort used Betty. Yet according to Yvonne Lime Fedderson, who was married to Don Fedderson from 1969 until his death in 1994, the two remained good friends.

"She's been a very dear friend of ours through the years," said Lime Fedderson. "I was not married to Don at the time he did the show, but I don't know if you know this, my friend and I started an organization for abused children many years ago, and she's one of our ambassadors. She's done a lot for us, and I just adore her. She's a wonderful human being."

Biding Betty's Time in Variety

An unfortunate byproduct of *The Betty White Show* was an apparent exile for Betty from the variety show genre for nearly two decades. Producers largely overlooked or forgot her talents, and she appeared only in rare exceptions.

Candid Camera was not the classical definition of a variety show, but the series did have several comic segments. The difference was the humor came from people unaware they were being filmed as part of a prank. On April 16, 1961, Betty played an undercover ticket seller at a theater showing the movie *The Misfits*. She made weird requests to customers, such as making a man pledge he would not tell the ending and having a woman promise to wear her shoes at all times.

Betty had a substantial role on *That's Life*, which was nominated for an Emmy as Outstanding Variety Series in the 1968–1969 season. Undeservedly running just one year, *That's Life* had Robert Morse and E.J. Peaker as newlyweds Robert Dickson and Gloria Quigley Dickson in a weekly musical comedy hour detailing the progress of their relationship.

In "Buying the House" on October 22, 1968, the Dicksons contacted a real estate owner named Honeywell, played by Paul Lynde. "That's my first name," he smarmily announced. "Guess you can't guess my last name. It's Rocccco, spelled with four C's. The third is silent!" After Robert and Gloria rejected several communities, Honeywell sang a song suggesting they buy a lot and build a new home. When Honeywell learned they couldn't afford their planned addition, he sang about how he hated people, while finding them a promising home.

In the next scene, Mrs. Adams (Betty) and her husband Frank Adams (Sid Caesar) showed their home of fifteen years to Robert and Gloria. The Adams had increasingly testy exchanges they tried to hide, as they desperately wanted to sell their property. As Mrs. Adams showed Gloria the laundry room, Frank pressed Robert on items like the plumbing. "I want you to have my pipes!" Frank exclaimed. Robert and Gloria's concerns about the house's looks and costs upset Frank. He told Robert to kick the fireplace to show how strong it was. The fireplace collapsed.

An enraged Frank threw them out while his wife implored to the couple, "Don't give up the enchanted castle!" But when Robert made an offer, Frank agreed immediately, in part because the Dicksons were the first potential buyers. Honeywell sold the home to the Dicksons who then sang about finding a place to live. Several hilarious lines delivered expertly by Lynde and comic bits by Sid overshadowed Betty's solid work in a limited role.

Betty's assignments vaguely related to variety remained slim the next seven years. She was a guest on three specials for the *ABC Wide World of Entertainment* late night series, "Phyllis Diller's 102nd Birthday Party" on May 15, 1974, "The Great American Game Show" on January 16, 1975 and "The Monty Hall Roast" on February 12, 1975.

Monty Hall cohosted "The Great American Game Show" with Betty, who joined Monty and Ralph Edwards, Art Linkletter, Bob Barker, and Mark Goodson for some banter and game playing. She pressed Goodson about the lack of women emcees. "Actually, I think it's coming," he said. "I think that it's not been done up to now—we have tried, as you know, a couple of times. There's been an enormous prejudice, and there are problems, as you know, with women being hosts, partly because the person in charge has got to be in charge without seeming—that sounds terrible—shrill ..."

For her part, Betty said, "The bottom line of the whole thing is I don't think—and I'm really going to get shaken by my sisters out there —I don't think women belong as emcees of game shows, for the very reason Mark mentioned. It's not that they can't do it, but the sound of that voice. An emcee has to talk a lot." Ironically, Betty would become the first solo female daytime game show emcee and get an Emmy for her work in 1983 on *Just Men!*

The mood was lighter on "The Monty Hall Roast," where Betty told Monty, "You've never looked better, which is kind of sad." She added, "Spending a night with Monty—let me rephrase that—spending time with Monty is really exciting. He doesn't always make it till nighttime but ..." Applause and laughter followed.

Of his game show *Let's Make a Deal*, Betty said, "It starts at 7:30 sharp, ends at 8 dull. It's the kind of show you have to watch over and over. You can't believe it the first time you see it. Who else in our business could become a millionaire and really be a giant star of our industry doing what he does? Almost any idiot could, Monty!"

Betty ended with "Getting back on Monty, getting back *to* Monty ... I've held him in something, I think it's been high esteem ... I haven't found a way to gift wrap a yawn." She got a round of applause at the end.

Glad to Have Time with Carol
Betty's involvement with variety shows got a huge boost when she guest starred on what many consider among the best in the genre, *The Carol Burnett Show* (1967–

1978). Visiting November 22, 1975, Betty stood out in the show's recurring sketch "The Family." She played Ellen Harper, the spoiled, bitchy sister of Carol's Eunice Higgins, who argued with her at the birthday party of their mother, played by Vicki Lawrence. Playing her nastiest character ever on TV, Betty's Ellen got to call Carol's Eunice a jackass twice and earned applause from the audience for her work.

Chris Korman, son of *The Carol Burnett Show* co-star Harvey Korman, said he believed this show was the first time his father worked professionally with Betty. "He just loved working with Betty," he said. "It was like Carol. These are professionals who came to play. There was no ego with Betty. Betty had a strong idea of what she wanted to do."

Betty returned to play Ellen on *The Carol Burnett Show* December 11, 1976 and March 5, 1978, as well as sing, dance, and portray other characters. All were top episodes. She and Allen Ludden waved goodbye to Carol on camera near the end of the finale, which aired on March 29, 1978.

Burnett alluded to Betty's work by reading a fake review on the 2012 special *Betty White's 90th Birthday: A Tribute to America's Golden Girl*. "'As another season of *The Carol Burnett Show* comes to a close, the highlight of the year was once again Carol Burnett's friend Betty White.'" Burnett grimaced, then continued. "'It's a real compliment to Carol that she doesn't seem to mind being upstaged time and time again by a superior and prettier actress.' Well, I wonder who wanted me to read that one!" Burnett then threw the "article" away to Betty's amusement.

A Bonanza for Betty

The Carol Burnett Show began a deluge of variety shows and specials using Betty during the mid to late 1970s. On *The Rich Little Show* on NBC February 23, 1976, Betty played Betty Ford to Little's Gerald Ford, who tried doing jokes from a comedy writer and bombed miserably. Betty scolded him with "You have to be very careful what you say on television." He responded, "Look who's talking!" When Little said, "Well, I'll admit, I'm not as funny as Alan King!" Betty answered, "You're not even as funny as Allen Ludden!" then gave a direct look into the camera.

Later, she hosted "Reduce-A-Rama Beauty Spa" and made statements undercut by Charlotte Rae holding signs in the background as commentary. When Betty boasted her spa helped people lose weight through a unique diet, Rae displayed the words "Dog food" and made a tongue sign.

At the finale, she said, "I'm Helen Dinah, and I used to be famous! Do you remember the big bands of the forties?!" She paused to silence, then continued with resignation. "Well, they had these big bands in the forties, and I used to sing with them!" She promoted an album called "623 Great Hits" where Little, Rae and Julie McWhirter imitated other singers. Betty also had this great line: "If you act right now, you'll get a bonus record of a brand new song written by Charlie Rich and Paul Anka. It's called 'Hey, Did You Happen to See Who's Having My Baby?'" At the end, Betty said she had the only copy of the album and implored some man to come see her to get the record—and more. *The Rich Little Show* ended five months later.

On *The Diahann Carroll Show*, the summer replacement series for *The Carol Burnett Show*, Betty did a couple of sketches on the August 21, 1976 installment on CBS. The segments were nothing special, as the emphasis was on Diahann Carroll singing solo and in musical numbers with guests Jim Nabors and George Benson. Similarly, Betty had little impact guest starring on the second show of *Cos*, a variety series aimed for children on ABC starring Bill Cosby. Her episode aired September 26, 1976, not long before the series died opposite *60 Minutes* on CBS

Betty made her only sketch appearance with Allen Ludden in *The Peter Marshall Variety Show*, seen in syndication on October 23, 1976. They played a couple married six years sitting at a bar where men made passes at Betty while Allen pledged his love. Betty and Ludden then talked to Peter about their "perfect marriage," before giving scripted answers to supposedly spontaneous questions from the audience and the host. When Marshall asked, "Can an extramarital affair ruin a marriage?" Betty shot back, "It can certainly help from time to time!"

Soon thereafter, Betty made a cameo on *The Paul Lynde Halloween Special*, telecast on ABC on October 29, 1976. As Miss Halloween of 1976, Betty spent a minute belittling Lynde, who then noted, "She has a striking resemblance to Betty White But then, so many witches do!" Betty worked with the host again on *Paul Lynde at the Movies*, a special on ABC on March 24, 1979.

As *Sonny & Cher* ended its last season on CBS in 1976–1977, Betty appeared twice. On November 7, 1976, she was billed as "Special Guest Star trying to take over the show" along with Ed McMahon. Betty first played Cher's desperate mother, pushing her homely daughter on a video dating service with a musical number to the tune of "The Continental." At the end, when client Sonny Bono said he wanted to meet the woman with the good-looking legs, Betty eagerly barged in and pushed Cher aside to date Sonny. Next, she appeared as one of several W.C. Fields impersonators with a putty nose and top hat and did a credible accent while cracking bad jokes. Cher joined them as Mae West. Both skits ran about ten minutes and were not worth the effort.

In a shorter and better bit, Betty played the disinterested housewife of a Rudolph Valentino sheik (Sonny). Wearing an apron around a dress that made her look like Sue Ann Nivens—she even referenced *The Mary Tyler Moore Show*—Betty avoided and belittled his advances. Her delivery was so strong that one could hear real guffaws in the studio apart from the laugh track to lines like "I wake up in the morning and find you've used all my mascara!" She reappeared on the series on January 21, 1977, a few months before the series ended.

Betty was on what turned out to be the series finale of *The Jacksons* on CBS March 9, 1977. The Jackson brothers wrote the opening theme, "On the Wall," and sang the tune accompanied by the Anita Mann Dancers and the Rick Wilkins Orchestra as Betty came on stage to sign a large scrim. She enjoyed dancing with Michael Jackson before the number ended. Unfortunately, the rest of her bits were a waste of time for her and the viewers.

In quick, unfunny skits, Betty played a saloon gal and then a spy on a street corner giving news to another agent who was Michael Jackson in a trash can. "There's this new television show about a short rodent who lives on a steamboat," she whispered to Michael. "What's it called?" he asked. "Little Mouse on the Ferry!" she answered as Michael deservedly groaned.

Later, Betty was the "Funky Godmama" to Janet Jackson's Cinderella. "We ain't going to no stiff ball!" she told Janet. "We are making it to a Stevie Wonder concert!" An excited Janet left with her as Betty exclaimed, "We're going to boogie tonight!" Her final shot had her as the spy with Michael to deliver another punchline with no punch. Betty was on screen for less than three minutes. Incidentally, contrary to some reports, Betty was not on the February 9, 1977 show.

Introduced by "ringleader" Lucille Ball, Betty did the special *Circus of the Stars* on CBS September 5, 1977. She worked with Valentine, a dromedary who picked up Betty's hat, lifted its front legs, retrieved a dumbbell, knelt to the ground, and lied down. "Of course, it's not too difficult with Hollywood actresses," Betty drily noted of the latter stunt. After prodding, Valentine stood up and took a phone off the receiver, where Betty pretended to hear a producer say he had seen the act and wanted to hire Valentine alone. The camel picked up the phone again twice, with good ad-libs by Betty before a stagehand took the prop away. The segment ended with Valentine opening the gate lock with his mouth. Betty reappeared on the third edition of *Circus of the Stars* on December 10, 1978, this time with an elephant.

For *The John Davidson Christmas Special* on ABC December 9, 1977, Betty was a beggar woman and fellow guest star Tim Conway played Charles Dickens in one sketch. Betty also sang and danced to "Turkey Lurkey Time" from the musical *Promises, Promises* and joined Davidson in performing "The Master's Christmas Party."

Dallying with *Donny & Marie*

In 1978 Betty got five guest shots on *Donny & Marie*, starring the wholesome brother and sister singing duo of Donny and Marie Osmond. Starting in 1975 on ABC, *Donny & Marie* relied on gaudy visuals and canned laughter over sharp writing to generate supposed excitement and laughter. Betty made the most of what material she received, which was quite variable.

In her first appearance on *Donny & Marie*, January 27, 1978, Betty played straight man to Paul Lynde's snooty gift exchange clerk, which was nothing special. Paul and Betty reteamed as boss and secretary at the Mediocre Modeling Agency, which sought dreary types. Espying Betty with her glasses on, Paul murmured, "You're average!" "Oh, you're just saying that, I'm really quite exceptional!" demurred Betty. To show he believed she was homely, Paul said he would cancel their date for the night. "You really know how to turn a girl's head!" cooed Betty. This cute sketch unfortunately had a stupid ending.

The finale was a 1958 high school prom led by Betty and Lynde who did his "Kids" number from the musical *Bye Bye Birdie*. He and Betty sang and danced to "The Stroll" with Donny and Marie. Betty also danced to Andy Gibb singing "The Great Pretender" and sang "The Birds and the Bees." She showed fine footwork for "At the Hop" at the end, too.

After making cameos on the September 22, 1978 and October 13, 1978, shows, Betty returned on December 1, 1978, with Lynde. A sketch with Lynde, Betty and Marie as snooty people bedeviling Donny in the outdoors went nowhere, as did Betty as a teacher befuddled by converting measurements to the metric system. Worse was Betty, Marie and two other women as hillbilly sisters who wanted to become rock stars with Lynde as their manager. Her only bearable bit was Betty and Lynde as aerialists bickering under their smiles to the audience. "The last time you cooked a dinner, the geek ran away from the circus!" Lynde said. "Yes, and I'm sure you miss your father!" Betty answered.

Betty reappeared on December 29, 1978, doing a somewhat amusing scarf trick. Then in "Daze of Their Lives," Betty played Donny's wife as they and other characters, played by Marie and Johnny Dark, learned who their true selves were in a fast yet tiresome bit. Betty and Marie played female honor guards as part of a "Provo Press" musical skit where she was more energetic than the lines she received. In another sketch, she was the worried mother of Christopher Columbus who agreed with Donny that Johnny Dark was dead despite Dark's protestations. Under such bad scripting, *Donny & Marie* went off the air in 1979.

Also in 1978, Betty was the very last star introduced on *CBS On the Air* on March 26, 1978, the network's celebration of its first fifty years on the air. She also participated when the network celebrated a quarter century of broadcasting during the live special *CBS at 75* on November 2, 2003. Betty gave another network equal time by appearing on *NBC's 60th Anniversary Celebration* on May 12, 1986 and *NBC 75th Anniversary Celebration* on May 5, 2002. Betty was the only star to appear on two network retrospective specials on both CBS and NBC.

You've Got to Have Hope
In the early 1980s, Betty's variety guest shots were largely unimpressive. She did the syndicated series *Big City Comedy*, taped in Canada starring John Candy, on November 15, 1980, *Norm Crosby's The Comedy Shop* on January 3, 1981, and *Laugh Trax* on October 16, 1982. She even showed up on the syndicated amateur contest *Star Search* on January 4, 1986.

For NBC, she did the short-lived series *The Big Show* on April 8, 1980 and was on the *NBC Star Salute to 1981* special airing before the Tournament of Roses Parade on New Year's Day 1981. In two season opener previews, Betty's talents were wasted in *NBC All Star Hour* on September 12, 1983 and *The Third Annual NBC All Star Hour* on September 16, 1985. On *A Comedy Salute to Baseball*, airing July 15, 1985 before the All-Star Game, she played Babe Ruth's daughter Shelley, writer of "Bambino Dearest."

Redeeming Betty in this blah period was her work with the king of TV comedy variety specials. Betty finally did one of Bob Hope's top-rated shows on November

22, 1981, *Bob Hope's Stand Up and Cheer National Football League's 60th Year*. More than ready for the appearance, Betty smartly played a counselor fooled by three NFL coaches faking insanity and the wife of Howard Cosell who was equally verbose as her sportscaster husband.

She didn't show up again with Hope until *Happy Birthday Bob* on May 16, 1988, which celebrated him turning eighty-five. Betty performed in a number that its writer, James Lipton, replayed when she visited Lipton's talk show, *Inside the Actors Studio*, on September 28, 2010.

Betty made four other appearances on Bob Hope specials thereafter. She movingly recounted her memories of Lucille Ball on *Bob Hope's Love Affair with Lucy* on September 23, 1989. On March 14, 1992, she helped the star recount his early years in show business in *Bob Hope and Other Young Comedians*. Betty delved into Bob's history again on *Bob Hope: The First 90 Years* on May 14, 1993, as she recalled highlights of his work on radio for another birthday special.

Sadly, when Betty made her last appearance with the comedian on *Bob Hope's Birthday Memories* on May 11, 1994, he looked unfocused and tired. On a set representing Bob's home, Phyllis Diller asked Betty for help in selecting a dress for Bob's party. Betty rejected several outfits before Diller pulled out a tiger print and said, "When I wear this, guys just want more!" "What, more Bromo Seltzer?" said Bob as he entered. Diller told him she wanted to do a love scene. "Didn't the two of you have a love scene in *Road to Morocco*?" Betty asked. "No, that was a camel!" Diller snapped back.

Betty and Diller had more dialogue before Bob recounted working with Lucille Ball in the movie *The Facts of Life* in a slow, gravelly voice. The bit concluded with Betty encouraging Diller to pick whatever outfit she wanted. Diller left, then after some clips aired, Betty talked to Bob briefly about his start as a dance instructor, leading into more clips. Not much else happened on this sad, low-rated effort shot without a studio audience.

Women's Comedy and Betty

As comedy created by women in variety specials increased in the 1980s, Betty came along for the ride. The results were mixed at best, even though Betty survived the results.

On April 6, 1982, Betty guest starred on the first of three specials called *The Shape of Things*. Executive producer George Schlatter had aired a special with the same name on CBS on October 19, 1973, which emphasized sketches and jokes on daily life from a feminist perspective. Schlatter sold the concept to NBC nearly a decade later. Betty was a hostess along with Morgan Fairchild, Sarah Purcell, and Lynn Redgrave, who also was on the 1973 special.

But while the 1973 *Shape of Things* used several women in its creation, the 1982 edition's key personnel were mainly men, and just three of the eight writers were women. The result was a lumpy show with a bloated cast that included the Chippendale Dancers gyrating and stripping to the opening number sung by the hostesses. Betty pushed aside Purcell to kiss one hunk.

In the opening sketch, Betty played a distaff equivalent of General George Patton gruffly barking out plans for equality. "If he likes the kids, threaten to take them away from him!" she huffed. She and the other women swapped jokes about infidelity. The spot was tiresome, as was the "Attaboy Awards" for men, such as John McEnroe disliking women umpires, with the ladies ringing cowbells after each announcement. After doing a mock torch number for Secretary of the Interior James Watt, Betty's other big duty was introducing Redgrave singing and enacting the Kenny Rogers song "The Gambler" with the Chippendale Dancers. She sang an empowering closing number with the other hostesses before the lumbering show mercifully ended.

Betty was better as a guest in the audience for the special *Pudgy!*, airing on Showtime July 26, 1982. Videotaped on the Queen Mary, celebrity guests sat in the audience to interact with its star, insult comedienne Pudgy (real name Beverly Wines). The hostess told Betty she recalled watching *Life with Elizabeth*, then looked at her wardrobe and said, "I remember that dress from that show! … That's nice, because you can keep washing and wearing it, you know?" Later, when Betty hit a high note during an audience singalong, Pudgy cracked, "I like her on game shows, I'm going to be honest, but she's rubbing me the wrong way tonight, okay?"

Somehow Betty got involved in *Joan Rivers and Friends Salute Heidi Abromowitz*, a special on Showtime June 14, 1985, so disastrous the director took his name off the production. Performed largely at Caesars Palace in Las Vegas, this frenetic "tribute" to Rivers' imaginary best friend Heidi Abromowitz, the "Tramp of the Century," tried too hard to be funny and often missed. Among many celebrities who were taped telling tired jokes about Heidi's promiscuity, Betty said, "Kraft named a spread after her!" She then disappeared from this mess.

Games and Disney

Betty was much better back on familiar turf in the special *Those Wonderful TV Game Shows*, seen on NBC February 27, 1984. Host Carl Reiner introduced Betty as one of the few women to host a game show. Because the show didn't have access to clips from Goodson-Todman game shows, she claimed of all her game shows, 'I think I'd have to say the most fun to do was *Liars Club*, because it gave us a chance to be funny and to polish up and hone our lying skills."

After some *Liars Club* clips aired and a mention of her game show *Just Men!*, Betty talked about Allen Ludden. "I really think the secret of Allen Ludden's success was that he truly enjoyed what he was doing. Whatever it was, he loved it." After clips of *General Electric College Bowl* and the finale of *Stumpers*, Betty said, "That was one classy fellow" and got misty-eyed.

Less enjoyable was Betty's outing on "Walt Disney World's 15th Anniversary Celebration" on *The Wonderful World of Disney* that aired November 9, 1986, on ABC. She and Bea Arthur were superimposed on previously recorded backgrounds while supposedly on their way to the party. Both behaved like their *Golden Girls* characters while telling the history of the Magic Kingdom and EPCOT. The only sparkling moment for Betty was when she joined a group of dancers at the Italy and Mexico pavilions and sang "I Love Paris" at the French pavilion at EPCOT.

Betty did another turn with Disney on October 9, 1988 on NBC. Hosting a special preview of *The Magical World of Disney* series, she spoke in a living room set about NBC and Disney's traditions of quality family entertainment. Next, Betty introduced some of the upcoming movies and new episodes on the series in a negligible appearance.

Much better was *A Conversation With Betty White*, a one-woman variety special on the Disney Channel October 15, 1989, taped at what was then the Disney-MGM Studios Park in Florida. The question-and-answer session with audience members was akin to what Carol Burnett did at the start of *The Carol Burnett Show*. In fact, Burnett was an executive producer. After receiving a standing ovation, Betty praised recently departed Lucille Ball as a comic actress and friend amid the questioning. "I must say, whenever you called on Lucy as a performer and as a friend, she was right there." On getting through Allen Ludden's death in 1981, she said, "I had three little dogs who helped me. Because you pretend, you dissemble ... I could cry in front of them, and I could get it out of myself."

The session ended on a happy note when Betty answered, "If there could be a fifth Golden Girl, who would be your selection?" "Well, there's a good question," she said. "Carol Burnett, I think. (applause) Can't you just see stirring Carol into that equation and the havoc she could wreak?" The special's only flaw was a few too many clips of *The Golden Girls*, *The Mary Tyler Moore Show*, and *Mama's Family* that could have been dropped in favor of hearing more from Betty.

Betty reunited with Burnett on the latter's variety repertory series *Carol & Company* on NBC November 3, 1990. In "Trisha Springs Eternal," Betty was Trisha Durant, a woman who moved next door and became the self-professed best friend of Rosalind Burke (Burnett). The behavior of her "new pal" forced Rosalind to take action to avoid being smothered by Trisha.

Betty the Go-To Retrospective Woman

Starting with *Funny Women of Television: A Museum of Radio & Television Tribute*, on NBC on October 24, 1991, Betty popped up often on historical profiles of her favorite medium. As this variety-documentary retrospective genre proliferated, usually Betty was part of the presentation.

She shared memories of *The Mary Tyler Moore Show* on *Behind the Laughs: The Untold Stories of Television's Favorite Comedies: A Paley Center for Media Special* on May 27, 1998, on Fox and *The 70s: The Decade That Changed Television: The Museum of Television & Radio* on September 7, 2000, on ABC. On the latter, she said, "Hi, I'm Betty White, and of course I've been on television every decade since the Neanderthals. During the seventies, I played a very unconventional woman on *The Mary Tyler Moore Show*. My character, Sue Ann Nivens, was a study in contrasts. She hosted a TV show about the joys of homemaking, yet she was unmarried herself. And quite well-known for playing the field." She introduced a segment on women's rights and the portrayal of females on TV, in a well-produced collection of obscure footage.

Betty also was on *The Museum of Television and Radio Presents: Great Women of Television Comedy* on April 15, 2003, on NBC and *TV's All-Time Funniest Holiday Moments: A Paley Center for Media Special* on November 26, 2010, on Fox. Her last blast into the past was on *TV's Funniest of the Funniest: A Paley Center for Media Special* on September 1, 2013, on NBC.

Other variety appearances for Betty were rooted in nostalgia. *Happy Birthday Hollywood* was a salute to America's entertainment capital, airing May 18, 1987, on

ABC. Betty was among many female dancers auditioning to impress director Busby Berkley, played by Gregory Harrison. Like most of the special, the presentation was well done but overlong and ultimately exhausting.

Another nostalgia special involving Betty was *The Great Love Songs* on August 9, 1995, on PBS. Betty hosted a musical salute with Skitch Henderson, the New York Pops Orchestra, Jack Jones, Maureen McGovern, John Raitt, Dionne Warwick, Cleo Laine, and Margaret Whiting.

The Fan Hits the Shat

Betty's sweetness image went by the wayside when she participated on *The Comedy Central Roast of William Shatner* on August 20, 2006. As a selected "roaster" of the veteran actor, Betty told and heard jokes much rawer than any other comedy she had performed on television.

"We decided to, you know, make some moves and take some chances in her career," said Jeff Witjas, Betty's agent since 2000, in explaining the assignment on the 2018 PBS documentary *Betty White: First Lady of Television*. "It really started taking off when she guested on the William Shatner roast for Comedy Central. Roasts are very risqué at times, and they wrote a lot of material that Betty decided to go with. … It opened things up."

"I was doing *Boston Legal* when I got asked to do the roast, and I read the material," she told Frank Bruni during a "Times Talk" event in 2011. "Sure, it's risqué. Sure, it's raunchy. It's not offensive to the point that it's going to do harm." Even so, the DVD showed footage of Betty during the rehearsal politely rejecting some suggested lines from the producers as too crude.

On the special, after getting a standing ovation, Betty went for the kill starting with the emcee. "Jason Alexander, you are such a treat! I was expecting you to be just dreadful. Well, in all fairness, I was basing that on everything you've ever done."

Among Betty's printable comments were the following jokes:

• "It always makes me laugh to see Artie Lange on stage, knowing I'm going to outlive him."

• "Oh, Bill. All your friends are either dead or they hate you! To be fair, I'm a little bit of Column A and a little bit of Column B."

• "But you look great! You know, they make one percent milk now!" Shatner kept chortling as she added, "Darling, you were supposed to explore the galaxy, not fill it!" •

- "I was so excited when I found out that I would be working with you on *Boston Legal*," Betty concluded, then added, "Till I worked with you on *Boston Legal*. Night!"

Betty became a target for jokes, as well, from other roasters, like this line from Lisa Lampinelli: "Betty White is so old that on her first game show ever, the grand prize was fire!"

"Bill called me the next day," Betty told Bruni in concluding her story of the roast. "He said, 'Did you live through it?' I said, 'Yeah, did you?' He said, 'Just!' He's a great guy."

After Shatner Was Shattered, Betty Was Boosted

Betty's best variety guest shot after the Shatner roast was accepting the Screen Actors Guild Lifetime Achievement Award on January 23, 2010. In a funny, warm speech, Betty told those assembled, "From the bottom of my bottom, thank you for whatever! (laughter)." She joked about "plain girl" Sandra Bullock, then mentioned her love of show business and being eighty-eight.

"I am still to this day starstruck. I look out in this audience and see so many famous faces. But what really boggles my mind is that I actually know many of you. And I've worked with quite a few. Maybe had a couple. (laughter and applause) And you know who you are." She concluded, "This is the highest point of my entire professional life. To the Screen Actors Guild, to each and every one of you, thank you from the bottom of my heart." She got another standing ovation.

While Betty received a prestigious award from her peers, a campaign was underway to give her a memorable variety show appearance later in 2010. The unlikely, unassuming crusader behind the movement was an associate director of training at AT&T, born when Betty was fifty-eight.

Facing a Campaign on Facebook

David Mathews became a fan of Betty's when his grandparents took him to Disney MGM Studios in 1989. "And one of the tours happened to have the house they used outside for *The Golden Girls* show. And I was very starstruck, whatever you want to call it. I was a little nine-year-old kid, and it stuck with me. And from that point on, I was always a *Golden Girls* fan.

"And then as I got older into young adulthood, I latched onto *The Golden Girls*, and for lack of a better word, I became a superfan. ... It was just to all of my friends, it became almost a part of my identity. They always knew me as a *Golden Girls* fan. Betty White was one of *The Golden Girls*, therefore I was a Betty White fan."

Little came of Mathews' obsession until he connected Betty to NBC's long-running, late night comedy variety series *Saturday Night Live* in December 2009. "I had made some random post that said, 'Betty White should host SNL.' I don't know where that came from. I don't know if we just latched onto the episode of *The Golden Girls* where she's had a heart attack or something and she's in the hospital bed and makes a joke of 'Live from New York, it's Saturday Night!' I wish I could pinpoint it, but I can't.'

Later that month, in advance of their fifth anniversary, Mathews and his husband took a road trip. One stop was in Washington, D.C., for a college friend of his husband. "And one night, we were sitting in his condo drinking pisco, which was an apéritif from South America, and probably way too much wine. And yet somehow, our mutual fandom of *The Golden Girls* came up. And I made a bet with this guy to do a Facebook page to get Betty White to host *Saturday Night Live*. The bet was that my Facebook page would get 2,000 likes. And for that work, I needed 2,000 people to think, 'Hey, this is a good idea.'"

The bet initially was a joke, since Mathews was not a big fan of *Saturday Night Live*. "I didn't dislike it. I was ambivalent toward it. I didn't watch it often."

But Mathews intended to try the challenge after he and his husband arrived in Atlanta, Georgia. "It was New Year's Eve from 2009 going into 2010, and I was just thinking, we had been tired of driving all day, and it was that night, New Year's Eve, that the *Saturday Night Live* show had popped on, and that's when I made the Facebook page. It took me all of ten minutes."

Mathews launched his campaign by sending invitations to all his friends on Facebook. "Over the next five weeks, slowly but surely, it grew incrementally, going from people to other people. And it had gotten over 2,000 within that first month. And I started to see sort of really obscure folks, like celebrities I didn't really hear or know about, that were signing on to it. I want to say, I don't know if it was Cloris Leachman or somebody of that era or generation who was a pioneer, liked it. I remember Rosie O'Donnell, I asked her to like it, and she said, 'Okay!' And then I said, 'Oh wow, this is starting to get attention.'

"At the first part of February, it was at 8,000 likes. It was becoming a thing. And we were selling our house in Austin and moving to San Antonio, and we had to drive back into Austin to close on our house. We went in the morning, and by the evening when we got back in our new home in San Antonio, it had gone from 8,000 up to 40,000 in one day. I went, 'Oh, wow! Okay! It's crossed whatever threshold it needs to cross.'"

Mathews said when the *USA Today* website and blogger Perez Hilton mentioned the campaign on the same day, "That's when the interviews began, and then in a few days it went over 100,000. The next thing I knew, it was a major network interview with Diane Sawyer and it went exponentially after that. And I think it topped off just shy of 600,000."

Pressure Builds for Betty
On February 17, 2010, Diane Sawyer of ABC News interviewed Mathews and Betty about the campaign separately. "I don't know where that came from," Betty said. "I'm such a technological spaz. I don't understand any of that stuff. And all of a sudden, all this stuff has come in, and I'm just watching it in awe." She later added, "I'm having the time of my life. I've never been this busy in my life. At eighty-eight years old, you don't expect to be this busy." She also thanked Mathews.

That same day, Betty appeared on *The Bonnie Hunt Show*. Hunt wondered why *Saturday Night Live* executive producer Lorne Michaels had not contacted Betty yet. "I'm sure they're probably trying to make sure that their material is of the utmost quality before they even bother you," she said. "Oh sure, that's what they probably do, I'm sure," Betty deadpanned to Hunt's audience.

Betty didn't reveal initially she had been approached to host the series previously. "I turned it down three times earlier in my career," she told Frank Bruni during a *Times Talk* in 2011. "It's such a New York-oriented show, and I'm such an obvious Californian that I was afraid I'd feel like a fish out of water, you know, I wouldn't fit in. I was scared, is what I was, frankly."

By this time, Betty's agent Jeff Witjas had heard about Mathews and the campaign. "He had reached out to me, and I don't remember exactly how we got in contact … He had let me know that they were actually talking to *SNL* and told me something might be coming from it." Betty's friend Rob Howe told Mathews in early March that the appearance was a done deal.

"I talked to Lorne Michaels, and we talked about who was going to come back from the cast," said Witjas in the 2018 PBS documentary *Betty White: First Lady of Television*. "Lorne was making it more of a Mother's Day show, which was very special."

Michaels also talked directly to Betty about his plans and she said no to hosting again, but Witjas overruled her. Still, Witjas knew even with returning cast members as extra guests, Betty would have to do a considerable amount of work during the show.

"Betty rehearsed vigorously all week," said Witjas. "Thursday. Betty looks at me with a look that I've never seen before. And she says, 'Never again.' Maybe I pushed her a little too far and a little too much. Because I was pushing her out of her comfort zone. And then she said it, she looked, [and] went right back into the regular Betty White right after she said it."

Betty disliked using cue cards and having script updates throughout the week. The planned quick costume changes were jarring, too. "Did you ever make a change in a minute and ten seconds? Wigs and everything. People are tearing your clothes off and others and, well. I've done that before," she joked to the hostesses of *The View* on June 14, 2010, when recalling her hosting gig.

To top it off, Betty had a busy promotional week, as well. On *Late Night with Jimmy Fallon* on May 6, 2010, the host asked her about Mathews. "Do you know this guy? Have you met him?"

"I've not met him, and when I do, I'm going to kill him," she answered with a fake glare to laughter from the audience and Fallon.

Meanwhile, Mathews got conflicting reports from NBC officials about whether he and his husband could attend in person until he heard "yes" from a representative. "Eventually, as we got closer to May, she said, 'We've got a couple of tickets for you.' But we had to pay our own way to get up there, foot our own bill for the hotel, all that fun stuff. And I asked if there would be a chance I could meet her. She said, 'There's no guarantees. I can't promise.' And I got it. If it can happen, it can happen. So they got front row seats for us in the balcony, which was really great."

And on May 8, 2010, what started as a whim in Mathews' mind became a reality nationwide. At age eighty-eight, Betty became the oldest host ever of *Saturday Night Live*.

Betty Goes Live from New York

Most viewers who saw Betty were surprised at how much she did as host. She did virtually every sketch, an impressive feat even with a couple of segments taped in advance and some time taken up by performances by musical guest Jay-Z.

"Even after fifteen-hour rehearsals, Betty White was running circles around that young cast," said returning cast member Amy Poehler in the 2012 special *Betty White's 90th Birthday: A Tribute to America's Golden Girl*. "But that was because she was trying to cop a feel," she joked.

Mathews praised Betty's work. "In my honest opinion, she was fantastic. I mean, right out of the gate with her monologue, the way she made fun of Facebook, we were roaring with laughter." Like many critics, he felt some writing fell short of Betty's performances in the sketches.

Betty won an Emmy for Outstanding Guest Actress in a Comedy Series for this show, which became her fifth nighttime statuette. She was not the oldest Emmy winner. Norman Lear won for producing in the Outstanding Variety Special in 2019 at age ninety-seven. But Betty did become the oldest actress to win the award thanks to this appearance.

After the show, Mathews and his husband got to go backstage. "And we were waiting in this little hallway outside her dressing room along with a bunch of A- and B-list folks we all know. Sigourney Weaver was there, and Matthew Broderick, and Penny Marshall, and a bunch of other folks from *SNL*. And we're all standing there, and I was too nervous to say anything, right? I'll never forget, I took out my phone to make a video, and Matthew Broderick was sitting across from me to my left, and he looked down at the camera being on, and I felt so ashamed. I don't want to be that guy!

"And before I turned in to go into her dressing room, Sigourney Weaver and Victor Garber were walking out, and I was walking in. And of course, I was on cloud nine. I knew that she was there, and she looked back at me and smiled, because I looked like this giddy kid."

Mathews had seen what Betty said on *Late Night with Jimmy Fallon* about his instigating the campaign. "So, when I walked in and saw her, the very first thing that I did is I pointed to either cheek and said, 'Which side do you want to punch?' And she looked up to me—I'm a short guy, only five foot seven, and she's what, five foot one?—and she was probably full of adrenaline herself, having just finished the show.

And she said, 'You know, up until this moment, I did want to slap you. Now that you're here, I just want to hug you.'

"So she gave me a big hug, and we made some small talk. And Jeff Witjas was right there, and he was the one who I had been speaking to, so I said hi to him. We posed for a couple of pictures, and that was it. And that was all there was. It was an amazing experience."

The show earned the highest rating for *Saturday Night Live* in a year and a half. Despite her trepidations, Betty enjoyed the experience enough to return on the *Saturday Night Live 40th Anniversary Special* on February 15, 2015. In "The Californians" sketch, Betty played a woman believed to have died in a balloon accident. She said the balloon operator, played by Bradley Cooper in a blonde wig, saved her life and made out with him to audience hysteria.

Copycat Facebook campaigns appeared in the wake of Betty's appearance, with Lorne Michaels vowing he would never have anyone host his show in that manner thereafter. One separate push to get Betty to host the Academy Awards in 2011 failed to capture the moment or widespread appeal of the original effort. Mathews was not surprised by this failure and similar ones.

"It was probably the first time that social media had had that kind of a pop culture connection, fan-induced impact," Mathews said. "You couldn't repeat that or duplicate that if you tried."

Paying Tribute to All, Including Herself

Besides appearing on fluffy specials like *25 Years of Sexy: People Magazine's Sexiest Man Alive* on ABC November 17, 2010, Betty made a few memorable visits on televised honorary events in the 2010s. First, she appeared on stage in *Tina Fey: The Mark Twain Prize* on PBS on November 9, 2010, and said, "I'm probably the only one here who actually dated Mark Twain. And I can tell you that they didn't call him Samuel Longhorn Clements for nothing!

"Tonight's not about me. Or my seven Emmys. Or about all I do for charity that I don't want people to know about. Speaking of my Emmys, I never would've gotten the seventh Emmy—the most important one, of course—if it wasn't for Tina."

Betty concluded by saying Fey deserved this honor but grimaced, "And the fact that she's only been in the business for five minutes (laughter) makes her achievement even more special!" She added, "And the wonderful thing is Tina Fey never had to sleep with anyone to get where she is. She just put out because she's a nymphomaniac!"

For *Kennedy Center Mark Twain Prize for American Humor: Celebrating Jay Leno* on PBS November 23, 2014, Betty appeared on tape on the set of *Hot in Cleveland*. She joked that she would give context for his career like she did for Tina Fey in 2010 and Mark Twain in 1910. "I'd call it a top ten list, but the last thing I'd need is Dave [Letterman] ticked off at me," Betty joked. As she did her monologue, her co-star Jane Leeves crossed her on the set and said, "Hi Jay!" Betty muttered "Bitch!" before congratulating Leno and enduring Leeves once more.

Betty outdid herself on *AFI Life Achievement Award: A Tribute to Morgan Freeman* on June 19, 2001, on TV Land. She emerged from the backseat of a black car driven onstage to insinuate that she had an affair with the honoree. "Morgan and I do have a lot in common though," she said. "We both starred in *Hello, Dolly!* on the stage. I was in a local production, but Morgan was the head waiter on Broadway in an all-black cast." A picture of Freeman from that picture appeared with the leading lady. "Yeah, that was Pearl Bailey as Dolly. I should've had that part. (laughter) I mean, I auditioned for it, but I didn't get it. Probably because of my last name. (laughter)"

Betty performed the musical's title tune as "Hello Morgan," with six black male singers and hilarious new lyrics like "Let's all clap, Morgan/Even though you've made some crap, Morgan." Freeman loved the bit and was the first one on his feet to give Betty a standing ovation.

But Betty's biggest variety special was *Betty White's 90th Birthday: A Tribute to America's Golden Girl*, airing on NBC January 16, 2012. Taped at the Biltmore Hotel in Los Angeles, the special began with Betty greeting guests riding in her limo. Naturally, they were pet dogs.

Amy Poehler cracked up the honoree with "Betty, you're going to hear a lot of jokes tonight about your age, but take comfort in the fact that come tomorrow, you won't remember any of them." Poehler added, "I wrote a fan letter to Betty White over twenty years ago, when I was just starting out in comedy. When I was five." She said Betty wrote back with "Dear You. Thanks for your letter. I have a lot of dogs, and I need something to line their cages with. Your incredibly absorbent letter did the trick. My advice to you is to stay out of the business. I don't need another blonde sniffing around my stuff. Leave now, and don't let my Emmys hit you on the way out."

Several tapes of celebrities aired, including President Barack Obama saying he needed a long-form copy of her birth certificate and pretending to listen to "Thank You for Being a Friend." Back at the ceremony, Zachary Levi came to Betty's table for an amusing bit of flirtation.

Carol Burnett got laughter by saying, "Like many of you, I first heard about Betty from the wonderful stories told to me by my grandmother. I would sit on her lap and listen to her stories about Betty and the Golden Age of Television, so you can only imagine how thrilled I was when I got to work with Betty on my show later in life on *The Carol Burnett Show*." A few clips appeared before Burnett concluded to applause, "All I want to look forward to—not all I want to look forward to—but I do want to look forward to ten years from now, being here on this stage saluting you on your hundredth. And I don't doubt that it's going to happen."

Mary Tyler Moore discussed Betty as Sue Ann Nivens. "She was so perfect that the original idea of having her appear in only one episode ended up with Betty joining our cast for our last four seasons. And in so doing, she created one of the great television characters in situation comedy history."

Joel McHale recounted Betty's game show career. After clips aired, Vicki Lawrence and Valerie Harper played a mock game of *Password* against Ed Asner and Gavin MacLeod with McHale as host. Each celebrity gave tributes to Betty afterward, starting with Lawrence. "Many, many years ago we went to dinner at Betty's house. And on the way home, my husband Al said to me, 'I don't want you to take this wrong, sweetie, but if anything ever happens to us, I would date Betty White.' And I said, 'Honey, if anything ever happens to us, I would date Betty White!'"

Harper and MacLeod thanked Betty sincerely. Then Asner joked, "Betty, I'm not going to try to suck up to you like other people! I'm mano a mano with you. Wipe that smile off your face!" McHale topped them all by saying, "Betty, I don't know who you are, but you seem very lovely. I am going to go on IMDB [Internet Movie Database] and find out."

Wendie Malick, Jane Leeves, and Valerie Bertinelli blew kisses to Betty before they introduced a clip from their series with Betty, *Hot in Cleveland*. Carl Reiner emerged to a standing ovation and said, "You're a national treasure because you're all goodness. I have never seen the meanness. Allen Ludden might have, I'm not sure!"

At the finale, eight chorus men singing special lyrics by Jerry Herman to the tune of "Mame" brought Betty on stage to do a final round of thanks. After a rapturous amount of applause that clearly humbled her, she kissed the sky.

"Oh my dears, I just—talk about milking it! You've had such an overdose of me lately. I've been the luckiest old broad on two feet to have all the jobs that I have had. And tonight, you have had the ultimate overdose. But you've been so warm and so wonderful. And weren't they all wonderful? (applause) I simply can't tell you what it means to have the kind of friendship and the kind of privilege that I have in this business.

"I don't know where the breaking point comes. When you're ninety years old, you know, you're bragging about it. But where does the breaking point come in there in the time when you just as soon people don't know how old you are? And then all of a sudden, there's a breaking point where you start to brag about it. I don't know when that happened, but boy, is it happening now! (laughter and applause)

"It has been such a privilege, and to look around this room and see all my wonderful friends who've been up here tonight. It's a privilege, and I'm not going to get heavy about it. But I want you to know that I appreciate it more than I can possibly express. Because, to be able to spend a lifetime in a business you love with the people you love—and get away with it!—it's just marvelous. Thank you, my dears, so much!" Then the male chorus led everyone in singing "Thank You for Being a Friend" as she hugged the presenters on stage.

Betty White's 90th Birthday: A Tribute to America's Golden Girl finished eighth in the ratings. Seen by nearly 14 million viewers, its success inspired NBC to have a similar special the following year, *Betty White's Second Annual 90th Birthday* on February 5, 2013. Betty was too sick to attend the festivities but appeared in taped segments afterward thanking the attendees.

The 2012 special also led into the number twelve show of the night, which was the debut of Betty's next series—*Betty White's Off Their Rockers*.

Betty Rocks On

Essentially *Candid Camera* using mature actors for setups—with hunky young men showing up at times to make its star happy—*Betty White's Off Their Rockers* gave Betty her sixteenth credit as a regular on a national TV series.

"It was a very popular show in Europe, it started in Belgium, in Brussels," Betty said of her latest program on *The Late Show with David Letterman* on May 16, 2012. "And it's one of those hidden camera shows where the older people, you know, senior citizens, prank younger people. They'll stage a situation or something that the youngster thinks is real, and it's not."

She added with a wink, "We want to make them as uncomfortable as possible."

The show also used younger actors pretending to be part of the AARP set for the gags. Between the gags, Betty appeared in short comic segments, usually running no more than two minutes. Her director of photography was Hisham Abed, who would win an Emmy in 2019 for Outstanding Directing of a Reality Program for *Queer Eye*.

"The two people that were the most scrutinizing of my work on the set were Betty's hair and makeup artists," said Abed. "I loved them. They were so nice and had been with her so long. Once they knew that I was going to treat Betty kindly with the lighting and everything … we established a good relationship, and we were off and running." Abed got the job through his friendship with the original director, Guy Shalem.

Though Betty's contributions looked like they came from a studio, Abed said that was not the case. "All three seasons were shot on location at certain large estates in and around Los Angeles. All the comedic segments. The first house was in Pasadena, the second Encino, something like that." He and the rest of the crew had a tight schedule to follow.

David Letterman asked Betty about filming both *Betty White's Off Their Rockers* and *Hot in Cleveland* in 2012. "How do you do two shows? It's impossible for me to do one show!"

"It's not impossible, David. You manage to muddle through!" she said to laughter and applause.

"The first couple of seasons, we were only able to get Betty on her off days when she wasn't working on *Hot in Cleveland*," said Abed. "So, we filmed maybe a couple of days a week over the course of four weeks for a total of eight to ten days, I can't remember exactly.

"Then the last season, when I directed, we were able to get her at a clear block of time. I think we have five days. and we shot every little segment we could in that amount of time. … We were double the amount of the work the season I directed in the same amount [of time filming as the first two seasons]."

The changes occurred because NBC dropped *Betty White's Off Their Rockers* in its second season, on July 9, 2013. After its strong debut, the series had poor ratings.

Even so, the Lifetime network accepted new episodes of *Betty White's Off Their Rockers* to air in 2014, produced on a smaller budget and even tighter schedule than on NBC.

As director, Abed emphasized a personal approach with Betty. "When I sat down next to the camera to do the first take of directing with her, she saw I was right there, and she so appreciated it. She verbalized as much, the feeling that she had someone there who has her back, and she really appreciated it.

"Sometimes she'd say things directly to the camera, then when actors were in a scene, she'd play to them. I remember at one point, she had a question whether she had to address the camera or not. I said, 'Yeah, this portion is going directly to the camera.' She looked at the camera and said, 'Oh yeah, my friend!' She must've had in her head that on the other side of the camera was her admiring friend. That simple statement said so much about how she projected herself."

The production company also made concessions as Betty's mobility decreased. "We did everything we could to make her life easy," said Abed. "By the time we got her in the third season, she wasn't doing much walking. But we always agreed to get her in and out on time. We started working shorter days than we had the previous seasons. And she gave her all, all the time."

The Lifetime episodes had a new executive producer who sped the pace on screen. "We had a great showrunner, Lee Hupfield, who had come from England," said Abed. "We wrote a lot of segments to be shorter, kind of like, not quite one-liners but sort of a one-two punch instead of longer scripted segments. And that helped A, satisfy the network's requirements for content that we needed to deliver, but also B, it's a lot easier to shoot if the segments could be shorter and we could run through them faster. It was an absolute necessity at the time, virtually the only way to do it."

Some memorable moments didn't make it to air, according to Abed. "My assistant clapper person dropped a slate in front of her, and as he recovered and walked away, she reached to pinch his butt. Not really. She was just joking around.

"And one time she got us all. This was also filming closeups. The clapper person clapped the slate as normal, he pulled it out right away, and right when it had clapped, she went 'Oww!' She grabbed her nose and everybody went, 'Oh, no!' but she was faking."

Lifetime ended airing *Betty White's Off Their Rockers* on June 20, 2014. Betty earned three consecutive Emmy nominations as Outstanding Host for a Reality or Reality-Competition Program for every season of the series, giving her twenty-three national Emmy nominations total. She also established a record sixty-four-year stretch between her first Emmy nomination and her last, having gotten her first nod in 1950. Carl Reiner would tie that length, having earned his first Emmy in 1954 and his last in 2018.

After *Betty White's Off Their Rockers*, Betty still had the drive to do one more series as a regular, a revival of *To Tell the Truth*. She was returning to another favorite genre, game shows, one she learned would offer her even more opportunities from the 1970s onward.

John Schuck was ready to play against Betty in the fourth week of *Stumpers*, a daily game show hosted by Allen Ludden in 1976 on NBC. She returned in the week before Christmas in 1976 and would compete again against Schuck on *The $100,000 Pyramid* in 1991. Courtesy of the Adam Nedeff Collection.]

Chapter Six
Betty, The Game Show Goddess Part II

Betty's involvement with game shows began to go into overdrive in 1972 when CBS installed a new daytime program vice president, Donald "Bud" Grant. Longtime game show director Mike Gargiulo believed Grant was the best programmer for that position by far.

"The three networks, with the exception of Bud Grant, very few network executives in that era really understood game shows," he said.

Grant previously oversaw NBC's daytime lineup and was intent on revitalizing CBS's schedule. In the mornings were reruns of CBS nighttime sitcom hits *The Lucy Show*, *My Three Sons*, and *Family Affair*. Those repeats came at escalating prices from when CBS started using them in the 1950s due to increases in residuals secured by professional unions.

Additionally, the sitcoms attracted more preschool viewers than stay-at-home mothers, making them unappealing to sponsors. To top things off, the prekindergarten set began having a decided preference for the public television daily show *Sesame Street* over the sitcoms.

"We're going to shoot for the young female audience that is tuned to NBC's games," Grant told Richard K. Doan in *TV Guide* of his plans. Grant's new slate from 10-11:30 a.m. was *The Joker's Wild*, *The (New) Price is Right*, and *Gambit*. All were hits, and within a year NBC cancelled its competing game shows *Concentration* and *Sale of the Century*.

Replacing *Concentration* was *Baffle*, where Betty was a guest star during its run starting in 1973. But Grant provided two more pivotal opportunities for Betty that year. The first was the chance to host her own game show, *Hollywood's Talking*. That story will be covered shortly.

The second opportunity was becoming a semiregular on *Match Game 73*, with the last two digits reflecting the year it was shown. This looser and wilder revival of *The Match Game* allowed Betty plenty of leeway to show off her natural sense of humor. Its success spurred many celebrity-laden imitators over the next twenty years, and Betty appeared on almost all of them.

As in Chapter Four, the following summaries of game shows with Betty run chronologically by her first appearance. This list omits previously discussed revivals from 1973 onward of *What's My Line?*, *To Tell the Truth*, *I've Got a Secret*, *Masquerade Party*, *You Don't Say!*, *The Price is Right*, and *He Said She Said*, which was retitled *Tattletales* from 1974 through 1978. Exceptions are for new versions of *The Match Game* and *Password*, because each was substantially different and Betty had extensive involvement in the renditions cited here.

Hollywood's Talking (March 26, 1973–June 22, 1973)
April 2, 1973 (guest interviewee)
Airing on ABC daytime February 6, 1967–December 29, 1967, *Everybody's Talking* challenged three players to be the first to determine what subject people on film were discussing. With his success hosting and producing *The Joker's Wild* on CBS in 1972, Jack Barry revived his creation as a pilot for the network called *Hollywood's Talking*, using only celebrity interviewees.

"The story we heard—and it has a Betty punchline coming—was that when Jack sold the show to Bud Grant and then Freddie Silverman—then head of CBS—Jack said, 'We're going to have thirty-six different celebrities on,'" said Mark Maxwell-Smith, a writer on *Hollywood's Talking*. "And we really did, but that was over the course of six weeks, because they would go out a couple of days to Beverly Garland's hotel in North Hollywood to do the interviews. So, for the course of a week or maybe ten days, we made a deal and used all the facilities at Beverly Garland's.

"And when you think about it, every time you turn the camera six inches, it's a different background. And you did it inside, you did outside, you did it in a playground, by the pool. And they had thirty-six celebrities. We had enough material for six weeks.

And then we writers—you know, the easy part was coming up with the questions. The hard part was screening all this raw footage and coming up with a montage that we hoped would elicit some laughs."

Barry also wanted Betty to host the series. "I know that Jack Barry was madly in love with Betty White's ability to be a host," said Maxwell-Smith. "He knew just what a remarkable talent she was and is to this day. But he ran up against what was then the supposed 'smart' opinion that women could not host a game show because, according to research, they would be deemed too bossy if they were the ones saying 'Oh no, you can't do that' or 'Yes, you can do this.'

"So, Bud Grant made the following accommodation. He didn't say 'You can't do a pilot with her.' He said, 'You have to do two pilots. You have to pick somebody else to do the other one.'"

The "other one" was Al Lohman, half of the top-rated Los Angeles morning radio team Lohman and Barkley with Roger Barkley. "What I remember so clearly is that Al Lohman decided he wanted to come out during the warmup and ingratiate himself with the audience," said Maxwell-Smith of Lohman's pilot for *Hollywood's Talking*. "We shot the show at CBS Television City at Beverly and Fairfax, at that point one of the most densely Jewish populated neighborhoods in the city. And Al Lohman proceeded to talk about Adolf Hitler.

"From that moment on, all of us on the set had smiles on our faces, because quite frankly—and while we did nothing to undermine him, we were supportive of him—everyone wanted Betty White to be the host of the show. And my recollection was she did a brilliant job. And we left the studio that night knowing it was a fait accompli that Betty White would be the host."

Betty recalled her *Hollywood's Talking* pilot on "The Great American Game Show," a 1975 special on the *ABC Wide World of Entertainment* late night series. "That night, everyone was very excited about finally the breakthrough, the gal was going to be the emcee. And I thought I had a job. I really did. And the next day, I thought I had a job. And then they sent it out for testing. And I tested well personally. And they liked other things that I had done. But they did not want to see me in that position. So, Geoff Edwards went in and got the show."

Disappointed with the outcome, Betty nonetheless agreed to be an interview subject on the series. Maxwell-Smith said she was easier to talk with than some celebrities. "The fact of the matter is that with the exception of some people, a lot of these people really did have to be coaxed and goaded because quite frankly, many of them ... have only one main interest, and that's themselves. It's difficult to get them to talk about something else."

With all the effort expended on the project, *Hollywood's Talking* ran only a third as long as *Everybody's Talking*. Maxwell-Smith explained why. "So, the punchline to all of this was supposedly—because the numbers were decent—but Freddie [Silverman] just didn't like Jack [Barry], I think, and said, 'Well, you said we were going to have thirty-six stars each week, and it's the same thirty-six over six weeks, so thanks and goodbye.'

"We got word on a Friday or whenever that the show was not going to get picked up. And Ken [Johnson, the producer and director] called us all in the office to tell us. And while we were there, he said, 'I better call Geoff,' meaning Geoff Edwards. And I wish I could take credit for this, but somebody else said, 'You realize right now if we'd got numbers, you'd be calling Betty White.'"

For her part, Betty said on "The Great American Game Show" if she had hosted *Hollywood's Talking* and saw it cancelled after thirteen weeks, she would have blamed herself for its failure.

Maxwell-Smith thought Edwards was fine hosting *Hollywood's Talking* but added, "Betty White would've been a brilliant host of that show. Whether the show would've lasted, I don't know."

Baffle (March 26, 1973–March 29, 1974)
May 7–11, 1973 (Beverly Garland)

Baffle was the new name for *PDQ*, a daily syndicated game from 1965 to 1969 from producers Merrill Heatter and Bob Quigley. Game show historian Steve Beverly said the main purpose of *PDQ* was to run on NBC's owned and operated stations from 1-1:30 p.m. daily when the network didn't offer programming. "They were looking for something inexpensive and took a chance on it," he said. "The numbers were enough that it successfully had a four-year run."

Betty never appeared on *PDQ*. But she did its revival in a week playing with mothers in advance of Mother's Day. As with the original, *Baffle* had celebrities pick three letters at a time from a phrase and tried to get their noncelebrity partners to identify the saying in the shortest amount of time. Beverly suspected that the name changed to *Baffle* to make the property appear new.

Robert Noah, an executive producer of *Baffle* with Heatter and Quigley, barely recalled working on *Baffle* apart from enjoying its host, sportscaster Dick Enberg. But he agreed that having *Baffle* go to an all-celebrity format on September 27, 1973, was not smart. "If the basic show doesn't work, it can be made better, but it's not a good sign," he said. *Baffle* ended six months later.

Match Game 73–79/PM (July 2, 1973–April 20, 1979; 1975–1982; July 16, 1990–July 12, 1991)
Semiregular 1973–1982; July 23–27, 1990; November 5–9, 1990; May 6–10, 1991
"We had such a good time doing that show," Goodson-Todman production manager Andrew J. Selig said of the 1973–1982 revival of *The Match Game*. So did many viewers. In its first season, *Match Game 73–74* became the number one series on daytime TV and remained the top daytime game show for the next four years. Betty was along for the ride roughly every month.

Match Game 73 (the series changed its two digits based on the year) had two players trying to match answers with six celebrities who arranged three apiece on two tiers. After two rounds, the player with the most matches played the "Super Match" to determine the most popular answers a studio audience gave to a phrase with a missing word. The player picked three celebrities to suggest possible responses. Matching the top answer won $500, the second most popular answer won $250, and the third most popular answer got $100. The player then picked a celebrity to play for ten times the amount won during the Super Match. Players continued until defeated.

What made *Match Game 73* stand out was the use of questions that implied double entendres. Also, because host Gene Rayburn walked across the set with a microphone rather than stand behind a podium, he could goof around with the celebrities and players constantly. The series developed a party atmosphere, which viewers loved to watch on CBS 3:30-4 p.m. daily.

Betty made the pilot on May 19, 1973 with Bert Convy, Arlene Francis, Jack Klugman, Jo Ann Pflug, and Richard Dawson. She asked why her response to "John's daughter came home from college with a BLANK" of "friend" got buzzed for not matching the player's answer of "boyfriend" while Convy got a match with "boy." Questions about what judges would allow as matching answers were a recurring challenge for the revamp. In the "Super Match," Betty gave the top answer to "Red BLANK" with "red, white, and blue."

When *Match Game 73* became a series, Betty came on the third week of the show along with Brett Somers and Charles Nelson Reilly. Somers and Reilly would become regulars and sit in the middle and end seat of the top tier respectively. Betty would sit on the end of the bottom tier next to the other regular, Richard Dawson. Guests would appear in the first seats of each tier.

The show was still finding its way and occasionally used questions straight from the 1960s show like "Name a musical instrument." But signs of what the series would become did appear. One question was, "When John saw this girl at the cocktail party, he could tell by the way she was dressed that she was a BLANK." Betty matched the contestant's answer of "swinger." Another leading question was "Mary has never seen John's BLANK." On the last day of the week, Betty wrote "bosoms" for the first time, which would become a popular answer written as "boobs."

By Betty's fifth visit on October 22–26, 1973, the wild, festive nature was solidly in place. When a handsome chaplain constantly picked Betty for the Super Match, Reilly griped on October 23, "They are so obvious with their relationship! … It's like a train wreck, it's so subtle!" The next day, a question referred to Dumb Dora, who became a running gag on the series.

Dick DeBartolo said he and other *Match Game* writers repeatedly used such characters as Dumb Dora and Old Man Periwinkle for convenience in creating the large amount of questions needed. "And the funny thing is, I had bought this incredible, expensive electronic typewriter. It was just before computers came in, and it was $700. And I remember I paid an extra $100 because there was a port in the back that, if you bought a computer, this typewriter could end up being the printer. And there were seven memory keys. And memory key number one was 'Dumb Donald was so dumb that.' And memory key two was 'Dumb Dora was so dumb that.'"

As for getting material passed the censor, DeBartolo said, "The thing you would do with *Match Game* was to write some out-and-out filth for questions, so that then the other stuff didn't look so bad. A joke question I wrote actually made it on the air. This, to me, was one of the fun things I wrote, thinking they would just laugh and say, 'Oh, we can't do this.' But they did it.

"Unlucky Louie was one of our characters, and the question was, 'Unlucky Louie was so unlucky that he went on a diet and lost two inches. But he didn't lose it on his waist. Unlucky Louie lost two inches off his BLANK.' And they did. Now, if it was the current *Match Game*, they would just say 'his boner,' 'his penis,' 'his johnson.'"

Betty caught on to the changes and supplied joke answers easily. During the week of November 5–9, 1973, one question was "The sultan's fifty wives went on strike saying, 'We really need more than one BLANK.'" The contestant said "husband," while Betty said "John" to laughter.

Still, Betty was human and could miss some obvious answers. On November 20, 1973, the Super Match question was "Pass BLANK." The contestant picked Betty first. "Oh, honey, I may have blown my best bit!" she said. "Remember to whom you're married!" said Somers. "Passover," Betty answered to groans. Dawson said "pass out," while McLean Stevenson said "passbook." When the contestant went on his own and said "Password," Betty hid under her desk. The player won $500 and Rayburn said, "And you're all invited to Betty White's divorce!" Betty redeemed herself by helping the player win $5,000 as she wrote "wink" for "quick as a BLANK."

Her commentary to wrong answers during the game often was amusing. On November 21, 1973, the question was, "Methuselah's wife said, 'My husband really is 900 years old. Just look at his BLANK.'" Betty said, "Look at his 'body.' and I don't want to discuss it," prompting applause.

So was her interplay with the host. When Rayburn saw Betty's outfit on the October 31, 1974 show and told her, "You've got little lions on your thing," she said, "No, but I have on my jacket!" to audience laughter. On September 6, 1976, when Rayburn asked the panel, "Shall we have a go at it?" Betty responded, "Should we do the show first?"

She also had a catty relationship with a *Match Game* regular. Betty asked on December 13, 1973, "Gene, what's our gift for the losers? Is it a weekend with Brett Somers?" She told Rayburn on March 7, 1974, "You and Brett buy your hair from the same place. I think it's adorable!"

Betty's quick wit was ready for anything Somers said. On January 22, 1974, when Rayburn congratulated Betty about working on *The Mary Tyler Moore Show*, Somers cracked "An older person is always good on a show!" "You should know!" Betty joked in response to applause.

The first of many questions that referenced Betty herself began April 1, 1974. "Betty White said, 'Every time I go streaking (audience laughter and Betty cracked up), Allen Ludden makes me wear his BLANK," said Rayburn. The player said "shorts," but Betty said "glasses" to applause.

The next day, on a question that said, "Little Orphan Annie cried and cried because her dog Sandy had eaten her BLANK," Somers crowed, "I'm the first one finished." "You were finished a long time ago, sweetheart," Betty responded to applause and even laughter from Somers.

The following week, Allen Ludden made his *Match Game* debut. Rayburn brought down three bad answers Ludden gave to Betty sitting in the studio audience. She tore them up. Rayburn also kissed Betty several times, causing Ludden to say, "Not only does he have the number one show in the country, he's now getting my wife, for heaven's sake!"

Regarding Ludden, among the many questions about him and Betty that appeared when she played, the funniest may have been the following on July 14, 1975: "At a barbecue at Betty White's, Betty made this statement: 'Folks, I've got good news and bad news. The bad news is, Allen Ludden's on fire. The good news is, I've got plenty of BLANK.'" The player said "booze," while Betty said "chicken" to applause.

Betty and Ludden appeared together on the panel for the first time August 4–8, 1975. On the last day, one player said, "I haven't tried Betty yet." "I've tried Betty," said Rayburn with a grin, prompting Ludden to mock threaten the host while Betty laughed and the audience applauded.

By that appearance, the series had started a weekly syndicated nighttime version called *Match Game PM*. To compensate for contestants playing on only one show, *Match Game PM* had two Super Match games. That way, contestants could try for up to $10,000 instead of $5,000.

According to Roger Dobkowitz, scorekeeper for the show, this point is where problems started to occur as producer Ira Skutch recycled questions from the daytime *Match Game* to use on *Match Game PM*. Indeed, Skutch reused at least five questions related to Betty alone.

Still, *Match Game PM* was a hit, and Betty contributed some great moments starting with the second show. "Marc Antony said, 'Times are so bad here in ancient Egypt that yesterday, I saw Cleopatra standing on the banks of the Nile selling her BLANK,'" said Rayburn. The contestant answered "barge." Betty quipped, "Her asp was half-priced. She was just 'half-asped,'" before giving her answer of "asp."

On the seventeenth *Match Game PM* show, Rayburn said, "When Betty White's husband Allen Ludden answered the phone and heard heavy breathing on the other end, he turned to Betty and said, 'It's BLANK.'" The contestant answered, "one of your dogs." Betty's response was "your mother" and added, "That could be a match, if you think about it!"

A bigger problem became apparent on the daytime show on October 26, 1977. Betty had her usual fun, taking tissues Rayburn gave to her and stuffing them in her blouse. "You don't need them there!" he laughed. As usual, Betty was upset about a question implying killing an animal and disliked being in the last seat, since she usually determined whether a contestant won.

The discord came as Rayburn informed viewers that CBS was moving the series to 11 a.m. effective November 7. Charles Nelson Reilly was irked about the switch, as were others.

"It just died," remembered writer Dick DeBartolo. "Because kids loved it after school."

Betty was on the show for its debut in the new time slot. When she returned in December 1977, the show moved to 4 p.m. Eastern on the fourth show after six weeks of bad ratings.

The show tried to regain its momentum with a few adjustments. On January 20, 1978, Rayburn told the panel about a new camera angled over the end of the top tier. Betty turned around, smiled, hiked up her skirt, and nodded her head in a come hither look to applause and whistles.

The time between when Rayburn asked questions and the celebrities wrote the answers was edited out, as well. That often meant some good banter between the panelists and with Rayburn was lost.

The biggest problem emerging in 1978 was Richard Dawson. The man sitting next to Betty had long been a favorite for players to match given his wit and creativity in answers. But he got to host his own game show in 1976, *Family Feud*. When that series surpassed *Match Game* a year later as the top daytime game show, he often seemed aloof and detached on *Match Game*.

"Richard had an ego, and it really came through when he did *Family Feud*," said production manager Andrew J. Selig.

The tipping point for Dawson was when Rayburn unveiled a star wheel contestants spun with all the celebrities' names on June 28, 1978. Landing on the name would determine which celebrity the player would try to match to win ten times what he or she earned in the Super Match. Having usually been picked in this portion, Dawson found the addition an affront and sulked more.

The last time Betty did a show with Dawson, on August 16, 1978, he claimed he had a lingering eye infection forcing him to wear sunglasses on the show. He left *Match Game* soon thereafter.

The daytime show already was in bad shape before he departed. *Broadcasting Magazine* reported from January through August 1978, *Match Game 78* was a low number eighteen in daytime, virtually tying its competition, *The Edge of Night*, on ABC. In contrast, *All in the Family* reruns airing before *Match Game* ranked at number five.

The daytime *Match Game* ended the following year. Betty stayed with the syndicated version, which during the 1979–1980 season was available both as a daily offering and a nighttime weekly show. Some future celebrities were contestants when Betty appeared, including actress Kirstie Alley and TV commentator Donny Deutsch in 1979–1980.

In the last three weeks of shows for the 1980–1981 season, Brett Somers got a role in a play and couldn't do the show. Betty sat in Somers' seat for the last week and exclaimed in mock horror, "I hate this! I absolutely hate these character parts, playing these older women!" That same week, upset when Rayburn said the panel missed an obvious answer, Betty switched places with him to host and read a question. She pretended to hike up her skirt to laughter.

Though no one knew it, the last taped episode of *Match Game* for the 1981–1982 season was the series finale, too. The show began with Charles Nelson Reilly pretending to be affectionate with a female mannequin. "Well, that's the dummy they use, 'Zelda,' to balance out all the color values on each camera," said Rayburn. "Yeah, but who's the blonde?" joked Betty in response.

Later, one female contestant kissed McLean Stevenson even though he had a cold, which prompted Betty to quip, "May I suggest that she take that and pass it along to Richard Dawson?" "Yes, splendid idea," laughed Gene, who still smarted from Dawson's departure. Betty did not do much after that, but it was a lively episode to end the series.

Match Game would be revived several times later, including most recently with Alec Baldwin as host on ABC every summer since 2016. Betty only did a version on ABC at noon from 1990 to 1991 for three weeks, where the magic clearly was gone for her with the series. Given the increasingly vulgar and single entendre answers, the split was a good decision for her.

Celebrity Sweepstakes (April 1, 1974–October 1, 1976; 1974–1977)
April 29–May 3, 1974; March 18–21, 1975; March 29–April 2, 1976; possibly more in syndication

Six celebrities sat in a row decorated with a horse racing gate motif on *Celebrity Sweepstakes*. After host Jim MacKrell read a question, members of the studio audience bet which of the celebrities could answer the query correctly. The two competing contestants saw the odds for each star generated by the votes and placed their bets accordingly, with higher possible payouts for stars with higher odds having the right answer.

Betty did the show only a few times because *Celebrity Sweepstakes* tried to use many different stars, MacKrell said. "We had a lot of them. The problem is, beyond their marquee value, which is great, then you've got to play the game and understand it and understand what it is you're doing. Many of the stars that we booked were not game show veterans and really didn't understand the game itself. They played, but they just didn't get into the spirit of it. It happened a few times. Fortunately, we had a cast of six up there, so you could avoid the ones that didn't get it."

Celebrity Sweepstakes was so popular daily on NBC that a syndicated version began in the fall of 1974. MacKrell said its demise began when Madeline David replaced Lin Bolen as NBC's vice president of daytime programs on February 1, 1976. "When she replaced Lin, she cancelled most of the shows that Lin had something to do with. She wanted to set her own agenda, I think."

MacKrell remembered one night his wife Cathy took a message from David, and he returned the call. "And she said, 'How are you?' And I said, 'I'm terrific. How are you?' She said, 'I'm great. I wanted to call you to tell you that we want you to do a pilot for us. Now, nothing is wrong with *Celebrity Sweepstakes*. We love it. But this is our way of keeping you at the network.' I said, 'Okay, that's great! I'll be glad to do that. Thank you very much.'

"And we said goodbye, and I turned to Cathy and said, 'We've just been cancelled.' Doesn't it sound to reason, if you hear that from the network? I did two pilots for them, and that went another way." *Celebrity Sweepstakes* went off NBC seven months after David became the head of daytime. The game show's syndicated version ran an additional year, while David was out of her job by the time Fred Silverman took over all programming at NBC in 1978.

"That era of game shows for me, at the time *Celebrity Sweepstakes* was on, was just an absolutely charmed time," said MacKrell. "I just had a wonderful, wonderful time."

Showoffs (June 30, 1975–December 26, 1975)
August 18–22, 1975; September 29–October 3, 1975
Goodson-Todman took the game of charades and had two trios of two celebrities and a noncelebrity contestant compete in conveying the same list of words within a minute on *Showoffs*. Naturally, one trio was offstage and unable to overhear the other team play.

The trio with the most correct identifications after two rounds played a bonus game. There, the winning contestant had ten seconds to convey one word to the two celebrity partners for $1,000, another ten seconds for a different word for $2,000, and a third word in fifteen seconds for $5,000. The contestant could stop at any time during these three rounds if desired.

Showoffs replaced *Password* on the ABC daytime schedule. Betty appeared with Allen Ludden opposite George Maharis and Conny Van Dyke the first week and Ron Masak and Lee Meriwether the last week.

The Magnificent Marble Machine (July 7, 1975–June 11, 1976)
October 13-17, 1975 (Earl Holliman); January 26–30, 1976
The Magnificent Marble Machine ran on NBC opposite *Showoffs*. Some regard the former series as a bigger flop even though it lasted longer. The game's set certainly was larger than that of *Showoffs* or pretty much anything else on TV in 1975.

"*The Magnificent Marble Machine* featured a fifty-foot-long pinball machine which, when it came to its clamorous life with its many flashing lights and bells, buzzers and other noisy sound effects, aroused the audience into a frenzy," host Art James wrote in his unpublished autobiography. "Unfortunately, the excitement in the studio was never transmitted to those watching across the country." Two celebrity-contestant pairs played a word game to win the right to play the machine.

Robert Noah was co-executive producer of *The Magnificent Marble Machine* with Merrill Heatter and Bob Quigley. He said Heatter created the concept but left others to produce the shows. Noah agreed with James about the set's appeal to studio audiences. The problem was that people enjoy playing more than watching pinball games. "How is it when you can't play, when you have to watch other people play?" he said.

The Magnificent Marble Machine did have some amusing moments. In December 1975, Florence Henderson accidentally busted a pinball while trying to launch it with her body strength behind the oversized plunger. "You're not the first girl who's done that to a guy," quipped her celebrity opponent David Brenner. But as James noted, "The remark was edited out, and the viewing audience was robbed of witnessing a hilarious, spontaneous moment on television."

Like *Baffle*, *The Magnificent Marble Machine* went the all-celebrity players route on January 19, 1976, in an unsuccessful attempt to stave off cancellation. Five months later, NBC edited *The Magnificent Marble Machine* from its schedule. A clip of the series appeared in the 1979 movie *The China Syndrome*. James estimated he received 100 residual checks from TV showings of the film. Collectively, those checks amassed to a magnificent one dollar.

Cross-Wits (1975–1979)
January 5, 1976; March 1, 1976; May 1, 1976; September 13, 1976; November 8, 1976
When *Truth or Consequences* ended in 1974, one of its writers, Jerry Payne, made a deal with its executive producer Ralph Edwards for a new game show. *Cross-Wits* would have two teams, each composed of two celebrities and one noncelebrity contestant, solving crossword puzzles. Each answer would, in turn, serve as a clue to the secret topic of the puzzle to be identified to win money. To flesh out the concept, Edwards held a meeting with Payne, Mark Maxwell-Smith, another former writer on *Truth or Consequences*, and Bruce Belland, a development executive.

"And I think it was probably Bruce who said, 'You know, one of the big hits now is *Match Game*, and there's *Hollywood Squares*. And they all have jokes. So how can we incorporate jokes into *Cross-Wits*?'" recalled Maxwell-Smith. Edwards had Maxwell-Smith and Belland write setup clues with punchlines for each on cue cards for stars to read. A star could deliver the joke to host Jack Clark before he or she had seven seconds to give the correct answer.

Maxwell-Smith eventually found this approach burdensome and favored having Clark ask an open-ended question with possible humorous ad-libs to follow by the celebrities. "That is, the answer that we were going for might have just been 'actress.' And the clue would be like "This is something that a lot of people would call Roseanne Barr!'" he said. "It got to the point where there were two sets of material on the show."

He did acknowledge that Betty was among the performers who could do either kind of joke well on *Cross-Wits*. "I won't say they were smarter, but as a guy who wrote, I'd say easily fifty percent of the material the first four years of the show, I would do some dreadful pun setup, and somebody like Betty would get it." The show aired weekly in nighttime syndication.

Maxwell-Smith also noted how competitive Betty was on *Cross-Wits*. "When the questions were poorly written, Betty couldn't divine the answer, she'd say, 'What's wrong with myself? What do I know about what I'm talking about myself?' And she'd do it with elegance and charm."

Cross-Wits ran five years in syndication. Betty didn't do a syndicated revival in 1986–1987.

Stumpers (October 4, 1976–December 31, 1976)
October 25–29, 1976 (John Schuck); December 20–24, 1976
Two teams, one each with a celebrity, competed on *Stumpers*. One team member reviewed three clues for a mystery noun and tried to pick the least helpful clue to give to an opposing team member. The player had a few seconds to guess as many possibilities for an answer. A correct guess on the first clue won fifteen points, ten points on the second, and five on the third. Three missed opportunities stumped a player and gave opponents the chance to win fifteen points with a correct response. The "Double Up" round followed, with both team members picking clues and guessing together to get thirty points on the first clue, twenty on the second, and ten on the third.

The first team to seventy won and played a bonus round. There, the celebrity tried to pick the best clue of three to help his or her partner connect the word or words to a famous personality. Each name identified won $100, and if all ten were correct, the player won $10,000.

Executive producer Lin Bolen helped create this game after she left as head of daytime programming at NBC. Regarding her selection of host, game show historian Steve Beverly said, "She took so much criticism because of that quote that ended up in the *Newsweek* article of her calling her morning show hosts 'my studs.' And then when she got her production deal, she said, 'How would you have thought of anybody any more distant from a stud than Allen Ludden?'"

Despite Ludden at the helm, *Stumpers* died opposite *The Price is Right* on CBS.

"The game was not that good," added Beverly. "It was a show that Allen did the best that he could with it."

Betty's second appearance was an all-star week where she and Joanna Barnes faced Peter Bonerz and Dick Gautier. By then, the series was a lost cause. *Stumpers* went off the following week.

The Hollywood Squares (October 17, 1966–June 14, 1980; 1986–1989; 1998–2004) December 27–31, 1976; August 28–September 1, 1978; September 4–8, 1978; September 15–19, 1986; December 1–5, 1986; March 16–20, 1987; October 5–9, 1987; January 25–29, 1988; April 11–15, 1988; September 12–16, 1938; November 28–December 2, 1988; February 27–March 3, 1989; September 13–17, 1999; November 3–7, 2003

The Hollywood Squares had two contestants play tic-tac-toe with celebrities in every square. The object was to get three stars in a row horizontally, vertically, or diagonally. Players captured a square by determining whether a celebrity's answer to a question from host Peter Marshall (for the 1966–1980 NBC daytime version), John Davidson (for the 1986–1989 syndicated version), or Tom Bergeron (for the 1998–2004 syndicated version) was correct. The winner of the best two of three games played a bonus game, which varied over the years.

Betty came to *The Hollywood Squares* rather late in part because of her association with its rival in spirit, *Match Game*. And while that show encouraged ad-libbing, *The Hollywood Squares* had scripted gag lines. For example, in her last appearance during Game Show Week II in 2003, Bergeron asked, "Does Dr. Joyce Brothers say that for guys, watching football is a healthy substitute for sex?" Discerning viewers knew a writer had Betty joke, "Well, during both of them, you can hear, 'It's up! It's good!'"

Even so, *The Hollywood Squares* did give Betty some leeway to drop her own characteristically clever remarks. Learning on the same show, one male contestant engaged in "combat grappling," she quipped, "I haven't done that since ... What time is it?" She was also likely the only celebrity to appear on the series over four decades.

Password Plus (January 8, 1979–March 26, 1982)
February 5–9, 1979 (Dick Martin); March 5–9, 1979 (Robert Pine); May 21–25, 1979 (John Philip Law); October 15–19, 1979 (Joanna Gleason); January 14–18, 1980 (Greg Morris); March 31–April 4, 1980 (Dick Gautier); May 5–9, 1980 (Greg Morris);

June 9–13, 1980 (John Astin); July 28–August 1, 1980 (Bill Cullen); September 23–29, 1980 (Gene Rayburn); December 17–23, 1980 (Dick Martin); January 23–29, 1981 (Wesley Eure); March 2–6, 1981 (Lucille Ball, Desi Arnaz Jr., Dick Martin); April 24–30, 1981 (Dick Martin); September 14–19, 1981 (Dick Martin); December 16–22, 1981 (Pat Sajak); February 18–23, 1982 (Regis Philbin)

After runs on CBS and ABC, *Password* went to NBC daytime in a rendition called *Password Plus*, with Allen Ludden still as host. The pairs of celebrity and noncelebrity partners now had only four chances to guess a word. That word would then appear on a board as one of five clues in the "Password Puzzle." The puzzle answers could be a person, place, or thing. The first team to correctly identify two puzzles played "Alphabetics," a bonus round where the celebrity gave clues to ten words arranged alphabetically. Contestants could play up to seven times.

Lew Retrum, the grand champion of *Password* from 1971 to 1975, had a bad experience with the revamp. "I kept in touch with [*Password* producer] Howard Felsher, and he called and hired me. Asked me to come in and write *Password Plus*. My association was short-lived. They wanted to pay me $100 for an entire week's worth of material. It wasn't like the greatest writing ever.

"I came up with one they thought was too complicated. It was 'Valley Forge,' and it was 'freezing,' and I don't remember what the other clues were. To me, it was obvious to anybody who went through fifth grade. The other guys there didn't know what it was, never heard of Valley Forge. 'You're too Eastern!' they said."

Retrum felt the puzzles were "dumbed down," too. "One of them was 'big,' 'red,' 'country.' It was 'Russia.' That to me was ridiculous. I mean, 'big,' how hard is it to get that? 'Little,' 'big.'

"So, I said, 'Listen, if I'm going to do this, I'm going to need more money. I'm not asking for much. Just something reasonable.' And Howard flew off the handle with the word 'reasonable.' Didn't like that. Fired me on the spot. And that was the end of that."

Betty had no such misgivings. She was in good spirits doing the show again and bantering with her husband, the host, even when she twisted her ankle going down the stairs with Robert Pine in 1979. When on that same show Ludden asked, "You know, Betty, people keep asking me, do you play *Password* at home?" she deadpanned, "Well, I have to do something, you know!" As the audience applauded, Ludden murmured, "I don't know why I asked that."

That same week, when one contestant was a Naval officer, Ludden said, "I can't recognize two stripes as a lieutenant, right?" and told Betty, "I know you could." She responded, "You haven't spent as much time in the Navy as I have!" 'I don't even want to hear about it!" he said back.

Ludden also told Betty, "You play delightfully, and it's good to have you here." "At the house or here?" she asked. "Well, she plays pretty good at the house too, I have to tell you," he allowed.

On October 16, 1979, Ludden really stepped into trouble when Betty played opposite Joanna Gleason and each had female partners. "Here I am with three beautiful ladies," he said. "I know which one he's leaving out," cracked Betty in response to audience applause.

But her jokes ended in 1980, when Betty and Ludden learned he had incurable stomach cancer. Bill Cullen filled in temporarily as Ludden recuperated from surgery in March and April 1980. Ludden came back to host *Password Plus*, then suffered a stroke in October 1980. Cullen was then hosting another NBC game show, *Blockbusters*, and couldn't reprise his role. The producers of *Password Plus* contacted another host to replace Ludden effective October 27, 1980.

"They called me and they said, 'Tom, would you come in and sub for Allen Ludden?'" said Tom Kennedy. "I said, 'It would be my sole pleasure only if he approves of me.' And they said, 'Well, he's the one who told us to call you.' So I said, 'That'll do it!'

"And so, I came in merely as a replacement and said, 'How's he doing?' They said, 'Well, he's doing better, and we're hoping he'll be back soon. We don't know how long you'll be doing it. Is that okay with you?' I said, 'Anything's okay with me. It's my pleasure. I hope he gets well soon.

"As we know, a couple of years later, he passed away. It turned out he had cancer and I didn't even know it … I didn't bother to enquire because Betty and Allen had their plate full. I would just say to Betty, 'How's he doing?' and she said, 'Honey, he's doing just fine.' She's Miss Positivity."

In a classy move, when Betty did the show three months after Kennedy took over, he introduced her as "Betty 'Mrs. Allen Ludden' White" and hugged her as the audience gave her a standing ovation. She got misty-eyed, but when Tom gave her a handkerchief, she said, "I'm not going to do that! I'm going to be a good kid! I really am! That's a, you really know how to throw a girl!"

During the show, when Betty correctly guessed "sousaphone" from the first clue of "tuba," a stunned Kennedy said, "Good to see you back, Betty!" When she combined "sousaphone" and the previous clue "yellow" to correctly guess "brass" in the Password Puzzle, Kennedy joked, "It's unmitigated cheating is what it is! She is absolutely brilliant!"

Later that week, Betty, Kennedy, and Dick Martin had a laughing fit when Dick gave "France" as an illegal clue for "French." Betty had a similarly raucous time with Martin and Lucille Ball and the latter's son Desi Arnaz Jr. during an all-star charity week in 1981. Lucy complained so much about Betty's clue "Caligari" for "cabinet," as in the film *The Cabinet of Dr. Caligari*, that Betty said, "Lucy, be sweet!" The TV legend then pasted a big artificial smile on her face to the audience's amusement. Betty cracked Lucy up by adding, "I didn't say be sickening!"

At the end of the week, Kennedy announced Betty had won the most money for her charity, the Los Angeles Zoo, and a $5,000 bonus. After Ludden's death on June 9, 1981, she returned to *Password Plus* three more times before the series ended.

Liars Club writer Shelley Herman noted her friend, Fred Wostbrock, represented Ludden's estate for royalties earned from his reruns of *Password* and *Password Plus* on GSN, also known as the Game Show Network. He received commissions from Betty for his work. "And she would send him checks as Betty White Ludden. It wasn't 'Betty White.' The commission checks, she personally used 'Ludden,' which I was just astounded when he showed me.

"And it was always a handwritten note thanking him for something he had done. Handwritten notes from Betty White Ludden." Betty had made sure to carry on her husband's legacy.

Mindreaders (August 13, 1979–January 11, 1980)
September 10–14, 1979 (Bill Daily); November 19–23, 1979 (Nipsey Russell)
A guessing game pitting men against women, this daily show on NBC had two teams compete. A celebrity captain had to guess which of two possible answers each of his or her three contestant members gave to a question. A right answer won fifty dollars, but a wrong one gave the other quartet the same amount and the celebrity captain a chance to win more money by guessing the remaining opposing contestants' answers correctly.

The first team to amass $300 played "Judge the Jury," where the three contestants of the winning team decided how many out of ten studio audience members reacted to a question. The correct number won $500, while matching the right number within two either way netted $200. After one round of guessing, the three contestants on a team played "Celebrity Turnabout," which could multiply their accumulated earnings to that point by ten times. A majority of the trio had to vote correctly on their leader's reaction to a question to win the money.

Driven by gut instinct with no other talent involved, *Mindreaders* ended after five months. While claiming Dick Martin did fine as host, game show historian Steve Beverly added, "I just think that it was not a great game, and you had to have a great game to go in at noon."

Whew! (April 23, 1979–May 30, 1980)
March 31–April 4, 1980 (John Saxon)

Whew! started with two players competing before adding celebrity partners on November 5, 1979. A noncelebrity challenger chose one of two categories his or her team would charge or block on a board. The board had five rows, each with five boxes from ten to fifty dollars, and a top tier with boxes of $200, $350, and $500. The "chargers" were in a soundproof room as the other pair told host Tom Kennedy what six blocks to hide behind individual boxes that would give the chargers a five-second delay if picked. The "blockers" could place one block on the top tier and no more than three on any other row.

The chargers had to scale the board within a minute to win the round. Otherwise, the blockers would win and get any cash amounts from blocked boxes the chargers had selected. The pair of chargers alternated in amending a blooper revealed behind a box on each level to ascend to the next row. For example, in the category of Movies, Betty had this underlined blooper: "Jurors were locked in a hot jury room in 'Twelve Sweaty Men.'" She correctly answered "Angry."

If the pair was running out of time, the noncelebrity charger could yell out "Long shot!" and automatically go to the top row. The move also allowed the blocker to place a block on one of the boxes. The charger had to guess the right box without a block and answer it correctly to win.

The first team to win two rounds played "The Gauntlet," which converted every hundred dollars earned in those rounds into additional seconds to add to a minute in playing time. The set pulled away to reveal upstage a jaw-dropping lineup of ten villains exquisitely designed by James J. Agazzi. The pair had to solve bloopers again to get past a pirate, a witch, and so on and win $25,000, with the noncelebrity choosing whether to face the first or last five villains.

Betty's appearance here was excellent. Her humor set the tone during her introduction. As John Saxon promoted his films *Beyond Evil* and *Battle Beyond the Stars*, she quipped, "He's doing 'Beyond' movies!" Mentioning how she and Allen Ludden would do the season premiere of *The Love Boat*, she said, "He's in love with his horse and I'm in love with his friend. No, that's not it!" As her contestant partner told Kennedy his plans if he won $25,000, she interjected, "Are you interested in older women at all?" Naturally, Betty helped him win, and he gave her two bear hugs and a kiss to celebrate while Tom congratulated her for a beautiful job.

"It was a well-constructed show, I want to say that," Kennedy said. "However, it was so fast and so dynamic that I felt the home audience didn't have a chance to properly digest the material that was being dealt with. And it turns out, I was right. A lot of people kind of watched it, but they just didn't come back, because you had to labor to keep up with it. So, when they added celebrities, I figured that the ratings were going down, and that they were doing that to goose it back up."

The production company taped at least three pilots in 1978 before *Whew!* joined the CBS lineup in 1979. Though the game show ended only a year later, *Whew!* still amassed the longest run of any daytime game show introduced on CBS between 1975 and 1982, for whatever that's worth.

Chain Reaction (January 14, 1980–June 20, 1980)
March 10–14, 1980; April 28–May 2, 1980; June 16–20, 1980
In *Chain Reaction* two teams, each with two celebrities and one noncelebrity player, attempted to name six words related in some way to each word proceeding and following them. Players asked for a letter in the answer either before or after a word as a clue. Correct answers won the same amount of points as the number of letters in the word except for two words per game where correct answers were worth double their points. The first team to get fifty points played an end game where the contestant could win $10,000 if he or she could identify ten subjects in ninety seconds. The two celebrity partners alternated in giving one word at a time to form a question as a hint for each subject. One celebrity switched teams for the next round of regular games.

Betty's first appearance had her teamed with Brian Patrick Clarke opposite Allen

Ludden and his partner Anita Gillette. When the opposing player incorrectly guessed "tower" in front of "lights," Betty got laughs for singing the tune "Harbor Lights" with "tower" in place of "harbor."

On the finale with Jay Johnson, Ron Silver, and Joyce Bulifant, Betty promoted her appearance with Ludden on the season opener of *The Love Boat*. She and Joyce won $500 for their partner. In the second end game, Betty called Ron "my hirsute friend" as they won $10,000 for their partner. Everyone then played a game for the Children's Village charity while alternating chairs and winning $700. The final puzzle's answers read from top to bottom, "Chain-Reaction-Audience-Viewers-Nielsen-Number-Cancellation-Good-bye."

Chain Reaction ended due to tepid ratings and the need of NBC's programming chief to cancel three daily game shows to add *The David Letterman Show*. "Freddie Silverman thought that David was going to be the next Arthur Godfrey," said *Chain Reaction* director Bruce Burmester. Ironically, Burmester initially directed *The David Letterman Show* before Hal Gurnee took over. The show ran four months before ending on October 24, 1980.

Burmester thought another factor hurt *Chain Reaction*. "You had to have a good vocabulary, you had to be able to unravel the associations between the words and things like that. One of the things you have to say about [executive producer] Bob Stewart's shows is that they always tended to be more about word problems, and again I hesitate to say intellectual. Whereas with *The Newlywed Game* and shows like that with much more visceral, emotional type of shows, Bob's were always kind of more cerebral."

Battlestars (October 26, 1981–April 23, 1982; April 4, 1983–July 1, 1983)
October 26–November 13, 1981 (three consecutive weeks); November 23–27, 1981; January 4–8, 1982; April 5–9, 1982; June 20–July 1, 1983 (two consecutive weeks)

"It was obviously a knockoff show of *Hollywood Squares*," game show historian Steve Beverly said of *Battlestars*. "They tried to give it more of a futuristic look with the set, et cetera. But plain and simple, it was a knockoff show. And if you're going to do a knockoff show, it better be really, really, really good." Few who have seen *Battlestars* would agree with that assessment.

Instead of nine celebrities in squares, *Battlestars* had six celebrities in interconnected triangles. The three triangles on the top row pointed up, and the three on the bottom pointed down. One of two contestants used plungers to stop on one of ten numbered vertices surrounding the stars. If a vertex connected to more than one star, the player could choose which star to answer a question. When a star had all three vertices deactivated, the player "captured" the celebrity. The first player to capture three stars played a bonus round. Executive producer Merrill Heatter sold the series after his ex-partner Bob Quigley retired, and yes, they had created *Hollywood Squares*.

Betty supplied some much needed humor. When host Alex Trebek noted Debbie Reynolds had celebrated turning another year older on April Fool's Day in 1982, Betty said, "Did you know it's been my birthday, too?" "When?" he asked. "January," she said with a poker face, garnering laughter and applause. She also was the punchline for a great joke. After a question revealed any woman with a yellow card meant she was a prostitute in old Russia, Rip Taylor pretended to be on the phone saying, "I have Betty's yellow cards, now shut up!"

Battlestars ended after six months, only to reappear a year later. Rather than face *The Price is Right*, NBC executives thought *Battlestars* had a better shot against *The Young and the Restless*.

"They didn't have anything better, and the thought was, 'Okay, well, maybe if we changed the time slot,'" said Beverly. "And they promised a heavy promotional campaign for it, which didn't work." Bringing back a lemon in the ratings so quickly was a disaster. The second go-round, dubbed *The New Battlestars*, ran only three months.

Betty did both *Battlestars* eight times total over nine months, more than half of the number of visits she made on *Hollywood Squares* over twenty-five years. Draw your own conclusions from that fact.

Celebrity Bullseye (1980–1982)
Two weeks in May 1982

Bullseye was a syndicated daily game show whose title came from three spinning circles that stopped when one of two competing players pressed a button. The top circles revealed two different categories and dollar amounts in hundreds for the player to choose. The bottom circle indicated the number of questions from host Jim Lange that needed to be answered correctly to win money. A player won a game by being the first to reach $2,000. The contestant winning two out of three games played a bonus round and competed against a new player.

Ratings for *Bullseye* worsened midway through the second season. "There was a note from stations who renewed it a second year that you better do something with this thing or we're not going to take a third year," recalled game show historian Steve Beverly. Converting the game to *Celebrity Bullseye* and having stars like Betty play for charities failed to prevent its cancellation.

The $25,000 Pyramid (September 20, 1982–July 1, 1988)/**The $100,000 Pyramid** (1985–1987; 1991)/**Pyramid** (2002)

October 11–15, 1982 (Charles Siebert); June 6–10, 1983 (Soupy Sales); October 24–28, 1983 (Ed Begley Jr.); January 16–20, 1984 (Earl Holliman); March 26–30, 1984 (Mike Farrell); June 25–29, 1984 (Nipsey Russell); November 12–16, 1984 (Dick Cavett); January 21–25, 1985 (Nathan Cook); May 20–24, 1985 (Joel Brooks); February 17–21, 1986 (David Graf); May 5–9, 1986 (Mitchell Laurance); August 4–8, 1986 (Jamie Farr); June 1–5, 1987 (Bill Cullen); April 4–8, 1988 (David Graf); September 23–27, 1985 (Nathan Cook); April 21–25, 1986 (Barry Jenner); Sept. 14–18, 1987 (David Graf); January 14–18, 1991 (Tom Villard); May 27–31, 1991 (John Schuck); November 25, 2002 (Dick Clark)

Bob Stewart left Goodson-Todman in 1964 after having created *To Tell the Truth*, *The Price is Right*, and *Password*. The executive producer had his biggest solo hit with what began as *The $10,000 Pyramid* on March 26, 1973, on CBS. Like *Password*, two pairs of celebrities and their partners competed, but the pace was more intense. Each partner had to convey seven items linked in some way in thirty seconds, such as "Describe these parts of a car." Players could use body language and say as many words for clues except part of the word or phrase.

After three rounds, the team with the highest score went to the Winner's Circle. One partner gave only a list of items related to six subjects, like "Directors." The subjects appeared behind six boxes shaped like a pyramid. Players who got all six categories in a minute won $10,000.

Original director Mike Gargiulo said he was instrumental in getting Dick Clark to host his first game show since *Missing Links* ended in 1964. Stewart had interviewed at least five candidates when Gargiulo was editing a parade he taped in Toronto hosted by Clark a few weeks earlier to be part of *The CBS All-American Thanksgiving Day Parade* in 1972.

"And I came back to New York and saw Bob," Gargiulo said. "We had time together to do several things. And I said, 'Well, I've got a guy who would work.' 'You mean the guy who does the dance thing in the afternoon [*American Bandstand*]? What does he know about anything?' I said, 'Well, he's pretty good.'" Clark auditioned for Stewart and got the job.

Gargiulo's successor, Bruce Burmester, added, "Very early on, Dick learned that Bob Stewart and the people he had working for him would never do a thing on the show that would put Dick in a bad light. And once that happened, he just kind of sat back and said, 'Okay, I don't have to protect myself anymore. All I have to do is come in and do the job.'"

The $10,000 Pyramid moved to ABC in 1974 and adjusted its top prize in 1976 to become *The $20,000 Pyramid* before ending on June 27, 1980. Two years later the series returned to CBS and gave players a five-day limit to win $25,000. Clark rejoined as host, and because the series now was taped in Los Angeles rather than New York City, Betty made her debut.

"This is your first time you've played Pyramid?" a surprised Clark asked Betty in 1982. She told him, "I played a lot of the other games, but you were always doing them from New York, and I could never quite schedule them." Clark joked she was the reason they moved to Los Angeles.

Betty was a natural for *The $25,000 Pyramid*, playing with charm and tenacity. She won a rare double tiebreaker against Mike Farrell to go to the Winner's Circle in 1984. On her last day with Bill Cullen in 1987, Betty broke a tiebreaker with one second to spare for the first game, then lost a tiebreaker on the second one. This was the last TV appearance of Cullen, who coincidentally had hosted the syndicated version of *The $10,000 Pyramid* from 1974 to 1979.

The $25,000 Pyramid ended on CBS in 1988. The syndicated version, *The $100,000 Pyramid*, also went off in 1988 after three years and a trio of guest shots by Betty. Clark hosted that show, too, which meant a hectic production schedule. Burmester said the normal pattern for *The $25,000 Pyramid* was to work two days every other week. "And when we did the syndicated version, we would go in, and we would work five shows on Thursdays and come in Friday and do five network shows and then do five syndicated shows," he said. "So, that was a long day."

Despite the circumstances, Burmester rarely had to stop taping or do extensive editing. He credited that achievement to the confidence Clark and Stewart had in each other since the show started in 1973. Clark was not infallible, however. Betty laughed on her first time on *The $100,000 Pyramid* when he gave out the year of a new car prize as 1958 and not 1985.

Betty did revivals of the property in syndication in 1991, where new host John Davidson said, "She's the best games player in all of television." and in 2002, with Donny Osmond as host. Appropriately, she faced off against Dick Clark in her last appearance on the game show.

Betty held the microphone she would use to let the male celebrities be heard in *Just Men!* She taped the series while doing a recurring role on *Mama's Family*, also on NBC in 1983. Courtesy of the Adam Nedeff Collection.

Just Men! (January 3, 1983–April 1, 1983)
Regular hostess
After Betty lost the hosting job on *Hollywood's Talking* in 1973, two other women co-hosted game shows. Sarah Purcell emceed *The Better Sex* with Bill Anderson from July 18, 1977 through January 13, 1978, while Leslie Uggams joined Peter Marshall

on *Fantasy* from September 13, 1982 through October 28, 1983. Betty finally became the first solo daytime game show hostess with *Just Men!*

The show's creator, executive producer, and writer was Rick Rosner. He created the hit cop drama *CHiPs* from 1978 through 1983 for NBC. "The story was I told—and I cannot say I was in the room when this happened, so if somebody else denies it, I'm not going to say no—Rick Rosner, who later went on to produce a version of *Hollywood Squares*, said, 'Oooo! I can make *Hollywood Squares* even better. Let's have it be all men, and it's daytime TV, it'll be all studs,'" said Mark Maxwell-Smith. "And I don't know if he said immediately there'll be a female host, but that's how he pitched it.

"And the first title he wanted for it was *STUDS*—*S*tars *T*alking *U*p *D*own *S*ideways. Remember, he did *CHiPs*. He was told, 'Oh, that's far too risqué,' so that's when they came up with the title *Just Men!*

"Now, Betty White did the pilot of *Just Men!* and apparently it didn't test all that well. This is the story I was told. Rick Rosner—and he should not be faulted for this, he has to be credited for being a good salesman—he either called or flew to New York, I don't know which, and got a meeting with Grant Tinker [then head of programming at NBC] and said, 'It's Betty White! You love Betty White! How can you not put Betty White on the air?' And so Betty White—and this is what's important to your book—Betty White was the reason that show was given a series order."

To address the pilot's kinks, NBC's West Coast head of daytime programming, Susan Simons, asked Maxwell-Smith to serve as a consultant for the series, based on his game show experience going back to 1969. "Rick said, 'Hi, how are you doing? Hello,' and then didn't say anything to me the next six weeks. Every once in a while, there would be something so egregious that I would say, 'Here's an alternative. How about if we do this?' And sometimes he said, 'Yeah, okay, fine.' And then he'd say—and I'd think it was because he didn't understand—he'd ask me to go and tell Betty directly. And then she graciously would take the note, and she'd do it that way. So it was not so much the actual structure, but it would be a moment about delivery. Do you reveal the contestant's guess first or the answer first, or whatever it might be."

This wobbly working relationship gave a rough start to *Just Men!* In the game, seven male celebrities greeted the audience before taking their seats. Betty followed by mixing one key that started a car with six others, then distributed the keys individually among the men. After interviewing two female contestants, Betty turned over a board with the show's logo to reveal on the other side a topic and a number, usually two, next to the word yes or no.

Betty revealed to the contestants the question the men had, such as "Are you a health food nut?" The number indicated how many answered yes. Contestants alternated for a minute in asking the men prepared questions. The answers were to serve as hints on whether each man was pro or con on the topic. A correct guess as to what man agreed to the desired response won the contestant that celebrity's key in the first round and froze that celebrity. In the second round, an incorrect guess for a question for the five remaining men gave the star's key to the opposing contestant.

The final round let the contestants ask only one question to the remaining four men and predict whether that celebrity said yes or no. A correct guess won that star's key and allowed the contestant to steal one of her opponent's keys. However, a wrong guess meant the opponent got the key and could steal one from the woman guessing at the time. The contestants interviewed all four men unless one player won all seven keys. The winner got to try two of the keys on the car. If one worked, she won the car. If not, she had up to six more chances to return and try to win.

Maxwell-Smith found several problems with *Just Men!* One was a failure to have at least one regular recurring panelist to play a certain role in spicing interest in the game. The closest the series had was three appearances by Steve Sax, shortstop for the Los Angeles Dodgers, who unimpressed Maxwell-Smith. "They thought he was the sexiest guy or something."

More irksome to him was the format. "There seems to me there was a point in the development of the game whether there was going to be a question about Steve Sax instead of just answering the question. But that said, when you go to Steve Sax, you don't want to just hear him say, 'I knew it' or 'I didn't know it.' You want business. Otherwise, you can have a picture of Steve Sax.

"Betty tried to the best of her ability—because I remember she'd go up and down, she'd go right next to those people with the mike—and she was attempting to establish a rapport. And some of these people were not 'rapport,' they were just poor. They could only rap poorly, or whatever."

Indeed, Betty did plenty of walking fast on the multileveled set depending on what celebrity the contestant chose, as she had the only working microphone. Amid all the movement, she managed to get in some good quick asides to the panelists.

"Do you sleep in pajamas, Gene? I can't remember," she once asked Gene Rayburn, implying sexual activity.

Poor ratings led to an early demise for *Just Men!* On the finale, Betty said, "This is our last show now here on this network (audible awwws), and we cannot thank you enough for all the wonderful help and fun and joy and letters and everything that you've brought. We hope we're back again very soon someplace somewhere. And we're going to find you. And you know why we're going to be here, because it's just men!" Everyone cheered, but a revival never happened.

What did occur was Betty earned an Emmy for her work. "The Daytime Emmy Awards ceremony was held in New York, and I didn't make the trip because, once again, my chances were somewhere between zero and zilch," she recalled to Morrie Gelman and Gene Accas in *The Best in Television: 50 Years of Emmys*. " Imagine my astonishment when they called that night to say I had won. It was a gender-oriented choice, I'm sure, but I wasn't about to argue." Betty became the first host to win an Emmy for a game show that ran only thirteen weeks.

What's more, because *Just Men!* fell into the 1984 ceremony's eligibility period, Betty got another nomination as Outstanding Game Show Host that year. She lost to Bob Barker for *The Price is Right*, as did Richard Dawson for *Family Feud*. Dawson had also lost to Betty in 1983 along with Dick Clark for *The $25,000 Pyramid*, but both had won in the category, Dawson in 1978 and Clark in 1979. Despite the loss, Betty became the only game show host to get two separate Emmy nominations for a thirteen-week series.

"Even though after a couple of weeks you could smell [failure] in the studio, she did her all," said Maxwell-Smith. "Which is why she got that Emmy. She proved to me—and I've seen other examples of this—that somebody who's a real talent can take something that's mediocre and try to make it the best. She could've after all just kind of phoned it in. She tried her best."

Maxwell-Smith concluded his thoughts on the series by saying, "Ultimately, Betty proved to be the winner in all this. She's beyond an icon. And you know, another part of it is, having her as a host, you lose some of the beauty of what she is, because she's such a great game player."

Family Feud (1977–1985; 1988–1995)
November 14–18, 1983; March 1, 1984 (ABC nighttime special); February 11–15, 1985; February 6–10, 1995

Family Feud featured two quintets of people, related in some way, competing to name the most popular answers from 100 audience members surveyed. A toss-up question occurred between a member of each team to determine control. The toss-up winner decided whether his or her team would play. Host Richard Dawson then read the question to each member of the quintet at play and asked for an answer. Three misses or "strikes" let the other team steal if they gave a matching answer remaining on the board.

Teams earned all the points representing the total number of people who said the displayed answers. The first team to 200 points won. Later, the goal was 300 points. The victors played Fast Money, where two members had to give different answers to five survey questions under twenty seconds each. If their responses tallied 200 points total, the team won $5,000 or more.

Begun on ABC daytime July 12, 1976, *Family Feud* was an immediate hit, and a nighttime version launched in syndication in 1977. The show considered any grouping of five persons a "family." Such was the case in 1983 when the All-Star Game Show Hosts week had Betty as part of the "Magnificent M.C.s" with Nipsey Russell, Bob Eubanks, Jim Perry, and Bill Cullen. Opposite them was the "Heavenly Hosts" team of Tom Kennedy, Jim Lange, Peter Marshall, Leslie Uggams, and Bert Parks. Betty's team won $32,868 for the United Negro College Fund and the Special Olympics, with Betty contributing to one of the Fast Money wins. There were many cute references to Betty's recent Emmy win as best game show host on *Just Men!*

Betty reappeared in 1984 on the Second Annual Battle of the Perfect Tens hour nighttime special on ABC. She competed as the leader of "Betty's Bruisers," with Douglas Barr, Anthony Geary, Wolfgang Puck, and Bruce Jenner, against Bert Convy and his "Bert's Beauties," Rita Moreno, Charlene Tilton, Jayne Kennedy, and Shelley Smith.

As the series neared its end in 1985—both in syndication and ABC daytime, where its final show was on June 14, 1985—Betty appeared on a week of shows featuring celebrities with stars on the Hollywood Walk of Fame. Joining Betty were Arlene Dahl, Gloria DeHaven, Audrey Meadows, and Dorothy Lamour. They competed against Mark Goodson, Rod McKuen, Cesar Romero, Rory Calhoun, and

Keenan Wynn. Introducing her team on the first show, Betty cracked up Dawson and the audience by looking at the men and saying, "It's funny, they've all got gray hair and none of us has, I don't know why!" On the last show of the week, Betty won Fast Money and the women amassed $41,534 for the Pearl S. Buck Foundation for Amerasian Children.

Family Feud returned in syndication three years later. Dawson rejoined that version in 1994, which now used four players instead of five. A year later, Betty and Carol Burnett, faced off. "This is so special for me," Dawson said at the top of the fourth show after the audience gave the players a standing ovation. "There are two women in my life who mean everything to me, my wife Gretchen and my child, little girl, Shannon Nicole. If they were ever rivaled by another woman, they're both on the stage right here. These ladies are talented, they're warm and they're funny and they're kind and they're magic." Carol, her daughter, her son-in-law, and the latter's mother played opposite Betty and members of the "Pico Poker Club," Henry Polic II, Brenda Thomson, and Tony Pandolfo.

The jackpot for each team started at $5,000, with face-offs to add $1,000, $3,000, and $5,000 respectively to a team if a person could buzz in first and give the top answer. In the third show's face-off, Betty answered, "Something that gets dumped" with "a boyfriend," and got a strike, prompting her to say, "Well, you haven't been to my house!" Carol's team got $27,000 for the Hereditary Disease Foundation, while Betty's won $17,000 for the Los Angeles Zoo and the Morris Animal Foundation. At the end, Richard proclaimed the event "The best week I ever had."

Go (October 3, 1983–January 20, 1984)
October 10–14, 1983 (Fred Grandy); January 2–6, 1984 (Robert Mandan)
Executive producer Bob Stewart had tried having players make questions a word at a time to help their partners identify a subject at least as far back as 1972 with a pilot for ABC called *$10,000 Sweep*. After some revisions, including serving as the end game for *Chain Reaction* in 1980, *Go* became a competition between two teams of five players, each led by a celebrity captain. Four players, including the celebrity, sat at a table where individual monitors showed them a subject. Two players had to alternate one word at a time, creating a question for the fifth player to guess the subject. When correct, the fifth player moved to another chair where one of the previous players joined another player to generate another question for another subject. Essentially, the

fifth player moved to his or her left twice and then right twice to finish with the same two players where he or she started, with one being the celebrity captain.

The first team to score five correct answers in the least amount of time won that round's points. The first round was worth 250 points, the second 500, the third 750, and the fourth 1,250. A team needed at least 1,500 points to win the game and a chance for a $10,000 jackpot.

Host Kevin O'Connell spent almost as long explaining these rules as teams needed to play a game. Even more tiresome was the jackpot. Four team members, including the celebrity, stood behind one seated player. That player needed seven correct answers in a minute, using questions formed by the others, one word at a time. The first would be formed by all four, the second three players, the third two, the fourth just one player, the fifth two, the sixth three, and the seventh all four. Players who weren't needed to convey any question ran off stage and then rejoined as needed during the jackpot, which made this process a very disjointed endgame to watch.

Betty won at least one jackpot during her guest shots and joked about the fact that the only question missed was the first one she gave solo. The line was funnier than watching the game.

Stewart said the best game shows have viewers yelling clues back to their screens. He failed to heed his advice here. Playing along was hard if someone started a question with "How ...?" when a viewer expected "Why ... ?" instead. Disinterested viewers tuned out, and after a sixteen-week run, *Go* stopped and was gone.

Dream House (April 4, 1983–June 29, 1984)
May 14–18, 1984
Dream House was pretty much what its name implied, the top prize for two competing couples. Betty apparently made a guest shot one week as a promotional spot. She later worked with host Bob Eubanks on *Trivia Trap* and his assistant Debbie Bartlett on *Animal Crack-Ups*.

Body Language (June 4, 1984–January 3, 1986)
July 2-6, 1984 (Ed Begley Jr.); August 27–31, 1984 (Anson Williams); February 6–8, 1985 (Jamie Farr); November 25–27, 1985 (Jamie Farr)

The object of *Body Language* was to pantomime five words in a minute to help a partner fill a sentence with blanks that served as a clue to a puzzle. Even if the partner got all five words, two words in the sentence were missing to add to the difficulty of solving the puzzles. A miss could let the other team steal a win. The first two puzzles were worth $100 and the next two $250. The first team to reach $500 played a game where the contestant won $100 for each word identified in a minute from the celebrity partner's pantomiming. The contestant could multiply ten times the amount won by guessing three more pantomimes by the celebrity in twenty seconds.

In her second week on the show, when Betty pretended to be a striptease artist after learning she could not talk, host Tom Kennedy cracked, "This is where the past really pays off!" Betty guessed one puzzle correctly with only three words. In another contest, she got all five clues from her partner, and in one bonus round, she got all ten possible identifications.

"It is what it is, a basic pantomime show, and I was doing nothing at the time, so they came at me with this thing and I said, 'Why not?'" recalled Kennedy of *Body Language*. "And Mark [Goodson] figured, and he was right, it was just an old chestnut, we can do it right."

Kennedy taped the pilot nine months before the premiere. More than four years after *Body Language* ended, Goodson taped a pilot for ABC with another celebrity charades variant called *Body Talk*, hosted by Vicki Lawrence, but it didn't sell. Between *Body Language* and *Body Talk*, Kennedy also hosted a failed pilot for another celebrity charades show, *Star Play*, under Carol Burnett's production company. Finally, a clip of *Body Language* appeared on Betty's sitcom *Hot in Cleveland* in 2012 as part of a flashback sequence for her character Elka.

Super Password (September 24, 1984–March 24, 1989)
November 5–9, 1984 (Jon Bauman); June 3–7, 1985 (Vicki Lawrence); January 13–17, 1986 (Richard Simmons); April 21–25, 1986 (Charles Shaughnessy); July 21–25, 1986 (Howard Morton); January 12–16, 1987 (Lucille Ball, Ann Dusenberry, Estelle Getty); April 6–10, 1987 (G. Gordon Liddy); October 26–30, 1987 (Dick Martin); February 29–March 4, 1988 (Dick Cavett); June 20–24, 1988 (Carol Channing); November 7–11, 1988 (Lucille Ball, Carol Channing, Dick Martin); February 16–17 and 20–22, 1989 (McLean Stevenson); March 20–24, 1989 (Christopher Hewett)

Super Password was *Password Plus* modified. The set had the podium and playing table float onto center stage after the guests and host Bert Convy came through the main entrance. Clues appeared on monitors for players rather than in wallets, and there was no pass or play option.

Also, the winner of the $200 puzzle played the "Ca$hword," where a word, appearing in a viewing device called a "magic toaster," had to be guessed with three clues. The jackpot started at $1,000 and increased by $1,000 every time the Ca$hword was missed.

The installation of the Ca$hword coupled with a leisurely pace under Convy meant that some episodes of *Super Password* had no time to play Alphabetics. More disconcerting was Convy's tendency to accidentally blurt out the password or the puzzle clue, such as revealing the final word in the puzzle on Betty's show with Howard Morton on July 23, 1986. These elements made some *Password* fans feel this edition was the show's weakest one.

Adding to that sense were some surprising missteps by the Goodson production team. (Bill Todman had died in 1979.) One was the taping and airing of the *Super Password* All-Star Special in early 1987 after Lucille Ball's attempted comeback sitcom, *Life with Lucy*, had been cancelled. Those circumstances made the pairing of her and former co-star Ann Dusenberry seem odd against Betty and her *Golden Girls* castmate Estelle Getty. For her part, Lucy laughed a lot at Betty's comments.

Another error was having Betty play *Super Password* against its most controversial guest celebrity ever, convicted Watergate felon G. Gordon Liddy. "Well. this is, I hope and think, an interesting week," Convy said at the top. Regarding Betty, Liddy tried to joke, "I wiretapped her dressing room. But I'll never tell." "We erased the tape already," Convy slyly shot back. Incredibly, despite the uneasy week, the show would bring Liddy against Marcia Wallace October 3–7, 1988. These two appearances would be his only ones as a guest on a game show.

Betty survived these mishaps and had a few memorably funnier moments on the series. During her first week with Jon Bauman, a male contestant gave the clue "bull," which cracked up Betty. "Don't you dare! Don't you dare!" warned Convy as he covered her mouth. "I've known you too long. I don't want you to do that." She guessed "frog," when the answer was "whip."

The first time two women competed on *Super Password* was in 1985 with Vicki Lawrence. "I don't know if I can play over here," said Lawrence, sitting on what had been considered the "man's side." "Oh, she can play anywhere," quipped Betty. Then, after playing the password "lusty," Betty noted, "I haven't known anybody lusty in so long."

155

During Dick Cavett's week in 1988, Betty said of her busy career, "As long as they keep asking me, I keep saying yes. And I do a lot of television, too!" Cavett responded, "Well, I'm not like her. I can't turn anything into a raunchy remark."

Super Password stayed on NBC daytime for four and a half years despite low ratings. Network executives knew cancelling the series probably meant local affiliates would claim the noontime slot for their own programming, which is what happened when the series ended. On its finale, Convy teared up thanking the crew before letting Betty speak. "I just have to say, Bert, that this is the fifth last *Password* that I've done. So the phoenix shall rise again, just get out of the way, we'll be back in a minute!" she said before hugging Convy.

Betty was right about *Password* returning again, although it would not be until nearly two decades later. And of course, Betty was there, ready to play *Million Dollar Password* in 2008.

Trivia Trap (October 8, 1984-April 5, 1985)
December 10–14, 1984
Betty joined Jayne Meadows and Vicki Lawrence against Tom Poston, Jamie Farr, and Bill Cullen in an all-star charity edition of *Trivia Trap*, a Goodson game show on ABC mornings. After choosing between two rows of possible responses, team members had to remove the three wrong answers among the chosen row's four possibilities. Identifying one wrong answer won $50, two $100, and all three $300.

After two rounds, teams competed in a trivia race to $1,000, where every question was worth $100 until after the tenth question, when a correct answer netted $200. Each team had three chances to guess. If all guesses were incorrect, the other team got to pick a question under three topics. The winning team played for a chance to win $10,000 individually. The women won the first two days and the men won the last three shows.

Betty had a good line on the fourth show when she answered who recorded the album *Cats Without Claws* with "Pussy Galore." Also, on the last day, asked what the final word in Lincoln's Gettysburg Address was, she cracked up Lawrence and host Bob Eubanks by saying, "Thanks and good night."

All-Star Blitz (April 8, 1985–December 20, 1985)

July 1–4, 1985

All-Star Blitz grew out of a pilot taped on September 28, 1984 called *Hot Numbers*. "They were playing different rules," recalled Chris Korman, whose father Harvey Korman participated in that show with host Peter Marshall. When finally airing, *All-Star Blitz* featured four celebrities underneath two rows of three screens. Two players competed to solve a word puzzle hidden by the screens, with each screen containing anywhere from one to four letters of a name or phrase.

Each celebrity sat below three vertices of the screen, top, middle, and bottom. To reveal a screen's contents, players had to light up all four vertices surrounding each screen. Contestants did so by picking a star and one of his or her vertices and correctly agreeing or disagreeing about the celebrity's answer to a question. A wrong answer failed to win the vertex and also gave control to the opposing player to ask questions until he or she was wrong. Each game began with four random vertices already lit and ended when a player identified the mystery phrase.

The first player to win two games won the right to play the bonus round. In "Blitz Bonanza," the winning contestant spun a wheel that would land to reveal the letters in one of the six screens. After four spins, the stars wrote down their guesses to the word puzzle and revealed them along with the player. Complicating matters was that the wheel spin could land on a screen already revealed and thus waste a turn to uncover the phrase. Players competed for $10,000 the first time, $15,000 their second, $20,000 their third, and $25,000 their fourth and final try.

Betty appeared with Ted Shackelford, Sherilyn Wolter, and Robert S. Woods two months after the show debuted and was its only amusing celebrity. When asked whether waking up a sleepwalker could shock them, Betty noted, "It depends on who wakes you up!" About whether an average person is more sensitive to touch on their outer thigh or their loins, Betty suggestively giggled and told Marshall, "Would you care to find out?"

Marshall also wished Betty luck on her upcoming series *The Golden Girls*. Otherwise, there was relatively little interaction between the host and the stars and relatively little fun either. A flop replacement for *Trivia Trap*, *All-Star Blitz* fizzled out of the ABC morning lineup less than six months after Betty's guest shot.

Double Talk (August 18, 1986–December 19, 1986)
August 18–22, 1986 (Stuart Damon)
In *Double Talk,* two teams, each with a celebrity and a noncelebrity partner, competed to decode four phrases disguised by synonyms. Both players on a team had to solve half of each phrase. For example, when host Henry Polic II read the show's first mystery phrase "Panhandlers can't be pickers," the noncelebrity said, "Beggars can't ..." and Betty followed with "... be choosers." Correct answers won ten points each, but if a pair guessed incorrectly, the other team could solve it for five points. One team started each board of four phrases, and if the pair solved all four, they played for a jackpot phrase worth $1,000.

Teams competed to get the highest score after four boards, with the last two boards awarding twenty points for correct answers. The winning pair played a bonus game for $10,000 to identify nine phrases within a minute. The only clues for the noncelebrity were the first initials and an incomplete sentence from the celebrity partner, who saw the answers on a private monitor. For example, with the letters "B" and "M" showing, Betty gave the clue, "If somebody is very rude, they're showing awfully ..." and the contestant correctly answered, "Bad Manners." Only one try and one answer were allowed, but a team could pass and return if time permitted. Betty missed the bonus on the first episode but won it on the second show of the debut week.

Double Talk combined elements of *Password, Pyramid,* and *You Don't Say!* and felt derivative as a result. By the seventh week it was retitled *Celebrity Double Talk,* as if not knowing stars played the game was the problem. This Bob Stewart creation went off the air less than two months later.

Wordplay (December 29, 1986–September 4, 1987)
January 19–23, 1987; May 4–8, 1987
In *Wordplay,* two players competed in finding the definitions for six out of nine words on a board. Lines connected the words so players could build on the dollar amounts won for correct answers, which started at twenty-five dollars and increased after every two words.

The winner played "Double Definition." The object of that round was to connect boxes from left to right on a board of four rows and six columns by answering clues correctly in forty-five seconds. Each box hid two definitions of a single word, and a correct answer won the box. For example, "Asian country/fancy dinnerware" were the clues for "China." An incorrect answer or a pass made it a block on the path and forced a player to go up or down that column to continue. The jackpot started at $2,500 and increased by that amount every day a player failed to win the round. Contestants played a maximum of three days.

Betty did the pilot on October 12, 1986, with Pat Sajak and Stuart Pankin, and Peter Tomarken as host. Given the word "kismet," she broke up Tomarken by saying, "Again, it's from ancient mythology, but so many of us were." Betty was the only star from the pilot to do the series.

Series host Tom Kennedy said *Wordplay* was a copy of *Oh My Word*, a 1966–1967 syndicated game show on which Kennedy guest starred. "All I know is they came to me with an offer, and I looked the show over and agreed to do it. The fact that Betty was on the pilot, I didn't know that, but it doesn't surprise me. Every producer in town, when they had a pilot, they all went for Betty, the queen of them all. She's ugly as hell, but what the heck?" he joked.

This is Your Life (April 19, 1987)

Guest

One of Betty's best TV appearances was the nighttime NBC special *This is Your Life*, a warm remembrance of her life and career by many of those closest to her. Host and executive producer Ralph Edwards went to a rehearsal hall where *The Golden Girls* did a photo shoot for a magazine. Told there was something on her bouquet of flowers, Betty joked, "It's a tarantula." She read a note saying she had a secret admirer. Edwards revealed he was the one and shouted, "This is your life!"

As Betty entered the TV studio, the audience gave her a standing ovation. Her first guest was her high school acting teacher, Professor Robert Witten, who noted she starred in *Pride and Prejudice*. "I was Pride," said Betty. Her co-star from that production, Larry Rose, also appeared. Jack Paar showed up as did Mark Goodson, who remembered meeting Betty on *Make the Connection*. "Betty was so wonderful, Ralph, that we booked her whenever we could after that," Goodson said. He also recounted Allen Ludden courting Betty.

Ed Asner, Cloris Leachman, Gavin MacLeod, Valerie Harper and Georgia Engel came out in a group hug like the finale of *The Mary Tyler Moore Show*, and Betty eagerly joined them. "No matter what the public thinks, I never slept with Betty,"

Asner said, then added, "Yet!" Moore joined them by satellite from New York and showed off her pet dogs. Betty got emotional as Edwards mentioned the passing of Ludden and her mother, then brightened up as Johnny Grant told her a new star on the Hollywood Walk of Fame would be in honor of Ludden. Former NBC chairman of the board Grant Tinker added, "I'm here tonight just simply because I will go anywhere that people gather to express their love for this lady." He said Allen's star would be next to hers. A grateful Betty then thanked all who joined her for this touching tribute.

Win Lose or Draw (September 7, 1987–September 1, 1989; 1987–1990)
September 7–11, 1987 (nighttime); July 17–21, 1989 (daytime); At least two other weeks daytime; At least seven other weeks nighttime

A game show Betty can take partial credit for creating was *Win Lose or Draw*. Burt Reynolds gave the backstory on the series' nighttime syndicated debut in 1987 to his business partner and host of the game show, Bert Convy. He and friends, including Betty and Allen Ludden, would play charades at parties, but one special invited guest, Fred Astaire, declined to participate.

"He was very, very shy," said Reynolds. "So, we tried to figure out a way to get him up. And the way to get him up, we found out, was he would draw. And so we came with a blackboard, and he got up and did—Were you there that night, Betty? He did *The Fleet's In* ..."

"*Follow the Fleet*," Betty corrected him. Reynolds showed how Astaire drew tiny sailors as clues.

"And he was so furious that we couldn't get it, because it was so obvious to him," Betty said.

"And it was so much fun that we decided to play it every week," said Reynolds. "And then one day Merv Griffin told me how much money he made on *Jeopardy!* and I said, 'Whoa, howdy!'"

From there, *Win Lose or Draw* became a series. The object was to convey names and phrases by drawing without using numbers or letters. If a team member said part of the answer, the player doing the drawing could write the word on the paper. The drawing team member had a minute to convey the clue and win $200. A doorbell sound at the halfway mark indicated the "artist" could switch out with another team member to finish drawing clues for the remaining team member. A correct answer after the switch won the team $100, but if missed, the other team could get $100 with the right guess. The final "Speed Round" gave each team ninety seconds to identify as many words and terms as possible, with team members allowed to switch twice as needed. Team members not drawing kneeled in front of the easel where the drawing player did his or her work.

On the nighttime syndicated debut, Betty, Annie Potts, and a female noncelebrity contestant faced off against Reynolds, Dom DeLuise, and a male noncelebrity contestant. The series officially began its nightly appearance on September 7, but some stations also played its pilot—billed as a "sneak preview"—on the weekend before its debut. Betty was there too along with Loni Anderson versus Reynolds and Tony Danza. In that preview, Convy said the game had always been a battle of the sexes and Betty agreed. "I've always played against the men," she nodded to laughter.

Betty flirted with Convy before playing the game as the first drawer and got her team to identify "Olive Oil" within ten seconds in the preview. Betty also got Loni's drawing of "Kiss of the Spider Woman" with two seconds left. She was always a top player, including on the daytime edition of *Win Lose or Draw* on NBC, hosted by Vicki Lawrence, which ran two years.

Animal Crack-Ups (August 8, 1987–September 1, 1990)
October 10, 1987; November 28, 1987; December 12, 1987; January 9, 1988; March 12, 1988; March 19, 1988; April 16, 1988; May 21, 1988; June 4, 1988; July 2, 1988; August 27, 1988

Billed as a "friend to animal lovers everywhere," Betty was one of four celebrities who competed to win $2,500 for a favorite animal charity on *Animal Crack-Ups*. The object was to correctly answer questions from host Alan Thicke like "Can a tree kangaroo walk like a man?" Footage shot by the Tokyo Broadcasting System revealed the truth after each celebrity revealed his or her choice. A match won a celebrity a stuffed hedgehog from Thicke's assistant, Debbie Bartlett.

The second round had Thicke ask celebrities individual questions and two other group questions. A last round with a group question followed. The celebrity with the most hedgehogs won $2,500 and a stuffed chimp from the World Wildlife Fund. Ties split the $2,500 evenly. Also seen was "Reggie the Heggie," a hedgehog puppet manipulated by Lisa Sturz and voiced by Susan Blu.

Animal Crack-Ups began on ABC Saturday nights in the summer of 1987 before moving onto the network's Saturday morning lineup. "This is one of those shows that could have never been successful as a prime time show," said game show historian Steve Beverly. "It was good for that summer tryout. When it moved to Saturday mornings, they tried to suggest it was on Saturday nights just to introduce it to the whole family."

Airing for three seasons, *Animal Crack-Ups* had the longest run of any Saturday morning network game show. "It stayed there because it was extraordinarily inexpensive," said Beverly. "It was less cost to do that show than to do a cartoon." Betty appeared only in its first season.

Wheel of Fortune (1983-present)

December 8, 1988

This syndicated nighttime game show was formerly a network daytime show from 1975 to 1991. Three contestants played Hangman by spinning a wheel to determine how much they could win by guessing a consonant in the puzzle. Vowels cost money. During Pet Lovers Week, after a player solved the puzzle "The Golden Girls," host Pat Sajak introduced Betty, who greeted Pat's assistant Vanna White before hugging Pat. "Thank you, and I love all your dogs around the set. I wasn't pointing to Vanna when I said that!" she joked. Betty said she wanted to bring her Golden Retriever Pontiac, a "career change guide dog," but worried about the set's slippery floor for his paws. She then left to applause.

Sweethearts (1988–1989)

At least two weeks

Based on a 1987 British game, *Sweethearts* was another *To Tell the Truth* rip-off. A trio of celebrity judges tried to find which one of three couples were actual lovebirds. Each couple that fooled a celebrity won $500, and if all three stars missed, the real couple won $1,500 plus a special "second honeymoon" vacation. With only one game played per show versus the two or three *To Tell the Truth* had averaged, *Sweethearts* came off in comparison as a drawn-out affair—pardon the pun—and lasted only a year in syndication with Charles Nelson Reilly as host.

3rd Degree! (1989–1990)

October 31, 1989; Two other weeks 1989

Betty and a female star competed against two male celebrities in *3rd Degree!*, a nightly syndicated game reminiscent of *Make the Connection*. The stars had to get the relationship between two guests. Teams alternated in up to two rounds of yes-or-no questioning, with the first turn of each team lasting a minute and the second lasting thirty seconds. Each wrong guess after a round of questioning collected the guests $250. If the subjects stumped the panel after four rounds, each guest got $1,000. Host Bert Convy interviewed the guests after each game.

The show's veracity seemed questionable given how both Betty and Loni Anderson and Burt Reynolds and Charles Nelson Reilly failed to identify Bob Carroll and Madelyn Davis for writing *I Love Lucy* on one show. "I was on the lot, for heaven's sake! ... I'm getting blind and stupid, not necessarily in that order!" said Betty. A later spot was better, as Loni identified two men as the inventors of the Edsel car. Burt Reynolds and Bert Convy packaged the series.

Scattergories (January 18, 1993–June 11, 1993)
May 24–28, 1993
Based on a board game, *Scattergories* had quartets of men and women competing. In the first round, both quartets tried to list as many items as they could beginning with the same letter in fifteen seconds. For example, given "Things men use to seduce women" with the letter "L," the male team said "love," "liquor," and "limousines." Members of the playing quartet individually picked four of five celebrities they hoped would have different answers from what they had given to add to their point total. If a celebrity's answer matched what the foursome had said, the team had a point subtracted.

After two rounds, the team with the most points won $500. In the bonus game, host Dick Clark read a category like "Habits that are hard to break" and team members held up their hands to give two potential answers per celebrity. Each celebrity had an answer that started with a different letter. The team had twenty-five seconds to give two possible responses for all five celebrities. By missing three celebrities, a team could win $4,000. An in-studio "jury" of five—both men and women—ruled what items given by players failed to meet the category criteria as answers.

Betty appeared on film for a week of the game along with Mark DeCarlo, Nicole Eggert, Adam West, and Robin Quivers. When a member of the male team picked Betty, Clark effused, "This is one of the most brilliant women you'll ever meet. She's had every line thrown at her. She's got one of the most fantastic minds in the world."

NBC executives let local stations air *Scattergories* and *Scrabble* in any one-hour block. "They had very bad clearance problems," said game show historian Steve Beverly. "And it was one of those shows that they were hoping that maybe they could get stations back with a format like *Scrabble* as the lead-in show—that at least had a six-year run behind it—and *Scattergories*, it had a name brand as a home game. They thought that maybe they could get some traction." Still, many affiliates declined to carry *Scattergories*.

Betty was among the last celebrities to appear on *Scattergories*, which ended two weeks after her visit. *Scattergories* marked the last network daytime game show to use celebrities regularly, providing an appropriate end to Betty's incredible thirty-three seasons of daytime game shows.

Game$how Marathon (May 31, 2006–June 29, 2006)
June 22, 2006 ("Match Game")
Game$how Marathon, the official spelling per the series' logo, was a weekly competition wherein six celebrities played classic TV game shows to win $100,000 for their charity of choice. This episode pitted Kathy Najimy against Lance Bass in the semifinal round for a spot in the finals. The hostess was Rikki Lake, and the panelists were George Foreman, Kathy Griffin, Bruce Vilanch, Adrianne Curry, Adam Corolla, and Betty.

"I like these celebrities more than the old celebrities on *Match Game*," said Bass, prompting an indignant Betty to respond, "Thanks a lot!" He tried to cover himself by adding, "And I love Betty the best!" Of the "old celebrities," by 2006 Richard Dawson was retired, while fellow 1970s panelists Brett Somers and Charles Nelson Reilly would die a year after this show aired.

Lake asked Betty her thoughts about doing *Match Game* again. "You're prettier than Gene Rayburn, I've got to tell you that!" Betty answered. She admired how the design replicated the set down to the orange carpet and joked that in the 1970s the celebrities came in drunk.

Even though Betty didn't match in the main game, she came off well. As she would often in the 1970s show, she did a mock belly dance at the end of one round. In the second Super Match, Betty got the top answer for "Purple BLANK" as "Purple Rain." Najimy won, by the way.

Despite often winning its Thursdays 8-9 p.m. time slot, CBS didn't renew

Game$how Marathon. A decade later, *Match Game* returned as a recurring summer series on ABC without Betty.

Million Dollar Password (June 1, 2008–June 14, 2009)
June 12, 2008 (Susie Essman); December 28, 2008 (Adam Corolla)
Taped in New York City, *Million Dollar Password* felt more like *Pyramid*. At the start of her first show, host Regis Philbin noted how Betty fell in love with Allen Ludden during the series' first run. "I slept with the host of *Password* for all those years," she said to laughter. Then to his amusement, she laid her head in the palm of her hand and asked, "What are you doing, Regis?"

In the elimination round, celebrities on *Million Dollar Password* had thirty seconds each to get five correct answers from their partners and vice versa, then the same process occurred by switching celebrity partners.

The noncelebrity player with the most correct answers played the million dollar round. Players competed for $10,000, then $25,000, $50,000, $100,000, $250,000, and finally a million dollars in getting five passwords within ninety seconds at each level. The contestant had to give the celebrity partner one less clue at each higher level of money. So, players started with trying to get five correct answers out of ten passwords for $10,000 and ultimately had to solve all five passwords at the million dollar level. The difficulty levels of the words increased, and a player could not return to a word he or she had passed. Not surprisingly, no one won the top prize.

Still, Betty had her moments. Given the show's theatre in the round layout, Betty told the encircling audience on her debut, "Pardon my back. Pardon my front." When her contestant said she was getting a little nervous, Betty said, "I'll have a vodka on the rocks!"

Betty won a tiebreaker in the second game of her first show and helped her partner reach $100,000. "I'm too old for this!" she mock protested to Regis before her partner saw the first five passwords for the $250,000 level and decided not to continue to play.

On her second show, Betty's first partner, Justin Root, said, "This is twenty years in the making. I told my elementary school—because I wasn't on the football team or baseball team, I couldn't get anything like that—so I lied to them and I said that my grandma was friends with you and that one day she was going to fly me out to California to play *Password*."

Betty laughed about the memory before Justin added, "So, the moral of the story is to lie."

"That's right, that's right," Betty agreed. "I've been getting by on it for sixty years on television." Then Regis showed a replay of Betty and Ludden on their first *Password* show after getting married, and Betty blew a kiss to the image of Ludden.

Justin won his round and got to fulfill his dream to play with Betty. "And now if I screw up, I'm really in trouble!" she joked. "Don't you dare mess up around him!" chimed in Regis.

Before Justin tried for $100,000, he told Regis, "You know, honestly, my prize was playing with her today." Regis stepped away from his podium and told Betty and Justin, "You know, I don't know about you, but I'm really enjoying these love scenes you two carry on! It's a bit much."

"I've been with a lot of people, and no one's ever said that to me before!" Betty grinned.

They didn't win $100,000, but Justin was fine with $25,000 and thanked Betty profusely again. Betty played the second game bonus, as well, and when she missed the word "hickey" while winning the $25,000 level, Regis pretended to give her a hickey on stage. "The last *Password* host who did that to me, I married!" she announced afterward.

Both of Betty's shows finished at number seven. The other *Million Dollar Password* shows finished in the top twenty-five during its six-week run from June 1 through July 6, 2008, and its sporadic run six times from December 18, 2008 to June 14, 2009. But it attracted few younger viewers, so CBS cancelled the game show after a year.

Nonetheless, by doing this series and then the 2016 revival of *To Tell the Truth*, Betty marked seven decades on television being a celebrity on game shows, a record unlikely ever to be surpassed. If there was any doubt Betty was the queen of game shows, this activity sealed the title for her.

Chapter Seven
Betty the Scene Stealer

Sue Ann Nivens, 'The Happy Homemaker," grinned at Phyllis Lindstrom, played by Cloris Leachman, who had to process that Sue Ann seduced her husband in "The Lars Affair," the 1973 season opener of *The Mary Tyler Moore Show*. Intended just as a guest shot for Betty, she played the role so well that she became a regular on the hit sitcom and won two Emmys for her work on the series.

Courtesy of Everett Collection.

During the twentieth century, only two actresses were regulars twice in different sitcoms that won the Emmy for Outstanding Comedy Series while they claimed a statuette for their work in both. Those women were Mary Tyler Moore and Betty White.

Coincidentally, one occasion occurred for both with the same series—*The Mary Tyler Moore Show*. Betty enjoyed best comedy series and best actress in a comedy Emmys later on *The Golden Girls*, while Mary previously achieved those double honors on *The Dick Van Dyke Show*. All three series were top ten ratings hits during their runs, as well.

The Mary Tyler Moore Show came along at the right time for Mary and Betty, though for somewhat different reasons. Let's start with what the program provided for its titular star.

Escaping Laura Petrie

Moore scored a triumph on *The Dick Van Dyke Show*, which debuted on CBS in 1961. As Laurie Petrie, the devoted young wife of Dick Van Dyke's lead character Rob, she won two Emmys and seemed poised for more success when *The Dick Van Dyke Show* ended in 1966. Although the series was still a top twenty hit, Van Dyke ended it to try his hand at movies, and so did Mary.

But apart from 1967's *Thoroughly Modern Millie*, Mary struggled for success. Then she reteamed with her former co-star on *Dick Van Dyke and the Other Woman*, a 1969 special on CBS. Network officials admired Mary's comic timing on display. Noting their interest, Mary's husband, former NBC programming executive Grant Tinker, got a guaranteed order of thirteen shows starring his wife in a sitcom for CBS's fall 1970 TV schedule Saturdays at 9:30 p.m.

Making Mary Richards

To produce *The Mary Tyler Moore Show*, Tinker enlisted James L. "Jim" Brooks and Allan Burns. Brooks created the ABC sitcom *Room 222* in 1969, winner of the Outstanding New Series Emmy, and Burns produced and wrote four of its episodes. However, they hadn't worked together as a team until Tinker drafted them for his wife's new series.

Brooks and Burns initially crafted Moore to play a divorced gossip columnist. CBS hated the notion, so the two men regrouped. Their revised pitch had Moore as

Mary Richards, a plucky single woman rebounding from a recent failed relationship to pursue a career in Minneapolis.

Supporting Moore was a cast of mostly unknowns. Playing her co-workers at the fictional WJM Channel 12 newsroom were Ed Asner as Lou Grant, the newscast's producer, supported by Mary Richards as associate producer; Gavin MacLeod as friendly Murray Slaughter, the news writer who sat next to Mary; and Ted Knight as Ted Baxter, the vain and shallow news anchor. After work, Mary hung out with her wisecracking pal Rhoda Morgenstern, played by Valerie Harper. Their landlady, Phyllis Lindstrom, was a well-meaning but sometimes an oppressive busybody, played by Cloris Leachman.

As filming for *The Mary Tyler Moore Show* commenced in the summer of 1970, cheering in the audience at every taping was Betty White. She and Allen Ludden had been friends with Mary Tyler Moore and Grant Tinker since 1962, and the couples supported each other's ventures. Even though Mary had fared well on *The Dick Van Dyke Show*, the fate of *The Mary Tyler Moore Show* was uncertain until it debuted, so she appreciated any kind of help.

Mary Makes a Monster Hit

The premiere episode of *The Mary Tyler Moore Show* on September 19, 1970 finished sixth for the week, the highest-rated new series debut on the 1970 fall network TV slate. The following week, the series finished twenty-third overall. It stayed around that spot most of the season.

For the 1971–1972 season, programming head Fred Silverman kept the series at Saturdays 9:30-10 p.m. and installed a new lead-in with Mary's former co-star—*The New Dick Van Dyke Show*. At the same time, Silverman moved *All in the Family*, the series that beat *The Mary Tyler Moore Show* for Outstanding Comedy Series, to lead off Saturday nights, followed by a sitcom starring Sandy Duncan called *Funny Face*, airing at 8:30 p.m. before *The New Dick Van Dyke Show*.

This CBS Saturday night lineup was a smash, with all four sitcoms in the top twenty. *Funny Face* went out of production when Duncan needed eye surgery, so Silverman moved *The Mary Tyler Moore Show* into the 8:30-9 p.m. slot. *The Mary Tyler Moore Show* finished the season at tenth place.

For the 1972–1973 season, Silverman moved *The Mary Tyler Moore Show* to 9 p.m. Saturdays, where its ratings stayed strong and it finished at number seven. While in that slot, Mary and company planned their fourth season opener—a doozy of a show called "The Lars Affair."

Creating Sue Ann Nivens
"We had never shown Lars, the husband of Phyllis, played by Cloris Leachman, in the show," Burns told Rose Dosti in *The Los Angeles Times*. "For four years Lars was a mysterious creature, always talked about but never seen. We wanted to do a show in which Lars had an affair with another woman, and it was during a story conference that someone came up with the idea of having a 'happy homemaker' type, the antithesis of Phyllis, a pseudo-liberated female, as the 'other woman.' It would be the ultimate irony.

"We kept talking about a 'Betty White' type but no one dared think of asking her. She was, after all, Mary's close friend."

As Betty recalled in the documentary "Eight Characters in Search of a Sitcom" on *The Mary Tyler Moore Show, The Complete Second Season* DVD, Sue Ann Nivens was "icky, sickening, yucky" but also had to be convincing and amusing as a jezebel. Reportedly ten actresses auditioned for the part and failed to capture all those facets Burns and Brooks desired.

Desperate, Burns and Brooks acquiesced to the original recommendation from the series' casting director, Renee Valenti. She had endorsed using Betty White in part because the sweet side of the character reflected Betty's TV persona. Of course, Sue Ann was the opposite of Betty in terms of being selfish. But the player and the character did share a bawdy sense of humor.

"Just give the part to Betty," Valenti told the executive producers. "It's only a one-shot [appearance], and she's been around long enough that she won't hurt you."

Betty did anything but hurt the show. As Burns told Dosti, "It was hilarious from the beginning. Betty brought things into the part we would have never dreamed of doing. And she came to the show in the nick of time—just when two strong people, Rhoda and Phyllis, left. She's added great strength to the show since."

That simple casting decision had a big impact on both Betty and *The Mary Tyler Moore Show*. Neither would be the same after "The Lars Affair" on September 15, 1973.

Meet the Neighborhood Nympho

Series writer Ed. Weinberger began his script as Mary wound down a party with Sue Ann Nivens, a woman with a daytime household hints series at WJM called *The Happy Homemaker*. Sue Ann told Mary, "I just feel terrible going off and leaving you with all this cleaning up to do." "Oh no, please, don't worry about it," Mary responded. "But it just seems so wrong to run off," Sue Ann said. "No, Rhoda will help," Mary insisted.

Then Sue Ann unleashed the following verbal volley of unsolicited help to Mary: "All right, if you insist, but remember, dear, do try a little iodine for that scratch on the desk. And baking soda will bring that grease up out of the carpet like nothing. Oh dear, dear!" As a stunned Rhoda looked up and held a coffee filter in Mary's kitchen, Sue Ann told her, "Don't throw away those coffee grounds. They're the perfect plant food for Mary's geraniums."

Back to Mary, Sue Ann instructed, "Now, if you want to tidy up in a hurry, think of your living room as a big clock. Start at midnight, and then go around the room working clockwise toward the kitchen. You'll be done in two shakes of a lamb's tail!"

Delivering the monologue rapid fire in less than twenty-five seconds, Betty exited the scene to applause. From there, Phyllis learned Lars drove Sue Ann home when the latter left. Two and a half hours later, Lars called Phyllis to say he had a car accident but luckily an all-night body shop is fixing his vehicle, and he will be home soon. Self-centered Phyllis accepted his explanation, much to the surprise of Mary and Rhoda, who witnessed the call.

When Mary saw Lars hanging out with Sue Ann at work, she was reluctant at first to believe a rumored affair between them. "She seems the kind of woman you leave for someone else!" she told Rhoda. Indeed, Sue Ann was just as self-centered and occasionally oblivious as Phyllis, which probably appealed to Lars, but whereas Phyllis offered her unsolicited advice to others because she thought she could help them, Sue Ann was all about what helped only herself.

Days passed, and Phyllis confessed to Mary and Rhoda she was upset about Lars being away from her so often. She baked an apple pie for the first time, which she knew was horrible despite the women claiming they liked it. "I've become such an object of pity that even Rhoda is being kind!" Phyllis moaned about her occasional nemesis. She knew that Lars and Sue Ann were an item in part because his clothes were cleaner coming home than when he left for work.

Blaming herself for the affair, Phyllis told Mary and Rhoda, "I'm afraid I've been just too much of a real woman." She described reading a book on the life of a bee where once the male bee has "serviced" the queen, he dies. "All in all, not a bad system!" she exclaimed before leaving.

Eventually Phyllis confronted Sue Ann on the latter's TV kitchen set. Sue Ann claimed she was too busy to talk as she rehearsed cooking with a chocolate soufflé in the oven. An enraged Phyllis slammed the oven door, causing the delicacy to deflate. "Oh, my poor baby!" Sue Ann exclaimed, taking out the soufflé and using her knee to shut the oven door. Betty improvised the move after director Jay Sandrich said the scene was looking bad with the gaping oven exposed.

Amid their disagreement, Mary arrived on the set and told Sue Ann she would be fired if station management learned of the affair. A satisfied Phyllis got a last bit of revenge by flinging some chocolate soufflé on Sue Ann before leaving.

"The Lars Affair" was a pivotal episode in several respects. The show earned Cloris Leachman her first Emmy for her pitch-perfect work. She won a second consecutive Emmy for Outstanding Supporting Actress in a Comedy in 1975 for "Phyllis Whips Inflation," which coincidentally was the only other time Phyllis and Sue Ann met on the series. "Didn't she threaten to rip Sue Ann's face off the next time she saw her?" Ted warned Mary in a failed effort to prevent the standoff. Desperate for employment to get more money, Phyllis planned to attack when she made amends with Sue Ann by begging, "Tell me, are there any jobs on your show?!"

Meanwhile, a subplot in "The Lars Affair" about Mary's boss, Lou Grant, having an argument with his wife set a storyline for the season wherein she eventually divorced him. This separation left Lou under the amorous gaze of Sue Ann, who would spend the rest of the series pursuing him. What was intended to be just a guest appearance became a recurring character as Betty's work at wringing laughs out of a potentially off-putting character role impressed the producers.

Betty modestly credited Sandrich for making Sue Ann palatable to the studio and home audiences for "The Lars Affair." "Jay had all the other people be amused by her, not be irritated by her," Betty said in the documentary "Eight Characters in Search of a Sitcom." "If the rest of the cast had been irritated by her, the audience would've been."

The return of the "neighborhood nympho," as Betty called Sue Ann, occurred November 17, 1973. That show defined her character even more as a help and a hindrance to Mary Richards.

Timing Veal Prince Orloff for Eight O'clock

As with "The Lars Affair," Ed Weinberger wrote "The Dinner Party." Mary had a day to get ready to host a celebration for Representative Margaret Geddes, played by Irene Tedrow, at her apartment at 119 North Weatherly. Rhoda recommended that Mary keep the event small to avoid a disaster. Lou told Mary, "You give rotten parties … My wife and I broke up at one of your parties, remember?" The only sympathetic advice came from Murray, who recommended that Mary use Sue Ann to help with the food. He said his wife replicated what she did on a recent show and it was "Great. The best frank and beans I ever had."

On her show's set, Sue Ann took out a strawberry swirl from the oven and plopped the soggy contents onto a plate. Exaggerating the start of the second word to imply she wanted to say a profanity, she exclaimed, "Oh, surely that isn't how a strawberry swirl is supposed to look like!" Sue Ann smiled, checked the device and laughed as she added, "Somebody forgot to plug in the oven. Well, I guess that just goes to show that anybody can make a mistake, even your Happy Homemaker. Now, don't you go away, we'll be right back after this commercial message!" After getting the clear sign, Sue Ann scowled and announced, "All right, who the hell is responsible for this?!" The audience reacted hysterically to Betty's sharp delivery of this line.

After the commercial, Sue Ann said on her next show, she will demonstrate how to feel fresh fruit. The statement generated more laughter, as did Sue Ann's benediction: "This is your Happy Homemaker saying, 'God couldn't be everywhere, so He made mothers.' Bye bye!" She then saw Mary, who said she didn't want to impose. "Nonsense! I'll be done chewing out the crew in two shakes of a lamb's tail!" said Sue Ann, who was as good as her word. She invited herself to Mary's party and promised to prepare six portions of Veal Prince Orloff, one for every guest. "Now, if you'll excuse me, I have to rake someone's tail over the coals!" she said before leaving.

Mary had another glitch when Ted Baxter asked when she wanted him and his somewhat flighty, but adorable, girlfriend and future wife Georgette, another new regular played by Georgia Engel, to be at her party. When Mary said she didn't have room for them, a bitter Ted said he had a party with the man of her dreams and she wasn't invited as retaliation before leaving.

At the night of the party, Sue Ann told Mary, "I have timed my Veal Prince Orloff for eight o'clock" and added, "Mary, my dear, I'm sorry, but if we don't eat at eight o'clock, we might as well take my delicious dinner and flush it right down the toilet." Rhoda arrived with her friend, Steve Waldman, played by Henry Winkler, who had just got fired and could use a pick-me-up. Sue Ann interrupted their exchange with "Mary, we eat in four minutes!" Rhoda said Steve could sit at the upstairs small table while Sue Ann kept giving time checks.

Luckily, all guests arrived in time. Congresswoman Geddes loved the conversation and food and, as Mary readied dessert, Rhoda noted that the party was a hit because "It's nine o'clock, and everybody's still here!" Unfortunately, Ted showed up, sheepishly peered at the surroundings, and convinced Mary to let him enter. He recounted his life of disappointment to Geddes, making the party a bomb. However, the studio audience found it all very amusing.

From here onward, Sue Ann appeared on *The Mary Tyler Moore Show* more frequently and never as far between episodes as her first two times. Part of this reason came from a strategic shift of having Sue Ann starting to pursue Lou romantically, beginning with her next appearance.

"I Have to Go Stuff a Duck"
"Happy Birthday, Lou" on December 22, 1973, had Mary planning a surprise party for her boss when Sue Ann arrived in the newsroom and accosted Lou. "Do you wear your sleeves up because you know what wonderful arms you have?" cooed Sue Ann. An uneasy Lou responded, "I just keep them up so I don't get any stuff on them" and left as she followed him.

Visiting the newsroom and watching the scene, Rhoda said to Mary, "Don't tell me the Happy Homemaker has eyes on Lou?!" "I think so," grinned Mary. "He meets all her requirements. He's a U.S. citizen between 18 and 55."

As Lou left for lunch with Rhoda, Sue Ann asked Mary, "Isn't it funny how hypermasculine men feel threatened by very feminine women?" "Gee, I hadn't noticed that," said Mary. "I have," said Sue Ann. "I threaten a lot of them!"

Hearing about Mary's planned party, Sue Ann thought Lou deserved something "super special" and offered to help. "And Mary, I promise you I can show you a thousand and one tricks that can turn any gathering into an affair." "I'll bet you can," Mary slyly responded. As Sue Ann left by saying, "I have to go stuff a duck," Mary responded, "I was just going to suggest you do that."

At the party, Sue Ann suggested a kiddie theme for the event, as she did for one of her viewers who had a birthday party for her grandfather. "Tell me, how did

Grandpa feel when they put him up on the pony to get his picture taken?" snorted Rhoda.

Sue Ann returned four weeks later. "The Co-Producers" on January 19, 1974, had Mary and Rhoda collaborate on a potential Sunday afternoon talk show. To their horror, Lou and the station owner wanted Ted and Sue Ann to co-host because they were under contract. Mary and Rhoda's worries about the egos and vanity of those talents collaborating proved to be right. The conversation devolved to where Sue Ann and Ted left and announced plans to become their own producers of the show. Revealing this news to Mary and Rhoda, Ted's girlfriend, Georgette, said, "Boy, are they gonna bomb!"

In "Lou's Second Date" on February 16, 1974, Mary became sick, so Rhoda went with Lou to a formal event in her place. Hearing of Mary's illness, Sue Ann suggested Lou send over a bowl filled with goldfish. "They're so practical, frolicking in their little bowl. They're jolly, cheerful friends! And then afterward, when they're dead, they make wonderful fertilizer!" she added.

Lou said he had fun with Rhoda, and when visiting Mary, Sue Ann learned the two had dated again. "Dear Lou, he can't say no to anyone!" fretted Sue Ann. When Mary returned to work, gossip spread about Lou and Rhoda being an item. "Oh, I don't blame Rhoda," Sue Ann said. "Any single girl is attracted to an older man."

When Lou and Rhoda decided to stay only friends, Sue Ann wondered if she and Lou could get together. He said they could go hit a bucket of golf balls after work. "Silly me. I'd love to, but I just remembered I have a big show tomorrow," responded an uneasy Sue Ann. "I have to go bread crumb my chicken parts!"

In five episodes during the 1973–1974 season, Betty White's Sue Ann character ranged from incidental to substantial in the plots as needed. This pattern would repeat in the following seasons, only with more appearances by Sue Ann. In the remaining forty episodes, audiences got to know more about her character, and the insights often made them laugh harder as a result. This growth in air time occurred in part because *The Mary Tyler Moore Show* spun off other female supporting characters in two new series entitled *Rhoda* and *Phyllis*, each named for their title characters, in 1974 and 1975 respectively.

Betty told Cecil Smith in *The Los Angeles Times* how she thoroughly relished Sue Ann. "I've been waiting all my life for a part like this," she said. For his part, Smith called the casting of Betty as Sue Ann "an act of sheer genius."

Know Your Happy Homemaker Better

Sue Ann's background came out over the next few seasons. In "Mary's Delinquent" on November 1, 1975, Sue Ann claimed to have loved home economics at an early age. "I guess it's no secret that I was a child prodigy. I was reading cookbooks at two, I start pickling at six. When I was twelve, I was quite heavily into sauces."

In "What Are Friends For" on November 16, 1974, Sue Ann said her first professional on-air credit occurred in Chicago. "It was a cooking show—*Let's Talk About Meat*." According to "A Girl Like Mary," on December 14, 1974, she mentioned her long tenure as "The Happy Homemaker" on WJM to Mary Richards. "I have done that job every day since July 1963. You know what that means, Mary? It means I've been smiling for eleven years!"

As far as her family, Sue Ann said in "Not a Christmas Story" on November 16, 1974, that she always taped her Yuletide show in advance so she could join her sister in Florida in December. "She's kind of a creep, but she's got a pool," Sue Ann added. She allowed that her sister was younger in "Mary's Delinquent," and added, "Naturally, she resented being the ugly one!"

Most of those statements turned out to be lies, because on "Sue Ann's Sister," on October 9, 1976, Sue Ann clearly was jealous of her sister Lila, played by Pat Priest. Five years Sue Ann's junior, Lila visited Minneapolis on leave from hosting a cooking show in Augusta, Georgia.

"We've only seen each other a few times in the last twenty years," Sue Ann said. "This will give us a chance to get reacquainted." "Oh, you must really be looking forward to it," Mary said. "Yes, like cramps," responded Sue Ann. "Oh Mary, I know it's awful to talk about one's sister that way, but as far back as I can remember, I've always felt that Lila was a rival. I used to be afraid to have boys pick me up at the house. I'd fear they'd see her. I used to have my dates pick me up on the streets."

To make matters worse, Lila connected with Lou at Sue Ann's birthday party hosted by Mary. An envious Sue Ann said, "I'm sorry, Mary, but I'm afraid there's only one thing for me to do under the circumstances. Now, I don't mean to break up your party, but I really think it would be better all around if I went out there and pushed her off the balcony."

Mary prevented Sue Ann from taking that action as Sue Ann and Lila made amends. Then Lila told Sue Ann, "I've been offered a chance to audition for *The At Home Show* on Channel 10, right here in Minneapolis. Isn't that fabulous?! And if I get it, we'll be together just like when we were kids! Oh, come on, I'll buy you dinner and we'll celebrate." Sue Ann congratulated her and told her she would meet her in the lobby, then let out a blood-curdling scream to Mary.

When Lila called Sue Ann to say she won her audition, Mary, Lou, Ted, and Murray offered congratulations. "Why are you all so happy for my sister? You like her better, don't you?" responded Sue Ann before she ran home sobbing. The crew came to her residence to cheer her up as Sue Ann acted like Camille on her bed. To their shock, her boudoir resembled a bordello.

"Nobody misses a vain, selfish, egotistical, middle-aged shrew," Sue Ann sighed. "Of course we do!" Mary awkwardly responded before bringing in Murray, Ted, and Lou to apologize. "I really love your bedroom, Sue Ann. You decorate yourself, or did you have a sex maniac come in?" Murray asked. Ted discovered her overhead mirror and a remote that made her bed vibrate. Sue Ann used the latter when she had Lou sit beside her, generating audience hysteria.

Lou forced a few compliments, but what turned Sue Ann around is when Lila arrived and told Sue Ann if she was unhappy about competing against her, she would give up her new job. "You don't have to do that. You can call them from here!" Sue Ann said as she grabbed her phone.

With that, Sue Ann went back to being her normal self. That activity included being the primary female friend and enemy for poor Mary Richards. Sue Ann could be kind to Mary, but her antagonistic side came out more often simply because it was better for comic effect.

Coveting Mary's Boyfriends, Dismissing Her Décor

Mary endured much grief from Sue Ann, especially if she had a hot date. Sue Ann's most unbridled lust for another man she thought Mary wanted was in "Mary Gets a Lawyer" on November 13, 1976. When Sue Ann saw an attorney, played by John McMartin, sitting at Mary's desk, she exclaimed, "Mary's got a hunk! Can I help you with something?" Sue Ann read his note to Mary. "I've been looking through my briefs and it's important that we talk as soon as possible." She smiled and giggled, "I certainly hope you're a lawyer!"

Introducing herself as "Mary's dearest friend," Sue Ann offered to serve as a character witness for Mary in the case just to get closer to the attorney. She told him, "Sometimes I wish I could be more like her. But no, I'm stuck with being wildly unpredictable, passionate, and just about the best time a fellow could have!" After the trial ended in Mary's favor, a cop gave the lawyer a letter to open from Sue Ann. It simply said, "I didn't want to tell you this till the trial was over, but I find you terribly attractive, and I must have you before nightfall or else I'll explode!"

Generally, however, Sue Ann considered Mary a loveless loser. In "Not With My Wife, I Don't" on January 3, 1976, Sue Ann discussed an upcoming show with Mary. "Tomorrow, my helpful hint for single girls is what turns a man on. Of course, I know lots of ideas on how to get a man interested myself, but I thought you might know a couple we could actually talk about on the air."

"I'm really very busy, and I haven't the vaguest idea what turns a man on," Mary said. "Well, I realize that, dear!" answered Sue Ann. "I just thought if I asked you, I might make your day!"

When Mary recounted a disastrous date in "Lou Dates Mary" on March 12, 1977, Sue Ann responded, "Ah, that's too bad, dear. Perhaps you should think about changing your escort service!" And in "Mary and the Sexagenarian" on February 12, 1977, Sue Ann told Mary to date Murray's father. "Of course, you may not get much action, but then again, you never did!"

Finally, Sue Ann attempted to have an unwilling Mary sample some of her food in "Murray Takes a Stand" on January 31, 1976, with this statement: "Oh, come on, Mary, you'll love it! One of the cheeses is bland, American, untouched by human hands—not unlike you!"

Sue Ann also critiqued Mary's taste often. In "Lou and That Woman" on October 5, 1974, she felt Mary's decorating plans for the building were outdated. "That's why I'm not going to say one word about that cruddy wallpaper in the men's bathroom," Sue Ann added. "Did you crash the men's room?!" Mary exclaimed. "Of course not! I went as somebody's guest!" Sue Ann said.

In "A Girl Like Mary" on December 14, 1974, Sue Ann visited Mary's apartment. "I love what you've done to it," she said. "I haven't done anything to it," Mary said. "I know, that took guts!" said Sue Ann.

Sue Ann complimented Mary on a recent party in "Lou Douses an Old Flame" on November 15, 1975, with "I couldn't have done better myself!" She then told Murray, "A tactful lie is no sin." Having overheard this, Mary said, "Well, Sue Ann, in that case, I enjoyed having you!"

A more cutting Sue Ann emerged in "Mary Moves Out" on September 20, 1975.

Missing Phyllis and Rhoda and feeling she was in a rut, Mary invited Sue Ann to her apartment. Sue Ann's idea of sympathy was saying, "If I can be bored with my life, Lord knows how you must feel about yours!" Mary surreptitiously moved a lamp to block more of Sue Ann as the latter kept talking.

"You know, dear, the first thing we're going to have to do is decorate your apartment," said Sue Ann. "You mean redecorate," responded Mary. "You mean it's been done before?!" asked Sue Ann. "Well, don't feel bad. I mean, what can one expect when one rents a furnished apartment." "Sue Ann, all of the furniture here is mine," Mary said. "I knew that, Mary. I was just trying to give you a graceful way out!" Sue Ann exclaimed.

She continued with, "You see, dear, an apartment should express the personality of whoever lives there. Why, take mine, for example. The minute you walk in, the décor says Sue Ann Nivens." "Right, early American!" retorted Mary. "Oh Mary, poor dear, sweet, adorable Mary," cooed Sue Ann. "If it makes you feel better to spew forth your filthy venom, go right ahead!"

Mary did move to a new apartment, and Sue Ann was at her most caustic there in "Mary Midwife" on September 25, 1976. As Georgette went into labor, her husband Ted said, "It's okay. There's no rush. The doctor said this could drag on for days." "Apparently he's been to Mary's parties," shot back Sue Ann. Later, regarding Georgette's birth in Mary's bedroom, Sue Ann said, "It's probably the most exciting thing that will ever happen in there."

Vanity, Thy Name is Sue Ann Nivens

Sue Ann could envy Mary professionally at times. In "A Girl Like Mary" on December 14, 1974, Sue Ann planned to audition for a spot on the newscast from a woman's point of view. When Sue Ann learned Mary would be auditioning too, she called her "A two-bit, double-crossing fink!" Sue Ann auditioned and told Ted, "Just cue me and then stick a sock in it!"

Her monologue hilariously missed the mark, with Sue Ann covering mudslides in Alaska in her regular drippy style. "Apple-cheeked housewives bustling down the cobbled streets were swept away by slithering mounds of mud! Let's all hope that survivors know that stubborn grime can be removed with a blend of warm water and cornstarch. Victims plucked gagging from the slime were treated at the high school gym, stunningly decorated for that night's prom, the theme of which is 'Fun on the

Farm.' Volunteers dressed as cows and chickens, circulated among the injured, passing out hand-embroidered tea towels." When she finished her speech, Ted Baxter, the bombastic newsman, looked perplexed by her efforts.

When Sue Ann did show sympathy to Mary, she was self-centered in doing so. In "Will Mary Richards Go to Jail?" on September 14, 1974, she discussed Mary facing a possible sentence for hiding the name of a source by saying, "I know what it's like to take a stand for a principle. I remember when a sponsor came to me, demanding that I incorporate their product in my Thanksgiving special ... But I took a firm stand on the principle of artistic integrity and told them to take their frozen giblets and ram them right up their nose!"

Sue Ann suggested holding a party for Mary with other friends before going to jail. "We'll have a prison motif. We'll serve our drinks in little tin cups and everyone can bang them on the table!" At the party, Sue Ann told Mary, "If you don't have a good time, no one else will!" Even with all this insensitivity, Sue Ann was truly distressed to see Mary having to wear handcuffs.

Even more poignant was "What Are Friends For?" where Sue Ann went with Mary to Chicago for a convention. Sue Ann blackmailed Mary to go out with two fun-loving morticians. To her chagrin, both men liked Mary much more than Sue Ann. A humiliated Sue Ann later confessed problems in her love life to Mary in detail. She broke down, and Mary consoled her. Still, such moments were rare exceptions to the rule in their humorously awkward relationship.

In This Corner, Sporting a Bald Pate, Murray Slaughter

No sympathy ever showed between Sue Ann and wisecracking Murray Slaughter. The two were constant comic antagonists to each other, with Murray mocking her sex life and Sue Ann zinging him back about his lack of follicles. Their first repartee occurred in the 1974 season opener, "Will Mary Richards Go to Jail?" After Ted impersonated James Cagney with "I'm not going to eat this slop" as part of a guessing game, Murray says it's "Sue Ann's first husband." She forced a laugh and slapped Murray's knee before remarking that "Bald people are always so jolly!"

In "Not with My Wife, I Don't," when Mary reminded Sue Ann that she was single too, Sue Ann responded, "Oh yes, but that's only because I don't happen to place my love life above my profession." "I thought that was your profession," shot back Murray. Sue Ann returned fire with "Jokes fall from your lips almost as fast as hair falls from your head."

In "Lou Douses an Old Flame," Sue Ann described her book on household hints, "How to Please a Man," when Murray interjected, "Well, like they say, those who can do, and those who can't teach." "Oh, Murray!" intoned Sue Ann. "Funny Murray! Witty Murray! Shiny Murray!" Later, when Sue Ann said, "I've been to several," in reference to a bachelor party the gang threw for Ted, Murray added, "Yeah, but this is the first time you've entered through the door!"

When Lou took Sue Ann on a test ride in a van in "Mary and the Sexagenarian," she said the vehicle was so roomy that "If I had to, I could put a bed in it." "If you had to, you could put a bed on a motorcycle," responded Murray. "I understand your dad's in town. Does his forehead go back to his ankles too?" Sue Ann chirped back.

In "One Producer Too Many" on October 30, 1976, Sue Ann proposed doing a restaurant review on the newscast. As she described the choices to Mary, "One week an Italian, the next week a German, then a Chinese, and a Hungarian," Murray entered in the middle of the conversation and asked, "What's up, Sue Ann? You taking a room at the U.N.?" Shortly thereafter, she responded, "Oh, Murray, you're so lucky. Other men get dandruff. You get waxy yellow buildup!"

During "The Critic" on January 8, 1977, Lou groused to Murray about their big baseball game loss to Channel 10 when Sue Ann said, "Lou, you are so adorable when you're childish!" "I imagine at your age, everyone seems childish," Murray responded. Sue Ann's words back to Murray included, "Right now, I have an overwhelming urge to diaper your head!"

For "Edie Gets Married" on September 13, 1975, Sue Ann told everyone she saw Lou eating with his ex-wife Edie and added, "I must confess, it baffles me why Lou would want something he's already had, when he can have something fresh and new and exciting. I mean, why buy day-old bread when he can have a beautiful cupcake piping hot from the oven?" She got applause for staring down a laughing Ted after Murray retorted, "But how many times has it been reheated?"

Murray and Sue Ann were particularly viperish in "Mary's Delinquent." "I have just been nominated Twin Cities TV Woman of the Year!" she announced. "What year?" he responded. She wanted him to type her resume, but he said she knew how to do that. "I know, but it's so difficult with these nails!" Sue Ann said. "I always thought they were retractable!" he responded. Looking over her resume, Sue Ann mused, "Let's see, what other unselfish things have I done to aid mankind?" "Did you include the time the Shriners were in town?" Murray snarled back.

Lots of vitriol also appeared in "A Reliable Source" on February 21, 1976. When Sue Ann appeared in a newspaper, Ted asked, "Murray, did you see the spread on Sue Ann?" "Oh yeah," Murray said. "But you don't notice it so much when she sits down!" After glaring at Ted, Sue Ann claimed that she wouldn't trade insults with Murray before she stared at his bald head and intoned, "Just checking my lipstick, dear!"

Learning Sue Ann made more money than he did, Ted asked, "Mary, do you know what Sue Ann takes home every week?" "Three sailors, a tree surgeon, and a boy in the mailroom," Murray said. Later, Sue Ann told Mary about an encounter with Lou. "He called me last night. I think he may have been drinking." "What makes you think that?" Mary asked. "He called her, didn't he?" Murray quipped.

The most degrading way Sue Ann treated Murray was in "What Do You Want to Do When You Produce?" on December 20, 1975. When Sue Ann hired Murray as her new producer, he soon regretted the job. The menial tasks Sue Ann made Murray perform culminated in forcing him to model a "stylishly stout wedding gown," in Sue Ann's words. "No veils, Sue Ann. A producer does not wear veils," he said. Sue Ann offered him to sit down and discuss things. He responded by plopping her on top of a large wedding cake. "Now if you will excuse me, I have a luncheon date with my wife," he said to applause, while Sue Ann tasted a piece of the cake and quipped, "Could use a little more vanilla!" Lusty Sue Ann decided to date her next producer instead.

What's most interesting about Sue Ann's relationship with Murray is that, while she joked constantly about his bald head, she didn't do so with the equally hairless pate of Lou Grant. For him, Sue Ann only had eyes for him in the bedroom, much to his chagrin.

Lust for Lou

What Sue Ann said to Lou often could be construed as sexual harassment by today's standards, but on *The Mary Tyler Moore Show,* her quips generated laughs as audiences watched the gruff newshound flustered by the horny homemaker. Several shows had at least one moment of Sue Ann making suggestive moves and statements toward an uncomfortable or even disgusted Lou.

In "Ted's Wedding" on November 8, 1975, when Lou arrived for the ceremony, Sue Ann said, "Lou, dear, do you think today might give you any dangerous ideas about me?" "Depends on how much whiskey they have," he responded. "Why, you charmer!" she answered. He shrugged and said, "There's not that much booze in the world!"

In "A Reliable Source," Sue Ann said, "Lou, you were so cute when you called me last night." "Oh, I called you by accident," he responded. "I didn't know it was your number written on the wall." "They say it doesn't pay to advertise!" she giggled back before leaving.

When Lou bought Mary a bouquet to perk her up in "Mary Moves Out," Sue Ann said, "Flowers aren't what Mary needs. I know what Mary needs! … A different kind of man than Mary has ever known before. One who would bring out the animal in her." She stared at Lou, who reacted uneasily.

In "Mary Midwife," Lou said at a party, "Mary thinks I should lose weight." "Nonsense, Lou! Your body's perfect," cooed Sue Ann in response. "I wouldn't touch it. If I did, I wouldn't stop!"

Sue Ann disdained and envied other women who hit on Lou. In "Lou Douses an Old Flame," she said she was happy when she learned Lou had received a message from a former lover who wanted to see him. "I'm just wondering who the cheap little tramp can be!" she added. Later at a party at Mary's apartment, Lou was morose, so Mary asked him, "Could I see you in my bedroom?" "If I'd only known it was that easy!" Sue Ann responded to laughter and applause.

On two occasions, Sue Ann's interactions with Lou went beyond flirtation. Lou and Sue Ann had a real date in "The Happy Homemaker Takes Lou Home" on December 6, 1975. Sue Ann told Lou she knew he really was attracted to her. "That's why you're always avoiding me. Because you know if you get too close, you're afraid the little pilot light of desire that flickers within you might turn the whole oven on!" He acknowledged that he refused to partner with her for the company sack race last year because "I didn't want to get into the sack with you!"

Lou unwittingly accepted Mary's offer to set him up on a date with Sue Ann. He ate a lot to avoid getting romantic with her, but that plan backfired. "There is nothing more rewarding than giving pleasure to a man," Sue Ann said, touching him as he grimaced. After dinner, she squeezed next to him on the couch, kissed him, and exclaimed, "Go ahead, Lou, you're stronger than I am, press your advantage!" She grabbed him by the tie to smooch again.

Initially overwhelmed physically by Sue Ann, Lou pressed her off himself. She was upset. "I went for broke on this date! What went wrong?! Is it me?!" she asked. "Yes," he said, then clarified with "You're much too good for this. Chasing men, throwing yourself at them, that's not you, Sue Ann." Though he called her a treasure who should not do the hunting, Sue Ann said, "You just rejected me, and I feel like a million dollars. Thanks, Lou." He told her maybe they would date again sometime. "When?!" she asked expectedly.

Lou never answered, but they reconnected in "Once I Had a Secret Love" on January 17, 1976. He confessed to Mary he got drunk with Sue Ann and spent the night at her apartment. When Sue Ann entered the newsroom to return Lou's coat, she told an unknowing Ted Baxter that "I didn't sleep a wink all night. I feel wonderful!" She greeted Lou with "It's opportunity knocking again!" and told him she felt "Like a glorious flower finally opening her petals to the sun!"

Flustered, Lou pleaded that Sue Ann keep the incident secret, but that didn't stop her from coming back to the newsroom to say, "Oh Lou, I just wanted to give you your socks back. They're all laundered. I put lemon juice in the water. Don't they smell all nice and fresh?" He thanked her and she answered, "I'll be happy to do it—any time!"

When Lou visited Sue Ann's set to say he was sorry about their night of passion, she told him, "Apologize for what?! You were wonderful! Let me put it this way: If you were a soufflé, you'd rise high in the pan! If you were crêpes suzette, your flame would light a whole room!"

Seeing her reaction, Lou proclaimed, "I don't know how to tell you this, but what happened the other night can never happen again." "Sure, it can!" Sue Ann implored. "No, no, it can't." he responded. She accused him of taking advantage of her and casting her aside until he offered to buy her two dinners and a lunch, to which she said, "You've got yourself a deal!" Alas, that was as far as Lou would take things romantically thereafter with Sue Ann.

Producer Allan Burns told Rose Dosti in *The Los Angeles Times* in 1976 that "The only bad comments we get are from people who generally object to the pushy one-off romance Sue Ann has with Lou Grant, Mary's boss in the show." He estimated that ninety-eight percent of the comments about the character were favorable otherwise.

Thoroughly Shallow Sue Ann

Sue Ann's control freak tendencies were on full display in "Ted's Wedding." Georgette had an impromptu marriage ceremony at Mary's apartment. As Mary rounded up the gang, Sue Ann emerged ready to go in the rush. She brought floral arrangements, a bouquet, a boutonniere for Ted, a veil for Georgette, and more amid applause and laughter. Sue Ann stopped her whirlwind of activity to get everyone in line, saying, "Now, what are you people all standing around with your thumbs up your noses for? We've gotta get this show on the road. Move it!"

She generated gales of laughter when Georgette asked about an outfit to go with her veil, "Does it have to be white?" and Sue Ann responded, "Let's see— Married in white, sailor's delight.' No, that isn't it." She even bullied the newly ordained minister who hadn't officiated a wedding previously. When Ted and Georgette finally kissed, immediately Sue Ann trilled "The Wedding March," threw rice at the newlyweds, and even snatched the bouquet Georgette threw toward Mary. This show may have been Betty's best work stealing scenes as Sue Ann.

Sue Ann was at her most ruthless in "A New Sue Ann" on October 26, 1974. Mary's friend, Gloria Munson, played by Linda Kelsey, insisted on meeting Sue Ann, her idol. Sue Ann let Gloria be her stand-in and helper, but when the station manager agreed with Gloria's idea to demonstrate calisthenics on Sue Ann's show, the Happy Homemaker went berserk.

"Little Miss Muffet is after my job!" she told Mary. Sue Ann even thought Gloria was having an affair with the station manager, to which Mary asked, "Why does that necessarily mean she's going to get your job?" "How do you think I got it?" Sue Ann said to laughter and applause.

When Gloria did a baking demonstration on Sue Ann's show, the latter dispensed the goodies Gloria cooked to everybody. "What are you up to?" asked a suspicious Mary. "Mary, can't you just accept the fact that I'm bowing out gracefully?" said Sue Ann. "No!" responded Mary.

She was right, as the newsroom came down with stomach pains. Sue Ann entered and said, "Good news, people! I think we got food poisoning!" "From what?!" exclaimed Mary. "Cream fillings. Apparently, they were left unrefrigerated," said Sue Ann. She did the dirty deed to undercut Gloria. Mary was livid about the news, but Sue Ann noted, "Mary, I ate it too! For the good of the show!"

Sue Ann was more egocentric in "You Can't Lose 'em All," on February 15, 1975. Nominations were out for the Teddys, short for Television Editors, a fictional awards program for broadcasters in Minneapolis. "I have been nominated for a Teddy Award and no one else at the station was!" Sue Ann proclaimed. Mary downplayed the achievement, but Sue Ann said, "I've worked twenty years for this award! I've baked and basted and fricasêed and hammed and flounced and puckered my fingers off for this lousy award!"

Sue Ann tied with the Rev. Dannenbrink, a TV priest played by Fred Grandy. She jubilantly kissed him along with Lou and the award ceremony host. The priest began his acceptance speech with "It would be presumptuous of me to thank you for this award, since in a much larger sense, you cast your ballots not for me, but for someone with whom I am unworthy to share it." "Oh, thank you, Father!" interrupted Sue Ann to laughter. "This award confers great honor. It also carries certain financial benefits. It will be contract time very soon. Thanks to you, this year Father Dannenbrink and I can really put the screws to the big shots!"

In "Sue Ann Falls in Love" on February 28, 1976, the Happy Homemaker got another Teddy Award nomination and a new, young boyfriend named Doug, played by James Luisi. "He was on my show last week when I was demonstrating how to cook without a kitchen," Sue Ann said. "And I've been teaching him the joy of the great indoors!" She told Lou that she could not go with him to the Teddy Awards as she promised last year by breezily saying, "How can I make this easy for you? I've met someone better!"

Sue Ann and Doug arrived at Mary's apartment prior to the ceremony. When Sue Ann stepped out, Doug kissed Mary, who smacked him and hissed, "You are despicable!" She mentioned the incident when Sue Ann announced plans to form a corporation with Doug. Sue Ann broke up with Doug and, as her category was read, she moped and cried, "I wish I were dead!" Named the winner, Sue Ann slowly trudged to the lectern and appeared to be hurting when she spun around, smiled and said, "Ladies and gentlemen, ..." as the audience laughed and applauded.

Directing "Sue Ann Falls in Love" was ironically another Doug—Doug Rogers, a Broadway choreographer and director who came out to Hollywood on the behest of Valerie Harper. He gave Harper her first piece of dialogue on the New York stage.

"She said, 'Someday, I'll pay you back,'" he recounted decades later. "Well, she went to California—in fact, I drove her to the airport when she was going to do *The Mary Tyler Moore Show*. The rest was history.

"As you know, she did a show called *Rhoda*, which was a spin-off, and one time Valerie called me. She said, 'You could do this show. Want to come out here?' And so I went out there, and she introduced me to everybody. Well, I had only done Broadway, off-Broadway, live shows like that as a director, so I had a lot to learn. Shooting with four film cameras and directing the actors was not a problem. She introduced me to the people and they allowed me to observe, which I did for quite a while. That was my college of learning process.

"Eventually the executive producers of *Rhoda* said, 'We have a script you might like. Do you want to read it?' I read it and I said, 'This is great.'" He directed "The Marty Morgan Story," which aired on February 9, 1976.

"Afterwards I was sitting on the soundstage with the actors, just talking about what had happened and thanking them, and … Valerie danced across the stage and said, 'That's my payback.'"

The episode went so well that Rogers got the offer to direct "Sue Ann Falls in Love" for *The Mary Tyler Moore Show*. He remembered how the star set the tone upon his arrival.

"The first day of rehearsal of *The Mary Tyler Moore Show*, now, you've got to understand Mary Tyler Moore was also a dancer. And she came up and said, 'You know, Doug, we've been doing this show for a while here'—and she had known I was a choreographer. She said, 'If you have any new ideas, don't hesitate to tell us, because we're pretty used to doing it one way.' Which was wonderful. It was her way of turning the show over to me, which was fantastic. So, I did that show. It went very well. It was a big success, and that was it."

"Sue Ann Falls in Love" earned Betty her second consecutive Emmy for playing Sue Ann. Allen Ludden also won in 1976 for Outstanding Host or Hostess—Game or Audience Participation Show for his work in *Password*. Betty and Allen were the second married couple to both win Emmys after Alfred Lunt and Lynn Fontanne claimed statuettes for their work in the special *The Magnificent Yankee* in 1965.

Sending Off Sue Ann

As Betty accepted her Emmy in 1976, Mary Tyler Moore planned to end her series the following year for other opportunities. Betty and other cast members understood Mary's plans but were sorry to hear the decision.

"I know for a fact that we all would've gladly signed on for an eighth year or more if they had chosen to do that," recalled Ed Asner. "We were quickly and easily gobbled up for our own spinoffs. But I would've forsaken mine, I know, to keep doing the show. But the call didn't come."

187

The writers created some episodes that final season to round out the characters' relationships and lives. Sue Ann played a key role in several shows, and Betty handled every line expertly as ever.

In "Murray Can't Lose" on November 27, 1976, everyone in the newsroom received a Teddy Award nomination. When Sue Ann won her third consecutive Teddy in daytime programming, she accepted it with, "I really don't deserve your lovely tribute. The real credit should go to Tom, an eighteen-pound Butterball turkey who gave his life so that I might stand here tonight and say, 'Thank you.'"

After the ceremony, everyone celebrated except Murray, who was the sole loser. When he gave Sue Ann a drink, she remarked, "Isn't it a glorious night? Except of course for you, dear." Even so, she and the others were moved when he read his planned acceptance speech showing them how much he cared for them. Incidentally and inexplicably, Gavin MacLeod was the only regular on *The Mary Tyler Moore Show* never nominated for an Emmy.

Sue Ann's win didn't prevent her daytime show from being cancelled in "Sue Ann Gets the Ax" on January 29, 1977. She decided to work out her contract with WJM before adding, "The program manager will try to get me to quit by making my life miserable, but I'm determined not to buckle." Sue Ann wanted a job in the newsroom, but Mary rejected the notion. That decision left Sue Ann reduced to doing the "Uncle Bucky" children's show, where she played Aunt Daisy with huge petals around her face working with two cranky puppeteers. She quit and asked Lou to change Mary's mind about her working in the newsroom.

"Okay, so she's not perfect," Lou told Mary in front of Sue Ann. "So she's a pain in the rump, a gossip, throws herself at every pair of pants she sees." "Maybe I should send in a resume," Sue Ann interjected to laughter and applause. Lou continued and stunned Sue Ann as he told Mary, "Look at this woman! In twenty years, this could be you!" As Sue Ann cried, Mary capitulated and added her occasional nemesis to the newsroom.

Here's Johnny

"Mary's Big Party" on March 5, 1977, was a fond farewell to Mary's lousy get-togethers at her apartment. Congresswoman Margaret Geddes forgave Mary for what happened in "The Dinner Party" three years earlier and offered Mary to host a soirée in honor of Johnny Carson, who was coming to emcee a show with the politician. All was well until the power went out in Mary's building, her flashlight battery was dead and no one could find candles. As Mary vowed the lights would come back on, Sue Ann said, "And believe me, dear, even if they don't, it's no reason why we can't all have a good time." "Sue Ann knows, Mary. When it comes to entertaining people in the dark, she's an expert," chimed in Murray.

In the dark, everyone recalled Mary's previous bad parties in flashbacks. Later, Mary called out Sue Ann for being on the floor with the bartender she hired, which generated applause from the audience. When Geddes arrived with Carson in the pitch-dark apartment, Mary introduced everyone. Sue Ann apparently was getting more romantic with the bartender away from the living room, as she shouted out, "We're in here, dear!" When Sue Ann greeted Carson, he asked, "Mary, do you have a dog?" "No," she responded. "Well, in that case, one of your guests just licked my face!" Johnny left, and Lou told Mary this was the worst party ever. Perhaps, but it was also one of the all-time funniest episodes of *The Mary Tyler Moore Show*, as well.

"You know, I had more fun doing that," Carson told Betty on *The Tonight Show* on December 1, 1977. "They called me—Ed. Weinberger, who used to work for *The Tonight Show*, called me one day. And he said, 'Would you come over? We've got a funny idea for *The Mary Tyler Moore Show*.' And that's one of the best shows, if not the best situation comedy on television. I said, 'What is it?' And he said, 'Well, you're not seen.' I said, 'Well, that doesn't sound too ego satisfying, Ed, could you tell me a little more about it?'"

Johnny added, "It was the strangest feeling, working in the dark and getting laughs. No, I've done that before!" Betty laughed and added, "Just reminiscing!"

The Tearful Finale

The appropriately titled "The Last Show" on March 15, 1977, ended the series with a surprise: The new station manager fired everyone but Ted, the news team's most incompetent member. In the newsroom, Sue Ann said, "They just told me I was being let go along with the rest of you. Is that true?" "Being fired is like being violated," Murray sighed. "Leave it to Murray to find a bright spot," Sue Ann responded.

Sue Ann did find a job, telling everyone, "There's this elderly gentleman who's taking a cruise to the Mediterranean. I'll be traveling with him as sort of a practical nurse." "That ought to be a nice change for you, Sue Ann. Cruising at sea," joked

Murray one last time. Her final shot back to him included saying, "I'll never see your scalp turn to silver."

But the jokes ended as all the regulars huddled in the newsroom for a final time. Lou broke down, and Mary embraced him as he looked at everyone and choked out the words, "I treasure you people." A group hug ensued, and everyone cried.

Then Mary said, "Last night I thought, 'What is a family anyway? They're just people who make you feel less alone and really loved.' And that's what you've done for me. Thank you for being my family." As the last one to leave, Mary smiled as she turned out the lights in the newsroom.

The tears and emotions flowed naturally from the cast members in the finale. They really were a family of actors who loved each other despite occasional disagreements. "When you're in a close cast like that, if you like each other, and if the vibes are right, I mean, you would die for each other," Betty said in the documentary "Eight Characters in Search of a Sitcom."

At the curtain call, the studio audience gave a standing ovation as Mary introduced "the best cast ever," which naturally included Betty. The show finished sixth in the ratings that week.

Never Can Say Goodbye to Mary

The Mary Tyler Moore Show won three Emmys in 1977, including its third consecutive win for Outstanding Comedy Series to tally up twenty-nine statuettes, a record number for a sitcom at the time. In an unprecedented move for any series at the annual event, the cast of *The Mary Tyler Moore Show* came out to take a bow.

Covering the activity, *The L.A. Herald Examiner* erred tremendously in calling this occasion "perhaps their last on-camera appearance as a television family." Instead, there were TV reunions, first when Betty was honored on a *This is Your Life* special in 1987 followed by specials on CBS in 1991 and 2003. An ABC TV-movie in 2000, *Mary and Rhoda*, updated the saga of the two titular characters without talking about the other regulars. The cast, including Betty, also sat at the head table for *CBS at 75*, the network's anniversary special in 2003.

Betty and *The Mary Tyler Moore Show* crew reunited on the Screen Actors Guild Awards in 2007 to present the best comedy series ensemble award to *The Office*. That series' cast members appeared more ecstatic about meeting their idols than getting the statuette. In 2008, Betty and the regulars showed up on *The Oprah Winfrey Show* for a reunion that included reconstructing the sets for the newsroom and Mary's apartment. Winfrey was a devoted fan.

A final reunion of the female regulars occurred on an episode of *Hot in Cleveland* in 2013. That series was one of many Betty did as a regular after *The Mary Tyler Moore Show* established her as a bona fide actress in demand and not just another TV personality. The series was that important to Betty's career. To paraphrase the last line of the show's theme song, Betty had made it after all.

Georgia Engel, John Hillerman, and Betty White were all smiles on *The Betty White Show* in 1977 until the ratings started falling. Courtesy of Everett Collection.

Chapter Eight
Betty the Shining Star

When *The Mary Tyler Moore Show* ended, three cast members starred in their own series in 1977. Ed Asner played a continuation of his character on *Lou Grant*, a one-hour dramatic spin-off. The notion came directly from the creators of *The Mary Tyler Moore Show*. "It was Allan Burns and Jim Brooks," said Asner. "They decided on their own to take it into the hour and to have Lou returning to his first love, print journalism."

Gavin MacLeod starred in *The Love Boat*, a sixty-minute comedy. Then there was Betty White in *The Betty White Show*.

Lou Grant ran five years. *The Love Boat* set sail for nine seasons. But *The Betty White Show* was off the air within four months.

The Betty White Show of 1977–1978, not to be confused with *The Betty White Show* of 1950–1951, 1952–1953, 1954 or 1958, was expected to be a hit. Reviewing the new series for the fall of 1977, the Dancer Fitzgerald Sample advertising agency survey gave *The Betty White Show* high marks for sponsors. She was a featured guest on the hour preview special *CBS Galaxy* on September 5, 1977, as well.

Yet *The Betty White Show* became a huge letdown critically and commercially. Many observers debated how and why this situation occurred, including Betty herself. Most of the participants did bigger and better projects later, again including Betty. She learned being a leading TV star in the 1970s required some adjustments from the luxuries she had enjoyed as a supporting act on *The Mary Tyler Moore Show*.

Betty Goes Undercover

Three writers and producers of *The Mary Tyler Moore Show* approached Betty with the idea of doing her own series as the sitcom wound down in 1977. Ed. Weinberger, Stan Daniels, and David Lloyd first decided Sue Ann Nivens wouldn't work as a main character, based on what happened with *Phyllis*. A previous spin-off from *The Mary Tyler Moore Show*, the series' ratings slid in its second and final season while formulating Betty's new project.

"*Phyllis*, with Cloris Leachman, was a wonderful example of what happens when you take a caustic character and try to refine her for a new series," Betty recalled to Phyllis Battelle in *The Daily News*. "They had to knock off the rough edges, and it took away something.

"Sue Ann would have been the same problem. She was rotten, and she couldn't be that rotten for that long—and then what would you have left? So, having said goodbye to Sue Ann—which was a mini trauma in itself because the role was the best thing to ever happen to me and it was hard to let her go—we had to decide, okay, what will I be?

"The first thought was that I would play a salty nun. But I didn't think there would be much room to grow in a character like that. Then we came up with the middle-aged actress concept. A middle-aged actress being directed in her TV series by her ex-husband."

Betty wanted the series within a sitcom to parody science fiction which, along with westerns, was the only genre in television in which she never acted. Weinberger, Daniels, and Lloyd vetoed the idea because they were unfamiliar with science fiction.

Instead, Betty became Joyce Whitman, the star of the CBS cop drama "Undercover Woman." Georgia Engel, who played Georgette on *The Mary Tyler Moore Show*, was her roommate, Mitzi Maloney. As a concession for animal lover Betty, Mitzi worked in a pet store.

Comparing Joyce with her previous character, Betty told Battelle, "Sue Ann was promiscuous. Joyce was not. Sue Ann went for the jugular. Joyce has a bitchy side, but she doesn't attack, she defends. Most important, my new character is vulnerable. Deep down, she loves the enemy and has a good sense of humor. Sue Ann had none."

John Hillerman played Joyce's acidic ex-husband and director, John Elliot, a man with a pencil-thin mustache, a cigarette holder and a dry, understated delivery. Cast members on "Undercover Woman" would be Carla Borelli as Joyce's vain co-star Lisa

Vincent, who played a fellow cop, and Barney Phillips as Fletcher Huff, a fretful, aging actor who played Joyce and Lisa's police chief. Other regulars were Charles Cyphers as Hugo Muncy, Joyce's beefy stunt double who wore a blonde wig, and Alex Henteloff as Doug Porterfield, the liaison from CBS.

With everyone in place, Betty and crew went to work. She had many fans in the audience for the test show, which, unlike *The Mary Tyler Moore Show*, would be videotaped rather than filmed.

"When we were doing *Liars Club*, it was when Betty did her pilot for *The Betty White Show*," recalled Shelley Herman, a writer and researcher on *Liars Club*. "It was taped over at CBS Television City, and we all went down to be supportive of Betty, to watch the pilot. Not that she needed us, of course, but it was something for young kids to do at the time.

"Taping a pilot, there's a lot of stop and start. I could see Betty was working really hard to make it successful, because they kept changing the lines, and it was a long night doing the pilot. And Allen [Ludden] was there. He was kind of pacing around. He wasn't seated with us.

"But at a certain point, I went over to talk to him. He was standing with his arms folded and those big glasses and the biggest smile on his face. He was staring at her and saying, 'Isn't she just marvelous?' Wow. To have a partner like that, who not only would say something like that but genuinely felt that way about her. He was so, so proud of her."

Also attending the pilot taping were two of Betty's co-stars on *Match Game 77*, Richard Dawson and Brett Somers. They wished her well on that series, as well as in person.

The good vibrations from all worked. *The Betty White Show* sold. CBS installed the series on Mondays 9-9:30 p.m., which had become a trouble spot during the 1976–1977 season when *Maude* occupied the slot. The sitcom had been a top ten hit since its debut in 1972 but slipped considerably. In fact, *Maude* became the first CBS series airing Mondays 9-9:30 p.m. not to finish in the top thirty since the debut of *I Love Lucy* in 1951.

More troubling for the series' future was the departure of Weinberger and Daniels for other projects after the pilot. Lloyd stayed on as executive story editor and also was credited as developer for *The Betty White Show*, while Weinberger and Daniels were listed as creators. Bob Ellison, another veteran producer of *The Mary Tyler Moore Show*, became executive producer while other creative talents joined the series, including George Tibbles, Betty's old writing pal on *Life With Elizabeth* in the 1950s, as story consultant.

"I think the scripts are marvelous, but will the audience think so?" Betty told Phyllis Battelle in *The Daily News* before *The Betty White Show* began. "What do I know? I'm just an amateur."

A Sparkling Start Goes South
The Betty White Show debuted on September 12, 1977, with Joyce Whitman ecstatic to get the lead in the series "Undercover Woman." "A weekly paycheck! I won't be dependent upon alimony checks from Old Picklepuss!" she crowed to her roommate Mitzi. Her joy collapsed when her ex-husband John, "Old Picklepuss," informed her he was the series' director.

The next day, John introduced the cast members. Lisa Vincent, a statuesque brunette, didn't endear herself to Joyce by saying, "I've admired you for years and years." Joyce disliked Lisa even more when the actress added how easier it would have been to copy *Charlie's Angels* and *Police Woman*. "You know, hire someone gorgeous and voluptuous, sexy and young. Finally, television has come out with a star that the middle-aged frumpy housewife can identify with!"

Doug Porterfield said he had just become vice president in charge of prime time dramatic development a day after working in the CBS mailroom. "The first time is always special," said Lisa about Doug's first day in his job. "What a memory you have!" purred Joyce to applause.

Seeing how considerate and caring John was on the set, Joyce thought about rekindling their relationship that ended after five years of marriage. But he was a cold fish. When she placed a flower in her cleavage, he responded, "I was hoping it was growing there." He lied about being married to avoid being with Joyce, which infuriated her when she found out. She manifested her displeasure in a series of visual gags that culminated in the set wall falling down around John.

At the end of the show, John shaved off his moustache. Joyce told him she liked him better with the moustache. "Then I did the right thing," he said with a smile.

After filming the pilot, the show dropped Carla Borelli's Lisa Vincent in favor of Caren Kaye as Tracy Garrett, Joyce's partner on "Undercover Woman." Kaye had just finished playing a blonde bombshell on the short-lived ABC sitcom *Blansky's Beauties* in the spring of 1977.

"I met Betty White on *The Mary Tyler Moore Show*," Kaye recalled later. "I played a sportscaster and got to know her there." Betty didn't appear on that episode, which was "What's Wrong with Swimming?" which first aired October 16, 1976, but she did attend the taping.

"I had been guest starring on MTM on all of their shows, so I wasn't that surprised when Betty put a show together that we might work again," Kaye added "Which is really a lovely testament to her generosity."

Tracy was a conniving, buxom blonde. "It was kind of like the play *All About Eve*," Kaye said of her character. "She was trying to kick her way to the top. I was also a great foil to Betty, because she was that person—who I was playing—on *The Mary Tyler Moore Show*, where she was the foil for [Mary]. So it was nice to have Betty on that other end, and to be the 'Betty White' to Betty White."

In her first appearance, Tracy claimed she had a great idea to improve one "Undercover Woman" script. "What if I cry during a scene and wear a bikini?" Her relationship with Joyce became sharper subsequently. When Tracy said, "You know, Joyce, with you driving a car, it's just not safe to walk the streets," Joyce shot back, "What streets do you usually walk, dear?"

Other times Tracy served as Joyce's verbal punching bag. After Hugo said, "The world is full of people who want weird stunts performed," Joyce asked, "Well, that takes care of you and Tracy, but what about the rest of us?"

While these bits were amusing, the numbers for *The Betty White Show* were not. The show's debut was in the top ten, but ratings soon sank. What caused the falloff was a matter of debate.

Kay Gardella, TV critic at *The Daily News* in New York City, blamed ratings woes on rival network ABC "pandering to the lowest common denominator" with its sitcoms targeted at teenagers. "Programs like *The Betty White Show*, intelligently produced with a certain amount of sophistication and adult appeal, are suffering the consequences," she wrote.

Other reviewers thought the show had problems that discouraged audiences from watching. David Handler of the Newspaper Enterprise Association praised Betty. "What a treat to have a star who bristles with bitterness, who is out-and-out nasty."

But he thought the ongoing feud between Joyce and John "was funny the first week, but after a while it's quite tiresome."

Indeed, the give-and-take between Joyce and John on their love life predominated over the plots. The second episode had Mitzi's cousin Wilma, played by Janis Paige, transformed from a schlub to a dazzler after dating John.

"The only problem I had with the show was the writing wasn't funny enough," said Doug Rogers, who directed this and two other episodes of *The Betty White Show*. "Also, you've got to remember, her character on *The Mary Tyler Moore Show* was very well-established, and almost everything she did there got a laugh because of the writing and the character. But we didn't get that kind of writing, and I never thought the show reached its full potential."

Indeed, there was a two-part story about John discovering that he and Joyce were not legally divorced. He then decided to make romantic overtures to Joyce, a tired plot going back to 1930s screwball comedy movies. The second part was really awful, as Joyce and John escalated a war of nerves in pretending to be back in marriage to irritate each other. Joyce reached Sue Ann Nivens' level of meanness by intentionally feeding John cat food.

The explanation by Joyce of her behavior was rather ridiculous. "If I hold John to something out of spite, I'll just drive him further away. If I have any thought, however remote, that we might get back together someday, I have to give him the divorce he wants now," she told Mitzi. "Oh! Your marriage is standing in the way of your romance!" said Mitzi. "Exactly!" said Joyce. She then had a party with other regulars to celebrate her real divorce with John.

Two shows stood out at exceptions to the general mediocrity. The eighth episode, "Good Night Sweet Fletch" on October 31, 1977, had an uproarious script by Glen Charles and Les Charles, who would later write and produce *Taxi* and *Cheers*. Doug said CBS wanted a big ratings grabber for "Undercover Woman" like a wedding. "Oh, I'd like that," said Joyce. "Some gorgeous hunk falls in love with me, asks me to be his wife." "Ah, what a great idea!" said Tracy. "Thanks," said Joyce. "I've always loved science fiction," responded Tracy.

Meanwhile, Fletcher was thrilled by the new script that gave him lots of lines. "My cup runneth over!" he exclaimed. "But what about me?" said Tracy as she looked for her part. Joyce responded, "Tracy, your cups are …" before John cut her off.

Ultimately, Doug suggested that Fletcher's character die to boost ratings. But viewers bombarded CBS to voice their displeasure of the chief's death. The solution was to have Fletcher return to play his twin brother. "He talked about you all the time!" enthused Joyce's character.

Three episodes later, "Joyce's Wedding," written by Bill Idelson, had the actress fall into a whirlwind romance with race car driver Larry Bennett, played by Philip Carey. The following exchanges were golden:

• "Dating a race driver, that must be fun!" said Tracy. "You wouldn't like it. Their cars don't have back seats," retorted Joyce. "Oh, right!" added Tracy.

• "Joyce, you know I don't take no for an answer," Larry said. "That's okay, Joyce doesn't give no for an answer!" responded John.

• "Boy, riding on the back of a motorcycle, that's one thing a guy could never get me to do," said Tracy. "Well, at last we found something!" shot back Joyce.

On the wedding day, Larry fled to Brazil. Joyce offered to reconcile with John. He was more concerned about his wedding gift. "Joyce, can I have my picture frame back?" he asked. As Joyce said goodbye to guests at the planned reception, Tracy said, "Joyce, you look so beautiful standing there. You remind me of my mother." "Oh, were you at her wedding, too?" snapped back Joyce.

But a couple of good shows can't outweigh mostly unsatisfactory ones. With NBC putting up big movies as competition, soon *The Betty White Show* sunk to third in its time slot. The series was not a distant third, but the results were far from what CBS wanted.

The Betty White Show last aired in its original time slot on November 28, 1977. A week later, CBS flipped the series with *Maude*, the sitcom that was following *The Betty White Show* Monday nights and previously held the 9-9:30 slot. Between those points, network executives decided to cancel *The Betty White Show*.

The Long, Slow Goodbye

Betty learned of the cancellation on December 1, 1977. The announcement was quite a surprise, as she along with Caren Kaye were promoting the series during a hiatus in taping episodes.

"I was on tour for *The Betty White Show* when it got cancelled," Kaye recalled. "So, they cancelled the interviews immediately. It was such a good show, it was so surprising it wouldn't be picked up. They'd started sending people on publicity runs about the show.

"And I was staying in New York, where I'm from, and I was told that it was not going to be picked up. That was really weird. It was so sad, because everybody on it was so happy."

Kaye remained friends with Betty. "I got to see her a lot after that," she said. "First of all, we lived in the same area, and I would run into her in restaurants and stuff. ... She is what she is. She can take that humor and really extend on it. She really is that person. Lovely, great."

Meanwhile, Betty was on *The Tonight Show* that evening. "You were mentioning at the beginning of the show that CBS had cancelled four shows," she told host Johnny Carson. "Make that five."

"Oh, no," said Carson.

"Yes, Betty's bitten the dust," she said. She joked whether she could still stay on *The Tonight Show*, and Johnny pretended to throw her off. Then Betty got serious about what had transpired.

"Let's face it. It's a whole new ballgame. They're fighting for their lives, all three of the networks are fighting, you know, terribly competitive, and, but, oh we were disappointed. And it hurts. I'd like to say, 'Well, that's the business,' but it hurts. Because you're so excited and you've got so many plans and we had so many changes."

Betty also told Carson she was going to star in a TV movie based on the life of Velma Johnston, also known as Wild Horse Annie for her defense of free-ranging mustangs. The project never got produced, nor did a planned version in 2011 starring Wendie Malick for The Hallmark Channel. Ironically, by that time Betty and Wendie were co-stars on the series *Hot in Cleveland*.

Although cancelled, the series kept airing for a few more weeks. In a not-so-subtle tweak at CBS, the last episode dealt with rumors of the impending cancellation of "Undercover Woman." At a party, Joyce and company pandered to Mr. Chase, played by Paul Marin, a network representative. Chase said he reluctantly would keep "Undercover Woman" on the air only because one of the chimps on its planned replacement series died.

The Betty White Show ended on January 9, 1978. The next week, *Maude* moved to Saturdays while CBS transferred *M*A*S*H* from Tuesdays to Mondays 9-9:30 p.m. The installment of that sitcom brought the network back into having a hit in that time slot through 1983.

"*The Betty White Show* was not outstanding," Betty wrote in her book *Here We*

Go Again. "I can't even say it was one of my all-time favorites, but we had given it our best shot, and one does get emotionally involved with the group of people, each time." The exception was one regular actor who, when told by Betty the series was ending, said he was glad because he didn't think he was being used properly. The actor wasn't John Hillerman, whom Betty said loved *The Betty White Show* more than anyone else.

Reporter Elliot Wald provided a postmortem report on the failure of *The Betty White Show*. Wald cited a poor lead-in—the western *Young Dan'l Boone*, axed after airing three times before *The Betty White Show*—the competition, and "a discernible decline in quality." He also noted some observers faulted CBS for making a rash decision to cancel.

"Did the end come too soon? Many believe it did, and statistics bear them out. CBS killed the show just nine weeks into its run. It had been on the plus side of the thirty percent barrier three of those weeks—though not the four weeks before cancellation—and averaged a 28.2 share. In the averages for the first thirteen weeks of the season *The Betty White Show* finished a respectable thirty-third, above such CBS perennials as *The Waltons, Good Times, The Jeffersons, Kojak,* and even *Maude*." The top thirty shows are generally thought of as cancellation-proof.

Wald also included a quote from Grant Tinker, head of the MTM production company and Betty's friend. "The show was never given a chance to develop," he said.

The switch to Mondays 9:30-10 p.m. caused more ratings erosion. The series ended the season tied for the forty-ninth position, which still put it slightly ahead of two other sitcoms that CBS renewed, *The Jeffersons* and *Good Times*.

Bud Grant, ex-daytime programming head turned vice president for programming for CBS entertainment, defended his network's actions on *The Betty White Show* to George Cashman in *The Berkeley Gazette*. "The first week, we had a thirty-five percent share of the audience. It dropped to twenty-seven the next week. Then we preempted it for the Elvis Presley special and got a fifty share. The following week Betty White was down. Apparently people would sample the series and not find it as appealing as we thought it would be."

Like *The Betty White Show, Maude* also ended in the 1977–1978 season. Its star, Beatrice Arthur, would team with Betty White seven years later to give them both a hit that equaled, if not surpassed, their successes on *Maude* and *The Mary Tyler Moore Show*—*The Golden Girls*.

The cancellation of *The Betty White Show* had a few other implications. Based on the advanced prognostications the series would be a smash, the star got featured on a special on rival network NBC.

The Dean Martin Celebrity Roast: Betty White took place in the MGM Grand Hotel in Las Vegas in 1977. Host Dean Martin introduced guests who told mild and variable jokes about Betty. "And like so many other people in America, Betty does have black roots!" Jimmie Walker said. She grinned at the remark about her hair. Bonnie Franklin said she had never met "this over-dimpled star" who took in actors down on their luck. "And it's great, if you don't mind being wormed and neutered," she added. Red Buttons said Betty once quipped to Allen Ludden, "Not tonight, unless you know the password!"

"Betty has everything that Miss America has. Unfortunately, they served her child's portions," cracked Phyllis Diller. "If it wasn't for her hickey, she'd have no figure at all!" Georgia Engel said Betty's driver's identification said, "For covered wagons only." Foster Brooks played Betty's ex-fiancé and called her "The old broad I used to mess around with." Milton Berle said Betty went out with the Tommy Dorsey Band even though she was not a singer.

The final roaster was Allen Ludden, who said, "When I proposed to her, the first thing she said was 'Sit up and beg!' … On our honeymoon, she rolled over and played dead!" He then introduced "The blue ribbon woman in my life." and Betty roasted all on the dais. She thanked Dean for a great evening and kissed him at the end.

The Dean Martin Celebrity Roast: Betty White aired May 31, 1978, four months after the cancellation of *The Betty White Show*. Because of the delay, references to *The Betty White Show* and *The Sanford Arms*, a spin-off of *Sanford and Son* starring guest LaWanda Page that went off in a month in 1977, were anachronistic. The show was such a debacle that Dean Martin stopped doing celebrity "roast" specials until six years later.

By the time *The Dean Martin Celebrity Roast: Betty White* did air, Betty had already tried another potential series. Regardless of what had happened on *The Betty White Show*, she had secured a lead role on another pilot with an old friend.

A "Fawlty" Pilot

After rising to international prominence in the sketch comedy series *Monty Python's Flying Circus*, John Cleese enhanced his comic standing in 1975 with *Fawlty Towers*. The wildly hilarious sitcom starred Cleese as Basil Fawlty, a hotel operator in rural England whose vanity, incompetence, and obnoxiousness led to hysterical complications among his staff and guests.

The BBC in the United Kingdom and on PBS in the United States repeated *Fawlty Towers* frequently long after the initial airing of its twelve episodes. As several 1970s hit sitcoms in America were adaptations of British series, *Fawlty Towers* was an obvious target for a similar treatment. Dean Hargrove and Roland Kibbee, formerly writers and executive producers for the hit mystery series *Columbo*, wrote and produced a script they called *Snavely* and cast Harvey Korman and Betty White as the leads in the spring of 1978.

Chris Korman, Harvey's son, was on the set during the taping on *Snavely*. He thought the pilot would be a hit for his father and Betty. "Mind you, I was ten or eleven years old, but I could tell they were having so much fun together, and you actually thought they were married. And I thought that would've been the key if the show would've gone forward. You could tell that Betty and Dad really loved working together, that they genuinely loved each other. They didn't have to fake it."

The modification of *Fawlty Towers* had Korman as Henry Snavely and Betty as his wife, Gladys Snavely. Their resort, Snavely Manor, had a wait staff consisting of Petro, played by Frank LaLoggia, an Albanian refugee who didn't speak English; and Connie, played by Deborah Zon, a waitress trying to earn a credit in hotel management. Under Henry's erratic leadership, Connie probably learned the wrong lessons in her field. A regular customer in their dining room was the semi-senile former local police chief, played by Ivor Francis.

Snavely began with Gladys giving Petro a roll of toilet paper to bring to a guest who requested the item an hour earlier. "Take up," she said, which made him look at the ceiling. She finally conveyed the meaning to Petro, but he accidentally transported a tray of food instead.

Henry arrived in the back room with a stuffed mountain goat's head to the dismay of Gladys. "We are in the hotel business," she said. "God, how I hate it!" Henry responded.

At the empty front desk, Mr. Bishop, portrayed by Jack Dodson, rang the bell repeatedly for service. Henry arrived and snapped, "Stop that racket! You'll be taken care of, just wait your turn!" His mood turned when he learned three inspectors from the International Hotel Guide are in town. Thinking Bishop could be one of them,

Henry accommodated the guest's extravagant demands and even gave him the room where he and Gladys lived, much to his wife's disgust.

Other disasters ensued. Gladys flirted with a guest who was a priest, played by Brad Trumbull. When the Snavelys discovered Bishop only sold hardware, Henry believed another guest, Mr. Foley, played by George Pentecost, was the real inspector. As Bishop got knocked out and planned to sue the hotel, Henry decided to impress Foley with a practice fire drill from his staff. Petro accidentally started a real fire during the drill and Henry used the fire extinguisher on Foley before learning he was not an inspector.

Bishop and Foley left Snavely Manor furious at Henry. He returned their vituperation loudly in the lobby without realizing the real inspectors had arrived and unceremoniously dismissed them. As Henry worried about his egregious error, Gladys consoled him by saying, "Why don't you hang your goat?"

Videotaped before a studio audience, *Snavely* didn't become a series. The pilot ran as an *ABC Comedy Special* on Saturday, June 24, 1978, from 8:30-9 p.m.

Industry speculation was either the result paled in comparison to the original or Betty and Harvey's recent failures made ABC executives wary about its potential. While Betty had the disappointment of *The Betty White Show*, Korman had recorded six episodes as the lead of a sitcom starring himself. Judging the results as poor, ABC aired *The Harvey Korman Show* irregularly from January 31, 1978 through August 3, 1978. "Both their track records for starring on their own weren't good," admitted Chris Korman.

Additionally, ABC had few slots available in its fall 1978 lineup. Its programmers picked up only two sitcoms to add to the schedule, *Mork & Mindy*, the biggest hit of the season, and *Apple Pie*, the biggest bomb. *Apple Pie*, which coincidentally starred Betty's *Golden Girls* pal Rue McClanahan, ran for only two shows, the quickest sitcom cancellation on ABC until *Emily's Reasons Why Not* in 2006.

Meanwhile, two versions of *Fawlty Towers* turned up later. Betty's other future *Golden Girls* co-star, Bea Arthur, was in *Amanda's*, which ran on ABC February 10, 1983–May 29, 1983. "Bea Arthur's was awful," opined Korman. Arthur shared the sentiment and hated doing the series so much that she nearly turned down *The Golden Girls*. Sixteen years later, John Larroquette was the title character in *Payne*, which ran on CBS from March 15, 1999–April 28, 1999.

During and after these attempts, *Fawlty Towers* continued to be popular and ranked among the best British sitcoms in several surveys. As is often the case, the original is still the greatest.

Another Missed Opportunity: *Stephanie*

On January 16, 1978, CBS aired *Fighting Nightingales*, a failed comedy pilot. The show was the creation of writer-producers Alan Uger and Michael Kagan.

"Alan Uger and I had been writing and producing partners for a few years and had a development deal with MTM Productions," said Kagan. "We had worked together on a pilot at Fox which was a female version of *M*A*S*H*, told from the nurses' point of view. It starred Adrienne Barbeau, but Stephanie Faracy stole the show. Alan and I became immediate fans of Stephanie and vowed to one day give her the shot she deserved."

That shot came after Faracy finished some movie roles and a regular part in the CBS sitcom *The Last Resort* from 1979 through 1980. "We saw her as a combination of Lucille Ball and Carol Burnett," said Kagan. "We created a show for Stephanie, pitched it to Grant Tinker [president and CEO of MTM Productions], who liked the idea, and we all went to pitch it to CBS, who bought it."

Stephanie would be shot like *The Mary Tyler Moore Show*, on film using multiple cameras and a studio audience. The pilot's plot had the titular character become the host of a TV newsmagazine show despite reservations from, and friction with, its prickly creator, Agnes Dewey. "Before we ever shot the pilot, Alan and I had written over a dozen episodic storylines for the series," said Kagan. "All were based on Stephanie being burdened by Agnes' demands, finding herself in over her head at work or struggling for a balanced personal life."

When it came to crafting the pilot itself, Kagan said. "We were discussing casting ideas with Grant Tinker one day when he mentioned how concerned he was about Betty White. Grant and Mary Tyler Moore were close friends with Betty and Allen Ludden. At the time, Allen was hospitalized at Cedar-Sinai Hospital battling stomach cancer.

"We suggested Betty for the role of the boss, Agnes. Grant thought having a job might just be what Betty needed as a distraction from her personal woes. Betty loved the script but was unsure about dividing her time between her husband and a new pilot. It was Grant who talked her into it, suggesting the distraction might be healthy for her. She read the script again and consented to play Agnes."

Beside Stephanie and Betty, others in the regular cast included Jeanetta Arnette, Robert Hitt, Alvy Moore, and Kent Perkins. "When you shoot a pilot, you hope that every actor meets your expectations. However, until you begin rehearsing and filming, you can't determine things like chemistry between actors, comic timing, camera presence, etc.," noted Kagan. "If the series had been picked up as a series, we would have made a few casting changes. All the ancillary actors in the pilot were friends of ours. [Guest star] Steve Landesberg was starring in *Barney Miller* at the time."

Kagan and Uger also realized, as they prepared the *Stephanie* pilot, how determined an actress Betty was given her circumstances. "Although we knew Allen Ludden was ill, we really had no idea how critical his condition was," said Kagan. "As for accommodating Betty, we created a rehearsal schedule around Cedar-Sinai visiting hours. Betty would shuttle back and forth between the studio and the hospital all day.

"We could all see the emotional toll it was taking Betty, but she was always remarkably professional when working. Upon returning to the studio, she would shake off her own emotions and plunge into the work of creating comedy. She could find the 'funny' in any line or situation. It was impossible to work with Betty White and not fall in love with her."

Kagan said *Stephanie* got lots of laughs from CBS executives but ran into huge hurdles to make the 1981 fall schedule. "In our case, CBS had produced fifty-three pilots with only three or four time slots to fill, so the competition was furious and the odds nearly insurmountable. Although I've never been a proponent of audience testing, the networks believed in the practice to help cover their asses. So, the pilot did not get picked up for a series because it didn't test as well as we hoped, *Stephanie* was liked but not loved in the show, and CBS didn't have a time slot for it."

Despite *Stephanie* not making the grade, Kagan enjoyed working with Betty. "Betty White always was, and still is, a truly remarkably gifted woman. Her talent and comedic instincts are only eclipsed by her heart and soul as a human being. She's one of the best examples of how to leave the world a better place than you found it. Betty enriches the lives of everyone she meets or works with.

"Allen's death left a hole in Betty's heart that will never be filled. But her love of animals and humans alike are an inspiration to all who are blessed to know her."

Stephanie aired as a special on CBS Tuesday 8:30-9 p.m. on September 8, 1981. By that time, Allen Ludden had passed away. To keep herself occupied in his absence, as she had done during his cancer treatment, Betty kept working on other potential

TV series projects. One was a proposed spin-off from a sitcom reteaming her with former co-star, Gavin MacLeod, in his series that was a hit in 1977 while *The Betty White Show* floundered.

Boarding *The Love Boat* with Carol Channing

The Love Boat docked on the ABC schedule September 24, 1977 after two TV movies served as pilots for the series on September 17, 1976 and January 21, 1977. MacLeod got the lead role of Captain Merrill Stubing after Harvey Korman rejected it because he was tired after a decade on *The Carol Burnett Show*, according to Korman's son Chris. "He also really didn't have a great desire to run around a soundstage dressed as a captain."

Betty made five guest appearances during the show's nine-year run. That quintet made *The Love Boat* the scripted series with the most guest visits by Betty, discounting any series where she was a semiregular. Four of the five times, she and Carol Channing portrayed recurring characters.

Their first outing was on October 17, 1981 in a ninety-minute special episode. Betty was flamboyant Betsy Boucher opposite Carol Channing's equally outrageous Sylvia Duvall. Betsy and Sylvia were stage actors and singers. Sylvia was the aunt of cruise director Julie McCoy, played by *Love Boat* regular Lauren Tewes. Secretly, Sylvia and Betsy were in cahoots to con the onboard wine tasting contest's sponsor, Elliot Banning, played by Douglas Fairbanks Jr.

"Carol and I played a couple of ex-Follies girls on the take, and the show seemed to work," Betty said of their initial teaming to Bob Thomas of the Associated Press. "I nearly didn't do it. Allen [Ludden] was desperately ill, and I didn't think I should leave him. The doctor said, 'You have to do it, both for yourself and for Allen.' I finished the show on Saturday. Allen died on Monday."

Ironically, Allen Ludden had made his last TV appearance when Betty debuted on *The Love Boat* on another special ninety-minute episode on November 22, 1980. Betty played Louise Willis opposite Ludden's Paul Willis, a jockey paying more attention to his racehorse, Joyce, than his wife. As a result, Louise accepted the invitation from Cliff, played by David Doyle, to go out dancing while Paul tended to Joyce. Learning of the potential romance, Paul sold Joyce to Cliff with the condition that he give up any interest in Louise. Betty looked smashing in a white nightgown in one sequence.

Betty's second *Love Boat* visit was well-received, so she and Carol reprised their roles on December 11, 1982. The two characters butted heads this time as Betsy acted as executrix of the estate of Sylvia's late husband and held the purse strings tightly to limit Sylvia's spending.

The third go-round for Betsy and Sylvia on January 7, 1984 had Betsy trying to sell her memoirs to book publisher John Drake, played by Cesar Romero, but he was more interested in Sylvia's body. Also guest starring was Rue McClanahan when both she and Betty were appearing on *Mama's Family*. Oddly, NBC had moved that series to run opposite the last half hour of *The Love Boat* starting with this episode.

In their last appearance on November 23, 1985, Betty and Sylvia billed themselves professionally as "B and B" and performed "Bosom Buddies" from *Mame* with the Love Boat Mermaid dancers in a delightful sequence. Sylvia now was a star on a soap opera and Betsy wanted to join the show while avoiding Sylvia's lecherous co-star, Roger Garrett, played by Louis Nye.

As the personal friendship between Betty and Carol blossomed in these shows, they considered working together professionally full time. In 1983 Betty and Carol appeared on *The Merv Griffin Show* to promote their idea of a sitcom together tentatively titled "Friends Like Us." They played Carol Compton and Betty Abernathy, with Carol as owner of "La Woman" magazine and Betty as its editor. Both had their own advice columns in the publication, lived in the same apartment building and even shared the same husband. Betty had three children with Brick before they divorced and he wed Carol. Following that, Brick left Carol after eight years.

Betty believed in premarital sex. "Well, crackers only get stale on the shelf! Practice makes perfect! If you want virgin wool, look for an ugly sheep!" Carol believed otherwise. "A man is so grateful if you let him know that he's the first. It works every time!" The women were arch competitors who nevertheless loved each other.

The "Friends Like Us" concept never sold. Channing went back to playing *Hello, Dolly!* on stage while Betty occupied herself with a new recurring role that was actually an old one.

Ellen and Eunice and Mama

Betty's first acting job after Allen Ludden's death in July 1981 involved a funeral. With the popularity of *The Carol Burnett Show* reruns in syndication, Burnett decided to have a comedy-drama special called *Eunice* depicting members of the recurring sketch "The Family." Burnett would resume her role as Eunice Harper Higgins, a woman dominated by her mother, Thelma Harper, played by Vicki Lawrence. Although she played the character only three times on *The Carol Burnett Show*, Betty popped up again as Eunice's snobbish sister Ellen Harper Jackson.

To encourage Harvey Korman to return as Eunice's husband, Ed Higgins, he became co-director of *Eunice* with Roger Beatty. Harvey's son Chris Korman said Beatty directed the cameramen while his father worked with the cast on line readings.

"She [Burnett] knew that my dad knew the character. He played just the third act part to pay his condolences. He reluctantly did it because he hated playing Ed. I don't mean to beat a dead horse, but he didn't know what to do with that character. He didn't like to play bumpkins very well. He didn't like the characters in 'The Family' anyway."

Eunice aired Monday, March 15, 1982 from 9:30 to 11 p.m. on CBS. The special began in 1955, with Eunice as a teenager. Ellen was absent until the last third of the show, after Mama died in 1978. After making Eunice laugh about how an aunt cracked chairs at Mama's funeral, Ellen's congenial mood with her sister changed when Ellen asked their brother, Phillip Harper, played by Ken Berry, how long he intended to stay in town. His suggestion that the family should have frozen Mama cryogenically to be revived later worsened a tense situation. The final straw for Eunice was to hear her ex-husband Ed had a new love.

When Ellen admired a lamp at Mama's house, Eunice snapped, "You want me to gift wrap that for you?!" She accused Ellen of wanting every possession in the house. "Look, sister dear! I know you've had a rough day, but that doesn't mean I have to take this!" Ellen responded. "I took enough when we were kids!" Ellen rejected Eunice's protests that she suffered more as a youth, especially after Eunice accidentally spilled a beer on Ellen's dress.

"You are an embarrassment to be around!" yelled Ellen to Eunice. "You always have been! No wonder your husband and kids headed for the hills!" Eunice demanded Ellen get out of "my house" before Ellen reminded her that both of them and Phillip owned the property. "Then get out of my sight!" she told Ellen.

Before Ellen left in a huff, she told Eunice, "And I have a bulletin for you about your precious Fluffy. You remember the day he disappeared? Well toots, that wasn't fried chicken we had for dinner that night!" Ellen added that Mama took it to the butcher after being tired of cleaning it up. "Oh, heaven's sake, Eunice! If we hadn't eaten him, that damn rabbit would've been dead of old age by now anyway!" she said to applause. The storyline was a repeat from Betty's guest shot on *The Carol Burnett Show* on December 11, 1976.

Eunice was a hit, finishing eighth in the ratings. But even before that fact came out, producer Joe Hamilton, Carol Burnett's husband, was pedaling the concept as a series. Executives at CBS and ABC rejected the proposal, but not NBC. Two days after *Eunice* aired, the network announced that *Mama's Family* would be added to its schedule.

"It should've ended right there," said Chris Korman. "How do you explain Mama's dead? Now you're going to resurrect her and bring her back? I mean, really?!"

But NBC badly needed comedies on its schedule, so Mama was revived as *Mama's Family*. And Betty was part of "The Family" again.

Ellen Mellows with Mama

NBC planned to air *Mama's Family* in the fall of 1982 on Saturdays at 9 p.m. But at the last minute, the network added to its lineup *Taxi*, which ABC had dropped after four years. NBC decided to put *Taxi* on Thursdays at 9:30 p.m., where it had aired on ABC, and move the new sitcom *Gimme a Break!* to Saturdays at 9 p.m. With that change, *Mama's Family* had to wait until midseason to debut.

"Our problem is a problem of plenty," NBC Entertainment President Brandon Tartikoff told Val Adams in *The Daily News*. "We haven't had so many schedulable comedy series available to us at the start of the season in seventeen years." Indeed, during the beginning of the 1965–1966 season, NBC had nine sitcoms on its schedule. As 1982–1983 dawned, NBC had eight sitcoms.

Mama's Family debuted on January 22, 1983. The only regulars returning from the special were Vicki Lawrence and Ken Berry, who now played Thelma's son Vinton "Vint" Harper. Vint's wife Mitzi had left him to become a cocktail waitress in Las Vegas. He flirted with Naomi Oates, played by Dorothy Lyman, the floozy next door to Mama, as he moved into Mama's house with his son Buzz, played by Eric Brown and daughter Sonja, played by Karin Argoud.

The relocation upset Vint's Aunt Fran, played by Rue McClanahan, Thelma's sister, who wrote for the local newspaper at Raytown and lived with Thelma as a paying guest. Betty's Ellen Harper Jackson came over to help clear out personal possessions and make room for Vint and his kids. She found her old composition book and enjoyed reading excerpts. As with *Eunice*, this bit was a repeat from Betty's guest shot on *The Carol Burnett Show* on December 11, 1976.

Betty signed only to be an occasional guest on *Mama's Family*. Creators and frequent writers Dick Clair and Jenna McMahon were producers of the series, while Joe Hamilton was executive producer. Harvey Korman and Roger Beatty were the main co-directors. With his primary role to stage the actors on the series, Korman was willing to play Ed for two episodes of *Mama's Family*. According to his son Chris, his biggest difficulty was with one of the regular actresses.

"He had a problem with Rue [McClanahan]. My Dad didn't like Rue. Rue was always, 'Why should I do this? What is my motivation?' My Dad said, 'Your motivation is we pay you a lot of money to do this role. What other motivation do you need, Rue!?'"

Korman said his father did like playing Alistair Quince, the ostensible host of every episode of *Mama's Family* on NBC. "He loved doing it because he got to be Harvey. Smart and cute. Affluent, very snobby, erudite." The introductions disappeared in syndicated reruns of *Mama's Family* but were restored on the DVD sets of the series.

Additionally, Korman helped Lawrence modulate her performance as Mama to smooth out the character's rough edges and generate more humor. Oddly, the same mellowing happened to Betty's Ellen as well, going from bitchy to bedeviled over the course of the series.

Ellen's softening on *Mama's Family* began with her storyline on the two-part wedding of Vint and Naomi. Fearing her husband Bruce was committing adultery, Ellen told Mama he was making her look like a fool. Then when Eunice arrived at the rehearsal ceremony, Ellen derided her sister for wanting to sing at the event. "Eunice, will you give up?" asked Ellen. "You had no talent as a child and as an adult you have even less!" Eunice shot back with confirmation that Bruce was having an affair with his secretary, to Ellen's horror.

On the wedding day on Part Two, Mama warned Eunice to be nice to Ellen. Ellen came in grinning because she got a new car from Bruce and a promise to end his affair. Eunice reserved her anger for Mama giving away her father's ring to Naomi. The slightly inebriated Eunice got to sing offkey and confronted Mama about how she favored Ellen as a child. "I was a straight A student! I earned every one of those bikes!" Ellen retorted. Ed finally took a drunk Eunice home.

Ellen seemed harder for the writers to fit into *Mama's Family* thereafter, staying as comic support and getting only a few lines. The exception during the first season was when Vint told Ellen, Mama, Naomi, and Buzz that they had tickets to fly to Hollywood and play *Family Feud*. Vint told an unimpressed Ellen she and him were the smart ones to answer questions. "You know what you get when you put your brain and my brain together? My brain," she snorted to Vint. When playing the game and meeting the other family, Ellen described that clan as "So know-it-all, so superior. I wish I was on their side!"

In the second season of *Mama's Family*, Ellen went from intimidating to insubstantial. When named "Woman of the Year" at Raytown's Country Club, Ellen convinced Mama to give her Grandma's brooch. However, Ellen was upset when Mama, Vint, and Naomi showed up as a surprise by request of Mayor Tutweiler, portrayed by Alan Oppenheimer. Her family members' uncouth manners appalled Ellen. "I'm going to the ladies room," she said. "Can I go with you?" Mama asked. "No, I'm just going to slam the lid on my head!" Ellen responded.

Ellen tried unsuccessfully to break up Mama from dancing with the mayor and complaining about garbage pickup. The mayor then asked Mama to say a few words about her daughter. "I will say, for snooty people, some of you ain't bad!" she prefaced to their amusement and Ellen's horror. For the first time, Ellen ended an episode without having the upper hand.

The old Ellen was back in "Rashomama," a very amusing episode where Naomi, Ellen, and Eunice presented their own perspectives on how Mama got hospitalized while they helped her make jam on a hot day. In Naomi's version, Eunice complained how Ellen passed her twice while she was parked on the side of a highway with a disabled car. "I didn't even see you!" exclaimed Ellen. "And take my word, I would know that dress anywhere!" She and Eunice accidentally hit Mama fighting over a stewpot. Ellen told a story where she was the savior homemaker who hugged Eunice and got complimented by Mama. She claimed Naomi and Eunice fought over the stewpot to hit Mama. Eunice denied that allegation and told a tale where Ellen acted like a mean queen who tried to kill her and ruin Mama's jars.

The last great appearance for Betty's character on *Mama's Family* was "Ellen's Boyfriend," but now even Mama threatened her. After divorcing Bruce, Ellen went to a lonely hearts club and met Glen, played by Gary Hudson, a hunk twenty years her junior. She loved him but was worried about Mama's reaction. Indeed, when Ellen later confronted Mama and told her Glen was a successful businessman who could have any woman he wanted, Mama asked snidely, "Then what the hell is he doing with you?" "Anything he wants, Mama! Anything he wants!" shot back Ellen. Mama revealed she was jealous of her daughter. The storyline was intriguing and Betty played the romance well, but unfortunately there was no follow through with Glen.

Ellen showed some of her old spunk in "Mama Learns to Drive" by belittling Naomi when the latter encouraged Mama to keep practicing how to handle a car. When Naomi advised, "You know what they say. If you fall off a horse, you're supposed to just climb right back on it again!" and hugged Vint, Ellen stared unimpressed. She then said, "Spoken like a woman with saddle sores." Ellen also told Naomi not to belittle Mama "Just because tricks don't come as easily to her as they do to you."

Otherwise, Ellen was mostly wasted in shows like a two-part episode where Ellen convinced Mama to host a press conference for the reelection of Mayor Tutweiler, who Ellen now dated. During the event, Mama made cutting remarks about the mayor's failures for senior citizens and then put him on the defensive about his lack of accomplishments. Upset, Tutweiler dared her to run for mayor and she accepted.

Outside Thelma's house, a reporter and others gathered to hear Mama speak. Ellen arrived and tried to break things up, claiming Mama was not really running for mayor. "You're only confusing her. Can't you see she is old and feeble?" Ellen told the reporter. Enraged and energized, Mama affirmed her candidacy. She escalated her campaign with the help of everyone in her family except Ellen, who organized a debate with Tutwiller to discredit Mama.

In the second part, Thelma won the mayoral race, but the responsibilities of the job so overwhelmed her that citizens threatened her with impeachment. Hearing the news on morning radio, Ellen convinced Tutwiller in their bed to intervene, which he did.

Seeing Ellen plead for her mother across two episodes was quite a character switch and neutered her appeal. But at that point, such alterations didn't matter. *Mama's Family* had finished sixty-sixth in its second and final season on NBC. The last network episode aired April 7, 1984.

Two years later, *Mama's Family* reappeared with new episodes in syndication. Joining Lawrence, Berry, and Lyman as regulars were Beverly Archer as Mama's neighbor Iola and Allan Kayser as Eunice's son Bubba Higgins. Betty made one early guest shot where Ellen brought Mama a present to apologize for not attending Aunt Fran's funeral. Mama was unmoved. The next day, Mama learned Ellen was having surgery at the hospital. She, Vint, Naomi, and Bubba irritated Ellen in her hospital room so much that Ellen had the nurse throw them out. But Mama returned and admitted Fran's death and the arrival of Bubba had made her tense. The women bonded until Mama learned Ellen was having a fanny tuck. Still, Mama confessed Ellen was her favorite child.

That so-so show marked the last time Betty was Ellen. She had no more time for *Mama's Family* because she was working on a new series that would offer a better showcase for her. That series would do the same for Rue McClanahan, which is why Aunt Fran had been written out of *Mama's Family*.

Betty had become a Golden Girl. Her career—and even television—would never be quite the same.

Chapter Nine
Betty The Rose in Bloom

Rose Nylund (Betty White) and Dorothy Zbornak (Bea Arthur) looked at Dorothy's mother Sophia (Estelle Getty) telling a story that begins, "Ficture it: Sicily, 1922," with Blanche Deveraux (Rue McClanahan) standing over Sophia's shoulder in a 1980s episode of *The Golden Girls*. All that was missing was the traditional cheesecake on the table. Photo Copyright Touchstone Television / Courtesy of Everett Collection.

As the COVID-19 pandemic affected the world in 2020, the BBC Culture website fought the gloomy atmosphere in an interesting way. "In these uncertain times, we need to take solace in the arts more than ever," the website announced April 1, 2020, as it launched essays from its writers about what pieces of culture brought them joy.

From a wealth of deserving candidates, the first pick was Betty's series *The Golden Girls*.

"*The Golden Girls* was fiercely funny, unashamedly soppy, brazenly glamorous [with an abundance of '80s shoulder pads and hairspray], and bravely outspoken—and there has never been a better time to treasure its legacy," noted writer Arwa Haider for an article titled "*The Golden Girls*: The most treasured TV show ever."

The truth was that its legacy had been cherished ever since it ended its seven-year run in 1992. What Haider called "arguably one of the greatest TV shows of all time" had created its own industry, with the following tie-ins spun off from the series and its characters:

- An off-Broadway puppet production
- An off-off-Broadway musical
- Hot sauces
- Breakfast cereal
- A set of underwear
- Eight-inch action figures
- Tiki cocktail cups
- A windshield sun shade
- A coloring book
- Shirts of all types, shapes, and sizes
- Protective masks as the COVID-19 pandemic spread

There was also a *Golden Girls*-themed Rue La Rue Cafe that opened in New York City in February 2017 with a wall devoted to Betty White, who toured and approved of the spot. Unfortunately, mismanagement caused the cafe to go out of business before the end of the year.

The Golden Girls has become so omnipresent in twenty-first century pop culture through clips, images, memes, and associated paraphernalia that some people may not recall a time without the series. For those persons, and even those who do remember, let's go back to its genesis.

Mining the Gold

An unexpected highlight came from two middle-aged actresses on August 24, 1984, during the taping of the annual fall preview special to highlight new series coming on the NBC schedule. Selma Diamond from *Night Court* and Doris Roberts from *Remington Steele* discussed their excitement about an upcoming show called "Miami Nice." Actor Don Johnson corrected the ladies and said his program was called *Miami Vice* while the women ogled the star.

Noting the enthusiastic reception for the spot, NBC Entertainment president Brandon Tartikoff and NBC Vice President for Series Warren Littlefield thought the concept had potential for a series. That notion was on their mind when they met with Paul Junger Witt and Tony Thomas. The two executive producers were behind the hit ABC sitcoms *Soap* (1977–1981), and its spin-off, *Benson* (1979–1986).

When Witt and Thomas unsuccessfully pitched an idea to Tartikoff and Littlefield, the executives gave a counteroffer. Come up with a sitcom about women around sixty who are having a lively social life, and get a guaranteed commitment of thirteen episodes.

They presented the concept to Susan Harris, who was Witt's wife. She had loathed ABC officials' creative interference with her sitcom *Hail to the Chief*, which ran seven episodes in early 1985, and refused to renew her exclusive contract with the network. A disgusted Harris vowed to write for movies thereafter, but the new offer changed her mind.

"I had to write *Golden Girls*," she told reporter Aljean Harmetz in 1986. "I've never gotten excited about a network idea before, but this was compelling. I could write grown-ups."

Harris created four primary characters in her script. Dorothy Zbornak was an opinionated divorced substitute teacher from Brooklyn, New York. Rose Nylund was a well-meaning but often dense widow from fictional St. Olaf, Minnesota, who worked as a grief counselor. Fellow widow Blanche Devereaux was a very Southern belle from Georgia with a high sex drive who rented out her house in Miami, Florida, to Dorothy and Rose. Sophia Petrillo, a Sicilian immigrant who was Dorothy's mother, moved in with the trio when her rest home, named Shady Pines, burned down.

In the script, Blanche had an engagement that went awry, and her roommates consoled her in the aftermath. Harris called the show *The Golden Girls*.

Tartikoff and Littlefield loved the script, as did Witt and Thomas. Excited by the planned series, the executive producers took the unusual step of sending out a teaser letter announcing their upcoming project to actresses under consideration for the parts. They mentioned Harris would join them as executive producer and Jay Sandrich would take time away from NBC's big hit, *The Cosby Show*, to direct the pilot. One letter recipient was Betty White.

Given her success as vixen Sue Ann Nivens on *The Mary Tyler Moore Show*, Witt, Thomas, and Harris considered Betty a natural for Blanche. Likewise, they thought Rue McClanahan was ideal for Rose given her nice, decent characters of Vivian Harmon on *Maude* and even Aunt Fran on *Mama's Family*.

But when McClanahan read as Rose for Sandrich, he didn't buy her as being an innocent from the Midwest. He told her to try Blanche, which McClanahan secretly desired to play. Impressed, Sandrich encouraged the executive producers to switch the roles between her and Betty.

Betty was taken aback. Sandrich told her he suggested the change because her playing Blanche struck him as simply a rehash of Sue Ann. To address her uncertainty about how to play Rose, he explained to Betty the character took the meaning of what people said too literally. Betty connected with the part from that talk and discovered she could draw from herself to play Rose.

"I was sure I was Sue Ann Nivens!" Betty joked of her change in characterization on *Sally Jesse Raphael* in 1988. "But there's an awful lot of Rose in Betty. I tell long, boring stories. I want everything to have a happy ending. I believe that everything is going to turn out swell.

"It's scary, there's so much Rose in me. But I like her because she's not dumb. She's just a little naive."

Betty appreciated the switch for another reason. "It's really worked out because Rue is finding marvelous things to do with Blanche," she told Bettelou Peterson of the Knight-Ridder News Service. "If I'd played her, no matter what stops I pulled out, you'd have found echoes of Sue Ann."

Rue and Betty weren't the first ones to secure their parts. Estelle Getty, primarily a stage actress, bowled over everyone who saw her spit out lines as the spirited, sharp-tongued Sophia. After auditioning several times in February 1985, she was Sophia.

The only role not cast was Dorothy. The toughest character proved the toughest to nail down.

The Dorothy Dilemma

In her script, Harris had called Dorothy "a Bea Arthur type" and wanted the actress in the pilot. But after *Maude*, Arthur had bad experiences starring in the 1983 sitcom *Amanda's* and doing a 1984 sitcom pilot with Charles Durning called *P.O.P.* Arthur passed on participating.

Looking for a replacement, NBC Senior Vice President of Talent and Casting Joel Thurm suggested Broadway veteran Elaine Stritch. Like Arthur, she specialized in playing comic types with a slightly abrasive delivery. But Stritch had not done American television regularly since starring in the 1960–1961 sitcom *My Sister Eileen* on CBS. She had worked on television more in the United Kingdom, including, ironically, a British version of *Maude* in 1980.

Thurm secured a reading for Stritch for the role. The meeting turned out to be a showdown between the prospective star and the author.

In her 2001 one-woman stage show, *Elaine Stritch at Liberty*, the titular star offered a caustic take on her audition before network executives and Susan Harris. "Oh yes, the writer. With the heavily sprayed Doris Day hairdo and an attitude. She didn't like me on sight, and I knew it."

Knowing that "It was a damn good script," Stritch offered to add an expletive to her lines to amuse Harris during the first reading. "She didn't think it was funny at all. Oh well. The hell with it. Who cares? And who knew, you know?"

"Well, I mean, how could I know? What I mean is, how could I know then? And even if I did know then, who cared? Yeah, who really gave a shit about playing some old broad who settles in Miami with two other old broads and her mother?"

Stritch concluded in her show, "I blew a thirty-five, forty, fifty—if they wanted me badly enough—thousand-dollar per episode for the first thirteen and after that who knew job. I blew it! I blew a multimillion, zillion dollar, international, syndicated, residual grabbing, boff-a-rooney, smash-a-rooney, television situation comedy titled *The Golden Girls!*"

Recovering from the debacle, Stritch later earned three Emmys as she did more TV in the 1990s through 2010s, including one for a televised version of *Elaine Stritch at Liberty* in 2004. But that rejection left *The Golden Girls* still without a Dorothy.

Hearing about Arthur's reticence, McClanahan called up her former *Maude* colleague and asked why she was holding out from the project. Arthur said she had no interest in playing "Maude and Vivian meet Sue Ann Nivens." McClanahan told her plans had changed and now Betty was Rose and she was the slut. That concept did intrigue Arthur, who signed for the pilot.

Betty, Arthur, McClanahan, and Getty taped the first *Golden Girls* on April 17, 1985. The show was an easy sell to NBC executives, who then went into overdrive publicizing the series in the summer of 1985 with a barrage of commercials. Some participants thought the promotions were overkill, including its creator.

"It's a little nerve-wracking at first because you're afraid you're not going to live up to expectations," Susan Harris told Michael Dougan in *The San Francisco Examiner*.

Such fears vanished once *The Golden Girls* finally made it to air.

Going Gaga Over the Girls

The Golden Girls debuted on September 14, 1985, on NBC Saturdays 9-9:30 p.m. While that time slot had been successful for *The Mary Tyler Moore Show* on CBS in the 1970s, the same fortune didn't befall any series airing there since *NBC Saturday Night at the Movies* ended in 1978. Seven years of bombs followed until *The Golden Girls* immediately became a top ten hit.

"The early success of *The Golden Girls* has been phenomenal," Betty told Scott Blakey in *The San Francisco Examiner*. "And it has taken me longer these days to get from any point A to point B. People stop and talk about Rose or one of the other characters on the show, or just talk. The age of the people who have responded is very wide. I think almost everyone can identify with at least one of those four women."

She added, "No one can say the network hasn't given *Golden Girls* the proper buildup and promotion. In fact, in the beginning we were worried the program might be oversold … In all the hundred years I've been in this business, I'd never seen that kind of hype."

One quick sign of its popularity Betty noticed in her own neighborhood. The bag boys at Betty's supermarket in Brentwood formed a fan club for her a month after *The Golden Girls* debuted.

Trying to explain the series' appeal, Betty told a reporter with United Press International, "Well, older people don't fall off the edge of the planet after they hit fifty-five. But you wouldn't know if you watch a lot of television, especially comedy. We're not ready to be swept under the rug.

"Middle and old age are wonderful areas to explore, and I don't mean wheelchairs bumping into each other either. Funny is funnier with a perspective based on an older frame of experiences. We've all been there and back.

"And we're bawdy because we can get away with it. There are no smirks or attempts to be licentious, which might be the case if some of the scenes were played by girls in their twenties."

Betty felt no apologies for playing storylines seen as racy for 1985 network TV, such as Rose being afraid of having sex with her boyfriend in "Rose the Prude" on September 28, 1985. "Let's face it, if we did the ladies right down the middle, they'd be nice ladies but dull," Betty told Bettelou Peterson of the Knight-Ridder News Service. "We have to draw on a larger canvas with a wider brush. Hopefully, if you don't like one thing, you'll like another.

"We're under the spotlight because we're coming at it from another frame of reference. But we can get away with a lot youngsters can't." She noted *The Golden Girls* got more fan mail from teenagers and children than people might have expected for a series on middle-aged actresses.

The series' popularity stunned its creator. "The fact that people love the show as much as they do surprises me," Susan Harris told Michael Dougan in *The San Francisco Examiner*. "I'd never had that happen before. Even *Soap* [which Harris created and wrote every episode from 1977–1981 on ABC] during its best innings never got the numbers that *The Golden Girls* gets."

Her interviewer seemed more assured of the series' place in TV history. A month after its premiere, Dougan wrote, "*The Golden Girls* is certainly in the same class as *I Love Lucy*, *The Mary Tyler Moore Show* and *M*A*S*H*."

For their part, NBC executives were so happy with the success of *The Golden Girls*, they made an unusual request to produce one extra episode than the standard twenty-four in the first season. The producers readily fulfilled that offer

The commercial and critical acclaim was reassuring for the cast and crew. They had survived a difficult period of discord as they started working on their first episodes in July. In fact, some of the personnel worried *The Golden Girls* was going to become a leaden loser.

Getting Bad Direction

After Jay Sandrich directed the pilot, he declined performing the duties for the series, as he was committed to direct *The Cosby Show*. So the executive producers looked for another director.

"And they brought in Paul Bogart, who had worked with Bea and Rue on *Maude*," said Lex Passaris, an editorial assistant with Witt-Thomas Productions since 1982 who would later direct *The Golden Girls*. "They didn't really know him, but they thought he'd be a good choice."

Bogart cut his directorial TV teeth on New York productions in the 1960s, winning Emmys for his work on *The Defenders* and the *CBS Playhouse* series of specials. In the 1970s he turned to comedy and directed *Maude* and *All in the Family*. Bogart earned one Emmy win and two Emmy nominations for his work on *All in the Family*.

But on *The Golden Girls*, Bogart clashed often with Witt, Thomas, and Harris. Besides being a director, Bogart negotiated to get the title of supervising producer on the series.

"There was a lot of tension there," said Passaris. "And Paul had recently gotten through a divorce, so he would extend the days as long as he possibly could, just so he wouldn't have to go back to an empty place, which is not a good idea ... And he was very tough on Betty."

Passaris said the director ultimately lowered morale for the cast and crew. "Frankly, during the Bogart episodes, everybody was in a little panic. When we had done the pilot, you could feel the energy all around the set. People knew that they had a hit. Then all of a sudden, it was rocky."

Witt and Thomas so disliked Bogart that they delayed the first episode he directed, "Job Hunting," from airing after the pilot as originally planned. Instead, the show ran on March 8, 1986, by which time he had departed. His work on "Guess on Who's Coming to the Wedding?" did air as the second episode. Bogart's other two shows were "Transplant," airing October 5, 1985, and "Break In" on November 9, 1985, before his dismissal after just four episodes.

Ironically, when *The Golden Girls* won the Emmy for Outstanding Comedy Series, Bogart claimed a statuette because his early credit as supervising producer was on the nomination. Even so, Bogart never directed another sitcom before retiring in 1995.

"Then Jim Drake came in," said Passaris. "He was one of the unsung heroes in a lot of ways. Jimmy brought the show back on its feet. Unfortunately, he and Bea, their styles clashed a little bit." Drake left after eight episodes, even though he got an Emmy nomination for Outstanding Direction in a Comedy Series for "The Heart Attack," which aired on November 23, 1985.

The third time was the charm when an unlikely candidate appeared as director. Terry Hughes spent nearly seventeen years with the British Broadcasting Company, starting as a director trainee and culminating with being head of entertainment. Then Hughes spent a year as a freelance director of commercials in the United Kingdom before moving to the United States to lead comedy development for the EMI studio.

Hughes developed and produced *Report to Murphy*, a CBS sitcom that ran two months in the spring of 1982. He moved more into directing thereafter but had done no sitcoms when he was asked to do some assignments for *The Golden Girls*.

"I saw *The Golden Girls* and I loved it," Hughes told Jerry Buck of the Associated Press in 1987. "It had that English edge to it and I responded to that. I directed two of the shows in the middle of the first season. Then they asked me to direct the rest of the season ... I'm in the middle of the third season and will do all of the fourth season. It doesn't come much better than that."

Passaris said Hughes was a hit with the cast from the start. "They had lunch and all sat down, and it was like finding Cary Grant. All four of them were absolutely in love with him from that day on. ... Terry understood the players involved, the rhythm of the show. He just got the whole thing. And his demeanor and his presence was very calming. He'd console, but not in a bad way."

In her 1987 Emmy acceptance speech, Rue McClanahan said, "And there's our secret weapon, the fifth Golden Girl, Terry Hughes. He makes us happy to come to work every day, every week, every year." Passaris agreed with that assessment, as did Betty. So did members of the Academy of Television Arts and Sciences, who awarded Hughes an Emmy for Outstanding Directing of a Comedy Series in 1987 along with nominations for the series in 1986, 1988, 1989, and 1990.

In 1990 Hughes left the series when offered to direct his first theatrical film, *The Butcher's Wife*. The result was such a critical and commercial failure that Hughes went back to directing TV comedies solely for the next three decades. In the meantime, Passaris had moved up from associate director to becoming the main director for the last two seasons of *The Golden Girls*.

A Rose-y Time for Betty

As Betty worked on *The Golden Girls* in its first season, she discovered more than just a pleasant working set with Hughes as her director. She grew to love Rose as the character displayed more facets during the season.

"Sue Ann was such a bag of wind, all talk and no fight," Betty told Bettelou Peterson of the Knight-Ridder News Service. "She was the most fun I'd ever had. Until Rose. I enjoy Rose more. With Sue Ann, you barged in, bump, bump, did your joke and left. You never really had a chance to build a character with a second or third dimension. Every once in a while, Rose gets her back up, and you see another side of her entirely."

Betty also recognized how Rose challenged her as an actress. "It was a long time since I was able to play honest," she told Scott Blakey in *The San Francisco Examiner*. "Rose is a more difficult part partly because of my own widowhood, I think. Also, here is a character without guile, not too swift on the uptake, innocent, grieving for a husband fifteen years dead, yet a funny woman without a vicious bone in her body. There are few theatrical tricks to fall back on."

Her toughest times involved dialogue where Rose missed her late husband Charlie, which reminded Betty of losing Allen Ludden. "A couple of speeches Rose makes get me by the throat," Betty told Aljean Harmetz. "All I have to do is substitute 'Allen' for 'Charlie,' Rose's husband."

However, for the most part, Betty delivered comic lines for Rose with her customary pluck. Her running gag was to dredge up weird events from her childhood. Any story where Rose began "Back in St. Olaf …" soon made Blanche, Dorothy, and Sophia roll their eyes while they solved their problems eating cheesecake in the kitchen. Those stories often incorporated native names and phrases devised by the writers for Rose to say with ease.

"They throw these Scandinavian names this long … and they mean nothing, but you have to memorize them exactly," said Betty on the 1989 Disney Channel special *A Conversation with Betty White*. "And it's a challenge. A couple of times, we've gotten so broken up, we've had to do it about four times before I can spit the words out." She added that although St. Olaf was a fictional municipality, she received memorabilia, such as jackets from St. Olaf College in Minnesota, and that institution's seventy-person choir came in mass to see a *Golden Girls* taping.

During its first season, *The Golden Girls* won the Emmy for Outstanding Comedy

Series while Betty also nabbed a statuette for Outstanding Lead Actress in a Comedy Series. In accepting her award, Betty said, "I am the lucky one who gets to come up and pick up this beautiful golden girl. But Estelle and Rue and Bea and I all thank you. We're a matched set, you can't split us up.

"We want to thank the network for taking a chance on four old broads, er, ladies [laughter], and I want to thank, of course, Paul Witt and that wonderful Susan Harris and Tony Thomas. And I'm not going to go down the list of names because if I miss anybody, it will break my heart. It's just the happiest experience, and the most wonderful people it's ever been my privilege to be with. Thank you."

Betty would get an Emmy nomination for Outstanding Lead Actress in a Comedy Series every year thereafter throughout the run of *The Golden Girls*. Her consecutive seven-year streak of Emmy nominations in that category matched the record Mary Tyler Moore compiled on *The Mary Tyler Moore Show*. Betty also earned four consecutive Golden Globe nominations for Best Performance by an Actress in a Television Series—Comedy or Musical from 1986–1989.

With *The Golden Girls*, Betty had found a regular home for her talents for the first time since *The Mary Tyler Moore Show*. Like that series, Betty always credited the writers for making Rose such a joy to watch. Though Susan Harris wrote the pilot, others were in charge of supervising the scripts. Here is how the writers and others put together episodes of *The Golden Girls*.

Applying the Gilt to the Girls
In advance of the first few seasons of *The Golden Girls*, married head writers Kathy Speer and Terry Grossman, supervising producers Barry Fanaro and Mort Nathan, and producer Winifred Hervey discussed at least twenty potential ideas for scripts The quintet typically took weeks to flesh out concepts and include an "A" and "B" story. The "A" story was the main focus for the show, while the "B" story was the subplot.

"We all draw on other people in our lives—parents, grandparents," Grossman said of the writing process to Nancy Mills of *The Los Angeles Times* in 1987. "Part of the reason for the show's popularity is that these are very vital people. The very same story you've seen 100 times on every sitcom takes on new light with characters in this age group. That makes life easier for us.

"Also, these four actresses are sensational. To have the entire cast be able to give you such high-caliber performances means you don't have to adjust your material.

You write the material, and they deliver. If they can't make it work, there's something wrong with the material."

Four sets of writing partners and two individual writers were on staff, as well. Occasionally, the producers took work from freelancers.

On Mondays, Betty and the other actors saw the script for the first time. The cast and guests sat on one side of eight tables arranged in a rectangle opposite the writers. After the first table read, the writers, producers, director, and an NBC programming executive discussed any script revisions needed.

From there, Speer, Grossman, Fanaro, Nathan, and Hervey went on changing lines. In the first two seasons, entire scenes were thrown out, and up to an estimated seventy-five percent of the first draft of a script was lost. By the 1987–1988 season, the producers and writers had a better idea of what worked for the ladies, so fewer changes were the rule.

On Tuesdays the cast read a revised script, followed by rehearsals and new lines on Wednesdays. Dress rehearsals occurred Thursday afternoons, by which time Betty and the other actors tried to have their lines memorized.

Fridays were taping days. "The way tape night was structured, much like others, we did two full audience shows," said director Lex Passaris. "So the first one, we called dress, it was straight through unless you had some real delays, and generally you could do that within an hour."

Following dress was a ninety-minute dinner break, where the cast received notes on new lines being added as needed for the second taping. Passaris said rewrites at this point usually were minimal. "And then generally the rule was that we did [each scene] twice. Very rarely would we do a whole third take."

The biggest problem Passaris said he had as director was with Estelle Getty missing her lines or marks during the tapings. "We would move on and then later on in the night, after the audience had left, we would pick up and do her parts. And if you go through and look it at, there's a lot of scenes like that."

Passaris added, "Except for Estelle, those four ladies only worked well in front of an audience. Bea would hold it back, which there's nothing wrong with that. It's one of my complaints with the modern system at work, that producers and networks want to see it on Tuesday."

The show shut down production every four weeks to give the cast and crew a break. Passaris said the overall atmosphere on the set of *The Golden Girls* was fun yet professional.

"Everybody came to work. Everybody knew their job," he said. "The younger among us got an education that no one could get anywhere else. Everybody was relatively pleasant to one another."

Like most others who worked with Betty, Passaris said she was a joy to direct. "Betty was the kind of a person who had an unbelievable technical skill about her in addition to everything else. We would get asked to do promos all the time to do at the end of an episode, PSAs for animal rights or whatever. Betty, there was a little bit of vanity on Betty's part. She needed glasses to see better. So her rule was 'Remember the copy ahead of time.' ... She'd do it dead on, one take, perfect length. That technical skill came from doing six days live when she started."

Even so, one person didn't have the same affection for Betty. That person was the one playing opposite her in every show.

Bea Versus Betty

Though all the actresses put on a happy face in public about working together, Betty and others on the set later acknowledged Bea Arthur was not a fan of Betty. Arthur didn't hate her colleague, but they had distinctly diverging approaches of working.

In the 1989 Disney Channel special *A Conversation With Betty White*, Betty denied any rumors she and her castmates didn't get along. "We're a joyful bunch," she said. But Betty obliquely mentioned their differences on *Sally Jesse Raphael* a year earlier. "I dance around and make jokes and fancy dance, and Bea puts up with it just so long and then finally says, 'Please!' ... She gets the most stage fright ... She really is uptight about what she does so beautifully."

"The way I kind of figured it was, Betty is a morning person," said Passaris. "Not a single day went by that you didn't show up on the set and Betty was, 'Glad you're here. How are you?' And so on. Bea walked in and wanted to get to work. And that was it."

Any problems Bea had with Betty were well hidden at the time and probably overblown in retrospect. The actresses consoled each other when they each lost their mothers a few months after *The Golden Girls* went into production, and they never criticized each other publicly.

"Better Late Than ... ?"

One person who loved working with both Arthur and Betty was Jim MacKrell. He guest starred in "Grab That Dough," which aired January 23, 1988, as game show host Guy Corbin. Ironically, MacKrell had his biggest TV success as host of *Celebrity Sweepstakes*, a game show where Betty had been a guest in the 1970s.

"I had worked with Marsha Posner, the producer for the show," said MacKrell in remembering his involvement on the series. "I had worked for that whole company, Witt-Thomas, quite a bit, and I think I did most of their shows .... She called me up and asked me to do *The Golden Girls*, and I was so delighted. I was just thrilled to death.

"So, I went down and of course was reunited with Betty, who was just gracious and wonderful. I met the other ladies, and it was a spectacular, wonderful week. It was the best."

"Grab That Dough" was the title for the fictional game show as well as the episode. The ladies got on each other's nerves during the game show to the point where Rose and Sophia competed against Dorothy and Blanche. MacKrell had a memorably unfazed, slightly smarmy delivery of a line after Blanche and Rose argued.

"Oh, shut up, Nylund!" Blanche said.

"You shut up!" Rose responded.

"Why don't you both shut up and answer this next question?" said Guy. Then he asked, "Finish this phrase: 'Better late than ... ?'"

"Pregnant!" Blanche answered. The audience broke up into hysteria.

MacKrell said the part he had the hardest time keeping a straight face involved Dorothy getting ready to "grab that dough" in the Magic Money Machine isolation booth.

"When we played 'Grab That Dough' and Bea Arthur was in the thing, as we led into it, I would say, 'Okay ladies, which one of you is going to grab that dough?' And Bea Arthur said, in that typical way, 'I'll grab, Guy.' And I'd go up. Every time she said that, I would fall on the floor. And it got to where they were kind the first two times, but every time she said it, man, I was gone! I just couldn't handle it.

"I realized it's not funny anymore, it's getting to be ridiculous. So, I bit the inside of my lip. Bit it through, making sure that I didn't laugh."

MacKrell also had a fond memory offstage during the episode. "The thing most endearing to our family is that we have a special needs son who's fifty and has hydrocephalus, and he's in love with Betty. And Betty, when I did 'Grab That Dough' with all the Golden Girls, he came down to the set and stayed with us. And all of them, especially Betty, treated him wonderfully. I mean, they just went out of their way to be nice to Jimmy. And it just thrilled me very, very much."

"Grab That Dough" was so ingrained as a top episode of *The Golden Girls* that Legos included a version of MacKrell as part of a line devoted to the series. When MacKrell heard about the set, he got a copy for himself.

"I have a spectacular young daughter. She's our baby. And she's grown. ... And she found on the internet that Lego and tracked down the artist and said, 'Hi, I'm Catie MacKrell, I'm Jim MacKrell's daughter, and he played Guy on *The Golden Girls*, and we will pay you. I'd like to have a copy of that.' He said, 'Oh, no, it would be my pleasure!' So he made a miniature copy of that. So I've got it in the office and thought, 'Man, you really made it when you became a Lego!'"

The Golden Girls got other celebrities to guest star, including Mickey Rooney, Burt Reynolds, Bob Hope, Dick Van Dyke, and Debbie Reynolds. But the producers couldn't convince at least one star to join Betty and the ladies.

"You know, I never miss your show, and I'm not just saying it because you happen to be on this network," Johnny Carson told Betty on *The Tonight Show* on February 3, 1988. "That is one of the best crafted shows and ensembles I've ever seen working."

After the audience applauded, Betty said, "We would give our souls and our sordid old bodies to get you on that show."

"You know, I thought about it once," Carson said. "I actually talked to somebody from your show. And then I got scared. And I said, 'I better stay and do something I know for sure rather than go over there.'"

Betty told Carson they could block and tape his segment without an audience. "They have a funny idea for you. And if there's any way—I'll take my clothes off again!" she joked. But Carson never did *The Golden Girls*.

She did tell Carson, "Can you imagine backing into a hit at this late date in your career? I still can't get it through my head and it's just, it's so wonderful."

Letting Rose Sprout Up Everywhere
With the popularity of *The Golden Girls*, NBC tried to exploit the characters in other venues. In 1988, the series spun off *Empty Nest*, with Richard Mulligan playing Dr. Harry Weston, a neighbor of Rose, Dorothy, Blanche, and Sophia. Also seen were

Kristy McNichol and Dinah Manoff as his daughters Barbara and Carol Weston; Park Overall as nurse Laverne Todd; and David Leisure as their neighbor, Charley Dietz. A few crossover episodes happened on both series, and Rose turned up three times on *Empty Nest*.

In "Strange Bedfellows," Rose returned pamphlets on every windshield in the neighborhood to Harry. "It took me most of the morning, but I think I got them all," she said. "I saw your address on the bottom, and I figured you wanted them back." He told her the leaflets were supposed to be on the windshields, which confused Rose. "How are you supposed to read them going back and forth like that?" she asked while miming windshield wipers in motion. "Although maybe on the slower speed, they might be easier. But no, that would still distract you from your driving. Maybe intermittent speed ..." Betty got applause for her delivery as she left.

Rose and Harry had a fender bender on "Rambo of Neiman Marcus" in 1989. Luckily, both were insured, with Rose using the "chapped hands" people from a small company in St. Olaf. She read its instructions. "Rule number one: Check to see if any livestock are damaged."

Harry told her not to get the insurers involved, but Rose insisted she would get his car fixed and pay for the repairs. She later visited his office and told Laverne that she almost became a nurse too but "My hat kept falling off."

Rose told Harry the car shop wanted $1,800 to repair a small dent on his vehicle. "I think they may be taking advantage of you," he told Rose. "Oh, no. When they heard a doctor was paying for the repairs, they couldn't have been more helpful!" she said.

Harry proposed that Rose take the vehicle to his repairman but also wanted to know what Rose had pasted on her car's windshield. "Oh, those are stickers of dead bugs! ... As a warning. So other bugs will see them and not smash into the window!" she said.

"I've seen this before. I'm guessing inbreeding," quipped Laverne.

At the end, Rose drove her fixed car to Harry's house, but she had another accident while missing Harry's neighbor Charley.

In "Dr. Weston and Mr. Hyde" in 1992, Rose had a hysterical exchange with Harry. "I'd like to ask your opinion about something, as a man of science. I mean, I'm not a man of science. I'm the one asking, you're the man of science!" she said. "Do you believe in full moons?"

"Absolutely not," retorted Harry.

"Well then, what's that big, round, shiny thing?" she said, pointing to the sky.

"Well, Rose, I know that full moons exist," Harry backtracked.

"Well, sure you do know now!" she shot back.

She followed up by asking, "Suppose you found out someone had kissed your boyfriend. Would you believe it was the full moon's fault?"

"Who knows?" shrugged Harry.

"Thank you, Harry! That clears things up!" She asked to use his phone, he said yes and she took the device and said, "I'll bring it back tomorrow."

In 1991, *Empty Nest* had its own spin-off, *Nurses*. Rose turned up there, too. "Begone with the Wind" featured Rose as a candy striper helping nurse Julie Milbury, played by Mary Jo Keenen, on her rounds. Milbury told Rose they should play "good cop bad cop" for a patient who refused to share his gift basket with others during a hurricane. So, Rose entered the room of Mr. Crandall, played by Patrick Cronin, pretended her fingers were a pistol, and yelled, "Freeze, scum!" Milbury tried to correct her, but the second time, Rose blurted, "Listen, pus bag!"

Rose even showed up on *Time Warner Presents the Earth Day Special* which ran on NBC April 22, 1990, on the twentieth anniversary of the environmental observation event. One segment cut to the Golden Girls watching the show and Dorothy noting how the fictional Burgers by Leroy packs its food in nonbiodegradable polystyrene foam, whose chemicals can be toxic.

"Well, it'd be nice if they'd stop making polystyrene foam altogether. But until they come up with something better or safer, people shouldn't throw it away. It can be reused, too," Rose said. She added, "Burger places should have recycle bins, because polystyrene foam can be used for lots of things. Park benches, cases for videotapes …" Having Rose pose as a fount of ecological knowledge indicated how poorly designed this special was.

A month later on *Night of 100 Stars III* on NBC, May 21, 1990, Betty and her *Golden Girls* co-stars, Bea Arthur, Estelle Getty, and Rue McClanahan, opened the special playing their characters missing their plane and instead arriving on the stage of Radio City Music Hall in a car. They got a rousing reception when they emerged in appropriately golden gowns.

Throughout all this, *The Golden Girls* stayed a top ten hit most of its run. The series was still in the top thirty when Bea Arthur announced she was leaving at the end of the

1991–1992 season. She had fulfilled her seven-year contract and was ready to pursue other projects. On the final episode of *The Golden Girls*, Dorothy married Blanche's cousin Lucas Collingsworth, played by Leslie Nielsen, after a quick courtship and moved with him to Atlanta.

Director Lex Passaris thought Arthur made the right decision. He noted the cast was the same four people with the same recurring ancillary characters, such as Stan Zbornak, played by Herb Edelman, Dorothy's bald, flailing ex-husband, and Miles, played by Harold Gould, Rose's boyfriend. To Passaris, after seven years, *The Golden Girls* was getting stale.

"The sets never changed," he said. "The location never changed. It was pretty solid. So, I would kind of agree with Bea. She really did everything she could with the character."

But executive producers Paul Junger Witt, Tony Thomas, and Susan Harris had an idea for a spin-off without Arthur. They had a receptive audience with their remaining cast.

"The ladies really didn't want to stop, especially for Rue and Estelle," said Passaris. "Rue had had some bad instances with business managers who had not treated her well."

Given those conditions, plans went into place for a pilot called *The Golden Palace*.

Tarnishing the Girls
The spin-off pilot script from Harris had Blanche, Rose, and Sophia sell their home to become owners of a forty-two-room hotel, The Golden Palace, on Miami Beach. To their dismay, the girls learned there is no housekeeping staff and Blanche's representative had lied about other terms in the hotel's contract. In addition, Roland, the hotel operator, played by Don Cheadle, who has a foster son named Oliver, played by Billy L. Sullivan, informed Blanche they had to make a payment within a week to stay solvent.

"Oh my God!" exclaimed Rose after learning that news. "This is it. This is my worst nightmare. Oh, I wish Dorothy were here!"

"Oh, honey, I'm afraid even she couldn't help us out of this," Blanche responded.

"No, but she could beat the crap out of you!" retorted Rose.

Rose had to serve as a waitress, a room cleaner, and a front desk operator. In the latter role, when a man in a ski mask attempted to rob the hotel, Rose thought he was a guest who wanted to store his gun in the vault. She told him she didn't know the vault's location, and he left frustrated.

Meanwhile, Sophia reached a truce with the hotel chef Chuy Castillos, played by Cheech Marin, and let him cook some Mexican food along with Italian. As visiting travel agents recommended the hotel, enough customers started making reservations to help the girls have enough money to cover their debts.

Passaris noted many problems occurred with this pilot, including a casting change at the outset. British comic actor Alexei Sayle was the original chef in the pilot and second episode of *The Golden Palace*, then Passaris was told to reshoot Sayle's scenes. "All I knew when I walked in to start episode two, they said, 'Oh, by the way, we're going to replace Alexei,'" said Passaris.

He offered to coach Sayle to get whatever improvements the producers wanted from him. "But they had given up. It was a very odd thing. And I was a fan of Alexei. I wanted to talk more with him and all that." Passaris dutifully redid the scenes with Cheech Marin in his place.

More problematic to Passaris was the series' setup. "The best reason I ever heard was the underlying premise [of *The Golden Girls*] was, at some point, you're going to be in your sixties. You'll lose some loved ones either through divorce or death or whatever. But you'll find a group that will help you have a roof over your heads, have friends, and have an exciting life."

In contrast, Passaris noted, "The message of *The Golden Palace* was that seven years later, you're going to find yourself falling for a bad investment. You're going to get into a situation where you're going to have to work your ass off to survive."

CBS executives overlooked that deficiency as they secured *The Golden Palace* on their schedule by guaranteeing a full season of episodes. The series ran Fridays from 8-8:30 p.m. starting September 18, 1992. What followed was a year that tarnished the legacy of what *The Golden Girls* had achieved and represented.

Malice Toward the Palace

While the chef situation was resolved quickly, another problem emerged to the creative team regarding the character of Oliver. None of the producers wanted to keep the kid, even though they liked the actor portraying him, Billy L. Sullivan.

"The backstory on that, it was episode three we shot, but it aired as episode fourteen," said Passaris. "We shot the episode. Tony [Thomas, one of the executive producers] looked at it and said, 'This is unairable. We've got to fix it.' And it went on the shelf for half a season." The show in question had Sophia and Oliver go on a joy ride with a guest's car.

Passaris thought adding Oliver was an edict from CBS executives to the producers to appeal to a younger demographic. "They stuffed him in, and even then, we were sitting on the sidelines going, 'Um, where is Health and Human Services? Did they forget the kid?' Nothing made sense."

The producers hated the situation and took action. "So, basically, Billy gets minimized. He was only signed for half the episodes anyway. And then halfway through the season, they came up with this idea of how to write him out, as the mother—who was Joely Fisher, before anyone knew who she was—she came in out of the blue. So we just had this little side scene with her." Oliver was never seen nor mentioned after he left on January 15, 1993.

More interference from CBS officials irked Passaris. "The network had this idea at the time of 'No one could sit.' That was their directive at the time. And we'd just done seven years of people who went into a room, they sat down, and they told funny stories, and everybody loved it.

"I looked at [the executives] and said, 'Now, wait a minute. They were in the sixties when we started and they're in their seventies now.' And Betty would never not do what they asked her to do. But it would wear her down." Passaris held firm, and the seating scenes remained.

For her part, Betty thought the absence of Bea Arthur as Dorothy threw the series' chemistry off, like taking a leg from a table. She also noticed big problems with the writing.

"With [*The Golden*] *Palace*, far too often we would start out with one script Monday, with major changes on Tuesday, and several times we received a whole new, unrelated script on Wednesday," Betty wrote in *Here We Go Again*.

These difficulties resulted in most episodes of *The Golden Palace* being passable at best. Even worse, when two recurring characters returned, the results were unsatisfying and even irritating.

In "Miles We Hardly Knew Ye," Rose made romantic insinuations to her old boyfriend Miles. "It's been a long time since we've 'played cards,'" she said, adding "If I don't get my deck shuffled soon …" But Miles admitted he was cheating on her, and she told him to leave. A later episode, "Rose and Fern," revealed Rose still called Miles at times despite breaking up with him. She gave up that activity when he married Fern, portrayed by Nanette Fabray.

And Dorothy's ex-husband returned in "One Angry Stan," where Blanche told Sophia the latter's ex-son-in-law had died after making love. "Oh, poor Stan. There's nothing worse than dying alone," Sophia sighed. Rose topped that with "At least we know he went quickly!" But the humor dissolved when Stan appeared to Sophia and explained he had to fake his death. The episode seemed further in error as Stan's funeral occurred without Dorothy attending.

Dorothy did return in "Seems Like Old Times," a two-part episode which easily represented the best shows of *The Golden Palace*. Amid much applause, Dorothy greeted the girls with a group hug and became a temporary and temperamental waitress, which was hilarious. Dorothy wanted Sophia to come back with her to Atlanta rather than work at the hotel, prompting a fight with Rose and Blanche. Sophia went to a rebuilt Shady Pines before deciding to go back to work at the Golden Palace. Dorothy reluctantly agreed.

"I really didn't think you could run this hotel," she told the others. "I thought you, Blanche, would lose interest and you, Rose, would marry Miles, and then Ma would come home.

"But I forgot what special people you are. I apologize for not having enough faith in you, and I just want you to know that I'm very, very proud of all of you."

Rose and Blanche gave Dorothy a lifetime pass to the Golden Palace. "This card entitles Dorothy Zbornak Collingsworth to stay in any room at the Golden Palace and eat cheesecake, tell dirty jokes, and have at least two friends who will listen to her cry, complain, and laugh for the rest of her life." The audience applauded. Then they went back to work, and after Dorothy surveyed the activity, she quietly departed in a touching farewell.

A few other episodes were above the usual mediocrity of *The Golden Palace*, such as "Say Goodbye, Rose." A hotel guest, Bill Douglas, played by Eddie Albert, resembled Rose's late husband Charlie. When Bill was leaving, she told him it reminded her of losing Charlie. Bill told her to pretend she was saying goodbye to Charlie. "Charlie, the thirty years that we spent together seemed like a day. When you died, part of me died, too. I love you, and I miss you," Rose said. Sophia took Rose to see George Burns, whose comedy routine cheered Rose up.

Otherwise, the meager enjoyment of *The Golden Palace* came from a few jokes reminiscent of the much better original series. In "Heartbreak Hotel" Taylor, played by Dick Van Patten, said upon meeting her, "Rose! What a beautiful name!" "You should see the flower!" she responded.

Also, when restaurant critic Gerald Davenport, played by Eric Christmas, died after eating at the Golden Palace in "You've Lost That Livin' Feeling," an unaware Blanche had a news crew visit. Asked what Davenport thought of his meal, Rose said, "Two bites and he was in heaven!"

The Golden Palace finished the season in sixty-sixth place and last aired August 6, 1993. But that occasion didn't mark the last time Betty would be associated with Rose on television. Popular demand wouldn't allow that to happen.

Still Thanked for Being a Friend

Betty played herself on *The John Larroquette Show* on March 12, 1996, in "Here We Go Again." In a spoof of *Sunset Boulevard*, bus station manager and writer John Hemingway, portrayed by John Larroquette, interviewed Betty in her hotel room, where she bragged she's been in twenty-eight *TV Guide* Closeup articles. "I'm tied with that freak Richard Chamberlain," she grumbled.

John learned Betty was working on *Golden Girls: The Musical*. "We can mount it here and ultimately do it on television. If that isn't worth a *TV Guide* Closeup, I don't know what is!" she said. Estelle Getty served as Betty's assistant and told John, "Get out while you still can!"

Reading the play, John realized the script was horrible. However, Betty promised him an interview in *People* magazine if he worked on the musical. John's girlfriend Catherine Merrick, played by Alison LaPlaca, agreed to help him and play Dorothy in the production. Meanwhile, Betty admitted to Estelle during a game of poker she planned to marry John.

Betty tried to get John to work at her hotel and showered him with gold objects. She also forced John to dress up as Dorothy because Catherine was locked in a broom closet backstage. Rue McClanahan joined Betty and Getty to reprise their *Golden Girls* roles along with John.

After the musical ended, Betty made a pass at John. When he said he loved only Catherine, Betty pushed him into a kiddie pool in the lounge, leaving his body floating down in the water like William Holden in *Sunset Boulevard*. Betty ascended a staircase until Rue told her *TV Guide* was here. "Tell them I'm ready for my closeup box!" she said.

For masterfully mocking her image, Betty won an Emmy for Outstanding Guest Actress in a Comedy Series. The statuette was her first since getting an Emmy in 1986 for *The Golden Girls*.

That same year at the 1996 MTV Movie Awards, Betty, Rue McClanahan, and Estelle Getty joined forces once again to parody the movie *Clueless* in a filmed segment that ran over just two minutes. The women played middle-aged versions of the teen stars from the movie instead of their Golden Girls personas, but elements of the latter were in place.

Talk remained strong about taping a *Golden Girls* reunion special throughout the late 1990s and early 2000s. "They tried several times," Betty told Frank Bruni during a 2011 "Times Talk" interview. "They wanted to do a movie. You know, a 'Golden Girls: Where Did They Go From Here?' And all of that. Bea [Arthur] wouldn't do it. And she may have been right. ... Quit while you're ahead. That's a great argument."

In June 2003, the Lifetime network aired a tribute special, *The Golden Girls: The Greatest Memories*, with comments from Arthur, McClanahan, and Betty. Getty was too ill to participate *The Golden Girls* repeats began on Lifetime in 1997. By the time this special ran, the sitcom appeared seven times weekdays and twice Saturdays on the network and drew an estimated 13 million viewers per week.

Asked about her thoughts on the show's staying power, Betty told David Bauder of the Associated Press that the credits went to the writing and the series serving as a "surrogate family" to younger viewers. "A lot of households now don't have grandmothers," she said. "I think they get a kick out of the fact that we're still viable."

"It's going to be rerun fifty years from now, I guarantee you," Lifetime's research director Tim Brooks told Bauder. "It's a show that isn't specific to its time and is very much about people."

Brooks' prediction appeared correct. On December 2, 2010, Betty told host George Lopez on *Lopez Tonight* how popular *The Golden Girls* remained in reruns globally. "We're in forty-nine countries. We're all over the world. We get mail from Bangladesh, Sri Lanka, Paris. Will you tell me what they see about four old broads in Bangladesh?! I don't know, but it's wonderful."

Hulu announced exclusive streaming rights for the series on February 13, 2017. "*The Golden Girls* has really stood the test of time and is still resonating with audiences.

So, when the opportunity came up to license it, we knew we had to take it," a Hulu spokesperson told CNBC.

With all that attention for a series where only one cast member was still alive—Getty died July 22, 2008, Arthur died April 25, 2009, and McClanahan died June 3, 2010—rumors surfaced about possible revivals of the series. In 2018 creator Susan Harris told *Entertainment Weekly* she adamantly opposed that possibility.

The series' staying power and influence was in evidence again in 2020, when British actress Cleo Rocos wrote her memoirs. She claimed that one afternoon in the late 1980s, she joined Princess Diana of Wales, singer Freddie Mercury, and comedian Kenny Everett in drinking champagne and watching *The Golden Girls* at Everett's home, where they improvised their own "naughtier storylines" over the top of muted episodes. The occasion represented how *The Golden Girls* was a worldwide pop culture item even among 1980s icons.

More than thirty-five years after its debut, *The Golden Girls* was a cultural phenomenon. Its importance to Betty's career is incalculable. The series certified her as a TV superstar and helped her avoid typecasting. She also proved she deserved to be a leading actress in her favorite medium. *The Golden Girls* was a career changer for a woman who had earned its resulting benefits for decades of hard work, and the series will stand as a testament to her talent.

The series has become a classic, and its star has become a legend. Long may they both wave.

Chapter Ten
Betty the Boss and Grandmother

Betty, Marie Osmond and Craig Ferguson found themselves stuck in the 1995 ABC sitcom loser *Maybe This Time*. Ferguson left the series before its cancellation and later joked about his work there when Betty appeared on his CBS late night talk show.
Courtesy of Everett Collection.

For a decade after *The Golden Palace* ended, Betty had regular roles in three failed sitcoms—*Bob*, *Maybe This Time*, and *Ladies Man*—and a recurring one in a hit—*That 70s Show*. Her parts were as a boss in *Bob* and as a grandmother in the rest.

If this summation doesn't sound inspiring, neither were the jobs overall. *Bob* was the best in showcasing Betty's talent, although the series fell short of the lofty heights Betty reached on *The Mary Tyler Moore Show* and *The Golden Girls*. *Maybe This Time* and *Ladies Man* had serious flaws in how they presented cast members, including Betty. *That 70s Show* was more consistently funny than *Maybe This Time* and *Ladies Man*, but Betty seemed peripheral to much of the action.

Reviewing this ten-year stretch, one had the nagging feeling that apart from *Bob*, the series' executive producers were fine relegating Betty to supporting roles with boring plots. Her fans watching these shows probably wondered more about what she was doing between shooting scenes than enduring her work on screen.

This unsatisfying time in her TV career including a sitcom pilot, *Me & Henry*, that would have made Betty portray yet another grandmother. Whether it was typecasting or coincidence, the years 1993–2003 provided Betty with several disappointing regular TV acting roles.

Hi, *Bob*

When *The Golden Palace* went off CBS in 1993, Betty White encountered a peculiar situation. Rather than search for a regular job in another series, she was already drafted for one.

The show was *Bob*, starring comedian Bob Newhart. Ironically, *The Golden Palace* had aired on CBS Fridays just ninety minutes before *Bob* at the beginning of the 1992–93 season.

Bob started as Newhart's third consecutive sitcom on CBS on September 18, 1992. *The Bob Newhart Show* stayed on CBS six seasons from 1972 to 1978. *Newhart* began on CBS in 1982 and ran eight seasons until 1990. Given that, expectations were high at the network that *Bob* would be another hit. But *Bob* didn't appeal to the masses the way its predecessors had done.

The failure also surprised its creators and executive producers, Phoef Sutton and the husband-and-wife team of Bill and Cheri Steinkellner. "Me and Bill and Cheri Steinkellner, we were just coming off *Cheers*, a hit NBC sitcom from 1983 to 1992, when we got the opportunity to do a show with Bob Newhart," recalled Sutton.

"We had all worshipped him, and he had done two successful series before that, so it seemed like he would be prime for another one."

When *Bob* debuted, Newhart played Bob McKay, an ex-greeting card artist now working in comic books who lived in Chicago with his wife Kaye, played by Carlene Watkins, and their adult daughter Trisha, played by Cynthia Stevenson. They were the only characters to survive a second season. Newhart played a tougher character at first than on his earlier sitcoms, but Sutton thought the bigger problem for the audience to accept was the setting.

"We were a little bit ahead of the curve to be interested in the comic book world," he said. "It seemed like a pretty cool thing to have this old comic book guy, this Bob Kane type guy, who is in the world of the modern comic books, which are more edgy. So, if we had done this ten years later, we would've been right on the pulse of popular culture.

"But as it was, it was way before then. Everybody was kind of like, 'What the hell is this? This is kind of strange.' And we went to Comic-Con in San Diego when it was just Comic-Con for comic books there. We had a great cast, it was a great show, but you know, it just didn't quite click enough."

Despite a switch midseason to follow the top twenty hit sitcom *Evening Shade* on Mondays, *Bob* finished its inaugural season at number seventy-two in the ratings. That performance generally meant cancellation for a series, but Sutton and the Steinkellners came up with a plan in the spring of 1993 to convince CBS to give *Bob* a second shot with a revamped format.

"So, we went to New York, and we knew it was going to get cancelled," Sutton recalled. "This is the upfronts when they make decisions. We were pretty sure we were getting cancelled. And we felt bad that it had a really great cast.

"We felt like we had real possibilities for sure, but we figured, 'We know we're going to get cancelled anyway, so why don't we throw a real hail Mary, and we'll claim we want to revamp the show entirely? He's going to leave the comic book world, go back to the greeting card world, work for Betty White as a greeting card king, and changes in the supporting cast and all that.' Which we figured 'They won't go for it, but at least we'll have tried.' We did that and they said, 'No, no, sorry, it's cancelled.'

"So, we flew back to L.A., going through the seven stages of grief on the airplane. When I got home I got a call from the network saying that they'd decided to pick the show up again. And so we had to do all those changes that we had not really intended to do. So, it just goes to show to be careful what you ask for."

Another factor helped get *Bob* a slot on the CBS fall 1993 schedule. Linda Bloodworth-Thomason, producer of the sitcom *Hearts Afire*, objected to a plan to move her series to Friday nights in its second season. CBS executives accommodated her request and relocated the sitcom to Wednesdays, but the network still had a gap on Fridays. *Bob* was the answer.

As Sutton and the Steinkellners processed their renewal, word leaked out from the CBS executive suite to the media that Betty White was joining *Bob*. This announcement surprised Betty and her agent, Tony Fantozzi. They checked out the news with the executive producers, who fortunately had thought ahead to flesh out a character presentation to Betty. Sutton claimed they presented another enticement to have Betty become part of the series.

"We had Bob Newhart, who was a big draw," he said. "Everybody wants to work with Bob, he's both an incredibly gifted comedian and a really great guy. The nicest guy in the world. And she is, too, so we really just had to offer it to her, and she came on board. She was great."

Actually, Betty was receptive to a point. She and Fantozzi realized *Bob* would be a third consecutive sitcom with her as a regular in nine seasons, and they worried viewers would burn out from seeing too much Betty White. So they proposed a compromise.

"I said, 'I can do guest shots, but I can't really sign up with the show,'" she told the syndicated TV information series *Entertainment Tonight*. She added she was enticed in part by her character having a pet white Poodle called Gypsy Rose Dog on the series.

The parties reached a deal where Betty agreed to appear six times and be billed as a special guest star on *Bob*. As it turned out, she didn't even get to do six shows on the series.

It's the Schmitt

At the outset of the second season opener on October 22, 1993, Bob had lost his comic book job. He returned to the Schmitt Greetings card company, where he had worked as an artist for twenty years prior to his comic book assignment. When he arrived, he learned his former boss Lester Schmitt had run off to Samoa with Tammi, a dental hygienist. Left behind was Lester's wife, Sylvia Schmitt, played by Betty, who was cutting out and burning Lester's face in old photos.

"It's my life for the very first time. Spank my rear and watch me go!" Sylvia proclaimed to Bob as she coped with the separation. Learning that Bob was out of work, she offered him to take over Lester's role as president. As she told him, "Deep down, you're a real Schmitt!" Sylvia's son Pete, played by Jere Burns, pouted about Bob receiving the position over himself.

The next episode, "For Pete's Sake," delved into Pete's unhappiness. Like his mom, his spouse had recently left him. Sylvia was only slightly sympathetic. She told Bob she resented delivering Pete as a baby. "Ten hours I pushed and screamed. I have a very narrow pelvic cavity."

But when Sylvia met Trisha, she considered Bob's daughter a perfect romantic partner for Pete. She invited Bob, Kay, and Trisha to her swanky apartment with Gypsy Rose Dog. Sylvia's matchmaking efforts were obvious, like making Trisha and Pete sit in the same chair together. Pete complained to his mother that she couldn't force a relationship on him, before he and Trisha bonded when stuck accidentally on Sylvia's balcony.

Betty returned two episodes later in "Speechless in Chicago," where Sylvia declined to see Pete accept a salesman of the year award because her estranged husband, Lester, also planned to attend. "He's only doing this to hurt me," she said. At Sylvia's urging, her pregnant bookkeeper Chris Szelinski, played by new *Bob* regular Megan Cavanagh, added, "Dirty bastard!" Sylvia finally relented and appeared, only to discover that Lester decided to go snorkeling instead of coming to the ceremony.

By this time, more viewers watched *The X-Files* on Fox opposite *Bob*, and CBS canned the series. One more episode without Betty aired on December 27, 1993. That was it for *Bob* on the network.

On March 23, 1997, the TV Land cable channel aired three previously unaired episodes of *Bob*, and two of them had Betty. In "Michiana Moon," Bob's best friend, Uncle Buzz Loudermilk, played by frequent *Bob* director Dick Martin, targeted Sylvia as his next romantic conquest. "It's a date!" she said in accepting Buzz's offer of a date, adding that "I haven't said that in a while ... Eisenhower administration." Bob, Kaye, Trisha, and Pete searched fruitlessly for Sylvia and Buzz at a wine tasting, then found them at a hotel where Sylvia rejected Buzz's sexual advances and refused to let him in her room.

In Betty's other episode, "Better to Have Loved and Flossed," Sylvia learned at Chris's baby shower that dental hygienist Tammi, played by Beverly Leech, had returned to Chicago without Sylvia's ex-husband Lester. Sylvia confronted Tammi with a baseball bat while, coincidentally, Bob was having a crown replaced. The whole situation wound up with Tammi making relative peace with Sylvia, even after Pete made a pass at Tammi.

Watching these episodes were like seeing a soufflé being made and the resulting dish falling flat. The ingredients were in place for hilarity, but they never quite jelled together effectively. "In that incarnation of the show … it was still a good show," Sutton said. "It just limped along."

The cancellation of *Bob* meant that Betty White would enter the 1994–1995 season with no regular or semiregular role on a sitcom, a situation that hadn't existed since 1981–1982. That problem didn't arise in 1995, though, as Betty got her seventh regular role in a sitcom.

Making a Package with William Morris

In the fall of 1994, Michael Jacobs and Bob Young, executive producers of the ABC sitcom *Boy Meets World*, met with Lee Rosenberg, their agent at William Morris. Jacobs and Young had a commitment for another series on the ABC schedule, and Rosenberg wanted to package the deal. He presented the duo with some celebrity names that also were clients of William Morris.

Jacobs took interest when Rosenberg mentioned Marie Osmond. "I felt that was a real interesting name, particularly in this political climate," Jacobs told Greg Braxton and Daniel Howard Cerone in *The Los Angeles Times*.

Some ABC executives also liked Marie Osmond's work starring in a touring stage production of *The Sound of Music* in 1994. Others questioned their judgment, as Osmond had rarely acted on television up to that time apart from appearances on variety and music specials. And while she did have success cohosting *Donny & Marie* from 1975 to 1979, she followed that series with two flops, *Marie* in 1980 and *Ripley's Believe It or Not* from 1985 to 1986.

Regardless, Jacobs also liked the idea of pairing Marie with Betty White. However, Betty was preparing a pilot for an hour daytime syndicated informational show called *The Betty White House*. But as that proposed series would be for Disney, the owners of ABC, all parties agreed to work on a schedule where she could do both series, just as she had done on TV previously. As it turned out, *The Betty White House* didn't become a reality.

To seal the deal, Jacobs and Young also picked a third actress client of William Morris, Ashley Johnson. She was under contract with ABC after coming to prominence playing the youngest daughter on the hit sitcom *Growing Pains* from 1990 to 1992.

"From a political and creative standpoint, it made a lot of sense," Jacobs said.

Yet another William Morris client, Susan Estelle Jansen, producer of *Boy Meets World* in 1994, joined Jacobs and Young to develop the series concept. She became the supervising producer while Jacobs and Young served as executive producers. Also added was David Trainer to produce and direct the series. He was a William Morris client, too. The series would be named *Maybe This Time*.

For packaging the deal, William Morris relinquished its usual ten percent commission on clients' fees in favor of five percent of the license fee paid by ABC to air *Maybe This Time* and five percent of backend revenues, including overseas sales and possible reruns in syndication. The latter potential never happened. Instead, plenty of discord followed.

Maybe Not This Time
In *Maybe This Time*, Marie Osmond played Julia Wallace, a divorced operator of a coffeehouse in Philadelphia. Assisting Julia was her mother, Shirley Wallace, played by Betty. Their co-worker was Logan McDonough, played by Craig Ferguson. Julia's twelve-year-old daughter and Shirley's granddaughter was Gracie Wallace, played by Ashley Johnson. Shirley's friend Kay Ohara, played by Amy Hill, oversaw a nearby pawn shop. The coffeehouse was at the corner of South and Lancaster, an impossible intersection if meaning South Street and Lancaster Avenue.

The location wasn't the only aspect that perplexed some observers. As a member of the Church of Jesus Christ of Latter-Day Saints, Osmond's character would be serving a beverage not condoned by her religion. She rationalized her situation by saying the series' establishment to her was more like a restaurant.

"Everybody has to eat, and we serve more than coffee ... To me, sitting around with food is a wonderful time to just vent," she told Mike Hughes of the Gannett News Service.

Hughes accepted that explanation better than reviewing the overall series. "In truth, it's bland," he wrote. "Producer Michael Jacobs—who needs to slow down and get a second wind—throws together his usual blend of gags and hugs, always pleasant and rarely exceptional."

The opener, "Please Re-Lease Me," definitely didn't perk like the drinks Julia and Shirley served. Kay gave Logan a golf club. "What degrading, soul-killing thing do you want me to do?" he asked Kay. "Which I'm guessing you've done before," interjected Shirley. "Oh, most certainly," he said. "I want you to go out with my niece and to make her fall in love with you," said Kay. "Oh, I could do that with my eyes shut," he said. "You may have to," smirked Shirley.

Meanwhile the landlord for the coffeehouse's property, Henry Witherspoon, played by Elliot Reid, reminded Shirley it was time to renew the rental agreement. She flirted with Henry to keep the payment down, which appalled Julia. The latter tried to negotiate with Henry while Shirley went to dress up in a Little Bo Peep outfit to entice Henry. When Shirley emerged, Julia had to confess her discussions with Henry led him to want $500 more per month, which the Wallaces couldn't afford. Henry's daughter Lorraine, played by Alicia Brandt, planned to raise the rent even more until Shirley got Logan to flirt successfully with Lorraine and save the day.

"*Maybe This Time* is offensively routine," opined Howard Rosenberg in *The Los Angeles Times*. "Osmond doesn't offer much, nor does the entire premiere beyond the skilled veteran White, who could get through this kind of sitcom in her sleep. Unfortunately, so could viewers."

"Please Re-Lease Me" aired Friday, September 15, 1995, with the next episode airing the following day in its regular time slot. As work on subsequent shows progressed, the set's mood grew dim. Hill told author Bob Leszczak in *Single Season Sitcoms of the 1990s* ABC executives forced Michael Jacobs to include her as a regular. Perhaps as a result, Hill found the executive producer dismissive in trying to develop her character, among other problems with the series.

"He was also very unkind to Marie," Hill told Leszczak. "She had some difficulty memorizing large amounts of dialogue and he was rather cruel to her about that. To get through it, she wrote lines on her hands, on the props, on tables, etc. Plus, they were always rewriting her lines."

Hill's only enjoyable memory of *Maybe This Time* was working with Betty. "She saved me every day," Hill noted. "She was funny, kind, smart, encouraging, sweet—pure genius. She's amazing."

As for Ferguson, he did the pilot in his early thirties as his first job in America from Scotland. He grew to hate the series, as plots focused more on the romantic entanglements of the Wallaces.

"He wasn't given much of anything to do on our show and felt frustrated," Betty wrote in *Here We Go Again: My Life in Television*. After muttering his discomfort, Ferguson had his request fulfilled to be released after taping the first thirteen episodes.

Betty reunited with her co-star ten years later when he hosted *The Late Late Show with Craig Ferguson*. Ferguson had Betty on as a guest from 2005 until his finale in 2014. On his December 11, 2011 show, he asked Betty why *Maybe This Time* wasn't a hit. "Well, I'll tell you why. We had this Scotsman (laughter), but we gave him nothing to do." She noted how he muttered about being misused and joked, "Somehow, we became friends. I guess it was pity on my part!"

Replacing Ferguson by January 1996 was comedian Dane Cook as Kyle, an ex-athlete sporting a mullet who worked at the Wallaces' shop. Its location now was said to be in nearby Haverford, Pennsylvania. No major changes in scripting occurred, however, and Betty's Shirley seemed relegated to incidental work in all the plots.

For example, in "Lucky Puck" on January 20, 1996, Shirley's function was to give the right answer to a trivia question to win tickets for the fictional Philadelphia Glaciers hockey game. As Julia romanced a hockey player and kissed his stick for good luck, Shirley charged customers more for their drinks if they wanted a cup with a kiss from her daughter. "It's never over till the rich lady sings!" Shirley crowed to her daughter while waving money collected.

In "St. Valentine's Day Massacre" on February 10, 1996, Shirley tried to help Kyle balance two dates at the same time by claiming his lady from France was a new pastry chef. The farcical situation was nowhere as effective or funny as what Betty did previously on *The Golden Girls*.

By that point, *Maybe This Time* had been cancelled. The show already was in jeopardy when Cloris Leachman turned up as Ferguson's mother to spar with Betty, as they did on *The Mary Tyler Moore Show*, in the episode "Beasy Body" on October 28, 1995. That event brought few new viewers to an already limping show.

Runnings Saturdays from 8:30 to 9 p.m., *Maybe This Time* finished in 108th position for the 1995–1996 season. It was the lowest-rated sitcom on ABC's lineup when it ended on February 17, 1996. Betty took a two-year hiatus this time before shooting another pilot.

Betty and Melanie

In April 1998, Betty taped a show planned to launch on CBS in the middle of the 1998–1999 season called *Me & Henry*. The multicamera sitcom came from Witt-Thomas Productions, who had produced *The Golden Girls* for Betty. She played the mother of a character portrayed by Melanie Griffith, who was a successful executive who needed White's help in raising her baby.

Rumors about Griffith's performance soon surfaced. "There have been reports that the prospective series' chances were badly hurt by the actress suffering from a bad case of stage fright when faced with working before a live audience for the first time," wrote newspaper columnist Marilyn Beck.

Regarding those claims, Betty told Beck, "Melanie was really scared as the taping approached, because it was so different from what she had done. She got me nervous worrying about how she would be. But when we did the show, Melanie came out and talked to the audience beforehand, told them she was scared to death, but she knew they'd be with her .... I stood backstage, listening, thinking, 'She's going to be fine.' And she was. They loved her and I was very proud of her."

Even so, by October, sources reported Griffith had negotiated an exit from the series as the producers questioned whether she was the right fit for the sitcom. As CBS executives considered if and how to add a new leading woman into the series, co-star Jeffrey Tambor got a deal to star in another Witt-Thomas sitcom, *Everything's Relative*. *Everything's Relative* ran only four times on NBC in 1999, but that was better than *Me & Henry*, which never aired.

That distinction scarcely mattered to Betty because, at the time *Everything's Relative* was bombing, Betty was working on yet another pilot for CBS. This effort sold. That statement is about the best many critics said about the series.

Betty Gets "Man"-handled

The premise behind *Ladies Man* copied that of *The Tom Ewell Show*, which aired on CBS from 1960 to 1961. The titular star lived with his wife, mother-in-law, and three daughters. *Ladies Man* provided only a slight contrast to that setup.

Played by Alfred Molina, Jimmy Stiles wanted a baby boy from his pregnant wife, Donna Stiles, played by Sharon Lawrence, to counterbalance a house with his mother, Mitzi Stiles, played by Betty White, and daughters Wendy Stiles, played by Katie Volding, and Bonnie Stiles, played by Mariam Parris. Jimmy also contended with visits from his ex-wife, Claire, played by Park Overall, who was Bonnie's birth mother, and his mother-in-law, Peaches, played by Dixie Carter. His friend Gene played by Stephen Root, served as a sounding board to Jimmy's concerns.

Carter appeared as Peaches on the pilot as a favor to Molina, an old friend. Her repartee with Betty so impressed the producers that they implored her to come back as a semiregular when not shooting her new show *Family Law*. Carter did so as her schedule permitted.

Their interplay was about the only saving grace of the pilot, which aired September 20, 1999. Among the lowlights, when Peaches arrived to say she had bought the daughters digital cell phones, an indignant Mitzi glared at Peaches and exclaimed, "You have one grandmother who doesn't feel the need to buy your love!"

Later, talking to Donna, Mitzi, and Peaches in the kitchen, Jimmy denied he hated women. Mitzi had her doubts, saying her husband loathed her the last twenty years of their marriage and thought the feeling could be hereditary. "He referred to me in his will as 'That bitch who killed me,'" she said.

Looking for consolation, Jimmy talked to Gene, who said he married four times because "Truthfully, it's because I don't have what it takes to be gay." Gene expounded on the advantages of being homosexual when another guy in the locker room overheard him and smiled. "What are you looking at, Nancy?!" growled back Gene, who later said that his son "went gay."

In the meantime, after Van Nuys police officers arrested her for shoplifting, Bonnie asked to move in permanently with Donna and Jimmy. All the women in the family met to discuss the situation, where Peaches revealed she had vodka in her purse. "What a surprise!" smirked Mitzi. "I'd offer you some but I know you prefer to hide your drinking from the children. Whoops, surprise!" snarled Peaches. The conversation devolved to the point where Mitzi said of Jimmy, "He used to spit my breast out of his mouth!" and Claire added, "You, too?!"

After accidentally calling the very pregnant Donna bloated, Jimmy's wife wanted him to make love to her. A superimposed title implied Donna went into labor three minutes after they began making out and delivered a baby boy. "You're not alone anymore," she told Jimmy about the new addition.

Critic Tim Goodman of *The San Francisco Examiner* called *Ladies Man* a dud where "the jokes are wincingly bad and predictable, as well." Molina feeling intimidated by the women made no sense to Goodman. Neither did the involvement of creator, executive producer, and writer Chris Thompson, who previously had participated in creating two of Goodman's favorite series.

"Clearly written by a man—but how can it be the same guy who created *Action* and helped guide *The Larry Sanders Show*? Apparently, that's a bigger mystery than women," Goodman said in summing up *Ladies Man*.

Producers recast the daughters by episode two, with Alexa Vega as Wendy and Shawna Waldron as Bonnie. Unfortunately, the writing only worsened. At home, Mitzi said the new baby boy looked like Jay Leno and told Donna, "He has your pretty pink nose." "That's my nipple," Donna said. "I'll just get my finger off it then!" answered Mitzi.

Mitzi added, "Jimmy nursed until he was four years old. Four years! He sucked me dry! … By the time he was finished, my breasts just hung there, like loaves of pita bread!"

Jimmy wanted to name their son Tiger Iggy, after Tiger Woods and Iggy Pop, but Donna preferred Chester, her late father's name. "Why don't you just call him Fancy Fancy Princess Nancy?!" responded Jimmy. "That was your nickname, wasn't it, Jimmy?" Mitzi interjected. "Oh, that's right, it was Sissy Sissy Little Missy!"

Until they could decide on a name, Mitzi said the baby ought to be called Richard Chamberlain like she did with Jimmy's father. "If you had to climb in the sack with a drunken, hairy-backed fish salesman every night, you'd be thinking about Richard Chamberlain, too!" That declaration stunned Jimmy, which made Mitzi say, "Oh, grow up, Missy!"

Later, Mitzi said she and her late husband had laughed at Jimmy playing Little League baseball. "It's how we bonded." Looking over Jimmy's pornographic magazine, Mitzi assessed the breasts in the centerfold were fake. Gene agreed with her and also flirted with Mitzi to her enjoyment.

The plots and the dialogue stayed poor over subsequent episodes. Betty had relatively little to enact in each installment except give a snappy line to show how sassy a grandmother she was.

On "Regarding Eric," on October 4, 1999, Mitzi boasted to Donna she held off sex with her husband for nineteen years for his refusal to apologize to her. "And on his deathbed, I flashed him and said, 'This could've been yours, you bastard, I win!'" she said.

The following episode, Peaches and Mitzi argued who was the first man in space when Mitzi cracked, "You were taking men around the world years before NASA was!" On the next installment, Mitzi asserted, "I've seen enough *Matlock*s to know that there's always some dumb eyewitness in the wings!" Gene then entered the room.

Later shows included the following bits of Mitzi business:

• Mitzi proclaimed her affection for a new boyfriend by saying, 'He's got both of his original hips and can drive at night!"

• As Claire discussed a wrinkle cream, Peaches said, "Mitzi could use it! Myself, I have always been blessed with skin like fine porcelain." "Yes, like a bus station sink!" shot back Mitzi.

• Mitzi said she had a boyfriend she loved in high school before another woman stole him from her. "Rot in hell, Barbara Bush!" she proclaimed.

• On Thanksgiving, Peaches said, "Hey, everybody! Guess what I have out in the car!" "A case of vodka and a change of underwear?" asked Mitzi. When Peaches said of her other daughter Delilah, "There's always one cub in the pride who favors the lioness," Mitzi zinged her with, "Yes, and there's always one puppy in the litter who favors the bitch!"

• Mitzi got a job at Dom DeLuise's Barbecue Barn and told her family, "Dom came by and personally showed me the secret to his beans!"

• At Christmas, Jimmy asked Mitzi, "Mom, what were you always saying was the best thing Dad ever did for you?" "Passing away before they invented Viagra," she said. Mitzi later added, "Your sister was conceived when I deboned a fish!" Also, Mitzi got drunk at the airport as the family's flight to Hawaii got delayed.

Wil Shriner, who had worked with Betty on his own talk show in 1987, came to *Ladies Man* to direct its episode "Bad Muthas." "I was just starting to direct television. Kelsey Grammer had given me my first opportunity [on *Frasier*]. But my second episode was *Ladies Man*.

"Betty was very gracious. I had a scene where she came through the door, and Sharon Lawrence said something about, 'Do you have anything with you?' And the line was, 'Do you want to pat me down?' And I went to Betty and said, 'Why don't you throw yourself against the doors, spread your hands and legs like a policeman would do to you?' She said, 'Great idea!'

"We did it. It got a big, big laugh, and the producers and everybody else looked at me and said, 'Oh, this guy adds to the funny!' Which, as a TV director, is great. But

Betty didn't go, 'No, that was my idea.' She was very gracious and said, 'No, that was Wil's idea.'"

Shriner declined to speculate what was wrong with *Ladies Man*. "You come in as a director, you're not the writer, you're not the show runner," he said. "Chris Thompson was a pretty good show runner for several shows. And Alfred Molina was a big star. And Sharon was a pretty big actress … So I don't know what the problem with that show was."

After "Bad Muthas" came the first season finale, "Romance," where Betty reunited with *Golden Girls* co-star Rue McClanahan as Mitzi's sister, known to the family as Aunt Lou. The two fought over a suitor played by George Hamilton. Also appearing was Estelle Getty as Sophia Gates. The surname prevented the series from copyright infringement with *The Golden Girls*, but the comparison was obvious.

Ladies Man aired on CBS Mondays 8:30-9 p.m. after *The King of Queens*, another domestic sitcom. Despite the compatible lead-in, ratings were shaky and its prospects were uncertain. "We're all sticking pins in our renewal dolls," Betty said in February 2000. She claimed the ratings were moving up and added, "A whole new slew of writers came in a few weeks, and it's made a big difference." She concluded with, "It's the happiest ship I've ever been on, and having done *The Mary Tyler Moore Show* and *The Golden Girls*, that's saying something."

But having a happy workplace and producing congenial results on screen can be mutually exclusive. The only encouraging news the series received for a time was Betty getting an Online Film and Television Association nomination as Best Actress in a New Comedy Series.

Eventually, *Ladies Man* barely earned a renewal after finishing at number fifty-seven in the ratings for the 1999–2000 season. The series was planned to be a midseason replacement in 2000–2001, but ultimately CBS burned off eight of the twelve episodes in June 2001.

Airing two episodes back-to-back Wednesdays from 8-9 p.m., the second season of *Ladies Man* dropped Peaches and Claire and added a third actress to play Wendy Stiles, Kaley Cuoco. Cuoco later became the female star of the CBS sitcom *The Big Bang Theory* from 2007–2019. Jimmy teamed with fellow architect Sabrina, played by Elizabeth Beckwith, to work on remodeling a house for Alex Trebek, who was heard in voiceovers. Gene got a regular girlfriend named Terry, played by Kathleen McClellan. They all disappeared after four weeks on June 27, 2001.

The cancellation of *Ladies Man* was a blessing for Betty. *Ladies Man* was a bad initial concept replete with unappealing dialogue, characters, and situations, and the writing made her character often embittered and harsh. Betty deserved better treatment than this debacle and got it, but not with her next big role.

That 70s Grandmother

Running on Fox from 1998 to 2006, *That 70s Show* was an affectionate look back at living in the "Me Decade" through the eyes of teenager Eric Forman, played by Topher Grace, and his family and friends in Wisconsin. The show frequently incorporated actors who were 1970s stars as guests. Typically these visits were fun and clever. Yet Betty's four times on *That 70s Show*—her most appearances on a sitcom since *Ladies Man*—were an exception. Playing a somewhat cold character, she had few lines to deliver in two shows, and her comic potential was wasted.

Betty's first episode was "Heartbreaker" on October 29, 2002 as Bea Sigurdson, the loud mother of Eric's mother Kitty Forman, played by Debra Jo Rupp. Bea's husband Bert, played by Tom Poston, imbibed a lot, perhaps in response to his wife's behavior. Bea's big moment on the show was insisting that she never went through menopause.

"Thank You," on December 3, 2002, had Kitty telling Bea on Thanksgiving, "I know that we have had our ups and downs, but in honor of this special day, I would like to tell you that I am thankful that you are my mother and I love you." Bea responded by saying she wanted more tea. The holiday dinner conversation revealed Eric was flunking math, prompting Bea to say, "Kitty, I'm sure he did the best he could, for someone who was held too long as a baby." Bea also liked how her granddaughter Laurie, played by Lisa Robin Kelly, yelled to wake up Bert.

Bert and Bea made a surprise visit in "Your Time is Gonna Come" on January 29, 2003, after Bert bought an ostrich farm next to a coyote farm, and the latter feasted on the former. "He lost all our money," said Bea. "We had to sell the house in Phoenix, which is why we're here." She later moaned, "Ah, it's always difficult for the beautiful women. You never understood that, Kitty." Bert suddenly died, and Bea went in denial. "He never thought about anybody but himself and those damn ostriches!" she exclaimed. But when Kitty came to Bea's bedroom and saw her crying, she broke down and wept, too, holding onto her son Eric. The moving moment promised to give Betty's character more depth, but alas, Bea would last only one more episode.

On "Babe I'm Gonna Leave You," on February 5, 2003, Kitty wanted to talk about Bert with Bea, who objected. Instead, Bea told Eric how important it is to tell people you love them before taking a walk. Devastated by her mother's apparent rejection, Kitty locked herself in her room, while Eric later told Bea that he was engaged to his girlfriend, Donna Pinciotti, portrayed by Laura Prepon. "Well, I guess this is a small town," an unimpressed Bea said before leaving.

Fretting that Bea disliked her, Donna tried to suck up to Bea. "I'm sure you're the nicest girl Eric has met so far," Bea said. At the coda, as Kitty and her husband Red, played by Kurtwood Smith, headed out to dinner, Bea asked, "Is that what you're wearing?" Kitty retreated back to her room in response. That was the last time Bea was seen.

Thankfully, Betty would bounce back from this and other unimpressive sitcoms she had endured for a decade. In fact, Betty's contributions as a recurring guest on a nighttime and daytime drama the rest of the aughts of the twenty-first century rank among her best work ever. Some producers knew Betty was ready to rise to a challenge, and she magnificently surpassed what most people expected from her in those parts.

Chapter Eleven
Betty the Drama Queen

The still that launched a thousand memes: Betty's character Catherine Piper brandished a gun at a store clerk just to get attention from her lawyer on the *Boston Legal* episode "Too Much Information," which aired January 24, 2006. Photo: Ron Tom / Copyright Fox / Courtesy: Everett Collection.

After being co-producer and writer of the upscale drama *L.A. Law* on NBC from 1987 to 1994, David E. Kelley created *The Practice* to depict lawyers in the struggling Boston firm of Young, Frutt and Berluti. Premiering on ABC March 4, 1997, *The Practice* was a critical favorite that climbed into the top ten in its fourth season, 1999–2000. During its run, *The Practice* won two Emmys for outstanding dramatic series in 1998 and 1999—the first double win for any ABC drama—and compiled eight Emmy wins for guest actors and actresses.

But in the 2002–2003 season, as ratings dropped, ABC cut the next season's licensing fee for *The Practice*. Kelley secretly took the opportunity to spend the 2003–2004 season preparing for a spin-off by introducing the morally dubious lawyer Alan Shore into Young, Frutt and Berluti. Shore would be fired and retaliate with a successful wrongful termination suit to force the firm's lawyers out of business. He also joined another law firm headed by Denny Crane, played by William Shatner. Kelley created Alan Shore with its portrayer, actor James Spader, in mind.

"David asked me to join *The Practice*, with six episodes left in the last season, to consult with him to turn it into what became *Boston Legal*," said Bill D'Elia. "I directed two of the last six, becoming a consulting producer, to get a feel for the new setting and characters. At the time, all David wanted for the new show was for it to be funny, as well as dramatic, and for it to take place in a big corporate law firm. We didn't know what it would be called or who precisely would be in it.

"William Shatner was a guest star in those last few episodes. James Spader only had a one-season deal for the final season of *The Practice*, so his involvement was not necessarily guaranteed. It was like having six episodes to develop a show as opposed to the usual practice of only having one pilot episode. The result became *Boston Legal*."

To set up the conflict between Shore and his partners at Young, Frutt and Berluti, Kelley incorporated a case where Shore's work led to a breaking point with his superiors. A key element of the three-story arc was the addition of Betty White, who had worked with Kelley in 1999 in the movie *Lake Placid* and an episode of *Ally McBeal*. Her character was a pushy, opinionated witness threatening Shore as he attempted to mount a defense of his client.

"David definitely had Betty in mind when he created the role," said D'Elia. "David Kelley has a unique ability to tap into an actor's strengths. He saw something in Betty that caused him to just dig deeper."

Indeed, Catherine Piper was quite unlike any woman Betty had portrayed on TV to that point. Kelley gave Betty a unique character which she imbued with unpredictability and subtlety.

Playing the Piper

First seen on January 25, 2004, Catherine Piper was walking her pet chihuahua at night as Dr. Paul Stewart, played by Patrick Dempsey, sped away in his car. He had seen the body of Brenda Wilbur, with whom he had an adulterous affair. Alan Shore, Paul's lawyer and childhood friend, knew Brenda, too. Paul's mother Victoria Stewart, played by Jill Clayburgh, told Alan that Brenda tried to extort Paul as he worked on the case.

Meanwhile, Catherine recognized Alan when he was a child in her neighborhood and shook his hand with dog excrement in her glove, to his disgust. She did it because she remembered how he played a similar Halloween prank that damaged her shoes.

"You were a crazy old bitch then. I can see nobody's adjusted your medication," he snarled.

Catherine told Alan she saw Paul leave Brenda's house at 10:30 p.m. the previous night. "I refer, of course, to dead Brenda, the slut all you boys wanted to screw in high school. Many of you went on to do it, I'm sure," she said with an evil twinkle in her eye and a giggle.

Noting she hadn't revealed that information to the police, Catherine added, "Tell Victoria if she pays me $1.3 million, I won't put her precious little baby in jail."

Alan didn't know about the nighttime visit, while no one else knew that Alan had slept with Victoria when he was sixteen. Victoria proposed bribing Catherine to keep her quiet, which Alan rejected. But when he followed up to meet with Victoria, she invited Catherine over, as well.

"What is she doing here?" he asked.

"Why, I'm here to suck on one of Victoria's shriveled nipples, of course. Is that why you're here, Alan?" she coyly responded.

Alan pleaded with Victoria that Catherine was unstable, but Victoria believed her testimony would be damaging to the case. Victoria directed Catherine to commit perjury, which prompted Catherine to ask for more money and excoriate Victoria for how she treated those not in the upper class.

In the next episode, Catherine entered Alan's law office and commented, "Wow, from the fancy suits, I'd never have guessed you worked in such a craphole!" Attorney

Jamie Stringer, playing by Jessica Capshaw, was to take Catherine's testimony until the latter said, "I'm sure you're good, darling, but your mouth looks like a drive-thru window for oral sex."

Meanwhile, Judge Marcus Winnaker, played by Ed Asner, recommended in his chambers that Alan plead voluntary manslaughter because the buzz in the jury pool was that Paul was guilty. After Alan objected and left, Winnaker warned District Attorney Harvey Clarke, played by Rick Hoffman, that Alan would be a tough defense attorney to challenge.

Yet Alan struggled to pick the right jurors, and Victoria asked for $50,000 more to silence Catherine from testifying. Alan and Victoria argued, and their back and forth led Catherine to say, "This give and take is a little like tennis, isn't it? You know, the game where you play with a racquet and two balls? Actually, I've got your balls. And if you don't want me to be making a racquet, you'll tell Victoria to get that extra fifty to me by tomorrow." Then Catherine told D.A. Clarke that Victoria paid her $600,000 not to reveal she saw Paul leave the scene of the crime.

For the third episode and trial finale, Alan pointed out in court that Detective Kevin McCarley, portrayed by Michael Reilly Burke, only investigated Paul for the murder and no other suspects. After Alan's grilling of the detective, Catherine told him, "I want you to know, I don't mind being a suspect at all! It gives me edge." She also warned him her testimony was up next.

On the stand, Catherine claimed she saw Paul return before 10 p.m., prompting Alan to object. "From my interview with the witness, I believe she's misspoken," he said.

"No, I haven't," Catherine said. The judge allowed her to finish. She told of receiving $600,000 from Victoria and added, "I'm not the noblest of people. I'm obviously not above extortion or even lying. But I just couldn't lie to help someone get away with murder."

Alan cross-examined Catherine on her negative opinions of Victoria and the victim to paint her as vengeful and judgmental with limited success. Paul's testimony on his behalf didn't help either, as D.A. Clarke pointed out a hammer was missing from Paul's toolbox.

So, when Victoria took the stand, Alan mentioned their tryst decades earlier and implied Victoria made love to him because she had incestuous feelings for Paul. In his closing remarks, Alan called Catherine a lunatic who hated the victim as much as

Paul. The jury found Paul not guilty, and a disgusted Catherine let out, "Boo! Boo!" as people filed out of the courtroom. Afterward, Alan admitted the incest angle was trial strategy—and discovered Paul was the real murderer.

"I had so much fun," Betty told Maria Elena Fernandez of *The Los Angeles Times* about her role on *The Practice*. "It has been my favorite show for years, and I'll miss the regular people like mad. But [becoming *Boston Legal* is] an interesting way of moving on and changing but keeping a sense of reference, the orientation for the audience. It's an interesting twist."

For her portrayal, Betty earned an Emmy nomination for Outstanding Guest Actress in a Drama Series, losing to Sharon Stone, who won ironically for a role on *The Practice*. Betty also got to participate in the "interesting twist," as Catherine reappeared on *Boston Legal* the next season.

While unsure exactly why David Kelley brought her back, his consulting producer partner Bill D'Elia said, "I know that David loved it when Betty was both sweet and nasty. If the network would have allowed it, she would have cursed profusely. I recall many first drafts where Catherine's lines were filthy, so we could know what he really wanted her to say."

Witness Turned Assistant

While Kelley decided to bring back and incorporate Catherine into *Boston Legal*, the series' writers came up with the cases in which she was involved. Phoef Sutton, who joined *Boston Legal* as consulting producer in 2005, explained the process of putting together the program.

"Every episode kind of had three stories … And it was the ongoing stories that David used to do, and there were the additional cases we would follow. Basically what you'd do is you'd read the newspaper, and you'd send him a slew of ideas for stories. And then he would pick and say, 'Well, why don't you write that?' A writer would write that story, but just that part of a script.

"And then he would take it and put it together, so you often were like, 'Oh God, I wrote an episode with Laurence [Broch]! I didn't know I was writing that!' So he would tend to 'Frankenstein' them together. That was generally the way it worked.

"There were some years where he was less involved, when he had more shows on the air. In that case, [co-executive producer] Janet Leahy was running the show, and she would tend to take a little more then. But often he would come back and rework stuff and do pretty extensive rewrites on things. So that added the 'David Kelley touch' to it."

Catherine's reintroduction on January 16, 2005 coincided with Alan's diminutive client Bernard Ferrion, played by Leslie Jordan, having avoided a jail term for killing his mother due to a technicality. Bernard then killed his neighbor who claimed to overhear the murder. An incensed Alan refused to represent Bernard again. His partner, Tara Wilson, played by Rhona Mitra, kept Bernard from going to trial.

At the same time, Catherine successfully applied to be Alan's new assistant despite telling him things like "Deep down, you really are a douchebag." She also met Bernard saying goodbye to Alan and found him to be a cute man.

Catherine was comic relief in the next few episodes, first as she greeted the firm's staff by handing out cookies and opinions in equal measure. When law partner Lori Colson, played by Monica Potter, said she disliked comments about her hair color, Catherine devilishly purred back, "I was just trying to make conversation, and I assumed you didn't want me to go anywhere near your eyebrows."

She tried to suck up to the firm's leader, Shirley Schmidt, portrayed by Candice Bergen, by standing next to her. When Shirley asked why, Catherine said, "With me by your side, dear, you almost look young."

"I have no idea who you are, but I like you," Shirley responded.

On the next episode, Catherine told Alan that while one of his appointments fell through, two policemen were ready to arrest him for instigating a bar fight the previous evening. As the men took Alan away, Catherine crowed, "Not to worry, dear, I'll cancel the rest of your day!"

Catherine became more enmeshed in drama in the following episode, as a nervous Alan told her to prevent a visit by his murdering former client Bernard. She wanted Bernard to come to her church and convert to Christianity. Learning of her offer, Alan warned Catherine not to befriend Bernard based on his previous behavior, cruelly adding that "If there was ever a person who deserved a whack on the head …" Catherine grimaced and walked away.

When Bernard came to take Catherine out to eat later in the episode and Alan objected, Bernard yelled, "Go screw yourself!" Catherine told her boss to leave Bernard alone. But Alan dismissed Bernard as a serial killer, much to Catherine's disgust.

Catherine the Killer

In the *Boston Legal* second season opener on September 27, 2005, Alan warned Catherine again about Bernard. "Your little boyfriend is twisted," he said. "Trust me when I tell you he's not finished killing." Those words rang in her ears in the next episode as she and Bernard watched coverage of a murder trial on TV.

"I must say, I always fantasized about my murder trial," Bernard said. "I was a little disappointed I didn't get one."

"You want to go to prison?" asked Catherine.

"No, but the excitement, being at the center of it. I think next time I'll leave little clues, like that BTK killer. Maybe little hints to make it fun."

"What do you mean, next time?" said Catherine, her voice and eyebrows simultaneously rising.

"Oh, I just like to daydream," said Bernard. "It's my little Walter Mitty self, I guess."

"Bernard, you seriously don't think you'd ever kill again, do you?"

"Of course not! But I miss—it was very empowering, taking a life. It's godlike," he said. Catherine appeared stunned by that statement. "I wouldn't do it again, of course," he added as she looked disturbed.

Catherine reported his statements to Detective John Stephenson, played by John Thaddeus, and added, "The whole reason I introduced him to God was to go in another direction." But the detective said the information was problematic, given her relationship with Bernard could be considered an extension of attorney-client privilege.

When Bernard ate with Catherine later that week, he detected an edge in her demeanor. "What are you going to do, whack me on the head?" she growled at him.

Bernard claimed his "godlike" statement was in jest, but she disagreed and added "I think maybe our friendship should take a little break."

"You can't do that," Bernard responded. He protested that he needed her in his life.

Catherine gave him a reprieve. Another night later they watched more murder trial coverage and Bernard remarked, "See, the thing is, once you got the taste of it, it's really hard to go back to an ordinary life. That's what I struggle with, I think."

Suddenly Catherine smashed the back of his head with a skillet. "Better?" she cooed.

As Bernard staggered to sit up, Catherine hit him again and killed him. "As God is my witness—my only witness," she murmured.

On the next episode, detective Stephenson asked Catherine when she last saw Bernard, who had vanished for a week. She said she decided to end her friendship with him at that time.

Catherine then told Shirley Schmidt about her relationship with Bernard and added, "I bludgeoned him with his own skillet."

"Catherine, you killed a man?!" Shirley responded with astonishment.

"Yes, dear! If only your prolonged staring could bring him back!" said Catherine, dripping with condescension.

Shirley consulted with her partners, who recommended Catherine confess to the murder. She refused. "Because the worst thing that could happen to this firm is for it to become public that one of your employees murdered a client, and you sat on the information," Catherine said. "I may not be a lawyer, but it seems to me that if I confess, it might make things easier for you."

Catherine demanded Alan represent her. She was upset when Shirley said Alan was vacationing in Canada while she was locked in jail and charged in the murder.

In the meantime, Shirley pled self-defense for her client and asked for a speedy trial given Catherine's age. The hearing's tense atmosphere broke when Catherine raised her hand and asked the judge, "Is it possible to request the Robert Blake jury?"

Defending Catherine

When Alan returned, he defended Catherine first by poking holes in Stephenson's claim of telling "the whole truth" about the case. He then put Catherine on the stand to explain why she befriended Bernard.

"I felt at his core he wasn't evil. I also thought I could help him by introducing him to Jesus Christ our Savior."

"Was he open to that?" Alan asked.

"Not terribly. He thought it would make him look like a bad Jew."

Catherine recounted how she went to the police with no help and thought that he might track her down if she left. "The way he talked, Bernie had a third strike coming," she added.

The judge allowed D.A. Valerie Murrow, played by Lisa Kaminir, to make Catherine reenact the murder. She knocked the mannequin's head into Alan's hands with the pan. He then recommended that she plead guilty. "Catherine, I'm not sure I can win this," he said. Catherine asked him to keep trying.

In his summation, Alan said, "Catherine Piper tried law and order. She was scared for her life. She did fear for the safety of others. And in the heat of that fear, she swung that skillet, accomplishing in the process something the police couldn't. She got the bad guy."

He clarified that he was not endorsing becoming a vigilante, just that Catherine at her age shouldn't be jailed. "Catherine Piper, in all her fear, acted in a very human way. She's here now, asking you to do the same," he concluded.

When Alan returned to his seat, Catherine whispered, "I thought you'd be better." But waiting for the verdict, she did thank Alan. The jury found Catherine not guilty.

"I think I might actually cry," she said. "You know, in all the time I've known you, Alan, I don't think I've hugged you."

"We need to fix that," he said as they embraced. He told his boss Denny Crane afterward he really cared about Catherine.

"There was a trial case on *Boston Legal*," recalled Phoef Sutton of Betty on this episode. "And David Kelley would always give huge speeches in that James Spader would have a two-page monologue ... And of course, she had a huge speech because she was on trial for murder. And everybody would go up constantly on the lines, because you can't remember that much stuff. Everybody except her. She did not go up. Ever. And I don't know how old she was at that time, but she was way older than everybody else. She was such a pro."

Catherine Returns as a Client

The joy of acquittal did not last long for Catherine. In the next episode, Shirley Schmidt fired Catherine as Alan's secretary without his knowledge. "However willing we are to relax the rules around here, we simply cannot have administrative staff killing clients," she said.

"Alan, I've been Schmidt-canned!" Catherine exclaimed when she saw her attorney.

He confronted Shirley, who said, "She needed to be fired. I decided to spare you the dirty work. Alan, she went to the police to turn in a client she subsequently murdered. If we're to maintain any integrity as a law firm ..." Alan interrupted Shirley, but she insisted it was better that she fire Catherine so that the latter would always cherish him.

That belief came to fruition a few months later. Catherine brandished a gun at a clerk, robbed a convenience store and deliberately smiled into the surveillance camera. After calling Alan as her attorney when arrested, she told him, "In a way, I suppose, this is all your fault."

An indignant Alan asked how he was responsible. "You said you would hire me as your personal assistant after the firm fired me. And I took you at your lying word!" she shot back.

He apologized but questioned why she committed a crime. "What else was I going to do? A gal's got to eat," she said. "And robbery isn't as bad as killing a man. And you got me off on that!"

Alan bribed the clerk and then talked with Catherine the next day. "Can we use osteoporosis as a defense?" she asked, adding she could fake the condition.

He later told her he dismissed her case and gave her a check for $3,000. "I hope you're not expecting sex for this!" she said indignantly.

"I am not. Consider it back pay," he responded.

That night, Catherine robbed the same store again and got in jail. "I certainly have a lack of impulse control," she told Alan when he visited her cell.

Alan told Assistant D.A. Holly Raines, played by Ana Ortiz, the reason behind Catherine's recent attempted larcenies. "It was about getting my attention," he said. "And she got it."

Holly agreed to give Catherine probation if Alan got her a job interview at his law firm. At dinner, he told Catherine he found her a better job. She became the firm's new sandwich cart vendor.

Catherine returned a month later on March 21, 2006, and forced Alan to intervene again when she attempted to liberate her friend Adele Freeman, played by Norma Michaels, from an assisted living center. A conservator, Donald Wharton, played by Matt Malloy, had gained control of Adele's estate without her permission.

"Catherine, if you knew this injustice was being done to Adele, why didn't you simply call me before you attempted to kidnap her?" he asked.

"Well, dear, you'd helped me out on those two convenience store robberies, not to mention the murder. I didn't want to think I was becoming a bother," replied Catherine.

Donald didn't know Adele's eye color or her late son's name but insisted she needed his help for clinical depression. A judge assigned Adele a court-appointed psychiatrist to examine Adele and reconvene six weeks after the examination. Alan objected, particularly with Donald remaining as her conservator.

After the hearing, Donald told Alan he would get his own high-priced lawyer using Adele's money to fight for her custody. Adele then told Catherine and Alan that Donald was trying to sell her house.

"This man is pure evil!" Catherine said. "Alan, you've got to get that creative brain of yours to work and stop him."

"Yes, I do," he responded smoothly.

That night, two thugs tied up Donald and stole some file boxes. Alan arrived with a release form for Donald to sign if he wanted to be free. The scared conservator acquiesced.

The ethically dubious Alan was surprised how swiftly and violently he made the quick fix and wondered who he was becoming as a person. But that issue didn't bother Catherine, who was happy he helped her once again.

Catherine's Last Stands on the Stand

Apart from a cameo on October 10, 2006, Catherine didn't show up on *Boston Legal* until two years later during its final season. Producer-director Bill D'Elia said the disappearance wasn't due to any complaints about the character, as "Most viewers loved her." Even so, given the large ensemble of regulars, they didn't consider making Catherine a regular character on the series.

On October 27, 2008, with Alan out of town, Shirley had to defend Catherine, who claimed she was a victim of "terrible malpractice" from a hospitalized doctor. "I only meant to set fire to his office," Catherine said. "How would I know he would run back inside?"

"So, basically you committed murder," said Shirley.

"Well, aren't you a defendant's dream?" snarked Catherine.

As the physician didn't die, Catherine was charged with attempted murder. She claimed her doctor gave her a drug that gave her a heart attack while getting kickbacks from the drug maker. She asked for a speedy trial. "After all, I'm old. As you are, dear," she told Shirley.

Shirley won the case, as the jury found Catherine not guilty by reason of temporary insanity. "Thank you, Shirley! You've been almost like a big sister to me," said Catherine.

"I'm touched," Shirley winced in response.

Catherine's final appearance was on December 1, 2008. After some repartee with Carl Sack, played by John Larroquette, a relatively new senior partner, Catherine said she was desperate for activity but couldn't find work due to her age. "I was thinking, if I were to come up with something I could sue for, something legitimate, and it could make the firm money ...." she said.

After some back and forth with Carl, he considered suing the TV networks for not catering to people over fifty. He argued before Judge Clark Brown, portrayed by Henry Gibson, that the demographic was ignored despite huge buying power.

"All the networks want to do is skew younger. Kids' shows for kids. The only show unafraid to have its stars over fifty is *Bos* ..." Carl caught himself before adding and looking directly into the camera, "Gee, I can't say it. Would, umm, break the [fourth] wall."

Catherine flirted with the judge during lunch to his shock until Carl intervened and apologized. Moved by Carl's arguments against ageism, Judge Brown ruled in favor of Catherine.

"You know, old people have active sex lives, too. My trailer or yours?" Catherine grinned as Carl left and the episode ended. The series went off ABC the following week.

Ironically, consulting producer Phoef Sutton said the demise of *Boston Legal* in 2008 was in part due to older viewers. "The network never really embraced the show. I think they were always looking for a reason to cancel it, partially because it skewed kind of older and because it was a show on ABC and they didn't own the show."

With the cancellation of *Boston Legal*, Betty ended playing a character she admitted she enjoyed. Piper has lived on since then. The image of her waving a gat at the clerk from 2006 has become a popular meme to show Betty as a tough old lady who takes no guff.

"Working with Betty was a remarkable experience," said producer-director Bill D'Elia. "She was always prepared and pleasant on set. No matter the hour—and we worked some late nights—she was always the consummate professional. She knew her lines, knew her character, took direction, and constantly belied her age and was full of energy. If she were ever to forget a line of dialog, she apologized to everyone and was embarrassed to have done so. Everyone loved her. Directing her was a joy."

Catherine Piper was endearing, infuriating, and unsettling to watch because of Betty's hard work. Even though not a regular, Betty played an integral role in the progression of *Boston Legal*. Her last few appearances as Piper concurred with Betty playing an even more dramatic TV role.

Getting Bold and Beautiful

Until January 1988, Betty had avoided acting in daytime soap operas. With low ratings for its serials, NBC added a contest featuring the star of its nighttime hit *The Golden Girls* to entice viewers to watch. "Where's Betty?" required players to count the number of episodes with guest appearances by Betty acting on *Days of Our Lives*, *Another World*, and *Santa Barbara* that month. The players whose correct answers were drawn won some color televisions and a trip to Hawaii. Unfortunately for the network, the event didn't boost the shows' ratings in the long term.

That promotion was all Betty did in the genre for nearly nineteen years afterward until she accepted an offer from *The Bold and the Beautiful* in 2006. The serial stood out from its competitors at the time in two ways: The show ran thirty minutes daily rather than an hour, and its setting was a real place.

"It really is supposed to take place in Los Angeles," noted Michael Stich, the primary director for *The Bold and the Beautiful* from 1987 through 2019. "And because of that, we have a lot of different guest stars on the show. Sometimes we would call them by their real names, like Charlton Heston was on as a neighbor."

As Stich recalled, the notion to approach Betty to be part of *The Bold and the Beautiful* came directly from Bradley Bell, the show's executive producer and head writer. "With Betty White, I might've heard it at a party that Bradley Bell knew her or met her before she was cast. And I knew he was trying to get her in something. It could've been anything, just a walk-on rather than something significant.

"So, I knew that she was coming on because he had called me at home and said, 'I found a great part for Betty White! What do you think?' And he started telling me."

The part was that of Ann Douglas, mother of Stephanie Douglas Forrester, who Susan Flannery had portrayed as the soap's matriarch since the start of *The Bold and the Beautiful*. Previously, Stephanie had claimed Ann was dead. Bell's idea was to reunite the women and explore the dynamics that had led to their decades of estrangement.

"I just thought it sounded like a great story," Stich said after hearing Bell's proposal. He thought it would be an easy sell for Betty, as well. "I knew she was going to be on. I knew it was going to be a great part."

When Betty agreed to play Ann, she signed on to do more than just her longest dramatic role on television. She also faced her most intense acting work schedule ever due to the tight requirements for producing a daily soap opera. Consider the work involved ahead of getting an episode of *The Bold and the Beautiful* on the air.

Prepping for Betty

By the time Betty joined *The Bold and the Beautiful* in 2006, the soap taped two episodes a day on a faster schedule than when Stich first joined the series. Although he was the primary director for the soap opera since it began in 1987, Stich had some assistance nearly two decades later.

"There was no way one director could do all the episodes," Stich said. "There were primarily three directors who did most of the shows. Other directors did a show or two a month. So, usually I did between two to four episodes a week."

That setup didn't mean Stich had a day or two off each week when he was not directing. "I would be prepping half of the time at home, blocking the scripts, getting everything ready before going into the studio," he said. "So I'd usually be in the studio for a couple of days out of the week and I'd be shooting two episodes each day when I went in. It was a pretty packed week."

Stich said preparation for future episodes was a crucial element for planning his direction on *The Bold and the Beautiful*. "There would be a production meeting once a week, and those production meetings would usually—because some people couldn't get in—they mostly ended up being a teleconference call, like in a boardroom with the other departments. And I would be at home … Everyone had a script discussing the following week's production. That would be a chance for any department to take care of things plot-wise, like lighting."

The creative producer of *The Bold and the Beautiful* originally was William J. "Bill" Bell. "He was great," Stich said. When Bill Bell died in 2005, his son Bradley Bell, took over as the soap's executive producer and head writer after having contributed scripts to the series from the start.

"The writers worked through him," Stich said of Bradley's role in the scripts. "And Bradley did the same thing that Bill used to do. Bill used to put out outlines for all the scripts. So, there was maybe a two-page description to the writer of what each scene should be, what the character development should be, what kind of things we wanted to make sure would unfold in the script.

"And so I would have those outlines in addition to the final script to be able to look at. So that would help a lot, to be able to understand. Sometimes maybe the writer didn't make it that clear that something needs to be noticed or addressed or concentrated on. I could at least know myself to make things important if I didn't see it in the script."

After the production meeting, Stich began blocking the script. "When I'm sitting at home, it's a very strange job, because when I'm blocking the script, I'm totally by myself. It's just me and the script. And it would take me twelve to fourteen hours to block each script.

"The way I like to do it is I like to do the whole thing in the actual order that the show is, because I think it's important to know what pace and energy should be happening in which particular scene … So I block each scene in my head. I write it all out. I do maps on the backs of pages to show where the characters are in the scene. And then we have to block all the camera shots."

Stich said this extensive preproduction became a necessity due to increased demands for producing more shows as quickly as possible. "It's one of those things where if we had more time, it wouldn't have to be so detailed. But as it got tighter and tighter on the budget in doing this kind of a show, I found that you had to be more precise, because there really wasn't time to play around.

"So I just got more into the details being written down, so I could at least remember when it was all broken down and then put that into the order I've been describing to you, doing a bunch of scenes in a row that would be spread out all over the show."

Stich added that regarding the production schedule for *The Bold and the Beautiful* "It's gotten much more—efficient, is the word they prefer to call it At the time, I didn't think we had enough time to do it properly, and now they're quicker than that. I was working with Betty probably shooting sixty pages a day. Now they'll shoot between ninety-five to 100 pages today, which is insane."

Betty's Workday as She Became Ann Douglas

When Betty came to tape *The Bold and the Beautiful* around 8 a.m. at Stage 32 at CBS Television City in Hollywood, one of the first persons she met was Stich. "I would see her once before makeup and hair and anything," he said. "And the next time I would see her, she was actually involved in shooting the scene."

Stich admitted being a little starstruck when he initially encountered Betty. "She's one of those people that when you see her, it's like, 'Oh my God, that's Betty White!' And literally that's what I said. ... She was sitting in a chair, and I walked up to her with all the crew and other people around me, and I said, 'You're Betty White!' And she said, 'Yes I am!' And I said, 'Glad to meet you.' She's just one of those people that puts a smile on your face. There's something about her. She's very unassuming."

With the pleasantries out of the way, Stich began the long day of shooting an episode of *The Bold and the Beautiful* by blocking the scenes to be shot by the cameras.

"The way we shot the show is, we would have all of the sets that were going to be used in those two episodes all set up in a single studio. So it was pretty tightly packed, but it was all set up so you could move from one set to another. Typically we would shoot every scene that was needed to be done in that set and then go to the next set. Sometimes we would go out of order, whatever would make it most efficient.

"So, what I would do is have a blocking meeting with the actors. The actors are not in wardrobe or makeup or anything like that. They're really just talking about basic things with the scene. You know, blocking is what ideas I have and what ideas they may have." Usually during this point, Stich came out of the control room to talk to the actors and crew and straighten out any issues they wanted to discuss.

"Then we go into each set, the actors would be there reading for me. And we would have a discussion about all of the scenes and anything they wanted to talk about to the writers or producers in blocking." Stich said Betty never complained or worried about anything asked of her.

Some soap opera directors give blocking instructions to actors based on their characters' names. Regarding his approach, Stich said, "I thought it was proper respect to call them by their real names. My notes to the camera operators would be the character names." So, he would say "Betty, go to the couch on that line" to the star and "Do a head shot of Ann before she goes to the couch" to a cinematographer.

"Then, the next time I would see them, they would actually be ready to shoot those scenes with the camera. After meeting with the actors, we would start shooting around 9:30 or 10 a.m. That's when the whole crew is there. You've got about ninety people on the crew involving all the departments."

Back into the booth to start shooting the scene, Stich aimed to tape each scene close to how it would run on air. "We would try to do it in one take. Sometimes we'd have to do pickups if we weren't able to get it in one take. We probably averaged three to four takes of each scene. We would usually want to do the whole thing top to bottom, but technical challenges sometimes occurred."

Even with all the planning and hard work by everyone for shooting, "It's usually a long day," Stich said. "It could go at least twelve hours, so you could be shooting until 9, 10 p.m. It's pretty typical. And we just kind of worked our way through all the scenes."

The First Meeting with Ann Douglas

Betty debuted as Ann Douglas on *The Bold and the Beautiful* on December 1, 2006. In that episode, Stephanie Douglas Forrester received psychiatric treatment from Dr. Taylor Hayes, played by Hunter Tylo. Stephanie had marital problems because her husband, Eric Forrester, played by John McCook, resented her desire to control everything.

Taylor diagnosed the root of Stephanie's problem as overcompensating for having dealt with an erratic, abusive father named John who left her feeling powerless. During their session, Stephanie revealed she had lied about Ann dying. Ann had blamed John's injuries to Stephanie on her daughter's behavior, so Stephanie cut her out of her family's life totally. "After my father died, I swore I'd never see her again," confessed Stephanie.

Stephanie also told Taylor that her sister, Pamela Douglas, played by Alley Mills, stayed with Ann in Chicago, Illinois, when their father died because Ann had no one else willing to do so. Taylor informed Stephanie that if she wanted to save her marriage, she had to confront her mother about her father's abuse. Stephanie agreed and phoned Pamela about coming to visit her and Ann and bringing Eric with her.

"I was wondering why Stephanie would decide to visit after all these years. Probably doesn't think I have much time left," a skeptical, bitter Ann confided to Pamela. She told Pamela not to put out the good china because "She's completely cut me off from her life, from my own grandchildren. Now, is that what family does?"

When Stephanie and Eric arrived, Ann acted civil until mentioning Stephanie's family. That topic prompted Stephanie to shock Ann by saying, "I told them you were dead, Mother." Pamela and Eric insisted Ann hear Stephanie out. A frank and somewhat bruising conversation ensued.

Initially Ann kept changing topics and even called Stephanie "morbidly sensitive" before the latter blurted out, "Why did you let him hurt me that way? Always when he drank, which seemed to be almost every night!"

"Back then, children disciplined their children when they deserved it. If your father ever struck you, you must've deserved it," Ann responded.

Pamela told Ann that she believed John abused Stephanie, but Ann remained steadfast in her denial. "Your father worked hard to give us a gracious life!" she exclaimed. She addressed Stephanie directly and said, "This fantasy of torture, this can only be for Eric's benefit."

"No child deserves that, Mother!" responded an angry Stephanie.

Ann accused Stephanie of trying to rob her memories of "the only man I ever loved, still loved." Stephanie retorted that she never got enough love from Ann, who then allowed that "It was a great disappointment to your father that his firstborn wasn't a son ... Your father wanted you to be a leader of men."

But Ann added to Stephanie, "You want to blame me—and worse yet your father, who can't defend himself—for the fact that you can't get along in life. Your husband can't manage you, you're a trial to your children. That's how you've always been ... Shame on you!"

"No, Ann, shame on you!" answered Eric. He defended his wife while Ann kept denying any abuse ever happened. "While you were plugging your ears and covering your eyes, she built herself from the ground up. And the real tragedy here is that you will never know what a magnificent job she did of it."

After Eric and Stephanie left, Ann told Pamela she would never forgive Stephanie for what she said about her father. She also requested that Pamela play her some music, and her daughter did so. Tellingly, the song was "Whatever Will Be (Que Sera Sera)."

"It's a pretty heavy story," director Michael Stich recalled of Betty's debut. "When Susan Flannery's character says these things to her about what happened to her as a child, she has to be very forceful. And the audience doesn't know whether Ann was saying the truth or Stephanie was saying the truth. Because she was so good at it. So, it was really important that she would be able to pull this off."

Acceptance and Denial for Ann

Ann reappeared unexpectedly on December 14, 2006, when Pam brought her to Los Angeles for a family visit. Stephanie was indignant as Ann asked for a civil conversation with her daughter.

While Ann got settled, Stephanie told Pam, "You ambushed me."

"You wouldn't have seen us if I told you we were coming," Pam said.

"You're damn right!" responded Stephanie.

"I know she's hurt you," Pam said. "You're angry. You have every right to be. And Mom knows it. She's been different since you came to Chicago. Your visit had a real impact on her, Steph."

Ann then told Stephanie her visit to Chicago had an impact. "The things you said really got to me, Stephanie. Truthfully, they bothered me, hurt me." She acknowledged that her husband did hit Stephanie and she was in denial about it and was scared.

"I couldn't look at your bruises, your welts. I should've said something. I should've done something." Ann apologized for her failures as a mother and begged for forgiveness.

Stephanie was not having any of it. "You actually said I should appreciate that he was strict with me," she said.

"Steph, she didn't mean that," Pamela said.

"She said it," Stephanie responded.

Ann said it was a shock for her to see Stephanie and couldn't tell the truth. She added that she just wanted forgiveness and to make peace. Stephanie stood firm.

"You had thirty years, Mother. You could've come to me. But you didn't. And when I finally came to you, what did you do? You denied it all over again."

"But I'm admitting now," Ann said.

"Well, the damage has been done. Not just to me, but to my family. My children. My children are my blessing, and you don't deserve to be part of our lives."

The back and forth culminated with Stephanie telling Ann, 'I don't want you anywhere near them [her grandchildren]." Stephanie proclaimed herself a Forrester and not a Douglas.

"I have accepted your apology," Stephanie said. "I can't forgive you. Now I want you to leave." Ann and Pamela did so.

Throughout the confrontation, Betty's Ann was thoroughly sympathetic while admitting to being flawed. Her dramatic interpretation and commitment to character impressed her director on *The Bold and the Beautiful*, Michael Stich.

"I didn't know when I first met her how she would be in this," he said. "I don't think anybody did. Because it's kind of a departure from other things she's done. It was a lot to play. And she was amazing.

"She had a script, was taking down notes, asking questions, talking about it. It was important to her that we get it right.

"And Susan Flannery is a very strong person in real life. It's not easy to do a scene bouncing off of her. You've got to hold your own, and she did. They respected each other."

Stich also complimented the work of Alley Mills as Stephanie's sister Pam. "It was great seeing the three of them working together, because they really wanted to make it work, and they knew that it was heavy stuff. It was a really great experience."

Twas the Season

Stephanie mistakenly believed Ann was out of her life when she addressed the Forresters' Christmas Eve party during an episode aired December 20, 2006. "The Douglases—my family—never bonded the way we have as Forresters," she told those assembled and added, "You're the only family I ever wanted."

Her jovial mood vanished when unbeknownst to her, Eric invited Pamela and Ann as Christmas guests. Ann told Stephanie, "I told you before, Stephanie, I need to tell you again. I am so sorry for what I did, sweetheart. I want to say it in front of your whole family. I am so sorry.

"And I shamed you for my failures as a mother. If the process of healing could begin, if there were something we could do. That's why, when Eric called, I allowed myself to hope.

"I knew it was unlikely. I knew you'd react this way. But I had to see you, darling. Every Christmas for thirty years, I've wondered what it would be like to celebrate with my family. Both my daughters. My beautiful grandchildren. My great-grandchildren."

Ann began to weep, but her grandson Ridge Forrester, played by Ronn Moss, sharply told her, "You lost your place here a long time ago."

"Just go, please," added Stephanie. "Just go."

But Ann stayed to plead her case. "It tore me up when your father hit you. I wanted so desperately to do something. But I was frozen. The dutiful wife. Never a question. Why didn't I go in that room and stop it? Taking out his drunken rage on my innocent girl. I know I don't deserve your forgiveness, but I can't live another day without you! You opened my eyes to the truth, the ugliness of the past. I refused to see it. But I see it now … God help me, I did nothing!"

Ann nearly collapsed, but Eric saved her. Eric implored Stephanie to forgive Ann, but Ridge objected. Dr. Taylor Hayes went to talk in private with Stephanie, her psychiatric patient, while Pamela addressed the Forresters.

"Do you think this is what your grandmother and I were hoping for? My mother has been separated from her daughter for over thirty years. Yes, I know, she should've protected Stephanie. I know she failed as a mother. But she's served her sentence. I know, because I served every day of it with her. My mother's not the monster. My father is."

Ann said she understood everyone blaming her because of Stephanie's strength. "Why couldn't I have been more like her?! Why?! I love your mother as much as you do, but I didn't, I couldn't, oh God, I'm so sorry!" she cried.

Stephanie finally relented on the December 22, 2006 episode, as she heard her family sing "What Child is This?" with Eric playing the piano and one of her grandchildren and, therefore, Ann's great-grandchild, held Ann's hand.

"All right, mother. All right. I forgive you," Stephanie said.

"Oh, my darling girl!" exclaimed Ann. She celebrated a joyous Noel with the Forresters.

Introducing the Mischievous Ann

After playing Ann on *The Bold and the Beautiful* for twelve episodes in 2006, Betty continued in the role for a few times early in the following year. These appearances allowed for a little of Betty's impish humor to seep into the characterization.

For example on February 8, 2007, Eric told Ann he wanted her and Pamela to move to Los Angeles, but Ann said no. In a clever *Golden Girls* reference, when Pamela mentioned she tried to get Ann a place to stay in Palm Beach, Ann scoffed, "At one of those golden years places? Oh, I can't abide old ladies!" Ann ended up convincing Eric to give her a car and a driver, a new wardrobe and even an appearance in one of his fashion shows.

Nearly three weeks later, Ann announced to Stephanie she was determined to stay with the Forresters in their house in Los Angeles rather than return to Chicago. Stephanie was resolute that while Pamela could do so, Ann could not.

"Well, I've done my penance. I have grandchildren and great-grandchildren who like and appreciate me. Why should I give that up?" argued Ann.

"There is no room for you in my home, mother."

"There is nothing but room!" Ann shot back.

Stephanie emphasized that she was head of the family. Ann responded by questioning the status of Stephanie's marriage with Eric. Sick of her mother's lying and controlling nature, Stephanie successfully forced Ann out.

Still, Ann and Stephanie had forged a bond with each other, and Ann made a couple of guest shots to help her daughter throughout 2007 and 2008. Then came a real shocker from *The Bold and the Beautiful* executive producer and head writer Bradley Bell in 2009: Ann was going to be killed off. And, in a television first, Betty White would be playing a death scene.

"We were joking to Brad, 'Don't do this to Betty! Don't do this to Betty!'" recalled director Michael Stich, who like the rest of the crew of *The Bold and the Beautiful* loved working with the actress. But Bell held firm and, as Stich admitted, "That was another great story to play."

The Passing of Ann

In a four-episode arc starting on November 18, 2009, Ann flew to California and took a cab to the Paradise Cove pier in Malibu, where Stephanie and Pamela had previously taken her to Christmas dinner. Ann dumped her prescribed drugs into the sea, then beckoned her daughters to join her and recounted the Christmas visit lovingly. "The moment I stepped on that pier, the ocean, the sea breeze in my face, that salty smell ..."

"So, you flew 2,000 miles just to smell the salty air?" asked Pamela.

"And to see my two wonderful daughters! In a place as close to heaven as I can imagine," Ann added. She then confessed her real reason, that she was dying of advanced pancreatic cancer.

"In the time I do have, I don't want any whining. I want some happy moments with my daughters. And the ocean, sea breeze in my face. Oh, and that smell." She had her daughters hold her hands while humming "Beautiful Dreamer."

Stephanie and Pamela insisted they needed to take her to see specialists, but Ann strenuously objected. "I've had enough of doctors and needles and pills. This is my life and my death, and I will handle it the way I want. I will not go to the hospital. That is my one wish, and you will honor it!"

As they planned to take Ann home, she winced, and they all stopped on a bench. Ann admitted that she had no more pain medication. "Maybe you can get me some of that medical marijuana," she said.

At home, Ann acknowledged to Pamela that she forced her to take care of her and waste her youth before she suddenly grimaced in pain. Medics called to the house told Pamela her mother was having a blood clot and needed to go to the hospital for treatment. Pamela reluctantly agreed.

Livid about Pamela violating the promise to their mother, Stephanie told Ann's attending physician Dr. Lewis, played by Yvette Freeman, "You're keeping her here against her will, Dr. Lewis. We are perfectly capable of making her comfortable at home."

"Can you really?" said Dr. Lewis, arguing that she was trying to save Ann's life and relieve the pain before allowing that to happen. Pamela had the legal power to move Ann home, but she decided to have Ann treated for the embolism in her lung first.

When Ann awakened, she told Stephanie, "I was an awful mother. If there is a hell, I don't think I'll go there if you forgive me." Dr. Lewis then confided to Stephanie and Pamela that a vessel had burst in Ann and the internal bleeding could not be stopped.

As Ann neared death, her daughters brought her to Paradise Cove. Regaining consciousness, Ann realized where she was and murmured, "Good girls."

"Don't leave us," whispered Pamela.

But Stephanie told her, "It's okay. You can go." Hearing those words, Ann closed her eyes and passed away. An ethereal vision of a woman appeared on screen walking down the pier before the episode ended.

"Brad wanted to do it and talked about it with us beforehand,' said director Michael Stich about directing the sequence with producer Cynthia Popp under the guidance of executive producer and head writer Bradley Bell. "It was a beautiful moment as opposed to a sad moment."

Stich added that Bell made some allowances in the production schedule, given Betty's advanced age, to film the death sequence on location. "He understood when certain things needed to take more time. ... I think all the scenes Betty was in were like that. They were heavy dramatic scenes, and they really required more time than normal to be right. And we were given that."

The beach footage was filmed in advance of Betty's home and hospital scenes.

"The actual last day was the hospital scene," said Stich. "She was great. And I really respected her as an actress. Talking to her between scenes, she was very into it.

"When she came back, now she was in this condition where she had to be taken care of and be in a hospital bed. It was interesting how she played that, because if you're truthful to the character, you see that's not easy to do. She was great at that. The whole ending was interesting, with her not wanting to die in a hospital room."

On her last day playing Ann, the crew of *The Bold and the Beautiful*, along with Susan Flannery and Alley Mills, threw a party for her. Susan noted that Betty would soon receive a lifetime achievement award from the Screen Actors Guild, as well as the Jane Goodall Foundation.

The crew also gave her a mockup photo of what a Douglas family picture would have looked like decades earlier using old pictures of Betty, Susan, and Alley. Betty loved it.

A few news outlets reported Betty ending her occasional role as a major entertainment story. In interviews, Betty downplayed her contribution to *The Bold and the Beautiful*. "I didn't realize I was a member of the OAS—the Over Acting Society," she cracked to Entertainment Tonight Canada.

But Stich was impressed by what Betty brought to the soap opera. "Of all the different guest stars we had on the show, without a doubt she had the biggest role to play, and she was great at it."

After her work on *The Bold and the Beautiful*, it looked as if Betty would go into the 2010s on a less grueling schedule. She would—but not for long. Despite her best efforts not to do so, Betty would be starting her seventeenth regular role on a national TV series after she turned eighty-eight years young.

Chapter Twelve
Betty the Added Attraction

Who else but Betty could look cool in a suit with drumsticks at age eighty-nine? Here her character Elka joined her housemates from left to right Joy (Jane Leeves), Melanie (Valerie Bertinelli), and Victoria (Wendie Malick) to compete in the "Battle of The Bands" episode of *Hot in Cleveland* that aired July 6, 2011.
Photo: Copyright TV Land / courtesy Everett Collection.

Three middle-aged women and one senior citizen lived together. Their love lives and misadventures formed the crux of the plots. Betty White was a regular.

The reason why *Hot in Cleveland* sounds akin to *The Golden Girls* is that the latter inspired the former. Suzanne Martin, a writer and producer who earned two Emmy wins in 1997 and 1998 as a producer on the sitcom *Frasier*, remembered the series due to a sad event that happened on July 22, 2008.

"I was driving to a meeting with Lynda Obst [a fellow producer] to talk about show development ideas, and there was a news announcement that Estelle Getty [who played Sophia on *The Golden Girls*] had died," Martin said. "I started thinking about *The Golden Girls* and how in my mind those women were in their eighties, but actually they were in their fifties and sixties. [Rue McClanahan was fifty-one in the pilot.]

"It got me thinking of what a contemporary *Golden Girls* might be like. And also how every new show was chasing after the same list of unavailable twenty-eight-year-old actors and how wonderful it would be to instead look at the very available list of actors over forty.

"Lynda and I met and talked about it. Also, about how we both liked shows about reinvention, and I said I was always intrigued about the idea that maybe there's some other place in the world you should be—somewhere where what you are is somehow valued more. Also, how people in L.A. feel like when they go home to the small towns they grew up in—they feel younger, thinner, more glamorous. And from that, I came up with the idea for the show.

"It was originally called *GILFS* and we pitched it to CBS Productions [not the network, the studio]. They laughed all the way through the pitch, but then said they couldn't sell it—a group of women over forty wouldn't sell. They asked if I could make them in their thirties, and that seemed silly to me, so I put the project aside.

"Later I had a meeting with Hazy Mills—Sean Hayes and Todd Milliner's production company—and gave them a laundry list of one-line pitch ideas. I left the meeting and a few weeks later got a call from them that they had sold the idea of the women who crash-land in Cleveland to TV Land on the one-line pitch. I wasn't even quite sure what TV Land was."

For those persons uncertain as well, TV Land was a cable and satellite channel launched in 1996 to carry vintage television series from the 1950s through 1970s. By the late 2000s, its shift focused to include more original programming to reach a younger audience, but those offerings were nondescript to most viewers and critics.

TV Land executives were on the lookout for original material that would draw bigger audiences than their initial wan efforts.

"I wrote the pilot for them, and the name was changed to *Hot in Cleveland*," Martin said. "Once we sold it to TV Land, Lynda was no longer involved, but was credited with being part of the creation of the show."

Besides being the creator of *Hot in Cleveland*, Martin was the writer for the pilot and executive producer. She shared the latter title with Sean Hayes and Todd Milliner, who liked the concept of women of a certain age appearing vibrant on TV, and as previously mentioned, Lynda Obst. Now, all they needed was a cast.

Lining Up the Hot Ladies

Milliner claimed to be the one who suggested Betty be part of the series' pilot in the 2015 retrospective episode "Hot in Cleveland: Hot Damn!" Her character, Elka Ostrovsky, would be an antagonist to the women, like Betty was on *The Mary Tyler Moore Show*. However, Elka was much more outspoken, sarcastic and shifty than Sue Ann Nivens ever was.

For the main cast, the executive producers met with actress Jane Leeves, who had worked with Martin on *Frasier*, then Wendie Malick, who had two Emmy nominations for her supporting role on *Just Shoot Me*. Finally, they approached Valerie Bertinelli, who had spent nearly a decade on the sitcom *One Day at a Time* from 1975 through 1984. When Bertinelli learned that "We have Betty White," her reaction to looking at the script was "Oh! I don't have to read it!" The other two actresses signed on, as well.

Betty did the pilot with the provision that it would be a guest shot. "It wasn't that I didn't love the girls or love the show," she explained to Frank Bruni in a 2011 "Times Talk." "There was just no room in my schedule for another series. No way.

"Well, sometimes you'll do a pilot in February and maybe you'll know whether it won or lost by May. Well, they got picked up in three weeks! And the company came to me and said would I do some more, and I said, 'Well, that was the proviso, that I would not.' And I have such a strong backbone. [audience laughter] They picked us up for ten [episodes], and would I do a couple more? I wound up doing all ten."

Without divulging how she, Hayes, and Milliner coaxed Betty to become a regular on *Hot in Cleveland*, Suzanne Martin said, "The ladies had so much fun the week of the pilot filming that there was no question in my mind that Betty would stay."

As for any concerns the producers had about Betty's advanced age handling the rigors of a weekly sitcom, Martin said, "When you cast an eighty-eight year old in a pilot, every single season you think it might be the last. But she kept going and is still going. We really didn't need to make accommodations for Betty. True story: Betty broke her back and was at the table read a few days later. She had difficulties hearing in the later years, so we positioned her close to other characters in scenes, and we had her seated where we could, but it really wasn't an issue."

With all those issues resolved, *Hot in Cleveland* debuted on TV Land on June 16, 2010.

Getting Hot: The First Show

The pilot opened with Betty saying, "*Hot in Cleveland* is recorded in front of a live studio audience." Specifically, the series was filmed in Stage 19 at CBS Studio Center in Studio City.

The first scene had three women from Los Angeles sitting in an airplane bound for Paris. While she was traveling, Melanie Hope Moretti, played by Valerie Bertinelli, learned her ex-husband had a hot new fiancée. She told the news to her on-board friends, Joy Scroggs, played by Jane Leeves, and Victoria Chase, played by Wendie Malick. "She's half my age!" Melanie said.

"Well, darling, that really isn't that young," replied Victoria.

"My *fake* age!" Melanie exclaimed.

"Oh my God, she's a child!" answered Victoria.

Engine trouble forced the plane to make an emergency landing in Cleveland. During the layover, the trio went into a local dive bar and noticed that the men stared at them.

"Everyone's eating and no one's ashamed." noted Victoria.

"I'm going to order chili fries!" said Joy.

Three men invited them to their table. Melanie bonded with Hank, portrayed by John Schneider, and told him she was an author and Joy was a beautician known as the "eyebrow queen of Beverly Hills." Victoria was a former daytime soap opera star.

In their hotel room, Melanie said she was moving to Cleveland after Hank, a plumber, showed her around Cleveland. She signed a lease on a house that cost the same as flying to Paris. Her real estate agent said, "Now, there's just one thing about this place I should mention …"

"Why are you renting to prostitutes?" interjected Elka Ostrovsky, played by Betty White, clad in an all-blue tracksuit. The agent explained that Elka was a caretaker for 50 years who came with the house and stayed in the guest cottage. She briefly told the ladies her life story and noted, "Escaping from the Nazis was the least of my worries."

A stunned Joy asked, "What are you, a hundred?"

"I don't like you," Elka struck back.

Joy mentioned she smelled pot. "What are you, a cop?" asked Elka.

"No."

"Then what's it to you?!"

When Melanie exalted about Hank calling her, Elka said, "That's shameful! I haven't even looked at another man since 1949. When a husband dies, you die." "But you're not dead," said Victoria. "Inside you die," Elka replied. "Oh, you still maintain the shell." She then showed off her body.

Regarding where Hank was taking Melanie, Elka said, "It's where whores go!" While Melanie went to see Hank, Joy and Victoria learned that he had a wife through an online search. "Well, who didn't see that coming?" dryly commented Elka as she walked by.

As Melanie learned the truth about Hank, Victoria was getting parts to play only grandmothers and Joy was losing her celebrity clients. Melanie told them they could change themselves by moving to Cleveland. "You're not going to become one of those women who like themselves, are you?" interrupted Elka. "Because everybody hates those women."

Joining the trio sitting in the porch swing, Elka assessed Melanie's problem of seeing a married man with, "When I was your age, we didn't get into that kind of trouble. My husband was the only man I ever dated."

"Well, didn't you ever want to try another one out? I mean, you know, to compare?" asked Victoria. Elka briefly looked away dreamily before retorting, 'Well, that's a sinful thought!"

"I say, I think we go to that bar where men think we're hot," said Melanie. "I'll drive," says Elka, getting the last word in the pilot.

"I loved the pilot because it was a magical week," said creator Suzanne Martin. "Everyone had so much fun, the audience went crazy. When Betty came out the first time, they applauded for a full three and a half minutes." Maybe that reaction convinced Betty to stay.

Getting Hotter: First Season Highlights

The second show took place the next morning Joy planned to date a younger man. "It's exciting!" she beamed. "It's disgusting!" replied Elka. "You're too old and creaky to be robbing the cradle." When Melanie entered crowing about a great night's sleep and a friendly greeting from a stranger, Elka deflated her bubble with "Who put a quarter in that one?!"

Melanie said she was selling her Los Angeles residence. Then she asked Elka, "How many guys gave you their number last night?" "One or two," Elka grinned, then flashed three fingers and added, "I had to wait till I was eighty-eight to find out that I have game!" Surveying her date prospects, Elka assessed, "Arthur can drive at night, and Larry has that nice full ring of hair. Sal has both original hips. Sexy as hell!"

That evening, Elka learned Joy had a boy when she was young and was worried she might be dating him. When Joy said her date told her she looks thirty-eight years old, Elka snapped back, "Your son is mentally challenged?" Elka snaps back.

In the closer, Joy mused, given her son's age, she may already have grandchildren. "Hey, maybe one of them is old enough for you to date!" said Elka. The girls glared as she asked, "Too soon?"

Melanie matched up Elka with Max, played by Carl Reiner, the only man who knew how to email her back from a senior center, on the third episode. They bonded over mocking Michael Bublé and comparing favorite medications. When he asked for salt, he said, "I'm impressed you can still use that." "Oh, I know how to shake what I've got!" she grinned.

Max kissed Elka. Later, she said she broke off an engagement with Max because he wouldn't go downtown—shopping and restaurants, that is. Then he came by to say, "I'm willing to try going downtown." "You are?" asked a happy Elka. "Only I hope I won't get lost down there!" he added.

Elka gave some choice one-liners in the fourth episode. She recommended Victoria be on top of her date during sex, "So your boobs don't flop to the side and get lost in your back fat." The audience laughed heartily. At the end, she said she could have made Liberace straight.

In the fifth episode, Elka dyed her hair bright red because Max invited her to the Senior Senior Prom. She was worried about fighting over him with Agnes Bradford. "Or should I say, Fat Ass Hagford!" What galled Elka particularly about Bradford was

"She takes hormone replacements. I can't compete with somebody who's doping. I had to take it up a notch."

After seeing how ridiculous her hair looked, Elka planned to avoid the prom until Joy gave her a better hairdo. Max picked her up in a tuxedo, and Elka looked beautiful with him in a new outfit.

Elka confessed in the seventh episode she had danced the previous night with Nick, played by Tim Conway, while she was still seeing Max. She tried to break the burgeoning affair off, but Nick overstimulated his pacemaker as he kissed her hand. He also sent her a poem with flowers.

"I've never been in a triangle before," she told Victoria and Joy. "You girls are slutty, what would you do?" When both Max and Nick invited her to a luau, she decided to go with neither of them.

The next day, the men argued over Elka. "When I get through with you, you'll be eating your bran muffin through a straw!" Max said. Elka broke up the fight and confessed she wanted Max more, but she did offer Nick to join them for the luau.

In the season finale, Elka had to let the women into her basement as a tornado hit, forcing Victoria to miss the Daytime Emmys. While in the basement, the trio saw a lot of jewelry Elka's husband stole as a fence for the mob. "He never let me in here," she said. "I thought he was hiding girlie magazines!"

Joy learned the reason why Elka had smelled like pot in the pilot was because of the smell of the "Polish polish" she used on the bric-a-brac. Meanwhile, Elka found out Joy had sex with a stranger earlier that day and asked, "How much did you pay him?" Joy says she was still shaken from the event, to which Elka responded, "Sounds like you didn't pay him enough!" Ignoring Elka's quips, Joy said she had received a message from her son she had put up for adoption.

Later, Victoria learned her rival, Susan Lucci, had accepted the Emmy Victoria had won. Melanie's cop boyfriend, Pete, arrived to say the storm had ended, but seeing the jewelry, he had to arrest Elka.

The mention of the Emmys in this episode was prescient. Betty earned an Emmy nomination for Outstanding Supporting Actress in a Comedy Series for this first season. Production designer Michael Hynes and set decorator Maralee Zediker won Emmys for their Outstanding Art Direction for a Multi-Camera Series, as well. Thereafter, the series would notch five more Emmy nominations without wins in technical categories.

Additionally, Betty won a Screen Actors Guild award for Outstanding Performance by a Female Actor in a Comedy Series and would be nominated in the same category in 2012 and 2013. With Bertinelli, Levees, and Malick, Betty also got a Screen Actors Guild nomination in 2011 for Outstanding Performance by an Ensemble in a Comedy Series.

The good news extended to the ratings. The premiere generated 6 million viewers. It finished the season at 4.3 million viewers, making *Hot In Cleveland* the top-rated cable sitcom of 2010.

The Evolution of Elka
At the *Hot in Cleveland* PaleyFest discussion in Beverly Hills on March 8, 2011, Betty described how Elka had progressed from the first season into the second one now underway. She also said she was trying to play her role as differently as possible from Sue Ann Nivens on *The Mary Tyler Moore Show* and Rose Nylund on *The Golden Girls*.

"Elka is a smart-ass character, and I'm trying to keep her away from the other two ladies, who I love very much. Thanks to Suzanne [Martin], she gives me such an opportunity. Because as she has evolved, Elka started out, she was sort of a heavy. She was a villain. As it evolved, she has gotten us hooked on these other ladies as they are on each other, so we're really a foursome, we're really a group that would stand up against the world to support each other."

Suzanne later added that she intended to delineate Elka's character development from the start. "It's nice in shows to have a rival, someone to go up against, but ultimately you want everyone to support each other and become a family," she said. "Before the women arrived from L.A., Elka was not really living much of a life, so, as much as she complained about them, they brought fun into her life."

At the start of filming the second season of *Hot in Cleveland*, *The Hollywood Reporter* noted Betty's impressive schedule. After returning from Atlanta, where she filmed the TV movie *The Lost Valentine*, Betty spent the last week of October 2010 recording promos for the series and for the Museum of Broadcast Communications in Chicago for friend and museum founder Bruce DuMont. Betty did these videos along with working for the Greater Los Angeles Zoo, appearing on the cover of *Parade Magazine* to support gay marriage, and performing other activities.

In the first week of November 2010, Betty rehearsed and filmed the second season debut of *Hot in Cleveland* while receiving the Charlie Chaplin Comedian Award at the Britannia Awards. She also released a voice message in support of Missouri's Proposition B on November 1, which would improve the conditions of dog-breeding farms. Voters in the state passed the proposition the next day.

Betty spent the first half of the next week flying to and from Washington, D.C. There, she attended a press conference where she became an honorary forest ranger, a dream she had as a child when women couldn't hold the position. She also participated in the taping of the PBS special *Tina Fey: The Kennedy Center Mark Twain Prize* before returning to California and completing another episode of *Hot in Cleveland*.

The third week in November was less hectic, at least by Betty's standards. All she had to do was tape another *Hot in Cleveland* show plus appear at an evening Screen Actors Guild screening and question-and-answer session about the series. *The Hollywood Reporter* ended its summary there, but presumably Betty took it even easier the next week, as it was the Thanksgiving holiday with no filming for *Hot in Cleveland*.

Elka was in jail in the second season opener with Diane, played by Mary Tyler Moore, who had a big "M" next to her bed. "It stands for murder," she said, adding that was what she was going to do to Elka if she didn't stop playing the harmonica. To make the nod to *The Mary Tyler Moore Show* even clearer, Diane also said she hates spunk, which is what Lou Grant told Mary Richards on the show's first episode.

Victoria complained her assets were frozen as her business manager was jailed when Elka interjected, "You've got to front up and bug down, bitch!" Elka added she now knew how to kill someone with a toothbrush.

The ladies held a garage sale to help raise bail for Elka while Joy faced a deportation challenge and got arrested. "Well, at least we know who the bitch is going to be," Elka told her in their cell.

An anonymous check got enough money for Elka and Joy to get out of jail. It came from their next-door neighbor, Rick, played by Wayne Knight. Joy got engaged to him to stay in the country. He paid bail because he had slept with Elka in the summer of 1997. "Blame it on Coolio!" she said.

In "Bad Bromance," Elka broke up with Max because his son was running for office and she worried that being charged with a crime would hurt his son's chances. She saved the day at the end and noted, "I signed up when my bender was over. That's my screen name, Bend Her Over!" A blooper of Betty laughing repeatedly at that line figured prominently in the series' highlights.

In "Hot for the Lawyer," Elka got an attorney for the mob, Kirk Stark, played by

Mark Deklin, and pretended she was senile as her legal defense during her hearing. Max showed up with Elka's foe Agnes Bradford, played by Millicent Martin, who said they were getting married. Upset with the way her roommates flirted on the stand with Kirk, Elka told the court she was competent for a trial and left to stop Max's wedding. She succeeded, and he proposed to Elka.

The quartet went to Los Angeles in a two-part episode where Elka stalked Robert Redford. In her quest, she got onto the stage of Jimmy Kimmel's show and luxuriated in the chair where Redford had sat. She and Melanie also worked as extras in a Redford movie before realizing they had no scenes with the actor.

In "LeBron is Le Done," a handsome basketball coach with the Cleveland Cavaliers, named Kevin, portrayed by Isaiah Mustafa, offered to buy Melanie a drink when Elka said, "Don't waste your money, she's good to go!" Elka coached Melanie on basketball lingo until Kevin revealed his reverse psychology on LeBron James, which inadvertently led to the latter leaving the team. "I'm going to kill that mother!" she yelled in Melanie's earpiece as Joy held her back. James was a comic topic of several episodes.

Elka broke up with Max in "Elka's Snowbird" after they agreed he wasn't ready for marriage. She had her trial in "Law & Elka," where she flirted with an elderly juror. Elka revealed on the stand that her late husband asked to hide the jewelry in the basement, then made out with the juror in a broom closet. "I'm desperate. Also, it's been a while!" she said to the women.

But the jury found Elka guilty, in part because she triggered the juror to have short-term memory loss by having sex with him. Before her sentencing, Elka went on the lam and hid out with the Amish when her car broke down while heading to Atlanta. The governor's wife, played by Amy Sedaris, pardoned Elka and gave Joy her green card in the following episode.

Joy met her abandoned son Owen, played by Michael McMillian, in "How I Met My Mother." A nervous Joy forced Melanie to switch places with her so Joy could pretend to be American. Victoria pretended to be Owen's British step grandmother and even Elka did a foreign accent to get in on the fun before Joy admitted the truth. Owen would become a recurring character.

Elka was especially spicy in "Battle of the Bands," where she played the drums as the quartet entered an amateur contest. When Melanie said, "And even if we don't

[win], it's an honor just to be entered," Elka responded, "That's what Joy said during Fleet Week!" and did a rim shot.

She was just as frisky when she joined the other women at a gay bar called Nice Buns in "Dancing Queens." Elka decked owner Lydia Domstrovsky, played by Doris Roberts. "Lydia was my best friend until the camping trip, when she slept with my husband!" Lydia admitted it was true and introduced Elka to the result of the affair, Lydia's son Elliot, played by Lex Medlin.

In "Indecent Proposals" Elka made a quick proposal to her friend Fred, played by Buck Henry, but he got pushed into a well. She said she wanted a simple wedding in the next episode until she got a bad spray tan and proclaimed, "I look like a f**king Oompa Loompa!" and became a bridezilla. Disgusted with her behavior, Fred called the wedding off until The Rev. Boyce "The Voice" Ballentine, portrayed by Cedric the Entertainer, and the women showed Elka an elaborate aisle walk. She apologized to Fred, saying she was scared about marrying again.

On "Elka's Wedding Day" she wanted a sign from her late husband that it was okay to marry Fred. When she learned that Fred had wanted the same from his late wife, Elka took that as the sign to wed. As she walked down the aisle, Elka suddenly got proposals from three men, one being Lester, played by Dick Van Patten, then Max, and then—to her shock—her dead husband Bobby, played by Don Rickles. He had been missing for forty years because the mob wanted to kill him and he had to fake his death. A stunned Elka didn't know what to do.

By the end of the second season, the success of *Hot in Cleveland* led TV Land executives to add other comedies designed to appeal to 25- to 54-year-old viewers. "We want to tell stories about characters in their forties and up who are reexamining their lives and starting new chapters," Keith Cox, executive vice president of development and original programming for TV Land, told T.L. Stanley in *The Los Angeles Times*. "And we're casting comedic icons that we know our viewers already love."

To that extent, *Hot in Cleveland* spun off Cedric the Entertainer's Reverend Boyce character into his own series, *The Soul Man*, which ran from 2012 to 2016. Betty appeared as Elka on the episode "All the Way Live" on March 28, 2014, where Elka brought two women as presents for another character's bar mitzvah. "Don't tell his parents, they're not children!" she told Reverend Boyce. In the same episode, Martin Lawrence's character, Rudy, wondered aloud if Elka was Betty White.

Hot Simmers Down Somewhat

By the third season, many viewers noted several guest stars on *Hot in Cleveland* came from classic TV sitcoms. Regarding this development, creator Suzanne Martin said, "Because we wanted Betty to date on the show, we were always on the hunt for age-appropriate men for her, and the ones who were still around were classics sort of by definition. We had so many great guest stars [young and older], and I think it became a fun thing for older stars to be a part of the show.

"And everyone wanted to work with Betty. The one I wish we could have gotten was Dick Van Dyke, but I think he thought some of our storylines were too racy for his brand."

The third season also was where *Hot in Cleveland* frequently reminded viewers of *The Golden Girls* to the former series' detriment. "I knew we would be compared, but I hoped we could do a good enough job to be compared favorably," said Martin. Yet the storylines often mimicked those of *The Golden Girls* very closely and usually fell short in comparison. Consider the following *Hot in Cleveland* plots against earlier *Golden Girls* episodes:

• "Beards" had Elka and the ladies pretend to be lesbians. Dorothy and Blanche pretended to be a couple for Rose's TV show in "Goodbye, Mr. Gordon," on January 11, 1992.

• On "Happy Fat," Elka went skydiving with her boyfriend Roy, played by John Mahoney, to be adventurous. Rose and Miles went skydiving to spice up their relationship in "The Bloom is Off the Rose," on January 5, 1991.

• Roy had a domineering parent who got in the way of his relationships on "One Thing or a Mother." Blanche's boyfriend had a mother interfering with her son's romantic life in "Mother Load," on October 26, 1991.

• Joan Rivers played Elka's twin sister Anka, estranged for forty years over an argument they didn't remember, in "By George I Think He's Got It." Sophia and her sibling Angela had not seen each other for decades over arguments that were misunderstandings in "The Sisters," on January 3, 1987.

• In "Storage Wars," Joy's big fake breasts are exposed, so to speak. Blanche's inflated bosoms popped during an audition in "The Actor," on January 17, 1987.

Between these redos and an unfulfilling season opener on November 30, 2011, where Elka broke up her relationship with Bobby without giving much for Don

Rickles to do, *Hot in Cleveland* appeared to be cooling down. At least one of the guests felt the same way, too.

In "Rubber Ball," Elka decided to get revenge on Jameson Lyles, played by Ed Asner, who operated a club and fired Elka as a waitress in 1947 for not going out with him. As an in-joke to their previous TV roles on *The Mary Tyler Moore Show*, Asner's Lyles quipped to Betty's Elka, "I can see you're not some happy homemaker." Lyles told Elka he dismissed her only because she was a bad waitress. At the end, Elka suggested they try to get together.

Though their chemistry was intact on screen Asner said this reunion with Betty was somewhat disappointing to him. "There wasn't enough contact," he said. "Betty's a contact-type performer, so I would've liked more contact."

A better *Mary Tyler Moore Show* reunion occurred in the third season as Georgia Engel became a semiregular as Elka's delightfully ditzy friend Mamie Sue. There were also nice visits by basketball player Baron Davis and Regis Philbin as Pierre, Elka's flirtatious hair stylist.

For viewers interested in going behind the scenes, "Some Like It Hot," on May 9, 2012, was invaluable. The schedule was much like that of *The Golden Girls*. The cast for that week's show did the table read Mondays followed by staging Tuesdays.

"We're more of a rehearsal process kind of show, where we will actually rehearse without any cameras, without any sound, without any technical aspects, just like we were doing a play," said director Andy Cadiff.

"The first couple of days, we carry a script, because the lines keep changing," said Betty. "But it's so much easier when you can put your script down and really play it."

"We are getting constant feedback on what's working and what's not working from table read to the tape night," noted executive producer Todd Milliner.

On Fridays, announcer Michael Burger warmed up the audience before introducing the cast. Betty and the women huddled with each other and had some laughs before taping, which normally took three to four hours.

Throughout the week, the atmosphere among cast and crew was loose and fun. "You'll walk by a cameraman, and he'll pat you on the shoulder," said Betty. "It's a delight."

About the only other distinctive episode in the third season was "God and Football," where Elka met idiotic Cleveland football kicker Jimmy Armstrong, played by Dan Cortese, in the locker room. "Can I squeeze your chest?" Elka asked. He said yes and she did so lustfully. At the hospital, after a doctor told Elka she was in such good shape that she could live forever, Victoria passed out after giving blood. She had a vision with Elka as God. Overhearing Victoria murmuring during her dream, Elka kept up the ruse and as "God" told Victoria to be kind and charitable without alerting the media.

At the end of the episode, the women celebrated Elka's ninetieth birthday. A coda included Betty getting her a real ninetieth birthday cake on the set. During the presentation, Betty cried and said, "I tell everybody that'll listen that I work on the happiest set I've ever worked on in sixty-three years in this business."

Fourth and Funnier Season
When new episodes of *Hot in Cleveland* began airing on November 28, 2012, the bad news was some episodes were still too much like *The Golden Girls*. "The Proposal" involved an engagement ring hidden in a dessert, which was reminiscent when Dorothy got hers from Stan in a baked potato in "There Goes the Bride," on February 2, 1991. "Pony Up" had Victoria inadvertently offering to donate a kidney, a similar dilemma Blanche faced with her sick sister in "Transplant," on October 5, 1985. Melanie discovered a man she had been dating was dead in "Corpse Bride," just like Rose did in "In a Bed of Rose's" on January 11, 1986.

Otherwise, by and large *Hot in Cleveland* improved markedly. Most notably was "It's Alive" on June 19, 2013. "Tonight, *Hot in Cleveland* is performed live in front of a studio audience, so I ought better watch my f*@king language!" Betty said in narration at the outset. The profanity was bleeped out, of course. The ladies were threatened because Elka and Mamie Sue had been selling pills to senior citizens at a discount by smuggling medicine from Canada. The funny story ended with the cast and guests William Shatner and Shirley Jones getting a standing ovation.

Carol Burnett turned up as Victoria's mother, Penny, in "Canoga Falls," an in-joke episode title as that fictional town was the setting for the recurring sketch "As the Stomach Turns" on *The Carol Burnett Show*. After getting word that Victoria's hometown in upstate New York planned to rename its town square after the actress, the women went to visit Penny, a local puppeteer. Victoria's sister Bess, played by Jean Smart, admitted the renaming announcement was a lie to make Victoria take more care of their mother.

Penny pretended to be a forgetful hoarder, but Elka saw through the ruse. "I know crazy. I live with crazy! And you're not crazy. What's your scam?" Penny told Elka she only wanted Victoria to stay longer with her, so Elka said, "Dial up the crazy!" The truth eventually emerged, and Penny went to Cleveland and connected with Elka's Nick, played by Tim Conway. "Oh Elka, I'm so glad we've had this time together," said Penny, echoing Burnett's famous closing line on *The Carol Burnett Show*. "Me too," grinned Elka as she moved on to two guys and Penny said to Nick, "You remind me of someone." Conway was a regular on *The Carol Burnett Show*.

Best of all might have been "Love is All Around," taking its name from the theme song of *The Mary Tyler Moore Show*. The show came together amid word that Valerie Harper had brain cancer, and the producers decided to make a tribute to her and the other women regulars on *The Mary Tyler Moore Show*. Elka and Mamie Sue reunited with the other members of Gorgeous Ladies of Bowling or GLOB—Angie, played by Harper, Peg, played by Cloris Leachman, and Diane, played by Mary Tyler Moore. "Did I like you?" Peg asked Angie, a veiled reference to their acrimonious relationship on *The Mary Tyler Moore Show*.

More references to the old show occurred. When Diane arrived, Elka said, "She made it after all!" Discussing themselves as bowlers, Elka exclaimed, "A classic!" "Every Saturday night, eyes were on us!" said Diane. "They even liked this one!" said Angie about Peg.

At the end, Peg asked a director, portrayed by Jesse Tyler Ferguson, "Why don't you do a show about us?" "I'm sorry, I don't see it," he responded. As the GLOB ladies toasted each other, a cat perched on a nearby window meowed like the end of *The Mary Tyler Moore Show*.

"I loved all episodes where the ladies fixed each other up on blind dates, especially 'Love Is All Around,' the episode that reunited all the ladies from *The Mary Tyler Moore Show*," noted series creator Suzanne Martin.

Martin added, "I thought the episode 'Cleveland Indians,' where Joy pretends to be Indian and it builds into a classic farce [written by classic *Frasier* farce writer Joe Keenan] was wonderful." While auditioning for the community theatre production of *The Importance of Being Earnest*, Elka impersonated being Joy's British mother in a sprightly show of misunderstanding.

While other episodes were not quite as outstanding, most of them did have some good lines and situations for Betty. In the season opener, Joy's son Owen, played by Michael McMillian, returned with a baby of his own named Wilbur, a moniker Elka loathed. Victoria took Wilbur onto the set of a movie audition and noted, "What parent doesn't want their child to be a star?" "Oh, right! Oh, those kids turn out great!" said Elka sarcastically.

"I went shopping at Forever 21," Joy said in "Method Man." "I'm guessing the Menopause Barn was closed?" Elka retorted.

Looking at Joy's wardrobe in "A Box Full of Puppies," Mamie Sue said, "I don't think I could pull off that skirt." "Many have!" Elka responded. When Joy doubted a guy was gay, Elka said, "Skintight jeans, a teacup pig. If only there had been some clues!" She also hugged a hunky firefighter named Sean, played by Eddie Cibrian, twice to audience amusement and encouraged Mamie Sue to hit on an older guy. "Look at that stride!" Elka said. "Original hips!"

"The Anger Games" had several references to *Wheel of Fortune* and *Jeopardy!*, which prompted Elka to quip at the end, "This never happens on *Password*!" The audience applauded and cheered the mention of the game show long associated with Betty.

In "Fast and Furious," the ladies attended a weight loss facility called Camp Shady Pines, the same name of Sophia's former nursing home on *The Golden Girls*. "I'm just here to lose a few pounds," Elka said. "At your age, who cares?" laughed Joy. Elka stared at Joy, then said, "Right back at you!" Elka also told the yoga counselor, played by Ed Begley Jr., "They moved here to get laid."

"I have a date with my gynecologist!" Melanie said in "The Fixer." "They're called appointments, dear," Elka responded. She later advised, "The best way to get over a man is to get under another one!"

There was also a show with clips called "Look Who's Hot Now" on August 7, 2013. The stars reminisced about the series with Kirstie Alley before the latter launched her own TV Land series, *Kirstie*. It lasted only one season, even with a crossover on *Hot in Cleveland*.

Off screen, the cast and crew observed what would have been Betty's fiftieth anniversary with Allen Ludden in 2013. "They threw a wonderful celebration on our set," Betty said on the CBS show *The Talk*.

Also in 2013 on the syndicated series *The Doctors*, the ladies showed the natural rapport they had on *Hot in Cleveland* while Betty admitted her nutrition could be better. "I still have hot dogs and French fries, what can I say?"

Down Somewhat in the Fifth

The producers of *Hot in Cleveland* took more risks in the fifth season, not all of which paid off. An ongoing storyline about Melanie successfully undergoing radiation treatment for a brain tumor for several episodes ran against the show's lighthearted tone and thus was unenjoyable.

Also off brand for the series was "The Animated Episode." The women became cartoon avatars of themselves when they entered Elka's house "built over a portal to another universe," she told them. With no laugh track, they toured the Rock and Roll Hall of Fame and met Steven Tyler, lead singer of Aerosmith, who made a pass at Elka. "Dream on!" she responded, referencing the title of an Aerosmith hit. The women got three wishes from Tyler that involved Elka as Wilhelmina Wonka in an unfunny musical fantasy. When Elka said at the end, "My advice is to forget it ever happened, or it'll make you crazy," plenty of viewers probably felt the same way.

The series further untethered itself from believable storylines as Elka ran a crazed campaign for city council against disabled black incumbent Powell, portrayed by Bill Bellamy. Elka beat him by drinking shots of vodka at one point, while Powell's opinionated aunt, played by Queen Latifah, endorsed Elka when she learned he was against dog parks. Following a bridge closing scandal like Governor Chris Christie faced in New Jersey, Elka won her seat.

Not all was lost, as the fifth season opener, "Stayin' Alive," was a strong if a little too broad an episode. Alex Trebek introduced the show to audience laughter with "First off and performing live, four women who are performing at the very peak of their craft. One of them is drunk." When Alex interrupted Victoria to update plot developments, Betty's Elka yelled, "We got this, Trebek!" to laughter and applause. After Elka and Mamie Sue talked about Steve Harvey being the funny one in *The Kings of Comedy*, the Reverend Boyce "The Voice" Ballentine, played by Cedric the Entertainer, one of the Kings of Comedy, told Elka, "Oh, the way Rue McClanahan was the funny one on *The Golden Girls*?" "I never saw that show," Elka grumbled. She and Mamie Sue made the same claim about *The Mary Tyler Moore Show* when Trebek said Cloris Leachman was that series' best actress.

"The live episodes were crazy, but so fun," recalled series creator Suzanne Martin. "We decided to do them to see if we could and to do something different and get attention. I would honestly say that the women worked so hard not to mess up that they didn't mess up enough! We actually changed a couple of lines at the last moment to throw them so it wouldn't look so perfect."

Elka's increasingly weird romantic life took prominence in several episodes. In "Elka Takes a Lover," she dated Luke, played by Chris Elliot, a Renaissance fair participant. "Elka and I role play. She's the village milkmaid," he said. "My milk churns bring all the boys to the yard," she added.

When Luke asked her, "What's the Wi-Fi password?" Elka proudly responded. "My measurements!" "Got those memorized!" Luke added to applause and laughter. She melted in his arms when he cooed, "Things are bound to turn hot when fire meets fire!" When she said, "Our souls touch," Luke added, "And everything else!" They even sang a duet before breaking up.

"The One with George Clooney"—George Clooney was the name of the women's dog—had Elka and Mamie Sue dating Elka's old flame Roy, played by John Mahoney. They acted like they were having a ménage à trois until Roy's domineering mother returned, inspiring both women to leave him.

In "Brokeback Elka," Elka pretended to be Victoria's online poetic cowboy lover "Nick Logan." "She makes me want to be a better man," Elka told Melanie about the ruse, adding "I think I'm in love with Victoria." Playing off the movie *Brokeback Mountain*, Elka later said, "I just can't quit her!" Seeing Betty play sapphic desires was pretty funny, especially since the truth never came out to Victoria. As Elka cheered Nick Logan, Victoria agreed and said he was "A man so perfect, only a woman could've invented him."

Elka retained her razor-sharp comebacks, too. In "Bucket: We're Going to New York," Joy said, "I never told you this, but when I first came to America, I auditioned for the Rockettes. Only I froze. I couldn't get my legs in the air." Elka's stare of curiosity after that line cracked up the audience, as did her follow-up of "You sure got over that one!"

"To me, orgasms are like donuts. Never had a bad one," Elka remarked in "Don Elka." "Even day-olds are just fine!" added Mamie Sue.

In "Playmates," Elka wrote and performed a stage comedy, "The Devil's Due," making fun of the women in her house. "You write what you know!" Elka told them when they complained, particularly Joy, about being played by a man. Morgan Fairchild played Elka on stage. At the end, Elka, as the on-stage narrator, said, "I realized these women hadn't ruined my life, they'd broadened it. And given it laughter. Sometimes, it's more fun to join the devil than to beat it."

That closing would have been a nice sentiment to end a fairly rocky season, but the producers instead went with "The Bachelors." Elka found her long-lost love Stan was now Olga, played by Marion Ross. "I guess you were the only woman I ever loved, too!" she announced, confused by the transition. Elka also met old flame Max, played by Carl Reiner, visiting from Florida. The episode ended with a cliffhanger on their future as "To be continued" flashed on screen.

Cooling Down *Cleveland*

By the sixth season, *Hot in Cleveland* had filmed over 100 episodes, enough to make the series attractive for local stations to rerun nightly. Ratings slid as well, making it likely *Hot in Cleveland* would be ending soon.

"It felt like the right time to conclude the series," said creator Suzanne Martin. "I actually knew from the pilot that I wanted to end the series with them on a plane. I like it when series end that everyone has their dreams come true, and that's what we tried to do for all the characters."

Unfortunately, as the series wound down, the need for more suspension of disbelief increased. Much semblance to reality dissolved as viewers were asked to accept ridiculous contrivances in many shows. In "Family Affair," a DNA test revealed Joy and Elka were distant blood relatives connected by a lesbian couple who raised their mutual ancestor.

Then Elka and Mamie Sue agreed to pose for a nude calendar to benefit the Cleveland Animal Shelter in "Cleveland Calendar Girls." "I drunk dialed that in," Elka added. She practiced being comfortable naked in their living room and got friends Helen, played by Jenny O'Hara, and Marcia, played by Marla Gibbs, to participate, as well.

Elka was breaking up with her latest love, Mayor Ted Deacon, played by Ben Vereen, in "One Wedding and a Funeral. "It's time for some goodbye sex with the mayor," she told Victoria and Melanie. "I don't understand why you didn't just end it after the steak dinner," Victoria interjected. "The man sprung for a forty-dollar filet!" exclaimed Elka. "So, you have to sleep with someone because they bought you a forty-dollar piece of meat?" asked Melanie. "I'm a lady!" Elka haughtily responded to laughter and applause.

The women were shocked as Elka announced, "The mayor is dead. In my bed! ... He was trying to impress me with how many pushups he could do. On top of me." They moved the body back to the mansion while Elka assumed the role of mayor. If that twist was hard to accept, the motivation on the next episode, "Scandalous," was even worse. After Joy's fiancé Bob, played by Dave Foley, tried to cover up the circumstances of the mayor's death. Elka confessed. The police decided not to arrest her due to potential fallout from the scandal for the city of Cleveland.

Most illogical of all was "Kitchen Nightmare." After the women converted their neighborhood bar into a restaurant, Pope Francis supposedly appeared to meet Elka. "Back in the day, popes got married!" she gushed. She then yelled to the women, "Where's the grub? My boyfriend's hungry!" Elka also told the religious leader she didn't like the idea of washing the feet of lepers. At the end, Elka told the women, "Well, I dumped the pope," as if that was any surprise.

The more realistic episodes were not much better. In "Bossy Cups," Elka hooked up with a hot guy named Jim, played by Robert Wagner, who turned out to be a boring, glass-wearing nerd. When she hid his glasses, he replaced them with dark shades and said he wasn't going to be able to talk for a few days, which turned her on more. In "Bad Girlfriends" Elka had to wear a tiger suit for a week after losing a bet with the Cincinnati mayor in a visual joke that was overdone. Victoria's father Alex Chase, played by Stacy Keach, dated Elka in a rather boring romance in "Say Yes to the Mess" before ending the relationship. "I'll never find another woman like you, Elka," he said. "That's true," she responded.

A few shows did harken back to better comedy that viewers expected from *Hot in Cleveland*. In "Tazed and Confused," Elka practiced the *Password*-style Secret Word Tournament with Melanie, a bad player. When the emcee, bartender Shane, played by Casey Washington, said, "I'm channeling Allen Ludden," Elka responded coolly, "I knew Allen Ludden. Allen Ludden was a friend of mine. And you, sir, are no Allen Ludden!" The audience laughed and applauded. Elka won when Melanie gave the clue of "flat" for "Joy," meaning Joy's chest.

In "Duct Soup," Joy's son Owen had a marriage rehearsal dinner where the cake had turrets shaped like penises. "I was excited to see the cake, but it looks like the cake is excited to see me!" Elka quipped. At the end of the ceremony, Elka offered Joy's ex-flame Simon, played by Craig Ferguson, to spend the night in her room. "What the hell? Let's give them something to talk about!" he said.

The best outing was "All About Elka," where Carol Burnett returned as Penny, Victoria's mother. She and Elka fought over playing a grandmother part in a play Victoria was producing. "You did a TV show with puppets!" snarled Elka. "I'll have you know that I can express more with one hand than most people can with their entire bodies," Penny responded, looking disdainfully at Elka's figure. "I can express how I feel about you with one finger!" Elka shot back.

Elka agreed to be the understudy but Penny warned, "Back off, blondie! I've never missed a performance." "I bet your audiences wished you had!" said Elka. Penny got back inside the theater after Elka locked her out, and both acted together on stage. Unfortunately, the producers couldn't resist injecting phoniness in *Hot in Cleveland* again and had Penny reveal at the end to Victoria that Susan Lucci was her half-sister due to an affair by Penny's late husband.

The one-hour finale had the women recalling their best times, worst dates, and more at Joy's bridal shower. "The best orgasm I ever had was when Joy said she was leaving," Elka said. The bridal party went to Las Vegas to pick up Joy and Bob's adopted baby. For various reasons, Melanie, Mamie Sue, Elka, and Bob's father Bob, played by Bob Newhart, got arrested but eventually were released.

Elka fell in love with the senior Bob, and they wed along with the junior Bob and Joy. "Oh my God, Elka is your mother-in-law!" Melanie told Joy after the double nuptials. "Call me Mom!" beamed Elka as a reluctant Joy hugged her old nemesis. Joy named her new adopted daughter Betty. "I never met a Betty I didn't like," she said. "And they're always so pretty!" chimed Elka.

The show ended with "You're My Best Friend" by Queen playing in the background five years later. All were married as they presented a birthday cake to Betty as she turned five. A note on screen read, "And everyone lived happily ever after in Cleveland. And Melanie, Joy, Victoria, and Elka still get together every Wednesday night." The show ended June 3, 2015.

Recounting her time with Betty on *Hot in Cleveland*, creator Suzanne Martin concluded, "Betty is everything you hope she would be and more. So talented, so lovely, so sweet, kind, and truly, truly funny—on and off camera. A hug from Betty was heaven. A compliment from Betty would make you happy for years.

"She and the other ladies adored each other, and she often said it was the most joyful experience of her career. Every member of the cast and crew was happy to be there. We really were. And she set the tone."

When *Hot in Cleveland* ended, Betty was ninety-three years old. She had become the oldest featured regular actress on a scripted TV series ever, and she had no intentions of extending that record. Instead, she remained active on television as a guest star. Let's take a deeper look at her work in that regard, which she had begun doing sixty years earlier.

Chapter Thirteen
Betty the Omnipresent

Betty made her last TV acting appearance to date in 2017 on the sitcom *Young & Hungry*. In the first of two guest shots, she admired Brandon Rush as a stripper who mistakenly performed for Betty and series star Emily Osment. Photo: Eric McCandless / Copyright Freeform / courtesy of Everett Collection.

Prior to joining *The Mary Tyler Moore Show* in 1973, Betty scarcely worked as an actress on television. Apart from her two 1950s sitcoms, she had only amassed six guest appearances on other comedies and dramas and played herself three of those times. *The Mary Tyler Moore Show* changed the perception of Betty as just a TV personality and, thereafter, Betty pretty much was able to choose guest acting shots. She was more in demand for work as she matured, and most of her guest acting jobs occurred in her seventies through nineties. Sometimes they aired close together. For one week alone in 2003, viewers could watch Betty in the drama *Everwood* on November 24, the sitcom *I'm With Her* on November 25, and the TV movie *Stealing Christmas* on November 30.

This chapter summarizes and reviews Betty's guest acting roles chronologically. For multiple shots on the same series, the entry under its title covers Betty's episodes starting with her first one. Each entry lists the episode title in quotes after the series title in italics, followed by the original air date and time in the Eastern time zone. Also given is the show's network or cable channel or syndication.

The cast and guest actors follow, based on the billing given on the show and note where Betty was given a special designation in the credits. To save space, abbreviations appear for an executive producer (EP), producer (P), director (D) and writer (W). For the same reason, the cast lists for most of the TV movies include only the key performers.

Star ratings appear at the start for entries viewed, which were all listed but *The U.S. Steel Hour*; *Lucas Tanner*; *Love, Sidney*; *The Dom DeLuise Show*; *Noddy*; *LA Doctors*; and *Providence*. Ratings represent the following assessments:

*****—The episode is classic material worth viewing again and again.

****—This effort is an almost perfect or above average show.

***—Roughly part of the show works well, but some deficiencies exist.

**—A lot more of the content is wrong than right here.

*—So much is wrong here that one wonders why Betty participated.

These ratings deal solely with the content of each show. From all programs viewed, Betty gave 100 percent regardless of the quality of material she received. For multiple appearances on a series, some ratings follow individual episodes due to varying quality, others after the title itself.

As a quick guide to these summaries, Betty's best appearances were on *The Odd Couple* (1972), *Ellery Queen* (1975), *Best of the West* (1981), *St. Elsewhere* (twice in 1985), *The Simpsons* (2000), *The Ellen Show* (2001), *Malcolm in the Middle* (2004),

Complete Savages (once in 2004 and once in 2005), *Community* (twice in 2010), and all of *Pound Puppies* (2010–13). Her worst were *Gary the Rat* (2003), *Glenn Martin, DDS* (once in 2009 and once in 2010), and *Save Me* (2013). Betty earned Emmy nominations for Outstanding Guest Actress in a Comedy Series for *Suddenly Susan* (1996), *Yes, Dear* (2002), and *My Name is Earl* (2009).

This chapter excludes the pilots *Snavely* and *Stephanie* from Chapter Seven. Also omitted due to prior mentions are Betty's guest shots as Rose Nyland from *The Golden Girls* on *Empty Nest*, *Nurses*, and *The John Larroquette Show*, and as Elka from *Hot in Cleveland* on *The Soul Man*.

The Millionaire, "Millionaire Virginia Lennart"**

October 17, 1956, CBS Wednesday 9-9:30 p.m.

Cast: Marvin Miller (Michael Anthony), Paul Frees (voice of John Beresford Tipton). Guests: Betty White (Virginia Lennart), Jacques Bergerac (Count Paul Lamada), Mabel Albertson (Emmy). EP: Fred Henry. P: Don Fedderson. W: Muriel Roy Bolton.

Michael Anthony was the executive secretary to the "fabulously wealthy" John Beresford Tipton, whose hobby was giving away $1 million tax free to people he never met. The latest beneficiary was Virginia, a waitress from Keokuk, Iowa. Approaching Virginia, Marvin said, "I'd like a few words." "Rare or medium? My words are very rare," she responded. He told her she would get a $1 million cashier's check if she signed a paper with conditions. "Who am I supposed to murder?" she asked suspiciously. Marvin said the money would be reclaimed if Virginia identified him as the source or investigated who he was. Additionally, she could only say she came into more money but not reveal how or how much.

With that in mind, Virginia convinced fellow waitress Emmy to tour Europe with her using money she claimed she inherited from rich relatives. When Virginia and Emmy met Count Lamada, Emmy told the unmarried Italian Virginia's lie about the latter's family. As the count romanced Virginia, she debated if she could fit in his family's aristocratic heritage and should reveal the truth. This melodrama offered limited pleasures beyond seeing a young Betty in an on-screen romance and having an enjoyable rapport with Mabel Albertson.

The U.S. Steel Hour, "Scene of the Crime"

June 27, 1962, CBS Tuesday 10-11 p.m.

Cast: Harry Townes (Martin Keller), Betty White (Betty Swan), Patricia Collinge (Amanda Fennel), Lester Rawlins (Ronnie Fennel), Anne Francine (Edna Thompson). Also: Edgar Stehli, Peggy Conklin, Doris Rich. D: Tom Donovan. W: Sidney Carroll, Brian Clemens (story).

Released from prison after twenty years, Martin Keller returned to the Green Mountain boarding house and proclaimed his innocence to fellow tenant Betty Swan. Martin said he was drunk at the time and had no memory of killing his then-girlfriend. Betty convinced Amanda Fennel, their landlady, to hear Martin's plea despite testifying against him in court. But when Amanda's statements produced some discrepancies with Martin's claims, Betty had to figure out who was telling the truth about the homicide. The live, dramatic anthology series ended its decade run almost a year after this episode aired. UCLA has a copy of this show in its collection.

Petticoat Junction, "The Cannonball Bookmobile"**

February 1, 1969, CBS Saturday 9:30-10 p.m.

Cast: Edgar Buchanan (Uncle Joe Carson), June Lockhart (Dr. Janet Craig), Linda Kaye Henning (Betty Jo Bradley), Mike Minor (Steve Elliott), Meredith MacRae (Billie Jo Bradley), Lori Saunders (Bobbie Jo Bradley), Frank Cady (Sam Drucker), Byron Foulger (Wendell Gibbs), Paul Hartman (Bert Smedley). Guest: Betty White (Adelle Colby). EP: Charles Stewart. Creator/P: Paul Henning. D: Ralph Levy. W: Charles Stewart, Dick Conway.

When Dr. Janet Craig's friend Adelle Colby arrived in Hooterville to establish a library, she attracted the eager attention of three of its middle-aged bachelors. These gentlemen were general store operator Sam Drucker, barber Bert Smedley, and Joe Carson, general manager of the Shady Rest Hotel. But train engineer Wendell Gibbs outdid them all by establishing the Cannonball Bookmobile on the railroad line, with its own car for Adelle to oversee book circulation. Wendell also read poetry to her, which won Adelle's heart, to the dismay of her other potential suitors. That plot is pretty much all this episode had to offer. Betty looked beautiful but had little to do in this rather inauspicious return to her acting in Hollywood after more than a decade.

Vanished***

March 8 and 9, 1971, NBC Monday 9-11 p.m. and Tuesday 9-11 p.m.

Cast: Richard Widmark (President Paul Roudebush), Skye Aubrey (Jill Nichols), Tom Bosley (Johnny Cavanaugh), James Farentino (Gene Culligan), Larry Hagman (Jerry Freytag), Murray Hamilton (Nick McCann), Arthur Hill (Arnold Greer), Robert Hooks (Larry Storm), E.G. Marshall (Arthur Ingram), Eleanor Parker (Sue Greer) William Shatner (Dave Paulick), Robert Young (Sen. Earl Gannon). Co-starring: Chet Huntley (Himself), Betty White (Herself), Stephen McNally (General Palfrey), Sheree North (Beverly West), Robert Lipton (Mike Loomis), Michael Strong (Pete Descowicz), Jim Davis (Captain Cooledge), Christine Belford (Gretchen Greer), Catherine McLeod (Grace Lally), Denny Miller (Big Bubba Touba), Don Pedro Colley (Mercurio), Russell Johnson (Clyde Morehouse), Hester Portinari (Ilka Windish), Martin Agronsky (Himself). EP: David Victor. D: Buzz Kulik. W: Fletcher Knebel, Dean Reisner.

 This two-part TV movie was an unsatisfying political drama set in Washington, D.C. Betty appeared at the start of its second part. Improbably, she and recently retired NBC reporter Chet Huntley played themselves as news anchors. They discussed the disappearance of Arnold Greer, the closest advisor to President Paul Roudebush. Betty said some thought Greer had defected to the Communist bloc, "Or kidnapping or, well, speculation, to coin a phrase, is rife." After the president's nemesis, Senator Earl Gannon, implied to reporter Martin Agronsky that Arnold was gay, "famed Washington, D.C., mystic," Hester Portinari, told Betty and Chet, "I see no sexuality in this." Instead, Portinari claimed the Chinese kidnapped Greer after failing to abduct the president. Betty, Chet, and Portinari then went away as the TV movie followed the effort of the president's friend, Gene Culligan, to obtain the truth. The interminable discovery led to a farfetched and anticlimactic resolution.

 Vanished somehow garnered eight Emmy nominations, winning for cinematography. Its other nods included Single Program of the Year, Writing and Lead Actor Richard Widmark, and Supporting Actor Robert Young. The latter starred at the same time on *Marcus Welby M.D.*, which vanquished *Vanished* in the ratings when the second part aired opposite the series.

O'Hara United States Treasury, "Operation: Lady Luck"**
January 14, 1972, CBS Friday 8-9 p.m.
Cast: David Janssen (Jim O'Hara). Guests: Ricardo Montalban (Rick Morris), Lyle Bettger (Layton Willard), Francine York (Diane Lazslo/Willard). Co-starring: Betty White (Undercover agent), Allen Ludden (Undercover agent), H.M. Wynant (Arnie Press), Colby Chester (Burt Hale), Henry Brandon (Ham Jason), Lyle Talbot (Art Prescott), Don Haggerty (Zig Halfer), Barney Phillips (Agent Alex Reid), Del Munroe (Mechanic), Marjorie Bennett (Agnes Howlitt). Creators: James E. Moser, Jack Webb. P: Leonard B. Kaufman. D: Sam C. Freedle. W: Bill Rega.

Federal agent Jim O'Hara convinced compulsive gambler Rick Morris to unwittingly lead him to top counterfeiters in New Orleans. Arnie and Zig intercepted the duo and took them to Art and Ham, who had a score to settle with Rick. Rick's old flame Diane tried to help him out while Jim planned for a transfer of money with the operation's head honcho, Layton Willard. Into this mix, Betty and Allen were two agents pretending to be an arguing couple joining Jim and Rick to wait for the hotel elevator. "Well, hello there!" cooed Betty's character to Rick as Jim and Allen unobtrusively switched briefcases. Betty and Allen's parts ran less than a minute yet played a pivotal plot point in this otherwise leaden slog, a *Mission: Impossible* imitation without that series' wit, style, and pacing. This episode aired opposite the debut of *Sanford and Son*, which would last five and a half years. *O'Hara United States Treasury* ended after just one year.

The Odd Couple, "Password"***
December 1, 1972, ABC Friday 9:30-10 p.m.
Cast: Tony Randall (Felix Unger), Jack Klugman (Oscar Madison), Al Molinari (Officer Murray Greshler), Elinor Donahue (Miriam Welby), Penny Marshall (Myrna). Guests: Allen Ludden (Himself), Betty White (Herself), Ronda Coplan (Mitzi Ferguson), Francine Greshler (Millicent Thomas). EP: Garry Marshall, Jerry Belson. P: Jerry Davis. D: Alex March. W: Frank Buxton.

Roommates Felix and Oscar were excited to play *Password* on TV until they learned their competitors were Millicent Thomas and Betty White. "She's an absolutely unbeatable player!" exclaimed Felix about Betty. Betty was not as impressed meeting Felix, accidentally calling him "Mr. Angle." Felix turned out to be a horrible player and a sore loser who had to be forcibly removed from the studio. A constant flow of belly laughs, including memorably awful clues from Felix, made this a classic. *TV Guide* ranked this show as the fifth-greatest TV episode ever in 1997.

Lucas Tanner, "The Noise of a Quiet Weekend"
February 26. 1975, NBC Wednesday 9-10 p.m.
Cast: David Hartman (Lucas Tanner), John Randolph (John Hamilton), Robbie Rist (Glendon Farrell), Alan Abelew (Jaytee Drumm), Trish Soodik (Cindy Damon), Kimberly Beck (Terry Klitsner), Michael Dwight-Smith (Wally Moore). Guests: Elisabeth Brooks (Gretchen), Henry V. Brown (Phil), Nicholas Colasanto (Mel), Jamie Farr (Police officer), Norman Fell (Abe Lydecker), Danny Goldman (Frankie), Lenore Kasdorf (Ann Callahan), Monte Landis (Waiter), Michael Lerner (Artie), Jaye P. Morgan (Judy Farrell), Tom Pedi (Police officer), Barbara Rhoades (Franny), Billy Sands (Bellhop), Jenny Sherman (Hostess), Betty White (Lydia Merrick). EP: David Victor. P: Jay Benson. D: Leo Penn. W: Jerry McNeely.

Missouri teacher Lucas Tanner had a weekend convention in New York City to attend along with his principal, John Hamilton. His neighbor, young Glendon Farrell, received permission to join them to see his aunt Judy Farrell, a singing star. Complications arose when Glendon got lost in the big city in his quest. UCLA has a copy of this show in its collection.

Ellery Queen, "The Adventure of Miss Aggie's Farewell Performance"**
October 19, 1975, NBC Sunday 8-9 p.m.
Cast: Jim Hutton (Ellery Queen), David Wayne (Inspector Richard Queen), Tom Reese (Sergeant Thomas Velie). Guests: Eve Arden (Vera Bethune), Nan Martin (Olivia Burns), John McGiver (Godfrey Pearl), Bert Parks (Larry Denver), Paul Shenar (Wendell Warren), Betty White (Louise Demery), John Hillerman (Simon Brimmer), Penelope Windust (Anita Leslie), Beatrice Colen (Mary Lou Gumm), Joseph R. Sicari (Gus Geropolis), Gerald Hiken (Alvin Burns), Nina Roman (Grace), Hilda Haynes (Nurse Frawley), Don Keefer (The Fence), Sidney Miller (Morgue attendant). EP: Richard Levinson, William Link. P: Peter S. Fischer, Michael Rhodes. D: James Sheldon. W: Peter S. Fischer (teleplay), Richard Levinson, William Link, Peter S. Fischer (story).

Vera Bethune starred as "Miss Aggie" on the radio serial "Every Day's Journey" when she collapsed from poisoning live on the air. After detective Ellery Queen visited her recuperating in the hospital, Vera was shot dead. Was her murderer one of the show's performers, Larry Denver or Anita Leslie? Announcer Wendell Warren? Sponsor Godfrey Pearl? Writers Olivia Burns or her husband Alvin, or both? Organist Mary Lou Gumm? Or Vera's agent, Louise Demery? To reveal who and how would spoil the fun. Let's just say that Betty had a great moment when pompous radio host Simon Brimmer planned to announce the killer on his show. Since most of the suspects were actors, he said he had paid them all to appear in the studio per union rules. That prompted Betty's character Louise to scoff in the control room, "He could pay more than scale, the tightwad!" This episode excelled in all departments, with the bonus of seeing Betty opposite John Hillerman two years prior to him playing her ex-husband on *The Betty White Show*. John McGiver appeared posthumously, having died of a heart attack on September 9, 1975.

With This Ring**
May 5, 1978, ABC Friday 9-11 p.m.
Tony Bill (Peter Turner), Tom Bosley (Edward Edwards), Diana Canova (Delores Andrews), Barbara Cason (Viola Andrews), Joyce DeWitt (Jilly Weston), John Forsythe (General Albert Harris), Scott Hylands (Tom "Bird Dog" Burkhardt), Donny Most (James Cutler), Dick Van Patten (Alvin Andrews), Betty White (Evelyn Harris), Deborah White (Kate), Mary Crosby (Lisa Harris). EP: Gerald W. Abrams. P: Bruce J. Sallan. W: Terence Mulcahy. D: James Sheldon.

Evelyn Harris told director of catering Edward Edwards she expected her daughter's upcoming wedding to be spectacular, as the president would be attending. For example, she wanted live birds in the cake so they would fly out when her daughter Lisa cut into it. But Lisa and her fiancé planned to postpone the event, though they were too scared to tell Evelyn. Evelyn also grated on the nerves of her ex-husband, Army General Albert Harris. She further complained about the reception area and thought the color scheme should change to red, white, and blue. Jill was ready to call off her wedding when Evelyn told her the president was coming. When Albert told Evelyn he thought Lisa was too young to get married, Evelyn argued that Lisa was very mature for her age. "Of course, you wouldn't know about that, since you were too busy to spend any time with her!" Evelyn snapped.

Later at dinner, Lisa told Evelyn that she wasn't getting married. Evelyn stormed off until Lisa told her, "We're just bored with each other." Suddenly sympathetic,

Evelyn agreed the ceremony shouldn't happen and told Albert she regretted pushing so hard for the marriage. These events led to a ridiculous conclusion in this insubstantial mess, which has two other would-be couples and their families getting ready for their big day in a contrived melodrama. Betty did as best as she could playing a humorless, pushy matriarch. This TV movie's working title was *Weddings*, which indicated just how generic it was.

The Best Place to Be*
May 27 and 28, 1979. NBC Sunday 9-11 p.m. and Monday 9-11 p.m.
Cast: Donna Reed (Sheila Callahan), Efrem Zimbalist Jr. (Bill Reardan), Mildred Dunnock (Rose Price), Betty White (Sally Cantrell), John Philip Law (Dr. Gary Mancini), Stephanie Zimbalist (Maryanne Callahan), Michael Shannon (Patrick Callahan), Gregory Harrison (Rick Jalowsky), Timothy Hutton (Tommy Callahan), Lloyd Bochner (Bob Stockwood), Madlyn Rhue (Emily Stockwood), Rick Jason (Paul Bellinger), Alice Backes (Kitty Rawlings), Peggy Converse (Tear Callahan), Leon Ames (William Callahan), Coleen Gray (Dottie Parker), Susan Walden (Betty Callahan), Liam Sullivan (Sean Callahan). P: Ross Hunter, Jacques Mapes. D: David Miller. W: Stanford Whitmore. Based on a book by Helen Van Slyke.

Monotonous and overextended, this two-part TV movie marked the lead's first Hollywood acting role since her sitcom *The Donna Reed Show* ended in 1966. Betty played Sally, a friend of Donna Reed's Sheila. Sally saw Emily Stockwood rendezvousing with Sheila's husband Sean, who died after making love with Emily. When Sheila learned Sean left her with no money to afford her house, Sally informed her that Sean was an adulterer. To Sally's shock, Sheila admitted she knew. Complaining that Sheila never confronted Sean with the truth, Sally snarled, "You have a turn-of-the-century mind that accepts every rotten double standard that men have been able to get away with!" Sally also boosted Sheila's morale by saying, "There will be another man. I guarantee you."

Improbably, Sheila somehow quickly got a job as a book seller and had a fling with young Dr. Gary Mancini, which Sally approved of but Sheila's mother, Rose Price, did not. Eventually, Sheila left Gary when he refused to divorce his wife and found new love with an old flame, author Bill Reardan. Sheila also dealt with her pot-smoking daughter Maryanne, her son Tommy hanging out with the hard-partying guys at a private school, and other manufactured melodramas. Apart from some clever quips, Betty's Sheila had relatively little to do as the plot progressed. Nevertheless, Betty promoted it on *The Tonight Show* and *Password Plus* the week before its first airing along with co-star John Philip Law.

Before and After***
October 5, 1979, ABC Friday 9-11 p.m.
Cast: Patty Duke (Carole Matthews), Bradford Dillman (Jack Matthews), Barbara Feldon (Penny), Art Hindle (Mike Farmer), Conchata Ferrell (Marge), Rosemary Murphy (Helen), Kenneth Mars (Ben Fryer), Randolph Powell (Lee), Betty White (Anita). EP: Frank Konigsberg. P: Sam Manners. D: Kim Friedman. W: Hindi Brooks.

Carole Matthews was desperate to lose the weight she gained since she married Jack. She struggled initially in an exercise class with her trim friend Penny before she connected with Mike Farmer, a hunky young artist. When Carole learned Jack attended an office party without her, she visited a meeting of Calorie Counters Anonymous along with Penny. The latter ran into Ben Fryer, an old flame who had lost seventy-five pounds. At this meeting, Anita, the group leader, had everyone sing weight loss lyrics to "Home on the Range." "I, too, used to be a porker, and look at me now!" she purred. When Anita learned a woman had gained pounds since the last meeting and asked her why, the woman said, "I don't know. I ate like a bird." "A vulture!" chimed in Anita to laughter. Anita made the poor woman wear a piggy mask. When she met Carol, Anita crowed, "We're going to turn you into a beauty queen! Even if it kills her." Anita's second pig masking infuriated Carol, who left. Carol had a more serious problem when Jack left and her vain mother Helen interfered. But Mike's continuing ardor in Carol sparked her to successfully lose weight and start dating him. Jack then wanted Carol back, Penny became anorexic after marrying Ben and other complications ensued. Despite considerable flaws, this production had an unconventional script to make it somewhat diverting nonetheless, and Betty and the cast gave it their all.

The Gossip Columnist**
March 21, 1980, Syndicated Various times (two hours)
Cast: Bobby Vinton (Marty Kaplan), Robert Vaughn (Mark Case), Dick Sargent (Alan Keyes), Kim Cattrall (Dina Moran), Conrad Janis (Ivan Bock), Joe Penny (Paul Cameron), Martha Raye (Georgia O'Hanlon), Bobby Sherman (Buddy Harwin),

Sylvia Sidney (Alma Lewellyn), Lyle Waggoner (Terry Anderson), Steve Allen, Jim Backus, Henny Backus, Jack Carter, Allen Ludden, Jayne Meadows, Rip Taylor, Betty White, David Sheehan (Themselves), Richard Deacon (Director). EP: Jon Epstein. D: James Sheldon. W: Michael Gleason.

Dina Moran dreamt she won the Pulitzer Prize for Journalism as she headed to Hollywood. To her dismay, managing editor Alan Keyes said she would cover entertainment at the fictional Los Angeles Sun newspaper rather than national politics. PR man Marty Kaplan told Dina he could give her an exclusive story if she interviewed amorous TV star Terry Anderson. He also introduced Dina to Betty White and Allen Ludden on a set. Allen told Marty and Dina they were working at Studio 32, to which Betty interjected, "I'm working. I don't know what he's doing!" Marty called the couple nice people before showing Dina the columnist she replaced, Alma Lewellyn. "She outlived her usefulness," Marty says. Alma said she was bored with Hollywood and wants to join Marty in PR. Meanwhile, Dina was upset with how Marty toyed with her, while Dina's concerned fiancé, Paul Cameron, arrived from Chicago, and on, and on, and on. Martha Raye's great dramatic performance kept this Tinseltown-themed timewaster from otherwise getting one star. The cameos by Betty and other celebrities meant to lend verisimilitude only made this TV movie look as unrealistic as *The Love Boat*.

Best of the West, "Mail Order Bride"****
September 24, 1981, ABC Thursday 8:30-9 p.m.
Cast: Joel Higgins (Sam Best), Carlene Watkins (Elvira Best), Meeno Peluce (Daniel Best), Valri Bromfield (Laney Gibbs), Tracey Walter (Frog Rothchild, Jr.), Tom Ewell (Doc Jerome Kullens), Leonard Frey (Parker Tillman). Special guest star: Betty White (Amanda Tremaine). Guests: Wil Albert (The Reverend), Art La Fleur (Dooley Wainwright), Erik Holland (Olaf Gunderson), Ronald F. Hoiseck (Sven Gunderson). Creator/EP/W: Earl Pomerantz. P: David Lloyd, Ronald E. Frazier. D: Doug Rogers.

In the late 1800s, crusty Doc Kullens fretted over his mail order bride's arrival because he had described himself as young and handsome to her. "Lies, lies, all my letters were full of lies!" he told his pal, Sam Best. "And now you're scared to face the truth," said Sam. "No, I'm scared all hers were, too!" responded Doc. Amanda Tremaine appeared at the Square Deal Saloon looking striking. Doc apologized for not revealing who he was to her earlier. "Those are love handles!" she said, kissing him long and hard to his amazement. As Doc left to fix an injured child's leg, Dooley Wainwright revealed that Amanda was really a prostitute from Kansas City. Sam debated with his wife Elvira whether to reveal the truth to Doc. At the wedding, the reverend recognized Amanda, so she told Doc her true profession, and he left the proceedings.

As Amanda left on the next stagecoach, she apologized to Doc. "You're a sweet man, Jerome. In a way, I'm glad it didn't work out. I was marrying you to get respectability. Marrying a man to get something from him, that's not much different from what I've been doing all my life. The only difference is up to now, I've always gone about it honestly," she said. Jerome felt that he couldn't match up to her other lovers. Amanda disagreed, and when Laney Gibbs announced that the stagecoach wouldn't leave until the following day, Amanda smiled and coaxed Doc to join her in her room. Betty provided a warm and funny portrayal to make this one of her best guest acting shots ever.

Love, Sidney, "Charlotte's Web"
January 13, 1982, NBC Wednesday 9:30-10 p.m.
Cast: Tony Randall (Sidney Shorr), Swoosie Kurtz (Laurie Morgan), Kalenna Kiff (Patti Morgan). Guests: Betty White (Charlotte Hogan), Michael Gross (Doctor), Tyra Ferrell (Nurse). D: Tony Mordente. W: Richard Baer.

Sidney's actress roommate Laurie feared Charlotte Hogan, the head writer of the soap opera "As Thus We Are," planned to eliminate Laurie's character. Worried this development would force Laurie and her daughter Patti to leave the apartment they all share, Sidney reluctantly agreed to a romantic dinner date with the amorous author to save Laurie's job. This episode was the ninth shown in this two-season sitcom where the lead character's homosexuality was underplayed.

Madame's Place, untitled episode**
October 14, 1982, Syndicated Thursday Various times (30 minutes)
Cast: Wayland Flowers (Voice/puppeteer of Madame, "The Man Behind the Woman"), Susan Tolsky (Bernadette, Madame's secretary), Johnny Haymer (Pinkerton, Madame's butler), Ty Henderson (Barney, Madame's producer), Judy Landers (Sara Joy, Madame's niece). Guests: Ronnie Schell (Federino Felluci), Betty White (Herself), Dick Hardwick (Himself), Doug Mattocks (Himself). EP: Brad Lachman. P: Don Van Atta, Bob Sand. D: Paul Miller. W: Bob Sand, Marc Warren,

Dennis Rinsler, Frank Mula, Tom Moore, Bob Howard, Greg Fields, Tony Garafalo, George Atkins, Wayland Flowers.

On the set of her talk show, hostess Madame introduced Betty with "And now I'd like to bring out one of the great ladies of show business. One of my dearest friends. The cute, the versatile, the incomparable, the candid, the positively splendid, Ms. Betty White!" Betty said, "I know talk show audiences are sick to death of gushy compliments between show people, but I can't tell you how wonderful I think you are!" Madame paid back the compliment, but the warmth dissolved as Betty noted, "My agent said the money was ridiculous, but I said I didn't care." "Well, Betty, the money isn't that bad. As a matter of fact, a little bird told me that you asked for the check the minute you got into your dressing room!" responded Madame. "Some blabbermouth said that? Well, I'm not going to let some offensive employee of yours spoil my enjoyment of being a guest on your show!" Betty shot back. As the conversation devolved, Betty called Madame "ripened" and mocked her nose and "grande dame illusions," and Madame jousted with Betty over their fashions. After each threatened to reveal the other's secrets, they reconciled and Madame called Betty "my dear, dear friend" as the latter left. Their bubbly exchange easily outshone the main flimsy plot, dully acted and directed, about Madame trying to get into the next movie of Italian director Federino Felluci.

Fame, "Sunshine Again"***
January 20, 1983, NBC Thursday 8-9 p.m.
Cast: Debbie Allen (Lydia Grant), Lee Curreri (Bruno Martelli), Erica Gimpel (Coco Hernandez), Albert Hague (Benjamin Shorofsky), Carlo Imperato (Danny Amatullo), Carol Mayo Jenkins (Elizabeth Sherwood), Valerie Landsburg (Doris Schwartz), Gene Anthony Ray (Leroy Johnson), Lori Singer (Julie Miller), Morgan Stevens (David Reardon). Guests: Carmine Caridi (Angelo Martelli), Madlyn Rhue (Mrs. Schwartz). Special Guest Appearances: Nancy Walker (Rachel Kaufman), Betty White (Catherine). Co-starring: Ann Nelson (Mrs. Berg), Ivor Barry (The maître d'). Featuring: Bronwyn Thomas (Michelle), Nia Peeples (Girlfriend). EP: William Blinn. P: Mel Swope. D: Harry Harris. W: Kelly Wood Adams, Renee Orin Hague.

Teacher Elizabeth Sherwood nagged her fellow instructor at New York's High School for the Performing Arts, cranky Benjamin Shorofsky, to date her friend Catherine. At dinner, Catherine confessed to Benjamin her real motive was to encourage him to do a benefit for the senior citizens activity center where she worked. He asked the students of choreographer Lydia Grant to perform there, but they had already planned to do a twenty-fifth work anniversary benefit for piano student Bruno's father, Angelo Martelli. When Angelo told Bruno that he didn't want the party with the students, the show was back on for the center. But plans went awry from there. This first-season episode of the musical drama needed a tighter script, but the cast's buoyancy compensated somewhat. Betty's future *Golden Girls* alumna Nancy Walker played Rachel Kaufman, a senior who liked the activities center and was the grandmother of student Doris Schwartz. Seeing her sing and Betty dance along with Debbie Allen provided a lively finale, especially for Betty's fans.

Hotel, "Outsiders"***
November 21, 1984, ABC Wednesday 10-11 p.m.
Cast: James Brolin (Peter McDermott), Connie Sellecca (Christine Francis), Shea Farrell (Mark Danning), Nathan Cook (Billy Griffin), Michael Spound (Dave Kendall), Heidi Bohay (Megan Kendall), Shari Belafonte Harper (Julie Gillette), Anne Baxter (Mrs. Victoria Cabot). Guest stars: Dick Cavett (Himself), Melinda Culea (Adrianna Dupre/"Agatha Deming"), Genie Francis (Jenny Bernard), Charles Frank (Nick Braithwaite), Betty White (Wilma Klein). Also: John Considine (Carl Bernard), Barbara Stuart (Frances Bernard). EP: Aaron Spelling, Douglas S. Cramer. P: Bill and Jo LaMond, Henry Colman. D: Kim Friedman. W: James Fritzhand.

Adrianna Dupre, author of the hit novel "Small Town Wives," attended a book fair at the St. Gregory Hotel. Her aunt and assistant, book editor Wilma Klein, became upset when she learned Adrianna misrepresented herself to pick up Nick and have a torrid affair with him. "Well, why didn't you tell him about your book?" asked Wilma. "And have him think I'm a nymphomaniac? It couldn't help," responded Adrianna. "It couldn't hurt," retorted Wilma. Neither realized that Nick was really vicious book critic Nick Braithwaite.

As Nick planned to interview Adrianna on TV, unaware of her fake identity, he had a heated discussion with Wilma. She snarled, "Being a smart critic doesn't begin to compensate for being born stupid!" But before the interview occurred, Adrianna passed out drunk after a Greek wedding and spent the night in Nick's room. Learning his real identity the next morning, she angrily left him. She recounted the incident to Wilma, who reacted with "Why, that sly old shark! I always thought he was only interested in a love affair with himself!" Then Nick discovered Adrianna's true self and tried to smooth things over with her, but she rejected him and planned to vacate an appearance with Dick Cavett along with Nick when Wilma convinced her to do otherwise. Adrianna confronted Nick with Cavett, and while he still disliked her book, he told her she had won him over personally.

This uneven episode of the dramatic series had a dreadful subplot where Genie Francis played James Brolin's troubled goddaughter. However, Betty delivered her dialogue with her usual panache and created a multidimensional character showing love, anger, disinterest, and more over the course of just a few scenes. Those factors, along with a few unexpected plot twists and Dick Cavett being Dick Cavett, helped merit this show three stars.

St. Elsewhere****

Cast: Ed Flanders (Dr. Donald Westphal), Norman Lloyd (Dr. Daniel Auschlander, director of services), Ed Begley Jr. (Dr. Victor Ehrlich), Stephen Furst (Dr. Elliot Axelrod, "Red, White, Black and Blue" only), Mark Harmon (Dr. Robert Caldwell), Eric Laneuville (Luther Hawkins), Howie Mandel (Dr. Wayne Fiscus "Red, White, Black and Blue" only), David Morse (Dr. Jack Morrison), Christina Pickles (Nurse Helen Rosenthal; "Red, White, Black and Blue" only), Cynthia Sikes (Dr. Annie Cavanero, "Red, White, Black and Blue" only), Denzel Washington (Dr. Philip Chandler), William Daniels (Dr. Mark Craig), Bonnie Bartlett (Ellen Craig, "Close Encounters" only). EP: Bruce Paltrow. P: John Masius, Tom Fantana.

"Red, White, Black and Blue"

February 13, 1985, NBC Wednesday 10-11 p.m.

Guest stars: Betty White (Captain Gloria Neal), Nancy Stafford (Joan Halloran), Herb Edelman (Richard Clarendon), Alan Fudge (Secret Service agent Knox), John Doolittle (Mr. Paley), Rhetta Greene (Ms. Wilkes), Ellen Bry (Nurse Shirley Daniels), Florence Halop (Mrs. Hufnagel). D: Eric Laneuville. W: Channing Gibson (teleplay), John Masius, Tom Fantana (story).

"Close Encounters"

November 20, 1985, NBC Wednesday 10-11 p.m.

Guest stars: Betty White (Captain Gloria Neal), Alfre Woodard (Dr. Roxanne Turner),

David Ackroyd (Colonel Chuck Cochrane), Jack Riley (Elliot Carlin), Oliver Clark (John Doe Number Six), Philip Sterling (Dr. Simon Weiss), Ramon Bieri (Gene Galecki), Suzanne Lederer (Yvonne Galecki), George Deloy (Ken Valere), Deborah May (Patti Valere), K Callan (Patty Galecki), Sagan Lewis (Dr. Jacqueline Wade), Linda Thorson (Jo Cochrane). D: Eric Laneuville. W: Norma Safford Vela (teleplay), John Masius, Tom Fantana (story).

St. Eligius was a last-minute pick to be a receiving hospital for a visit by the first lady in "Red, White, Black and Blue." Leading the charge was Captain Gloria Neal, one of the president's doctors. After she and Secret Service agent Knox reviewed protocol and plans for the event, Gloria joined Dr. Donald Westphal at home for dinner and exchanged pleasantries. Despite several complications, the tour by the chief executive's wife occurred smoothly the following day. As Gloria left, she said, "You know, Donald, back in med school, my knees used to get weak when I saw you. The feeling hasn't changed. I'm kind of sorry nothing happened last night." She kissed him, then the widower told his colleague Dr. Auschlander he had been inspired to make changes in his life. In an episode with a lot of plots unfolding, Eric Laneuville provided a firm directorial hand while being the only regular not seen here. And Betty's straight dramatic role went swimmingly.

Dr. Neal returned in "Close Encounters" to evaluate the mental condition of the hospital's patient, Colonel Chuck Cochrane, for NASA. Her diagnosis was unfavorable. "He's shouting from the mountaintop about walking with God. The public is going to think we're sending religious zealots into space. They'll lose confidence in NASA," she told Daniel. But Daniel favored Cochrane's attending physician, Dr. Jack Morrison, who recommended that Cochrane stay at St. Eligius before being handed over to the government for care. "Both times you've come to this hospital, I've never seen you function as a doctor," Daniel told Gloria. "And frankly, for all intents and purposes, I don't think you are one anymore." She gave him a handshake, then fretted, "This place is exactly the same" before leaving. As Gloria questioned Chuck's stability, in another part of the hospital Dr. Simon Weiss treated an amnesiac dubbed John Doe who thought he was Mary Richards of *The Mary Tyler Moore Show*. In one memorable moment, the patient saw Gloria and insisted she was Sue Ann Nivens. This wildly inventive episode packs a lot of emotions effectively into one hour, and Betty's confused reaction to being called Sue Ann was fantastic.

Betty told Tom Kennedy on the February 6, 1985, installment of *Body Language* that her first guest shot came when "I opened my big mouth on a *Tonight Show* [on April 19, 1983, with Joan Rivers] and said I had a big crush on Ed Flanders, and the next thing I know, they cast me in a script." She added, "We had a wonderful time. We also did the show!"

In 1986, Betty told Bettelou Peterson of the Knight-Ridder News Service that "They're working on another script" for Gloria to reappear on *St. Elsewhere*. That event never happened.

Who's the Boss?**
Cast: Tony Danza (Tony Micelli), Judith Light (Angela Bower), Alyssa Milano (Samantha Micelli), Danny Pintauro (Jonathan Bower), Katherine Helmond (Mona Robinson). EP: Martin Cohan, Blake Hunter. P: Bud Wiser.

"Eye on Angela"
February 19, 1985, ABC Tuesday 8:30-9 p.m.

Special guest star: Betty White (Bobbie Barnes). D: John Bowab. W: Ellen Guylas.

"Thanksgiving at Mrs. Rossini's"
November 26, 1985, ABC Tuesday 8-8:30 p.m.
Guests: Rhoda Gemignani (Carmella Rossini), Bill Erwin (Santa Claus), Ray "Boom Boom" Mancini (Joey Rossini), Ric Mancini (Joe Rossini), Donna Ponterotto (Theresa Rossini), Al Ruscc (Papa Joseph Rossini), Rosamarie Thomas (Gina Bonafetti), Betty White (Macy's Thanksgiving Day Parade voice). D: Asaad Kalada. W: Dawn Aldredge, Judith Bustany.

Seemingly sweet but actually conniving TV reporter Bobbie Barnes visited the home of Angela Bower. The advertising executive lived with her son Jonathan and mother Mona while having room for her live-in housekeeper Tony Micelli and his daughter Samantha. As the hostess of the local show "Eye on Hartford," she intimidated Angela during her initial run-through. That evening, the family watched a scary movie that gave them nightmares and prompted some changes in sleeping arrangements that inadvertently left Angela and Tony in bed together. Bobbie arrived early with her crew, Jonathan let them in and, of course, Bobbie discovered them leaving the room together.

"Would you like to tell us how you start your day?" leered Bobbie. "Well, you're really going to laugh when you hear this, but when Tony crawled into bed with me, he thought he was getting in bed with somebody else," she said. Bobbie asked if he meant to be with Mona, which flustered Angela in trying to respond to her. Tony tried his best to stop the tape from airing but said he would not sleep with Bobbie as part of his efforts, even though she told him, "It might work!" Then Mona intervened and threatened to blackmail Bobbie for having an affair, which forced Bobbie to drop the story. Betty enlivened this tiresome plot as much as she could, but her hard work and charm could not surpass the pedestrian dialogue and direction that made "Eye on Angela" a miss overall.

In "Thanksgiving at Mrs. Rossini's," Mona planned to attend the Macy's Thanksgiving Day parade while everyone else went to Brooklyn to enjoy the holiday at Tony's old pals the Rossinis. The men's sexism appalled Angela, while the sexy appearance of old school chum Gina Bonafetti stunned Tony. Midway through the show, everyone watched the Macy's Thanksgiving Day Parade, where Betty's voice intoned, "Here it is, folks. The moment you've all been waiting for, the Santa Claus float! I don't see Santa yet, but here's one of his elves!" The camera zoomed in on Mona smiling as Betty continued, "That's a mighty cute elf, but where's the big guy himself? Oh, here's another elf!" Another camera showed Mona from a different angle. "No, that's the same elf." "Tony should see this!" said Angela, and she ran into the kitchen finding Tony kissing Gina. In fact, Santa never appeared on TV during the parade, causing problems for Mona. A promising first half deflated fast in the second in this episode, and like most of the guest stars, Betty had relatively little to make amusing.

ALF Loves a Mystery**
September 12, 1987, NBC Friday 8-8:30 p.m.
Cast: Paul Fusco (Voice of ALF), Shannon Doherty (The Lady in Red), Stephen Furst (Max the Mole), Benji Gregory (Brian Tanner/Kid Cameron), Jackée Harry (The Countess), Danny Ponce (Frank Harty), Douglas Seale (The butler), Betty White (Aunt Harriet), Mary Wickes (Agatha Megpeace), Heidi Ziegler (Jo Harty). P/W: Joseph Maurer, Bradley Wigor. D: Tony Singletary.

ALF, which stood for Alien Life Form, previewed his new Saturday morning cartoon before his pal Brian Tanner encouraged him to write a private eye story. So, ALF transformed Brian into "Kid Cameron," a detective in a trench coat investigating a Hollywood mansion. The butler introduced Kid to Jo and Frank Harty. Kid's new client, the Countess, Max the Mole, and the Lady in Red. The Countess hired all the others to search for her lost fortune in the residence. For Kid and the Hartys, characters from NBC's fall 1987 Saturday morning lineup gave them clues where to find the treasure and showed clips from their cartoons. The Hartys and Kid also heard cries for help from the butler's Aunt Harriet, passing through on her way to a New Age convention in San Diego. She waved her hands over a crystal ball and insulted ALF appearing inside the ball before giving the trio a flashlight as they moved onward. "Here's looking at you, kid," intoned Kid. "What a guy!" heaved Aunt Harriet in response. When Kid and the Hartys found the jewels, Agatha Megpeace, the maid, revealed she was really an undercover officer and awarded the fortune to the Lady in Red. On screen less than three minutes, Betty enlivened an otherwise unexceptional promotional show using two characters from the NBC sitcom *ALF*, which aired from 1986 to 1990.

D.C. Follies, "Tammy Faye Bakker Debuts Her Latest Song"**

October 13, 1987, Syndicated Various times (30 minutes)

Regulars: Fred Willard, The Krofft Puppets. EP: Sid Krofft, Marty Krofft. D: Rick Locke. W: Mike Kirschenbaum, Bob Dolan Smith, E. Jeffrey Smith.

This flaccid attempt to satirize politics using puppets the way the superior *Spitting Images* did in the United Kingdom gave Betty a lousy part. Dolls representing Richard Nixon and Gerald Ford discussed getting a stripper for Jimmy Carter's birthday at D.C. Follies, a popular watering hole for politicos in the nation's capital. The ecdysiast was Betty sporting balloons on top of her clothes. "They call me the Hawaiian volcano," she cooed. "That's because I can cook pineapple dishes and erupt at the same time!" When the bartender recognized her from *The Golden Girls*, she replied, "A girl has to think of her future!" With lame lines and plotting, there was little here to like.

The Dom DeLuise Show, untitled episode

October 15, 1987, Syndicated Various times (30 minutes)

Cast: Dom DeLuise (Dom DeLuca), Lois Foraker (Blanche Maxwell). Guest: Betty White (Herself). EP: Greg Garrison.

Betty joined Hollywood barber Dom DeLuca in recalling the "good old days" while he and his girlfriend Blanche dreaded marrying each other. This poorly reviewed and little viewed sitcom lasted just one season before vanishing from circulation.

Matlock, "The Network"**
December 1, 1987, NBC Tuesday 8-9 p.m.
Cast: Andy Griffith (Ben Matlock), Nancy Stafford (Michelle Thomas). Special appearances: ALF, Jason Bateman, Corbin Bernsen, Rhea Perlman, Malcolm Jamal-Warner, Betty White (Themselves). Guest stars: Harris Laskawy (Larry Davis), Cameron Mitchell (Lane Lockletter), Jonathan Perpich (David Martin), Granville Van Dusen (Paul J. Bartel), Ann Gillespie (Linda Lewis), John Zarchen (Jordan Sanders), Larry Anderson (Doug August), Debra Sue Maffett (Terry McNeil). EP: Fred Silverman, Dean Hargrove. P: Richard Collins. Co-P: Jeff Peters. D: Christopher Hibler. W: Philip Mishkin (teleplay), Dean Hargrove and Joel Steiger (story).

TV producer Paul J. Bartel fought a charge that he literally stabbed in the back Greg Titlemen, a network programming chief. Doug August and Terry McNeil, hosts of the show "Hollywood Today," described the murder case to viewers and cut to celebrities giving their reactions, starting with Betty White on the set of *The Golden Girls*. "Greg wasn't the cold-hearted, impersonal executive everyone thought him to be," she said. "You know, the kind who did everything on the phone. To the contrary, he thrived on the personal touch. For instance, when he cancelled my first series, he personally told his assistant to call me. An actress remembers that kind of thoughtfulness, believe me."

That flat joke led into another lousy one by Corbin Bernsen before the show recounted the murder's circumstances and Bartel's defense by top lawyer Ben Matlock and his associate Michelle Thomas. More celebrity interviews with horrible punchlines occurred as Ben interviewed suspects like TV star Lane Lockletter, Westland Studios head Larry Davis, and Greg's successor David Martin and his assistant Linda Lewis. Despite the director's considerable efforts to punch up the proceedings, this limp mystery was pretty dull, even with a bit role by Aneta Corsaut, who previously was Andy Griffith's love interest, Helen Crump, on *The Andy Griffith Show*.

Chance of a Lifetime***
November 18, 1991, NBC Monday 9-11 p.m.
Cast: Betty White (Evelyn Eglin), Leslie Nielsen (Lloyd Dixon), Ed Begley Jr. (Darrel

Elgin), Michael Tucci (Randall), Ann Turkel (Tippi), Annabelle Gurwitch (Sherry), Lincoln Kilpatrick (Amos), Orson Bean (Fred), Elaine Stritch (Sybil), William Windom (Dr. Bill Edelman). EP/W: Lynn Roth. EP: Charles Fries. D Jonathan Sanger.

After Dr. Bill Edelman said she had only six months to live, demanding that drapery company president Evelyn Eglin pretend everything was fine to her son, Darrel. Seeing an infomercial for Café de Paradiso, a Mexican resort promising pleasure, Evelyn booked a trip. The widow's sudden move shocked her subordinates Randall, Sherry, and Amos. At the resort, pretentious young floozy Tippi flirted with distinguished Lloyd Dixon, but he only wanted Evelyn. Their relationship blossomed, and Evelyn even agreed to bungee jump from a balloon along with dining and sleeping with Lloyd. But when Dr. Edelman informed Evelyn she was misdiagnosed, she returned immediately to her workplace without telling Lloyd. A determined Lloyd tracked her down and, while Evelyn pretended to object and be uninterested in him, the truth finally came out. Betty clearly had fun here, as she got to dance energetically with Leslie among other activities. Though the script was unexceptional, the efficient direction and Stephen McNutt's rich cinematography emphasizing warm colors and lighting, made this frothy TV movie easy to watch.

Diagnosis Murder, "Death By Extermination"***
December 2, 1994, CBS Friday 8-9 p.m.
Cast: Dick Van Dyke (Dr. Mark Sloan), Scott Baio (Dr. Jack Stewart), Victoria Rowell (Dr. Amanda Bentley-Livingston), Michael Tucci (Norman Briggs), Delores Hall (Nurse Delores Mitchell), Barry Van Dyke (Steve Sloan). Guests: Susan Gibney (Genevieve Ducasse), Elyssa Davalos (Constance Wardell), Joel Polis (Larry Macklin), Kari Lizer (Lena Prosser), Betty White (Dora Sloan). Also: Jann Karam (Receptionist), John Walter Davis (Shep Cruikshank the exterminator), Sara Peery (Sarabeth), Robert Crow (Uniformed Man). EP: Michael Gleason, Dean Hargrove, Fred Silverman. F: Barry Steinberg. D: Christopher Hibler. W: Dan Wilcox.

Dr. Mark Sloan's overbearing older sister Dora visited and inconvenienced the physician on his day off while she waited for her new home to be sprayed for termites. As Dora showed Mark the house's walk-in closet, the body of her real estate agent, Harvey Wardell, fell out. Mark's son Steve, a detective, determined someone killed Wardell by drugging. He forbade Dora from moving in and told her to stay with

Mark in the meantime, to Mark's chagrin. At Dora's real estate company, Mark met the late man's secretary, Lena Prosser, while Dora enlisted Genevieve Ducasse as her new agent for the house. As the deceased also cheated on his wife, Constance Wardell, and faced threats from an unhappy client, Larry Macklin, they were suspects, as well. Meanwhile, Mark's colleagues Jack, Amanda, Norman, and Delores experienced Dora's opinions and nagging, and Amanda and Jack even endured Dora interfering in their investigative work.

Like many episodes on this series, which ran from 1993 to 2001, the mystery was too loosely constructed and presented, and the mixture of comedy and suspense was sloppy. The suspects were uninteresting compared to Dora, too. But making Betty so integral to the plot made up for lots of those shortcomings. Having her sing "For Me and My Gal" with Dick, speak Russian—or an approximation thereof—with a contact in Moscow, and help in unmasking the criminal made this a treat for Betty watchers.

The Naked Truth, "Elvis is Coming"**
September 27, 1995, ABC Wednesday 9:30-10 p.m.
Cast: Tea Leoni (Nora Wilde), Holland Taylor (Camilla Dane), Jonathan Penner (Nicky Columbus), Amy Ryan (Chloe Banks), Mark Roberts (Dave Fontaine), Darryl Savid (T.J.). Special appearance: Betty White (Herself). Guests: Larry Drake (Dr. Bryce Folger), Brighton Hertford (Lizzie). Creator/EP: Chris Thompson. EP: Brad Grey, Bernie Brillstein. D: Ted Bessell. W: Laurie Parres.

While driving her car, Betty was shocked by photographer Nora Wilde snapping pictures in her car. Apologizing for the ambush, Nora said, "I just need a couple of pictures. ... This is a new job, and the competition is so fierce, and you're so sweet on television. Do you mind?" "Don't be silly, dear!" said Betty with a smile. She invited Nora to sit in the front passenger seat, only to throw her out. "Bet you wouldn't have done that if I was a Cocker Spaniel!" exclaimed Nora. Betty disappeared after that teaser for a tasteless, joyless main plot about a doctor wanting to inseminate Nora with Elvis Presley's sperm. Despite what some sources claim, Betty didn't appear on this series' "Star and Comet Collide! Giant Bugs Invade!" episode that aired November 15, 1995.

A Weekend in the Country**

June 12, 1996, USA Network

Cast: Faith Ford (Susan Kaye), Christine Lahti (Ruth Oakley), Jack Lemmon (Bud Bailey), Richard Lewis (Bobby Stein), Dudley Moore (Simon Farrell), Rita Rudner (Sally Shelton), John Shea (Michael Kaye), Betty White (Martha). Also appearing: Joe Clarke (Delivery man), Dan Cortese (Thunder the masseur), Jennifer Elise Cox (Arista Farrell), Joseph Fusco (Flight attendant), Jim Kline (Paul), Lisa Mende (Christine), Donna Ponterotto (Flight attendant). EP: Larry Estes, Rob Kenneally, Jack Lemmon, Michael Rotenberg. P/D: Martin Bergman. W: Martin Bergman, Rita Rudner.

Sally Shelton's fellow airplane passenger Martha drank wine heavily as she learned that Sally was artificially inseminated. "How extraordinary! I always wondered about that. Was it … pleasant?" Martha grinned. She added, "I love modern women! They take everything into their own hands. Bravo!" When Martha said the latter, she accidentally spilled some wine on Sally. Martha then vanished while Sally arrived in Temecula, California, and stayed at the inn of New Age enthusiast Ruth Oakley. Also on Sally's flight and at Ruth's inn was comedian Bobby Stein, booked for a concert by cheap, boring promoter Bud Bailey. Bobby reconnected with Susan, his old flame now married to Michael Kaye. They lived next door to wine harvester Simon Farrell, who coincidentally was the sperm donor for Sally and the ex-husband of Ruth. The supposedly comic complications leisurely unfolded with little humor or excitement. Betty's role was just an extended cameo, and it's a shame that she didn't get to work with Jack Lemmon even though he was one of the executive producers. Star Rita Rudner co-wrote the screenplay with her husband, Martin Bregman, who served as producer and director, Martin Bregman. Originally planned for theatrical release first, this TV movie had Dudley Moore in his last acting role.

Suddenly Susan, "Golden Girl Friday"**

November 7, 1996, NBC Thursday 9:30-10 p.m.

Cast: Brooke Shields (Susan Keane), Nestor Carbonell (Luis Rivera), Kathy Griffin (Vicki Groener), Judd Nelson (Jack Richmond), David Strickland (Todd Stiles), Barbara Barrie ('Nana' Eileen Keane). Special guest star: Betty White (Midge Haber) Guests: Peg Phillips (Judge G. Campbell, incorrectly billed in the credits as "Judge Cameron"), Caroline Williams (Ms. Turner), Debbie James (Lacy), Cal

Gibson (George), John P. Griffin (Ernie), Elliot Woods (Lenny). EP and Developers: Gary Dontzig, Steven Peterman. Co-EP: Dan O'Shannon. Supervising P: Ian Praiser. Co-P: Perry Rogers. Consulting P: Mimi Friedman, Jeanette Collins. Consulting P: Korby Siamis. P: Frank Pace. Creator: Clyde Phillips. D: Shelley Jensen. W: Rick Singer, Andrew Green.

When her boss Jack looked for an assistant, Susan suggested hiring Midge. Susan's grandmother Nana had said that Midge, her taekwondo class partner, was a former corporate secretary who needed a job. But Midge fouled everything for Susan's coworkers, from taking unreadable phone messages for Vicki to parking on Todd's moped. When fired, Midge retaliated by suing Jack for age discrimination. On the stand, the seemingly befuddled Midge became well-spoken. Discussing her dismissal, she told the judge, "I just hope that I live to see the day when people are not judged by the color of their hair. Whatever it may be!" Midge's lawyer undermined the claims of Jack's staff on the stand, too.

After Midge left the court giggling, Susan confronted her in the bathroom. Midge discovered a tape recorder on Susan and said, "Don't ever try to con a con! You're such a bleeding heart, you and your Nana! And your hip, happening coworkers. You were the easiest marks I ever had!" Unbeknownst to Midge, the hidden Nana recorded the tirade.

At the end, Midge rolled her eyes as she posed for mug shots and a narrator intoned, "Midge Haber was convicted of perjury with intent to defraud and was sentenced to 500 hours of community service in the Milliken Avenue Day Care Center." The latter segment was the funniest bit in an otherwise largely unamusing show. Betty got an Emmy nomination for her sharp work, but her scenarios, pretending to be dense and her transformation to a savvy conniver, were flatly written and presented.

The Story of Santa Claus**
December 4, 1996, CBS Wednesday 8-9 p.m.
Voices: Ed Asner (Nicholas "Santa" Claus), Betty White (Mrs. Gretchen Claus), Tim Curry (Mr. Nostros), Miko Hughes (Clement), Kathryn Zaremba (Aurora), Jim Cummings (Mr. Minch). EP: Arnold Shapiro. D: Toby Bluth. W: Rachel Koretsky, Steve Whitestone.

In Europe "a long time ago," the childless, poor Clauses gave out free toys to children. When they sailed out to sea on a borrowed boat, a powerful storm propelled them to the North Pole, where they saved Clement the elf. Mr. Nostros, the wizard, granted the Clauses a wish in return. Santa wanted to make and deliver toys for free for children across the world on Christmas. Seeing Clement, Aurora, and other elves transforming into reality, what he thought was impossible, Nostros plotted to destroy their progress during the year. Even with low expectations for an animated children's special, this Yuletide yawner was humdrum rather than ho ho ho. Treacly music and lyrics by Marie Maxwell and John Thomas drew out the monotony. Worst of all, Mrs. Claus did little more than fret and swoon over her husband.

"I only had to do one day's recording; Ed [Asner] had to do several," Betty told Bridget Byrne of Entertainment News Wire about this special. "It was great working with him again."

The Lionhearts**
Voices: William H. Macy (Leo Lionheart Jr.), Peri Gilpin (Lana Lionheart), Natasha Slayton (Kate Lionheart), Cameron Finley (Spencer Lionheart), Nicolette Little (Judy Lionheart), Joe Pantalino (Various). EP: Paul Sabella, Jonathan Dern, Ruth Bennett. P/D: Byron Vaughns.

"Family Circus"
September 19, 1998, Syndicated Various times (30 minutes)
Guest voices: Harve Presnell (Leo Lionheart Sr.), Betty White (Dorothy). W: Ruth Bennett.

"... But Some of My Best Friends Are Clowns"
October 3, 1998, Syndicated Various times (30 minutes)
Guest voices: Tom Arnold (Shecky Bell), Andrea Martin (Lucy Bell), Wallace Shawn (Freddy the studio executive), Betty White (Dorothy). W: Greg Antonacci.

"Singin' in the Mane"
October 17, 1998, Syndicated Various times (30 minutes)
Guest voices: Flea (Iceberg), Richard Kind (Chorus Teacher), Jeffrey Tambor (Hank, the head of MGM), Betty White (Dorothy). W: Joanne Pagliaro.

"Brown Dog Day"
November 14, 1998, Syndicated Various times (30 minutes)
Guest voices: Karl Malden (Sekulovich the neighbor), Wallace Shawn (Freddy the studio executive), Betty White (Dorothy). W: Greg Antonacci.

"Leo's Diet"
November 21, 1998, Syndicated Various times (30 minutes)
Guest voices: Harve Presnell, Wallace Shawn (Freddy the studio executive), Jeffrey Tambor (Hank, the head of MGM), Betty White (Dorothy). W: Rick Gitelson.

In this animated series, Leo Lionheart was the big cat who roared at the start of MGM productions. At home, Leo coped with his loud guitarist son Spencer, his horse-loving daughter Kate, his impish toddler Judy and his wife Lana, an ex-circus acrobat. Helping him prepare for the camera was Dorothy, a makeup lady with poor vision whose service extended back forty-three years earlier to styling Leo's father. She gave him a rather messy mane while interacting with him and did little else. Betty is so wasted here that her character had just one line in "Singin' in the Mane" and just two in "Brown Dog Day." This aimless, useless trifle had the odd aim of promoting a movie studio brand primarily to preschoolers and ended after thirteen episodes. Betty would appear in another feline-based animated series in 2004 with similarly disappointing results, *Father of the Pride*.

Noddy, "Anything Can Happen at Christmas"
December 6, 1998, PBS Kids Sunday 10:30-11:30 a.m.
Cast: Sean McCann (Noah), Katie Boland (Kate), Kyle Kassardjian (Daniel "D.J." Johnson), Max Morrow (Truman), Jayne Eastwood (Aunt Agatha). Voices: Catherine Disher (Noddy), Karen Bernstein (Tessie Bear), Benedict Campbell (Santa and others). Guest: Betty White (Mrs. Santa Claus).

"Noddy" was the acronym of the officially named "Notions, Oddities, Doodads and Delights of Yesterday," an antique shop operated by Noah Tompkins. His grandchildren Kate and Truman hung out there often with their pal D.J. to enjoy the talking puppets and other magic in the store. The children also played with a doll, conveniently named Noddy, that they asked for advice on problems, which led to playing in an animated cartoon with Noddy and his friends facing a similar situation and teaching a moral. This Canadian production somehow got Betty to visit Truman at the shop and take him to the North Pole for its Christmas installment. Betty played Mrs. Claus for the second time in two years, following *The Story of Santa Claus* in 1996. She would reprise the role in 2010 for *Prep & Landing Stocking Stuffer*. This episode was unavailable for review as of this writing.

LA Doctors, "Leap of Faith"
December 7, 1998, CBS Monday 10-11 p.m.
Cast: Ken Olin (Dr. Roger Cattan), Matt Craven (Dr. Tim Lonner), Rick Roberts (Dr. Evan Newman), Sheryl Lee (Dr. Sarah Church), Joseph Ashton (Nick Newman), Coby Bell (Patrick Owen), Dierdre O'Connell (Susann Blum), Rebecca Rigg (Kelly Newman), Melora Walters (Felicity). Guests: Judith Scott (Nina Morris), Talia Balsam (Julie Lonner), Erica Jiminez-Alvarado (Eva Lonner), Vanessa Erica Jiminez-Alvarado (Christine Lonner), Betty White (Mrs. Brooks). D: Reynaldo Villalobos. W: John Lee Hancock.

Betty played a woman who refused to have Dr. Tim Lonner operate on her brain tumor because she thought it let her contact her late husband. This medical drama ran only from 1998 to 1999.

Disney's Hercules, "Hercules and the Tiff on Olympus"**
March 1, 1999, Syndicated Various times (30 minutes)
Voices: Tate Donovan (Hercules), Corey Burton (Zeus), James Woods (Hades), Robert P. Costanza (Philoctetes), Samantha Eggar (Hera), Frank Welker (Pegasus), Bob Goldthwait (Pain), French Stewart (Icarus). Guest voices: Richard Lewis (Neurosis), Betty White (Hestia), John Kassir (Charon). EP: Tad Stones. D: Phil Weinstein. W/ Story Editors: Richard Liebmann-Smith, Ken Koonce, Michael Merton.

In this one-season cartoon's finale, Zeus, the scheming brother of fellow god Hades, tried to undermine the marriage of Zeus and Hera and the confidence of their mortal son Hercules. To achieve the latter, he conjured up Neurosis, a creature who lives up to his name, to dampen the spirit of Hercules. Figuring into this turmoil was Hestia, a goddess party planner upset by how these developments cause havoc to her celebrations. Betty voiced a minor role in a minor series despite Disney having corralled considerable name talent to voice its characters. The problem was self-consciously "clever" writing with several jokes that probably went over the head of younger viewers—and weren't that funny either—while using juvenile plotting bored any adult viewers.

King of the Hill
Voices: Mike Judge (Hank Hill, Boomhauer, and others), Kathy Najimy (Peggy Hill), Pamela Segall Adlon (Bobby Hill and others), Jonathan Hardwick (Dale Gribble), Stephen Root (Bill Dauterive). EP: Greg Daniels, Mike Judge, Jonathan Aibel, Glenn Berger, Howard Klein, Michael Rotenberg. P: Richard Appel, Kit Boss, Dean Young, David Zucker, Mark McJimsey, Joe Boucher.

"Escape from Party Island"*
March 16, 1999, Fox Tuesday 8-8:30 p.m.

Voices: Brittany Murphy (Luanne Platter), Toby Huss (Cotton Hill). Also starring: Phil Buckman (Chad), Dave Buzzota (Waiter Frat Guy), Dena Dietrich (Tilly's friend), Beth Grant (Tilly Hill), Rich Rinaldi. Special guest voices: Phyllis Diller (Lillian), Uta Hagen (Maureen), Pauly Shore (Deejay), Betty White (Delia). D: Gary McCarver. W: Jonathan Collier.

"The Son Also Roses"*
December 8, 2002, Fox, Sunday, 8:30-9 p.m.
Special guest voices: Michael Clarke Duncan (Coach Webb/Morgan), Betty White (Dorothy/Ellen). Also starring: David Herman (Monroe), Phil LaMarr, Breckin Meyer (Joseph Gribble), Lauren Tom (Connie). D: Dominic Polcino. W: Dan Sterling.

Hank's mother Tilly Hill came to visit in "Escape from Party Island," taking him away from hanging out with Boomhauer, Dale, and Bill. He had to drive Tilly and her four friends to tour a miniature museum on an island off the Texas coast. The quintet exasperated Hank, especially Delia, a hot-tempered ex-nurse who, at one point, threw her wig at Hank in disgust. Adding to his hassles, MTV hosted spring break festivities at their hotel and forced them to curtail their activities. Betty had the best lines among the seasoned actresses voicing the mature characters, but some parts were forced and stereotypical, limiting the pleasure despite everyone giving their best.

In "The Son Also Roses," Hank wanted his bumbling son Bobby to play football at Tom Landry Middle School, and the latter got a job as a towel boy. Even that menial duty impressed Hank, but Bobby preferred growing roses. When Hank discovered his son's passion, Peggy encouraged him to let Bobby compete in a flower competition. Hank embraced the preparation for the judging strongly to Bobby's dismay. Betty had only four lines as a snickering rose contestant midway through the show and sources differ whether her character's name was Dorothy or Ellen. Regardless, this episode of the animated sitcom was a poor showing overall in more ways than one.

Ally McBeal, "Saving Green"***
November 8, 1999, Fox Monday 9-10 p.m.
Cast: Calista Flockhart (Ally McBeal), Courtney Thorne-Smith (Georgia Thomas), Greg Germann (Richard Fish), Lisa Nicole Carson (Renee Raddick), Jane Krakowski (Elaine Vassal), Vonda Shepard (Herself), Portia de Rossi (Nelle Porter), Lucy Liu (Ling Woo), Peter MacNicol (John Cage), Gil Bellows (Billy Thomas). Guests: Betty White (Dr. Shirley Flott), Gerry Becker (Myron Stone), Nicki Aycox (Kim Puckett), Holmes Osborne (Principal Figgins), Brad Wilson (Harold). Special appearance: Al Green (Himself), Gladys Knight (Herself). EP/W: David E. Kelley. Co-EP: Jonathan Pontell. P: Pamela Wisne, Steve Robin, Jeffrey Kramer, Mike Listo. D: Peter MacNicol.

Ally confessed to her new therapist, Dr. Shirley Flott, that she had visions of Al Green singing to her. The doctor suggested Ally use an antidepressant and added, "I'm on it!" Ally objected to using a mind-altering drug, but Dr. Flott insisted. "Mine comes in a suppository form. Gives me a little wriggle!" giggled the doctor. Returning to Dr. Flott, Ally told of having sex in a car wash with a stranger and kissing a woman and knew that she couldn't fall in love with either of them. "Does that make any sense?" she asked a stunned Shirley, who called Ally "vulgar" and insisted she do drugs. Ally refused and left. The hallucinations intensified as Ally saw her coworkers sing along with Al Green in a production number of "Let's Stay Together" featuring Gladys Knight leading a gospel chorus. "I think it was a transition fantasy," she told a disinterested Dr. Flatt, who gave her a prescription. "Mental health will soon be yours. And then the only problem you'll have left is whether or not your friends will recognize you!" said the doctor.

Worried about "killing" Al Green, Ally flushed the pills down a toilet, prompting Dr. Flott to accuse Ally of suffering from dementia. Noting how easily she gave the drugs to Ally in suppository form, she yelled, "Stick it up your ass!" and added, "Oh, go pick another theme song, you pissy little thing, I'm through with you." Dr. Flott threw out Ally with the latter's mouth agape. Ally had one last hallucination with Al Green dancing with her before vanishing. Like most episodes of *Ally McBeal*, this is the type of show whose quirks can either charm or grate on a viewer. At the very least, it's quite stylish, and Betty is mesmerizingly unpredictable throughout her part.

The Simpsons
Voices: Dan Castellaneta (Homer Simpson), Julie Kavner (Marge Simpson), Nancy Cartwright (Bart Simpson), Yardley Smith (Lisa Simpson), Hank Azaria (Various), Harry Shearer (Various), Tress MacNeille (Various).
"Missionary: Impossible" ****
February 20, 2000, Fox Sunday 8-8:30 p.m.
Special guest voice: Betty White (Herself). EP: Mike Scully, James L. Brooks, Matt Groening, Sam Simon. P: Bonita Pietila, Denise Sirkot, Richard Sakai. D: Steven Dean Moore. W: Ron Hauge.
"Homerazzi" ***
March 25, 2007, Fox Sunday 8-8:30 p.m.
Special guest voices: Jon Lovitz (Enrico Irritazio), J.K. Simmons (Editor), Betty White (Herself). Also starring: Pamela Hayden (Little girl), Karl Weidergott. EP: Ian Maxtone-Graham, Matt Selman, Tim Long. Co-EP: John Frink, Don Payne, Dana Gould, Kevin Curran, Michael Price, Bob Odenkirk, Marc Wilmore, Joel H. Cohen. D: Matthew Nastuk. Co-EP/W: J. Stewart Burns.

On "Missionary: Impossible," Homer Simpson and his son Bart were upset when Betty interrupted their British comedy show on TV. "If you like great PBS programs like 'Do Shut Up' and 'Shut Your Gob,' you'll want to support our pledge drive," she said. Betty added, "If you watch one second of PBS and don't contribute, you're a thief!" As Homer moaned, Betty noted, "We're only $10,000 away from returning to our show!" Homer made an anonymous pledge of that amount to get back to his program. To his shock, officials traced his call back to his house, and Betty arrived with the PBS Pledge Enforcement Van to pick up the money. Learning Homer couldn't pay, Betty led a mob after him.

Homer took refuge in the First Church of Springfield, where the pastor spirited him away to be a missionary in the South Pacific. A ham radio let him communicate w ith his family in Springfield, who told Homer he was now regarded as a humanitarian for his work. Bart pretended to be Homer at work, while Homer introduced the tribe to casino gambling and an ersatz form of beer. The activities corrupted the tribe members. A guilty Homer told them they were all sinners and needed to build a chapel to repent and .. well, to say there was a surprise ending involving Betty is an understatement. A deft spoof of the television industry and people's obsession with the medium, and to a certain extent Betty's image, this episode was a delight.

When an accident destroyed Marge's photo album in "Homerazzi," the family restaged the lost pictures. One new shot caught a celebrity tryst in the background. Homer sold the photo to a tabloid publisher for a sum that encouraged him to ambush stars with his camera. While at a dry cleaner, complaining that no star had acknowledged his existence, Betty greeted him. "Hello, Homer! Have you lost weight?" she asked. "Oh, like you care, Betty White!" he groused. "Oh, how's Maggie?" "Her name is Marge." "I was talking about your baby." "Uh, oh, she's looking very snappish!" he said, clicking a photo. "Thanks for taking my picture. If you want me to sign it, here's a stamped self-addressed envelope. And give Santa's Little Helper a big hug for me!" Betty said. "Yeah, that's right, just walk away!" Homer muttered as Betty left. Betty voiced herself smoothly in an episode that was fine but less layered than her previous outing on *The Simpsons*.

The Wild Thornberrys

Voices: Lacey Chabert (Eliza Thornberry), Tim Curry (Nigel Thornberry), Jodi Carlisle (Marianne Hunter Thornberry), Flea (Donnie Thornberry), Danielle Harris (Debbie Thornberry), Tom Kane (Darwin the chimp).

"A Tiger by the Tail"***

February 26, 2000. Nickelodeon Saturday Various times (30 minutes)

Special guest voices: Betty White (Grandma Sophie Hunter), Zoe Adnopoz (Kalia), Phil Proctor (Game host/bodybuilder), Alex Veadov (Yuri), Leeza Vinnichenko (Svetlana). Co-EP: Eryk Casemiro. D: Mark Risley. W: Adam Beechen, Kate Boutilier.

"A Family Tradition"**

November 22, 2000, Nickelodeon Wednesday Various times (30 minutes)

Special guest voices: Betty White (Grandma Sophie Hunter), Roscoe Lee Browne (Goulam). D: Mark Risley. W: Alice Miller, Kate Boutilier.

"The Anniversary" ***
December 11, 2000, Nickelodeon Monday Various times (30 minutes)
Special guest voices: Betty White (Grandma Sophie Hunter), Ed Asner (Grandpa Frank Hunter), Robert Ito (Asian Black Bear). D: Cathy Malkasian. W: Earl Hamner, Don Spies.

Grandma Sophie Hunter's dislike of exploring the outdoors made it difficult when she joined her daughter Marianne filming a salmon spawning run in Russia in "A Tiger by the Tail." The Thornberrys were nature documentarians, with Marianne as cinematographer and her husband Nigel as host. Marianne ordered Nigel and their daughters Eliza—who secretly could talk to animals—and Debbie, adopted infant son Donnie and pet chimp Darwin to make everything perfect for her mother. To everyone's surprise, Sophie had taken a great adventures class and now enjoyed the open country.

Inspired by the change, Eliza tried to get her friend Kalia, the Siberian tiger, to visit, but the creature turned on her. Eliza stayed away as the rest of her family filmed on the river near where Kalia lived, even when Sophie said, "We've got to stare down our nightmares." But Eliza was inspired by Sophie's bravery in rafting even though her grandmother had not done the activity before. "I'll never be as fearless as your Mother, of course, but you certainly can," Sophie told Eliza. Eliza summoned Kalia to save them during their trip, and she reconciled with the talking tiger. Sophie departed, happy that her daughter Marianne was becoming more domesticated. This animated cartoon series no doubt appealed to Betty with its love for wild animals, and her portrayal of this grandmother was endearing without being cloying.

The day before Thanksgiving, Sophie spoke to Eliza and Debbie through a short-wave radio to request the Thornberrys come home to celebrate with her in "A Family Tradition." Nigel and Marianne needed to get footage in East Africa for their foundation's next film, but they let their children and Darwin fly back to the United States. Goulam, a native, took the quartet to the airport, but the girls decided they would miss their parents. With Goulam gone, the girls tried to return to their campsite. But Nigel and Marianne decided to go home, too, before learning from Goulam that their children had missed the plane. Goulam located Eliza and company, and instructed them to go to the caves, where the family dramatically reunited amid the threat of crocodiles in the river. Marianne apologized to her mother on the radio for missing the dinner and Sophie graciously accepted. It would have been more interesting to see the Thornberrys eat rather than endure this episode's tiresome plot in the second half, especially to give more for Betty to do.

For "The Anniversary," Sophie and Frank Hunter celebrated their fiftieth wedding anniversary in Japan with a surprise visit to the Thornberrys. Determined to show he was still in shape at age seventy, Frank climbed Mount Fuji with Eliza and Darwin at night. But Frank got stuck under a tree limb hit by lightning, and after Eliza freed him, they returned to the camp, only to encounter an Asian black bear whose paw was trapped. As a veterinarian, Frank was able to treat the bear while Eliza communicated to the beast to be calm and trust her grandfather. Renewed by the experience, Frank and Eliza scaled the mountain. The next morning, Eliza and Frank returned to their family and brought the black bear for Nigel and Marianne to film for their next documentary. A touching meditation on the challenges of aging and the longevity of love, this episode allowed Ed to showcase his acting range extensively and make room for some nice moments by Betty.

In addition to these three episodes, Betty voiced Sophie in the 2002 theatrical movie adaptation of this series called *The Wild Thornberrys*.

The Retrievers**

July 30, 2001, Animal Planet Monday 8-10 p.m.
Cast: Robert Hays (Tom Lowry), Mel Harris (Karen Lowry), Alan Fachins (Ed), Alana Austin (Liz Lowry), Taylor Emerson (Widdy Lowry). With: Betty White (Angela Krisper), Robert Wagner (Durham Haysworth). Also: Kurt Johnson (Marcel), Cathy Fithian (Charlene Groper), Ken Tipton (Norman Groper), Josh Dennis (Marvin Groper), Desiree Yard (Brenda Groper), Cole Stratton (Phil), Ryan A. Allen (Fred), Leon Russom (Farmer Jenkins), Glenn Dunk (Frank Haddock), Katy Barnhill (Lulu Betts). EP: Steve Austin. P: Jonathan Bogner. D: Paul Schneider. W: Larry Ketron.

Arriving in a remodeled country home in Placerville, California, the Lowrys found a Golden Retriever who insisted on staying. They dubbed her Pilot. She gave birth to six puppies, which the family enjoyed while Tom worked overtime to design an advertising campaign to impress his client, billionaire Durham Haysworth. Eventually Tom, his wife Karen, daughter Liz, and son Widdy gave away the puppies. Those adopting the pooches included Angela Krisper. When Widdy told his family Pilot had run away and barked at houses to find her puppies, Tom said they needed to retrieve the retrievers.

They contacted Angela first. "Why, you're the people that gave me that horrible little dog!" she griped. She was glad to return her puppy because he had been destroying her furniture and chewing on everything. "I thought having a dog was supposed to reduce your stress level!" she added before surrendering her puppy and celebrating its removal. More complications abounded as the Lowrys continued their retrieval efforts, all pretty boring.

Filmed on location, this TV movie stressed cuteness over compelling characters and told a story too slender to interest most mature viewers. A few musical sequences to pad out the running time didn't help. Anyone interested in seeing Betty play a woman who doesn't bond with a dog for a change should know that she's in this film less than five minutes total.

The Ellen Show, "Missing the Bus"****
November 16, 2001, CBS Friday 8:30-9 p.m.
Cast: Ellen DeGeneres (Ellen Richmond), Jim Gaffigan (Rusty Carnouk), Emily Rutherford (Catherine Richmond), Martin Mull (Mr. Ed Munn), Kerri Kenney (Pam), Cloris Leachman (Dot Richmond). Special guest star: Betty White (Mrs. Connie Gibson). Guests: Dakota Fanning (Young Ellen Richmond), Porscha Coleman (Kid #1), Grady Hutt (Kid #2). EP: Mitchell Hurwitz, Carol Leifer, Ellen DeGeneres. P: Chuck Martin. D: Andrew D. Weyman. W: Ric Swartzlander (teleplay and story), Jim Gerkin (story).

Guidance counselor Ellen Richmond recognized Mrs. Gibson, her old school bus driver who has been active in her profession for forty-five years. She remembered Ellen was responsible for the only traffic ticket of her career, which put her on suspension for two weeks. Learning Mrs. Gibson had an upcoming birthday, Ellen planned a surprise party. To Ellen's horror, her principal Mr. Munn announced it was Mrs. Gibson's mandatory retirement party, as well, since she turned sixty-five. "Well, how did anyone know my age or even that it was my birthday?" an indignant Mrs. Gibson asked. Having revealed that fact, Ellen had to drive the bus before Mrs. Gibson took over the following morning. "You drove right over my heart, and you didn't even signal!" she fumed to Ellen. "If that's not a country song, it really should be," Ellen quipped before pledging to find extra money in the school budget to keep Gibson as a driver. After a slow start, great comic lines flourished in this show, all expertly delivered by a top cast.

And it was fun as always to see Betty face off against Cloris Leachman, here playing Ellen's mother. Unfortunately, the series lasted only thirteen episodes.

Disney's Teacher's Pet, "The Turkey That Came to Dinner"***
March 23, 2002, ABC Saturday 8:30-9 a.m.
Voices: Nathan Lane (Spot/"Scott Leadready"), Debra Rupp (Ms. Marilu Moira Angela Darling Helperman), Shaun Fleming (Leonard Helperman), Jerry Stiller (Pretty Boy), David Ogden Stiers (Mr. Jolly). Guest voices: Betty White (Grandma Rose), William Sanderson (Lurkey). EP: Gary Baseman, Bill and Cheri Steinkellner. D: Ennio Torresan Jr. W/Story Editors: Bill and Cheri Steinkellner.

A dog that wanted to be a boy, "Scott Leadready," hung out with his child owner, Leonard, pretending to be a neighborhood friend, as well as a fellow student. When Grandma Rose planned to visit, her pet allergy forced Scott to stay in the laundry room during Thanksgiving. Rose brought Leonard the vintage video game "Catch the Blog" and his mom a fresh, live turkey. The turkey, named Lurkey, had a southern drawl and needed Scott and Leonard's help to avoid his fate. Scott managed to escape and pretend to be a boy to Leonard's mom, Marilu Moira Angela Darling Helperman, and Grandma, while Lurkey dissuaded Rose from killing him. A great vocal cast of talent, including Betty, sounding older than her real age, and some unexpected twists made this passable animated cartoon enjoyable for viewers of all ages.

Yes, Dear, "Kim's New Nanny"**
October 21, 2002, CBS Monday 8:30-9 p.m.
Cast: Anthony Clark (Greg Warner), Jean Louisa Kelly (Kim Warner), Liza Snyder (Christine Hughes), Mike O'Malley (Jimmy Hughes), Anthony Bain (Sammy Warner), Michael Bain (Sammy Warner). Guests: Anna Gunn (Jessica), Betty White (Sylvia). EP: Alan Kirschenbaum, Gregory Thomas Garcia. D: Jeff Mayer. W: Alan Kirschenbaum, Gregory Thomas Garcia, Erik Shapiro, Patrick McCarthy.

Stay-at-home mother Kim Warner bonded with her new friend Jessica until the latter pawned off her daughter, Julia, and her nanny, Sylvia, to Kim as she went to work. When Kim learned that Jessica berated Sylvia, she offered to hire the nanny instead. But Sylvia was inept in carrying for Kim and Greg's young son Sammy. Soon, Kim found that all the other mothers in her class have handed off Sylvia to each other since they didn't have the courage to fire her. Betty tried her best to brighten this hackneyed plot and even got an Emmy nomination for her efforts. But given that the script defined Sylvia as being lazy, incompetent, and even dumber than Rose Nylund in *The Golden Girls*, it was a hopeless cause.

Providence, "The Heart of the Matter"
November 8, 2002, NBC Friday 8-9 p.m.
Cast: Melina Kanakaredes (Dr. Sydney Hansen), Seth Peterson (Robbie Hansen), Mike Farrell (Dr. James "Jim" Hansen), George Newbern (Owen Frank), Denis Arndt (Dr. Bill Augustine), Alex D. Linz (Pete Calcatera), Matt Champagne (Leo), Jeffrey Nordling (Dr. David Baylor). Guests: Paula Cale (Joanie Hansen), Tessa Allen (Hannah Hansen), Samaria Graham (Nurse Izzy Nunez), Lauren Holly (Darla Rosario), Betty White (Julianna), Dana Daurey (Heather Tupperman), Toni DeRose (Patrice), Cynthia Graham (Alice). EP: Monica Wyatt. P: Elle Triedman. D: Kevin G. Cremin. W: Rob Fresco.

Dr. Jim Hansen treated the pet of Julianna, a client for his veterinary practice. This episode aired a month before this family dramatic series ended a nearly four-year run from 1998 to 2002.

Return to the Batcave: The Misadventures of Adam and Burt**
March 9, 2003, CBS Sunday 9-11 p.m.
Cast: Adam West, Burt Ward, Lyle Waggoner, Frank Gorshin, Julie Newmar (Themselves), Lee Meriwether (Waitress in diner). Special guest star: Betty White (Herself). Also: Jack Brewer (Adam West), Jason Marsden (Burt Ward), Amy Acker (Bonnie Lindsey), Brett Rickaby (Frank Gorshin), Curtis Armstrong (Jerry the Butler), Jim Jansen (William Dozier). EP/D: Paul A. Kaufman. Co-EP: Larry Germain, Dawn Wells. W: Duane Poole.

This insubstantial TV movie reunion of principals from the 1966–1968 series *Batman* had Adam West and Burt Ward tracking down the Batmobile when stolen at a charity event. They recalled that their work on the show as younger actors recreated how they got cast on *Batman*, their offscreen lives at the time and more. One flashback they imagined was actually shot in 2003. As they scaled a building, Betty White opened a window wearing a shower cap. "Could you hold it down?! People are trying to sleep in here!" After they pledged to be quieter, she said, "All night long, people going up and down the walls. It's enough to drive you batty!" It's that kind of humor wearily woven throughout. Some DVDs and TV showings have subsequently listed this TV movie as *Back to the Bat Cave*.

Gary the Rat, "This is Not a Pipe"*
October 5, 2003, SpikeTV Sunday 9-9:30 p.m.
Voices: Kelsey Grammer (Gary Andrews), Billy Gardell (Mr. Harrison), Jonathan Cook, Robb Cullen, Vance DeGeneres, Spencer Garrett, Rick Gomez, Camille Grammer, Rob Paulsen. Special guest stars: John Corbett (Frank Siliogotoriettio), Betty White (Gary's mom). EP/W: Mark Cullen, Robb Cullen. EP: Kelsey Grammer, Arnold Rifkin. P: Joanne Asquith Weiss. D: Brian Mulroney.

Wall Street attorney Gary Andrews nonchalantly handled transforming one evening into a walking, talking six-foot rodent, doing his usual amoral business while ignoring his ailing mother on the phone. Here, while Gary defended Frank, a lawyer fired for having leprosy by the firm of Boywe, Cheatem, and Howe, he learned that Bugsy had kidnapped his mother from the hospital. She dug a tunnel under Bugsy's lair to help her and Gary escape. His mother told Gary it was about time for him to visit her. He said he had to return to court and for her to find her own way out. "I'm proud of you," she said sweetly to Gary. "I wish I could say the same," he said flatly before leaving and winning his case. Unfunny, unpleasant, and uninteresting, this animated cartoon series ran thirteen episodes with little attention. Betty had only a few lines, all unfunny, which makes one wonder why she agreed to do this series. It's arguably her least worthy TV credit ever.

The Grim Adventures of Billy & Mandy, "Who Killed Who/Tween Wolf"***
October 31, 2003, The Cartoon Network Friday 10:30-11 p.m.
Voices: Richard Horvitz (Billy), Grey DeLisle (Mandy), Greg Eagles (Grim), Vanessa Marshall (Irwin). Guest: Betty White (Old Mrs. Doolin) Creator/EP: Maxwell Atoms. W: Gord Zajac. D: Pat Shinagawa, John McIntyre, Randy Myers.

Billy accidentally tossed a pair of dice over the fence of Old Mrs. Doolin's property while playing a board game with his pal Irwin. He was afraid to retrieve the dice because the house was haunted. His friend Mandy disagreed, but their pal Grim, as in Grim Reaper, insisted that people who went beyond the fence all died. Fearless Mandy entered the ancient home and met an old woman in the shadows holding the dice. Mrs. Doolin sensed Mandy's stubbornness, so they practiced dueling with swords and then ate dinner. The formerly relaxed Mandy tensed up as Mrs. Doolin spoke of feeding her pet spider Frankie. "Somebody told me a story that you fed the bones of some kid to your pet spider and you're really a ghost," confessed Mandy. Mrs. Doolin cackled and said, "You must've been talking to that old bag of bones, Grim! Ever since I beat him in a staring contest, he's been making up all kinds of stuff about me!"

Mandy told Mrs. Doolin to keep the dice since Billy and Irwin would not let her play with them because she's a girl. This news infuriated Mrs. Doolin, so she and Mandy plotted revenge on Billy when he came to the old house. To say what happened next would spoil a clever twist ending. This animated cartoon geared to older preadolescents started slowly and could have been funnier, but it was satisfactory enough as a showcase for Betty.

Everwood***
Cast: Treat Williams (Dr. Andy Brown), Gregory Smith (Ephriam Brown), Emily VanCamp (Amy Abbott), Debra Mooney (Edna Harper), John Beasley (Irv Harper), Vivien Cardone (Delia Brown), Chris Pratt (Harold Brighton "Bright" Abbott), Tom Amandes (Dr. Harold Abbott). EP: Greg Berlanti, Mickey Liddell. P: Joan Binder Weiss.

"Unhappy Holidays"
November 24, 2003, The WB Monday 8-9 p.m.
Guests: Sarah Lancaster (Madison Kellner), Marcia Cross (Dr. Linda Abbott). Special Guest Star: Betty White (Carol Roberts). Guest stars: Merrilyn Gann (Rose Abbott), Paul Wasilewski (Tommy Callahan), Richard Herd (Herb Roberts), Evan Saucedo (Charlie Grey), Adam Beach (Mr. Grey Cloud), Steve O'Neill (Roger Murphy). D: Jason Moore. W: John E. Pogue.

"Your Future Awaits"
May 3, 2004, The WB Monday 8-9 p.m.
Cast includes: Nina Feeney (Stephanie Nizniki). Special guest star: Philip Baker Hall (Dr. Donald Douglas). Guest stars: Merrilyn Gann (Rose Abbott), Clyde Kusatsu (Edward Agawa), Richard Herd (Herb Roberts). Special appearance by: Betty White (Carol Roberts). D: Marita Grabiak. W: Wendy Mericle, Patrick Sean Smith.

In "Unhappy Holidays," general practitioner Dr. Andy Brown was livid that his sixteen-year-old son Ephriam was dating Madison Kellner, the twenty-year-old babysitter of Andy's other child and Ephriam's younger sister, Delia. Meanwhile, Andy's colleague, Dr. Harold Abbott, grimaced about his in-laws, Carol and Herb Roberts, coming for Thanksgiving. Carol often belittled how Harold raised his son Bright and daughter Amy and just about anything else. The first morning of her stay, Carol told Harold, "Well, that was just about the worst night of sleep I've ever had … I thought you'd be doing us a favor by letting us sleep in your bed, but I can't imagine the sleeper sofa's any worse." When Harold's mother Edna arrived, Carol indelicately asked, "You still married to the black man?" meaning Edna's husband Irv. During the family dinner, after Carol complained about the gravy, Harold mocked Amy's boyfriend Tommy Callahan, a paroled drug addict, prompting a blowup between Harold and Amy. Harold and Andy commiserated about their problems before Harold lost $7,000 at a casino.

Carol confronted Harold for failing the family. "You've lost Amy. And Bright'll never amount to much, because you didn't push him enough in the beginning. I knew when he was still little you weren't raising him right. And now you're a profited gambler to boot!" When Carol groused that her daughter Rose should have married someone else rather than drag the family legacy down, Rose told Carol to shut up and praised Harold as a good husband and even better father. Herb agreed with Rose and told Carol to pack up. The solid dramatic family episode gave Betty some choice scenes and lines, but more could have and should have been provided.

"Well, it's nice to see that nothing's changed around here," smirked Carol in "Your Future Awaits" as she and Herb arrived amid Harold arguing with his son Bright. The latter insisted he didn't want to go to his graduation, as he had been held back a year and had no immediate plans after high school ended. The next morning, Carol implied that Harold chewed noisily and added, "I heard on the news that most problems of kids today have to do with a poor male role model." Harold endured worse treatment when Carol insisted that he treat Herb's boils and the doctor had to hire actors to pretend to be patients for his uninsured practice. Upon arriving at Harold's office, Carol quipped, "Good thing you don't do the decorating at home. You should try to get one of those homosexuals from the TV to come in here and spruce the place up."

Harold's charade failed, but at least Bright did attend his ceremony to the delight of everyone, including persnickety Carol. Though the plot and situations were less meaty than Betty's previous episode, she had more chances to shine and be lovable in this installment, even while she behaved obnoxiously.

I'm With Her, "Meet the Parent"**
November 25, 2003, ABC Tuesday 8:30-9 p.m.
Cast: Teri Polo (Alex Young), David Sutcliffe (Patrick Owen), Danny Comden (Steve Johannson), Rhea Seehorn (Cheri Young). Special guest star: Susan Sullivan (Rosalyn Owen). Special appearance: Betty White (Herself). Co-starring: Ossie Mair (Doctor "Skippy"). Co-Creators/EP: Chris Henchy, Marco Pennette. EP: Jack Burditt. P: Faye Oshima Belyeu. W: April Pesa. D: Robby Benson.

Teacher Patrick Owen planned to do Thanksgiving with his movie star girlfriend Alex Young, her sister Cheri, and David's mother Rosalyn. His friend Steve cautioned David about introducing Alex to Rosalyn, the "beast from the East." David did so anyway, to his regret. As Alex mentioned her former co-stars, Rosalyn interjected, "Oh, what about Betty White?" "Betty White?" asked Alex. "Yeah. Did you ever work with her? Oh, I love her!" After Alex said, "I've actually never met her," Rosalyn then told Alex to end the latter's relationship with Patrick the Monday after Thanksgiving.

Distraught and trying to impress Rosalyn, the next day Alex got Betty to visit her and Rosalyn. "Would you like an autograph?" Betty asked. "Oh, you're not the *Murder She Wrote* lady," said Rosalyn. "Oh, no. That's Angela Lansbury," said Betty. "Oh, right! That's the one I like," responded Rosalyn. Betty gave a great disgusted look before Rosalyn told Alex that she didn't want her son to go "all Hollywood." "Oh, I'm sorry, I forgot your name," Rosalyn then said to Betty, who edgily repeated it to her. After Rosalyn left, Alex apologized to Betty, who responded, "Oh, don't worry, dear. I know what it's like. My boyfriend's mother is a pain in the ass, too!" In the end, Patrick defended his right to date Alex to Rosalyn. This episode of a one-season sitcom came to life only through the work of Susan Sullivan and Betty, who played herself as sprightly as ever.

Stealing Christmas**

November 30, 2003, Lifetime Sunday 8-10 p.m.

Cast: Tony Danza (Jack Clayton/"Oscar Burton"), Lea Thompson (Sara Gibson), Angela Goethals (Noelle Gibson), Betty White (Emily Sutton), David Parker (Harry Zordich), Malcolm Stewart (Doug Jennings), Alfred E. Humphreys (Officer Tim Hogan), Gwynyth Walsh (Jo the waitress). EP: Raffaella de Laurentiis P/D: Gregg Champion. P: Oscar Louis Costo. W: Greg Taylor (story), Lloyd "Lucky" Gold (screenplay).

Trapped at a department store before he could finish his heist, safecracker Jack Clayton dressed as Santa Claus to escape and took a bus ride out of town. At the final stop in the town of Evergreen, Noelle Gibson picked him up, thinking he's a Kris Kringle her mother Sara hired to work on their tree farm. Jack assumed the role under the pseudonym of Oscar Burton and stuck around when he saw another bank to rob. Next to the bank was the toy store of gentle Emily Sutton. To scope out the store, Jack said he wanted to buy her toy trains, but Emily refused to sell them because they were her late husband's favorite items. Suspicious newspaper owner Doug Jennings told police officer Tim Hogan to run a background check on Jack as the latter ingratiated himself with locals and revived the town's spirit.

Meanwhile, Jack got his henchman Harry Zordich a job as an assistant to Emily as part of their plot to break through her store's wall and rob the adjacent bank. Could the goodness of Sara, Emily, and other residents of Evergreen win Jack's heart over committing a theft? Who cares? Even Betty's usual brilliance couldn't spark enthusiasm for this Yuletide yawner of a TV movie with an improbable, irritating mix of sloppy suspense and slushy sentiment. Hopefully, at least Betty had a good time filming this production in Vancouver, British Columbia, Canada.

My Wife and Kids, "The Maid"***

May 5, 2004, ABC Wednesday 8-8:30 p.m.

Cast: Damon Wayans (Michael Kyle), Tisha Campbell-Martin (Jay Kyle), George O. Gore II (Michael Kyle Jr.), Jennifer Nicole Freeman (Claire Kyle), Parker McKenney Posey (Kady Kyle), Noah Gray-Cabey (Franklin Mumford). Special guest star: Betty White (June Hopkins). Creators/EP: Don Reo, Damon Wayans. EP: David Himelfarb, Dean Lorey. Co-EP: Eric L. Gold, Kevin Rooney, James Vallely. P: Craig

Wayans, Kim Wayans, Susan M. Crank. D: Damien Dante Wayans. W: Valencia Parker, Rodney Barnes (teleplay), Shane Miller (story).

June Hopkins was an energetic maid who arrived to help Michael Kyle, his daughters Claire and Kady, and his son Michael Jr. while Jay, Michael's wife, and the children's mother, left for a seminar. "Serving others is what makes me happy!" June said as she fixed everything and fulfilled virtually every wish the family had. June also told Michael how she helped Dr. James Naismith invent basketball. She even impressed Kady's brainy buddy Franklin by beating him at chess while cleaning the oven. Jay came home early and was stunned by June's efficiency. She thought she had no purpose to her family with June around. Michael and the kids agreed that June needed to be released to make Jay feel better. But June preempted Michael's dismissal by saying, "My work here is done." The implication that she was Mary Poppins was explicit at the end when Franklin claimed June opened her umbrella and flew into the sky.

Despite the plot's predictability, Betty made June endearing without being syrupy, so this was tolerable albeit inconsequential. The end credits showed a blooper where Damon Wayans accidentally called Tisha Campbell-Martin June instead of Jay and Betty cracked him up by quipping, "Gee, try to get it right, Damon!"

Malcolm in the Middle, "Victor's Other Family"**
May 9, 2004, Fox Sunday 9-9:30 p.m.
Cast: Jane Kaczmarek (Lois), Bryan Cranston (Hal), Justin Berfield (Reese), Erik Per Sullivan (Dewey), Frankie Muniz (Malcolm). Special guest stars: Cloris Leachman (Ida), Betty White (Sylvia). Guests: Adam Wylie (Scott), Maura Soden (Roberta), Andrew James Allen (Jerome), Tom Virtue (Peter Dietrich), Megan Hubbell (Jerome's Girlfriend). Creator/EP: Linwood Boomer. D: David Grossman. W: Eric Kaplan.

When Lois learned she had a half-sister living in Canada, she drove her sons Reese and Malcolm to meet their extended family. Reese, Malcolm, and Lois marveled how Scott, Malcolm, and Roberta were their happier doppelgängers. Also impressing them was Roberta's mother Sylvia, whose sweetness stood in contrast to Lois's mother, the Teutonic talking terror Ida. Just as all parties bonded, Ida arrived to wreak havoc and fight for her late philandering husband Victor's pension that she claimed Sylvia and her family got to support their lifestyle while she suffered for years. This fifth-season episode of the popular sitcom had the characters of Betty and Cloris briefly at odds again, and the script, acting, direction, and production were all solid and swift. The result was quite funny and unexpectedly moving at points, as well.

Higglytown Heroes***
Voices: Taylor Masamitsu (Eubie), Frankie Ryan Manriquez (Wayne), Liliana Mumy (Twinkle), Rory Charles Thost (Kip), Edie McClurg (Fran the squirrel). Creators/D/W: George Evelyn, Dennis Morella.

"First Snow"
September 14, 2004, Disney Jr. Tuesday 7-7:30 a.m. and 11:30 a.m.-noon
Guest voices: Betty White (Grandmama), Dee Bradley Baker (Pizza Guy).

"Two Bees or Not Two Bees"
July 22, 2005, Disney Jr. Friday 7-7:30 a.m. and 11-11:30 a.m.
Guest voices: Betty White (Grandmama), David Jeremiah (Grandpapa), Kate Pierson (Beekeeper hero).

"Something Ducky Going On"
June 24, 2007, Disney Jr. Sunday 7:30-8 a.m.
Guest voices: Betty White (Grandmama), David Jeremiah (Grandpapa), Bobby Holliday (House painter hero).

The title characters were animated, pear-shaped nesting dolls who learned life lessons in two segments per show. Calling themselves "Higgly kids" in honor of their hometown, they often interacted with adults. In her debut visit, Kip's Grandmama sang how she was a Higglytown hero herself and could knit the quartet of children any clothes they needed. "Two Bees or Not Two Bees" had Grandmama and Grandpapa recounting their courtship on a farm before finding out its berries had vanished. The heroes tried to track them down with the help of a beekeeper, who said the plants need time to pollinate first. And in Betty's last appearance, Grandmama and Grandpapa needed to remove the polka dots on the walls of their house that were scaring ducks, so they enlisted the help of a painter. These pretty entertaining presentations, designed to appeal to tots, were pleasant for adults to watch, as well, and hear Betty's beautiful voice in song.

Father of the Pride, "Donkey"**

September 21, 2004, NBC Tuesday 9-9:30 p.m.

Voices: John Goodman (Larry), Cheryl Hines (Kate), Orlando Jones (Snack the gopher), Carl Reiner (Sarmoti), Danielle Andrea Willis, David Herman, Julian Holloway, John O'Hurley, Daryl Sabara. Special guest voices: Wendy Malick, Garry Marshall, Eddie Murphy (Donkey). Unbilled: Betty White (Grandma Wilson). EP: Jeffrey Katzenberg, Jonathan Groff, Jon Pollack, Peter Mehlman. Co-EP: Joe M. Aguilar, Siegfried and Roy, Bernie Yuman, Cheryl Holliday, Mike Barker, Matt Weitzman. P/W: Ron Weiner P: Mary Sandell, Ken Tsumura. D: Bret Haaland.

Donkey, from the movie *Shrek*, came to Las Vegas to shoot a commercial, which excited the white lion family of Larry, his wife Kate, their children Hunter and Sierra, and Kate's complaining father Sarmoti. To impress Hunter, Larry promised to have Donkey appear in his class. But the creature's agent, Ellen the Pig, opposed the idea, so Larry, Sarmoti, and Snack kidnapped a lookalike to fool the kids. Larry also starred in the stage magic show of Siegfried and Roy, who were incensed about Grandma Wilson's bed and breakfast replacing their favorite restaurant. The duo protested the establishment, but the gentle, plump, little old lady remained unmoved until a desperate Siegfried slept with her and convinced her to end the business.

So much talent resulted in so little enjoyment in this overpromoted, overproduced, animated cartoon series. As the fourth episode of thirteen aired, the strain already showed in trying—and failing—to make the comedy appeal to adults and children. To top it off, Betty had relatively little to voice here.

Complete Savages****

Cast: Keith Carradine (Nick Savage), Andrew Elden (Sam Savage), Shaun Sipos (Jack Savage), Erik von Detten (Chris Savage), Evan Ellingson (Kyle Savage), Jason Dolley (T.J. Savage), Vincent Ventresca (Jimmy Savage). EP: Mel Gibson.

"The Man Without a Ball"

December 3, 2004, ABC Friday 8:30-9 p.m.

Special appearance by: Betty White (Mrs. Agnes Riley). Teleplay: W: Donick Cary.

"Saving Old Lady Riley"

May 27, 2005, ABC Friday 8:30-9 p.m.

Special appearance by: Betty White (Mrs. Agnes Riley). Guests: Kylie Sparks (Brenda), Steven Gilborn (Town councilman), Pat Finn (Reporter Chet Pringle).

In "The Man Without a Ball," rather than rake leaves, as told by Nick, their dad, Sam, Jack, Chris, Kyle, and T.J. played basketball until the ball went into the yard of "Old Lady Riley" next door. "Get out of my yard before I whack you with my cane!" she said to Kyle as he attempted to retrieve the ball. She hit him for talking back and kept the ball. When Kyle learned it was the game ball from their father's high school championship, the boys visited their neighbor and pleaded for its return. Mrs. Riley said they had to do chores first. "And clean up that gum," she said before spitting a wad out. When they finished, she claimed, "I'm an old woman. I have trouble remembering things! I have to lay down!" and left. They knew Mrs. Riley was faking it, but she came at them with a chainsaw laughing and saying, "Now, get out of here! Unless you want to lose a few more balls!"

Nick was angry for his sons losing the ball, so the boys trespassed into Riley's house and took her parakeet as hostage. She retaliated by doing the same to their pet dog. Learning of the standoff, Nick said, "Nobody terrorizes my kids but me! ... It's time somebody gave Old Lady Riley the bird!" He visited her house with the parakeet, but she was asleep in a chair. Nick saw his dog and motioned for him to grab the ball before leaving, but the dog tugged off Riley's artificial leg instead. She hopped up and cried out, "I'm coming for you, Savage! And your little dog, too!" Rick and Mrs. Riley reached a truce and swapped the leg and ball respectively. This episode was a pretty effective broad comedy, written, directed, and acted to the hilt by everyone.

All the Savage sons except Sam played field hockey and accidentally broke Mrs. Riley's window in "Saving Old Lady Riley." She demanded to speak to their father. "I'm sick of your smart mouths, your firecrackers in my mailbox, your ugly mutt pooping on my lawn! And most of all, I'm most sick of ...." and she collapsed. To revive her, the boys jammed an air pump into her mouth and massaged her chest with a toilet plunger. She woke up and said, "Last I recall, I was tearing you boys a new one " Nick told his sons to promote their first aid success in the news. When Sam found out his brothers lied about having performed CPR on Riley to reporters, Kyle said, "They wanted heroes, so we pretended to be heroes. That's what heroes do." A disgusted Sam nonetheless kept their dirty secret.

However, at an assembly honoring the boys, a playback of their emergency call revealed the truth. Riley stood up and said, "I hate these kids. I really do. They're noisy, surly, disrespectful, smelly boys. But I would not be up here today if it weren't for their reckless and stupid actions. So to me, they'll always be heroes." Back at her home, however, Riley made sure that the Savages cut wood, repaired her home, and made her tea sandwiches to repay their debts while holding a rifle. Though some viewers may have hated themselves for laughing so hard at Betty's expense, this dark comedy was quite funny overall and expertly delivered by everyone involved.

Annie's Point**

January 22, 2005, Hallmark Channel Saturday 8-10 p.m.

Cast: Betty White (Annie Eason), Richard Thomas (Richard Eason), Amy Davidson (Ellen Eason), Ellen Albertini Dow (Louise Tette), Robert F. Lyons (Jack Backis), John Dybdahl (Patrick Weller), Diane Robin (Brenda Trager), James Keane (Doug Gordon), Jay Underwood (Policeman), Garrett Strommen (Scott Tardy). EP: Larry Levinson, Robert Halmi Jr. P: Kyle Clark, James Wilberger. D: Michael Switzer. W: Mike Leonardo.

While her son Richard attempted to keep the family's real estate business afloat, widow Annie Eason convinced her granddaughter and Richard's daughter Ellen to join her on a trip. Annie left Chicago with Ellen bound for the California coast, where Annie planned to spread her late husband's ashes. Their unannounced departure upset Richard, especially with Annie's health worsening, and he drove in hot pursuit to intervene. But before he arrived, Annie had time to pretend to be a blind artist at a street fair, go skinny dipping with Ellen, get arrested and escape from jail, and do more mischief before a sentimental ending.

Betty flexed her dramatic muscles impressively in this TV movie and got plenty of screen time since the movie basically consisted of her, Amy Davidson, and Richard Thomas. Unfortunately, the script was plodding and thin, and the production values came up short. There were obvious process shots for Betty and Amy, as they pretended to be on country roads, and location shots supposedly in the Midwest were clearly taken in southern California. All told, there wasn't much of a point to watch this film.

Joey, "Joey and the House"**

October 13, 2005, NBC Thursday 8-8:30 p.m.

Cast: Matt LeBlanc (Joey Tribbiani), Andrea Anders (Alex Garrett), Paul Costanzo (Michael Tribbiani), Jennifer Coolidge (Bobbie Morganstern), Miguel A. Nunez Jr. (Zach), Gina de Matteo (Gina Tribbiani). Special guest star: Betty White (Margaret Bly). Guests: Tim Bagley (Leonard), Gina St. John (Susan Walters), Cathy Shambley (Prospective Buyer). P: Linda Videtti Figueiredo. D: Ben Weiss. W: Dave Finkel, Brett Baer.

Movie star Joey Tribbiani placed a bid on a home so that he could move out of his sister Gina and nephew Michael's home in Los Angeles. Susan Walters, the real estate agent, thought Joey and Gina were a young married couple, which was the type of buyer the seller, Margaret Bly, wanted for her house. Joey and Gina visited Margaret with an animatronic baby controlled outside the house by Joey's pal Zach. The "baby" caught on fire and had to be hidden from Margaret during the tour. Margaret agreed to sell Joey the house and then asked him and Gina, "Aren't you going to kiss?" They did so awkwardly with their eyes closed, which perplexed Margaret, but the sale continued.

One of many unsatisfying installments that helped sink this spinoff from *Friends* in its second year, "Joey and the House" sagged considerably due to its misuse of Betty. She came on screen more than halfway through the show and had only a handful of funny lines. Additionally, her character was alternately sweet, crazy, demanding, and ignorant. Betty deserved better than this.

Ugly Betty, "Bananas for Betty"**

December 6, 2007. ABC Thursday 8-9 p.m.

Cast: America Ferrera (Betty Suarez), Eric Mabius (Daniel Meade), Alan Dale (Bradford Meade), Tony Plana (Ignacio Suarez), Ana Ortiz (Hilda Suarez), Judith Light (Claire Meade), Christopher Gorham (Henry Grubstick), Ashley Jensen (Christina McKinney), Becki Newton (Amanda Tanen), Michael Urie (Mark St. James), Mark Indelicato (Justin Suarez). With: Rebecca Romijn (Alexis Meade), Vanessa Williams (Wilhelmina Slater). Guests: Freddy Rodriguez (Gio Rossi), John Cho (Kenny), Max Greenfield (Nick Pepper), Alec Mapa (Suzuki St. Pierre), Betty White (Herself), Ted Lyde (Security guard), Jeff Sumner (Gay couple Betty White Fan #1), Bruce Dent (Gay couple Betty White Fan #2), Ian Gregory (Attorney),

Patrick Cavanaugh (Morgue doctor), Candace Kita (Reporter #1), Richard Varga (Reporter #2). EP: James Hayman, Salma Hayek, Jose Tamez, Ben Silverman, Marco Pennette, Silvio Horta. P: Dawn DeKeyser. D: Michael Spiller. W: Tracy Poust, Jon Kinnally.

Vain fashion publisher Wilhelmina Slater grabbed a taxi hailed by Betty White and accidentally closed the door on Betty's fingers. Wilhelmina let Betty fall to the ground without realizing who she was and threw her some money callously to help out. A male couple who told Betty they had called emergency and recorded what had happened took a selfie with her even though she was in pain. The media accosted Wilhelmina, who realized this was a public relations disaster. Betty called Wilhelmina from her hospital room to say, "I'll be fine. I did lose blood, but it was my own fault. I stopped to sign a few autographs and almost bled out on the sidewalk." She added she adored her fans, "Except for the few sickos who write lesbian fan fiction about me and Bea Arthur."

Betty agreed to forgive Wilhelmina with reporter Suzuki St. Pierre. He asked, "Wilhelmina, what do you have to say to award-winning actress, animal rights activist, friends to gays everywhere—I love you. "Me too!" exclaimed Wilhelmina's assistant Mark St. James—Betty White?" As Wilhelmina touched Betty, she screamed, "Now she's going after my other hand!" To Wilhelmina, she said, "You hate me! What did I ever do to you?" An astonished Wilhelmina demanded the taping stop. Betty told her, "I'm sorry, honey, this feud is huge, and I'm going to milk it till it's dry!" She said she needed it because "That *Golden Girls* money went right into the slots." A defeated Wilhelmina plotted another strategy to take over rival Meade Publishing.

A weak script made much of the cast force their comic delivery here except for Vanessa Williams and, of course, Betty. She played the exaggerations well, but the setup's extreme artificiality limited its enjoyment, and the rest of the show was similarly disappointing.

My Name is Earl, "Witch Lady"***
March 19, 2009, NBC Thursdays 8-8:30 p.m.

Cast: Jason Lee (Earl Hickey), Ethan Suplee (Randy Hickey), Jaime Pressly (Joy Turner), Nadine Velasquez (Catalina), Eddie Steeples (Darnell Turner). Special guest star: Betty White (Grizelda Weezmer, the "Crazy Witch Lady"). Guests: Dale Dickey (Patty Weezmer), Mike O'Malley (Officer Stuart Daniels), Gregg Binkley (Kenny

James), Noah Crawford (Young Earl), Stacey Hinnen (Chuck), Randy Brenner (Cop). EP: Bobby Bowman, Greg Garcia. Co-P: Kim Hamberg, Matt Ward, Vali Chandraskeran. P: Jessica Goldstein, Chrissy Pietrosh, Hilary Winston, Jason Lee, Henry Lange Jr. W: Michael Shipley, Matt Ward. D: Eyal Gordin.

Earl and his brother Randy were shocked to see "Crazy Witch Lady," a woman in black with large eyeglasses and long, flowing gray hair. She was number 186 on Earl's list of people that he had wronged earlier in his life. When younger, Earl tricked Grizelda into gluing her hands onto a broom and made it appear like she was attacking him, causing a policeman to use a stun gun on her. After Earl apologized for the incident, Grizelda invited him over to drink tea at her house. She drugged him and locked him in her basement, telling Earl she was aggrieved at the way the town has treated her. Randy dropped by and Grizelda locked him up, too, because he threw a bucket of water on her to make her melt a few years earlier.

She also chained Earl's friends Stuart and Kenny, a gay couple, because Stuart once called Grizelda a whack job while policing her neighborhood. Also locked up in order were Earl's ex-wife Joy, her husband Darnell, everyone's friend Catalina, and Patty the daytime hooker, who revealed that Grizelda was her mother. Grizelda announced she planned to stab someone to death and told the group to decide who the victim would be. Earl intervened by noting how everyone was labelling each other just as they called Grizelda a witch rather than a real person. He didn't blame her for being driven to act crazy after the way people had treated her for twenty years. Overhearing his speech, Grizelda hugged him—and then stabbed him. She really was crazy, but she got rehabilitated.

This close-to-last episode of *My Name is Earl*, which ran from 2005 to 2009, varied widely in tone, and plenty of jokes failed to land. But Betty portrayed every aspect of her multifaceted character so perfectly that her unexpected detours are a marvel to watch, and she got an Emmy nomination, too. For those reasons, this show gets three stars.

Glenn Martin, DDS*

Voices: Kevin Nealon (Glenn Martin), Catherine O'Hara (Jackie Martin), Judy Greer (Wendy Park), Jackie Clarke (Courtney Martin), Peter Oldring (Conor Martin). EP: Michael Jamin, Sivert Glarum, Eric Fogel, Leslie Sole, Malcolm Dunlap, Michael D. Eisner, Steven A. Cohen, Noel Bright.

"From Here to Fraternity"
August 31, 2009, Nickelodeon Monday 8-8:30 p.m.
Also starring: Brian Huskey (Peter), Dawnn Lewis (Nurse), Sam McMurray (Tucker Wade), Betty White (Dora), Thomas Dekker, Phyllis Yvonne Stickney. W: Adam Pava. D: Dave Barton Thomas.

"Step-Brother"
September 17, 2010, Nickelodeon Friday 10:30-11 p.m.
Also starring: M.C. Hammer (Himself), Rachael Harris (Melissa, the wedding planner), Phil LaMarr (Grandpa Bert), J.B. Smoove (Curtis/Uncle Dexter), Betty White (Grandma Sheila Martin). W: Brian Behar, Steve Baldikoski. D: Ken Cunningham.

To impress his son Conor and show how cool he is, mobile dentist Glenn Martin went with his wife Jackie to their class reunion at Bearden University in "From Here to Fraternity." Joining them were Conor, their daughter Courtney, and Courtney's business assistant Wendy. Glenn met his old foe, ex-football star Tucker Wade. To Jackie's horror, her old sorority house was now a convalescent home. Undaunted, she made its residents act like her former housemates, so the elderly Dora got into a swimsuit and asked, "Who's up for the bikini car wash?" which made her nurse vomit. Betty had only six lines in this unpleasant, unfunny installment, where the alleged comedy included having her character's glass eye and false teeth knocked out when she was spanked with a board.

In "Step-Brother," as Glenn's mother Sheila planned to marry Bert, Glenn and his wife and children met Bert's successful son Curtis. Sheila called Curtis "Doodlebug," her same nickname for Glenn. Curtis threatened to usurp Glenn as Sheila's favorite by giving her a new car—"It's so funky fresh!" Sheila cooed—and doing other favors. Meanwhile, Jackie upset Sheila by modifying the latter's grandmother's address, so Sheila denied her as a bridesmaid. And Bert disinvited Curtis from the wedding after seeing his son destroy Glenn's artwork. Almost every joke died in this lifeless outing. Betty had more to say than her last visit to this cartoon but little more to enjoy.

30 Rock, "Stone Mountain"**
October 29, 2009, NBC Thursday 9:30-10 p.m.
Cast: Tina Fey (Liz Lemon), Tracy Morgan (Tracy Jordan), Jane Krakowski (Jenna Maroney), Jack McBrayer (Kenneth Parcell), Scott Adsit (Pete Hornberger), Judah

Friedlander (Frank Rossitano), Alec Baldwin (Jack Donaghy). Special guest stars: Jeff Dunham (Rick Wayne), Jimmy Fallon (Himself), Betty White (Herself). Guests: Katrina Bowden (Cerie), Keith Powell (Toofer), John Lutz (Lutz), Sue Galloway (Sue), Blaine Horton (Sacha), Jonathan Dickson (Male Newscaster), Carson Elrod (Travis), Nick Sullivan (Emcee), Melissa Wood (Attractive woman). EP: Tina Fey, Marci Klein, David Miner, Robert Carlock. P: Alec Baldwin, Paula Pell, Don Scardino, Jerry Kupfer. D: Don Scardino. W: John Riggi.

When Tracy Jordan heard two celebrities had died, he worried that he would be next based on the belief that "These things happen in threes." Taking action, Tracy called Betty and yelled "Boo!" in an effort to scare her to death. "Tracy! I haven't seen you since that rapping grandma movie we did! You were so funny as the rapping grandma," she said. Betty soon ascertained Tracy's real reason and asked, "Is this a rule of threes call?!" "No," Tracy meekly responded. "Nice try, Jordan, but I am going to be at your funeral. I will bury you!" she said. Betty filmed her scenes in California away from the cast in New York. Her delivery was the highlight of an otherwise disappointing sitcom episode, playing largely off tired stereotypes of gays and rural residents. In fact, she was much better and funnier playing herself than Jimmy Fallon was doing the same here.

The Middle, "Average Rules"****
May 19, 2010, ABC Wednesday 8:30-9 p.m.
Cast: Patricia Heaton (Frankie Heck), Neil Flynn (Mike Heck), Charlie McDermott (Axl Heck), Eden Sher (Sue Heck), Atticus Shaffer (Brick Heck). Special guest star: Betty White (Mrs. Nethercott). Guests: Andy Milder (Principal Shaolin), Greg Cromer (Coach Emerson), Dale Raoul (Guidance counselor), Mary Passeri (Mrs. Seabrook), Kiva Jump (Mrs. Thomas), Blaine Saunders (Carly), Adrienne Berry (Cross-country girl). Creators/EP/W: Deann Heline, Eileen Heisler. D: Wendey Stanzler.

Frankie and her husband Mike were upset with their children's performances at the end of the school year. That included their son Brick, who Orson Elementary School librarian Mrs. Nethercott threatened to hold back a year for missing books. She told him, "For years, I have watched as you've checked out book after book after book and brought them back covered with syrup and yogurt. That is, if they even came back at all!"

Mrs. Nethercott warned Brick he could not advance to third grade until he returned all thirty-one books he checked out by Walt Whitman's birthday. He met the deadline for all books except for an atlas. "If only you had a map to find it!" smirked Mrs. Nethercott, who gave him until Sir Arthur Conan Doyle's birthday to produce the book. So Brick checked out the atlas in the municipal library and returned that version to Nethercott instead. This episode was a moderately amusing take on what adults expect from their children, and though her work was only a subplot, Betty made a vivid and enjoyable impression as always.

Community****

Cast: Joel McHale (Jeff Winger), Gillian Jacobs (Britta Perry), Danny Pudi (Abed Nadir), Yvette Nicole Brown (Shirley Bennett), Alison Brie (Annie Edison), Donald Glover (Troy Barnes), Ken Jeong (Ben Chang), Chevy Chase (Pierce Hawthorne).

"Anthropology 101"

September 23, 2010, NBC Thursdays 8-8:30 p.m.

Special guest star: Betty White (Professor June Bauer). Guest stars: Jim Rash (Voice of Dean Pelton), Dino Stamatopoulos (Star-Burns), Richard Erdman (Leonard), Abigail Marlowe (Female Britta, fan number one), Sara Van Horn (Female server), Angela Malhotra (Female student), Kelsey Gunn (Student number one), Angela Trimbur (Student number two), Ken Schumaker (George Clooney impersonator).

"The Psychology of Letting Go"

October 7, 2010, NBC Thursdays 8-8:30 p.m.

Special guest star: Betty White (Professor June Bauer). Guest stars: John Oliver (Professor Owen Duncan), Patton Oswalt (Nurse Jackie), David Jean Thomas (Chief Umbootu), Pat Crawford Brown (Voice of Pierce's mom). Co-starring: Amber Lancaster (Christine), Natalina Maggio (Hot girl), Patrick O'Neil (Christine's boyfriend), Bill Parks (Dude number one), D.C. Pierson (Mark Millot), Justin Alston (Dude number two).

Set at fictional Greendale Community College, this sitcom kicked off "Anthropology 101," its second season opener, with returning students Jeff, Britta, Abed, Shirley, Annie, Troy, Ben, and Pierce meeting a new anthropology teacher. Professor June Bauer began her class asking, "What is it exactly that separates men from animals?" "Divorce," cracked student Star-Burns. Disgusted, she shot a dart into his cheek with a blow gun, which impressed Abed and Troy. In a later class, she assigned work to students when Jeff interrupted her to proclaim his love of Britta. "This is making me sick," quipped the professor.

Outside the class, the group was shocked to learn that after temporarily breaking up with Britta a few months earlier, Jeff had kissed Annie. Jeff attempted to correct the discord with Britta in Professor Bauer's class by saying the most important tool to human survival was respect, and without it, mankind will go instinct. "Well, that's one answer," said the teacher. "Here's the one I had in mind. Combining all nine tools, you get this. A deadlier weapon than any one item in the box." Bauer revealed a crossbow and added, "So, I'm going to use this to attack you, and you use respect to defend yourself!" Her shot missed his head, but she knocked him down and attempted to choke him to death. Bauer got suspended while the class got automatic A's on their assignment, and Jeff's recovery inspired everyone to bond together.

In the outtakes for "Anthropology 101," Betty bobbled one line and said, "I was acting here!" to the crew's amusement. She also joked that her character was a closet cougar sitting between Danny Pudi and Donald Glover when filming the closer as the trio sang Toto's "Africa" and the credits rolled. For that segment, Betty learned the lyrics on the set the day of the shooting, amazing everyone. Her scene needed only five takes. Otherwise, Betty nailed every line in two takes.

The DVD commentary indicated that it took the writer and producers of "Anthropology 101" a month to figure out how to resolve storylines from the previous season and give quality time for Betty on screen. "We knew that Betty White probably was going to be just a one-off—you know, she would go crazy and try to kill Jeff at the end of the episode," writer and co-executive producer Chris McKenna said.

Betty's character reappeared at the closer two episodes later, where Professor Owen Duncan said Bauer had been put on administrative leave with pay. The bit showed her in the Congo talking to Chief Umbootu and explaining the premise of the movie *Inception*. This closer was nowhere near as amusing as Betty's previous show, but both episodes were generally well written and acted overall and a solid asset on Betty's resume. Additionally, Betty snagged a People's Choice Award nomination for Favorite TV Guest Star as Professor Bauer.

Pound Puppies**
"Rebound"
November 5, 2010, Friday The Hub Various times (30 minutes)
"My Fair Rebound"
August 13, 2011, Saturday The Hub Various times (30 minutes)
"Zoltron"
October 15, 2011, Saturday The Hub Various times (30 minutes)
"Bone Voyage"
November 12, 2011, Saturday The Hub Various times (30 minutes)
"The Fraud Princess"
June 9, 2012, Saturday The Hub Various times (30 minutes)
"The Ruff Ruff Bunch"
July 14, 2012, Saturday The Hub Various times (30 minutes)
"The Accidental Pup Star"
August 25, 2012, Saturday The Hub Various times (30 minutes)
"Pound Preemies"
December 1, 2012, Saturday The Hub Various times (30 minutes)
"Beauty is Only Fur Deep"
August 10, 2013, Saturday The Hub Various times (30 minutes)
"The Truth is in Hear"
September 14, 2013, Saturday The Hub Various times (30 minutes)
"Little Monster"
October 5, 2013, Saturday The Hub Various times (30 minutes)
"Rebound's First Symphony"
October 12, 2013, Saturday The Hub Various times (30 minutes)
"Lord of the Fleas"
October 19, 2013, Saturday The Hub Various times (30 minutes)
Voices: Eric McCormack (Lucky), Rene Auberjonois (Leonard McLeish), Yvette Nicole Brown (Cookie), John DiMaggio (Niblet), Michael Rapaport (Squirt), Alana Ubach (Strudel), M. Emmet Walsh (Olaf), Betty White (Agatha McLeish), Brooke Goldner (Rebound).

Living together in a shelter, Lucky, Cookie, Niblet, Squirt, and Strudel, also known as the Pound Puppies, were eager to help their fellow pets get adopted. The arrival of the adorably hyperactive pup Rebound coincided with a visit by dog catcher Leonard McLeish's crotchety mother Agatha, who didn't know his profession but hated canines. But Rebound won her over, and Agatha adopted her. Agatha returned several times thereafter. She trained Rebound to be a show dog, left Rebound with Leonard while she went on a cruise, with Gavin MacLeod voicing the captain, and unwittingly dealt with a con artist posing as a beau, voiced by Tim Conway. Most hilariously, she had an extended spat with a new neighbor. For an animated cartoon aimed at preadolescents, Betty got a lot of lines in most episodes, and she was beautifully funny and expressive each time.

Prep & Landing Stocking Stuffer**
December 7, 2010, ABC Tuesday approximately 8:50-8:57 p.m.
Voices: Betty White (Mrs. Claus), Dave Foley (Wayne), Derek Richardson (Lanny), Sarah Chalke (Magee), W. Morgan Sheppard ("The Big Guy"). EP: John Lasseter. P: Dorothy McKim. D/W: Kevin Deters, Stevie Wermers-Skelton.

Subtitled "Operation: Secret Santa," this animated short had elves Wayne and Lanny meet clandestinely with a mystery contact who turned out to be Mrs. Claus. She offered the elves hot chocolate before saying she needed their special skills to retrieve a wooden box tucked away inside Santa's office. Wayne and Lanny snuck down the chimney and followed Mrs. Claus's instructions to discover her husband's secret workshop. Their trek and its aftermath were quite entertaining albeit not as impressive as the original *Prep & Landing* TV movie in 2009. Betty's rich, warm vocals were a big asset here. Added to fill out the overflow of the perennial *A Charlie Brown Christmas* special rerun, *Prep & Landing Stocking Stuffer* won the Emmy for Outstanding Short-Format Animated Programming in 2011.

Hallmark Hall of Fame: The Lost Valentine**
January 30, 2011, CBS Sunday 9-11 p.m.
Cast: Jennifer Love Hewitt (Susan Allison), Betty White (Caroline Thomas), Sean Faris (Lucas Thomas), Billy Magnussen (Neil Thomas), Megharn Fahy (Young Caroline Thomas), Nadia Dajani (June Oliver), Will Chase (Andrew Hawthorne), Mike Pniewski (Craig Warren), Helmar Augustus Cooper (Joseph Williams), Ron Clinton Smith (Western Union delivery man), Tom Nowicki (Glenn Billings), Nita Hardy (Anne Billings), Andy Stahl (Senator Max Irving), Gregalan Williams

(Chaplain Richard Brady), Mitch Grant (C.P.O. Harris), Muni Zano (Mr. Morang), Alexis Camins (Young Morang), Gil Gerard (Neil Jr.), Victoria Loving (Maggie), Lori Beth Edgeman (Jenny), Robert Pralgo (David Oliver), Justin Greer (Jeff Billings), Carlos Lopez (Matt Figueroa), Phi-Long Nguyen (Calderas), Richard Marrero (Rios), Nick Stephens (Little boy), Richard Van Arsdale (Japanese soldier). EP: Jennifer Love Hewitt, Brent Shields. P: Barbara M. Gangi, Andrew Gottlieb. D: Darnell Martin. W: Maryann Ridini Spencer, Barton Taney (teleplay).

Based on a book by James Michael Pratt and filmed on location in Atlanta, *The Lost Valentine* began with a flashback of Caroline Thomas saying goodbye to her husband Neil as he took a train going to war in 1944. He died in combat, and she spent every subsequent Valentine's Day visiting the depot where he had shipped out. TV producer Craig Warren pitched the story to news anchor Susan Allison to cover. She was unmoved until she realized Caroline's grandson Lucas had overheard her. Susan apologized and then visited Caroline. Gradually, Susan learned Caroline's love story while she in turn developed her own passion for Lucas.

After Caroline had a minor heart attack while recounting her story, Susan pursued Glenn Billings, whose father's life was saved in World War II by Neil. The discovery led to finding another survivor, Mr. Morang, who did a satellite interview with Caroline recounting the last days of her husband in combat. Morang helped the U.S. Navy find Neil's body and give Caroline Neil's personal effects. At the end, when Betty kissed and hugged the casket of her husband draped with the U.S. flag, the moment was incredibly moving.

In an interview with CBS News in Atlanta, Jennifer Love Hewitt said, "I took a picture of Betty and I the first day, and I sent it out to all my friends, and I was like, 'I've fallen in love, and you're just going to have to accept it.' She's amazing."

For her part, Betty confessed that "Through the years, people have always asked me, 'Is there something you've never done in this business that you'd like to do?' And in the back of my head—I didn't always say it—but in the back of my head, it was always a Hallmark Hall of Fame."

The Lost Valentine finished third in the ratings for the week and was the highest-rated Hallmark Hall of Fame TV movie in four years. And Betty earned a Screen Actors Guild nomination for Outstanding Performance by a Female Actor in a Television Movie or Miniseries.

The Client List, "Past is Prologue"**

June 17, 2012, Lifetime Sunday 10-11 p.m.

Cast: Jennifer Love Hewitt (Riley Parks), Loretta Devine (Georgia Cummings), Colin Egglesfield (Evan Parks), Rebecca Field (Lacey Jean Locklin), Alice Lagano (Selena Ramos), Kathleen York (Jolene), Brian Hallisay (Kyle Parks), Cybill Shepherd (Linette Montgomery). Guests: Paul Dooley (Earl Hudson), Elisabeth Rohm (Taylor Berkhalter), Desi Lydic (Dee Ann), Trevor St. John (Nathan). With: Greg Grunberg (Dale Locklin), Betty White (Ruth Hudson). Co-starring: Tyler Champagne (Travis Parks), Cassidy Guetersloh (Katie Parks), Hazel Sepenuk (Twinkle Berkhalter). EP/D: Jennifer Love Hewitt. W: Barbara Nance (teleplay).

Abandoned by her husband Kyle, mother of two, Riley Parks, made ends meet at a day spa, The Rub, in Sugar Land, Texas. Her boss Georgia told her that certain clients expected sex as part of their services. Though horrified, her desperation led her into prostituting herself for work. In this episode Kyle re-entered Riley's life a year after leaving, much to the disgust and distrust of Riley's mother Linette, her friend Lacey Jean, and even Riley's brother Evan. At the same time, Riley's client Earl Hudson died on the massage table. His wife Ruth was his emergency contact number.

When Riley told Ruth of his passing, she laughed and said, "It's the best news I've had in fifty years!" She explained her love for him had vanished and she had a longtime affair with another man she could now marry. In a scene wisely deleted but contained as an outtake on the DVD set, Earl somehow came back alive and planned to file for divorce. Betty's impressive timing with her few lines made her work much better than the muddled melodramatics involving Riley. This episode was the first season finale of a series that would run only one more year.

Save Me, "Holier Than Thou"*

June 13, 2013, NBC Thursday 8-8:30 p.m.

Cast: Anne Heche (Beth Harper), Michael Landes (Tom Harper), Alexandra Breckinridge (Carly McKenna), Madison Davenport (Emily Harper), Heather Burns (Jenna Dennings), Diedrich Bader (Dr. Elliot Tompkins), Joy Osmanski (Maggie Tompkins). Guests: Betty White (God), Stephen Schneider (Pete Dennings), Orlando Jones (God). P: Joanne Tell, Anne Heche. D: Scott Winant. W: Raphael Bob-Waksberg, Joanna Calo, Julie Durk.

Beth Harper believed the Lord told her to prevent the closing of Eastside Park

Hospital in Cuyahoga County, Ohio, where Beth gave birth to her daughter, Emily. She set up a race to raise funds, but no one wanted to help. On race day, Beth had a fever but insisted God needed her to run. Beth passed out on the course and woke up in a movie theater with God disguised as Betty White. "Just an identity I threw on," "she" said. "My Betty outfit always puts people at ease."

God, as Betty, showed Beth a film of the latter's childhood, where God appeared as a black student in her class, and later as a stripper who helped Beth pick her husband. These interactions confused Beth about what she should do, which prompted God, as Betty, to respond, "You want holier than thou. That's my least favorite emotion ... Just lead by example. That's all I want you to do."

Returning back to life, Beth apologized for pressuring everyone to assist her cause. Her efforts left the hospital still $7,000 short. When she went to sleep, a different God, looking like the black student as an adult, appeared and told her the hospital needed to be destroyed. He showed her how her friends became inspired by her passion, which is how she really made a difference.

This clunky sitcom mixed frenetic slapstick and banal banter with reverent moments. Beth didn't exhibit traditional Christian behavior, and the endings showing her impact in following the supposed word of God were mawkish and flat. Betty's appearance was a missed opportunity, too, with no real reason given for Orlando Jones replacing her in the second dream sequence.

This was the series' seventh and final episode. Given its quality, it was no big loss.

Bones
Cast: Emily Deschanel (Dr. Temperance "Bones" Brennan), David Boreanz (FBI Special Agent Seeley Booth), Michaela Conlin (Angela Montenegro), Tamara Taylor (Camille Sorayan), T.J. Thyne (Dr. Jack Hodgins), Brian Klugman (Dr. Oliver Wells, 2015 only), John Boyd (FBI Special Agent James Aubrey). EP: Randy Zisk, Michael Peterson, Jonathan Collier (2017 only), Stephen Nathan, Barry Josephson, Hart Hanson (Creator). Co-EP: Jan DeWitt, Karine Rosenthal (2017 only). P: Joe Hortua (2015 only), Gene Hong (2015 only), Keith Foglesong, David H. Jeffery, David Boreanz, Emily Deschanel, Kathy Reichs.

"The Carpals in the Coy-Wolves" **
October 22, 2015, Fox Thursday 8-9 p.m.
Special guest star: Betty White (Dr. Beth Mayer). Guests: Tyler Francavilla (Jamie Wetchil), Erin Cahill (Ashlie Smith), Paul Johansson (Craig Smith), Tom Lenk (Chris Winfelder), Ronde Barber (Lou Divers), Greg Bryan (Mitch), Joshua Rush (Bradley). D: Randy Zisk. W: Gene Hong.

"The Radioactive Panthers in the Party" ***
March 14, 2017, Fox Tuesday 9-10 p.m.
Special guest star: Betty White (Dr. Beth Mayer). Guests: Michael Grant Terry (Wendell Bray), David Faustino (Himself), Rebecca Metz (Linda Martin), Charlie Saxton (Kirby Lee), Fred Stoller (Allen Peppermelt), Meeghan Holaway (Barb Martucci), James Earl (Gordy), Matthew Jones (Dwayne Haskins). D: Michael Lange. W/Supervising P: Keith Foglesong.

Noted forensic anthropologist Dr. Beth Mayer joined Dr. Wells, Dr. Hodgins, Bones, Angela, and Camille to find the source of a decomposed murder victim in "The Carpals in the Coy-Wolves." The six-times married Dr. Mayer told FBI investigator Seeley Booth she was a fantasy football enthusiast like the deceased. "Oh, I love a good trash talking!" she said. She also encouraged Dr. Wells to go out in nature to help his erectile dysfunction. This episode was dysfunctional, as well. The mystery was sluggish, the badinage between Hodgins and Wells about the latter's condition was tiresome, and Betty had few lines except for a nice final scene inspiring confidence in Bones.

In "The Radioactive Panthers in the Party," Seeley and Bones ran into Dr. Mayer, who told them she had forsaken forensics to study prairie dogs. Meanwhile, Bones deduced a man who fell from a bridge onto a passing car was murdered. Her further discoveries identified the corpse as a man who was trying to direct his first film. Seeley and James investigated the victim's former employee, Linda Martin; the man who took over directing the film, Kirby Lee; the owner and trainer of a panther, Dwayne Haskins; and even the movie's star, David Faustino. Amid that activity, Bones spotted Dr. Mayer reading one of Bones' five dissertations and asked the expert how she learned her passion for forensics had vanished. "If you're used to the electricity dancing through your veins, and suddenly it's not there, you notice," Dr. Mayer said.

This mystery was better and the humor more appropriate than Betty's first visit to *Bones*, and her scenes had more emotional resonance even though she appeared less than the previous episode. The show marked Betty's last straight dramatic role on TV.

SpongeBob SquarePants, "Mall Girl Pearl/Two Thumbs Down"***
March 12, 2016, Nickelodeon Saturday 7:30-8 p.m.
Voices: Tom Kenny (SpongeBob SquarePants and more), Roger Bumpass (Squidward Tentacles and more), Lori Alan (Pearl Krabs), Jill Talley (Marina and more), Clancy Brown (Mr. Krabs and more), Sirena Irwin (Nixie). Special guest star voices: Betty White (Beatrice), Aubrey Plaza (Nocturna). W: Claire O'Kane. P: Jennie Monica. EP: Stephen Hillenburg, Paul Tibbett.

Learning her friends Marina, Nocturna, and Nixie were working at Bikini Bottom Mall, Pearl Krabs went to find a job there. She pleaded with Beatrice, the mall manager, after being rebuffed at every store. Beatrice hired Pearl to work at Grandma's Aprons. But Marina, Nocturna, and Nixie mocked her for working at an "old people's store." "Don't let those bobble-headed nincompoops get to you, Pearlie!" Beatrice told her new employee. "We all go through difficult times at some point."

Beatrice showed Pearl the joys of knitting, making cookies, and more. Still, Pearl's trio of friends disdained her work, so Beatrice cried out, "Granny power," had her false teeth chattering away to attack the ladies and knitted a scarf to tie them together. Beatrice released Marina, Nocturna, and Nixie after they agreed to apologize and be nice to Pearl. Pearl told them she enjoyed acting like a grandmother, but Beatrice cautioned her to enjoy being young, as well. Though only seen in the first half of the animated cartoon and barely interacting with the title character, Betty's outing was a fun installment for her and enjoyable for all ages to watch.

Crowded, "The Fixer"***
April 17, 2016, NBC Sunday 9-9:30 p.m.
Cast: Patrick Warburton (Mike Moore), Carrie Preston (Martina Moore), Miranda Cosgrove (Shea Moore), Mia Serafino (Stella Moore), Stacy Keach (Bob Moore), Carlease Burke (Alice Moore). Special guest stars: Betty White (Sandy), Jane Leeves (Gwen). Guests: Sterling Knight (Nate Johnson), John Colella (Dr. Matthews). EP/Creator: Suzanne Martin. EP: Sean Hayes, Todd Milliner. D: Andy Cadiff. W: Chelsea Myers.

Martina recounted to Dr. Matthews how she counseled the bickering mother-daughter pair of Sandy and Gwen. Sandy drank, partied late, and brought home men. "I'm just having a little fun!" protested Sandy, who also mocked her daughter's "stupid accent" that came from Sandy marrying a Briton and raising Gwen in London. "Can you even understand her?" griped Sandy to Martina. Sandy also claimed Gwen was back to being a virgin. "It can lapse, like a driver's license!" and confided to Martina that "There are cobwebs down there."

While Martina took a break from the session to help her daughters with their own dilemmas, Sandy went to the bed of Martina's sick husband Mike and rubbed down his hairy chest. Sandy also made him chocolate chip pancakes. Then Sandy moved into Martina's already crowded house with her daughters Shea and Stella and her in-laws Bob and Alice. Soon Shea, Stella, and Bob asked Sandy for advice, while Stella transformed into an attractive, vibrant woman. "You look beautiful and happy," said Sandy, who left with Gwen to go to a warehouse party. Assessing what Mike and Martina had told him, Dr. Matthews recommended that Mike attempt to reconnect with his birth mother.

Sporadically funny, this sitcom's seventh episode out of fourteen aired let Betty roam freely from bubbly to bitchy throughout. There also was a nod to the previous working relationship between Jane Leeves and Betty on *Hot in Cleveland* when Gwen asked Sandy if she looked like a hooker from Cleveland.

Young & Hungry[***]
Cast: Emily Osment (Gabi Diamond), Jonathan Sadowski (Josh Kaminski), Aimee Carrero (Sofia Rodriguez), Kym Whitley (Yolanda), Rex Lee (Elliot Park). EP/Creator: David Holden. EP: Eric Tannenbaum, Kim Tannenbaum, Ashley Tisdale, Jessica Rhoades, Caryn Lucas, Andy Cadiff. P: Jason Wang. D: Andy Cadiff.

"Young & Valentine's Day"
March 20, 2017, Freeform Monday 8-8:30 p.m.
Guests: Betty White (Ms. Bernice Wilson), Bryan Safi (Alan), Jonathan Schmock (Maître d'), Brandon Rush (Male stripper), Jackie Joyner (Future Mrs Stein), Carlo Mendez (Gorgeous guy). W: Rachel Sweet.

"Young & Las Vegas, Baby"
May 8, 2017, Freeform Monday 8-8:30 p.m.

Guests: Betty White (Ms. Bernice Wilson), Carl Reiner (Bernie Schwartz), David Douglas (Cashier). W: Joshua Corey, Brian Kratz.

Though in love with Josh, Gabi planned to just hang out with her pals Sofia and Yolanda on "Young & Valentine's Day." But when her friend Elliot spied a gift box with a dinner she made for him on behalf of his husband Alan, she claimed instead it was a present for Josh. Many complications ensued, culminating with Gabi thinking Josh was proposing to her at a fancy restaurant. Worried, she ran back to her apartment and went down her fire escape.

Seeing an open window, Gabi entered the room of Ms. Wilson, who sat on a couch in a white wedding dress and threatened to shoot the young woman. After Gabi explained her situation, Ms. Wilson muttered, "Did I ask?" Gabi offered to cook Ms. Wilson a meal but saw the brisket in the freezer had expired in 2003. "So did Harry," said Ms. Wilson. "Was Harry your husband?" asked Gabi. "No, it was the cow! You're a natural blonde, aren't you?" smirked Ms. Wilson.

The older woman revealed Harry was her fifth husband and that she loved weddings more than husbands, which is why she wore her gown. "I wear it every Valentine's Day," she said before advising Gabi to "Put it on, it answers all your questions." After Gabi donned the gown, Josh had gone down the fire escape and saw her in the window. Now he thought Gabi was ready to marry him. Sofia, Yolanda, and Alan joined Josh in confronting Gabi, who got everything straightened out with Josh while Mrs. Wilson lusted after him. This fast and furious farce featured Betty delivering her lines with élan, and she even got to lust after a male stripper at the end.

In "Young & Las Vegas," upset about turning twenty-five, Gabi found out when she received flowers meant for Ms. Wilson that they shared a birthday. The error led Sofia to ask the senior citizen who her secret admirer was. "I don't know. Maybe my CrossFit trainer?" she replied before saying it could be Bernie Schwartz. "He's a man I met in Vegas twenty years ago when we were married. And not to each other."

The note said Bernie wanted to meet her in Sin City, so Ms. Wilson drove with the girls from San Francisco until she got stopped for speeding. Ms. Wilson paid off the cop with $500 she planned to use for gambling. "It wasn't my first offer," she grinned, implying that she had flirted first.

Unfortunately, that left her and the girls with no money when they arrived at a convenience store. "Oh well, I guess I won't be feeling the Bern," sighed Bernice. But

Gabi put some quarters her late mother gave her as a gift into a slot machine and won a big enough payout to get them to Vegas.

At the honeymoon suite, the trio opened the door to see Josh, Yolanda, and Elliot, who arrived earlier on a jet. They all waited for Bernie, but he appeared to be a no-show. Bernice was happy, nonetheless. "I got to drive. I got to Vegas. And I won a jackpot. It's the best night I've ever had!" Bernie then arrived and delivered flowers. "Thank God he's still jacked!" she grinned. The old lovebirds forced the rest of the group to leave, as Gabi reconciled with Josh.

In a promotional video about the episode, star Emily Osment said, "I was a huge fan of *The Mary Tyler Moore Show* when I was a kid growing up, so I always watched Betty on *The Mary Tyler Moore Show* … She's so wonderful and so sharp and funny and kind to everybody, and we're very lucky to have her." In the same video, Betty commented, "It's a joy to work on this set. I love, well, everybody. It's just a pleasant, happy set. There's not a grouch on it."

As of this writing, this show marked Betty's last TV acting role. Apparently and thankfully it was a happy one, too.

Epilogue

"Are you going to interview Betty White?"

Nearly everyone asked me that question when I told them about this book. While I said I hoped to do so, the question actually had two different answers.

First, I had met Betty in July 2007 at the Game Show Congress at the Garland Hotel in North Hollywood, California. When she was introduced, I, like many other attendees, started chanting "Bet-ty! Bet-ty!" in honor of her decades-long contributions and devotion to game shows. Betty was there to help honor game show creator Bob Stewart with the Bill Cullen Career Achievement Award. Game show expert Steve Beverly surprised Betty with the inaugural Arlene Francis Panelist Award, as well. The event also marked the first time I met my lifelong friends Steve Beverly and film historian Stu Shostak in person.

Cut to the Game Show Congress on November 14 and 15, 2009. Beverly, Shostak and I reviewed our plans for the weekend, as I was helping Shostak cover the event live on the internet and Beverly was an event organizer. One challenge was making sure Beverly could escort Betty easily and swiftly from Shostak's interview platform in the back of the auditorium to the front of the stage. Betty, who had been at every Game Show Congress except 2005 due to a scheduling conflict, would be accepting the Bill Cullen Career Achievement Award on behalf of her late husband, Allen Ludden.

Overhearing our conversation was Shostak's friend, former child actor Frank Bank, best known as Lumpy Rutherford on *Leave It to Beaver* from 1957 to 1963. "He said, 'Can I come to this thing on Sunday?'" recalled Beverly. "And I said, 'Yeah, it's open to anybody.' He said, 'I just want to come because I've never met Betty White before.'"

Betty's arrival was even crazier than Shostak, Beverly, and I imagined. Somehow, through the throng of attendees, Betty got to Shostak's booth. I helped her enter and exit safely each way. She was what everyone said about Betty—warm, delightful, funny, adorable. From there, Beverly had to lead Betty forward.

"I came back and got her, I'm bringing her down the aisle, and at that point in time, she was getting mobbed," Beverly said. "I remember she never failed to have a smile for everybody. Somebody could've been uncomfortable about that, but she would stop for people to take her picture. She gave a few autographs.

"And when I got up to the row right behind where we were going to bring her up front, Frank Bank was there, because he had asked us at Stu's house that night. So, Frank comes down to the end of the aisle, because he wants to meet her, and I stop right there. And he said, 'Betty, I bet you don't know who I am, but I'm Lumpy!' And all of a sudden she looked at him, and she said—without batting an eyelash, she'd never seen him before except maybe on TV—she said, 'Where's Eddie [Haskell, Lumpy's pal on *Leave It to Beaver* played by Ken Osmond]?' I will never forget that. It broke Frank up, because he was not expecting that at all."

My second hidden answer to the question of interviewing Betty was I knew the event would be a long shot when I started the project. The effects of time had taken their toll on Betty's mobility and voice.

By 2019, Betty was rarely on TV. No interviews occurred for her ninety-seventh birthday even though ABC News and other outlets profiled the event. She had not appeared on any entertainment program since the seventieth Emmy Awards presentation on September 16, 2018, either.

The exceptions were two promotional pieces in August 2019. First, she voiced a public service announcement for Smokey Bear's seventy-fifth birthday. Next, before the opening of the hundredth season on the NFL on September 5, 2019, Betty taped a part in a thirty-second ad for *Sunday Night Football* on NBC. Host Al Michaels pretended to be at the podium for a news conference mentioning the significance of the milestone. "I don't think there's anybody out there who could possibly put that into words," he said.

"I can!" exclaimed Betty in a raspy voiceover.

"Betty White?" Michaels responded.

"Al, B-Dawg's talking now!" said Betty as the camera cut to her in what appeared to be a setup in her own home. "One hundred years of NFL history. The Packers and the Bears. There's only one thing more badass than this year's kickoff, and you're looking at her!"

Most of the latter part of the script didn't show Betty on camera. The advertisement tried to present Betty in the best possible light, yet one could tell she was not the dynamo she used to be.

"She uses a walker at home, and she obviously has to hold onto somebody when she's in public now," said David Mathews, who started the Facebook campaign for Betty to host *Saturday Night Live*, in early 2020. "She's still sharp, but her voice is losing its timbre. It's a little cracky-er."

Everyone around Betty knows that if she was healthy enough to do more TV, she would. She has always understood the realities of the business and adjusted her expectations accordingly.

"I hear people say, 'Oh, but there are no roles for women anymore, you know? Once you pass a given age, nobody wants you,'" she said in a 2005 interview for the American Comedy Archives at Emerson College. "Yes they do, but you've got to take what comes by. You can't say, 'Well, I'm waiting. No, I don't want to play mothers. No, I don't want to do this.' You take the role that comes by.

"And sometimes, it isn't the best. If it's one you really hate, then avoid it. But if it's not one you're thrilled with or it's too small a role or you think for some reason or other it's not your cup of tea, do it anyway. Because it's a growth situation. You may never want to do that again, but at least you tried it, and it kept you alive in the minds of not only the audience but the people doing the casting."

"I am amazed that I'm still on television, they still let me come back," she stated in the 2018 PBS documentary *Betty White: First Lady of Television*. "And I'm not saying that coyly, I mean it. It's such a privilege to still be able to work in this business."

In the 2017 HBO documentary *If You're Not in the Obit, Eat Breakfast*, Betty told host Carl Reiner she planned to be as active as she could in her later years. "I don't want to be a burden to anybody. Except possibly Robert Redford," she joked.

Betty is not a burden as of this writing. She still has her agent of twenty years, Jeff Witjas, who I contacted several times for an interview that never got confirmed amid the COVID-19 pandemic outbreak in 2020. False reports came out that Betty contracted the virus in March 2020. Two months later, Betty was said to be safely quarantined at her home and doing well.

Also, in May 2020, a news release said Betty would be starring in a movie for the Lifetime network pay channel set to air in December 2020. The release said Betty would play a woman who "helps whip would-be Santas into shape, spreading the true meaning of Christmas and leading everyone to wonder: is she secretly Mrs. Claus?" This project did not occur due to the ongoing COVID-19 pandemic.

Whatever does happen in the future, the specter of mortality is not a concern for Betty.

"Everybody says, 'What about death?' And that's coming closer," she said in the special *Barbara Walters 10 Most Fascinating People of 2010*, having no idea she would still be alive a decade later. "My mother had a wonderful philosophy. She said, 'Nobody knows what happens at that moment,' so whenever we lose anyone in the family, Mom would always say, 'Now he knows the secret!' So, I kind of find myself thinking, 'I'm curious, and I'll know a secret!'"

As for her legacy, Betty has downplayed her impact. In 1997, her agent at the time, Tony Fantozzi, asked, "How do you want to be remembered?"

"I don't even know that I'd be remembered," she modestly answered. "I would just like to have [known] somewhere along the line that I made people laugh, and I made them think a little bit. And the two parts of my life, the animal part and the television part—and I worked them together as much as I can.

"By doing all the game shows and by doing all the talk shows, and by doing situation comedies and the diversity that I've done, the audience never—had I done Sue Ann Nivens as my first show, I would have been typed forever. But I haven't, so the audience [said], 'Oh, it's Betty being silly again.' That's what I'd like to be remembered, as Betty, their good friend they invited into their home."

She will be recalled for much more than that, of course. For a final perspective, I'll leave you with these words, from a man who has known her personally and professionally since 1953.

"Wes, when you said you were doing a book on Betty, and you asked me if I would mind chatting, I immediately said yes," said Tom Kennedy. "But I thought about it and said, 'This is going to be the dullest show in the world!'

"Because the only thing I can say about Betty is she's the greatest. Period. That's the end of it. No matter what you're talking about—personality, singer, dancer, comedienne, and human being. The best. She's the best.

"What else do you want to talk about?"

When someone makes comments like that, it's hard to think of what else to say. Except thanks again, Betty, for giving us decades of laughter, tears, excitement, joy, and fun. No one else will ever be able to match what you have done on television for so long in so many ways.

Dave Letterman could have been telling a shaggy dog story about this item in front of him while Betty and John Amos look things over on *Liars Club* circa 1977. Betty was a regular on the 1969 version and a semiregular on the 1970s revamp. Courtesy of the Adam Nedeff Collection.

Appendix
Betty By the Numbers

National TV series as a regular performer—Seventeen[1]
Life with Elizabeth (1953-55, Syndicated)—starring actress
The Betty White Show (1954, NBC)—hostess
Make the Connection (1955, NBC)—panelist
Date with the Angels (1957-58, ABC)—starring actress
The Betty White Show (1958, ABC)—hostess
Liars Club (1969, Syndicated)—panelist
The Pet Set (1971-72, Syndicated)—hostess
The Mary Tyler Moore Show (1973-77, CBS)—supporting actress
The Betty White Show (1977, CBS)—starring actress
Just Men! (1983, NBC)—hostess
The Golden Girls (1985-92, NBC)—starring actress
The Golden Palace (1992-93, CBS)—starring actress
Maybe This Time (1995-96, ABC)—supporting actress
Ladies Man (2000-02, CBS)—supporting actress
Hot in Cleveland (2012-15, TV Land)—supporting actress
Betty White's Off Their Rockers (2014, NBC and Lifetime)—hostess
To Tell the Truth (2016, ABC)—panelist

---

[1] The most regular national TV series of any American female personality as of 2020; the runners-up are Cloris Leachman with fourteen and Pat Carroll with thirteen. Ahead of Betty are Bill Cullen with thirty-three and Dennis James with eighteen. Dick Clark and Bert Parks are tied with Betty at seventeen, followed by Carl Reiner at sixteen. Betty worked with all of these talents on TV at least once.

National TV series as a semiregular—Nine
Tonight Starring Jack Parr (1959-62, NBC)—frequent guest, at least seventy shows
Match Game 73-79/PM (1973-82, CBS and Syndicated)—frequent panelist, at least 104 weeks
Liars Club (1976-78, Syndicated)—frequent panelist, at least thirty-two times
Mama's Family (1983-86, NBC and Syndicated)—fifteen episodes out of sixty episodes
Bob (1993, CBS)—four out of six episodes aired
The Lionhearts (1998, Syndicated)—five times out of thirteen episodes
Boston Legal (2005-08, ABC)—eighteen times over three years
The Bold and the Beautiful (2006-09, CBS)—twenty-three shows over three years
Pound Puppies (2010-13, The Hub)—thirteen times out of sixty-five episodes[2]

Emmy wins—Seven
Most Outstanding Female Personality, for *Life with Elizabeth*, 1952 (Los Angeles area Emmy award)
Outstanding Continuing Performance by a Supporting Actress in a Comedy Series, for *The Mary Tyler Moore Show*, 1975 and 1976
Outstanding Host or Hostess in a Game or Audience Participation Show, for *Just Men!*, 1983 (Daytime Emmy award)
Outstanding Lead Actress in a Comedy Series, for *The Golden Girls*, 1986
Outstanding Guest Actress in a Comedy Series, for *The John Larroquette Show*, 1996
Outstanding Guest Actress in a Comedy Series, for *Saturday Night Live*, 2010

Emmy nominations without wins—Seventeen[3]
Best Actress, for *The Betty White Show*, 1951
Outstanding Continuing Performance by a Supporting Actress in a Comedy Series, for *The Mary Tyler Moore Show*, 1977
Outstanding Host or Hostess in a Game or Audience Participation Show, for *Just Men!*, 1984 (Daytime Emmy award)
Outstanding Lead Actress in a Comedy Series, for *The Golden Girls*, 1987, 1988, 1989, 1990, 1991, 1992
Outstanding Guest Actress in a Comedy Series, for *Suddenly Susan*, 1997
Outstanding Guest Actress in a Comedy Series, for *Yes, Dear*, 2003
Outstanding Guest Actress in a Drama Series, for *The Practice*, 2004
Outstanding Guest Actress in a Comedy Series, for *My Name is Earl*, 2009
Outstanding Supporting Actress in a Comedy Series, for *Hot in Cleveland*, 2011

---

2   Two of these were game shows, two were sitcoms, two were cartoons, one was a talk show, one was a drama and one was a soap opera.

3   Betty also won a Lifetime Achievement Award from the Daytime Emmys in 2015.

Outstanding Host for a Reality or Reality-Competition Program, for *Betty White's Off Their Rockers*, 2012, 2013, 2014

Aired pilots—Two, both sitcoms
Snavely (June 24, 1978, ABC)
Stephanie (Sept. 8, 1981, CBS)

Guest acting shots, miscellaneous—Three
ALF Loves a Mystery (Sept. 12, 1987, NBC)
D.C. Follies (Oct. 13, 1987, Syndicated)
Noddy (Dec. 6, 1998, PBS)

TV movies—Twelve
Vanished (March 9, 1971, NBC)
With This Ring (May 5, 1978, ABC)
The Best Place to Be (May 27 and 28, 1979, NBC)
Before and After (Oct. 5, 1979, ABC)
The Gossip Columnist (March 21, 1980, Syndicated)
Chance of a Lifetime (Nov. 18, 1991, NBC)
A Weekend in the Country (June 12, 1996, USA Network)
The Retrievers (July 30, 2001, Animal Planet)
Return to the Batcave: The Misadventures of Adam and Burt (March 9, 2003, CBS)
Stealing Christmas (Nov. 30, 2003, Lifetime)
Annie's Point (Jan. 22, 2005, Hallmark Channel)
The Lost Valentine (Jan. 30, 2011, CBS)

Guest shots, dramas—Twenty
The Millionaire (Oct. 17, 1956, CBS)
The U.S. Steel Hour (June 27, 1962, CBS)
O'Hara United States Treasury (Jan. 14, 1972, CBS)
Lucas Tanner (Feb. 26, 1975, NBC)
Ellery Queen (Oct. 19, 1975, NBC)
Fame (Jan. 20, 1983, NBC)
Hotel (Nov. 21, 1984, ABC)
St. Elsewhere (Feb. 13, 1985, NBC)
St. Elsewhere (Nov. 20, 1985, NBC)
Matlock (Dec. 1, 1987, NBC)
Diagnosis Murder (Dec. 2, 1994, CBS)
L.A. Doctors (Dec. 7, 1998, CBS)

Ally McBeal (Nov. 8, 1999, FOX)
Providence (Nov. 8, 2002, NBC)
Everwood (Nov. 24, 2003, The WB)
Everwood (May 3, 2004, The WB)
Ugly Betty (Dec. 6, 2007, ABC)
The Client List (June 17, 2012, Lifetime)
Bones (Oct. 22, 2015, FOX)
Bones (March 14, 2017, FOX)

Guest shots, cartoons—Twenty
The Story of Santa Claus (Dec. 4, 1996, CBS)
Disney's Hercules (March 1, 1999, Syndicated)
King of the Hill (March 16, 1999, FOX)
The Simpsons (Feb. 20, 2000, FOX)
The Wild Thornberrys (Feb. 26, 2000, Nickelodeon)
The Wild Thornberrys (Nov. 22, 2000, Nickelodeon)
The Wild Thornberrys (Dec. 11, 2000, Nickelodeon)
Disney's Teacher's Pet (March 22, 2002, ABC)
King of the Hill (Dec. 8, 2002, FOX)
Gary the Rat (Oct. 5, 2003, SpikeTV)
The Grim Adventures of Billy & Mandy (Oct. 31, 2003, The Cartoon Network)
Higglytown Heroes (Sept. 14, 2004, Disney Jr.)
Father of the Pride (Sept. 21, 2004, NBC)
Higglytown Heroes (July 22, 2005, Disney Jr.)
The Simpsons (March 25, 2007, FOX)
Higglytown Heroes (June 25, 2007, Disney Jr.)
Glenn Martin, D.D.S. (Aug. 31, 2009, Nickelodeon)
Glenn Martin, D.D.S. (Sept. 17, 2010, Nickelodeon)
Prep & Landing Stocking Stuffer (Dec. 7, 2010, ABC)
Spongebob SquarePants (March 12, 2016, Nickelodeon)

Guest shots, sitcoms—Forty-two
Petticoat Junction (Feb. 1, 1969, CBS)
The Odd Couple (Dec. 1, 1972, ABC)
The Love Boat (Nov. 22, 1980, ABC)
Best of the West (Sept. 24, 1981, ABC)
The Love Boat (Oct. 17, 1981, ABC)
Love, Sidney (Jan. 13, 1982, NBC)
Madame's Place (Oct. 14, 1982, Syndicated)

The Love Boat (Dec. 11, 1982, ABC)
The Love Boat (Jan. 7, 1984, ABC)
Who's the Boss? (Feb. 19, 1985, ABC)
The Love Boat (Nov. 23, 1985, ABC)
Who's the Boss? (Nov. 26, 1985, ABC)
The Dom DeLuise Show (Oct. 15, 1987, Syndicated)
Empty Nest (Feb. 4, 1989, NBC)
Empty Nest (Nov. 11, 1989, NBC)
Nurses (Nov. 9, 1991, NBC)
Empty Nest (Feb. 29, 1992, NBC)
The Naked Truth (Sept. 27, 1995, ABC)
The John Larroquette Show (March 12, 1996, NBC)
Suddenly Susan (Nov. 7, 1996, NBC)
The Ellen Show (Nov. 16, 2001, CBS)
Yes, Dear (Oct. 21, 2002, CBS)
That 70s Show (Oct. 29, 2002, FOX)
That 70s Show (Dec. 3, 2002, FOX)
That 70s Show (Jan. 29, 2003, FOX)
That 70s Show (Feb. 5, 2003, FOX)
I'm With Her (Nov. 25, 2003, ABC)
My Wife and Kids (May 5, 2004, ABC)
Malcolm in the Middle (May 9, 2004, FOX)
Complete Savages (Dec. 3, 2004, ABC)
Complete Savages (May 27, 2005, ABC)
Joey (Oct. 13, 2005, NBC)
My Name is Earl (March 19, 2009, NBC)
30 Rock (Oct. 29, 2009, NBC)
The Middle (May 19, 2010, ABC)
Community (Sept. 23, 2010, NBC)
Community (Oct. 7, 2010, NBC)
Save Me (June 13, 2013, NBC)
The Soul Man (March 28, 2014, TV Land)
Crowded (April 17, 2016, NBC)
Young & Hungry (March 20, 2017, Freeform)
Young & Hungry (May 8, 2017, Freeform)

Guest shots, variety—Eighty
Candid Camera (April 16, 1961, CBS)
The Jerry Lewis Show: From This Moment On (November 1962, Syndicated)

That's Life (Oct. 22, 1968, ABC)
"Phyllis Diller's 102nd Birthday Party," ABC Wide World of Entertainment (May 15, 1974, ABC)
CBS Bicentennial Minute (host, Sept. 15, 1974, CBS)
"The Great American Game Show," ABC Wide World of Entertainment (Jan. 16, 1975, ABC)
"Monty Hall Roast," ABC Wide World of Entertainment (Feb. 12, 1975, ABC)
The Carol Burnett Show (Nov. 22, 1975, CBS)
The Rich Little Show (Feb. 23, 1976, NBC)
The Diahann Carroll Show (Aug. 21, 1976, CBS)
Cos (Sept. 26, 1976, ABC)
The Peter Marshall Variety Show (Oct. 23, 1976, Syndicated)
The Paul Lynde Halloween Special (Oct. 29, 1976, ABC)
Sonny & Cher (Nov. 7, 1976, CBS)
The Carol Burnett Show (Dec. 11, 1976, CBS)
Sonny & Cher (Jan. 21, 1977, CBS)
The Jacksons (March 9, 1977, CBS)
CBS Galaxy (Sept. 5, 1977, CBS)
Circus of the Stars (Dec. 5, 1977, CBS)
The John Davidson Christmas Special (Dec. 9, 1977, ABC)
Donny & Marie (Jan. 27, 1978, ABC)
The Carol Burnett Show (March 5, 1978, CBS)
CBS On the Air (March 26, 1978, CBS)
The Dean Martin Celebrity Roast: Betty White (May 31, 1978, NBC)
Donny & Marie (Sept. 22, 1978, ABC)
Donny & Marie (Oct. 13, 1978, ABC)
Donny & Marie (Dec. 1, 1978, ABC)
Circus of the Stars III (Dec. 10, 1978, CBS)
Donny & Marie (Dec. 29, 1978, ABC)
Paul Lynde at the Movies (March 24, 1979, ABC)
The Big Show (April 8, 1980, NBC)
Big City Comedy (Nov. 15, 1980, Syndicated)
NBC Star Salute to 1981 (Jan. 1, 1981, NBC)
Norm Crosby's The Comedy Shop (Jan. 3, 1981, Syndicated)
Bob Hope's Stand Up and Cheer National Football League's 60th Year (Nov. 22, 1981, NBC)
Eunice (March 15, 1982, CBS)
The Shape of Things (April 6, 1982, NBC)
Pudgy! (July 26, 1982, Showtime)
Laugh Trax (Oct. 26, 1982, Syndicated)
NBC All Star Hour (Sept. 12, 1983, NBC)

Those Wonderful Game Shows (Feb. 27, 1984, NBC)
Joan Rivers and Friends Salute Heidi Abromowitz (June 14, 1985, Showtime)
A Comedy Salute to Baseball (July 15, 1985, NBC)
The Third Annual NBC All Star Hour (Sept. 16, 1985, NBC)
Star Search (Jan. 4, 1986, Syndicated)
NBC's 60th Anniversary Celebration (May 12, 1986, NBC)
Walt Disney World's 15th Anniversary Celebration, The Wonderful World of Disney (Nov. 9, 1986, NBC)
Happy Birthday Hollywood (May 18, 1987, ABC)
Happy Birthday Bob (May 16, 1988, NBC)
The Magical World of Disney (Oct. 9, 1988, NBC)
Bob Hope's Love Affair with Lucy (Sept. 23, 1989, NBC)
A Conversation With Betty White (Oct. 15, 1989, The Disney Channel)
Time Warner Presents the Earth Day Special (April 22, 1990, NBC)
Night of 100 Stars III (May 21, 1990, NBC)
Carol & Company (Nov 3, 1990, NBC)
Funny Women of Television : A Museum of Radio & Television Tribute (Oct. 24, 1991, NBC)
Bob Hope and Other Young Comedians (March 14, 1992, NBC)
Bob Hope: The First 90 Years (May 14, 1993, NBC)
Bob Hope's Birthday Memories (May 11, 1994, NBC)
The Great Love Songs (Aug. 9, 1995, PBS)
Behind the Laughs: The Untold Stories of Television's Favorite Comedies: A Paley Center for Media Special (May 27, 1998, FOX)
The 70s: The Decade That Changed Television: The Museum of Television & Radio (Sept. 7, 2000, ABC)
NBC 75th Anniversary Special (May 5, 2002, NBC)
The Museum of Television and Radio Presents: Great Women of Television Comedy (April 15, 2003, NBC)
CBS at 75 (Nov. 2, 2003, CBS)
Comedy Central Roast of William Shatner (Aug 20, 2006, Comedy Central)
Dreams Come True: A Celebration of Disney Animation (Dec. 4, 2009, ABC)
Saturday Night Live (May 8, 2010, NBC)
Tina Fey: The Mark Twain Prize (Nov. 9, 2010, PBS)
25 Years of Sexy: People Magazine's Sexiest Man Alive (Nov. 17, 2010, ABC)
TV's All-Time Funniest Holiday Moments: A Paley Center for Media Special (Nov. 26, 2010, FOX)
AFI Life Achievement Award: A Tribute to Morgan Freeman (June 19, 2011, TV Land)
Betty White's 90th Birthday: A Tribute to America's Golden Girl (Jan. 16, 2012, NBC)
Betty White's Second Annual 90th Birthday (Feb. 5, 2013, NBC)

TV's Funniest of the Funniest: A Paley Center for Media Special (Sept. 1, 2013, NBC)
Kennedy Center Mark Twain Prize for American Humor: Celebrating Jay Leno (Nov. 23, 2014, PBS)
Saturday Night Live 40th Anniversary Special (Feb. 15, 2015, NBC)
If You're Not in the Obit, Eat Breakfast (May 19, 2017, HBO)
Little Big Shots: Forever Young (June 21, 2017, NBC)
Betty White: First Lady of Television (Aug. 21, 2018, PBS)

Selected talk show guest shots—100[4]
The Steve Allen Show (Oct. 7, 1964, Syndicated)
The Merv Griffin Show (April 21, 1966, Syndicated)
Dinah's Place (March 2, 1972, NBC)
The Tonight Show Starring Johnny Carson (Dec. 25, 1974, NBC)
Dinah! (Nov. 13, 1975, Syndicated)
Dinah! (Jan. 29, 1976, Syndicated)
The Tonight Show Starring Johnny Carson (March 17, 1976, NBC)
Dinah! (April 13, 1976, Syndicated)
The Tonight Show Starring Johnny Carson (Dec. 1, 1977, NBC)
The Tonight Show Starring Johnny Carson (Aug. 16, 1978, NBC)
The Tonight Show Starring Johnny Carson (Oct. 5, 1978, NBC)
The Merv Griffin Show (guest hostess, Oct. 10, 1978, Syndicated)
The Tonight Show Starring Johnny Carson (Dec. 22, 1978, NBC)
The Tonight Show Starring Johnny Carson (Feb. 8 and 9, 1979, NBC)
The Tonight Show Starring Johnny Carson (May 4, 1979, NBC)
The Merv Griffin Show (guest hostess, July 17, 1979, Syndicated)
Dinah! (Aug. 8, 1980, Syndicated)
The Tonight Show Starring Johnny Carson (Aug. 14, 1981, NBC)
The Tonight Show Starring Johnny Carson (Nov. 12, 1981, NBC)
The Tonight Show Starring Johnny Carson (Dec. 2, 1982, NBC)
The Tonight Show Starring Johnny Carson (April 19, 1983, NBC)
Donahue (Sept. 1, 1983, Syndicated)
The Tonight Show Starring Johnny Carson (Sept. 7, 1983, NBC)
The Tonight Show Starring Johnny Carson (Sept. 28, 1983, NBC)
The Tonight Show Starring Johnny Carson (June 1, 1984, NBC)
Late Night with David Letterman (Oct. 5, 1985, NBC)
The Merv Griffin Show (Nov. 5, 1985, Syndicated)

---

4 Betty did hundreds of talk show guest shots. This list is just a sample of confirmed appearances.

The Tonight Show Starring Johnny Carson (Feb. 18, 1986, NBC)
The Tonight Show Starring Johnny Carson (guest hostess, Sept. 8, 1986, NBC)
The Tonight Show Starring Johnny Carson (April 1, 1987, NBC)
The Tonight Show Starring Johnny Carson (Oct. 7, 1987, NBC)
The Wil Shriner Show (Oct. 14, 1987, Syndicated)
The Tonight Show Starring Johnny Carson (Feb. 3, 1988, NBC)
The Pat Sajak Show (Feb. 27, 1989, CBS)
The Pat Sajak Show (May 1, 1989, CBS)
The Tonight Show Starring Johnny Carson (Sept. 25, 1990, NBC)
The Late Late Show with Tom Snyder (July 1, 1997, CBS)
The Martin Short Show (Oct. 4, 1999, Syndicated)
The Martin Short Show (April 12, 2000, Syndicated)
The Late Show with David Letterman (May 8, 2000, CBS)
The Daily Show with Jon Stewart (May 11, 2000, Comedy Central)
The Ellen Degeneres Show (Sept. 10, 2003, Syndicated)
The Late Late Show with Craig Ferguson (Oct. 19, 2005, CBS)
The Late Late Show with Craig Ferguson (Oct. 19, 2005, CBS)
The Late Late Show with Craig Ferguson (May 9, 2006, CBS)
The Late Late Show with Craig Ferguson (Dec. 4, 2006, CBS)
The Late Late Show with Craig Ferguson (July 13, 2007, CBS)
The Late Late Show with Craig Ferguson (June 9, 2008, CBS)
Late Night with Jimmy Fallon (June 11, 2009, NBC)
The Late Late Show with Craig Ferguson (Dec. 21, 2009, CBS)
The Bonnie Hunt Show (Feb. 17, 2010, Syndicated)
Lopez Tonight (May 5, 2010, TBS)
Late Night with Jimmy Fallon (May 6, 2010, NBC)
The View (June 14, 2010, ABC)
The Daily Show with Jon Stewart (June 14, 2010, Comedy Central)
The Late Late Show with Craig Ferguson (Aug. 11, 2010, CBS)
The Late Late Show with Craig Ferguson (Sept. 23, 2010, CBS)
Barbara Walters 10 Most Fascinating People of 2010 (Dec. 9, 2010, ABC)
The View (Jan. 18, 2011, ABC)
The Late Show with David Letterman (Jan. 18, 2011, CBS)
Late Night with Jimmy Fallon (Jan. 19, 2011, NBC)
The Late Late Show with Craig Ferguson (Jan. 26, 2011, CBS)
The Late Show with David Letterman (May 4, 2011, CBS)
The View (guest hostess, May 3, 2011, ABC)
The Late Late Show with Craig Ferguson (May 17, 2011, CBS)
The Late Show with David Letterman (June 13, 2011, CBS)

Late Night with Jimmy Fallon (June 14, 2011, NBC)
Jimmy Kimmel Live! (Aug. 15, 2011, ABC)
Late Night with Jimmy Fallon (Nov. 28, 2011, NBC)
The Daily Show with Jon Stewart (Nov. 29, 2011, Comedy Central)
The Late Late Show with Craig Ferguson (Feb. 14, 2012, CBS)
Conan (Feb. 28, 2012, TBS)
The Late Show with David Letterman (May 16, 2012, CBS)
The View (May 17, 2012, ABC)
The Late Late Show with Craig Ferguson (Dec. 11, 2012, CBS)
Late Night with Jimmy Fallon (Jan. 7, 2013, NBC)
The Doctors (Feb. 13, 2013, Syndicated)
The Late Late Show with Craig Ferguson (June 6, 2013, CBS)
The Tonight Show with Jay Leno (June 13, 2013, NBC)
The Talk (June 17, 2013, CBS)
The Talk (Dec. 2, 2013, CBS)
Queen Latifah (Jan. 14, 2014, Syndicated)
The Tonight Show with Jay Leno (Feb. 3, 2014, NBC)
Conan (March 4, 2014, TBS)
The Talk (March 18, 2014, CBS)
The Late Late Show with Craig Ferguson (March 24, 2014, CBS)
Queen Latifah (May 19, 2014, Syndicated)
The Late Late Show with Craig Ferguson (May 27, 2014, CBS)
The Late Late Show with Craig Ferguson (Dec. 17, 2014, CBS)
The Talk (Jan. 14, 2015, CBS)
Jimmy Kimmel Live! (April 16, 2015, ABC)
The Late Late Show with James Corden (April 21, 2015, CBS)
Conan (May 18, 2015, TBS)
The Late Late Show with James Corden (June 9, 2015, CBS)
Conan (July 8, 2015, TBS)
The Late Late Show with James Corden (Jan. 12, 2016, CBS)
The Late Late Show with James Corden (May 10, 2017, CBS)

Betty towered above the men in the 1984 NBC special *Those Wonderful Game Shows*. Joining her amid the balloons from left to right were fellow game show emcees George Fenneman, Carl Reiner and Ralph Edwards. Courtesy of the Adam Nedeff Collection.

Confirmed game show guest shots—338[5]
What's My Line? (June 19, 1955, CBS)
What's My Line? (June 26, 1955, CBS)
To Tell the Truth (June 10, 1958, CBS)
To Tell the Truth (June 17, 1958, CBS)
To Tell the Truth (June 24, 1958, CBS)
I've Got a Secret (July 23, 1958, CBS)
I've Got a Secret (Aug. 13, 1958, CBS)

---

[5] Doing a week's worth of a game show is counted as one appearance here. Counting each individual day on a week of game shows, Betty appeared on at least 1,235 game show episodes as a guest. This does not include game shows where she was a regular or semiregular.

I've Got a Secret (Sept. 24, 1958, CBS)
To Tell the Truth (Dec. 23, 1958, CBS)
To Tell the Truth (Dec. 30, 1958, CBS)
To Tell the Truth (Feb. 3, 1959, CBS)
To Tell the Truth (Feb. 10, 1959, CBS)
To Tell the Truth (Feb. 17, 1959, CBS)
To Tell the Truth (Feb. 24, 1959, CBS)
To Tell the Truth (March 3, 1959, CBS)
To Tell the Truth (March 10, 1959, CBS)
To Tell the Truth (March 17, 1959, CBS)
To Tell the Truth (May 5, 1959, CBS)
To Tell the Truth (May 12, 1959, CBS)
Keep Talking (July 1, 1959, CBS)
Masquerade Party (Aug. 6, 1959, NBC)
What's My Line? (March 13, 1960, CBS)
To Tell the Truth (Dec. 5, 1960, CBS)
To Tell the Truth (Dec. 26, 1960, CBS)
To Tell the Truth (Jan. 2, 1961, CBS)
To Tell the Truth (Jan. 9, 1961, CBS)
What's My Line? (March 5, 1961, CBS)
To Tell the Truth (March 27, 1961, CBS)
To Tell the Truth (April 3, 1961, CBS)
To Tell the Truth (April 10, 1961, CBS)
To Tell the Truth (April 17, 1961, CBS)
To Tell the Truth (April 24, 1961, CBS)
To Tell the Truth (May 1, 1961, CBS)
To Tell the Truth (Sept. 18, 1961, CBS)
To Tell the Truth (Oct. 9, 1961, CBS)
To Tell the Truth (Oct. 16, 1961, CBS)
Password (Oct. 16-21, 1961, CBS)
To Tell the Truth (Nov. 20, 1961, CBS)
To Tell the Truth (Dec. 4, 1961, CBS)
To Tell the Truth (Dec. 11, 1961, CBS)
To Tell the Truth (Dec. 18, 1961, CBS)
To Tell the Truth (Dec. 25, 1961, CBS)
To Tell the Truth (Jan. 8, 1962, CBS)
To Tell the Truth (Jan. 15, 1962, CBS)
Password (Jan. 29-Feb. 2, 1962, CBS)
To Tell the Truth (March 12, 1962, CBS)

To Tell the Truth (May 21, 1962, CBS)
To Tell the Truth (June 25, 1962, CBS)
Password (July 23-27, 1962, CBS)
Play Your Hunch (July 31, 1962, NBC)
Your First Impression (Sept. 24-28, 1962, NBC)
To Tell the Truth (Nov. 19, 1962, CBS)
Password (Nov. 26-30, 1962, CBS)
Your First Impression (Dec. 24-28, 1962, NBC)
Your First Impression (Dec. 31, 1962-Jan. 4, 1963, NBC)
Your First Impression (Jan. 7-11, 1963, NBC)
The Match Game (Jan. 28-Feb. 1, 1963, NBC)
Password (Feb. 17, 1963, CBS)
You Don't Say! (April 1-5, 1963, NBC)
Your First Impression (April 8-12, 1963, NBC)
Your First Impression (April 15-19, 1963, NBC)
Your First Impression (April 22-26, 1963, NBC)
Your First Impression (June 10-14, 1963, NBC)
Your First Impression (June 17-21, 1963, NBC)
What's My Line? (June 23, 1963, CBS)
Password (June 24, 1963, CBS)
To Tell the Truth (July 3, 1963, CBS)
To Tell the Truth (July 22, 1963, CBS)
The Match Game (Aug. 5-9, 1963, NBC)
The Match Game (Sept. 2-6, 1963, NBC)
To Tell the Truth (Sept. 23, 1963, CBS)
Your First Impression (Sept. 30-Oct. 4, 1963, NBC)
Password (Oct. 14-18, 1963, CBS)
Password (Oct. 28-Nov. 1, 1963, CBS)
Missing Links (Nov. 11-15, 1963, NBC)
The Match Game (Nov. 18-21, 1963, NBC)
Password (Dec. 30, 1963-Jan. 3, 1964, CBS)
Your First Impression (Jan. 6-10, 1964, NBC)
Your First Impression (Jan. 13-17, 1964, NBC)
The Match Game (Jan. 20-24, 1964, NBC)
The Price is Right (Feb. 14, 1964, ABC)
The Match Game (Feb. 17-21, 1964, NBC)
Get the Message (March 3-April 3, 1964, ABC)
To Tell the Truth (April 6, 1964, CBS)
To Tell the Truth (April 20-24, 1964, CBS)

The Match Game (April 27-May 1, 1964, NBC)
Password (May 28, 1964, CBS)
Get the Message (June 1-5, 1964, ABC)
The Match Game (June 15-19, 1964, NBC)
The Match Game (Aug. 3-7, 1964, NBC)
The Match Game (Sept. 14-18, 1964, NBC)
Password (Oct. 24-28, 1964, CBS)
To Tell the Truth (Aug. 31, 1964, CBS)
Get the Message (Aug. 31-Sept. 4, 1964, ABC)
Get the Message (Sept. 21-25, 1964, ABC)
Get the Message (Oct. 26-30, 1964, ABC)
Password (Nov. 30-Dec. 3, 1964, CBS)
The Match Game (Dec. 14-18, 1964, NBC)
What's This Song? (Jan. 25-29, 1965, NBC)
The Match Game (Feb. 8-12, 1965, NBC)
Password (Feb. 22-26, 1965, CBS)
The Match Game (April 19-23, 1965, NBC)
Password (May 20, 1965, CBS)
The Price is Right (July 12-16, 1965, ABC)
Password (July 26-30, 1965, CBS)
The Match Game (Aug. 2-6, 1965, NBC)
Call My Bluff (Aug. 9-13, 1965, NBC)
What's This Song? (Aug. 30-Sept. 3, 1965, NBC)
What's My Line? (Sept. 5, 1965, CBS)
Password (Oct. 25-29, 1965, CBS)
The Match Game (Dec. 6-10, 1965, NBC)
What's My Line? (Dec. 12, 1965, CBS)
Concentration (Dec. 24, 1965, NBC)
Password (Jan. 3-7, 1966, CBS)
Password (March 21-25, 1966, CBS)
The Match Game (March 28-April 1, 1966, NBC)
You Don't Say! (May 2-6, 1966, NBC)
Password (May 30-June 3, 1966, CBS)
The Match Game (June 27-July 1, 1966, NBC)
Chain Letter (July 4-8, 1966, NBC)
Password (Aug. 1-5, 1966, CBS)
To Tell the Truth (Aug. 15-19, 1966, CBS)
What's My Line? (Aug. 28, 1966, CBS)
You Don't Say! (Oct. 24-28, 1966, NBC)

The Match Game (Nov. 28-Dec. 2, 1966, NBC)
The Match Game (Dec. 26-30, 1966, NBC)
Password (Jan. 9-13, 1967, CBS)
You Don't Say! (Feb. 6-10 1967, NBC)
Password (March 5, 1967, CBS)
The Match Game (March 13-17, 1967, NBC)
Password (April 3-7, 1967, CBS)
Snap Judgment (April 10-14, 1967, NBC)
You Don't Say! (May 8-12, 1967, NBC)
Snap Judgment (June 5-9, 1967, NBC)
Password (June 12-16, 1967, CBS)
The Match Game (July 24-28, 1967, NBC)
Password (Sept. 11-15, 1967, CBS)
The Match Game (Sept 25-29, 1967, NBC)
You Don't Say! (Oct. 30-Nov. 3, 1967, NBC)
The Match Game (Nov 27-Dec. 1, 1967, NBC)
Snap Judgment (Jan. 15-19, 1968, NBC)
The Match Game (April 8-12, 1968, NBC)
You Don't Say! (April 29-May 3, 1968, NBC)
Snap Judgment (June 3-7, 1968, NBC)
Win With the Stars (Oct. 16, 1968, Syndicated)
You Don't Say! (Oct. 28-Nov. 1, 1968, NBC)
You Don't Say! (March 10-14, 1969, NBC)
Win With the Stars (May 29, 1969, Syndicated)
It Takes Two (July 28-Aug. 1, 1969, NBC)
You Don't Say! (July 23-Aug. 1, 1969, NBC)
You Don't Say! (Aug. 18-22, 1969, NBC)
What's My Line? (Sept. 18, 1969, Syndicated)
The Match Game (Sept. 22-26, 1969, NBC)
It's Your Bet (Oct. 13, 1969, Syndicated)
Beat the Clock (Oct. 29, 1969, Syndicated)
He Said She Said (Nov. 23, 1969, Syndicated)
Beat the Clock (Jan. 19, 1970, Syndicated)
It's Your Bet (Feb. 9 1970, Syndicated)
He Said She Said (April 13, 1970, Syndicated)
What's My Line? (May 31-June 4, 1970, Syndicated)
Beat the Clock (Oct 19, 1970, Syndicated)
Password (Aug. 16-21, 1971, ABC)
It's Your Bet (Jan. 3 1972, Syndicated)

Password (Jan. 10-14, 1972, ABC)
It's Your Bet (May 8, 1972, Syndicated)
Password (Aug. 28-Sept. 1, 1972, ABC)
I've Got a Secret (Oct. 31, 1972, Syndicated)
What's My Line? (Nov. 23, 1972, Syndicated)
Password (Jan. 15-19, 1973, ABC)
I've Got a Secret (Jan. 16, 1973, Syndicated)
Hollywood's Talking (April 2, 1973, CBS)
Password (April 9-13, 1973, ABC)
Baffle (May 7-11, 1973, NBC)
Password (June 11-15, 1973, ABC)
Password (Sept. 24-28, 1973, ABC)
Password (Nov. 26-30, 1973, ABC)
Password (March 11-15, 1974, ABC)
Tattletales (March 25-29, 1974, CBS)
Celebrity Sweepstakes (April 29-May 3, 1974, NBC)
Tattletales (May 13-17, 1974, CBS)
Password (June 24-28, 1974, ABC)
Password (July 15-19, 1974, ABC)
Password (July 22-26, 1974, ABC)
Tattletales (Aug. 13-17, 1974, CBS)
Password (Sept. 16-20, 1974, ABC)
Password (Sept. 23-27, 1974, ABC)
Masquerade Party (Oct. 6, 1974, Syndicated)
Tattletales (Oct. 14-18, 1974, CBS)
Password All-Stars (Jan. 27-31, 1975, ABC)
Password All-Stars (Feb. 17-21, 1975, ABC)
Password (March 10-14, 1975, ABC)
Celebrity Sweepstakes (March 18-21, 1975, NBC)
Password (March 24-28, 1974, ABC)
Password (June 27, 1975, ABC)
You Don't Say! (July 21-25, 1975, ABC)
You Don't Say! (July 28-Aug. 1, 1975, ABC)
You Don't Say (Aug. 11-15, 1975, ABC)
Showoffs (Aug. 18-22, 1975, ABC)
Showoffs (Sept. 29-Oct. 3, 1975, ABC)
The Magnificent Marble Machine (Oct. 13-17, 1975, NBC)
You Don't Say! (Nov. 3-7, 1975, ABC)
Cross-Wits (Jan. 5, 1976, Syndication)

The Magnificent Marble Machine (Jan. 26-30, 1976, NBC)
Tattletales (Feb. 9-13, 1976, CBS)
Cross-Wits (March 1, 1976, Syndication)
Celebrity Sweepstakes (March 29-April 2, 1976, NBC)
Cross-Wits (May 1, 1976, Syndication)
Cross-Wits (Sept. 13, 1976, Syndication)
Stumpers (Oct. 25-29, 1976, NBC)
Cross-Wits (Nov. 8, 1976, Syndication)
Stumpers (Dec. 20-24, 1976, NBC)
The Hollywood Squares (Dec. 27-31, 1976, NBC)
Tattletales (Jan. 31-Feb. 4, 1977, CBS)
Tattletales (Sept. 19-23, 1977, CBS)
Tattletales (Nov. 20, 1977, Syndicated)
Tattletales (Jan. 9-13, 1978, CBS)
The Hollywood Squares (Aug. 28-Sept. 1, 1978, NBC)
The Hollywood Squares (Sept. 4-8, 1978, NBC)
Password Plus (Feb. 5-9, 1979, NBC)
Password Plus (March 5-9, 1979, NBC)
Password Plus (May 21-25, 1979, NBC)
Mindreaders (Sept. 10-14, 1979, NBC)
Password Plus (Oct. 15-19, 1979, NBC)
Mindreaders (Nov. 19-23, 1979, NBC)
Password Plus (Jan. 14-18, 1980, NBC)
Chain Reaction (March 10-14, 1980, NBC)
Whew! (March 31-April 4, 1980, CBS)
Password Plus (March 31-April 4, 1980, NBC)
Chain Reaction (April 28-May 2, 1980, NBC)
Password Plus (May 5-9, 1980, NBC)
Password Plus (June 9-13, 1980, NBC)
Chain Reaction (June 16-20, 1980, NBC)
Password Plus (July 28-Aug. 1, 1980, NBC)
Password Plus (Sept 23-29, 1980, NBC)
Password Plus (Dec. 17-23, 1980, NBC)
Password Plus (Jan. 23-29, 1981, NBC)
Password Plus (March 2-6, 1981, NBC)
Password Plus (April 24-30, 1981, NBC)
Password Plus (Sept. 14-19, 1981, NBC)
Battlestars (Oct. 26-30, 1981, NBC)
Battlestars (Nov. 2-6, 1981, NBC)

Battlestars (Nov. 9-13, 1981, NBC)
Battlestars (Nov. 23-27, 1981, NBC)
Password Plus (Dec. 16-21, 1981, NBC)
Battlestars (Jan. 4-8, 1982, NBC)
Password Plus (Feb. 18-23, 1982, NBC)
Battlestars (April 5-9, 1982, NBC)
Bullseye (early May 1982, Syndicated)
Bullseye (late May 1982, Syndicated)
The $25,000 Pyramid (Oct. 11-15, 1982, CBS)
The $25,000 Pyramid (June 6-10, 1983, CBS)
Battlestars (June 20-24, 1983, NBC)
Battlestars (June 27-July 1, 1983, NBC)
Go (Oct. 10-14, 1983, NBC)
The $25,000 Pyramid (Oct. 24-28, 1983, CBS)
Family Feud (Nov. 14-18, 1983, Syndicated)
Go (Jan. 2-6, 1984, NBC)
The $25,000 Pyramid (Jan. 16-20, 1984, CBS)
Family Feud (March 1, 1984, ABC)
The $25,000 Pyramid (March 26-30, 1984, CBS)
Dream House (May 14-18, 1984, NBC)
The $25,000 Pyramid (June 25-29, 1984, CBS)
Body Language (July 2-6, 1984, CBS)
Body Language (Aug. 27-31, 1984, CBS)
Super Password (Nov. 5-9, 1984, NBC)
The $25,000 Pyramid (Nov. 16-20, 1984, CBS)
Trivia Trap (Dec. 10-14, 1984, ABC)
The $25,000 Pyramid (Jan. 21-25, 1985, CBS)
Body Language (Feb. 6-8, 1985, CBS)
Family Feud (Feb. 11-15, 1985, Syndicated)
The $25,000 Pyramid (May 20-24, 1985, CBS)
Super Password (June 3-7, 1985, NBC)
All-Star Blitz (July 1-4, 1985, ABC)
The $100,000 Pyramid (Sept. 23-27, 1985, Syndicated)
Body Language (Nov. 25-27, 1985, CBS)
Super Password (Jan. 13-17, 1986, NBC)
The $25,000 Pyramid (Feb. 17-21, 1986, CBS)
Super Password (April 21-25, 1986, NBC)
The $100,000 Pyramid (April 21-25, 1986, Syndicated)
The $25,000 Pyramid (May 5-9, 1986, CBS)

Super Password (July 21-25, 1986, NBC)
The $25,000 Pyramid (Aug. 4-8, 1986, CBS)
Double Talk (Aug. 18-22, 1986, ABC)
The Hollywood Squares (Sept. 15-19, 1986, Syndicated)
The Hollywood Squares (Dec. 1-5, 1986, Syndicated)
Super Password (Jan. 12-16, 1987, NBC)
Wordplay (Jan. 19-23, 1987, NBC)
The Hollywood Squares (March 16-20, 1987, Syndicated)
Super Password (April 6-10, 1987, NBC)
This is Your Life (April 19, 1987, NBC)
Wordplay (May 4-8, 1987, NBC)
The $25,000 Pyramid (June 1-5, 1987, CBS)
Win Lose or Draw (Sept. 7-11, 1987, Syndicated)
The $100,000 Pyramid (Sept. 14-18, 1987, Syndicated)
The Hollywood Squares (Oct. 5-9, 1987, Syndicated)
Animal Crack-Ups (Oct. 10, 1987, ABC)
Super Password (Oct. 26-30, 1987, NBC)
Animal Crack-Ups (Nov. 28, 1987, ABC)
Animal Crack-Ups (Dec. 12, 1987, ABC)
Animal Crack-Ups (Jan. 9, 1988, ABC)
The Hollywood Squares (Jan. 25-29, 1988, Syndicated)
Super Password (Feb. 29-March 4, 1988, NBC)
Animal Crack-Ups (March 12, 1988, ABC)
Animal Crack-Ups (March 19, 1988, ABC)
The $25,000 Pyramid (April 4-8, 1988, CBS)
The Hollywood Squares (April 11-15, 1988, Syndicated)
Animal Crack-Ups (April 16, 1988, ABC)
Animal Crack-Ups (May 21, 1988, ABC)
Animal Crack-Ups (June 4, 1988, ABC)
Super Password (June 20-24, 1988, NBC)
Animal Crack-Ups (July 2, 1988, ABC)
Animal Crack-Ups (Aug. 27, 1988, ABC)
The Hollywood Squares (Sept. 12-16, 1988, Syndicated)
The Price is Right (Sept. 14, 1988, CBS)
Super Password (Nov. 7-11, 1988, NBC)
The Hollywood Squares (Nov. 28-Dec. 2, 1988, Syndicated)
Wheel of Fortune (Dec. 8, 1988, Syndicated)
Super Password (Feb. 16-17 and 20-22, 1989, NBC)
The Hollywood Squares (Feb. 27-March 3, 1989, Syndicated)

Super Password (March 20-24, 1989, NBC)
Win Lose or Draw (July 17-21, 1989, NBC)
3rd Degree! (Oct. 31, 1989, Syndicated)
Match Game (July 23-27, 1990, ABC)
To Tell the Truth (Sept. 24-28, 1990, NBC)
Match Game (Nov. 5-9, 1990, ABC)
To Tell the Truth (Nov. 26-30, 1990, NBC)
The $100,000 Pyramid (Jan. 14-18, 1991, Syndicated)
To Tell the Truth (Feb. 4-8, 1991, NBC)
Match Game (May 6-10, 1991, ABC)
The $100,000 Pyramid (May 27-31, 1991, Syndicated)
Scattergories (May 24-28, 1993, NBC)
Family Feud (Feb. 6-10, 1995, Syndicated)
The Hollywood Squares (Sept. 13-17, 1999, Syndicated)
Pyramid (Nov. 25, 2002, Syndicated)
The Hollywood Squares (Nov. 3-7, 2003, Syndicated)
Game$how Marathon (June 22, 2006, CBS)
Million Dollar Password (June 12, 2008, CBS)
Million Dollar Password (Dec. 28, 2008, CBS)

Bibliography

"ABC-TV Goal: Evening Lead by April," *Broadcasting*, Nov. 25, 1957, p. 56.
"ABC-TV Switching Three Shows," *Broadcasting*, Dec. 16, 1957, p. 10.
Adams, Val. "You can hail 'Taxi' at the same time," *The Daily News*, July 29, 1982, p. 62.
"All Out to Help Beef Up Angels," *Billboard*, Oct. 14, 1957, p. 9.
Ames, Walter. "Quiz Kids Video Show Moving to CBS Network; Betty White Hailed as TV's Busiest Gal," *The Los Angeles Times*, Nov. 6, 1951, Part I, p. 22.
———. "Palance's Dickering for TV Shakespearean Sponsor; Bill Williams in Rigid Training," *The Los Angeles Times*, Feb. 26, 1952, Part I, p. 26.
———. "Doris Day Guests With Bob Crosby; Dinah With Perry," *The Los Angeles Times*, Nov. 14, 1956, Part II, p. 12.
———. "Williams Sheds Cowboy Gear for Date with Betty," *The Los Angeles Times*, May 10, 1957, Part II, p. 10.
"'Angels' Moves to Live in Jan.," *Billboard*, Dec. 16, 1957, p. 2.
Ardmore, Jane. "Betty White: Look at the Girl Who Was Never Going to Marry!" *TV Dawn to Dusk*, November 1971, pp. 46-47, 80.
"Axe 'B-fast Club'; Betty White Set," *Variety*, Feb. 3, 1954, p. 26.
Battelle, Phyllis. "It's all right for Betty White," *The Daily News*, Sept. 9, 1977, p. XQ8.
Bauder, David. "Girls are getting golden the second time around," *The Santa Maria Times* [Santa Maria, California], June 29, 2003, p. C4.
Beck, Marilyn. "Tim Allen returns sober to film final season," *The St. Cloud Times* [Saint Cloud, Minnesota], June 28, 1998, p. 63.
Beck, Marilyn and Stacy Jenel Smith. "Decision Time for 'Ladies Man,'" *The Daily News*, Feb. 20, 2000, New York Vue section, p. 4.

Bender, Jack. "Password Passes Shadows' Ratings," *The Courier* [Waterloo, Iowa] *TV Showtime*, May 21, 1971, p. 5.

Berns, Samuel D. "Television Today: Hollywood, U.S.A.," *Motion Picture Daily*, Sept. 6, 1955, p. 10.

"Betty White | Interview | TimesTalks." YouTube, uploaded by New York Times Events, April 19, 2016, www.youtube.com/watch?v=Jd_y9W_m63k

"Betty White Loves Animals (and People)," *Daytime TV*, March 1972, pp. 43, 46.

"Betty White Unsold, Shifts to New Time," *Variety*, June 30, 1954, p.

"Betty White: TV's Cinderella," *The American Weekly*, Aug. 15, 1954.

Blakey, Scott. "Betty White: Color Her Golden as in 'Girls,'" *The San Francisco Examiner*, Oct. 13, 1985, Datebook section, pp. 50-51.

Braxton, Greg and Daniel Howard Cerone. "You're Under Their Influence," *The Los Angeles Times*, Sept. 10, 1995, Calendar section, p. 7.

Brooks, Tim, and Earle Marsh. *The Complete Directory to Prime Time Network and Cable TV Shows 1946-Present* (Ninth Ed.). New York: Ballantine, 2007.

Bruce, Leslie. "Just How Busy is Betty White?" *The Hollywood Reporter*, Nov. 30, 2010.

Buck, Jerry. "British, US humor are not oceans apart," *The Sacramento Bee*, Oct. 30, 1987, Weekend Scene section, p. 7.

Bukszpan, Daniel. "Why Hulu is hoping to turn old *Golden Girls* episodes into a goldmine." CNBC, Jan. 28, 2017, www.cnbc.com/2017/01/27/why-hulu-is-hoping-to-turn-old-golden-girls-episodes-into-a-goldmine.html

Byrne, Bridget. "Animated Betty White has a jolly time as Mrs. Claus," *The Sacramento Bee*, Dec. 4, 1996, p. D9.

Colucci, Jim. *The Q Guide to The Golden Girls*. New York: Alyson, 2006.

Curran, Ann. "Lady Luck," *The Desert Sun* [Palm Springs, Calif.], Feb. 17, 1996, p. C1.

Davis, Stephen. *Say Kids! What Time Is It? Notes from the Peanut Gallery*. Boston: Little, Brown and Company, 1987.

Doan, Richard K. "'Sesame Street' Ousts 'Lucy,' 'Family Affair,' 'Three Sons' Reruns," *TV Guide*, June 3-9, 1972, p. A-1.

Dosti, Rose. "Does TV Image Hurt? Home Economists and Sue Ann," *The Los Angeles Times*, May 6, 1976, Part VI, pp. 1 and 13.

Dougan, Michael. "Her first big hit," *The San Francisco Examiner*, Oct. 22, 1985, p. E-9.

Fernandez, Maria Elena. "'Practice' already practicing for fall," *The Los Angeles Times*, May 14, 2004, Calendar section, pp. E1 and E26.

Fischler, Grace. "Betty White: Call Me Wholesome," *TV Stage*, December 1954, pp. 28, 65-67.

Foreman, Bob. "Agency Ad Libs," *Sponsor*, April 19, 1954, p. 118.

Foster, Bob. "NBC to Launch Its 'Monitor' on Sunday," *The Times* [San Mateo, California], June 9, 1955, p. 27.

———. "TV-Radio," *The Times* [San Mateo, California], Feb. 7, 1958, p. 19.

Gardella, Kay. "CBS: Why Number 3?" *The New York Daily News*, Sept. 30, 1977, p. 66.

Gelman, Morrie and Gene Accas. *The Best in Television: 50 Years of Emmys*. Santa Monica, Calif.; General Publishing Group, 1998.

Goldberg, Lee *Unsold Television Pilots, 1955-1989*. Jefferson, N.C.; McFarland, 1990.

"'The Golden Girls' shows best new series promise," *The Hartfield Sentinel*, July 29, 1985, p. 13.

Goodman, Tim. "Coming up: A hit (maybe) and two misses," *The San Francisco Examiner*, Sept. 17, 1999 p. C-8.

Gross, Ben. "What's On?" *The Daily News*, July 23, 1955, p. 31.

"Guild Hearing Delayed," *Broadcasting*, Feb. 9, 1959, p. 53.

"Guild to Distribute Two New Film Series," *Billboard*, July 18, 1953, p. 10.

"Guild Wraps 39 'Liz' Pix," *Variety*, July 8, 1953, p. 22.

Hall, Claude. "Vox Jox," *Billboard*, May 23, 1970, p. 32.

Handler, David. "Bad Casting Hurts Betty White Show," *The Santa Ana Register*, Oct. 4, 1977, p. D4.

Harmetz, Aljean. "For Golden Girls, older is better," *The Sacramento Bee*, Oct. 6, 1985, TV Today section, p. 8.

Herman, Pinky. "Television—Radio," *Motion Picture Daily*, Jan. 25, 1956, p. 6.

Hoffman, Steve. "'Pet Set' Grows and Goes," *The Cincinnati Enquirer TV Magazine*, Jan. 31-Feb. 6, 1971, p. 1.

Huff, Richard. "CBS doesn't love this 'Bob'; dumps newest Newhart series," *The Daily News*, Nov. 15, 1993, p. 71.

Hughes, Mike. "Marie Osmond, Betty White star in coffee house sitcom," *The Desert Sun* [Palm Springs, Calif.], Sept. 15, 1995, p. E4.

Humphrey, Hal. "15th Rose Parade for Betty White," *The Los Angeles Times*, Dec. 25, 1968, Part IV, p. 30.

Hyatt, Wesley. *The Encyclopedia of Daytime Television*. New York: Billboard, 1993.

———. *Short-Lived Television Series 1948-1978*. Jefferson, North Carolina: McFarland, 2003.

———. *Emmy Award Winning Nighttime Television Shows, 1948-2004*. Jefferson, North Carolina: McFarland, 2006.

———. *The Carol Burnett Show Companion: So Glad We Had This Time*. Albany, Ga.: Bear Manor Media, 2016.

———. *Bob Hope on TV: Thanks for the Video Memories*. Albany, Ga.: Bear Manor Media, 2018.

"Inner Tube," *The Daily News*, Nov. 16, 1998, p. 84.

"Jack Webb, Betty White Prove Best in Any Show," *Billboard*, July 31, 1954, p. 4.

James, Art. *Let's Hear It For ...: Memoirs of a Genial Game Show Host*. Unpublished manuscript.

LaSalle, Mick. "He's Just Teasing," *The San Francisco Examiner*, Jan. 23, 2000, Datebook section, p. 44.

Leigh Scott, Kathryn and Jim Pierson (editors). *Dark Shadows Almanac: 30th Anniversary Tribute*. Los Angeles: Pomegranate Press, Ltd., 1995.

Leszczak, Bob. *Single Season Sitcoms of the 1990s: A Complete Guide.* Jefferson, North Carolina: McFarland, 2018.

Lowry, Cynthia. "Why All The Fuss Over a Parade?" *The Santa Cruz Sentinel*, Dec. 30, 1966, p. 6.

Maksian, George. "'Eunice's' Mama to be resurrected," *The Daily News*, March 17, 1982, p. 62.

Martin, Bob. "Viewers usually enjoy tube booboos," *The Independent* [Long Beach, Calif.], Jan. 1, 1973, p. B-12.

Michaels, Taylor. "TV Pipeline," *The San Francisco Examiner*, Sept. 5, 1999, TV Week section, p. 2.

Mills, Nancy. "'Golden Girls' Polishes Its Scripts," *The Los Angeles Times*, Oct. 30, 1987, Section VI, pp. 1 and 36.

Morris, Jane. "TV's New Queen: Salute to Betty White," *TV Star Parade*, September 1954, pp. 33-39, 67-68.

"Nat'l Telecasting Gets Good Result, Tho Tints Go Awry," *Billboard*, Jan. 9, 1954, p. 2.

Nesteroff, Kliph. "The Early Betty White 1947-1973." Classic Television Showbiz, April 4, 2010, https://blog.wfmu.org/freeform/2010/04/the-early-betty-white.html

O'Leary, Dorothy. "Life with Betty," *Radio-TV Mirror*, June 1954, pp. 40-41, 98-99.

Page, Don. "Betty White Queen of TV's Animal Kingdom," *The Los Angeles Times*, April 23, 1971, Section IV, p. 19.

"People," *The Record* (Hackensack, N.J.), Oct. 6, 1998, p. 2.

Peterson, Bettelou. "Capping her career: 'The Golden Girls' is fitting crown for Betty White," *The Times Advocate* [Escondido, Calif.], March 20, 1986, North County Magazine section, p. 29.

"Pinky & Betty," *Variety*, Feb. 10, 1954, p. 32.

"Plymouth Axes Anthony for 'Date' Series," *Billboard*, March 30, 1957, p. 2.

"Plymouth for 74 Wks. of 'Angels,'" *Billboard*, May 6, 1957, p. 13.

Rich, Allen. "The Listening Post," *The Valley Times* [North Hollywood, Calif.], Oct. 18, 1950, p. 26.

Rosenberg, Howard. "'Perfect,' 'Luck': Comedy Series, Science-Fiction Drama Shine," *The Los Angeles Times*, Sept. 15, 1995, p. F29.

Schwartz, David, Steve Ryan and Fred Wostbrock. *The Encyclopedia of TV Game Shows* (3rd ed.). New York: Checkmark, 1999.

Shalit, Sid. "What's On?" *The New York Daily News*, Feb. 8, 1954, p. 29.

Smith, Cecil. "After 25 Years, The 'Real' Betty White," *The Los Angeles Times*, Dec. 21, 1973, Part IV, p. 37.

———. "Busy Betty Builds a New Family," *The Los Angeles Times*, Oct. 9, 1977, TV Times supplement, p. 2.

Stanley, T.L. "It's a prime time for those of a certain age," *The Los Angeles Times*, Jan. 9, 2011, p. S6.

Tashman, George. "Tashman on TV," *The Berkeley Gazette*, Jan. 21, 1978, p. 21.

Tator, Joel. *Los Angeles Television*. Charleston, South Carolina: Arcadia, 2014.

Thomas, Bob. "Betty White's road back," *The San Francisco Examiner*, March 15, 1982, p. E10.
"$3,000,000 1954 Production Sked Set by Guild Films," *Variety*, May 5, 1954, p. 37.
Vernon, Terry. "Tele-Vues," *The Long Beach Independent*, July 30, 1950, p. 28-A.
"Vidpix Chatter—New York," *Variety*, Dec. 8, 1954, p. 39.
"Vitapix-Guild Combine Has 3 Keys to Success: Money, Stations, Show," *Billboard* Oct. 30, 1954, pp. 2 and 4.
Wald, Eliot. "Viewpoint," *The Los Angeles Times*, March 5, 1978, TV Times supplement, p. 18.
"Welles, Arnaz Join to Film 'Theater' Series," *Billboard*, April 14, 1956, p. 2.
"What's Troubling the Advertiser?," *Broadcasting*, Sept. 30, 1957, p. 115.
White, Betty. *Here We Go Again: My Life in Television*. New York, N.Y.: Scribner, 2010.
White, Tess, "My Daughter, Betty White," *TV Radio Mirror*, February 1955, pp. 29-31, 77-78.

Websites
Bobstewart.fandom.com
Classic TV Archive (ctva.biz)
Markgoodson.fandom.com
The TV Ratings Guide (www.thetvratingsguide.com)

Index

ABC Comedy Special 204
ABC Wide World of Entertainment (variety series) 81, 99, 125, 376
Abed, Hisham 119-120
Abelew, Alan 306
Abrams, Gerald W. 308
Accas, Gene 47, 150, 393
Acker, Amy 336
Ackroyd, David 316
Action (sitcom) 250
Adams, Val 210, 391
Adnopoz, Zoe 331
Adsit, Scott 350
Adventures of Kit Carson, The (western series) 52
AFI Life Achievement Award: A Tribute to Morgan Freeman (variety special) 116, 377
Agazzi, James J. 142
Agronsky, Martin 305
Aguilar, Joe M. 344
Aibel, Jonathan 328
Ainsley Harriott Show, The (informational show) 43
Al Jarvis Show, The (Los Angeles talk show) 14-15, 18, 46, 95
Alan, Lori 360
Alara, Cheche 67
Albert, Eddie 8, 16, 235
Albert, Wil 311
Albertini Dow, Ellen 346
Albertson, Mabel 303
Alda, Alan 68
Aldredge, Dawn 317
Alexander, Jason 109
ALF (sitcom) 319
ALF Loves a Mystery (children's special) 318-319, 373
All in the Family (sitcom) 132, 169, 222
Allan, Lane 11-12
Allen, Andrew James 342

Allen, Debbie 313-314
Allen, Marty 69
Allen, Ryan A. 333
Allen, Steve 40, 68-69, 311
Allen, Tessa 336
Alley, Kirstie 132, 294
All-Star Blitz (game show) 157, 388
Ally McBeal (drama series) 256, 329-330, 374
Alston, Justin 352
Amanda's (sitcom) 204, 219
Amandes, Tom 338
Ameche, Don 65
American Bandstand (variety series) 146
American Top Forty (radio show) 16
American Weekly, The (publication) 10-12, 19
Ames, Leon 309
Ames, Walter 13, 52, 391
Amos, John 370
Amsterdam, Morey 69, 82
Anders, Andrea 347
Anderson, Anthony 66
Anderson, Bill 147
Anderson, Larry 320
Anderson, Loni 161, 163
Andrews, Ralph 79, 88
Andy Griffith Show, The (sitcom) 320
Animal Crack-Ups (game show) 153, 161-162, 389
Anka, Paul 71, 101
Annie Oakley (western series) 50
Annie's Point (TV-movie) 346, 373
Another World (soap opera) 91, 267
Ansara, Michael 3
Antonacci, Greg 325-326
Appel, Richard 328
Apple Pie (sitcom) 204
Archer, Beverly 213
Arden, Eve 32, 307
Ardmore, Jane 12, 31, 391
Argoud, Karin 210
Armstrong, Bill 85
Armstrong, Curtis 336
Arnaz, Desi 54
Arnaz, Lucie 56
Arnaz Jr., Desi 138, 140
Arndt, Denis 336
Arnette, Jeanetta 206
Arnold, Tom 325
Arsenio Hall Show, The (talk show) 41
Art Linkletter's House Party (variety show) 17, 21, 71
Arthur, Bea 5, 34, 107, 204, 215, 219, 227-228, 231-232, 234, 348
As the World Turns (soap opera) 71
Ashton, Joseph 327

Asner, Ed 5, 117, 159-160, 169, 187, 193, 258, 291, 324-325, 332
Asquith Weiss, Joanne 337
Astaire, Fred 42, 160
Astin, John 138
Atkins, George 313
Atoms, Maxwell 337
Auberjonois, Rene 354
Aubrey, Skye 305
Austin, Alana 333
Austin, Steve 333
Aycox, Nicki 329
Azaria, Hank 330
Bachelor's Haven (TV series) 47
Back to the Bat Cave See *Return to the Batcave: The Misadventures of Adam and Burt*
Backes, Alice 321
Backus, Henny 311
Backus, Jim 59, 70, 311
Bader, Diedrich 357
Baer, Brett 347
Baer, Richard 312
Baffle (game show) 124, 126-127, 135, 386
Bagley, Tim 347
Bailey, Pearl 116
Bain, Anthony 335
Bain, Barbara 32
Bain, Michael 335
Baio, Scott 321
Baird, Jeanne 22
Baker Hall, Philip 338
Baldikoski, Steve 350
Baldwin, Alec 132, 351
Ball, Lucille 54, 56, 102, 105, 107, 138, 140, 154-155, 205
Balsam, Talia 327
Balter, Sam 14, 16
Bank, Frank 365-366
Barbara Walters' 10 Most Fascinating People of 2010 (talk show special) 1-2, 4, 6, 368, 379
Barbeau, Adrienne 205
Barber, Ronde 359
Barker, Bob 24, 32, 80-81, 99, 150
Barker, Dick 11
Barker, Mike 344
Barkley, Roger 125
Barnes, Joanna 90, 137
Barnes, Rodney 342
Barney Miller (sitcom) 206
Barnhill, Katy 33
Baron, Sandy 76
Barr, Douglas 151
Barrie, Barbara 323
Barry, Ivor 313
Barry, Jack 30, 79, 124-125
Bartlett, Bonnie 315

Bartlett, Debbie 153, 161
Baseman, Gary 335
Bass, Lance 164
Bateman, Jason 320
Batman (sitcom) 336
Battelle, Phyllis 194, 196, 391
Battersea, Wes 12-13
Battle Beyond the Stars (movie) 142
Battlestars (game show) 143-144, 387-388
Bauder, David 237, 391
Bauman, Jon 154-155
Baxter, Anne 314
Beach, Adam 338
Bean, Orson 66, 70, 76, 321
Beasley, John 338
Beat the Clock (game show) 71, 90, 385
Beatty, Roger 209, 211
Beck, Kimberly 307
Beck, Marilyn 248
Becker, Gerry 329
Beckwith, Elizabeth 252
Beechen, Adam 331
Before and After (TV-movie) 310, 373
Begley Jr., Ed 145, 153, 294, 315, 320
Behar, Brian 350
Behind the Laughs: The Untold Stories of Television's Favorite Comedies: A Paley Center for Media Special (variety special) 108, 377
Belafonte Harper, Shari 314
Belford, Christine 305
Bell, Bradley 267-268, 276-277
Bell, Coby 327
Bell, William J. "Bill" 268
Bellamy, Bill 295
Belland, Bruce 135
Bellows, Gil 329
Belson, Jerry 306
Bennett, Marjorie 306
Bennett, Ruth 325
Bennetts, The (soap opera) 17
Bennington, Bill 19
Benson (sitcom) 271
Benson, George 101
Benson, Jay 307
Benson, Robby 340
Berfield, Justin 342
Berg, Gertrude 15
Bergen, Candice 260
Bergen, Polly 64-65
Berger, Glenn 328
Bergerac, Jacques 303
Bergeron, Tom 137
Bergman, Martin 323

INDEX

Berkeley Gazette, The (publication) 201, 394
Berlanti, Greg 338
Berle, Milton 68, 202
Berman, Shelly 71, 76
Berns, Samuel D. 51-52, 392
Bernsen, Corbin 320
Bernstein, Karen 326
Berry, Adrienne 351
Berry, Ken 209-210
Bertinelli, Valerie 117, 279, 281-282, 286
Bessell, Ted 322
Best in Television: 50 Years of Emmys, The (book) 47, 150, 393
Best of the West (sitcom) 302, 311-312, 374
Best Place to Be, The (TV-movie) 33, 309-310, 373
Better Sex, The (game show) 147
Bettger, Lyle 306
Betty and Friends (book) 43
Betty White: First Lady of Television (documentary) 10, 13, 109, 367, 378
Betty White House, The (pilot) 244
Betty White in Person (book) 4, 38
Betty White Show, The (1950-51 Los Angeles talk show) 15, 193, 372
Betty White Show, The (1952 Los Angeles variety show) 17, 46, 193
Betty White Show, The (1954 daytime talk show) 2, 18-22, 50-51, 60, 193, 371
Betty White Show, The (1958 variety series) 28, 57, 95-98, 193, 371
Betty White Show, The (1977 sitcom) 192-202, 204, 207, 308, 371
*Betty White's 90th Birthday: A Tribute to America's Golden Girl (*variety special) 100, 114, 116, 118, 377
Betty White's Off Their Rockers (reality series) 118-121, 371, 373
Betty White's Second Annual 90th Birthday (variety special) 118, 377
Beverly, Steve 5, 28, 64, 66, 70, 75, 84, 88, 126, 136, 141, 143, 145, 162, 164, 365-366
Beyond Evil (movie) 142
Bieri, Ramon 316
Big Bang Theory, The (sitcom) 252
Big City Comedy (variety series) 104, 376
Big Show, The (variety series) 104, 376
Bill, Tony 308
Billboard (publication) 22, 50
Binder Weis, Joan 333
Binkley, Gregg 348
Bishop, Joey 69-70
Bixby, Bill 78, 93
Blakey, Scott 220, 224
Blinn, William 313
Blockbusters (game show) 139
Blondie (radio sitcom) 11
Bloodworth-Thomason, Linda 242
Blu, Susan 161
Bluth, Toby 324
Bob (sitcom) 240-244, 372
Bob Hope and Other Young Comedians (variety special) 105, 377
Bob Hope: The First 70 Years (variety special) 105, 377
Bob Hope's Birthday Memories (variety special) 105, 377

Bob Hope's Love Affair with Lucy (variety special) 105, 377
Bob Hope's Stand Up and Cheer National Football League's 60th Year (variety special) 105, 376
Bob Newhart Show, The (sitcom) 240
Bob Smith Show, The (daytime series) 20-21
Bob-Waksberg, Raphael 357
Bochner, Lloyd 309
Body Language (game show) 153-154, 317, 388
Bogart, Paul 222
Bogner, Jonathan 333
Bohay, Heidi 314
Boland, Katie 326
Bold and the Beautiful, The (drama series) 267-278, 372
Bolen, Lin 133, 136
Bolger, Ray 76
Bonanza (western series) 25
Bonerz, Peter 137
Bones (drama series) 358-360, 374
Bonnie Hunt Show, The (talk show) 43, 112, 379
Bono, Sonny 101-102
Boomer, Linwood 342
Boone, Richard 71
Boreanz, David 358
Borelli, Carla 194, 196
Bosley, Tom 305, 308
Boss, Kit 328
Boston Legal (drama series) 109-110, 255-256, 259-267, 372
Boucher, Joe 328
Boutilier, Kate 331
Bowab, John 317
Bowden, Katrina 351
Bowman, Bobby 349
Bowman, "Mama" Doris Day 67
Bowman, Lee 70
Boy Meets World (sitcom) 244-245
Boyd, Jimmy 16, 55, 95-96
Boyd, John 358
Bracken, Eddie 63
Bradley Baker, Dee 343
Brandon, Henry 306
Brandt, Alicia 246
Braxton, Greg 244, 392
Breakfast in Hollywood (daytime series) 17-18
Breckinridge, Alexandra 357
Brenner, David 135
Brenner, Randy 349
Brewer, Jack 336
Bridge, Loie 49
Bridges, Lloyd 76
Brie, Alison 352
Bright, Noel 349
Brillstein, Bernie 322
Broadcasting (publication) 54, 132, 391, 393, 395

Broch, Laurence 259
Broderick, Matthew 114
Brokeback Mountain (movie) 296
Brolin, James 314-315
Bromfield, Valri 311
Brooks, Elisabeth 307
Brooks, Foster 202
Brooks, Hindi 310
Brooks, James L. "Jim" 168, 170, 193, 330
Brooks, Joel 145
Brooks, Tim 237, 392
Brown, Clancy 360
Brown, Eric 210
Brown, Henry V. 307
Brown, Governor Jerry 35
Brown, Yvette Nicole 352, 354
Browne, Roscoe Lee 331
Bruni, Frank 31, 109-110, 112, 237, 281
Bry, Ellen 315
Bryan, Greg 359
Brynner, Yul 3
Buchanan, Edgar 304
Buck, Jerry 223
Buckman, Phil 328
Bulifant, Joyce 143
Bullock, Sandra 2, 110
Bullseye (game show) See *Celebrity Bullseye*
Bumpass, Roger 360
Burditt, Jack 340
Burger, Michael 291
Burke, Carlease 360
Burke, Michael Reilly 357
Burmester, Bruce 38, 143, 146
Burnett, Carol 33-34, 90, 92, 94, 99-101, 107-108, 117, 152, 154, 205, 207-211, 292-293, 299
Burns, Allan 168, 184, 193
Burns, George 235
Burns, Heather 357
Burns, J. Stewart 330
Burns, Jere 243
Burr, Raymond 24
Burton, Corey 327
Bush, Barbara 251
Bustany, Judith 317
Butcher's Wife, The (movie) 223
Buttons, Red 202
Buxton, Frank 82, 306
Buzzota, Dave 328
Byrne, Bridget 325, 392
Cachikis, Tess See White, Tess Cachikis
Cadiff, Andy 291, 360-361
Cady, Frank 304
Caesar, Sid 98

Cahill, Erin 359
Cale, Paula 336
Calhoun, Rory 151
Call My Bluff (game show) 83, 384
Callan, K 316
Calo, Joanna 357
Camins, Alexis 356
Campbell, Benedict 326
Campbell-Martin, Tisha 341-342
Candid Camera (variety series) 98, 118, 375
Candy, John 104
Capshaw, Jessica 258
Carbonell, Nestor 323
Cardone, Vivien 338
Carey, Philip 199
Caridi, Carmen 313
Carlisle, Jodi 331
Carlisle, Kitty 65-66
Carlock, Robert 351
Carmichael, Hoagy 63
Carol & Company (variety series) 108, 377
Carol Burnett Show, The (variety series) 5, 94, 99-101, 107, 117, 207-211, 292-293, 376
Carradine, Keith 344
Carrero, Aimee 361
Carroll, Bob 163
Carroll, Diahann 101
Carroll, Pat 68-69, 79, 371
Carroll, Sidney 304
Carson, Johnny 6, 15, 30, 34-41, 43, 65, 188-189, 200, 229,
Carson, Lisa Nicole 329
Carter, Dixie 249
Carter, Jack 311
Carter, Jimmy 319
Cartwright, Nancy 330
Cary, Donick 344
Casemiro, Eryk 331
Cason, Barbara 308
Cass, Peggy 66, 69, 77
Cassidy, Jack 84
Cassidy, Maureen 56
Castellaneta, Dan 330
Cattrall, Kim 310
Cavanagh, Megan 243
Cavanaugh, Patrick 348
Cavett, Dick 145, 154, 156, 314-315
CBS All-American Thanksgiving Day Parade, The (variety special) 26
CBS at 75 (variety special) 104, 190, 377
CBS Bicentennial Minute (informational spot) 376
CBS Galaxy (variety special) 193, 376
CBS On the Air (variety special) 104, 376
CBS Playhouse (series of specials) 222
Cedric the Entertainer 289, 295

Celebrity Bowling (game show) 61
Celebrity Bullseye (game show) 144-145
Celebrity Sleuth (publication) 39
Celebrity Sweepstakes (game show) 5, 145-146, 228, 386-387
Cerf, Bennett 62, 77, 82
Cerone, Daniel Howard 244, 392
Chabert, Lacey 331
Chain Letter (game show) 84, 384
Chain Reaction (game show) 142-143, 152, 387
Chalke, Sarah 355
Chamberlain, Richard 236, 250
Champagne, Matt 336
Champagne, Tyler 357
Champion, Gregg 341
Chance of a Lifetime (TV-movie) 320-321, 373
Chandraskeran, Vali 343
Channing, Carol 154, 207-208
Chaplin, Sidney 76
Charles, Glen 198
Charles, Les 198
Charlie Brown Christmas, A (animated special) 355
Chase, Chevy 352
Chase, Ilka 69
Chase, Will 355
Cheadle, Don 232
Cheers (sitcom) 198, 240
Cher 101-102
Chester, Colby 306
China Syndrome, The (movie) 135
Chippendale Dancers, The 106
CHiPs (drama series) 148
Cho, John 347
Christmas, Eric 236
Cibrian, Eddie 294
Cincinnati Enquirer TV Magazine, The (publication) 31
Circus of the Stars (variety special) 102, 376
Circus of the Stars III (variety special) 103, 376
Clair, Dick 211
Clark, Anthony 335
Clark, Dick 76, 145-147, 150, 163-164, 371
Clark, Jack 73, 135
Clark, Kyle 346
Clark, Oliver 316
Clarke, Brian Patrick 142
Clarke, Jackie 349
Clarke, Joe 323
Clarke Duncan, Michael 328
Clayburgh, Jill 257
Cleese, John 202
Clemens, Brian 304
Client List, The (drama series) 357, 374
Clinton Smith, Ror 355

Clooney, George 296, 352
Clueless (movie) 237
Cochran, Phil 29-30
Cohan, Martin 317
Cohen, Joel H. 330
Cohen, Steven A. 349
Colasanto, Nicholas 307
Colella, John 360
Coleman, Porscha 334
Colen, Beatrice 307
Colley, Don Pedro 305
Collier, Jonathan 328, 358
Collinge, Patricia 304
Collins, Jeanette 324
Collins, Richard 320
Collyer, Bud 64-65
Colman, Henry 314
Columbo (drama series) 203
Comden, Danny 340
Comedy Central Roast of William Shatner (variety special) 109-110, 377
Comedy Salute to Baseball, A (variety special) 104, 377
Comedy Shop, The See *Norm Crosby's The Comedy Shop*
Community (sitcom) 303, 352-353, 375
Complete Savages (sitcom) 303, 344-345, 375
Conan (talk show) 43, 380
Concentration (game show) 83-84, 123-124, 384
Conklin, Peggy 304
Conlin, Michaela 358
Connors, Chuck 56
Connors, Mike 78
Conreid, Hans 84
Considine, John 314
Conversation with Betty White, A (variety special) 107-108, 224, 227, 377
Converse, Peggy 309
Convy, Bert 89, 127, 151, 154-156, 160-161, 163
Conway, Dick 304
Conway, Tim 103, 285, 293, 355
Cook, Dane 247
Cook, Jonathan 337
Cook, Nathan 145, 314
Coolidge, Jennifer 347
Coolio 287
Cooper, Bradley 115
Cooper, Helmar Augustus 355
Coplan, Ronda 306
Corbett, John 337
Corey, Joshua 362
Corolla, Adam 164
Corsaut, Aneta 320
Cortese, Dan 291, 323
Cos (variety series) 101, 376
Cosby, Bill 101

Cosby Show, The (sitcom) 218, 222
Cosell, Howard 105
Cosgrove, Miranda 360
Costanza, Robert P. 327
Costanzo, Paul 347
Costas, Bob 42
Costo, Oscar Louis 341
Couric, Katie 6
Cox, Jennifer Elise 323
Cox, Keith 289
Cox, Wally 71
Cramer, Douglas S. 314
Crane, Bob 32
Cranston, Bryan 342
Crank, Susan M. 342
Craven, Matt 327
Crawford, Noah 349
Crawford Brown, Pat 352
Cremin, Kevin G. 336
Cromer, Greg 351
Cronin, Patrick 231
Crosby, Mary 308
Cross, Marcia 338
Cross-Wits (game show) 135-136, 386-387
Crow, Robert 321
Crowded (sitcom) 360-361, 375
Culea, Melinda 314
Cullen, Bill 24, 66, 68, 80, 84, 138-139, 145-146, 151, 156, 365, 371
Cullen, Mark 337
Cullen, Robb 337
Cummings, Jim 324
Cunningham, Ken 350
Cuoco, Kaley 252
Curran, Jan 33, 392
Curran, Kevin 330
Curreri, Lee 313
Curry, Adrianne 164
Curry, Tim 324, 331
Cyphers, Charles 195
Dagmar 70
Dahl, Arlene 151
Daily, Bill 140
Daily News, The (publication) 49, 194, 196-197, 210, 391, 393-394
Daily Show with Jon Stewart, The (talk show) 42, 379-380
Dajani, Nadia 355
Dale, Alan 347
Daly, John 62
Damon, Stuart 158
Daniels, Greg 328
Daniels, Stan 194-195
Daniels, William 315
Dann, Mike 17

Danza, Tony 43, 161, 317, 341
Dark, Johnny 104
Dark Shadows (soap opera) 91, 393
Date with the Angels (sitcom) 28, 45, 51-57, 95, 371
Daurey, Dana 336
Davalos, Elyssa 321
Davenport, Madison 357
David Letterman Show, The (daytime talk show) 38-39
David, Madeline 133
Davidson, Amy 346
Davidson, John 22, 102, 137, 147
Davidson, John S. 22
Davis, Baron 291
Davis, Jerry 306
Davis, Jim 305
Davis, John Walter 321
Davis, Madelyn 163
Dawson, Richard 68, 70, 93, 127-128, 131-132, 150-152, 164, 195
Day, Dennis 75
Days of Our Lives (soap opera) 267
Dayton, Danny 69
D.C. Follies (comedy series) 319, 373
De Laurentiis, Raffaella 341
De Matteo, Gina 347
De Rossi, Portia 329
Deacon, Richard 32, 54, 311
Dean Martin Celebrity Roast: Betty White, The (variety special) 202, 376
DeBartolo, Dick 26-27, 76-77, 89, 128, 131
DeCarlo, Mark 163
Defenders, The (dramatic series) 222
Degeneres, Ellen 43, 334
Degeneres, Vance 337
DeHaven, Gloria 63, 151
DeKeyser, Dawn 348
Dekker, Thomas 350
Deklin, Mark 288
D'Elia, Bill 256, 259, 265-266
DeLisle, Grey 337
Deloy, George 316
DeLuise, Dom 35, 161, 251, 319-320
Dempsey, Patrick 257
Dennis, Josh 333
Dent, Bruce 347
Dern, Jonathan 325
DeRose, Toni 336
Deschanel, Emily 358
Desert Sun, The (publication) 33, 392-393
Deters, Kevin 355
Deutsch, Donny 132
Devane, William 37
Devine, Loretta 357
DeVol, Frank 18, 49-50, 95

DeWitt, Jan 358
DeWitt, Joyce 308
Diagnosis Murder (drama series) 321-322, 373
Diahann Carroll Show, The (variety series) 101, 376
Diamond, Selma 217
Dick Van Dyke and the Other Woman (variety special) 168
Dick Van Dyke Show, The (sitcom) 168-169
Dickey, Dale 348
Dickson, Jonathan 351
Dietrich, Dena 328
Diller, Phyllis 99, 105, 202, 328
Dillman, Bradford 310
DiMaggio, John 354
Dinah! (talk show) 34, 378
Dinah's Place (talk show) 33, 378
Disher, Catherine 326
Disney's Hercules (cartoon series) 327-328, 374
Disney's Teacher's Pet (cartoon series) 335, 374
Doan, Richard K. 123, 392
Dobkowitz, Roger 130
Doctors, The (informational series) 294, 380
Dodson, Jack 203
Doherty, Shannon 318
Dolley, Jason 344
Dom DeLuise Show, The (sitcom) 302, 319-320, 375
Donahue (talk show) 40, 378
Donahue, Elinor 306
Donahue, Phil 40
Donald O'Connor Show, The (talk show) 30
Donna Reed Show, The (sitcom) 309
Donny & Marie (variety series) 103-104, 244, 376
Donny & Marie (talk show) 43
Donovan, Tate 327
Donovan, Tom 303
Dontzig, Gary 324
Dooley, Paul 357
Doolittle, John 315
Dorsey, Tommy 202
Dosti, Rose 170, 184, 392
Double Talk (game show) 158, 389
Dougan, Michael 220-221, 392
Douglas, David 362
Douglas, Paul 20
Doyle, David, 207
Drake, Jim 222-223
Drake, Larry 322
Dream House (game show) 153, 388
Dreams Come True: A Celebration of Disney Animation (variety special) 377
Duke, Patty 310
Duncan, Arthur 19
Duncan, Sandy 169
Dunham, Jeff 351

Dunk, Glenn 333
Dunlap, Malcolm 349
Dunnock, Mildred 309
Durk, Julie 357
Durning, Charles 219
Dusenberry, Ann 154-155
Dwight-Smith, Michael 307
Dybdahl, John 346
Eagles, Greg 337
Earl, James 359
Earth Day Special, The See *Time Warner Presents the Earth Day Special*
Eastwood, Jayne 326
Ed Wynn Show, The (variety series) 96
Eddie Albert Show, The (Los Angeles talk show) 16
Eddy, Nelson 10, 30, 36
Edelman, Herb 232, 315
Edge of Night, The (soap opera) 132
Edgeman, Lori Beth 356
Edwards, Douglas 66
Edwards, Geoff 125-126
Edwards, Ralph 99, 135, 159, 381
Eggar, Samantha 327
Eggert, Nicole 163
Egglesfield, Colin 357
Eisner, Michael D. 349
Elaine Stritch at Liberty (one-woman special) 219
Elden, Andrew 344
Ellen (talk show) 2, 43, 379
Ellen Show, The (sitcom) 302, 334-335, 375
Ellery Queen (drama series) 302, 307-308, 373
Ellingson, Evan 344
Elliot, Chris 296
Elliott, Gordon 66
Ellison, Bob 195
Elrod, Carson 350
Emerson, Taylor 33
Emily's Reasons Why Not (sitcom) 204
Empty Nest (sitcom) 229-231, 303, 375
Enberg, Dick 127
Engel, Georgia 159, 173, 192, 194, 202, 291
Engel, Roy 54
Entertainment Tonight (informational series) 242, 278
Entertainment Weekly (periodical) 238
Epstein, Jon 311
Erdman, Richard 352
Erlenborn, Ray 48
Erwin, Bill 317
Essman, Susie 165
Estes, Larry 323
Eubanks, Bob 151, 153, 156
Eunice (special) 208-211, 376
Eure, Wesley 138

Evans, Dale 19
Evelyn, George 343
Evening Shade (sitcom) 241
Everett, Kenny 238
Everwood (drama series) 301, 338-340, 373
Everybody's Talking (game show) 124
Everything's Relative (sitcom) 248
Ewell, Tom 311
Fabian 78
Fabray, Nanette 235
Face the Facts (game show) 71
Facts of Life, The (movie) 105
Fahy, Meghann 355
Fairbanks Jr., Douglas 91, 207
Fairchild, Morgan 106, 296
Fallon, Jimmy 43, 113-114, 351
Fame (drama series) 313-314, 373
Family Affair (sitcom) 97, 123
Family Feud (game show) 131, 150-152, 212, 388, 390
Family Law (dramatic series) 249
Family Theater (radio drama) 11
Fanaro, Barry 225-226
Fanning, Dakota 334
Fantana, Tom 315-316
Fantasy (game show) 148
Fantozzi, Tony 60, 242 368
Faracy, Stephanie 205
Farentino, James 305
Fargo, Donna 27
Faris, Sean 355
Farr, Jamie 145, 153, 156, 307
Farrell, Mike 145-146, 336
Farrell, Shea 314
Father of the Pride (cartoon series) 326, 344, 374
Faustino, David 359
Fawlty Towers (sitcom) 202-204
Fedderson, Don 18, 31, 46-47, 49, 51-52, 95, 97, 303
Fedderson, Yvonne Lime 97
Feeney, Nina 338
Feldman Chester 68
Feldon, Barbara 310
Feldstein, Al 26
Fell, Norman 307
Felsher, Howard 91-92, 138
Fenneman, George 381
Ferguson, Craig 43, 239, 245-247, 298
Ferguson, Jesse Tyler 293
Fernandez, Maria Elena 259, 392
Ferrell, Conchata 310
Ferrell, Tyra 312
Ferrera, America 347
Fey, Tina 115-116, 350-351

Field, Rebecca 357
Fields, Greg 313
Fighting Nightingales (sitcom pilot) 205
Finkel, Dave 347
Finley, Cameron 325
Finn, Pat 345
Fischer, Peter S. 307
Fischler, Grace 13, 392
Fisher, Joely 234
Fithian, Cathy 333
Flanders, Ed 315, 317
Flannery, Susan 267, 272, 274, 278
Flea 325, 331
Fleming, Shaun 335
Flockhart, Calista 329
Flowers, Wayland 312-313
Flynn, Neil 351
Foch, Nina 69
Fogel, Eric 349
Foglesong, Keith 358-359
Foley, Dave 298, 355
Follow the Fleet (movie) 160
Fontaine, Joan 77
Fontanne, Lynn 187
For Better or Worse (daytime dramatic anthology) 71
Foraker, Lois 319
Ford, Faith 323
Ford, Gerald 100, 319
Ford, Glenn 84
Ford, Tennessee Ernie 21
Foreman, Bob 20, 392
Foreman, George 164
Forsythe, John 24, 76, 308
Foster, Bob 96
Foulger, Byron 304
Francavilla, Tyler 359
Francine, Anne 304
Francis, Arlene 60, 62, 71, 127, 365
Francis, Genie 314-315
Francis, Ivor 203
Frank, Charles 314
Frank Sinatra Show, The (variety series) 55, 57
Franklin, Aretha 2
Franklin, Bonnie 202
Frasier (sitcom) 251, 280-281, 293
Frazier, Ronald E. 311
Freedle, Sam C. 306
Freeman, Jennifer Nicole 341
Freeman, Morgan 116
Freeman, Yvette 277
Frees, Paul 303
Fresco, Rob 336

Frey, Leonard 311
Friedlander, Judah 350-351
Friedman, Kim 310, 314
Friedman, Mimi 324
Friends (sitcom) 347
Fries, Charles 321
Frink, John 328
Fritzhand, James 314
Fudge, Alan 315
Full Circle (soap opera) 71
Fuller, Sam 17
Funny Face (sitcom) 169
Funny Women of Television: A Museum of Radio & Television Tribute (variety special) 108, 377
Furst, Stephen 315, 318
Fusco, Joseph 323
Fusco, Paul 318
Gabel, Martin 62
Gabor, Eva 32
Gabor, Zsa Zsa 47
Gaffigan, Jim 334
Galloway, Sue 351
Gambit (game show) 123
Game$how Marathon (game show) 164-165, 390
Gangi, Barbara M. 356
Gann, Merrilyn 338
Garafalo, Tony 313
Garagiola, Joe 27, 66, 88
Garber, Victor 114
Garcia, Greg 349
Garcia, Gregory Thomas 335
Gardell, Billy 337
Gardella, Kay 197, 393
Gardner, Hy 64
Gargiulo, Mike 5, 24-26, 60, 72-74, 76, 83, 123, 145-146
Garland, Beverly 32, 124, 126
Garrett, Spencer 337
Garrison, Greg 319
Garry Moore Show, The (variety series) 70
Garton, Dick 49
Gary the Rat (cartoon series) 303, 337, 374
Gautier, Dick 87-88, 137
Geary, Anthony 151
Gelman, Morrie 47, 150, 393
Gemignani, Rhoda 317
General Electric College Bowl (game show) 71, 107
Genevieve 62
Gerard, Gil 356
Gerkin, Jim 334
Germain, Larry 336
Germann, Greg 329
Get the Message (game show) 81-82, 383-384
Getty, Estelle 154-155, 215, 218, 220, 226, 231, 236-238, 252, 280

Gibb, Andy 103
Gibbs, Marla 297
Gibney, Susan 321
Gibson, Cal 323-324
Gibson, Channing 315
Gibson, Henry 266
Gibson, Mel 344
Gifford, Frank 71
Gilborn, Steven 345
Gillespie, Ann 320
Gillette, Anita 69, 143
Gilpin, Peri 325
Gimme a Break! (sitcom) 210
Gimpel, Erica 313
Girl Talk (talk show) 30
Giroux, Lee 22
Gitelson, Rick 326
Glarum, Sivert 349
Gleason, Joanna 137, 139
Gleason, Michael 311, 321
Glenn Martin, D.D.S. (cartoon series) 303, 349-350, 374
Glover, Donald 352-353
Go (game show) 152-153, 388
Godfrey, Arthur 22, 24-25, 143
Goethals, Angela 341
Gold, Eric L. 341
Gold, Lloyd "Lucky" 341
Goldbergs, The (sitcom) 15
Golden Girls, The (sitcom) 3, 5, 30, 34, 37, 51, 81, 107-108, 110-111, 155, 157, 159, 162, 168, 201, 204, 215-233, 236-238, 240, 247-248, 252, 267, 280, 286, 290-292, 294-295, 303, 314, 319-320, 336, 348, 371-372
Golden Girls, The: The Greatest Memories (documentary) 238
Golden Palace, The (sitcom) 81, 232-236, 240, 371
Goldman, Danny 307
Goldner, Brooke 354
Goldstein, Jessica 349
Goldthwait, Bob 327
Gomez, Rick 337
Good Morning America (talk show) 2
Good Times (sitcom) 201
Goodman, John 344
Goodman, Tim 249-250, 393
Goodson, Mark 60, 73, 76, 79, 81-82, 93, 99, 151, 154-156, 159
Goodson-Todman 60, 63-64, 68, 72, 74-76, 79-80, 83-84, 92, 107, 127, 134, 145
Goodwin, Bill 22
Gordin, Eyal 349
Gordon, Gale 76
Gore II, George O. 341
Gorham, Christopher 347
Gorshin, Frank 336
Gossip Columnist, The (TV-movie) 310-311, 373
Gottlieb, Andrew 356

INDEX

Gould, Dana 330
Gould, Harold 232
Grab Your Phone (Los Angeles TV series) 12-13
Grabiak, Marita 338
Grace, Topher 253
Graf, David 145
Graham, Cynthia 336
Graham, Samaria 336
Grammer, Camille 337
Grammer, Kelsey 251, 337
Grandy, Fred 152, 186
Grant, Beth 328
Grant, Cary 223
Grant, Donald "Bud" 123-125, 201
Grant, Johnny 160
Grant, Michael 359
Grant, Mitch 356
Gray, Coleen 309
Gray-Cabey, Noah 341
"Great American Game Show, The," *ABC Wide World of Entertainment* (variety special) 81, 99, 125-126, 376
Great Gildersleeve, The (radio sitcom) 11, 54
Great Love Songs, The (variety special) 109, 377
Green, Al 329-330
Green, Andrew 324
Greene, Lorne 23-25, 27, 31, 78
Greene, Rhetta 315
Greenfield, Max 347
Greer, Judy 349
Greer, Justin 356
Gregory, Benji 318
Gregory, Ian 347
Greshler, Francine 306
Grey, Brad 322
Griff (drama series) 27
Griffin, John P. 324
Griffin, Kathy 164, 323
Griffin, Merv 30-31, 65, 74, 160, 208
Griffith, Andy 320
Griffith, Melanie 248
Grim Adventures of Billy & Mandy, The (cartoon series) 337-338, 374
Grizzard, George 71
Groening, Matt 330
Groff, Jonathan 344
Gross, Michael 312
Grossman, David 342
Grossman, Terry 225-226
Growing Pains (sitcom) 245
Grunberg, Greg 357
Guetersloh, Cassidy 357
Guiding Light (soap opera) 17
Gunn, Anna 335

415

Gunn, Kelsey 352
Gurnee, Hal 29, 38-39, 143
Gurwitch, Annabelle 321
Guylas, Ellen 317
Gypsy Rose Lee Show, The (talk show) 30
Haaland, Bret 344
Hackett, Buddy 86
Hagen, Uta 328
Haggerty, Don 306
Hagman, Larry 305
Hague, Albert 313
Hague, Renee Orin 313
Haider, Arwa 216
Hail to the Chief (sitcom) 217
Hall, Delores 321
Hall, Monty 69-70, 74, 84, 90, 99
Hallisay, Brian 357
Halmi Jr., Robert 346
Halop, Florence 315
Hamberg, Kim 349
Hamilton, Bill 19
Hamilton, George 76, 252
Hamilton, Joe 210-211
Hamilton, Murray 305
Hamner, Earl 332
Hammer, M.C. 350
Hancock, John Lee 327
Handler, David 197, 393
Hanson, Hart 358
Happy Birthday Bob (variety special) 105, 377
Happy Birthday Hollywood (variety special) 108, 377
Hardwick, Dick 312
Hardwick, Jonathan 328
Hardy, Nita 355
Hargrove, Dean 203, 320-321
Harmetz, Aljean 217, 224, 393
Harmon, Mark 315
Harper, Valerie 117, 159, 169, 186, 293
Harris, Danielle 331
Harris, Harry 313
Harris, Mel 333
Harris, Rachael 350
Harris, Susan 217, 219-221, 225, 232, 238
Harrison, Gregory 109, 309
Harry, Jackée 318
Hart, Moss 65
Hartman, David 307
Hartman, Paul 304
Harvey, Steve 19, 295
Harvey Korman Show, The (sitcom) 204
Hatos, Stephen 84
Hauge, Ron 330

Hayden, Pamela 330
Hayek, Salma 348
Hayes, Sean 280-281, 360
Hayman, James 348
Haymer, Johnny 312
Haynes, Dick 12, 17
Haynes, Hilda 307
Hays, Robert 333
He Said She Said (game show) 88-89, 124, 385 See also *Tattletales*
Hearts Afire (sitcom) 242
Heaton, Patricia 351
Heatter, Merrill 126-127, 134, 144
Heche, Anne 357
Heisler, Eileen 351
Helfer, Ralph 32
Heline, Deann 351
Helmond, Katherine 317
Henchy, Chris 340
Henderson, Florence 135
Henderson, Skitch 109
Henderson, Ty 312
Henning, Linda Kaye 304
Henning, Paul 304
Henry, Buck 289
Henry, Chuck 40
Henry, Fred 303
Henteloff, Alex 195
Hercules See *Disney's Hercules*
Herd, Richard 338
Here We Go Again: My Life in Television (book) 4, 25, 30, 43, 57, 234, 247, 395
Herman, David 328, 344
Herman, Jerry 117
Herman, Shelley 33, 61, 85-87, 140, 195
Hertford, Brighton 322
Hervey, Winifred 225
Heston, Charlton 267
Hewett, Christopher 154
Hibler, Christopher 320
Hickman, Darryl 83
Higgins, Joel 311
Higglytown Heroes (cartoon series) 343, 374
Hiken, Gerald 307
Hill, Amy 245-246
Hill, Arthur 305
Hillenburg, Stephen 360
Hillerman, John 192, 194, 201, 307-308
Hilton, Perez 112
Himelfarb, David 341
Hindle, Art 310
Hines, Cheryl 344
Hinnen, Stacey 349
Hitt, Robert 206

Hoffman, Rick 258
Hoffman, Steve 31, 393
Hoiseck, Ronald F. 311
Holaway, Meeghan 359
Holden, David 361
Holden, William 56, 236
Holland, Erik 311
Holliday, Bobby 343
Holliday, Cheryl 344
Holliman, Earl 134, 145
Holloway, Julian 344
Holly, Lauren 336
Hollywood on Television (Los Angeles talk show) 3, 13-16, 19, 31, 47, 55, 95,
Hollywood Reporter (publication) 286-287
Hollywood Squares, The (game show) 61, 86, 135, 137, 143-144, 148, 387, 389-390
Hollywood's Talking (game show) 124-126, 147, 386
Home Show, The (talk show) 42
Hong, Gene 358
Hooks, Robert 305
Hope, Bob 104-105, 229, 376-377
Horta, Silvio 348
Horton, Blaine 351
Hortua, Joe 358
Horvitz, Richard 337
Hot in Cleveland (sitcom) 2, 116-117, 119, 154, 191, 200, 279-300, 303, 361, 371, 372
Hotel (drama series) 314-315, 373
Hour Magazine (talk show) 40
Hovis, Larry 85-86
Howard, Bob 313
Howe, Rob 112
Howie Mandel Show, The (talk show) 42
Hrysikos, Demetrios 6
Hubbell, Megan 342
Hudson, Gary 212
Hudson, Rock 34
Hughes, Felix 10
Hughes, Mike 245
Hughes, Miko 324
Hughes, Terry 223
Humphrey, Hal 22, 393
Humphreys, Alfred E. 341
Hunt, Bonnie 43, 112
Hunter, Blake 317
Hunter, Ross 309
Huntley, Chet 305
Hurwitz, Mitchell 334
Huskey, Brian 350
Huss, Toby 328
Hutt, Grady 334
Hutton, Jim 307
Hutton, Timothy 309
Hylands, Scott 308

INDEX

Hynes, Michael 285
I Love Lucy (sitcom) 47-48, 54-56, 83-84, 163, 195, 221
Idelson, Bill 199
If You Ask Me (And Of Course You Won't) (book) 40
If You're Not in the Obit, Eat Breakfast (documentary) 367, 378
I'll Bet (game show) 88
I'm With Her (sitcom) 302, 340, 375
Imperato, Carlo 313
Inception (movie) 353
Indelicato, Mark 347
Ingels, Marty 75, 82
Inside the Actors Studio (talk show) 105
Irwin, Sirena 360
It Takes Two (game show) 87-88, 385
Ito, Robert 332
It's Your Bet (game show) 87-88, 385-386
I've Got a Secret (game show) 68-69, 124, 381-382, 386
Jackpot (game show) 92
Jackman, Hugh 43
Jackson, Janet 102
Jackson, Kate 91
Jackson, Michael 102
Jacksons, The (variety series) 102, 376
Jacobs, Gillian 352
Jacobs, Johnny 96
Jacobs, Michael 244-246
Jacobs, Seaman 96
Jamal-Warner, Malcolm 320
James, Art 134-135
James, Debbie 323
James, Dennis 371
James, LeBron 288
James, Sheila 56, 96
Jamin, Michael 349
Janis, Conrad 310
Jansen, Jim 336
Jansen, Susan Estelle 245
Janssen, David 306
Jarvis, Al 3, 13-16, 46
Jason, Rick 309
Jay-Z 114
Jeffersons, The (sitcom) 201
Jeffery, David H. 353
Jeffreys, Anne 22
Jenner, Barry 145
Jenner, Bruce 151
Jensen, Ashley 347
Jensen, Shelley 323
Jeong, Ken 352
Jeopardy! (game show) 83, 160, 294
Jeremiah, David 343
Jerry Lewis Show, The: From This Moment On (variety special) 375

Jillian, Ann 56
Jim Nabors Show, The (talk show) 34
Jiminez-Alvarado, Erica 327
Jiminez-Alvarado, Vanessa Erica 327
Jimmy Dean Show, The (variety series) 71
Jimmy Kimmel Live! (talk show) 43, 287, 380
Joan Rivers and Friends Salute Heidi Abromowitz (variety special) 106, 377
Joanne Carson's VIPs (talk show) 30
Joey (sitcom) 347, 375
Johansson, Paul 359
John and Leeza from Hollywood (talk show) 42
John Davidson Christmas Special, The (variety special) 34, 103, 376
John Davidson Show, The (talk show) 40
John Larroquette Show, The (sitcom) 236-237, 303, 372, 375
Johnson, Ashley 245
Johnson, Don 217
Johnson, Jay 143
Johnson, Ken 126
Johnson, Kurt 333
Johnson, Russell 305
Joker's Wild, The (game show) 123-124
Jones, Carolyn 92
Jones, Jack 109
Jones, Matthew 359
Jones, Orlando 344, 357-358
Jones, Shirley 292
Jordan, Leslie 260
Josephson, Barry 358
Joyner, Jackie 361
Judge, Mike 328
Jump, Kiva 351
Junger Witt, Paul 217, 232
Just Men! (game show) 61, 99, 107, 147-151, 371
Just Shoot Me (sitcom) 281
Juvenile Jury (talk show) 30
Kaczmarek, Jane 342
Kagan, Michael 205-206
Kahn, Milt 47
Kalada, Asaad 317
Kamen, Milt 71
Kaminir, Lisa 262
Kanakaredes, Melina 336
Kane, Tom 331
Kaplan, Eric 342
Karam, Jann 321
Kasdorf, Lenore 307
Kasem, Casey 16
Kassardjian, Kyle 326
Kassir, John 327
Kate Smith Hour, The (daytime variety series) 17
Katzenberg, Jeffrey 344
Kaufman, Leonard B. 306

Kaufman, Paul A. 336
Kaufman, Reub 47, 51
Kavner, Julie 330
Kaye, Caren 196-197, 199-200
Kaye, Stubby 82
Kayser, Allan 213
Keach, Stacy 298, 360
Keane, James 346
Keefer, Don 307
Keenan, Joe 293
Keenen, Mary Jo 231
Keep Talking (game show) 69-70, 382
Keith, Brian 76
Kelley, David E. 256-257, 259-260, 263, 329
Kelly, Jean Louisa 335
Kelly, Lisa Robin 253
Kelsay, Bill 54
Kelsey, Linda 183
Kenneally, Rob 323
Kennedy, Jayne 151
Kennedy, Tom 49, 53, 79, 87-88, 91, 95, 139, 141-142, 151, 154, 159, 317, 368-369
Kennedy Center Mark Twain Prize for American Humor: Celebrating Jay Leno (variety special) 116, 378
Kenney, Kerri 334
Kenny, Tom 360
Kern, Janet 5
Ketron, Larry 333
Kibbee, Roland 203
Kiff, Kaleena 312
Kilgallen, Dorothy 62
Kilpatrick, Lincoln 321
Kimmel, Jimmy 288
Kind, Richard 325
King, Alan 76, 100
King, Larry 2, 51
King of Queens, The (sitcom) 252
King of the Hill (cartoon series) 328, 374
Kinnally, Jon 348
Kirschenbaum, Alan 335
Kirschenbaum, Mike 319
Kirstie (sitcom) 294
Kita, Candace 348
Klavan, Gene 63
Klein, Howard 328
Klein, Marci 351
Kline, Jim 323
Klugman, Brian 358
Klugman, Jack 37, 127, 306
Knebel, Fletcher 305
Knight, Gladys 329
Knight, Sterling 360
Knight, Ted 169

Kojak (drama series) 201
Konigsberg, Frank 310
Koonce, Ken 327
Kopelman, Jean 76-77
Koretsky, Rachel 324
Korman, Chris 5, 100, 157, 203-204, 207, 209-211
Korman, Harvey 5, 100, 157, 203-204, 207, 209, 211
Krakowski, Jane 329
Kramer, Jeffrey 329
Kratz, Brian 362
Krofft, Marty 319
Krofft, Sid 319
Krofft Puppets, The 319
Kulik, Buzz 305
Kulp, Nancy 53
Kupfer, Jerry 351
Kurtz, Swoosie 312
Kusatsu, Clyde 338
LA Doctors (drama series) 302, 327, 373
La Fleur, Art 311
L.A. Herald Examiner, The (publication) 190
L.A. Law (dramatic series) 256
Lachman, Brad 312
Ladies Man (sitcom) 240, 248-253, 371
Lagano, Alice 357
Lahti, Christine 323
Laine, Cleo 109
Lake, Rikki 163
Lake Placid (movie) 256
LaLoggia, Frank 203
LaMarr, Phil 328
LaMond, Bill and Jo 314
Lamour, Dorothy 151
Lampinelli, Lisa 110
Lancaster, Amber 352
Lancaster, Sarah 338
Landers, Judy 312
Landes, Michael 357
Landesberg, Steve 206
Landis, Joe 12
Landis, Monte 307
Landon, Michael 32
Landsburg, Valerie 313
Lane, Nathan 335
Laneuville, Eric 315-316
Lange, Artie 109
Lange, Jim 144, 151
Lange, Michael 359
Lange Jr., Henry 349
Lansbury, Angela 340
LaPlaca, Alison 236
Larroquette, John 204, 236, 266

INDEX

Larry King Live (talk show) 2
Larry Sanders Show, The (sitcom) 250
Laskawy, Harris 320
Lasseter, John 355
Last Resort, The (sitcom) 205
Late Late Show with Craig Ferguson, The (talk show) 43, 247, 379-380
Late Late Show with James Corden, The (talk show) 43, 380
Late Late Show with Tom Snyder, The (talk show) 42, 379
Late Night with David Letterman (talk show) 11, 14, 39, 378
Late Night With Jimmy Fallon (talk show) 43, 113-114, 379-380
Late Show with David Letterman, The (talk show) 39-40, 42-43, 118, 379-380
Later (talk show) 41
Laugh Trax (variety series) 104, 376
Laurance, Mitchell 145
Law, John Philip 137, 309-310
Lawrence, Martin 289
Lawrence, Sharon 248, 251
Lawrence, Vicki 42, 91, 93, 100, 117, 154-156, 161, 209-210
Lawrence Welk Show, The (variety series) 19
Leachman, Cloris 111, 159, 167, 169-170, 172, 194, 247, 293, 295, 334-335, 342, 371
Leahy, Janet 259
Leakes, NeNe 67
Lear, Norman 114
Leave It to Beaver (sitcom) 365-366
LeBlanc, Matt 347
Lederer, Suzanne 316
Lee, Jason 348-349
Lee, Rex 361
Lee, Sheryl 327
Leech, Beverly 244
Leeves, Jane 116-117, 279, 281-282, 360-361
Leifer, Carol 334
Leisure, David 230
Lembeck, Harvey 78
Lemmon, Jack 323
LeMond, Bob 20
Lenk, Tom 359
Lennart, LeRoy 49
Leno, Jay 39-40, 43, 116, 250,
Leonard, Jack E. 76
Leonard, Sheldon 76
Leonardo, Mike 345
Leoni, Tea 322
Lerner, Michael 307
Leszczak, Bob 246
Let's Make a Deal (game show) 99
Letterman, David 11, 14, 38-41, 43, 86, 116, 118, 131, 143, 370, 373-380
Levenson, Sam 70
Levinson, Larry 346
Levinson, Richard 307
Levi, Zachary 117
Levy, Ralph 304

423

Lewis, Dawnn 350
Lewis, Richard 323, 327
Lewis, Robert Q. 62, 66, 76, 77, 82
Lewis, Sagan 316
Leyden, Bill 75, 83
Liars Club (game show) 61, 85-87, 107, 140, 195, 370-372
Liberace 56, 284
Liberace Show, The (variety series) 47
Liddell, Mickey 338
Liddy, G. Gordon 154-155
Liebmann-Smith, Richard 327
Life with Elizabeth (sitcom) 2, 9, 16, 46-53, 57, 60, 63, 95, 106, 196, 371-372
Life with Lucy (sitcom) 155
Light, Judith 317, 347
Linden, Hal 93
Link, William 307
Linkletter, Art 62, 68, 99
Linz, Alex D. 336
Lionhearts, The (cartoon series) 325, 372
Lipton, James 105
Lipton, Robert 305
Listo, Mike 329
Little, Nicolette 325
Little Big Shots: Forever Young (variety series) 19, 378
Littlefield, Warren 217-218
Liu, Lucy 329
Live with Kelly and Michael (talk show) 43
Live with Regis and Kathie Lee (talk show) 41
Lizer, Kari 321
Lloyd, David 194, 311
Lloyd, Norman 315
Locke, Rick 319
Lockhart, June 24, 304
Lohman, Al 125
Long, Tim 330
Lopez, Carlos 356
Lopez, George 43, 237
Lopez Tonight (talk show) 2, 43, 237, 379
Lorax, The (direct-to-video cartoon) 4
Lorey, Dean 341
Los Angeles Times (publication) 13, 31, 52, 170, 175, 184, 225, 244, 246, 259, 289, 391-395
Lost Valentine, The (TV-movie) 286, 355-356, 373
Lou Grant (dramatic series) 193
Love Boat, The (sitcom) 142-143, 193, 207-208, 311, 374-375
Love of Life (soap opera) 75
Love Hewitt, Jennifer 355-357
Love Report, The (informational daytime show) 40
Love, Sidney (sitcom) 302, 312, 374
Loving, Victoria 356
Lovitz, Jon 330
Lowe, Rob 44
Lowry, Cynthia 22, 394

Lucille Ball-Desi Arnaz Show, The (sitcom) 56
Lucas, Caryn 361
Lucas Tanner (drama series) 302, 307, 373
Lucci, Susan 235, 299
Lucy Show, The (sitcom) 84, 123
Ludden, Allen 3, 29-31, 33, 35, 59, 61-62, 65, 71-73, 76, 78-80, 83-88, 90-91, 100-101, 107, 117, 122, 129-130, 134, 136, 138-140, 142-143, 159-160, 165-166, 169, 187, 195, 202, 205-208, 224, 294, 298, 306, 311, 365
Luisi, James 186
Lunt, Alfred 187
Lutz, John 351
Lyde, Ted 347
Lydic, Desi 357
Lyman, Dorothy 210, 213
Lynde, Paul 78, 98-99, 101, 103-104
Lyon, Ed 16
Lyons, Robert F. 346
Mabius, Eric 347
MacDonald, Jeanette 10, 36
MacKrell, Cathy 133
MacKrell, Catie 229
MacKrell, Jim 5, 133-134, 228-229
MacLeod, Gavin 4, 117, 159, 169, 188, 193, 207, 355
MacNeille, Tress 330
MacNicol, Peter 329
MacRae, Meredith 304
Macy, William H. 324
Macy's Thanksgiving Day Parade 23, 25-27, 317-318
Mad Magazine (publication) 26, 76
Madame's Place (sitcom) 312-313, 374
Maffett, Debra Sue 320
Maggio, Natalina 352
Magical World of Disney, The (variety special) 107, 377
Magnificent Marble Machine, The (game show) 134-135, 386
Magnificent Yankee, The (dramatic special) 187
Magnussen, Billy 355
Maharis, George 134
Mahoney, John 290, 296
Mair, Ossie 336
Make the Connection (game show) 60, 63-64, 159, 163, 371
Malcolm in the Middle (sitcom) 302, 342-343, 375
Malden, Karl 326
Malhotra, Angela 352
Malick, Wendie 117, 200, 279, 281-282, 286, 344
Malkasian, Cathy 332
Malloy, Matt 264
Mama's Family (sitcom) 5, 108, 147, 208, 210-214, 218, 372
Mancini, Ray "Boom Boom" 317
Mancini, Ric 317
Mandan, Robert 152
Mandel, Howie 315
Mann, Anita 102

Manners, Sam 310
Manoff, Dinah 230
Manriquez, Frankie Ryan 343
Mapa, Alec 347
Mapes, Jacques 309
March, Alex 306
March, Fredric 20
March, Hal 48, 87-88
Marcus Welby M.D. (dramatic series) 305
Marie (variety series) 244
Marin, Cheech 233
Marin, Paul 200
Marlowe, Abigail 352
Marrero, Richard 356
Mars, Kenneth 310
Marsden, Jason 336
Marshall, E.G. 305
Marshall, Garry 306, 344
Marshall, Penny 114, 306
Marshall, Peter 101, 137, 147, 151, 157
Marshall, Vanessa 337
Martin, Andrea 325
Martin, Bob 24
Martin, Chuck 334
Martin, Dean 202
Martin, Dick 137-138, 140-141, 154, 243
Martin, Millicent 288
Martin, Nan 307
Martin, Ross 71
Martin, Suzanne 280-281, 283, 290, 293, 295, 297, 299, 360
Martin Short Show, The (talk show) 42, 379
Martindale, Wink 82-83
Marvin, Lee 34
Mary and Rhoda (TV-movie) 190
Mary Tyler Moore Show, The (sitcom) 3-5, 24, 27, 51, 102, 108, 129, 159, 167-191, 193-195, 197-198, 201, 205, 218, 220-221, 225, 240, 247, 252, 281, 286-287, 291, 293, 295, 302, 316, 363, 371-372
Masak, Ron 134
Masamitsu, Taylor 343
M*A*S*H (sitcom) 200, 221
Masius, John 315-316
Masquerade Party (game show) 69-70, 124, 382, 386
Masters, Natalie 54
Match Game (game show) 24, 26-27, 61, 75-78, 84, 89, 124, 127-132, 135, 137, 164-165, 195, 372, 383-385
Mathews, David 110-115, 366
Mathis, Johnny 90
Matlock (drama series) 260, 320, 373
Mattocks, Doug 312
Maude (sitcom) 195, 199-201, 218-220, 222
Maurer, Joseph 318
Maxtone-Graham, Ian 330

Maxwell, Marie 325
Maxwell-Smith, Mark 124-126, 135-136, 148-150
May, Deborah 316
Maybe This Time (sitcom) 239-240, 245-247, 371
Mayer, Jeff 335
Mayo Jankins, Carol 313
McAvity, Tom 17
McBrayer, Jack 350
McCann, Doreen 55
McCann, Sean 326
McCarthy, Patrick 335
McCarver, Gary 328
McClanahan, Rue 204, 208, 210-211, 214-215, 218, 220, 223, 231, 236-238, 252, 280, 295
McClellan, Kathleen 252
McClurg, Edie 343
McCook, John 271
McCormack, Eric 354
McDermott, Charlie 351
McDowall, Roddy 71
McGavin, Darren 76
McGiver, John 307-308
McGovern, Maureen 109
McHale, Joel 117, 352
McIntyre, John 337
McJimsey, Mark 328
McKay, Jim 63
McKenna, Chris 353
McKenney Posey, Parker 341
McKim, Dorothy 355
McKuen, Rod 151
McLeod, Catherine 305
McMahon, Ed 75, 84-85, 101
McMahon, Jenna 211
McMartin, John 177
McMillian, Michael 288
McMurray, Sam 350
McNally, Stephen 305
McNeely, Jerry 307
McNichol, Kristy 230
McWhirter, Julie 101
Me and Henry (sitcom pilot) 240, 248
Meade, Julia 82
Meadows, Audrey 151
Meadows, Jayne 68, 156, 311
Medlin, Lex 289
Mehlman, Peter 344
Melville, Sam 91
Mende Lisa 323
Mendez, Carlo 361
Menkin, Larry 51
Mercury, Freddie 238
Mericle, Wendy 338

Meriwether, Lee 134, 336
Merman, Ethel 70
Merton, Michael 327
Merv Griffin Show, The (talk show) 30-31, 208, 378
Metz, Rebecca 359
Meyer, Breckin 328
Miami Vice (dramatic series) 217
Michaels, Al 366-367
Michaels, Lorne 2, 112-115
Michaels, Norma 264
Middle, The (sitcom) 351=352, 375
Mike Douglas Show, The (talk show) 30, 40
Milano, Alyssa 317
Milder, Andy 351
Miller, Alice 331
Miller, David 309
Miller, Denny 305
Miller, Marvin 303
Miller, Paul 312
Miller, Shane 342
Miller, Sidney 307
Milliner, Todd 280-281, 291, 360
Million Dollar Password (game show) 156, 165-166, 390
Millionaire, The (drama series) 52, 303, 373
Mills, Alley 271, 274, 278
Mills, Nancy 225
Milner, Martin 90
Mindreaders (game show) 140-141, 387
Miner, David 351
Minor, Mike 304
Misfits, The (movie) 98
Mishkin, Philip 320
Missing Links (game show) 75-76, 84, 145, 383
Mission: Impossible (dramatic series) 306
Mitchell, Cameron 320
Mitra, Rhona 260
Molina, Alfred 248-249, 252
Molinari, Al 306
Monica, Jennie 360
Monroe, Marilyn 11
Montalban, Ricardo 306
Montgomery, Elizabeth 90, 92
"Monty Hall Roast, The," *ABC Wide World of Entertainment* 99, 376
Monty Python's Flying Circus (variety series) 202
Mooney, Debra 338
Moore, Alvy 206
Moore, Del 48-49, 52, 57, 95-96
Moore, Dudley 323
Moore, Garry 66, 68
Moore, Jason 338
Moore, Mary Tyler 32, 117, 160, 168-169, 187, 225, 287, 293,
Moore, Steven Dean 330

Moore, Tom 313
Mordente, Tony 312
Morella, Dennis 343
Moreno, Rita 83, 151
Morgan, Henry 68-70, 76-77
Morgan, Jaye P. 307
Morgan, Tracy 350
Mork & Mindy (sitcom) 204
Morris, Greg 90, 137
Morris, Jane 11-12, 51, 394
Morrow, Max 326
Morse, David 315
Morse, Robert 98
Morton, Howard 154
Moser, James E. 306
Moss, Ronn 274
Most, Donny 308
Motion Picture Daily (publication) 51
Mula, Frank 313
Mula, John C. 86
Mulcahy, Terence 308
Mull, Martin 334
Mulligan, Richard 229
Mulroney, Brian 337
Mumy, Liliana 343
Muniz, Frankie 342
Munroe, Del 306
Murder She Wrote (dramatic series) 340
Murphy, Brittany 328
Murphy, Eddie 344
Murphy, Rosemary 310
Murray, Don 76
Museum of Television and Radio Presents: Great Women of Television Comedy, The (variety special) 108, 377
Mustafa, Isaiah 288
Mustin, Bert 54
My Name is Earl (sitcom) 303, 348-349, 372, 375
My Sister Eileen (sitcom) 219
My Three Sons (sitcom) 97, 123
My Wife and Kids (sitcom) 341-342, 375
Myers, Chelsea 360
Myers, Randy 337
Nabors, Jim 101
Najimy, Kathy 164, 328
Naked Truth, The (sitcom) 322, 375
Name That Tune (game show) 82
Nance, Barbara 357
Narz, Jack 48-49, 53, 88, 90
Nastuk, Matthew 330
Nathan, Mort 225
Nathan, Stephen 358
NBC All Star Hour (variety special) 104, 376, 377

NBC Saturday Night at the Movies (movie series) 220
NBC 75th Anniversary Special (variety special) 104, 377
NBC Star Salute to 1981 (variety special) 104, 376
NBC's 60th Anniversary Celebration (variety special) 104, 377
Neal, Roy 22
Nealon, Kevin 349
Neise, George 54
Nelson, Ann 313
Nelson, Barry 70-71
Nelson, Frank 96-97
Nelson, Judd 323
Nesteroff, Kliph 12, 15, 394
New Dick Van Dyke Show, The (sitcom) 169
New York Daily News, The (publication) 49
New York Pops Orchestra, The 109
Newbern, George 336
Newhart (sitcom) 240
Newhart, Bob 240-242, 299
Newlywed Game, The (game show) 88, 143
Newmar, Julie 336
Newsweek (publication) 136
Newton, Becki 347
Nguyen, Phi-Long 336
Nielsen, Leslie 232, 320
Night Court (sitcom) 217
Night of 100 Stars III (variety special) 231, 377
Nightlife (talk show) 41
Nixon, Richard 319
Noah, Robert 37, 76-77, 82-83, 127, 134
Noddy (children's special) 302, 326-327, 373
Noonday Show, The (talk show) 34
Nordling, Jeffrey 336
Norm Crosby's The Comedy Shop (variety series) 104, 376
North, Kedzie 26
North, Sheree 305
Nowicki, Tom 355
Nunez Jr., Miguel A. 347
Nurses (sitcom) 231, 302, 375
Nye, Louis 208
Obama, President Barack 116
O'Brian, Hugh 56
O'Brien, Conan 43
O'Brien, Pat 76
Obst, Linda 280-281,
O'Connell, Dierdre 327
O'Connell, Kevin 153
O'Connor, Donald 20
Odd Couple, The (sitcom) 302, 306-307, 374
Odenkirk, Bob 330
O'Donnell, Rosie 111
Office, The (sitcom) 190
O'Flaherty, Terence 10

INDEX

O'Hara, Catherine 349
O'Hara, Jenny 297
O'Hara United States Treasury (drama series) 306, 373
O'Hurley, John 70, 344
O'Kane, Claire 360
O'Leary, Dorothy 10, 394
Oldring, Peter 349
Olin, Ken 327
Oliver, John 352
O'Malley, Mike 335, 348
One Day at a Time (sitcom) 281
$100,000 Pyramid, The (game show) 122, 145-147, 388-390
One on One with John Tesh (talk show) 42
O'Neil, Patrick 352
O'Neill, Steve 338
Oppenheimer, Alan 212
Oprah Winfrey Show, The (talk show) 43, 190
Ortiz, Ana 264, 347
Osborne, Holmes 329
O'Shannon, Dan 324
Oshima Belyeu, Faye 340
Osmanski, Joy 357
Osment, Emily 301, 361, 363
Osmond, Donny 103, 147
Osmond, Marie 103, 239, 244-246
Osmond, Ken 366
Oswalt, Patton 352
Overall, Park 230, 249
Paar, Jack 28-30, 34, 38, 60, 62, 71-72, 159
Pace, Frank 324
Page, Don 31
Page, LaWanda 202
Pagliaro, Joanne 325
Paige, Janis 198
Palmer, Betsy 68
Paltrow, Bruce 315
Pandolfo, Tony 152
Pankin, Stuart 159
Pantalino, Joe 325
Parade Magazine (publication) 286
Parker, David 341
Parker, Eleanor 305
Parker, Valencia 342
Parks, Bert 65, 70, 151, 307, 371
Parks, Bill 352
Parres, Laurie 322
Parris, Miriam 248
Passaris, Lex 222-223, 226-227, 232-234
Passeri, Mary 351
Password (game show) 3, 5-6, 29-30, 43, 59, 61, 70-74, 79-80, 82, 84, 90-93, 117, 124, 129, 134, 137-140, 145, 154-156, 158, 165-166, 187, 202, 292, 298, 306, 310, 382-390
Password All-Stars (game show) 91-93, 386

431

Password Plus (game show) 137-140, 154, 310, 387-388
Pat Sajak Show, The (talk show) 33, 41, 70, 379
Paul Lynde at the Movies (variety special) 101, 376
Paul Lynde Halloween Special, The (variety special) 101, 376
Paulsen, Rob 337
Pava, Adam 350
Payne (sitcom) 204
Payne, Don 330
Payne, Freda 27
Payne, Jerry 135
PDQ (game show) 126
Peaker, E.J. 98
Peck, Jim 80
Pedi, Tom 307
Peeples, Nia 313
Peery, Sarah 321
Pell, Paula 351
Peluce, Meeno 311
Penn, Leo 307
Penner, Jonathan 322
Pennette, Marco 340
Penny, Joe 310
Pentecost, George 204
People (publication) 37, 115, 236
Peppard, George 92
Per Sullivan, Erik 342
Perkins, Kent 206
Perlman, Rhea 320
Perpich, Jonathan 320
Perry, Jim 151
Pesa, April 340
Pet Set, The (informational series) 6, 31-33, 85, 371
Peter Marshall Variety Show, The (variety series) 101, 376
Peterman, Steven 324
Peters, Jeff 320
Peterson, Bettelou 218, 221, 224, 317, 394
Peterson, Michael 358
Peterson, Seth 336
Petticoat Junction (sitcom) 304, 374
Peukert, Martha 92
Pflug, Jo Ann 127
Philbin, Regis 30, 40, 138, 165-166, 291
Phillips, Barney 195, 306
Phillips, Clyde 324
Phillips, Peg 323
Phyllis (sitcom) 175, 194
"Phyllis Diller's 102nd Birthday Party," *ABC Wide World of Entertainment* (variety special) 99, 376
Pickles, Christina 315
Pierson, D.C. 352
Pierson, Kate 343
Pietila, Bonita 330

Pietrosh, Chrissy 349
Pine, Robert 137-138
Pintauro, Danny 317
Pioneers of Television (documentary) 29, 46, 51
Plana, Tony 347
Play Your Hunch (game show) 74, 383
Plaza, Aubrey 360
Pniewski, Mike 355
Poehler, Amy 114, 116
Pogue, John E. 338
Polcino, Dominic 328
Polic II, Henry 152, 158
Polis, Joel 321
Pollack, Jon 344
Polo, Teri 340
Pomerantz, Earl 311
Ponce, Danny 318
Ponterotto, Donna 317
Pontell, Jonathan 329
Poole, Duane 336
P.O.P. (sitcom pilot) 219
Pope Francis 298
Popp, Cynthia 277
Ponterotto, Donna 317
Portinari, Hester 305
Posner, Martha 228
Poston, Tom 64-66, 71, 156, 253
Potter, Monica 260
Potts, Annie 161
Pound Puppies (cartoon series) 302, 354-356, 372
Poust, Tracy 348
Powell, Keith 351
Powell, Randolph 305
Practice, The (drama series) 256-259, 372
Praiser, Ian 324
Pralgo, Robert 356
Pratt, Chris 338
Pratt, James Michael 356
Prep & Landing (TV movie) 355
Prep & Landing Stocking Stuffer (cartoon special) 327, 355, 374
Prepon, Laura 254
Presley, Elvis 201
Presnell, Harve 325-326
Pressly, Jaime 348
Preston, Carrie 360
Price, Michael 330
Price, Vincent 78
Price is Right, The (game show) 72, 80-81, 123-124, 136, 144-145, 150, 383-384, 389
Prickett, Maudie 54
Priest, Pat 176
Princess Diana of Wales 238
Proctor, Phil 331

433

Providence (drama series) 302, 335, 374
Puck, Wolfgang 151
Pudgy! (variety special) 106, 376
Pudi, Danny 352-353
Purcell, Sarah 106, 147
Pyramid 145-147, 158, 164, 390 See also *The $100,000 Pyramid* and *The $25,000 Pyramid*
Queen (band) 299
Queen Latifah (actress) 295
Queen Latifah (talk show) 43, 380
Queer Eye (reality series) 119
Quigley, Bob 126-127, 134, 144
Quivers, Robin 163
Rachins, Alan 333
Radio-TV Mirror (publication) 10
Rae, Charlotte 100-101
Raffill, Stewart 6, 32-33
Rainbolt, Bill 86
Raitt, John 109
Randall, Tony 62, 90, 306, 312
Randolph, John 307
Raoul, Dale 351
Rapaport, Michael 354
Raphael, Sally Jesse 40, 218, 227
Rash, Jim 352
Rawlins, Lester 304
Ray, Gene Anthony 313
Ray Anthony Show, The (variety series) 53
Rayburn, Gene 63, 77, 83, 127, 129-132, 138, 150, 164
Raye, Martha 34, 310-311
Redford, Robert 288, 367
Redgrave, Lynn 106
Reed, Donna 309
Reed, Robert 71
Reese, Tom 307
Reeves, Richard 54
Rega, Bill 306
Regis Philbin Show, The (talk show) 30, 40
Reichs, Kathy 358
Reid, Elliot 83, 246
Reilly, Charles Nelson 37, 78, 128, 131-132, 162-164
Reiner, Carl 2, 69, 107, 117, 121, 284, 297, 344, 362, 367, 371, 381
Reisner, Dean 305
Remington Steele (drama) 217
Rennie, Michael 3
Reo, Don 341
Report to Murphy (sitcom) 223
Retrievers, The (TV-movie) 333-334, 373
Retrum, Lew 73, 91-93, 138
Return to the Batcave: The Misadventures of Adam and Burt (TV-movie) 336, 373
Reynolds, Burt 33-34, 86, 160, 163, 229
Reynolds, Debbie 144, 229
Rhoades, Barbara 307

Rhoades, Jessica 361
Rhoda (sitcom) 175, 186-187
Rhodes, Michael 307
Rhue, Madlyn 309, 313
Rich, Allen 15
Rich, Charlie 101
Rich, Doris 304
Rich Little Show, The (variety series) 100-101, 376
Richard Simmons Show, The (exercise show) 40
Richardson, Derek 355
Rickaby, Brett 336
Rickles, Don 289-291
Ridini Spencer, Maryann 356
Rifkin, Arnold 337
Rigg, Rebecca 327
Riggi, John 351
Riley, Jack 316
Rinaldi, Rich 328
Rinsler, Dennis 313
Ripley's Believe It or Not (informational series) 244
Risley, Mark 331
Rist, Robbie 307
Rivera, Geraldo 41-42
Rivers, Joan 36-37, 43, 106, 290, 317
Roberts, Doris 217, 289
Roberts, Mark 322
Roberts, Pernell 76
Roberts, Rick 327
Robin, Diane 346
Robin, Steve 329
Robinson, Charlie 84
Rocos, Cleo 238
Roddy, Rod 81
Rodriguez, Freddy 347
Rodriguez, Paul 37
Rogers, Doug 186-187, 198, 311
Rogers, Perry 324
Rogers, Roy 19
Rogers, Wayne 90, 92
Rohm, Elisabeth 357
Roman, Nina 307
Roman Holiday (movie) 17
Romero, Cesar 151, 208
Romijn, Rebecca 347
Ronstadt, Linda 35
Room 222 (sitcom) 168
Rooney, Kevin 341
Rooney, Mickey 229
Root, Justin 165-166
Root, Stephen 249, 328
Rose, Jalen 67
Rose, Larry 159

Rose, Si 96
Rose Marie 42
Rosenberg, Howard 246, 394
Rosenberg, Lee 244
Rosenthal, Karine 358
Rosner, Rick 148
Ross, Marion 297
Rotenberg, Michael 323
Roth, Lynn 321
Roth, Roxy 47
Rowell, Victoria 321
Roy Bolton, Muriel 303
Rudner, Rita 323
Rue La Rue Cafe 216
Rupp, Debra Jo 253, 335
Rusco, Al 317
Rush, Brandon 301, 361
Rush, Joshua 359
Russom, Leon 333
Russell, Nipsey 140, 145, 151
Rutherford, Emily 334
Ryan, Amy 322
Sabara, Daryl 344
Sabella, Paul 325
Sadowski, Jonathan 361
Safford Vela, Norma 316
Safi, Brian 361
St. Elsewhere (drama series) 302, 315-316, 373
St. John, Gina 345
St. John, Trevor 357
Sajak, Pat 33, 41, 70, 138, 159, 162
Sakai, Richard 330
Sale of the Century (game show) 123
Sales, Soupy 84, 145
Sallan, Bruce J. 308
Sally Jesse Raphael (talk show) 218, 227
Sampley, Mary 8, 14, 16
San Francisco Examiner (publication) 10, 220-221, 224, 249
Sand, Barry 41
Sand, Bob 312
Sandell, Mary 343
Sanders, Hugh 55
Sanderson, William 335
Sandrich, Jay 172, 218, 222
Sands, Billy 307
Sanford and Son (sitcom) 202, 306
Sanford Arms, The (sitcom) 202
Sanger, Jonathan 321
Santa Barbara (soap opera) 267
Sargent, Dick 310
Saturday Night Live (variety series) 2, 43, 111-115, 367, 372, 377
Saturday Night Live 40th Anniversary Special (variety special) 115, 378

Saucedo, Evan 338
Saunders, Blaire 351
Saunders, Lori 304
Savage, Paul 55
Save Me (sitcom) 303, 357-358, 375
Savid, Darryl 322
Sawyer, Diane 112
Sax, Steve 149
Saxon, John 141-142
Saxton, Charlie 359
Sayle, Alexei 233
Scardino, Don 351
Scattergories (game show) 163-164, 390
Schell, Ronnie 312
Schlatter, George 106
Schlitz Playhouse of Stars (dramatic anthology) 57
Schmock, Jonathan 361
Schneider, John 282
Schneider, Paul 333
Schneider, Stephen 357
Schneider, Tawny 40
Schuck, John 122, 136, 145
Schumaker, Ken 352
Scott, Judith 327
Scrabble (game show) 164
Scully, Mike 330
Scully, Vin 88
Seale, Douglas 318
Sedaris, Amy 288
Seehorn, Rhea 340
Segall Adlon, Pamela 328
Selig, Andrew J. 69, 81, 89, 127, 131
Selleca, Connie 314
Selman, Matt 330
Sepenuk, Hazel 357
Serafino, Mia 360
Serling, Anne 85
Serling, Rod 76, 85, 90
Sesame Street (children's series) 123
70s, The: The Decade That Changed Television: The Museum of Television & Radio (variety special) 108, 377
Shackelford, Ted 157
Shaffer, Atticus 351
Shalem, Guy 119
Shalit, Sid 49, 394
Shambley, Cathy 347
Shannon, Michael 309
Shape of Things, The (variety special) 106, 376
Shapiro, Arnold 324
Shapiro, Erick 335
Sharbutt, Del 18
Shatner, Will 109-110, 256, 292, 305

Shaughnessy, Charles 154
Shaw, Reta 96-97
Shawn, Dick 73
Shawn, Wallace 325-326
Shea, John 323
Shearer, Harry 330
Sheehan, David 311
Sheldon, James 307-308, 311
Shenar, Paul 307
Shepard, Vonda 329
Shepherd, Cybill 357
Sheppard, W. Morgan 355
Sher, Eden 351
Sherman, Bobby 310
Sherman, Jenny 307
Shields, Brent 356
Shields, Brooke 323
Shigeta, James 90
Shinagawa, Pat 337
Shipley, Michael 349
Shore, Dinah 33-34
Shore, Pauly 328
Shostak, Stu 365-366
Showoffs (game show) 134, 386
Shrek (movie) 344
Shriner, Herb 41
Shriner, Wil 41-42, 61, 251-252
Siamis, Korby 324
Sicari, Joseph R. 307
Sidney, Sylvia 311
Siebert, Charles 145
Siegfried and Roy 344
Sikes, Cynthia 315
Silver, Ron 143
Silverman, Ben 348
Silverman, Fred 38, 124, 126, 133, 143, 169, 320-321
Simmons, J.K. 330
Simmons, Richard 154
Simon, Sam 330
Simons, Susan 148
Simpsons, The (cartoon series) 302, 330-331, 374
Singer, Lori 313
Singer, Rick 324
Single Season Sitcoms of the 1990s (book) 246
Singletary, Tony 318
Sipos, Shaun 344
Sirkot, Denise 330
60 Minutes (newsmagazine) 101
Skutch, Ira 130
Slayton, Natasha 325
Smart, Jean 292
Smith, "Buffalo" Bob 21

Smith, Bob Dolan 319
Smith, Cecil 175, 394
Smith, E. Jeffrey 319
Smith, Gregory 338
Smith, Kurtwood 254
Smith, Patrick Sean 338
Smith, Roger 76
Smith, Ron Clinton 355
Smith, Shelley 151
Smith, Yardley 330
Smoove, J.B. 350
Snap Judgment (game show) 84-85, 385
Snavely (sitcom pilot) 203-204, 303, 373
Snyder, Liza 335
Soap (sitcom) 217, 221
Soden, Maura 342
Sole, Leslie 349
Somers, Brett 128-130, 132, 164, 195
Somerset (soap opera) 91
Sonny & Cher (variety series) 101-102, 376
Soodik, Trish 307
Soul Man, The (sitcom) 289, 303, 375
Spader, James 256, 263
Sparks, Kylie 345
Speer, Kathy 225-226
Spelling, Aaron 314
Spies, Don 332
Spiller, Michael 348
Split Second (game show) 88
Spongebob SquarePants (cartoon series) 360, 374
Sponsor (periodical) 20
Spound, Michael 314
Stafford, Nancy 315
Stahl, Andy 355
Stamatopoulos, Dino 352
Stanley, T.L. 289
Stanzler, Wendey 351
Star Search (variety series) 104, 377
Stark, Art 74-75
Stealing Christmas (TV-movie) 302, 341, 373
Steeples, Eddie 348
Stehli, Edgar 304
Steiger, Joel 320
Steinberg, Barry 321
Steinberg, David 341
Steinkellner, Bill and Cheri 240, 335
Stephanie (sitcom pilot) 205-206, 303, 373
Stephens, Nick 355
Sterling, Dan 328
Sterling, Philip 316
Sterling, Robert 22
Steve Allen Show, The (talk show) 30, 378

Stevens, Connie 73
Stevens, Morgan 313
Stevenson, Cynthia 241
Stevenson, McLean 34, 129, 132, 154
Stewart, Bob 72, 76, 80, 143, 145-146, 152, 158, 365
Stewart, Charles 304
Stewart, French 327
Stewart, Jon 42
Stewart, Malcolm 341
Stich, Michael 267-272, 274, 276-278
Stickney, Phyllis Yvonne 350
Stiers, David Ogden 335
Stiller, Jerry 335
Stoller, Fred 359
Stone, Sharon 259
Stones, Tad 327
Story of Santa Claus, The (cartoon special) 324-325, 327, 374
Stratton, Cole 333
Strickland, David 323
Stritch, Elaine 219, 321
Strommen, Garrett 346
Strong, Michael 305
Stuart, Barbara 87, 314
Stumpers (game show) 107, 122, 136-137, 387
Sturz, Lisa 161
Suddenly Susan (sitcom) 303, 323-324, 372, 375
Sullivan, Barry 78
Sullivan, Billy L. 232-234
Sullivan, Liam 309
Sullivan, Nick 351
Sullivan, Susan 340
Sumner, Jeff 347
Sunday Night Football (sports series) 366
Sunset Boulevard (movie) 236
Super Password (game show) 154-156, 388-389
Suplee, Ethan 348
Sutcliffe, David 340
Sutton, Phoef 240-244, 259, 263, 266
Swann, Lynn 66
Swartzlander, Ric 334
Sweet, Rachel 361
Sweethearts (game show) 162
Switzer, Michael 346
Swope, Mel 313
Talbot, Lyle 306
Talk, The (talk show) 14, 43, 294, 380
Talley, Jill 360
Tambor, Jeffrey 248, 325-326
Tamez, Jose 348
Taney, Barton 356
Tannenbaum, Eric 361
Tannenbaum, Kim 361

Tartikoff, Brandon 210, 217-218
Tashman, George 201, 394
Tattletales (game show) 88-89, 124, 386-387 See also *He Said She Said*
Taxi (sitcom) 198, 210
Taylor, Greg 341
Taylor, Holland 322
Taylor, Rip 144, 311
Taylor, Tamara 358
Teacher's Pet See *Disney's Teacher's Pet*
Tedrow, Irene 173
Tell, Joanne 357
$10,000 Pyramid, The (game show) 145-146
Tewes, Lauren 207
Thaddeus, John 261
Thanksgiving Parade Jubilee (variety special) 26
Thanksgiving Parade of Parades (variety special) 26
That 70s Show (sitcom) 240, 253-254, 375
That's Life (variety series) 98, 376
Thicke, Alan 161
Thin Man, The (sitcom) 57
Third Annual NBC All Star Hour, The (variety special) 104, 377
3rd Degree! (game show) 162-163, 390
30 Rock (sitcom) 350-351, 375
This is Your FBI (radio drama) 11
This is Your Life (game show special) 159-160, 190, 389
This Week in Sports (sports series) 50
Thomas, Bob 207
Thomas, Bronwyn 313
Thomas, Dave Barton 350
Thomas, David Jean 352
Thomas, John 325
Thomas, Richard 346
Thomas, Rosamarie 317
Thomas, Tony 217, 225, 232
Thompson, Chris 250, 252, 322
Thompson, Lea 341
Thomson, Brenda 152
Thorne-Smith, Courtney 329
Thoroughly Modern Millie (movie) 168
Thorson, Linda 316
Those Wonderful Game Shows (variety special) 107, 376, 381
Thost, Rory Charles 343
Thurm, Joel 219
Thyne, T.J. 358
Tibbett, Paul 360
Tibbles, George 15-16, 18, 46-47, 49, 51-52, 54, 95-96, 196
Tilton, Charlene 151
Time Warner Presents the Earth Day Special (variety special) 231, 377
Tina Fey: The Mark Twain Prize (variety special) 115-116, 287, 377
Tinker, Grant 148, 160, 168-169, 201, 205
Tipton, Ken 333
Tisdale, Ashley 361

To Tell the Truth (game show) 5, 64-68, 70, 74-76, 80, 83, 121, 124, 145, 162, 166, 371, 381-384, 390
Today (talk show) 1
Todman, Bill 60, 63-64, 68, 74-76, 79-80, 83-84, 92, 107, 127, 134, 145, 155
Tolsky, Susan 312
Tom, Lauren 328
Tom, Dick and Harry (Los Angeles TV series) 12
Tom Ewell Show, The (sitcom) 248
Toni Tennille Show, The (talk show) 40
Tonight! America After Dark (talk show) 28
Tonight Show Starring Johnny Carson, The (talk show) 6, 15, 30, 33-39, 41, 43, 75, 189, 200, 229, 310, 317, 378-379
Tonight Starring Jack Paar (talk show) 28-30, 38, 60, 372
Tony Danza Show, The (talk show) 43
Torme, Mel 82
Torresan Jr., Ennio 335
Tournament of Roses parade 21-25, 84, 104
Townes, Harry 304
Trainer, David 245
Trebek, Alex 66, 144, 252, 295
Triedman, Elle 336
Trimbur, Angela 352
Trivia Trap (game show) 153, 156-157, 388
Trumbull, Brad 204
Truth or Consequences (game show) 135
Tsumura, Ken 344
Tucci, Michael 321
Tucker, Forrest 82
Turkel, Ann 321
TV Dawn to Dusk (publication) 12, 31
TV Guide (publication) 5, 123, 236-237, 307
TV Stage Magazine (publication) 13
TV Star Parade (publication) 11-12, 51
TV's All-Time Funniest Holiday Moments: A Paley Center for Media Special (variety special) 108, 377
TV's Funniest of the Funniest: A Paley Center for Media Special (variety special) 108, 378
25 Years of Sexy: People Magazine's Sexiest Man Alive (variety special) 115, 377
$25,000 Pyramid, The (game show) 145-147, 150, 388-389 See also *The $100,000 Pyramid* and *Pyramid*
$20,000 Pyramid, The (game show) 146
Tylo, Hunter 271
Tyson, Mike 67
Ubach, Alana 354
Uger, Alan 205-206
Uggams, Leslie 147, 151
Ugly Betty (drama series) 347-348, 374
Underwood, Jay 346
Urie, Michael 347
U.S. Steel Hour, The (drama series) 302, 304, 373
USA Today (publication) 2, 112
Valenti, Renee 170
Vallely, James 341

Valley Times, The (publication) 15
Van Arsdale, Richard 356
Van Atta, Don 312
Van Dusen, Granville 320
Van Dyke, Barry 321
Van Dyke, Conny 134
Van Dyke, Dick 168-169, 229, 290, 321
Van Hartesveldt, Fran 11, 54
Van Horn, Sara 352
Van Patten, Dick 236, 289, 308
Van Slyke, Helen 309
VanCamp, Emily 338
Vance, Vivian 83
Vanished (TV-movie) 305, 373
Varga, Richard 348
Variety (publication) 17, 20, 25
Vaughn, Robert 310
Vaughns, Byron 325
Veadov, Alex 331
Vega, Alexa 250
Velasquez, Nadine 348
Ventresca, Vincent 344
Vereen, Ben 297
Vicki! (talk show) 41
Victor, David 305, 307
Videtti Figueiredo, Linda 347
View, The (talk show) 2, 44, 113, 379-380
Vilanch, Bruce 164
Villalobos, Reynaldo 327
Villard, Tom 145
Vinnichenko, Leeza 301
Vinton, Bobby 310
Virtue, Tom 342
Volding, Katie 248
Von Detten, Erik 344
Waggoner, Lyle 88, 311, 336
Wagner, Robert 298, 333
Wald, Elliot 201, 395
Walden, Susan 309
Waldron, Shawna 250
Walker, Jimmie 202
Walker, Nancy 313-314
Wallace, Marcia 155
Wallingford, Jimmy 22
Walsh, Gwynyth 341
Walsh, M. Emmet 354
"Walt Disney World's 15th Anniversary Celebration," *The Wonderful World of Disney* (variety special) 107, 377
Walter, Tracey 311
Walters, Barbara 1-4, 6, 368
Walters, Melora 327
Waltons The (drama series) 201

Wang, Jason 361
Warburton, Patrick 360
Ward, Burt 336
Ward, Matt 349
Warren, Marc 312
Warwick, Dionne 109
Washington, Casey 298
Washington, Denzel 315
Wasilewski, Paul 338
Watkins, Carlene 241, 311
Wayans, Craig 342
Wayans, Damien Dante 342
Wayans, Damon 341-342
Wayans, Kim 342
Wayne, David 307
Wayne, Frank 76
Wayne Brady Show, The (talk show) 43
We Love Lucy (special) 56
Weaver, Dennis 32
Weaver, Sigourney 114
Webb, Jack 306
Weekend in the County, A (TV-movie) 323, 373
Weidergott, Karl 330
Weinberger, Ed. 171, 173, 189, 194-195
Weiner, Ron 344
Weinstein, Phil 327
Weiss, Ben 347
Weitzman, Matt 344
Welker, Frank 327
Wells, Dawn 336
Wermers-Skelton, Stevie 355
West, Adam 163, 336
Weyman, Andrew D. 334
What's My Line? (game show) 60, 62-63, 68-70, 74, 124, 381-386
What's This Song? (game show) 82-83, 384
Wheel of Fortune (game show) 162, 294, 389
Whew! (game show) 141-142, 387
Whitcomb, Cliff 16
White, Deborah 308
White, Horace 9-10, 61
White, Tess Cachikis 9-10, 61, 407
White, Vanna 162
Whitestone, Steve 324
Whiting, Margaret 109
Whitley, Kym 361
Whitmore, Stanford 309
Who's the Boss? (sitcom) 27, 317-318, 375
Wickes, Mary 318
Widmark, Richard 305
Wigor, Bradley 318
Wil Shriner Show, The (talk show) 41-42, 379
Wilberger, James 346

Wilcox, Dan 321
Wild Thornberrys, The (cartoon series) 331-333, 374
Wile Jr., Frederick W. 17
Wilkins, Rick 102
Willard, Fred 319
Williams, Anson 153
Williams, Bill 52, 54, 57
Williams, Cara 56
Williams, Caroline 323
Williams, Gregalan 355
Williams, Treat 338
Williams, Vanessa 347-348
Willis, Danielle Andrea 344
Wilmore, Marc 330
Wilson, Brad 329
Wilson, Ernest C. 14
Win Lose or Draw (game show) 160-161, 389-390
Win With the Stars (game show) 82-83, 385
Winant, Scott 357
Winchell, Paul 69
Windom, William 321
Windust, Penelope 307
Winkler, Henry 174
Winslowe, Paula 55
Winston, Helen 19
Winston, Hilary 349
Winters, Jonathan 28-29
Wiser, Bud 317
Wisne, Pamela 329
With This Ring (TV-movie) 308-309, 373
Witjas, Jeff 109, 112-113, 115, 367
Witten, Robert 159
Wolf, Herb 69
Wolter, Sherilyn 157
Wood, Gene 90
Wood, Melissa 351
Wood Adams, Kelly 313
Woodard, Alfre 315
Woods, Elliot 324
Woods, James 327
Woods, Robert S. 157
Woody Woodbury Show, The (talk show) 30
Wordplay (game show) 61, 158-159, 389
Worley, Jo Anne 91
Wostbrock, Fred 33, 140, 394
Wyatt, Jane 71
Wyatt, Monica 336
Wylie, Adam 342
Wynant, H.M. 306
Wynn, Keenan 152
X-Files, The (science fiction series) 243
Yagemann, Bill 79

Yard, Desiree 333
Yes, Dear (sitcom) 303, 335, 372, 375
You Don't Say! (game show) 78-80, 124, 383-386
York, Francine 306
York, Kathleen 357
Young, Bob 244
Young, Dean 328
Young, Robert 305
Young & Hungry (sitcom) 361, 375
Young and the Restless, The (soap opera) 92, 144
Young Dan'l Boone (western) 201
Your First Impression (game show) 74-75, 383
Yuman, Bernie 344
Zajac, Gord 337
Zano, Muni 356
Zarchen, John 320
Zaremba, Kathryn 324
Zediker, Maralee 285
Ziegler, Heidi 318
Zimbalist, Stephanie 309
Zimbalist Jr., Efrem 309
Zisk, Randy 358-359
Zon, Deborah 203
ZooLife with Jack Hanna (informational show) 42
Zucker, David 328

www.ingramcontent.com/pod-product-compliance
Lightning Source LLC
Chambersburg PA
CBHW050158240426
43671CB00013B/2166